A system of international comparisons
of gross product and purchasing power

UNITED NATIONS INTERNATIONAL
COMPARISON PROJECT: PHASE ONE

A system of international comparisons of gross product and purchasing power

PRODUCED BY THE STATISTICAL OFFICE OF THE UNITED NATIONS, THE
WORLD BANK, AND THE INTERNATIONAL COMPARISON UNIT OF THE
UNIVERSITY OF PENNSYLVANIA

Irving B. Kravis • *Zoltan Kenessey* • *Alan Heston* • *Robert Summers*

with the assistance of SULTAN AHMAD, ALICIA CIVITELLO, SAMVIT P. DHAR,
MICHAEL McPEAK, ALFONSO PARDO-GUTIERREZ, LORENZO PEREZ,
ALFONSO UONG, DONALD WOOD, JR., *and* ANTONIO YU

PUBLISHED FOR THE WORLD BANK BY
The Johns Hopkins University Press • Baltimore and London

Copyright © 1975
by the International Bank for Reconstruction and Development
1818 H Street, N.W., Washington, D.C. 20433

Library of Congress Catalog Card Number 73-19352
ISBN 0-8018-1606-8 (cloth)
ISBN 0-8018-1669-6 (paper)

Library of Congress Cataloging in Publication data will be found on the last
printed page of this book.

Contents

Contents (Continued)

Preface

International comparisons of production, consumption, and investment are indispensable for the analysis of economic and social development. As a result of work over the past two decades by national statistical offices, the United Nations and other international organizations, data on national income and expenditure are becoming more and more comparable from the standpoint of statistical methodology.

However, even where standard methodology has been adopted to produce national estimates of these aggregates, a major limitation to comparability has been the inadequacy of official exchange rates for purposes of converting estimates in national currencies to a common basis of valuation. Careful estimates by other means require large resources and sustained effort; as a result only a few have so far been made. Studies, such as the pioneering comparisons of the Organisation for Economic Cooperation and Development under Gilbert and Kravis, and the work of the Council for Mutual Economic Assistance and the Economic Commission for Latin America, have been limited to relatively homogeneous groups of countries. Thus, at the end of the 1960s no adequate basis existed for comparisons on a worldwide scale.

The long-term aim of the work begun by the United Nations International Comparison Project in 1968 was to fill this important gap in international statistics by developing detailed intercountry comparisons for gross domestic product and the purchasing power of currencies. The results of the first stage of this effort are presented in this report. An extension of the project to cover additional countries is currently under way.

A number of sources have provided financial support for this work. We are pleased to acknowledge the major contribution made by the Ford Foundation to the initial phases of this project through a grant to the University of Pennsylvania as well as the continuing contribution of the Government of the Netherlands to the United Nations Trust Fund for Development Planning and Projections, which has helped to finance the work, and also directly to the project for its current extension. The International Bank for Reconstruction and Development (World Bank) has provided substantial assistance for the past several years, as has the United States Agency for International Development. Extensive assistance in kind has been provided by the Statistical Office of the European Economic Community. Other important contributors to the extension of this work are: The Danish International Development Agency; the German Bundesministerium für Wirtschaftliche Zusammenarbeit; the Norwegian Development Agency; and the United Kingdom Ministry of Overseas Development. We also wish to thank statisticians in all the participating countries for their very valuable contributions to this undertaking. Finally, we are especially pleased to introduce this report as the result of a joint effort of the United Nations and the World Bank.

HOLLIS B. CHENERY
Vice President, Development Policy
International Bank for Reconstruction and Development

JACOB L. MOSAK
Deputy to the Under-Secretary-General for Economic and Social Affairs
United Nations

Introduction

The past two decades have witnessed the rapid development of work at the national level on the estimation of product, income, and expenditure aggregates. As a result, an increasing number of countries in all regions of the world regularly publish such estimates.[1] These data are widely used at the national level for economic policymaking, planning, and research.

But as yet the use of the same data in the international context has been less successful. There are two main prerequisites for the successful use of the growing wealth of estimates of national product, income, and expenditure—at either the national or the international level—for country-to-country comparisons. The first prerequisite is the adoption of comparable methodological principles (standard definitions, classifications, frameworks, and the like by the estimators in the different countries, or the possibility of rearranging national estimates according to standard methodological procedures. The second is the introduction of comparable valuation with regard to the product, income, and expenditure aggregates, generally estimated in value terms of national currencies.

Significant results have been achieved, and much work is in progress to meet the challenge of the first prerequisite, especially in regard to the United Nations new System of National Accounts (SNA), which was issued at the end of 1968.

At the end of the 1960s, however, the situation was far less satisfactory with respect to comparable valuation. Because official exchange rates could not be relied upon to convert the estimates of different countries, a special effort was required to develop an intercountry set of comparisons of national accounts aggregates on a comparable basis of valuation.

The Statistical Commission of the United Nations, at its thirteenth session held in the spring of 1965 in New York, discussed at some length the conversion problem involved in comparing national accounting aggregates expressed in national currencies. In this discussion, the Statistical Commission agreed that this problem was important and that the solution obtained by using currency conversion rates based directly or indirectly on prevailing exchange rates was inadequate for many purposes. At that time, however, the Commission considered that the alternative of exhaustively repricing the relevant product and expenditure flows was not practicable for most countries, "although it might form the basis of a definitive solution for the statistically advanced countries if undertaken at relatively infrequent intervals."[2] Therefore, the Commission welcomed the proposal of the Secretariat to begin systematic work on this subject as resources permitted, and it recommended, as a first step, that a study should be made of all available experience and data in the field at the international, regional, and national levels, with the aim of formulating more specific proposals for this work.

The recommended study was undertaken in 1967, and a report entitled "International Comparisons of Production, Income and Expenditure Aggregates" was submitted to the fifteenth session of the Statistical Commission, held early in 1968 in New York. The purpose of the report was to outline a project on the subject, which was prepared for the years 1968-71, to carry out comparisons for a selected number of countries and develop, test, and describe suitable techniques for the more comprehensive comparisons to be carried out at subsequent stages of the work. Because of the limited resources available in the U.N. budget for statistical purposes,

---

[1] The 1970 United Nations *Yearbook of National Accounts Statistics* presented national accounts estimates for ninety-four countries and territories.

[2] U.N. Statistical Commission, *Report of the Thirteenth Session*, April 20–May 7, 1965 (New York: United Nations, 1965), para. 77.

members of the Commission considered that "the project might be organized on the basis of participation by additional international organizations and considerable assistance from Member States."[3]

The U.N. International Comparison Project, which began its activities later in 1968, indeed became a cooperative undertaking. The central project staff was organized in two units, one located at U.N. headquarters, the other at the University of Pennsylvania. To enable the creation of the latter unit, the Ford Foundation generously made a major contribution in the form of a grant to the university. The World Bank provided substantial financial aid, and the statistical offices of the participating countries made substantial and essential contributions in real terms. Financial support also was provided, mainly for the work in India, by the U.S. Agency for International Development and, for collaboration with Japanese statisticians, by the U.S. Social Science Research Council.

The director of the U.N. Statistical Office maintained general supervision over the development of the project. The immediate responsibility for the undertaking rested with the project director, located in Philadelphia, and the associate project director, located in New York, who were in continuous communication with each other. For the initiation of the work, helpful advice was obtained from an Advisory Board.[4]

Detailed proposals for the project, entitled "Plans for International Product and Purchasing Power Comparison," were issued as a separate document in August 1968. As a result of suggestions received from members of the Advisory Board and from statisticians in cooperating international agencies, as well as on the basis of the experience with the beginning of the practical work of the comparisons, an expanded and revised set of proposals was issued in September 1969 under the title "Methods for International Product and Purchasing Power Comparisons." These proposals were discussed at a meeting of the Advisory Board, held in October 1969 in Bellagio, Italy.

In the execution of the project, arrangements were made to draw upon the work and strength of numerous international organizations and bodies. Within the United Nations, personnel from the statistical divisions of the Economic Commission for Africa (ECA), the Economic Commission for Europe (ECE), and the Economic Commission for Latin America (ECLA) lent their experience and skills to certain stages of the work. The Statistical Office of the European Economic Community (EEC) agreed to coordinate closely its comparisons among the then six member countries of EEC with the U.N. International Comparison Project and to participate intensively in those comparisons of its member countries with the United States which were carried out in the U.N. project.[5] The Brookings Institution made available its experience in closely related work in Latin America.

In the countries reported on in the present volume, the following national institutions were most active in supplying materials for and participating in the work:

Colombia: mainly the Departamento Administrativo Nacional de Estadística, but also the Centro de Estudios Desarrollo Económico at the Los Andes University and the Banco de la República

Hungary: the Hungarian Central Statistical Office

India: the Central Statistical Organization of the Government of India

Japan: the Bureau of Statistics in the Office of the Prime Minister, the Economic Research Institute of the Economic Planning Agency, and the Institute of Developing Economies

Kenya: the Statistical Division in the Ministry of Finance and Planning

United Kingdom: the Central Statistical Office in the Cabinet Office, the Economic and Statistics Division of the Department of Trade and Industry, the Statistics Division of the Department of Employment, and the Department of Environment

United States: the Statistical Policy Division of the Office of Management and Budget in the Executive Office of the President, the Bureau of Labor Statistics, and the National Income Division of the Office of Business Economics

In respect to France, the Federal Republic of Germany, and Italy, the work was carried out in cooperation with the Statistical Office of the European Economic Community in Luxembourg.

It is not possible to acknowledge all the individuals who assisted in the work, but mention should be made of Dorothy Brady, Polibio Cordova, Alan Gleason, Pal Koves, Angus Maddison, Gyorgy Szilagyi, and L. Zienkowski, who rendered valuable advice in the formative stages of the project. In the course of the actual provision of the data, particular appreciation goes to Alvaro Velásquez-Cock, Jorge A. Celis, Ernesto Rojas-Morales, Germán Botero de los Ríos, Jaime Sabogal, Jesús M. Tello, Rafael Isaza, and Rafael Prieto of Colombia; Albert Racz, Margaret Mod, Jozsef Tar, Gyorgy Szilagyi,

[3]U.N. Statistical Commission, *Report of the Fifteenth Session*, February 26–March 8, 1968 (New York: United Nations, 1968), para. 42.

[4]The Advisory Board consisted of the following persons: P. J. Loftus, United Nations (chairman); W. Beckerman, Oxford University; R. Bowman, U.S. Bureau of the Budget; U. Chand, Central Statistical Organization, India; M. Gilbert, Bank for International Settlements, Switzerland; E. Krzeczkowska, Central Statistical Office, Poland; S. Kuznets, Harvard University; M. Mod, Central Statistical Office, Hungary; J. Mosak, United Nations; R. Ruggles, Yale University and U.S. National Bureau of Economic Research; R. Stone, Cambridge University; and S. Tsuru, Institute of Economic Research, Japan. The project director was Irving B. Kravis and the associate director was Zoltan Kenessey.

[5]The project methodology was discussed initially by the statistical experts of the EEC countries at a special meeting held in Luxembourg with the participation of the director and the associate director of the U.N. International Comparison Project.

Adam Marton, Szaboles Rath, and Mihaly Zafir of Hungary; B. W. Chavan, R. M. Chatterjee, L. N. Rastogi, N. K. Chandekar, Girdhar Gopal, and R. N. Lal of India; Sadanori Nagayama, Tsu-tomu Noda, and Mytsuru Ide of Japan; Parmeet Singh of Kenya; John Ayris, Bernard Brown, Peter Capell, John Dearman, Jack Hibbert, Rita Maurice, Bill Osborn, Alec Sorrell, and Laurence Surman of the United Kingdom; Milton Moss, John Musgrave, Janet Norwood, and Winifred Stone of the United States; and Guy Bertaud, Phillippe Goybet, Hugo Krijnse-Locker, Vittorio Paretti, and Silvio Ronchetti of the EEC.

Aid with the price collection in various countries was given by Najib Banabila, William Berry, Mary Lou Drake, Wilma Heston, Ethel Hoover, and Karren Wood. Assistance in the work of the central staff was provided by Jill Brethauer, Betsy Burton, Susan Colson, Beatrice Fitch, Mitchell Kellman, Kurt Kendis, Jean Kunkel, Linda Robson, Jane Samuelson, Michelle Turnovsky, and Carl Weinberg. Jorge Salazar and Stanley Braithwaite provided helpful links with the related work of the Brookings Institution and the Economic Commission for Latin America, respectively. Bela Balassa, Wilfred Beckerman, Abram Bergson, J. P. Hayes, Salem Khamis, Moni Mukherjee, Joel Popkin, Nancy Ruggles, and Richard Ruggles gave valuable advice on an earlier draft of this report. From the beginning to the final stage, Laszlo Drechsler was a thoughtful and constructive critic. Peter E. de Janosi of the Ford Foundation and John Edelman and Elinor Yudin of the World Bank provided sympathetic and effective liaison with these supporting organizations. The effective support of the directors of the U.N. Statistical Office, Patrick J. Loftus, Abraham Aidenoff, and Simon Goldberg, made possible the execution of the project.

The active participation of the various national and international authorities in the project and the gracious help continuously enjoyed by the central project staff from these colleagues and from their institutions were of the greatest importance for the success of the work and are most appreciatively acknowledged. Goddard W. Winterbottom provided thoughtful and professional editorial guidance and also prepared the volume's index. Responsibility for the methods applied and the results obtained, of course, rests entirely with the central project staff.

A system of international comparisons
of gross product and purchasing power

Part I

Objectives and main results

Chapter 1

The nature of the study and the main results

A. The Nature of the Study

THE PROBLEM

The lack of accurate data on comparative levels of output and income in different countries is an important gap in the knowledge of the world economy. When such comparisons are required, the usual practice is to convert the outputs of the various countries to U.S. dollars or some other common currency through the use of official exchange rates. But as any traveler knows, the official exchange rates do not reflect the relative purchasing powers of different currencies, and thus errors are introduced into the comparisons. These errors often may be small, as is probably the case between the currencies of the United States and Canada,[1] but they can be quite large as well. An earlier study found, for example, that US$1,000, when converted to sterling at the official exchange rate, bought a basket of U.K. goods 64 percent larger than the dollars could have purchased in the United States.[2] In the study reported upon here, the purchasing power of sterling was 52 percent greater in terms of the U.K. basket of goods in 1970.

The difficulties of using exchange rates to convert the output of different countries into a common currency are compounded when exchange rates themselves change. For example, in view of the 16.9 percent upward evaluation of the yen in the Smithsonian agreement of late 1971, the use of exchange rates to convert gross domestic product (GDP) of Japan to U.S. dollars would produce for the ensuing year a 16.9 percent increase in the estimate of Japanese per capita GDP relative to that of the United States even if no change had occurred in the per capita GDP of either country in terms of its own currency.

Reasonably accurate comparisons of intercountry differences in production, incomes, and purchasing power of currencies are required for a wide variety of purposes. They are useful in any effort to understand the process of economic growth and development. Because product, income, and expenditure aggregates are fundamental variables in most models of growth or development, the lack of internationally comparable data of this kind impairs the validity of cross-sectional comparisons of stages of economic development or judgments on the success of development efforts. This is true whether interest lies in savings or investment ratios, the composition of real output, growth rates, the role of government, or a number of other critical aspects of development.

Such comparisons also are useful for policy purposes at the international and national levels. For example, an appreciation of the differences in the level of income is important in the allocation of aid and in the judgment of its efficacy. It is relevant as well to international burden sharing, whether for current costs of international bodies or for developmental or military objectives.

At the national level, it is important for planning purposes that both developed and underdeveloped countries be able to anticipate the patterns of expansion in final demand as income levels rise. Without internationally comparable income, output, and expenditure indicators, it is difficult to use the experience of wealthier countries to anticipate the time pattern of the changes that may be expected to occur in the development of the poorer ones. And, as in Western Europe, Eastern Europe, and Latin America, income and price comparisons may help illuminate potential or actual problems created by regional economic integration.

One evidence of the widespread feeling of need for international comparisons of the kind offered here is the

---

[1] See Economic Council of Canada, *Second Annual Review* (Ottawa: The Council, December 1965), p. 51.

[2] M. Gilbert and I. Kravis, *An International Comparison of National Products and the Purchasing Power of Currencies* (Paris: Organization for European Economic Cooperation, 1954), pp. 22–23.

fact that so many organizations concerned with international economic problems have attempted to produce their own estimates of per capita income relationships between countries: for example, the U.N. Statistical Office, the Organization for European Economic Cooperation (OEEC),[3] the Council for Mutual Economic Assistance (CMEA), the International Bank for Reconstruction and Development (World Bank), the Economic Commission for Latin America (ECLA), and a number of governments, including those of Canada, the Federal Republic of Germany, Japan, the Soviet Union, and the United States. In addition, a number of estimates have been made by individuals, and many of these are in the public domain. Virtually all of the private estimates and some of the official ones are based on armchair calculations. Although many of these may come closer to the truth than the simple conversion at official rates of exchange, a more solid and consistent basis for the estimates nonetheless is to be desired. Unfortunately, estimates for which field work has been done vary widely in the intensity and quality of the effort.

From the world standpoint, the aggregate effort that has gone into these comparisons has not been as productive as a well-coordinated effort would have been. The coverage of countries is not narrow, but the studies have been so varied in time and method that an incomplete jigsaw puzzle of comparisons has been the result. No useful worldwide system of consistent, reliable comparisons covering a substantial number of countries has been produced. More than that, no uniform framework has been laid down that can be used as the basis for an expanded and continuing coverage of countries over time.

THE PURPOSE OF THE INTERNATIONAL COMPARISON PROJECT

The U.N. International Comparison Project (ICP) represents a cooperative effort, under the aegis of the U.N. Statistical Office, to establish such a system of comparisons of real product and purchasing power.

The initial phase of the ICP, reported in this volume, had two main purposes: first, to work out the methods for the system of international comparisons, and, second, partly an end in itself and partly an adjunct to the first purpose, actually to make such comparisons for a group of countries selected to provide a variety of countries with respect to income levels, systems of economic organization, and locations.

In light of the latter consideration, we were fortunate to have obtained the cooperation of the following countries for the initial set of comparisons: Colombia, Hungary, India, Japan, Kenya, the United Kingdom, and the

United States. In addition, the European Economic Community (EEC), which carried out a comparison among its six constituent countries and with some outside countries for the year 1970, coordinated its work closely with the ICP. The governments of France, the Federal Republic of Germany, and Italy authorized the EEC Statistical Office to provide the ICP with the necessary data for the comparisons. For expository convenience, these three countries are referred to as the "EEC countries," although the passage of time has made the United Kingdom an EEC country as well.

Thus, the countries in the first phase include several major developed market economies, several developing countries, and one centrally planned economy. From the regional point of view, Africa, Asia, Europe, Latin America, and North America are represented. The countries also differ widely with respect to population, area, climate, mores, and degree of dependence on other countries or trading blocs. Finally, the relative importance of the nonmarket sector varies significantly among the countries.

Real product and purchasing-power comparisons are presented herein for these ten countries for 1970 and for six of them for 1967 as well. The comparisons relate not only to GDP as a whole, but also to consumption, capital formation, and government.[4] The results for GDP and three main subaggregates for 1970 are summarized in later parts of this chapter. In following chapters, estimates are provided for a more detailed breakdown—for both the ten countries in 1970 and the six countries in 1967.

In addition to the methodological work itself, a manual for carrying out international comparisons has been prepared. The standardization and systematization thus proposed have important advantages. Standardization helps to ensure that the data for countries added to the system in subsequent phases will be comparable to the data for the first-phase countries. Systematization will reduce greatly the costs of introducing new countries into the present ten-country network of international comparisons. Country coverage already is being extended, and it is hoped that the network will be expanded at a more rapid rate in the future.

RELATION OF THE ICP TO ITS ANTECEDENTS

Behind the work of the ICP lies substantial progress in national accounts work in the world. Not only has the estimation and use of national accounts spread, but also there has been a notable movement toward the adoption of common methods (standard definitions, classifications, and the like) by national-income estimators in different countries.

---

[3]Now the Organization for Economic Cooperation and Development (OECD).

[4]For definitions of these terms, see p. 4.

In addition, a number of international comparisons have been made, at least for groups of relatively homogeneous groups of countries–namely, those of the OEEC,[5] the CMEA,[6] and the ECLA.[7] Some pioneering work in comparisons between centrally planned and market economies has been carried out as well under the auspices of the Conference of European Statisticians.[8]

The nature of past experience and the character of the new problems have several implications for the design of the ICP. The techniques developed in the past work related mainly to comparisons focusing upon one pair of countries at a time: that is, to "binary" comparisons. Thus, it seemed logical to begin with these kinds of comparisons, although at the same time the project deliberately undertook to deal with a heterogeneous group of countries.

The general framework of the binary comparisons follows the OEEC studies of the early 1950s, but several major improvements over these studies have been made. First, the more extensive cooperation of the countries has enabled ICP to make a larger number of price comparisons with far more control over the comparability of quality than in the earlier studies. Second, for rents and some durable goods, so-called hedonic regression methods of international price comparisons have been employed (see Chapters 8 and 9). These methods, made feasible by the advances in economic theory and statistics and the advent of computers since the OEEC studies, allow us to hold constant across countries a number of different quality variables and thus to improve price comparability. Third, for construction, reliance has been placed almost entirely upon price comparisons for entire construction projects rather than for measured units of building operations (such as the laying of a certain number of bricks), upon which major reliance was placed in the earlier work.

Although the experience gained in the earlier studies provided valuable guidance for the present work, new problems had to be solved. For one thing, the very heterogeneity of countries created some difficult problems. For example, a common list of items for which price comparisons could be made for all countries had to be ruled out. In addition, ways had to be found to meet the problems posed by the existence in some countries

of a large rural sector having a substantially different content of consumption from the more westernized urban sector.

The large number of countries eventually to be included in the network of comparisons made it clear that binary comparisons alone will not suffice. Binary comparisons between each pair of countries quickly reach an astronomical number; even the ten countries produce forty-five possible pairs (that is, $n(n - 1)/2$, where n is the number of countries). Therefore, it was important to design the binary comparisons so that they could be fit into a broader framework in which a large number of countries are compared simultaneously. An essential feature of these "multilateral" comparisons, as we refer to these simultaneous comparisons, is that the circular test, or transitivity requirements, is satisfied. That is, $I_{j/k} = I_{j/l} \div I_{k/l}$, where $I_{j/k}$ is a price or quantity index for the jth country relative to the kth country, and l is a third country. A set of binary comparisons, when each pair of countries is compared directly, will not necessarily possess this property. Chapter 4 returns to this question.

Another consideration arising out of the large number of countries eventually to be included—and also out of the need to keep estimates up to date—was the importance of cost reduction either through the development of shortcut methods or through greater efficiency.

TREATMENT OF DIFFICULT INDEX-NUMBER PROBLEMS

Like all makers of price and quantity indexes, ICP faced a number of methodological choices for which economic and statistical theory offers little or no guidance.

In meeting these issues, we had the benefit of the views of statisticians in the participating countries and in international agencies. These consultations helped the project to arrive at procedures that are more likely to find wide acceptance.

In some areas, however, particularly with respect to the multilateral comparisons, it was necessary to break new ground. The sanction of established usage cannot be claimed here, but, as we have suggested above, the need for a world system of comparisons requires some such development.

Our response to this situation has been along the following lines: First, we have tried to set out these problems, indicating the advantages and disadvantages of each of a number of alternative solutions and our reasons for the choices we made. Second, for the major aggregates, we show more than one set of results. Third, we provide far more detailed data than ordinarily would be regarded as publishable in order to furnish the building blocks for those who wish to handle the data in ways that are different from the ones we finally followed.

[5] Gilbert and Kravis, *An International Comparison;* M. Gilbert and Associates, *Comparative National Products and Price Levels: A Study of Western Europe and the United States* (Paris: 1958).

[6] See L. Drechsler, *Értékbeni mutatoszamok nemzetkozi összehasonlitasanak módszertang* (Budapest: Kozgazdasagi és Jogi Könyvkiado, 1966) (with Bibliography).

[7] "The Measurement of Latin American Real Income in U.S. Dollars," *Economic Bulletin for Latin America*, XII (October 1967), pp. 107–142.

[8] Conference of European Statisticians, *Comparison of Levels of Consumption in Austria and Poland*, Document WG. 22/19, mimeo. (New York: United Nations, 1968).

B. A Thumbnail Sketch of the Methods

The methods of the study, as already noted, form the subjects of subsequent chapters. In order to make the main results intelligible to the general user who does not intend to go into the details of the methods, however, a brief outline is provided here.

GENERAL CONCEPTS

Comparisons are made in terms of expenditures on GDP, its main subdivisions, and detailed subcomponents. The concepts underlying the price and quantity measurements conform closely to the definitions in *A System of National Accounts* (SNA).[9]

In the SNA breakdown of expenditures on GDP, the principle of classification for the main subaggregates is based on the type of transactor. The major transactors are (1) private households, (2) governments, and (3) enterprises purchasing on capital account; the (roughly) corresponding subaggregates are (i) private final consumption expenditure, (ii) government final consumption expenditure, and (iii) gross capital formation.[10] The use of this classification allows comparison for different countries of the real quantity of product purchased by households, the real quantity purchased by governments, and the real amount of capital formation. This is of great interest, of course, and the results on this SNA basis are presented in Chapter 13.

Within private final consumption expenditure, the SNA follows a familiar functional classification, dividing expenditures into such categories as food, clothing, and medical care. Where, as in most countries, both households and governments pay for some of the commodities and services in these functional categories, notably in the medical-care and education categories, the SNA calls for the inclusion of household expenditures only; government expenditure is included under government final consumption expenditure.

As a result, an international comparison of consumption categories that strictly followed SNA lines would not be especially informative for those categories in which the division of payments between households and governments varies from country to country. It would not allow a proper comparison, for example, of the total consumption of educational services by a society, but only of that part purchased by households in each country.

To obtain the desired aggregate amount of these general kinds of final expenditures—food, medical care,

and the like—regardless of the varying degrees to which they are paid for by households or governments, we have assigned each general type wholly to "consumption" or to "government" in a uniform manner from country to country. Expenditures for health, education, recreation, and housing have been assigned to ICP "consumption," more formally labeled "Final Consumption Expenditure of the Population" (CEP). Services providing physical, social, and national security—those activities which are found rather consistently to be carried on by public authorities and financed by tax revenues—have been allocated to ICP "government," or, to use the formal term, to "Public Final Consumption Expenditure" (PFC). The line of demarcation between ICP consumption and government is discussed in Chapter 3. The expenditures shifted from SNA government to ICP consumption are tabulated in Table 13.15.

The purchasing-power parities (PPPs) and the price indexes are based in general on market prices: that is, the prices paid by final purchasers. The main exception to this occurs in those areas of consumption in which both households and governments make expenditures. In these cases, an effort has been made to price services rendered at the full cost to society, including payments by households and governments where they have been made by both. Similarly, in housing, an effort has been made to add the governmental subsidy component of rent to the rents paid by tenants.

These matters of classification and definition affect the meaning of the results and the uses to which they may be put. In particular, it should be noted that the ICP PPPs, even for consumption, are not invariably those faced by households. If, for example, a comparison were desired of the per capita or per household incomes of two countries derived from household survey data in each, these PPPs, reflecting the full social costs of important subsidized services, would have to be adjusted to take account of the differences in the provision of free or subsidized goods in the two countries.

THE METHODS OF THE MULTILATERAL COMPARISONS

Multilateral per capita quantity comparisons and price comparisons for GDP, consumption, capital formation, and government for 1970 are presented in the following pages for ten countries. A more detailed report on the comparisons will be found in Chapter 14. The multilateral comparisons represent, in our judgment, the most generally useful estimates that can be produced. Other methods produce somewhat different answers. These alternative results for a number of other methods that have found favor in one place or another are given in Chapters 4 and 5.

The methods we have chosen to produce the multilateral results yield a unique cardinal scaling of countries with respect to GDP and each of its components. They are not influenced by the particular country selected as

---

[9] U.N. Statistical Office, *Studies in Method*, Series F, Number 2, Rev. 2 (New York: United Nations, 1968).

[10] Final expenditures represent purchases for the use of the buyer and not for resale or for embodiment in a product to be sold. "Gross capital formation" is defined for ICP purposes to include changes in stocks and net exports.

the base country. They enable us to present GDP in money terms in an "additive" matrix of numbers in which the rows represent components of GDP and the columns are countries. (By an additive matrix is meant one in which the numbers on any row indicate quantity relationships among the countries, whereas those in any column may be added to form GDP or some sub-aggregate thereof.) Finally, we have adopted methods based on a conception of the world price structure.

The world price structure comprises a set of average international prices based on the price and quantity structures of the ten countries included. Each of these ten countries plays a role in determining the structure of international prices, with allowances made for the extent to which each may be considered to represent excluded countries. The international prices have been used to value the quantities of each of the ten countries. The international prices and the product values they are used to obtain are expressed in "international dollars" (I$). An international dollar has the same overall purchasing power as a U.S. dollar for GDP as a whole, but the relative prices correspond to average "world" relative prices rather than to U.S. relative prices. Thus, the purchasing power of an international dollar over foot-wear or transport equipment, for example, is not the same as that of a U.S. dollar. As noted above, the results of the comparisons would have been the same if any other country had been taken as the numeraire country; if the currency of another country had been used as the basis for the computations, the numbers expressing the values of GDP and the like all would have been different only by a constant factor. The multilateral methods, summarized in this and the preceding paragraph, are explained more fully in Chapter 5.

C. The Main Results

THE MAJOR AGGREGATES IN NATIONAL CURRENCIES

Tables 1.1 and 1.2 show the major aggregates that usually are drawn upon for GDP comparisons. (Data for 1967 also are presented in these tables, although use will not be made of them until Chapter 13.) Table 1.1 shows GDP in national currencies, exchange rates, and popula-tion figures. These materials lead to the figures on per capita GDP converted to U.S. dollars by means of ex-change rates (column 9). According to these exchange-rate conversions, the 1970 per capita GDPs of the other nine countries (column 10) varied from 2 percent of that of the United States, in the case of India, to 64 percent, in the case of Germany.

Table 1.2 shows the composition of GDP with respect to consumption, capital formation, and government. Capital formation varied in 1970 from 17 to 20 percent of GDP in Colombia, India, Kenya, the United Kingdom and the United States to about 30 percent in France, the

Federal Republic of Germany, and Hungary and over 40 percent in Japan.

Government, defined according to the ICP concept described above, accounted for 14 percent of U.S. GDP in 1970 and from 5 to 11 percent in other countries. Although separate figures for defense expenditures have not been gathered in the ICP, it seems clear that rela-tively large U.S. defense expenditures play a significant role in producing the larger governmental share in that country.

THE MAJOR AGGREGATES IN INTERNATIONAL DOLLARS

The results of the ICP's multilateral per capita quantity comparisons and price comparisons for GDP, consumption, capital formation, and government are presented in Tables 1.3, 1.4, and 1.5. The ten countries in Table 1.3 have been arrayed from left to right in order of increasing 1970 per capita GDP. GDP per capita varied from I$275 in Kenya to I$4,801 in the United States (Table 1.3, line 4); in relative terms, the lowest per capita GDP, that of Kenya was 5.7 percent of that of the United States (line 12).

The results produced by the use of exchange rates are repeated from Table 1.1 for comparison (line 13). The extent of the difference between the ICP estimates and the exchange-rate-derived figures is indicated by the "exchange-rate-deviation index" (line 14), which is simply the ratio of the former to the latter.[11] The per capita GDP of India, for example, relative to the United States remains quite low when the product of both coun-tries is valued at international prices, but the ratio of the Indian to the U.S. per capita GDP is 3.5 times the ratio indicated by the use of exchange rates. The size of the exchange-rate-deviation indexes tends to decline with rising real GDP. The factors influencing the size of the index and time-to-time changes in it are discussed in Chapter 13.[12]

The investment, or capital formation, quantity ratios (line 10) are strikingly larger than the GDP ratios in the cases of Japan, the Federal Republic of Germany, and France. They are larger as well, though by smaller mar-gins, for Italy, Hungary, the United Kingdom, and Colombia. The ratios for government (line 11), on the other hand, are smaller than the GDP ratios, except for Kenya and India.

The composition of GDP in terms of the three main subaggregates when all quantities are valued at inter-national prices (lines 5–8) may be compared with the composition when each country's own prices are used to value quantities (Table 1.2). When all goods are valued at

[11] The use of this term is simply a matter of convenience and is not intended to express any judgment about the appropriate-ness of the exchange rate. The equilibrium exchange rate is determined by more factors than simply GDP purchasing-power parities. See the comments on this point below.

[12] See pages 186–188.

Table 1.1. Gross Domestic Product in National Currencies and in U.S. Dollars at Official Exchange Rates

	Currency unit	GDP in national currency	Official exchange rate to US$	GDP in US$ millions converted at official exchange rate $ millions	(U.S.=100)	Population (000)
	(1)	(2)	(3)	(4)=(2)÷(3)	(5)	(6)
1970:						
Colombia	P millions	130,591(F)	18.56	7,036	0.72	21,363(U)
France	Fr millions	818,392(F)	5.554	147,352	14.98	50,776(C)
Germany, F.R.	DM millions	687,466(F)	3.66	187,827	19.09	60,987(C)
Hungary	Ft millions	321,458(P)	30.	10,715	1.09	10,331(C)
India†	Rs millions	398,900(F)	7.5	53,187	5.41	541,839(C)¶
Italy	L billions	57,903(F)	625.	92,645	9.42	54,504(C)
Japan	¥ billions	74,577(F)	360.	207,158	21.06	103,499(U)
Kenya	Sh millions	11,556(P)	7.143	1,618	.16	11,247(C)
United Kingdom	£ millions	50,003(P)	.4167	119,998	12.20	55,989(U)
United States	$ millions	983,770(P)	1.00	983,770	100.00	204,900(C)
1967:						
Hungary	P millions	246,849(P)	30.	8,228	1.04	10,217(C)
India‡	Rs millions	324,670(F)	7.5	43,289	5.47	506,702(C)#
Japan	¥ billions	43,725(F)	360.	121,458	15.34	100,243(C)
Kenya	Sh millions	8,804(P)	7.143	1,233	.16	9,928(C)
United Kingdom	£ millions	39,707(P)	.3571§	111,193	14.02	55,112(C)
United States	$ millions	791,614(P)	1.00	791,614	100.00	198,700(C)

Sources: *GDP*: (F) refers to estimates based on the 1952 version of the U.N. System of National Accounts (SNA); and (P) to present (1968) version. See U.N., *A System of National Accounts*, Studies in Methods, Series F, No. 2, Rev. 3 (New York: United Nations, 1968). For the few cases among our countries in which estimates have been available on both the former and present bases, the GDP aggregates have differed by amounts ranging from around 0.3 percent to 1.7 percent, with neither version consistently yielding a higher aggregate than the other.

The GDP figures are those reported to the U.N. Statistical Office, except for the U.S. data for 1967, which were adjusted to present SNA concepts by the ICP staff; for France, Germany (F.R.), and Italy, for which the data were supplied by the Statistical Office of the European Economic Community; and for the 1970 Japanese data, which were provided by Institute of Developing Economies in Tokyo. For reasons explained in the text (see p. 23), rent subsidies have been added to the GDP figures reported by these sources. The amounts added were as follows:

	Currency unit	1967	1970
France	million francs		229
Germany, F.R.	million DM		506
Japan	billion yen	73.4	115
United Kingdom	million pounds	195	304
United States	million dollars	282	533

The figures for France and Germany (F.R.) used for 1970 actually pertain to rent subsidies in 1965, and the 1970 figure for Japan is an estimate.

Exchange rates: Par values as reported in IMF *International Financial Statistics*, January 1971, except for Hungary, which is from U.N. *Statistical Yearbook*, 1971, p. 605, and Colombia, which is annual average of end-of-month selling rates as reported in U.N. *Monthly Bulletin of Statistics.*

Population: Figures followed by (C) were provided to ICP by each country, except for United States, which is from national income issue of *Survey of Current Business*, July 1972, Table 7.6 (p. 46); and figures for France, Germany (F.R.), and Italy, which were provided to ICP by EEC Statistical Office. Figures followed by (U) represent an unofficial U.N. estimate.

†Reference year April 1970–March 1971.
‡Reference year April 1967–March 1968.
§Rate changed from .3571 to .4167 on November 18, 1967.

¶Reference date for population is October 1970.
#Reference date for population is October 1967.

a common set of international prices, the share of capital formation in total GDP is lower in Hungary and Kenya by 4 or 5 percentage points and by smaller amounts in Japan and India. International prices push the consumption share up in these countries, except for India, in which it is government that emerges with a substantially larger share. In the other countries, capital formation rises in relative importance in GDP at international prices, most notably in the Federal Republic of Germany, in which there is a 5-point difference from the share at national prices.

Because the estimates are transitive and invariant with respect to the base country, it is legitimate to compare any pair of countries among the ten. The figures for relative per capita GDP for all pairs have been presented in Table 1.4; they are based on line 4 of Table 1.3.

Purchasing-power parities—units of each currency required to purchase the same quantity of goods as a U.S. dollar—are presented in Table 1.5 (lines 1–4). They may be compared with the exchange rate in line 5. They may be converted, more conveniently, to price indexes relative to U.S. prices by dividing them by the exchange

	Per capita GDP		
	In national currency		In US$ at exchange rate
Units	Amount	($)	U.S.=100
(7)	(8)=(2)÷(6)	(9)=(8)÷(3)	(10)
P	6,113	329	6.85
Fr	16,118	2,902	60.45
DM	11,272	3,080	64.15
Ft	31,116	1,037	21.60
Rs	736	98	2.04
L(000)	1,062	1,699	35.39
¥(000)	721	2,003	41.72
Sh	1,027	144	3.00
£	893	2,143	44.64
$	4,801	4,801	100.00
Ft	24,161	805	20.27
Rs	641	85	2.13
¥	436	1,211	30.40
Sh	887	124	3.11
£	720	2,016	50.60
$	3,984	3,984	100.00

rate (lines 6-9). (The price index form expresses each country's price level—after conversion to dollars at the official exchange rate—as a percentage of that of the United States.) Prices for GDP as a whole varied from about 30 to 85 per cent of U.S. prices. Price levels for governmental services were even lower relative to the United States because of the importance of the compensation of governmental employees in this sector and because of the lower wage levels that prevail in lower-income countries.

The aggregate categories in Table 1.5 are too broad to enable much more to be said about international price relationships. In Chapters 13 and 14 it will be seen, for example, that prices in construction tend to be quite different from country to country, probably reflecting different wage levels, whereas prices for producers' durables tend to approach much closer to a common world level.

The broad picture of the quantity and price relations presented in Tables 1.3, 1.4, and 1.5 is similar in the main to that which emerges from the binary comparisons discussed in Chapter 4 and presented in Chapter 13. One of the more noticeable differences is in ranking of two of the countries with similar levels of per capita GDP, but the countries involved—the United Kingdom and Japan—have per capita GDPs that are so close that little significance can be attached to the rank of one relative to the other. (Compare line 12 of Table 1.3 with line 4 of Table 13.17.) The question of the relationship between pairs of countries other than pairs involving the

Table 1.2. Gross Domestic Product and Its Main Subaggregates, in National Currencies and Percent Distribution

| | Colombia (P million) | France (Fr million) | Germany, F.R. (DM million) | Hungary (Ft million) | India (Rs million) | Italy (L billion) | Japan (¥ billion) | Kenya (Sh million) | U.K. (£ million) | U.S. ($ million) |
	(1)	(2)	(3)	(4)	(5)	(6)	(7)	(8)	(9)	(10)
Part A. 1970										
In national currencies										
Consumption	97,727	523,108	405,077	194,226	301,030	40,414	38,059	7,913	35,517	670,380
Capital formation	26,006	236,691	208,910	102,290	66,320	13,261	30,664	2,322	9,937	171,524
Government	6,858	58,593	73,479	24,942	31,550	4,228	5,854	1,321	4,549	141,866
GDP	130,591	818,392	687,466	321,458	398,900	57,903	74,577	11,556	50,003	983,770
Percentage distribution										
Consumption	75	64	59	60	75	70	51	69	71	68
Capital formation	20	29	30	32	17	23	41	20	20	18
Government	5	7	11	8	8	7	8	11	9	14
GDP	100	100	100	100	100	100	100	100	100	100
Part B. 1967										
In national currencies										
Consumption				155,869	254,648		24,369	6,223	28,547	525,889
Capital formation				74,328	46,430		16,363	1,698	7,135	146,188
Government				16,652	23,592		2,993	883	4,025	119,537
GDP				246,849	324,670		43,725	8,804	34,707	791,614
Percentage distribution										
Consumption				63	79		56	71	72	66
Capital formation				30	14		37	19	18	19
Government				7	7		7	10	10	15
GDP				100	100		100	100	100	100

Table 1.3. Comparisons of Per Capita Gross Domestic Product, Consumption, Capital Formation, and Government, 1970

	Kenya	India	Colombia	Hungary	Italy	U.K.	Japan	Germany, F.R.	France	U.S.
Valuation at international prices (I$)										
1. Consumption	193	250	555	1,263	1,516	2,050	1,591	2,015	2,238	3,295
2. Capital formation	43	49	166	524	558	627	1,139	1,243	1,138	922
3. Government	39	43	42	148	124	218	222	327	223	584
4. GDP	275	342	763	1,935	2,198	2,895	2,952	3,585	3,599	4,801
Percentages distribution of GDP valued at international dollars										
5. Consumption	70	73	73	65	69	71	54	56	62	69
6. Capital formation	16	14	22	27	25	22	39	35	32	19
7. Government	14	13	5	8	6	7	7	9	6	12
8. GDP	100	100	100	100	100	100	100	100	100	100
Per capita quantity indexes based on international prices (U.S.=100)										
9. Consumption	5.84	7.58	16.8	38.3	46.0	62.2	48.3	61.2	67.9	100.0
10. Capital formation	4.65	5.34	18.0	56.9	60.5	68.1	123.6	134.8	123.4	100.0
11. Government	6.66	7.31	7.2	25.4	21.3	37.4	38.1	55.9	38.2	100.0
12. GDP	5.72	7.12	15.9	40.3	45.8	60.3	61.5	74.7	75.0	100.0
Conversion to US$ at exchange rates										
13. GDP (U.S.=100)	3.00	2.04	6.85	21.6	35.4	44.6	41.7	64.2	60.4	100.0
Exchange rate deviation index (12÷13)										
14.	1.91	3.49	2.32	1.87	1.29	1.35	1.47	1.16	1.24	1.00
Addendum										
Aggregate GDP (U.S.=100)†	.31	18.84	1.66	2.03	12.18	16.48	31.06	22.23	18.58	100.0

†Line 4 times population, relative to United States.

United States is examined in Chapter 14, and the reasons for preferring the multilateral results are given.

Chapter 14 also includes multilateral comparisons for Hungary, India, Japan, Kenya, the United Kingdom, and the United States for 1967. Binary comparisons involving the same countries and the same reference date can be found in Chapter 13.

A COMPARISON OF 1950 AND 1970

For four of the nine countries compared with the United States, the present results may be compared with 1950 results of the Gilbert–Kravis study. For this purpose, we draw on the binary comparisons because they are more comparable to the 1950 estimates. (It should be pointed out, however, that the 1950 estimates refer to GNP rather than to GDP.) As already noted, the differences between the multilateral results (summarized in Tables 1.3 and 1.5) and the binary figures are not great.

It can be seen from Table 1.6 that all four of the European countries have gained substantially on the United States in terms of per capita gross product. Gauged by the ideal index—the geometric mean of the U.S.-weighted and the own-weighted indexes—the per capita gross product of the four countries in 1970 ranged from one-half to three-fourths of the U.S. figure. This compares to a range from one-fourth of the U.S.

per capita to more than one-half, twenty years earlier. Italy and the Federal Republic of Germany improved their position relative to the United States the most, and the United Kingdom, the least. The United Kingdom, with the highest per capita of the four European countries in 1950, clearly is below France and the Federal Republic of Germany in 1970.

The relative rise in the GDP of all four European countries has been especially great in capital formation. It already has been noted that France and the Federal Republic of Germany, devoting nearly twice the proportion of GDP to capital formation as the United States in 1970 (Table 1.2), had substantially more real investment per capita than the United States—a sharp contrast with 1950, when per capita capital formation was only about 35 to 40 percent of the U.S. level. The quantity indexes for government services per capita, on the other hand, show consistent declines between 1950 and 1970.

Prices in the three EEC countries were not, in general, as far below U.S. prices in 1970 as they were in 1950. In the United Kingdom, however, 1970 prices were slightly lower in relation to U.S. prices than they were in 1950, perhaps continuing to reflect the impact of the 16.7 percent devaluation of sterling near the end of 1967.

It also may be of interest to compare the 1970 results with those obtained by extrapolating the 1950 estimates by the changes in real per capita GDP for the United

Table 1.4. Relative Gross Domestic Product Per Capita, All Pairs of Countries, 1970

Denominator country	Numerator country								
	Kenya	India	Colombia	Hungary	Italy	U.K.	Japan	Germany, F.R.	France
India	80.3								
Colombia	35.8	44.7							
Hungary	14.1	17.6	39.5						
Italy	12.4	15.5	34.7	88.0					
U.K.	9.5	11.8	26.4	66.8	76.0				
Japan	9.3	11.5	25.9	65.5	74.5	98.0			
Germany	7.6	9.5	21.3	53.9	61.3	80.7	82.3		
France	7.6	9.5	21.2	53.7	61.1	80.4	82.0	99.6	
U.S.	5.7	7.1	15.9	40.3	45.8	60.3	61.5	74.7	75.0

States and each other country. The figures are as follows:

	Per capita quantities (U.S. = 100)		
		1970	
	1950†	Extrapolated‡	ICP result†
France–United States	45	68	74
Germany–United States	36	67	74
Italy–United States	23	40	48
United Kingdom–U.S.	56	57	62

†Table 1.6.
‡Ratio of 1970 to 1950 real product, estimated by chaining figures in U.N. *Yearbook of National Accounts Statistics*, 1964 and 1970 editions. The ratios were: France, 2.722; Germany (F.R.), 3.629; United Kingdom, 1.727; and United States, 2.057. When these ratios were divided by the population change calculated from Table 1.1, the per capita ratios were: France, 2.248; Germany (F.R.), 2.824; Italy, 2.582; United Kingdom, 1.554; and United States, 1.508. The per capita ratios for the first four countries were divided by the U.S. ratio, and the results were used to extrapolate the 1950 figures to 1970.

The extrapolations understate relative French, German (F.R.), and U.K. products by 8 or 9 percent and relative Italian product by 17 percent.[13] There is no

[13]When the same extrapolators are applied to the U.S.-weighted 1950 indexes, the 1970 estimates come close to the

logical reason to expect identical results. The 1950 real product comparisons are based solely on 1950 prices, the 1970 ones solely on 1970 prices. The extrapolations are based on time series that in principle compare the 1950 and 1970 quantities in each country using current (1970) prices. Actually, data in constant 1970 prices or in the prices of any other single year were not available, and the twenty-year time series in each country had to be strung together from two or three subsets of years each of which had its own base-year prices. This further diminishes the likelihood that the extrapolators will yield answers which are similar to those produced by direct estimates.

Of course, all these comparisons, like the others presented in this study, are based on a single year. The year chosen may not be a representative one for some of the countries. For the United States, for example, 1970 was unusual in that real gross product actually declined slightly (by less than 1 percent). The impact of cyclical and other temporary influences upon the comparisons

1970 ICP results—within 6 percent in all four comparisons. The extrapolated 1950 own-weighted indexes fall short of the ICP results by about 15 percent for France, Germany (F.R.), and the United Kingdom and by 28 percent for Italy.

Table 1.5. Purchasing-Power Parities and Price Indexes for Gross Domestic Product, Consumption, Capital Formation, and Government, 1970

	Kenya (Sh)	India (Rs)	Colombia (P)	Hungary (Ft)	Italy (L)	U.K. (£)	Japan (¥)	Germany, F.R. (DM)	France (Fr)
	Currency units per US$								
Purchasing power parities									
1. Consumption	3.68	2.24	8.3	15.0	493	.312	233	3.32	4.64
2. Capital formation	5.30	2.74	8.1	20.8	480	.311	286	3.03	4.51
3. Government	2.55	1.15	6.4	13.7	526	.314	215	3.11	4.36
4. GDP	3.74	2.16	8.0	16.1	483	.308	244	3.14	4.48
5. Exchange rate	7.143	7.5	18.56	30.0	625	.4167	360	3.66	5.554
	U.S. prices=100								
Price index									
6. Consumption (1÷5)	52	30	45	50	79	75	65	91	84
7. Capital formation (2÷5)	74	37	44	69	77	75	79	83	81
8. Government (3÷5)	36	15	34	46	84	75	60	85	79
9. GDP (4÷5)	53	29	43	54	77	74	68	86	81

for the reference years may be greater for subaggregates such as capital formation. The difficulties of finding a "normal" year or of adjusting the data to offset the peculiarities of the selected reference year have led us to confine ourselves to calling attention to these problems.

D. A Note of Warning and Guidance

THE LIMITATIONS OF THE STUDY

It has already been made apparent that the international comparisons reported upon in this volume involve many problems concerning the availability and quality of data and concerning concepts and methods applied. Some of them are intractable. Nonetheless, improvements in the international comparability of national accounting magnitudes can be achieved, and they should not be delayed until the resolution of each and every one of these problems by the further development of statistical theory and practice. Obviously, the valid use of the comparisons depends on the understanding by the readers of both its possibilities and limitations. Use of the results of the comparisons in an inappropriate context or without an understanding of their limitations can lead to erroneous conclusions. A study of this sort reaches persons of varying backgrounds, not all of whom possess the special training in economics and statistics required for the full appreciation of the conceptual and empirical problems encountered in the work. In addition, some readers may not have the time to cover the detailed methodological discussions of the report. For these reasons, the attention of readers is called at this early point to a number of caveats.

First, in the case of the comparisons involving Hungary, the work represents the collaboration of the Hungarian Central Statistical Office and the U.N. ICP staff. For the rest, the study is published on the responsibility of the secretariats involved. The views expressed in it should not be attributed to other organs of the United Nations, the World Bank, or the participating governments. The generous cooperation of the countries in furnishing the data, providing expertise, and offering comments on the work should not be interpreted as approval of the results shown. A significant effort was made to obtain the views of the participating national statistical offices on the draft of the report, but an official approval of the results was neither sought nor received from the governments involved—in fact, it would have been inappropriate for a research project of this nature.

Second, it should be stressed that the purchasing-power parities calculated are not measures of equilibrium exchange rates and, therefore, cannot be relied upon as indicators of overvaluation or undervaluation of currencies for foreign trade analyses. Equilibrium exchange rates depend upon the supply and demand for each currency; such supply and demand for currencies depend in turn upon their relative purchasing power over some—but far from all—of the commodities and services that constitute GDP, upon transfer costs (including transport costs and the effects upon price of protection), and upon the direction and size of capital flows.[14]

Third, it must be pointed out that on the statistical side, the estimates are based upon a necessarily limited set of observations, and thus sampling errors must be reckoned with. Furthermore, despite extensive efforts to avoid them, some incomparabilities remain with regard to prices, quantities, expenditures, and even population sizes gathered from different countries. The quality of the data varies from one country to another, and fitting the country expenditure data into the ICP classification system sometimes required approximations for certain detailed categories. The combined effect of errors of observation and sampling errors is reduced when a number of detailed expenditure categories are aggregated to totals such as consumption or GDP.

Fourth, from the standpoint of economic theory, comparisons of income can be justified rigorously only in terms of the preference system of a given person at a given moment in time. The customary time-series uses within each country of GDP figures in constant prices already involve a large jump from this underlying theoretical formulation. When real GDP per capita rises from one year to the next, the country is regarded as better off in some significant sense. This involves the assumption that the utility of each dollar's (or other currency unit's) worth of GDP is identical for all persons in the country. It assumes also that welfare comparisons can be made legitimately for the populations at the two dates in terms of the price structure of a selected year. The inappropriateness of such an assumption increases as comparisons are made between more distant points in time. The position with respect to international comparisons is not different in principle. In practice, in country-to-country comparisons (India with the United States, for example) price structures deviate from each other—and therefore (for one or the other or both) from any base price structure that can be selected—to a greater degree than is likely to be true of short-term comparisons within a given country. This is not always the case, however; a comparison of real per capita GDP between France and the Federal Republic of Germany for 1970, for example, may involve less stretching of the

---

[14]The relationship between the purchasing power of currencies and equilibrium exchange rates is discussed in most textbooks on international economics. See, for example, C. P. Kindleberger, *International Economics*, 5th ed. (Homewood, Ill.: Irwin, 1973), pp. 390ff.

Table 1.6. Price and Per Capita Quantity Comparison for France, Germany, Italy, and the United Kingdom with the United States, 1950 and 1970

(U.S.=100)

ICP Aggregate	Price indexes			Quantity indexes		
	U.S. weights	Own weights	Ideal index	U.S. weights	Own weights	Ideal index
Gross Product						
France						
1950	89	64	75	53	39	45
1970	89	74	81	82	68	74
Germany, F.R.						
1950	86	60	72	43	30	36
1970	95	80	87	80	67	74
Italy						
1950	92	52	70	30	18	23
1970	83	66	74	54	43	48
U.K.						
1950	81	61	70	63	49	56
1970	78	66	72	68	58	62
Consumption						
France						
1950	90	63	75	53	39	45
1970	94	74	83	77	60	68
Germany, F.R.						
1950	91	62	76	42	28	34
1970	99	82	90	68	56	62
Italy						
1950	94	53	71	31	18	24
1970	86	66	76	55	42	48
U.K.						
1950	84	63	73	66	52	59
1970	80	66	73	70	58	64
Capital Formation						
France						
1950	92	79	85	41	35	38
1970	81	74	77	136	124	130
Germany, F.R.						
1950	81	61	71	39	29	34
1970	87	75	81	150	128	138
Italy						
1950	95	74	84	19	15	17
1970	75	68	72	68	60	64
U.K.						
1950	79	72	75	35	31	33
1970	79	72	76	70	64	67
Government						
France						
1950	74	52	62	90	62	75
1970	78	74	76	40	39	40
Germany, F.R.						
1950	57	46	51	70	57	63
1970	87	83	85	58	55	56
Italy						
1950	74	28	45	52	20	32
1970	73	64	68	28	24	26
U.K.						
1950	60	43	51	107	77	91
1970	63	51	57	55	45	50

Sources:
  1950: M. Gilbert and I. B. Kravis, *An International Comparison of National Products and the Purchasing Power of Currencies* (Paris: Organization for European Economic Cooperation, 1954).
  1970: Tables 13.16 and 13.18.

Note: The 1950 figures refer to GNP; 1970 figures to GDP.

underlying theory than a comparison for either country between 1950 and 1970. (For supporting evidence for this last statement, see Chapter 15.)

Fifth, comparisons between countries with levels of economic development and social system as similar as those of France and the Federal Republic of Germany may be considered more reliable than comparisons between countries differing as widely in these respects as the United States and Hungary or the United Kingdom and India. This familiar point is illustrated by the differences between the quantity indexes in Table 1.6 obtained when U.S. price weights are used and when each country's own price weights are used. To illuminate the implications of different assumptions, we present at various points in this volume, alternative estimates based on different methods with respect to weighting and other matters. Of the various estimates presented, the authors believe that the multilateral estimates summarized in Tables 1.3, 1.4, and 1.5 and presented in more detail in Chapter 14 are the ones most generally useful. The reasons for this view are set out in Chapter 5.

A GUIDE FOR THE READER

For the reader who wishes to probe beyond this summary of the results, it may be helpful to offer some guidance, beyond the topical table of contents, by drawing together and expanding a little on what already has been said.

Chapters 2 to 12 are mainly methodological. Their purpose is to explain as fully as possible the gathering and processing of data from the standpoint both of the governing principles and of the actual procedures. Where no clear-cut theoretical or practical grounds exist for selecting one procedure over another, we usually experimented with the alternatives. We try to state clearly the grounds, sometimes admittedly narrow, for choosing the method we adopted, and we often give the alternative results.

This series of chapters begins with a discussion in Chapter 2 of conceptual aspects of the comparisons, including problems in the definition of output and price. This is followed in Chapter 3 by a description of the data obtained from the countries and the methods of preparing the materials for the computation of index numbers. The classification system used in the ICP is presented in the Appendix to Chapter 3.

Chapter 4 deals with the methods of calculating the purchasing-power parities (PPPs) and the quantity indexes for binary comparisons. The text sets out, first, the desired properties for the indexes we seek to derive and, then, in the light of these criteria, describes the binary methods we chose. The results of some alternative methods are presented and, to compare them with the results of our preferred methods, some of the overall results of the preferred "original-country" binary com-

parisons are included.[15] (The latter are presented in full in Chapter 13 after all the methodological chapters have been set out.) The first set of alternative quantity indexes found in Chapter 4 (Table 4.1) are obtained by using the United States as a bridge country to derive comparisons between pairs of countries not including the United States. Also shown are original-country comparisons for the three EEC countries,[16] and the results of equal weighting and item weighting within detailed expenditure categories are compared[17]

Chapter 5 is concerned with the methods of multilateral comparisons. Once again, a consideration of the desired properties is followed by a weighing of alternative methods and the reasons for selection of the preferred method. Our method of deriving transitive PPPs for detailed expenditure categories—the "Country-Product-Dummy" method—is described and its results compared with the results of the binary comparisons in Sections B and C of the chapter. A number of alternative methods of combining price and quantity comparisons for the detailed categories into PPPs and quantity indexes for the major national accounts totals are described in Section D. We choose a formula offered some years ago by R. G. Geary and recently applied by S. H. Khamis.

In addition to the index number formula, the results of the multilateral comparisons depend on the weights assigned to each of the ten countries in deriving the average international prices.[18] Alternative weighting schemes are described and evaluated in Section E.

Throughout the discussion of the alternative methods of obtaining PPPs for categories and of weighting countries—Sections B, C, D, and E—the results both of the method selected and of those rejected are shown in connection with each problem considered. We carry over this practice into Section F, in which the results of aggregation formulas offered by Walsh, by Elteto, Koves, and Szulc (EKS), and by Van Yzeren are compared with the results for our version of the Geary-Khamis formula and with the results of the binary comparisons.

The last section of Chapter 5 discusses the degree of imprecision in the final estimates of relative GDPs per capita.

Chapters 6 through 12 are concerned with methods of comparison within specific expenditure categories: consumers goods (Chapter 6), medical care and education (7), automobiles (8), rents (9), producers durables (10), construction (11), and government services (12). Chapter 6 sets out general methods of quality matching that have applications throughout the study. Three of the other chapters also involve some general methodo-

---

[15] See pages 49–50.
[16] See pages 52–53.
[17] See pages 47–49 and 53.
[18] See page 5.

logical issues: the role of quantity comparisons (7) and the use of regression methods in price comparisons (8 and 9). These three chapters also contain alternative results for the categories with which they are primarily concerned. Chapters 8 and 9 will indicate that we have not hesitated to dwell at length on individual categories for which the methodological problems were particularly challenging. In these cases, the importance of the categories in expenditures is not necessarily proportionate to the length of their treatment.

Chapter 13 presents the binary results of the study in full product detail, and Chapter 14 does the same for the multilateral comparisons. Price and quantity comparisons are presented in those chapters for more than thirty subdivisions of GDP and for various aggregations.

Chapter 15 represents a reconnaissance into the possible analytical uses of the new data. We investigate, first, the extent of similarity of the price and quantity structure of the ten countries. Second, we engage in some limited explorations of demand relationships. The fuller exploration of both of these lines of inquiry must await the addition of more countries to the ICP system of comparisons.

In conclusion, it may not have escaped notice that we have been unable to avoid developing a certain jargon. The text is filled with terms such as "CPD method," "original-country binary comparisons," and others that are not exactly terms of everyday household parlance or even terms familiar in statistical offices and classrooms. But to avoid writing a descriptive sentence or two each time we wished to refer to one of these concepts, a resort to such labels became necessary. To give substance to this apology, a glossary is offered at the end of the book.

Part II

Methods

Chapter 2

Conceptual problems

We begin this discussion of some of the theoretical aspects of international comparisons by considering the case for the validity of such comparisons. (In view of the very existence of this book, it is unlikely to surprise anyone that we conclude that such comparisons may validly be made.) We then discuss briefly the alternative broad approaches to international comparisons of prices and quantities. Finally, we cover the definition of output and the concept of price—matters that are fairly standard in the context of the statistics of a single nation but that raise certain problems in the context of international comparisons.

A. The Validity of Making International Comparisons

The interest in international comparisons of real product on the part of major international organizations, governments, and individual scholars has been noted in Chapter 1. So, too, have their uses in judging comparative economic performance, for burden sharing, and for analytical purposes in setting growth targets and in studying growth processes.

The question sometimes has been raised, however, as to whether comparisons are justified in principle. To put in an extreme form a question that is sometimes asked: What meaning can be attached to numbers that purport to compare bundles of commodities and services consumed in the villages of Asia and Africa with the radically different bundles consumed in the cities of Europe and America?

This challenge to international comparisons (unless it is accompanied by an equal challenge to intertemporal comparisons) can be based only on the size of the gap between the quantities and prices in the situations being compared. Nothing in the logic of the objection fails to apply to some degree to comparisons between two closely adjacent periods for a given country. In rigorous theory, comparisons are justified only from the standpoint of a given person at a given moment in time. One can legitimately ask questions about differences in the

money income that would be required to leave a given individual indifferent between the price structure he actually faces at that moment in time and some alternative price structure or structures with which he might be confronted at the same moment. Even comparisons of the welfare of the same individual at two points in time cannot be made rigorously, because it cannot be assumed that his tastes remain identical as he passes through life.[1] Comparisons of the welfare of an entire nation at two points in time are still more difficult to justify.

These niceties, however, generally are ignored in intertemporal comparisons. Problems of interpersonal comparisons are put to one side completely, and money aggregations simply are compared at two points in time without regard to the distribution of gains or losses among individuals and the impact of these changes on aggregate welfare. Also, it is assumed that tastes remain unchanged, an assumption that few persons would regard as unreasonable when the comparison is confined to a short interval of time such as one year to the next or even a period of several years. The hemline may rise or fall and car fenders may change their shape, but if one is prepared to accept the desire for changes in style as an inherent part of the utility function once a certain level of income is reached, then such changes need not be regarded as changes in taste.

Over a longer period of time, however, the style of life appears to change in a more fundamental sense. The clothing worn is apt to be made of different materials; the entertainment enjoyed may be transmitted in different forms; travel from homes to places of work and to friends' homes may be by means of different forms of transport; and in many cases even the food purchased is different from that available in an earlier age.

How do the assumptions required for international comparisons differ? The aggregation assumption that

---

[1] See F. M. Fisher and K. Shell, "Taste and Quality Change in the Pure Theory of the True Cost-of-Living Index," in J. N. Wolfe, ed., *Value, Capital and Growth* (New York: Academic Press, 1968).

disregards the internal distributional effect on welfare is exactly the same. What is different is that the assumption of similar tastes places a still greater strain on credulity when a comparison is made between distant situations in space at a given moment in time. Are we really warranted in assuming that the taste structure of such different peoples as the French, the Japanese, the Indians, and the Americans are similar?

This question—and the related question involving long-term comparisons within a country—may be answered in two ways. On one level, stress may be placed on the differences in the physical forms of the things people consume in the different situations. French wine, Japanese saki, German beer, and American cola can be regarded as reflecting different tastes. So, too, can the relatively large quantities of automobiles, refrigerators, and other durable goods consumed by Americans as compared with the quantities consumed by people in other countries. Indeed, products can be found in some countries that have no single equivalent or no equivalent at all in the consumption pattern of other countries. For example, next to their persons the Kashmiris use a tiny stove, a *kangri*, filled with glowing coals to keep off the winter chill. An equivalent in other countries is difficult to think of; some combination of a blanket, pajamas, sweater, and warm stones would be required to serve the same purpose.

On the other hand, it is possible to regard the basic needs and desires of man as fundamentally the same in different periods and different places. In this view, what changes from time to time and what is different from place to place is not so much what men would like to have but what it is that the economy affords them. What differs is, first, the extent to which the economy is capable of satisfying their needs, and, second, the means by which they are satisfied—that is, the physical identity of the goods. Differences in technology and differences in relative factor prices have been mainly responsible for variations in the physical forms in which the economy produces goods that satisfy those basic wants which have remained substantially constant through time and over space.

There are reasons for believing that it is the latter view that, in the main, is the more valid approach to the international differences observed in the real income of nations. Support for this view can be found both in ordinary observation and, to a modest degree, in econometric analyses. Any traveler around the world cannot help but be struck by the similarity of goods found in the shops of the major cities. A person could be in a department store in Tokyo or New York and not be able to tell which was which, were it not for the differences in language and appearance of the people. As economic levels rise, plumbing facilities in housing and the possession of automobiles and other durable goods, once regarded as American idiosyncrasies, are becoming common in other parts of the world. Even in parts of Asia in

which material values often are thought to take a second place to the spiritual, emerging middle classes typically pursue the same patterns of consumption that people with equivalent income levels pursue elsewhere in the world.

A reasonable inference is that the consumption patterns of the peasant and subsistence sectors in less developed countries are different from those of middle-income urban dwellers in the same countries and from the consumption patterns prevalent in the richer countries, not because of differences in taste, but because of differences in opportunity. If this is the case, the measurement of relative income levels between the rural and urban sectors of the less developed countries and between the less developed countries as a whole and the wealthy countries as a whole is in principle a valid exercise. The problem then becomes one of finding criteria of equivalence between the different physical forms of goods that are used to satisfy similar wants. This is difficult but not objectionable in principle, and, as we argue subsequently, it is manageable in practice.

In the realm of econometric and statistical materials, no extensive evidence exists on either side on this issue, but the limited materials available support the general view that human tastes are more alike than not. One clue is given by the tendency for price ratios for subcomponents of consumption and of GDP in country-to-country comparisons to be correlated inversely with the quantity ratios.[2] This at least suggests the existence of international similarities in price and income elasticities In addition, several studies indicate that at least for the United States and the countries of western Europe, great similarities exist between consumption patterns; income elasticities of demand for various categories of goods and ownership patterns for consumers' durables seem to be alike.[3] Chapter 15 shows that the similarities in consumption patterns among France, the Federal Republic of Germany, Italy, the United Kingdom, and the United States at a given time (1950 or 1970) tended to be greater than the similarities for the patterns of individual countries at periods separated by 20 years (1950 and 1970). In addition, the simple "demand" equations we present in Chapter 15, based on quantity, price, and income data for our ten countries, including countries as diverse regarding income levels and consumption patterns as India and the United States, generally yield plausible coefficients for prices and incomes.

---

[2] See M. Gilbert and I. B. Kravis, *An International Comparison of National Products and the Purchasing Power of Currencies* (Paris: Organization for European Economic Cooperation, 1954), pp. 51–57.

[3] H. S. Houthakker and L. D. Taylor, *Consumer Demand in the United States* (Cambridge: Harvard University Press, 1966), pp. 167–172; and L. T. Wells, "Test of a Product Cycle Model of International Trade: U.S. Exports of Consumer Durables," *Quarterly Journal of Economics* 83 (February 1969), pp. 152–162.

B. Alternative Approaches to International Comparisons

If we focus for the moment on international comparisons of real product per capita, two basic approaches are available. The one followed by ICP and by most of its predecessor studies is to make the comparison in terms of expenditures on GDP and its major subdivisions (consumption, government, and capital formation) and minor subdivisions (food, clothing, and the like). The alternative is to make comparisons from the production aspect of GDP and its subdivisions (net product of individual industries).

The interest in—and significance of—comparisons on the product side would be great.[4] For countries with important industrial sectors, however, the statistical difficulties of performing such comparisons are much greater than in the case of the expenditure comparisons. A task of "double deflation" is involved, in which the price comparisons that have to be made for each industry must include comparisons both of output prices and input prices. The great difficulties that this involves made the statistical services of several of the more developed countries reluctant to attempt the production approach, although hope remains that this can be done at some future stage.

Another basic choice in the approach to international comparisons of real product is between "direct" and "indirect" quantity comparisons. In direct quantity comparisons, quantities are compared for each detailed subcomponent of GDP (milk, tractors, and the like) and are aggregated to give quantity ratios for food consumption and the like up to GDP by the use of expenditure weights. In the indirect approach to real product comparisons, price comparisons are made for the detailed subcomponents of GDP, and the resulting price ratios are divided into the corresponding expenditure ratios to derive the quantity ratios. That is,

$$\frac{p_{ij} q_{ij}}{p_{ik} q_{ik}} \div \frac{p_{ij}}{p_{ik}} = \frac{q_{ij}}{q_{ik}} \, ,$$

where p and q are prices and quantities, i refers to the ith commodity, and j and k are two countries.

Direct quantity comparisons are difficult to make for many categories of products. Apparel, for example, is so heterogeneous that quantity data for each type and quality of product usually are difficult to obtain. Even if quantity information about some variants is available in both or all the countries involved in the comparison, the quantity ratios may be expected to exhibit wide dispersion relative to the corresponding price ratios in the case of categories composed of such varied kinds of products.

The indirect approach to quantity comparisons, which relies as noted upon direct price comparisons, has two advantages. First, price ratios for individual products are easier to obtain. Second, the sampling variance of the indirect quantity ratios will be smaller than the variance of the direct quantity ratios. The latter point follows from the presumed relative sizes of the sampling variances of the price and direct quantity ratios. Primary reliance, therefore, has been placed on the price comparison approach in the ICP.

In a few detailed categories, however, quantity data lend themselves more readily to international comparisons than do price data. These are categories for which the quantity data are available on a comprehensive basis and in which the contents are relatively homogeneous, at least as far as can be measured for purposes of international comparison. These conditions are met in the service sectors for which national accounting conventionally measures output by the quantity of inputs, as in education.

Furthermore, quantity comparisons not only are possible in some of these cases but also are easier to make because price data pose special problems. For example, in all the countries we have dealt with, it is much easier to obtain information about the number of teachers than it is to obtain national average compensation data for them.

Direct quantity comparisons have been relied upon for personnel in the medical care and education sectors. In these instances, the direct quantity indexes and the indirect price comparisons have been used for purposes of aggregation to obtain quantity and price comparisons for consumption and GDP. (See Chapter 7.)

In some categories, both direct quantity and direct price comparisons can be made. If we had complete knowledge and accurate data, the direct quantity ratio times the direct price ratio would equal the expenditure ratio.[5] That is, the factor reversal test would be met. In most cases, however, these ideal conditions do not exist, and the product of the price and quantity ratios deviates from the expenditure ratio. This may be taken, as Irving Fisher observed long ago,[6] as a measure of the joint error of the two ratios. The reason is that the expenditure ratio (in the present context, j's expenditure in its currency as a ratio of k's expenditure in its currency) is a datum, whereas the price and quantity indexes are estimates that may be calculated by many different methods.

---

[4]The most notable work utilizing this approach is D. Paige and G. Bombach, *A Comparison of National Output and Productivity of the United Kingdom and the United States* (Paris: Organization for European Economic Cooperation, 1959).

[5]This is clearly true at the level of individual items. For a category in which two or more items have to be aggregated, it is true provided that an index-number formula is used that permits this condition to be satisfied.

[6]Irving Fisher, *The Making of Index Numbers* (Boston: Houghton Mifflin, 1922), pp. 77ff.

Where the product of the two direct ratios deviates from the expenditure ratio and no source of error can be uncovered, we have two choices. One possibility is to accept the inconsistency in order to obtain, as far as our knowledge permits, the best possible price ratio and the best possible quantity ratio. The alternative is to discard one of the direct ratios, whichever seems less trustworthy after the necessary checks, and to replace it by the one derived from the retained ratio and the expenditure ratio.

We have opted for the latter course. That is, in our main tables in Chapters 1, 13, and 14, we have presented price and quantity ratios that when multiplied together produce the expenditure ratios. With the exceptions mentioned three paragraphs above, the price comparison generally was retained, because the price ratios for individual commodities are subject, as noted earlier, to less dispersion; therefore, the estimates are subject to smaller sampling error than the quantity ratios. The convenience of having consistent price and quantity ratios seemed to be worth the small difference in the result that would be produced at the aggregative levels (for example, food, consumption, and GDP) if the independent price and quantity ratios each were retained consistently. The direct ratios, where both were available, are presented in Chapter 7.

Whatever approach is taken to international comparisons, the reliability of the results depends basically upon the careful matching of the commodities and services with respect to which price or quantity comparisons are made. This is as essential for direct quantity comparisons as for direct price comparisons, for comparisons using the product or income-originating approach as for those such as ours using the expenditure approach.

Another common feature of international comparisons, whatever the approach, is the need to base the work on a sample of representative goods. The sample is stratified by industry in the product approach (iron and steel or machine tools) and by function in the expenditure approach (food or clothing).

The classification of GDP in terms of which the sample is stratified must be common for all the countries compared. The classification used in the ICP is discussed in Chapter 3. We have broken down expenditures on GDP into more than 150 categories that, of course, can be aggregated to varying levels. These 150-plus categories, referred to as "detailed" categories, are the finest subdivision for which we offer any data in this report.

A completely different approach to the international comparison of real consumption is represented by what have come to be known as "shortcut" methods.[7] These methods have in common a reliance upon such various indicators as steel production, number of telephones, and stock of motor vehicles. They differ from one to the other in the selection of indicators, although there is a great deal of overlapping, and in the statistical methods used to derive measures of relative consumption from the indicators. In the work of Wilfred Beckerman, probably the best known of the researchers in this area, regression methods are employed.[8]

The attractiveness of the shortcut methods is, of course, that they are economical relative to the large resources required for comparisons such as those reported upon in the current volume. On the other hand, the relative merits of different shortcut methods and the validity of the results produced by them cannot be assessed without a set of benchmark data comprising consistent and careful comparisons for a sufficiently large number of countries to permit statistical testing. The high cost of the full comparisons brings a much richer set of data, of course, including quantity and price comparisons not only for GDP as a whole but also for a large number of subcomponents. Our effort in the next stages of the ICP, therefore, is to reduce the cost of adding additional countries to the network so that in the event that shortcut methods do not prove to be satisfactory or adequate, the full comparisons can be more economically done.

C. The Meaning of Output

CONVENTIONS ABOUT THE PRODUCTION BOUNDARY

The conceptual problems involved in defining GDP so that it constitutes an unduplicated aggregate that distinguishes the results of economic activity from non-economic activity have been discussed now for the better part of half a century. For some questions, the outcome has been a clear resolution based on underlying theoretical considerations; but for others, where theory could not resolve the issues, conventions commanding international agreement have been developed. These resolutions and conventions have been set out carefully and systematically in the System of National Accounts (SNA).[9]

In the concept of GDP that has emerged, it is well understood that many aspects of welfare are not measured. Gross domestic product tells nothing about such important aspects of welfare as the pleasantness or unpleasantness of working conditions, the net improve-

[7]A. Heston, "A Comparison of Some Short-Cut Methods of Estimating Real Product per Capita," *Review of Income and Wealth* (March 1973), pp. 79–104.

[8]W. Beckerman, *International Comparisons of Real Income* (Paris: OECD Development Center, 1966); and W. Beckerman and R. Bacon, "International Comparisons for Income Levels: A Suggested New Measure," *Economic Journal* 76 (September 1966), pp. 519–536.

[9]U. N. Statistical Office, *A System of National Accounts,* Studies in Methods, Series F, No. 2, Rev. 3 (New York: United Nations, 1968).

ment or deterioration of the environment, or the equities or inequities of the economic and social organization.[10]

What the GDP does is to measure in a reasonably satisfactory way the changes from time to time in the provision of satisfaction-yielding commodities and services, holding constant the production boundary marking off economic activity from other human activities. In the context of international comparisons, the GDP concept enables us to judge the relative flow of outputs of satisfaction-yielding products from the economies of two or more countries in a manner analogous to that in which the relative flows are compared for two or more time periods within a country.

A number of conceptual and practical problems remain, however, when it comes to international comparisons. The SNA, detailed and careful as it is, necessarily leaves some leeway in its practical application, and the possibility arises that two countries may conform to the SNA and still be left with some incomparabilities in their GDPs. International differences in GDP coverage that may be relatively unimportant for measuring time-to-time changes within countries may have to be taken into account in place-to-place comparisons. In addition, a number of problems of implementation of SNA concepts and procedures that have not been fully resolved in time-to-time measurements also are encountered in place-to-place measurement.

ENVIRONMENT AND OUTPUT

One set of problems relates to the environment, including both the impact of production on the environment and thereby on welfare, and the impact of the environment in its pristine state upon welfare.

Were there a way to measure them, the adverse effects of such unfavorable concomitants of high production and economic growth as high noise levels, polluted atmosphere, and congested transport arteries might be regarded as negative goods. As matters stand, our conventions governing the preparation of national accounts do not provide for any deductions from GDP for environmental deterioration, but they do lead to additions for some but not all expenditures designed to improve the environment or to prevent further deterioration.

Expenditures by government, households, or businesses on capital account to reduce pollution or otherwise protect the environment are counted as additions to final product. Expenditures for these purposes by businesses on current account, however, are not regarded as final product, but merely increase the prices of output. This means that efforts to offset the deterioration

[10] For a recent attempt to produce another welfare oriented measure, see W. Nordhaus and J. Tobin, *Is Growth Obsolete?* in National Bureau of Economic Research, *Economic Growth* (New York: Columbia University Press, 1972), pp. 1–80.

of the environment affect the GDP estimates of different countries according to their extent and to the transactors that carry on these efforts. Thus, as between two countries, one of which devoted substantial resources to attempts to combat environmental deterioration and another that used none of its resources for this purpose, the former—other things (resources, productivity, and other influences) being equal—would have a relatively smaller GDP if its environmental efforts were financed through business expenditures on current account. If, on the other hand, its efforts were conducted through governmental expenditures, the two countries would be shown to have equal GDPs.

Given the present stage of international comparisons, we make no effort in the ICP to deal with these problems. At a later point, if environmental costs continue to rise, as seems likely, it may be necessary for national-income statisticians to reconsider the treatment of such costs, for time-to-time measurements within the country as well as for country-to-country comparisons.

Differences in environmental conditions raise further questions about the comparisons of real product quite apart from the adverse effects of production. Some of these questions are relatively easy to answer. For example, a cold climate requires men to produce heat for residences and other buildings, but this is unnecessary in a warm climate. The production of heat is an economic activity that adds to welfare and must be counted as a part of the contribution the economy is making to welfare where the heat is produced. Thus, the income of a country that requires and produces heat is higher than the income of a country in a warm climate that does not require or produce heat, the production of all other products being equal in the two countries. It is equally clear, on the other hand, that added inputs or costs to attain a given level of welfare that are necessitated by a harsher environment do not represent more production. A potato remains a potato whether it takes one hour to produce in a rich soil in a hospitable climate or three hours in a barren soil in an unfavorable climate.

MEASUREMENT OF RELATIVE NEW CAPITAL FORMATION

A question arises, however, into which of these two reasonably clear-cut cases—the one representing added outputs necessitated by a cold climate, the other, merely added costs—we should place the extra inputs and costs that may be required to produce capital goods in an unfavorable environment. For example, a mountainous country may have to build largely curved highways at a steep incline, whereas a flat country may be able to build most of its highways straight and level. Is flat land for highways analogous to fertile land for potatoes and mountainous land analogous to barren land? In that case, we should take as our unit of output one mile of highway, regardless of its inclination. Alternatively, we may argue that a mile of mountain road is regarded as more output than a mile of flat road within each country and should be counted as such in comparisons between countries. Or, to take another illustration, suppose that in a cold climate a steam power plant has to be built with insulating walls around its boiler room and switchhouse, whereas in a warm climate both may be exposed to the weather. Assuming that all other characteristics are identical, shall we regard inputs and costs required for enclosed construction in the cold climate simply as added costs or shall we regard them as more output?

One line of reasoning in response to such questions is to regard the future flow of services that each capital good would produce in each country as the basis for evaluating the relative amounts of investment. This implies that an international comparison should be made of the present value of the increases in output—ultimately in the form of consumption goods—that new capital goods would contribute in each economy. In the real world, we have no dated list of consumer goods that eventually will flow from new investment, but only the value of investment and the prices of the capital goods themselves in each country's own currency. Furthermore, knotty problems would arise in isolating the differences in the future flow that could be attributed to the input of capital from the differences attributable to other elements, such as other factor inputs and environment. Therefore, it is too difficult to implement the future flow of services approach.

The most common method of measuring time-to-time changes in the quantity of new capital investment is based on the value of the physical inputs at constant prices. The current value series for capital formation is divided by a price index for capital goods, which usually is formulated in terms of changes in the production cost of base-period equipment. This has the disadvantage, both in the time-to-time context and in international comparisons, of ignoring differences in the productivity of capital goods. Capital goods are purchased not to obtain their base-year inputs, but rather for their productive capacity, and price comparisons should be based on the cost after adjustment for improvements in productive capacity.

If the capacity of each new machine or other form of investment to contribute to production could be measured in terms of one dimension, the task would be relatively simple. If, for example, the productivity of a steam power plant could be measured solely by the kilowatts it generates, we would have an unambiguous basis for quantity comparisons. Other things, of course, such as fuel economy, labor requirements, and reliability affect the net contribution of the power plant. The same is true of most other producers' durable goods.

For those kinds of producers' durables which are marketed in a variety of models, it is possible through statistical analysis to relate observed prices to the various physical characteristics that contribute directly (for example, the horsepower of a tractor) or indirectly (weight as a guide to durability) to the value of the good in production. That is, the presumption is that the prices producers are willing to pay for these characteristics reflect their contribution to production. For certain goods that are available in a variety of models, we have made price comparisons between different countries for models defined in terms of certain combinations of these characteristics. These methods, sometimes referred to as "hedonic indexes,"[11] are discussed in Chapter 8.

For other machinery and for construction, when no empirical evidence existed on the relative productivity of different variants, we based our price comparisons on equivalent physical specifications. In the case of highways, for example, we were not able to obtain any basis for assessing productivity; therefore, we compared prices for things with like physical specifications. The cost of a flat road of a given specification in one country was compared with the cost of a road of the same specification in another country, and likewise for a mountainous road. The effect, of course, was to treat the mountainous road as more output than a flat road; in a sense, an adverse environment in this instance required more production, just as low temperatures necessitated the provision of heat and warm clothing. Similarly, insulating walls for power plants in cold climates were regarded as part of output rather than mere additions to cost.

THE "GENERAL" QUALITY OF OUTPUT

The basic approach to the treatment of differences in quality for specific goods is to attempt to avoid such differences between goods for which comparisons are made or to adjust prices where goods of equivalent quality cannot be found. Thus, because quality differences of this type do not affect the output comparisons, they need not be discussed in connection with the definition of output. They are treated in Chapter 3 in Section C, entitled "The Matching of Qualities."

Some kinds of quality differences, however, are associated with the whole aggregate of goods rather than pertaining to specific products. For a given aggregate of goods, to have conveniently located, well-stocked stores with courteous and efficient sales personnel is more advantageous to the population than to be forced to search for supplies and to queue up for service. A similar point applies to such ancillary services as credit, delivery, right to return merchandise, and repairs and adjustments. Generally, a greater variety of goods also is to be preferred to a lesser variety.

A retail distribution system that provides all these conveniences and services is more expensive and absorbs more real resources than one that does not. The GDP of each country includes the value of such services to the extent that they are rendered. Our method of inter-

[11] Z. Griliches, ed., *Price Indexes and Quality Change* (Cambridge: Harvard University Press, 1971).

national comparisons, however, does not attempt to measure international differences in their provision. We simply compare the extent to which each economy delivered meat and potatoes, shoes and stockings, and the like to its residents without regard to the extent or nature of the accompanying services.

The direction of the bias that results from the omission of these general quality factors is difficult to judge. There are some reasons to believe, for example, that American output would be higher relative to that of other countries were it possible to measure and include these factors in our comparisons. Variety, availability of goods, convenience of shopping, and the provision of services, including credit sales, all appear to favor this point of view. On the other hand, Americans tend to buy in relatively large quantities, particularly with respect to foods and household supplies, with the consequence that a part of the storage function is transferred from retail establishments to households. In addition, the larger number of sales in small quantities that are more typical of other countries can be regarded as the provision of more distributive services for the same quantity of final product delivered to consumers. Thus, even if it is granted that U. S. shops are more convenient and provide more services in some respects than those of other countries, at least some offsetting factors exist.

D. The Concept of Price

THE USE OF MARKET PRICES

The definition of output and the concept of price are closely related. Thus, the decision to ignore all the differences discussed in the previous paragraphs and to define our commodities primarily in physical terms has direct implications for the concept of price. The concept of price used is influenced also by the final expenditure approach we follow and by SNA definitions.

To start with the latter point, purchasers' values (market prices) are used in valuing the final products that make up GDP.[12] The possibility of systematic factor-cost comparisons either in lieu of, or as supplementary to, the market price comparisons was considered and rejected. Even on theoretical grounds, the case for factor prices is not completely without blemish, because the quantities observed are responses to market prices. The operative reasons behind the decision against factor prices, however, were the great difficulty of ascertaining true factor costs in many countries.

These difficulties arose out of the extensive distortions of market prices from factor costs that characterize nearly all countries. The industrialized market economies subsidize their domestic agriculture, developing countries subsidize industrial production directly or

through the exchange rate system,[13] and socialist countries also have price structures reflecting the impact of public policies.

In some sectors in which governments paid for substantial portions of the total social cost of a commodity or service, however, we tried to estimate what may be regarded as the total market price—that paid by households plus that paid by governments. This was done, for example, in connection with housing services.

The reason for this treatment is that, in some countries, the use of prices paid by households alone would lead to a gross underestimation of the relative importance of certain categories of expenditures. In Hungary, for example, tenants pay less than 20 percent of the current costs of housing. Thus, in any aggregation of relative real product, the use of Hungarian weights based on tenant prices or expenditures would assign much less importance to housing than it should have.

Although other unusual differences exist between factor costs and market prices, notably in alcoholic beverages and tobacco, expenditures in these categories are much less important. In the OEEC comparisons,[14] such distinctions between factor prices and market prices affected the aggregate results little. These comparisons were for similar countries, but high taxation of alcoholic beverages and tobacco is common.

THE NATURE OF THE NATIONAL AVERAGE PRICES

The market price that is sought for each good is the average price for all the units of that product which entered into the nation's GDP in the reference year. As noted above, the way in which this average is estimated is closely related to the definition of the final product to which it applies. We have already ruled out variety and quality of distributive services as elements affecting the definition of the product. Apart from the problems of specifying quality, considered in Chapter 3, decisions have to be made also with respect to such aspects of product definition as seasonality, size of transaction, location, and own-account production.

The basic rule we have applied in all these cases was that products were defined within each country on the basis of their physical characteristics: a potato with given physical characteristics was treated not only as the same product but also as the same quantity, whether it was purchased in the country or in the city, in January or June, by the piece or by the bushel, and whether it was purchased or consumed out of own production. The price of the potato is apt to vary, of course, from one situation to another in each of the cases. The appropri-

---

[12] Final products are those bought by purchasers for their own use and not for resale.

[13] See B. Balassa and Associates, *The Structure of Protection in Developing Countries* (Baltimore: Johns Hopkins Press, 1971); and I. Little, T. Scitovsky, and M. Scott, *Industry and Trade in Some Developing Countries* (London: Oxford University Press, 1970).

[14] Gilbert and Kravis, *An International Comparison.*

ate price for the present study is an average in which the actual price of each unit entering into GDP is given an equal weight; if the country has followed the recommendations of the SNA, this average will correspond to that implicit in the expenditure figure.

Deviations from this a-potato-is-a-potato rule were permitted only when there was clear evidence that physically different products were equivalent in use in two or more countries. The criteria used to identify such cases are described in Chapter 3, in Section C, entitled "The Matching of Qualities."

With respect to the seasonal factor, the ICP takes the view that a country that uses extensive resources to produce fruit out of season simply is obtaining a final product in an expensive way: strawberries in January are not different from strawberries in June, simply more expensive. It can be claimed, on the other hand, that the rare or unusual is not just more costly but confers greater satisfaction, and that strawberries in January really involve more final product than an equal amount of identical strawberries in June. Although the latter point of view may be valid for some aspects of intertemporal measurement of real product within a country,[15] as a practical matter it has less to commend it in the context of international comparisons in which the objective is to compare the amount of product derived by different nations from whatever resources and climatic conditions they face. If one country chooses to use resources to produce some of its fruit under adverse conditions, it should not be counted as more product than an equal quantity of the identical fruit produced under more favorable conditions in another country. Otherwise, we should have to determine continually the conditions of production for each final product with a potentially seasonal character before we could say how much product it really was. We also would have to decide how various seasonals in different countries might be matched.

The treatment of products as identical without regard to international differences in the average quantity purchased per transaction may raise some questions. Many items, particularly foods and pharmaceutical products, are more expensive per unit when bought in small quantities. Rice in the United States, for example, cost 14 percent more per ounce when purchased in a sixteen-ounce bag than when purchased in an eighty-ounce bag. The price premium per unit on small purchases can be regarded as the price paid by the consumer for more distributive service, and it can be argued that the additional service should be treated as part of final product. Although this view has some validity, it can be argued against it that shoppers, especially those with high income, sometimes may buy larger quantities without any price incentive merely to economize their shopping time.

[15] See U.N. Statistical Office, *A System*, p. 61 (para. 4.68).

The practice we followed in implementing the physical definition of products was to obtain the average price paid per unit for the most common size transaction in each country. If, for example, a certain specification of soap customarily was purchased in packages of three in one country and in packages of six in another, we sought to compare the price per cake for packages of three in the first country with the price per cake for packages of six in the second. This treatment, by the way, has the merit of producing an average price for each country that is consistent with the expenditure figure in the national accounts.

PRICING SELF-PRODUCED GOODS

A special problem in the concept of national average price arises in connection with location, because it is closely related to the treatment of consumption of own production. Like the other price problems, this issue is linked directly to the concept of national product.

Under conditions of optimal resource allocation, goods that absorb more resources represent more output than goods that absorb fewer resources. Potatoes consumed in the city count for more output than potatoes consumed on the farm. This valuation, based on the conditions of static equilibrium, is embedded in national-income accounting practice, and to some extent it is carried over into the time-to-time measurement of changes in income. Thus, in national accounting statistics as usually prepared, a shift from farm to urban consumption, with farm and urban prices constant, raises real product. If we try to match this treatment in international comparisons, we will treat own consumption of potatoes and purchased consumption of potatoes as separate products. This implies pricing the former at producers' prices, the latter, at retail prices.

This method leads to a lower estimate of the relative product for a country with relatively high own consumption and with a relatively large spread between the producers' and retail prices. The following illustration may bring out the way the arithmetic works:

	Urbanized country			Rural country			Extensions	
	p_u	q_u	$p_u q_u$	p_r	q_r	$p_r q_r$	$p_u q_r$	$p_r q_u$
Own consumption of potatoes	5	10	50	2	100	200	500	20
Purchased potatoes	10	100	1000	8	10	80	100	800
Total		110	1050		110	280	600	820

Both countries consume 110 of potatoes, but with very different distributions between own consumption and purchased consumption. The quantity index with the urbanized country's weights is

$$\frac{\Sigma p_u q_r}{\Sigma p_u q_u} = \frac{600}{1050} = 57.$$

The quantity index with the rural country's weights is

$$\frac{\Sigma p_r q_r}{\Sigma p_r q_u} = \frac{280}{820} = 34.$$

If the difference in price spread is eliminated so that the retail (purchased) price in the rural country is 4 (that is, two times the own-consumption price as in the urbanized country), both indexes come to 57. (Or, if the common spread is four times the own consumption price—for example, p_u for purchased potatoes is 20—both indexes come to 34.)

Whether it is correct or not, to use a method that results in counting the same quantity of potatoes as less output because they are consumed on the farm depends on the reasons for the different distribution of populations between farm and city. In general, a population living close to its points of production will require less transport inputs and, all other things being equal, will enjoy more final product than a population dwelling at a greater average distance from its points of production. Distance involves a cost, and a greater need to overcome it should not be allowed to count as more output any more than the greater need to wrest production from a less fertile soil. Someone might wish to argue that urban dwelling (at a distance from production) is a result of choice rather than necessity, and that the greater costs entailed in this preference constitute a contribution to welfare. There may be an element of truth in this view: the attraction of cities all over the world seems to be powerful and only partly explicable in terms of greater economic opportunity. We cannot gauge the relative roles of choice and necessity in urban concentration, however. We are not trying to assess the relative utilities and disutilities involved in urban dwelling. We do not attempt to deduct the disutilities entailed in urban life such as pollution and commuting time, and we should eschew techniques that implicitly ascribe greater utilities in urban living. Counting an urban potato as more product than a rural potato because of the costs of transport and trade margins would be to ascribe more welfare to city than to rural dwelling. It seems preferable, for international comparison purposes, to regard a potato as a potato.

The way to achieve this is to combine own production and purchased output for each product into a single category. This still leaves open the question of how the national average price will be determined, particularly how own consumption will be valued for the purpose of estimating the national average price. There are two possibilities for the valuation of own consumption: one is to value it at retail, the other to value it at producers' prices. In the latter case, the national price is the weighted average of producers' and retail prices, using consumption weights. In either case, once the national average price is determined, both methods treat all units consumed so that they make an equal contribution to each country's relative product: a potato is a potato for comparison purposes, whether consumed on the farm or in the city. What is different is that the relative importance of the product—that is, the price weight assigned to the quantity—will be greater when own consumption is valued at retail prices. The quantity ratio for potatoes will be the same whichever prices are used, because all potatoes are treated as a single category.

There is, however, a clear case for valuing own consumption at producers prices and using a weighted average of producers and retail prices. First, the weighted average prices truly reflect the average resource input in each country. Second, they are the prices that are in each country's expenditure data (if the SNA is followed), and, therefore, they are the prices that will produce price ratios consistent with the appropriate quantity and expenditure ratios.

Chapter 3

Organizing the basic data

The actual work of international comparison falls into three main stages. First, there is the need to work out a common classification of GDP and to break down each country's GDP into the selected categories. This serves two purposes. From a technical standpoint, it provides a stratification within which the sample of commodities for price or quantity comparisons can be chosen. From the standpoint of the utility of the results, such classification enables comparisons to be made for subaggregates of GDP.

The second main task is to choose the sample of items and to match the qualities in different countries. Finally, the price or quantity comparisons made for individual items must be aggregated.

The methods followed in the ICP with respect to the first two of these steps are described in this chapter. The aggregation methods for binary comparisons are set out in Chapter 4 and those for the multilateral comparisons in Chapter 5.

A. The Classification System

The nature of the classification has been alluded to at several points in the foregoing chapters. It has been mentioned that the expenditures on GDP are subdivided into more than 150 detailed categories, and that with certain exceptions, the scheme follows that proposed in the SNA. These and related matters are set out more fully in the following paragraphs, and the classification system itself, with examples of items priced, appears as the Appendix to this chapter.

The SNA is an obvious reference framework for an international comparison of real products. It provides a standard set of definitions and classifications to which all cooperating countries can be asked to conform with respect to the way in which the detailed data necessary to carry out the comparisons are provided: that is, it gives guidance on what should be included and how. The production boundary defined by the SNA is sometimes helpful as well, serving as a reference source to determine in questionable cases what it is that should not be included in the comparisons.

We have felt it necessary, however, to introduce one deviation from the SNA concept of GDP. For reasons spelled out in Chapter 2,[1] we have added government subsidies for current housing services to GDP.

With respect to the classification of expenditures, aside from the need to define the detailed expenditure categories more precisely, the modifications in the SNA classification were intended (1) to improve the international comparability of the resulting estimates, (2) to increase the convenience with which the results could be presented, and (3) to facilitate the actual work of making the comparisons.

The modifications for the last two purposes were relatively minor. The main changes to simplify the presentation of results related to the definition of the aggregates into which GDP is initially broken down. For purposes of convenience in the presentation of results, the SNA categories "increase in stocks," "gross fixed capital formation," "exports of goods and services," and "imports of goods and services" (entered with a negative sign) have been consolidated into the ICP category "gross capital formation" (GCF). The other major aggregates used by the SNA are government final consumption expenditure and private final consumption expenditure. Price and quantity comparisons are presented for these three major aggregates drawn from the SNA.

The changes made to facilitate the work of international comparisons consisted chiefly of breaking down the categories shown in the SNA more explicitly into detailed and well-defined categories. The selection of the detailed categories from the SNA classification was guided by several criteria. One was the relative importance of different items in the expenditures of five or six countries for which information was at hand at an early stage when the classification had to be drawn up. Another was the desire to ease the problems of making price comparisons for the detailed categories. This objective could be promoted by defining the categories so as to minimize the dispersion of international price relatives within the categories.[2]

[1] See page 23.
[2] See page 30.

A somewhat greater departure from the SNA seemed necessary to make the aggregates and subaggregates more comparable in content from nation to nation. In the SNA, expenditures on final products are classified according to the type of transactor—household, non-profit institutions serving households, and government—as well as by functional type—food, clothing, and the like. The comparisons of the three major SNA aggregates corresponding to the main transactors enable us to compare the baskets of goods purchased by households and by governments, respectively. Some types of final products such as education, medical care, and recreation, however, often are paid for by both governments and households, mainly by the former in some countries, by the latter in others. As noted earlier, it seems important to make the country-to-country comparisons of these functional types of product invariant to the institutional arrangements governing their provision; whether they are paid for by households or governments should not affect the quantity comparisons or the weights these types of product receive in quantity comparisons or aggregates in which these types of products are included.

For this reason, each functional type of final product is assigned wholly to "consumption" (ICP's "Consumption Expenditure of the Population," or CEP) or to "government" (ICP's "Public Final Consumption Expenditure," or PFC) in a uniform manner from country to country. So assigning products requires an internationally uniform boundary line between "consumption" and "government."

Such a boundary is not easy to draw. One might look for guidance to materials on standards and levels of living, but soon it will become apparent that the concepts involved here are too broad to be helpful in the present context. An expert committee of the United Nations, for example, included conditions of work, the employment situation, and human freedom, as well as aggregate consumption, as components of the level of living. The other components, which perhaps can be regarded as overlapping with some categories of final product, were:[3]

- Health, including demographic conditions
- Food and nutrition
- Education, including literacy and skills
- Transportation
- Housing, including household facilities
- Clothing
- Recreation and entertainment
- Social security

Another possibility would be to take as the touchstone of consumption the individual character of the benefits derived from the final product. Commodities

and services that are consumed individually (or by individual households) would be regarded as constituting consumption, whereas those services which are provided to the society as a whole would be treated as government. Education and medical services, for example, provide direct service to immediately identifiable individuals, whether they are furnished by privately operated institutions or private practitioners or by a governmental agency with or without fees. On the other hand, the making of laws and their administration, including police protection, represent services that benefit the society on a group basis. Of course, the society as a whole benefits from the individual's consumption of educational and medical services and the individual is a beneficiary of the administration of justice. Nevertheless, consumption may be distinguished from government in that the individuals directly and immediately benefiting from each specific use of resources can be readily identified in the former case, whereas in the latter case, the main purpose is to serve the group as a whole rather than individuals as individuals.[4]

The notion of the relatively individual or personal character of consumption as contrasted with the social or group character of government can be carried an additional step by using the distinction between private goods and public or social goods that is made in the theory of public finance.[5] Goods that can be subdivided into units that in principle can be sold to individuals (or to individual households) and consumed by them without any benefit accruing to any other individual (or household) are regarded as private goods (a loaf of bread, a tooth extraction). Goods that cannot be so subdivided for exclusive consumption, goods that cannot be consumed by one individual (or household) without having some of the benefits spill over to others, goods whose use cannot be withheld from those who do not pay, are regarded as public or social goods (defense). If we equate consumption with private goods and government with public goods, all or most commodities and services in the food, clothing, shelter, education, medical care, recreation, and transportation categories would be consumption, whereas the resources devoted to the making of laws and their administration, including police protection, would fall under government. The identification of consumption with private goods would mean that education and medical services would be regarded as personal consumption under whatever arrangements they were provided and however they were paid for. Of

[3]United Nations, *Report on International Definition and Measurement of Standards and Levels of Living* (New York: United Nations, 1954), p. 80.

[4]Our line of reasoning here recently has been adopted in U.N. Statistical Commission, *A Draft System of the Statistics of the Distribution of Income, Consumption and Accumulation*, Document E/CN.3/425 (New York: United Nations, February 3, 1972), paragraph 146 ff.

[5]R. Musgrave, "Provision for Social Goods," in J. Margolis and H. Guitton, eds., *Public Economics* (London: Macmillan, 1969). See also the article in the same volume by Paul Samuelson, "Pure Theory of Public Expenditure and Taxation."

course, the distinction between private and public goods would not resolve all the difficulties, because questions of interpretation, particularly as concerns the administrative feasibility of instituting fees, still remain. In principle, some types of services such as those provided by roads could be withheld from persons who do not pay, and in some instances actually are, but the more usual situation is that they are open to all.

Although the criteria outlined in the three preceding paragraphs provide some helpful guidance, they are not completely consistent with one another, and each leaves open a number of questions of interpretation in actual application. Therefore, to avoid a degree of arbitrariness in the allocation of final goods between consumption and government is impossible. Fortunately, the most important allocations necessary to obtain internationally consistent coverage of "consumption" and "government" do seem fairly clear cut on any of the criteria. Thus, most expenditures on housing, health, education, and recreation seem to fall into the consumption category, whichever of the three bases is used. The inclusion in ICP consumption of current housing subsidies represents a net addition to total GDP as defined in the SNA; the other items involve merely transfers from government to consumption without affecting total GDP.

"Government" is viewed as comprising those final products which most societies, regardless of economic and social system, have found can best be provided through public organizations and financed by tax revenues. These final products take the form largely of services that provide citizens with physical, social, and national security. They include the making of laws, the administration of justice, and the establishment and maintenance of standards where necessary to promote the public welfare, as in foods and drugs, medical practice, and education.

It is less clear where insurance-type expenditures should be classified. Social security is included as part of the level of living by the U.N. experts, and some forms of security, such as life and health insurance, can be and are purchased individually in many western countries. On the other hand, it can be argued that the administrative apparatus required to provide social security is a hallmark of the "welfare" state, and that all states have become welfare states in this sense. In view of this identification of the bulk of these expenditures with governments in most countries, it would have been consistent to classify private and public insurance schemes with government in the International Comparison Project. In practice, household net expenditures— premiums minus benefits—on life insurance were left in consumption as a matter of expediency; in view of the small magnitude of these expenditures in most countries other than the United States, it did not seem worthwhile to make the necessary adjustments.

These definitions of "consumption" and "government" require an allocation between the two of the

expenditures on nonprofit institutions serving households. These are assigned in the last SNA consolidation to household consumption, but for purposes of the ICP, we have assigned to government their expenditures under the categories of professional and labor organizations and civic associations, research and scientific institutes, and welfare services (exclusive of expenditures for food, clothing, and the like for individual use). Their other expenditures (education, medical, recreational and cultural, religious, and miscellaneous) are allocated to the appropriate categories of consumption.[6]

These differences from the SNA are discussed in more specific detail in Chapter 12. For the most part, however, the definitions of the three main components of GDP follow the SNA, and the reader is referred to that source for further details.

For most purposes, the three major subaggregates of GDP are subdivided into detailed categories, as follows:

0	Consumption	110
1	Capital formation	38
2	Government	5
	Total	153

Some further disaggregation sometimes is employed, but when this is the case, explanations are given.

In almost every case, some reallocation was necessary of expenditures on GDP from the classification in use in the country, because the categories are more detailed than, and, in any case, slightly different from, those used in the country's own accounts. Resort to supplementary data such as household surveys and production statistics often was required.

An effort was made to obtain estimates of expenditures for each category in every country and to provide price and quantity ratios for each. This approach helped in the gathering and processing of the basic data in a way that left many alternatives open with respect to methods of aggregation.

The estimation of expenditures on SNA concepts and for the detailed categories pose special problems for countries using the Material Product System (MPS) of accounts.[7] The relation of the MPS to the ICP version of the SNA is discussed in a note immediately following the main text of this chapter and preceding the Appendix.

B. The Sampling of Price Ratios

SAMPLING PRINCIPLES

For each of the detailed categories, it was necessary to select a number of representative goods for which

---

[6] For a description of the composition of the expenditures of these institutions, see U.N. Statistical Office, *A System of National Accounts*, Studies in Methods, Series F, No. 2, Rev. 3 (New York: United Nations, 1968), p. 89.

[7] See U.N. Statistical Office, *Basic Principles of the System of Balances of the National Economy*, Studies in Methods, Series F, No. 17 (New York: United Nations, 1971).

prices for identical or equivalent specifications could be found in the countries being compared. Before describing what actually was done along these lines, it may be useful to consider what we would do if our resources were unlimited and our knowledge complete. It is convenient to think of these problems, at least initially, in terms of binary comparisons (that is, involving only two countries), although our ultimate objective is a set of consistent multilateral comparisons (involving many countries).

Let us begin with the population of the final purchases, unit by unit, of commodities and services in each of two countries in a binary comparison. Each population of transactions may be divided into those which are for commodities and services that are common to the other country and those which are for things that are not included in the other country's set. One way or another, it might be possible to establish equivalences between things in the nonoverlapping sets of the two countries, but for present purposes, we will ignore this possibility and concentrate on the items in the overlapping set.

In principle, then, an international price comparison would be based on a random sample of the price relatives—the ratio of one country's price to the other's price[8]—of the commodities and services found in the overlapping set. Of course, the character of such a random sample and of the population of overlapping items being sampled would be unambiguous only if the frequencies of the purchases of identical products were the same in the two countries. Actually, this is extremely unlikely, and the probability is that some items in the overlapping set are purchased more often in one country than in the other. Let us put this problem aside for the moment, however, and define the overlapping set to include not only the identical items in the two countries but also the identical numbers of each item. In effect, we take the highest common multiple for each item and put the excess into the nonoverlapping set.[9]

In a random sample of the population of identical items appearing with identical frequencies, each transaction in a final product would have an equal chance of being represented in the sample. Even this approach would have the disadvantage that, from the standpoint of a value aggregate such as GDP, it would lead to an oversampling of items of small value with numerous transactions relative to those of high value with few transactions. This would not bias the estimated purchasing-power ratios between currencies unless relative international prices varied systematically with the size (in value terms) of the transaction unit in which different goods typically are exchanged. It is more likely than not, however, that relative prices do vary in this way; one would expect durables that tend to come in units carrying larger price tags than do nondurables to be relatively cheaper in higher-income countries.

A more appropriate sampling frame would involve the substitution of values for physical quantities so that the population of final products being considered would be a population of dollars or pounds sterling or rupees worth of transactions. The difficulty here is that the evaluation of the overlapping set of commodities would depend upon which country's prices were used to value them. A valuation in the currency of either country—so as to obtain a sampling of the distribution of, say, dollars' worth or rupees' worth or other currency's worth of final product—would be an improvement over the sampling of the common list of physical items, although the result probably would be to produce higher relative prices for the country whose prices were used than would be produced if the other country's prices were used. This effect can be expected because of the tendency, referred to above, for relative prices to be inversely correlated with relative quantities. The use of one country's prices would tend systematically to assign lower transactions values to those kinds of goods which were most important in that country and therefore to diminish the sampling ratio for such goods.

A preferable way of dealing with the difference between the value and physical unit distributions would be to sample the physical unit distribution and then to weight the different price relatives according to their expenditure weights for one country or the other or for a combination of both countries.

In the real world, to approximate any such ideal scheme for random sampling would be difficult. For one thing, an existing stratification of the transactions is forced upon us. In reality, we are not confronted with a list of individual transactions, but rather with a classification of final expenditures divided into commodity groups that, although differing in detail, generally are similar from one country to another. There is, first, the division into government, households, and capital formation, and within each of these sectors there are fairly familiar subdivisions (food, clothing, and the like, in consumption). Although the widespread adoption of such a classification attests to its utility, there is little reason to believe that it is optimal from the point of view of international price comparisons. Some of the common classifications, such as dairy products, can be expected to comprise items for which the price relatives will be fairly uniform from one specification to another, whereas others, such as household furnishings (including furniture, household textiles, and household appliances), may contain price relatives that vary widely. We have some control, of course, over the commodity classification by our ability to combine groups—or what generally is more helpful but also more difficult, to subdivide

---

[8] That is, p_j/p_k, where p is the price of a given specification of a good and j and k are countries.

[9] This is similar to Keynes's "highest common factor." See J. M. Keynes, *A Treatise on Money*, Vol. 1 (London: Macmillan, 1950), p. 108.

them so as to obtain categories that are more likely to have homogeneous price relatives in them.

One suggestion that has been made is to use the dispersion of price relatives as a criterion for the classification of items into commodity groups.[10] The idea is to choose from among alternative classification systems that one which minimizes the variance of price relatives within categories relative to the variance between categories. This is an attractive objective, because small dispersions justify the use of unweighted averages within categories, a practice that sometimes is made necessary by the lack of data for weighting and that always is convenient.[11] If this objective were accepted, it might be implemented on an a priori basis by classifying consumer goods according to similarity in production rather than on a functional basis. Alternatively, experience with international comparisons might make it possible to modify the starting classification so as to reduce the dispersion of price relatives within categories. That progress along these lines will be easier in binary than in multicountry comparisons can be expected, particularly because in the latter, the maintenance of identical detailed categories merits higher priority than the reduction of within-category price dispersion.

A more feasible procedure is, first, to start with the basic classification suggested by the SNA and used by most countries; second, to modify it with some subdivisions designed to improve homogeneity; and, third, to cope with the remaining problems of heterogeneity within classifications by increasing the size of the sample within the more heterogeneous categories. Optimally, the sampling rate within each category would be proportional to the standard deviation of the price relatives in the category.[12]

SAMPLING PRACTICE

In light of the theoretical and practical problems facing us, we have worked along three lines in choosing specifications.

First, the classification basically follows traditional final-product classification lines, but it was modified

with a view toward reducing the dispersion of international price relatives within categories. As already noted, we did not know what the dispersion of price relatives would be in different categories, and we had to base this work on a priori expectations. Nevertheless, some changes in the SNA classification seemed clearly to promise some benefits on this account. For example, the category of purchased transport[13] was broken down into local-distance and long-distance transport, which was further disaggregated into train, bus, and airplane transport in the expectation that the price relatives for local transport would have substantially larger dispersion than the price relatives for other classifications, and that the subcategories would have less dispersion. In a few cases, where similar price relationships seemed likely to prevail, different SNA categories were consolidated. For example, the repair categories in furniture, furnishings, and household equipment and operation, which are included in the SNA separately for each subgroup (that is, for furniture, for appliances, and for other subgroups), were combined into one detailed category, thus reducing the need for pricing work.

Second, the target numbers of specifications for the detailed categories were determined initially on the basis of the relative importance of the categories in the GDPs of five or six countries for which information was available in the early planning stage. The roughly proportional sampling ratios then were modified in the light of the expected degree of dispersion of price relatives within the categories. For example, only one specification was provided for relatively homogeneous categories such as eggs and coffee, whereas five were called for in the case of a heterogeneous category such as men's and boys' hosiery, underwear, and nightwear.

Third, the selection of specific items within the detailed categories was governed by two principles. The first was the criterion of "concentrated selection": that is, the selection of the goods with the largest expenditure weights was adopted. The advantage of this rule is that it produces a large coverage of the expenditures within each category at a low cost, and thus it diminishes the likelihood of sampling error attributable to omitted items.

On the other hand, concentrated sampling has significant disadvantages for our purposes. In the first place, it yields an unambiguous rule for the selection of items only if applied to the expenditure of one country. When used in this fashion, however, it is likely to produce a sample of items some of which will fall outside the overlapping sets referred to above. Even if applied from the standpoint of one country to the items within the overlapping set, concentrated sampling will bias the price comparisons so as to produce lower relative prices for the country whose expenditures are used

---

[10]See T. Mizoguchi, "An Application of Variance Analysis for the International Comparison of Price Levels," processed (Tokyo: Hitotsubashi University, 1969); also in Committee for Comparative Research of Levels of Living in Japan and the United States, *Comparison of Levels of Living in Real Terms in Japan and the United States* (Tokyo: Japan Society for the Promotion of Science, 1971).

[11]The convenience arises from the fact that unweighted averages produce single price and quantity comparisons, rather than different ones for each set of weights. Single averages, it is true, can be produced by formulas that take into account the weights of more than one country, but they are less appropriate for bridge-country comparisons that, for example, derive the Country j/Country k comparison from the product of the Country j/Country l and Country k/Country l comparisons. (See Chapter 4.)

[12]See L. Kish, *Survey Sampling* (New York: John Wiley, 1965), p. 92.

[13]SNA category 6.3; see United Nations, *A System.*

as the basis for the selection of items.[14] The reason is, once again, the inverse correlation between price relatives and quantity relatives. The second disadvantage of concentrated selection is that it is likely to lead to an underrepresentation of the items of low importance within each group.[15] If the price relatives are markedly different for low and high volume items, this will bias the results, although it is more difficult to predict the direction of this bias in international comparisons.

The second principle governing the selection of items was that each specification chosen had to be important or at least in common use in the consumption of each country. The idea is to avoid the selection of items that, although they can be found in a given country, will be so uncommon as to provide an unrepresentative basis for price comparisons within the category in which they fall. This means that each specification should be typical for the category in each of the countries with respect to volume of sales, source of supply (domestic versus foreign), and any other factors that affect relative price formation. It means also that care must be taken to avoid price gathering in outlets catering to the minority of extremely high- or extremely low-income groups in the population. In the case of the United States, for example, goods that can be found readily in stores that cater to mass markets, such as mail-order houses, supermarkets, or department stores, can be taken as satisfying this criterion.

Although an effort was made to keep the representative goods similar as we extended the price collection effort to successive countries, the satisfaction of the criteria of concentrated selection and common use, as well as the practical need to make maximal use of data available without special field work, resulted in a variation from one binary comparison to another in the number and identity of the representative goods chosen for a given detailed category. For example, although four kinds of fish were priced in Japan, the list did not include carp, which was a common fish in Hungary and India, because, with few exceptions, the Japanese consume only sea fish. Again, broadcloth shorts were priced in the European countries, and cotton briefs in Kenya. In this case, both styles were common in both areas, but we took prices that were already available.

C. The Matching of Qualities

MATCHING PROCEDURES

After the decisions about the selection of specifications were made, each was subject to close scrutiny to ensure that qualities were really equivalent in the countries being compared.

The specification itself was the focal point for this work of quality matching. An example of a simple specification used in the ICP is the one for eggs: "Fresh chicken eggs, large size (weighing at least 680.4 grams per dozen), white or brown shell. Not the best quality, but close to it. The white is less thick and high than the best quality; the yolk must be firm, high, and not easily broken."

Sometimes, as in the case of the egg specification, it could be assumed that anything meeting the specification in one country could be considered equal in quality to anything meeting the specification in another country. This was true for most foods. For most other goods, no brief specification could define the product with sufficient precision to ensure such a result; each specification narrowed the range of products, to be sure, but it still covered a variety of qualities.

An important means of coping with this problem was to organize an interchange of price experts in which the experts from each country had the opportunity to visit the shops of the other country to examine the actual items.[16]

These visits helped also to clear away misunderstandings arising from differences in terminology. In Japan, for example, "cashmere" refers to a weave rather than to a yarn, as in the United States and Europe. Again, in England, "ox liver" is used rather than "beef liver," the American terminology.

In the course of their meetings, the experts decided which matchings they could agree upon and for what categories new specifications should be substituted for the ones which had been tentatively agreed upon in advance. Further specifications usually had to be prepared and new prices gathered after these meetings.

The experts often carried samples or sent them ahead, and returned with other samples to aid in the completion of the matching process. The samples usually were for grains, dried vegetables, tobacco, apparel, footwear, textiles, stationery, or small housewares. In the case of consumers' and producers' durables, the brochures of the producers played a large role. The aid of buyers for large stores, manufacturers, and trade associations also was obtained in determining matching specifications.

These efforts do not take long to report, but they were essential to the establishment of comparable quality. Even so, we are conscious of many deficiencies in our price comparisons, in terms both of doubtful matches of qualities and, more important, of inadequate samples of items within detailed categories. An iterative process would have been desirable: visits and revisits by consumer-goods price experts to check on supple-

---

[14] D. Brady and A. Hurwitz, Conference on Research in Income and Wealth, "Measuring Comparative Purchasing Power," in *Problems in the International Comparison of Economic Accounts*. Studies in Income and Wealth, Vol. 20 (Princeton: Princeton University Press, 1957).

[15] Brady and Hurwitz, "Measuring Comparative Purchasing Power."

[16] For two of the countries in which experience with specification pricing was less extensive, however, reliance was placed mainly on outside experts.

mentary specifications and to add further specifications. These deficiencies, however, can be diminished as the ICP is extended to new countries in the future, and as more experience accumulates in matching.

MATCHING METHODS

In the process of decision making about matching, several different methods were relied upon. These are set out in the following paragraphs.

Physical identity. The preferred method was to find goods that were physically identical in each of the countries. As already noted, this was substantially the situation for many foods. Among nonfoods, also, comparison of prices for physically identical goods sometimes could be made, particularly where the same models of a given brand or trademark were sold in the different countries. Commodities for which identity on the basis of brand names or trademark was established included pharmaceuticals, cameras, toys, and consumers' and producers' durables. In some of these cases, such as cameras, the trademark and model number were included in the specification; in others, such as toothpaste, a list was provided of brands or trademarks that met the specification.

Equivalence in quality. More usually, however, exactly identical commodities could not be found. In a number of cases, there were products in different countries that conformed to the same general specification but had small differences in design or composition that seemed to be relatively unimportant or offsetting with respect to cost. If such differences were deemed unlikely to affect the country-to-country price ratios, they were ignored. For example, a Japanese polyester cotton broadcloth with a thread count of 116 by 72 was taken as comparable to a U.S. one with a thread count of 128 by 72. Sometimes larger differences between specifications existed, but the best though incompletely researched judgment of our experts was that they were comparable in terms of relative costs and utilities. For example, a Japanese cocktail table made of verbena wood veneer from Southeast Asia was compared with a U.S. cocktail table of walnut, mahogany, or oak veneer. Ideally, more time and effort should have gone into the establishment of equivalence in certain cases of this kind.

Replication of product. In general, the end product was regarded as the touchstone in assessing equivalence in quality, and different prices were compared for equivalent goods even though different means of production were used in different countries. Ready-made men's suits, for example, are most common in the United States and are cheaper than tailor-made garments, whereas in India the opposite is true. In this case, we sought to identify a U.S. ready-made garment equivalent in quality to each Indian tailored garment. This effort involved an exchange of cloth samples and consultations with cloth manufacturers in both countries, tailors in India, and ready-made clothing manufacturers in the United States. A similar procedure was unnecessary in other countries, because ready-made garments appear to be displacing tailor-made clothing quite generally. In Japan, for example, two-thirds of the suits sold in 1967 were of the ready-to-wear variety.

The straddle method. In some instances in which the exact matching quality could not be found, prices for a slightly higher and a slightly lower quality product were averaged to make the match. For example, U.S. sliced bacon was regarded as equivalent of the average of "middle cut smoked" and "streaky smoked" in the U.K. price list.

Equivalence in use. A number of cases were encountered in which things were not physically identical but clearly served the same need or use. For example, in the United States, 120-volt light bulbs commonly are used, whereas in Europe, 220-volt bulbs are common. It appears that there would be little or no difference in the cost of production were the two types of bulbs produced under similar conditions in the same country, and because no difference exists in the utility afforded by them, they were treated as equivalent products. In some instances, the establishment of equivalence required a larger leap in judgment than in the case of light bulbs. For example, as is described more fully in Chapter 6, we equated Japanese noodles with U.S. spaghetti despite difference in their physical composition.

Taste equivalence. In a few cases, one variant of a product was cheaper than a second variant in one country, whereas the opposite price relationship prevailed in another country. We regarded these instances as attributable to taste differences, and we made a direct price comparison between the cheaper variants in each country. For example, a standard U.S. wheat sells at a discount in India relative to an indigenous wheat that makes better chapaties, even though, in the outside world, the U.S. wheat sells for a premium. The Japanese have a strong preference for short-grain rice, and there is not even a market for long-grain rice in the country, even though long-grain rice commands a price premium elsewhere. In these and similar cases, national tastes seem to have adapted themselves to a product that is regarded abroad as relatively low in quality. In taking such products as directly comparable to products regarded as higher in quality elsewhere, we are assuming that tastes in these cases are independent and not merely a reflection of relatively low incomes. If the Indians shift from the local wheat to American wheat and the Japanese from short- to long-grain rice as their incomes rise, this will prove to have been the wrong decision.

Price adjustment. In some cases in which qualities were not directly comparable, a price adjustment was made to raise or lower the price in one country by the amount appropriate to the difference in quality. The amount of the adjustment was based on differences between market prices or costs. Ideally, the adjustments should have been made in terms of each country's prices in turn, because the percentage difference in prices or costs between the two specifications would not necessarily be the same in the two countries. The required information generally was easier to obtain from U.S. sources, however, and the adjustments usually were made in terms of that country's prices. Costs were used widely in construction to adjust for such differences as the presence in the specification of a basement for which a price was estimated in one country and its absence in that of another country. Adjustments were made also on the basis of size, most systematically in construction, where cost estimates for buildings were placed on a per-square-meter basis. (In general, buildings of the same size were compared, but, on the advice of an architectural consultant, small differences such as that between a thirty-two-unit apartment building in the Common Market countries and an otherwise similar thirty-six-unit building in the United States simply were matched on a per-square-meter basis.)

Regression method. Regression methods are a means for achieving a broader and more systematic price adjustment to a common set of specifications for complicated products that appear on the market in many different models, each with its own mix of specifications. These methods are described in Chapter 8 and need not be discussed here.

But before leaving the subject of matching, reference should be made to the problems created for price comparisons when the same goods are packaged differently in different countries. For example, paper containers are cheaper for distribution of cream in the United States, where high wages make the collection and cleaning of used bottles expensive, and bottles are cheaper for distribution in Europe, where paper products are costly. Our solution to these cases was to treat cartons and bottles containing the same quality and quantity of cream as equivalent and directly comparable. This could be regarded as an instance of taste equivalence.

On the other hand, where two types of packaging of a product exist side by side in both countries, with one more expensive than the other in both countries, we treat the different packaging as representing different qualities. Rice, for example, is sold in both boxes and bags in Europe and the United States, with the box packaging consistently the more expensive. In such cases, the packaging was part of the specification, and prices were compared only for similarly packaged products.

UNIQUE GOODS AND EMPTY CATEGORIES

When price comparisons are made on the basis of a sample of representative goods of equivalent quality, as outlined above, expenditures on other goods in effect are transferred to the expenditure on the representative goods in the same category. In the case of the direct price comparisons the effect of such transfers is to raise the quantities of the representative goods by the same proportion as their expenditure has been increased. In the case of direct quantity comparisons, the quantities must be increased explicitly by the same proportion as expenditures; otherwise, the implicit price relationships would be distorted.

In an earlier study,[17] "unique" goods were defined as goods available only in one of the countries in a binary comparison. Because unique goods are omitted from the list of representative goods, expenditures on them are transferred to representative items, as described in the previous paragraph.

If unique goods are pervasive, special methods for handling them must be developed. Among the developed countries, few unique products are found that play any major role in consumption, and from the standpoint of international comparisons, it is fortunate that such goods are becoming less and less frequent—though it may make for a duller world. One of the few encountered in the developed countries included in the present report is Japan's bean cake, or *tofu*. (The fact that bean cake can be found in the Oriental restaurants and groceries of the United States and other countries does not alter this view of the product, because it is a mass-consumed item in Japan and a specialty item elsewhere.)

The unique-goods problem looms larger and appears in both directions in comparisons between developed and developing countries. The nonmarket sector of the developing country may have goods that are unique as far as the developed country is concerned, and some of the products found on the markets of the developed country may be unique as concerns the developing country. The market goods of the developed country almost surely will be found in the cities of the less developed country, however, and the rural sector may be brought into comparisons through the urban sector rather than directly. For example, rents may be initially compared between India and the United States, on the basis of overlapping types of dwellings found in the United States and in such large Indian cities as Bombay and Calcutta. The large-city rents then can be adjusted to national averages by comparisons of rents in the large cities with rents in small cities and in rural areas. The latter comparisons may be based on types of dwellings that can be found in both the large cities and the other areas in India, though not in the United States. It may be necessary, as in the case of India, to perform this linking operation in more than one step if such large differences exist between rural and big-city levels of living in the less developed country that overlapping specifications cannot be found; in such a case, the rural areas have to be compared with small cities and the small cities with the large cities. It may be desirable to extend this linking procedure to other categories, as was done in India.

[17] M. Gilbert and I. B. Kravis, *An International Comparison of National Products and the Purchasing Power of Currencies* (Paris: Organization for European Economic Cooperation, 1954).

When multilateral comparisons, those involving a number of countries at once, are considered, the number of unique goods is relatively small, and they are not likely to be important in the expenditure of any country. Small dwellings (with a floor area of, say, 15 square meters) not substantially built and without running water or electricity are unique to India in a binary comparison with the United States, but once the comparison is made multilateral and Kenya is included, the uniqueness disappears. In our multilateral comparisons, we have developed methods to include such specifications that are common to some countries though absent in others; these will be discussed in Chapter 5.

Sometimes, however, there may be no purchases in the entire category. Of course, one of the considerations in selecting the detailed categories was to make them broad enough to minimize this possibility. Nevertheless, any classification that gives reasonable expenditure breakdowns for the industrialized countries may produce some detailed categories that are empty of expenditures in small developing countries. This is particularly likely to happen in the capital-goods sector, because the expenditures of such countries for particular kinds of capital goods tend to be lumpy—that is, large expenditures in one year, zero in others. Thus, zero expenditures were found for some categories of transportation equipment, for example, in one of the developing countries.

The empty-category problem could be met by consolidating the detailed category for which there is a zero expenditure with another for which it is judged that comparative prices would be representative of those of the omitted items. The identical result will be achieved by assigning to the omitted category the price ratio observed for the one thought to be representative of it. We followed the latter method because it preserves the formal symmetry of the multilateral comparisons.

D. Processing the Basic Data

After the prices were received by the ICP, the first processing step was to convert them to a 1967 or a 1970 reference date or to both. Some of the prices already referred to these dates, but a large number did not. Prices collected especially for the ICP usually had to be converted, because usually they were gathered on a current basis in order to maximize the response rate in the field work. Each such price was extrapolated from its individual reference date to annual averages for 1967, 1970, or both by a price index for a similar item or, if such an index was not available, by an index for the category in which the item belonged. These indexes usually were obtained from the price series maintained by each country for its consumer or wholesale price indexes.

The next step, applicable to all the prices, was to subject them to two computer programs, CLEANSER

and COMPARE, devised to highlight errors. In CLEANSER, prices for all countries were printed out for each specification. The purchasing-power parity (PPP) —the ratio of the price in local currency to the dollar price—also was printed for each specification. Finally, the prices of the countries other than the United States were converted to U.S. dollars at the official exchange rate and expressed as percentages of the U.S. price. Any unusual price relationships within a particular specification stood out conspicuously for an investigation of possible clerical or other errors. In COMPARE, similar price ratios were printed out for any given pair of countries; here were displayed unusual price relationships from one specification to another for a particular binary comparison. Data cleaning for expenditures consisted chiefly of ensuring that the figures supplied for detailed categories added up correctly to the figures given for aggregates.

These data-cleaning operations helped to reveal clerical errors both at the sending and receiving ends. Equally important, they called attention to errors in matching that previously had escaped notice. Some of these problems could be straightened out by the ICP staff, but most required the advice and sometimes further information from the country's statistical office.

The value and quantity data were entered on a per capita basis, using midyear population estimates. This had the advantages of producing a greater degree of comparability across countries and of calling immediate attention to unusual relationships that might indicate errors or the existence of special problems. (In some instances, the source materials were such that per capita data, based on household surveys, actually were more reliable than aggregate data divided by rough population estimates.)

The concept of resident population, as defined in *A System of National Accounts,*[18] was used. It includes all persons "whose general center of interest is considered to rest in the given country." In general, all persons living in the domestic territory of the country are included, the main exclusion being tourists, temporary business visitors, foreign seasonal workers, and foreign diplomatic and military personnel.

A Note on Conceptual Adjustments Needed for MPS Countries

by Laszlo Drechsler, Economic Commission for Europe

To ensure comparability, data of countries using the Material Product System (MPS) must be adjusted to the SNA concepts adopted for the International Comparison Project. The necessary adjustments are close to those known as SNA-MPS intersystem adjustments. A document of the U.N. Statistical Commission describes in

---

[18] United Nations, *A System,* p. 93.

detail the conceptual relationship between the revised SNA and MPS.[19] This document gives a detailed inventory on the differences between the various SNA and corresponding MPS concepts and includes a set of adjustment tables, which provide the links between the different indicators of the two systems.

The main conclusions of the document with respect to expenditure categories, together with some further adjustment problems specific to the ICP, are summarized below.

The SNA concept of household consumption can be derived from the personnel (material) consumption of the population of the MPS. The following adjustments are necessary:

1. Add household's consumption of nonmaterial services, financed by themselves.
2. Add consumption (both material and nonmaterial) accruing to households, financed by others (enterprises, government, and so forth). This consists of the cost of these goods and services minus the amount paid by the population.
3. Deduct depreciation of dwellings.

Among the other possible adjustments with respect to consumption that must be considered are the following:

1. Adjustment from the "consumption in the domestic market" to the "consumption of resident households" basis. This might be negligible in some MPS countries.
2. Adjustment for business travel expenses (other than food) that are included in MPS personal consumption but not in the ICP consumption.
3. Adjustment for uniforms. The scope of the uniforms that are included in household consumption is different in the SNA and MPS.
4. Adjustment for tips. Tips are included in final consumption in the SNA but not in the MPS. It should be noted that this does not relate to the service charge, entered on the bills, because this is treated as final consumption in the MPS too.
5. Sales of secondhand goods by households. In the SNA, this is negative consumption, whereas it is not deducted in the MPS.
6. Import duties paid by households. In the SNA, they are included in consumption, but not in the MPS.
7. The term "nonmaterial services" is interpreted in a somewhat broader sense in the ICP than in the MPS. For example, lottery and gambling margins and banking services (but not interest) also are covered under this flow.

The concept of "gross fixed capital formation" can be derived from the net fixed capital formation as defined in MPS. The required adjustments are:

1. Add depreciation of fixed assets as defined in the MPS.
2. Add unforeseen losses in fixed assets. In the MPS, unforeseen losses are charged against capital formation, whereas in the SNA, they are treated as capital losses and do not decrease the capital formation of the given year.
3. Add work in progress in construction. In the MPS, this item is covered by the increase in stocks and not by the fixed capital formation.

There may be some further differences between the MPS and SNA concepts, but they cannot be determined on the basis of the definitions used in the two systems. It would be desirable to devote some attention to the borderline between current and capital repairs and to the borderline between outlays on development that are treated as capital formation and current outlays (treated as intermediate consumption). Differences in this field may exist between countries using the same national accounting system. Differences may exist also in the field of some military expenditures (in the SNA, all military expenditures are excluded from capital formation).

The "increase in stocks" concept can be derived from the same concept of the MPS (generally referred to as increase in material circulating assets). The following adjustments are necessary:

1. Deduct work in progress in construction. (In the MPS, this belongs to increase in stocks, whereas in the SNA, it is put with fixed capital formation.)
2. Add unforeseen losses in stocks. In the MPS, these losses are charged against capital formation, whereas in the SNA, they are treated as capital losses.

Some further possible differences may occur in connection with:
- The treatment of some military expenditures.
- The gold ingots and other financial gold, which are excluded in the SNA from capital formation—treated as financial assets—whereas in the MPS, presumably not.
- The valuation of the stocks.

Net exports—exports minus imports—can be determined from the corresponding MPS concept by adding the export and import of nonmaterial services in its broader sense. Further adjustments that may be necessary include:

1. Adjustment for purchase of nonresident households (for example, tourists) in the domestic market and purchase of resident households abroad. (In the SNA,

[19] U.N. Statistical Commission document E/CN.3/397/Rev. 1 (New York: United Nations, 1969). For a brief description of the MPS, see U.N., *Yearbook of National Accounts Statistics, 1970* (New York: United Nations, 1970).

these flows are covered by exports and imports, but not in the MPS.)

2. Adjustment for the differences in the treatment of financial gold. In the SNA, when industrial gold is converted to financial gold, it is recorded as an export, whereas when financial gold crosses the border, it is considered as a transaction in financial assets and liabilities and not as an export or import; in the MPS, financial gold is covered in export and import when it crosses the border.

There is no MPS concept corresponding to the SNA concept of government. The MPS "consumption of the non-material sphere serving community needs"—generally referred to as "consumption of non-material sphere II"—is, on the one hand, broader than the SNA government in that it covers also financial institutions, insurance, and the like, and, on the other hand, narrower in that it relates only to material cost.

The SNA concept of government consumption can be compiled from the following elements:

- Material cost (including depreciation) of these activities
- Purchase on nonmaterial services by these activities
- Wages and salaries, employer's contributions to social security, to pension funds in these activities[20]
- Minus: value of sales by these activities.

All of the foregoing relate to a restricted part of the non-material sphere II (excluding insurance, banks, and the like) but may include some activities that are in the non-material sphere I—for example, some community and welfare services.[21]

[20]If indirect taxes are paid by these activities, they should be included as well.

[21]In this connection, see the discussion on the borderline between "consumption" and "government" in this chapter.

APPENDIX TO CHAPTER 3

The international comparison project: *classification system*

The classification of final expenditures follows closely the classifications suggested in *A System of National Accounts* (SNA; United Nations, *A System of National Accounts*, Studies in Method, Series F, No. 2, Rev. 3 [New York: United Nations, 1968]). Some modifications have been necessary to meet the special requirements of the International Comparison Project; these are covered in footnotes indicated by letter superscripts. Actually it has been necessary to develop a more detailed classification than that given in the SNA, but in this process, the list of items given in the SNA classifications has been used as guidance. For producers' durables, use has been made of the International Standard Industrial Classification (ISIC; United Nations, *International Standard Industrial Classification Statistical Papers*, Series M, No. 4, Rev. 2, [New York: United Nations, 1968]) in order to obtain more detailed product breakdowns.

The main categories and their code numbers are as follows:

0 Final Consumption Expenditure of the Population[a]
  01. Food
  02. Clothing and footwear
  03. Gross rent, fuel and power[b]
  04. Furniture, furnishings, household equipment, and operations
  05. Medical care and health expenses[c]
  06. Transport and communication
  07. Recreation, entertainment, education, and cultural services[d]
  08. Other goods and services[e]
1 Gross Capital Formation[f]
  10. Residential buildings[g]
  11. Nonresidential buildings[h]
  12. Other construction[i]
  13. Land improvements and plantation and orchard development[j]
  14. Transport equipment
  15. Nonelectrical machinery and equipment

  16. Electrical machinery and equipment
  17. Other durable furnishings and equipment
  18. Increase in stocks[k]
  19. Exports less imports of goods and services
2 Public Final Consumption Expenditure
  20. Compensation of employees
  21. Expenditure on commodities

The most disaggregated categories, which together account for the total GDP, constitute what is referred to in the text as the "detailed categories." The more aggregative "summary categories," which also account for the total GDP are in italics. (Two sets of footnotes are used. The first, using numerical superscripts following category numbers, refers to special groupings of categories in the summary binary tables in Chapters 13 and 14. The second, using letter superscripts following category titles, refers to more detailed explanations of the categories themselves.)

0 *Final Consumption Expenditure of the Population*[a]

01.000 *Food, beverages, and tobacco*

  01.100 *Food*

    01.100 *Bread and Cereals*

      01.101 Rice, glazed or polished but not otherwise worked (including broken rice)

      01.102 Meal and flour of wheat, barley, and other cereals and, maize

      01.103 Bread and rolls

      01.104 Biscuits, cake, and other bakery products

      01.105 Cereal preparations, preparations of flour, starch or malt extract, used as infant food or for dietetic or culinary purposes; tarts and pies other than meat and fish tarts and substances other than meat

      01.106 Other cereals (macaroni, spaghetti, noodles, vermicelli, and similar products, whether cooked ready for consumption or not; rice cooked ready for consumption; malt, malt flour, malt extract, potato starch, sago, tapioca, and other starches; etc.)

01.110 *Meat*

01.111 Fresh beef and veal

01.112 Fresh lamb and mutton

01.113 Fresh pork

01.114 Fresh poultry

01.115 Other fresh meat (sheep, goats, horses, game, edible offal, frog meat, and meat of marine mammals such as seals, walruses, and whales)

01.116 Frozen, chilled, dried, salted, smoked, canned meat, meat preparations, bacon, ham, and other dried, salted, or smoked meat and edible offals; meat extracts and meat juices; sausages, meat pies, meat soups in liquid, solid, or powder form, whether or not containing vegetables, spaghetti, rice, or the like; paste products filled with meat, such as canelloni, ravioli, and tortellini

01.120 *Fish*

01.121 Fresh or frozen fish and other sea food

01.122 Canned and preserved fish and other sea food and fish preparation; tinned fish soup, snails, fish pie

01.130 *Milk, cheese, and eggs*

01.131 Fresh milk

01.132 Milk products (evaporated, condensed, dried milk, cream, buttermilk, whey, yogurt, cheese, curd)

01.133 Eggs, treated eggs, egg products

01.140 *Oils and fats*

01.141 Butter

01.142 Margarine, edible oils, peanut butter, mayonnaise, other edible oils

01.143 Lard and other edible fat

01.150[1] *Fresh fruits and vegetables* (other than potatoes and similar tubers)

01.151 Fresh fruits, tropical and subtropical (orange, tangerine, lemon, lime, grapefruit, banana, mango, pineapple, etc.)

01.152 Fresh fruits, other (apple, pear, cherry, grape, melon, plum, prune, nut, strawberry, etc.)

01.153 Fresh vegetables (beans, cabbages, carrots, cauliflowers, cucumbers, eggplants, garlic, ginger, onion, peas, pumpkins, squash, spinach, lettuce, tomatoes, edible seeds, herbs, lentils, pulses, mushrooms, rhubarb, truffles, etc.)

01.160[1] *Fruits and vegetables other than fresh* (excluding potatoes and similar tubers)

01.161 Dried, frozen, preserved fruits, juices, fruit peel, nuts, and parts of plants preserved by sugar

01.162 Dried, frozen, preserved vegetables, vegetable juices, vegetable soups without meat or meat abstract (or only traces)

01.170[1] *Potatoes, manioc, and other tubers* (potatoes, manioc, arrowroot, cassava, sweet potatoes, and other starchy roots; tinned and other products such as meal, flour, flakes, chips, except starches)

01.180[2] *Sugar* (refined sugar and other products of refining beet and cane sugar, not including syrups)

01.190 *Coffee, tea, and cocoa*

01.191 Coffee

01.192 Tea

01.193 Cocoa

01.200[2] *Other foods*

01.201 Jam, preserves, marmalades, jellies, syrup, honey

01.202 Chocolate, sugar confectionery, ice cream

01.203 Salt, spices, vinegar, prepared baking powders, sauces, mixed condiments and mixed seasonings; yeast; substitutes for coffee, tea, and cocoa; and other food n.e.s.

01.300 *Beverages*

01.310 *Nonalcoholic beverages* (mineral waters and other soft drinks)

01.320 *Alcoholic beverages*

01.321 Spirits

01.322 Wine and cider (including cider with low alcohol content)

01.323 Beer (including beer with low alcohol content)

01.400 *Tobacco*

01.410 *Cigarettes*

01.420 *Other* (cigars, tobacco, snuff, etc.)

02.000 *Clothing and footwear*

02.100 *Clothing other than footwear, including repairs*

02.110[3] *Clothing materials* (woolen materials and synthetic materials of woolen character; cotton materials and synthetic materials of cotton character; other materials, silk [natural and synthetic], synthetic fibres [other than woolen and cotton character], flax, hempen, and the like)

02.120[3] *Outer clothing other than leather and fur* (coats, suits, trousers, shirts, blouses, skirts, dresses, sweaters, etc., both ready made and custom tailored)

---

[1] In the summary binary tables, these categories are combined as Fruits and Vegetables.

[2] In the summary binary tables, these categories are combined as Spices, Sweets, and Sugar.

[3] In the summary binary tables, these categories are combined as Clothing, Leather Clothing; expenditures have been treated as a separate category only in the binary comparison of Hungary with the United States.

02.121   Men's (16 years and over)

02.122   Women's (16 years and over)

02.123   Boys' and girls' (15 years and under)

02.130[3]   *Hosiery, underwear, and nightwear*

02.131   Men's and boys'

02.132   Women's and girls'

02.140[3]   *Leather clothing and furs*

02.150[3]   *Other clothing* (haberdashery, millinery, aprons, smocks, bibs, belts, gloves and mittens other than rubber; handkerchiefs, except paper handkerchiefs; muffs, sleeve protectors, bathing suits, crash helmets, suspenders; accessories for making clothing such as buckles, buttons, fasteners, patterns, zippers, etc.)

02.160[3]   *Rental of clothing, repairs to clothing other than footwear*[1]

02.200   *Footwear including repairs*

02.210[4]   *Footwear* (includes rubbers, sport shoes [other than boots and shoes with ice or roller skates attached, gaiters, spats, leggings, puttees])

02.211   Men's (16 years and over)

02.212   Women's (16 years and over)

02.213   Children's (15 years and under)

02.220[4]   *Repairs to footwear* (including shoe cleaning)

03.000   *Gross rent, fuel and power*

03.100   *Gross rents*

03.110   *Gross rents* (excluding indoor repair and upkeep.[ac] All gross rent in respect of dwellings, actual and imputed in the case of owner-occupied houses, including ground rents and taxes on the property. In general, house rent will be space rent, covering heating and plumbing facilities, lighting fixtures, fixed stoves, wash basins, and similar equipment that customarily is installed in the house before selling or letting. Also included are payments for garbage and sewage disposal. Rents paid for rooms in boardinghouses, but not in hotels, are included. Rents of secondary dwellings such as summer cottages, mountain chalets, etc., also are included.)

03.120   *Expenditures of occupants of dwelling units on indoor repair and upkeep* (indoor painting, wallpaper, decorating, etc.)[m]

03.200   *Fuel and power*

03.210   *Electricity*

03.220   *Gas* (natural and manufactured gas, including liquefied, petroleum gases [butane, propane, etc.])

03.230   *Liquid fuels* (heating and lighting oils)

03.240   *Other fuels, water charges, and ice* (coal, coke, briquettes, firewood, charcoal, peat, purchased heat, hot water, water charges, and ice)

04.000   *Furniture, furnishings, household equipment, and operation*[n]

04.100[5]   *Furniture, fixtures, carpets, and other floor coverings*

04.110   *Furniture and fixtures* (beds, chairs, tables, sofas, storage units, and hallboys; cribs, high chairs, playpens; door and dividing screens; sculptures, carvings, figurines, paintings, drawings, engravings, and other art objects; venetian blinds; fireplace equipment; other furniture and fixtures)

04.120   *Floor coverings* (carpets, large mats, and linoleum; other floor coverings)

04.200[5]   *Household textiles and other furnishings* (curtains, sheets, tablecloths and napkins, towels, tapestries, bedding mattress, and other coverings, of all materials; furnishings such as ashtrays, candlesticks, and mirrors; awnings, counterpanes, and doormats; flags; garden umbrellas; garment and shoe bags, laundry hampers and bags, and shoe racks; mosquito nets; steamer and traveling rugs; wastepaper baskets and flower and plant boxes and pots)

04.300[5]   *Heating and cooking appliances, refrigerators, washing machines and similar major household appliances including fitting*

04.310   *Refrigerators, freezers, and cooling appliances* (refrigerators, food freezers, ice boxes, room air conditioners, and fans)

04.320   *Washing appliances* (dishwashers, other washing appliances)

04.330   *Cooking appliances* (cooking appliances, reflector ovens, camping stoves, and similar appliances, toasters, electric coffee makers)

04.340   *Heating appliances other than cooking* (clothes drying and ironing appliances)

04.350   *Cleaning appliances* (electric floor-scrubbing, -waxing, and -polishing machines, vacuum cleaners, water-softening machines)

04.360   *Other major household appliances* (sewing and knitting machines, garden tractors, power-driven lawnmowers, nonportable safes, water pumps)

04.400[6]   *Glassware, tableware, and household utensils* (pottery, glassware, cutlery, silverware; hand kitchen and garden tools (not power driven); all types of kitchen utensils; portable toilet and sanitary utensils for indoor use; electric bulbs, plugs, wire, cable, and switches; heating pads, saucepans, nonelectric coffeemakers; thermos bottles and flasks; watering cans, wheelbarrows, garden hose and sprinkling devices, lawnmowers (not power driven), and other garden appliances; portable money boxes and strong boxes; household scales; ladders; locksmith's wares)

04.500   *Household operation*

04.510[6]   *Nondurable household goods* (paper products, cleaning supplies [household soap, scourers, polishes, cleaning materials, shoe polish,

---

[4]In the summary binary tables, these categories are combined as Footwear.

[5]In the summary binary tables, these categories are combined as Household Furniture and Appliances.

[6]In the summary binary tables, these categories are combined as Household Supplies and Operations.

mops, brooms and brushes, dyes for dyeing clothing and household textile furnishing; washers, insecticides, fungicides, and disinfectants] others [matches, candles, lamp wicks, clothes hangers, clothespins, rope, string and twine, nails, nuts and bolts, screws, tacks, hooks, knobs, needles, pins, aluminum foil, and so on])

04.520[6] *Domestic services* (total compensation, including payments in kind to domestic servants, cleaners, etc.; includes payments in cash and in kind to babysitters, chauffeurs, gardeners, governesses, tutors, etc.)

04.530[6] *Household services other than domestic* (includes cleaning, dyeing and laundering; hire of furniture, furnishings and household equipment, including payments by subtenants for the use of furniture, etc.; service charge for insurance of household property against fire, theft, and other eventualities; payments for services such as chimney cleaning, window cleaning, snow removal, exterminating, disinfecting and fumigating, etc.)

04.600[6] *Repair to furniture, furnishings, and household equipment* (repairs to all items in categories 04.100 through 04.500)

05.000 *Medical care and health expenses*[aa]

05.100[7] *Medical and pharmaceutical products* (includes medical and pharmaceutical products, whether directly purchased by consumers or by hospitals and independent practitioners, etc., for use in the care of patients)

05.110 *Drugs and medical preparations* (medicines, vitamins and vitamin preparations, cod and halibut liver oil)

05.120 *Medical supplies* (clinical thermometers, hot-water bottles and ice bags; bandage materials, first aid kits, elastic medical hosiery, and similar goods)

05.200[7] *Therapeutic appliances and equipment* (major appliances and equipment, whether directly purchased by consumers or by hospitals and independent practitioners, etc., for use in the care of patients: eyeglasses; hearing aids; glass eyes, artificial limbs, orthopedic braces and supports; surgical belts, trusses and supports; medical massage equipment and health lamps; wheelchairs and invalid carriages, motorized or not)

05.300[7] *Services of physicians, dentists, and nurses and related professional and semi-professional personnel* (compensation of employed persons and net income of independent practitioners for services performed, both in and out of the hospital)

05.310 *Physicians*

05.320 *Dentists*

05.330 *Nurses, physiotherapists, technicians, midwives, etc.*

05.400[7] *Current expenditures of hospitals, laboratories, clinics and medical offices, n.e.c.* (expenditures other than those covered in 05.100, 05.200, and 05.300; includes professional expenses of independent practitioners: expenditures related to physical facilities; personnel other than medical and related practitioners; service charges on accident and health insurance)

06.000 *Transport and Communication*

06.100 *Personal transport equipment*

06.110 *Passenger cars*

06.120 *Other*

06.200 *Operation of personal transport equipment*

06.210 *Tires, tubes, other parts and accessories*

06.220 *Repair charges*

06.230 *Gasoline, oils, and greases*

06.240 *Other expenditures* (parking and garaging; bridge, tunnel, ferry, and road tolls; driving lessons; hire of personal transport equipment, service charges on insurance of personal transport equipment)

06.300 *Purchased transport services*

06.310[8] *Local transport* (fares on trains, buses, and cabs; includes: service charges for special transport accident insurance)

06.320[8] *Long-distance transport* (fares on transport; fees for transporting personal transportation equipment, for baggage transfer; storage and excess charges; tips to porters; service charges for baggage)

06.321 Rail

06.322 Bus

06.323 Air

06.330[8] *Miscellaneous transport* (household moving and water transport)

06.440 *Communication*

06.410 *Postal*

06.420 *Telephone and telegraph*

07.000 *Recreation, entertainment, education, and cultural services*

07.100[9] *Equipment and accessories, including repairs*[o]

07.110 *Radio, television sets, and phonographs* (radio, television sets, phonographs, tape recorders, radio transmitting and receiving sets for amateur radio stations, clock radios)

07.120 *Major durables for recreational, entertainment, and cultural purposes* (airplanes; boats and outboard motors; cameras, projection equipment, other photographic equipment, binoculars; microscopes and telescopes; pianos, organs, violins, cornets, and other major musical instruments; typewriters; power-driven equipment for woodworking, metalworking, etc.; horses; swimming pools that are not permanent fixtures)

07.130 *Other recreational equipment and goods* (semidurable and nondurable goods; harmonicas

---

[7] In the summary binary tables, these categories are combined as Medical Care.

[8] In the summary binary tables, these categories are combined as Purchased Transport.

[9] In the summary binary tables, these categories are combined as Recreation.

and other minor musical instruments; records; flowers; all sports equipment and supplies except sports clothing and footwear; camping equipment; films and other photographic supplies; used postage stamps for philatelic purposes; children's outdoor play equipment; pets other than horses; feeding stuffs for pets; exercising equipment)

07.200[9] *Entertainment, religious, recreational, and cultural services* (excluding hotels, restaurants, and cafes)[ad]

07.210 *Public entertainment* (private and public expenditure on places of public amusement and recreation, including theaters, cinemas, sports, museums, art galleries, historical monuments, botanical and zoological gardens, parks, ski facilities, and the like)

07.220 *Other recreational and cultural activities* (expenditure on private entertainment such as hiring musicians, clowns, etc., for private parties; bridge, dancing, and sports lessons; gambling; portrait and other services such as film developing and print processing furnished by photographers; hire of radio and television sets, airplanes, boats, horses, and other recreational equipment; veterinary and other services for pets; radio and television licenses where government broadcasting stations exist; religious activities)

07.300[9] *Books, newspapers, magazines, and stationery*[p]

07.310 *Books, newspapers, magazines, and other printed matter*

07.320 *Stationery supplies* (ink, paper clips, pens, pencils; typewriter carbon and stencil paper; pencil sharpeners, paper punches, hand stamps and seals; typewriter ribbons; slide rules, drawing sets, and similar instruments)

07.400[10] *Education*[ab]

07.410 *Compensation of employees* (total expenditure for personnel, whether paid by governments or institutions or directly by households)

07.411 Teachers for primary and secondary school, and administrative personnel with teaching qualifications such as principals and deans should be classified with teachers)

07.412 Teachers for colleges and universities.

07.420[10] *Expenditures of educational institutions related to physical facilities*

07.430[10] *Other expenditures of educational institutions*

07.431 Books, stationery, and related supplies

07.432 Other

08.000 *Other goods and services*[e]

08.100[11] *Services of barber and beauty shops, baths, massage parlors, etc.*

08.200[11] *Goods for personal care*[q]

08.210 *Toilet articles and preparations* (including shaving equipment; electric hair driers and hair clippers, electric or not; permanent wave sets for home use; tooth and toilet brushes)

08.220 *Personal effects* (jewelry, watches, rings, and precious stones; travel goods, handbags, and similar goods; umbrellas, walking sticks and canes; pipes, lighters, tobacco pouches; pocket knives, sunglasses; clocks; baby carriages)

08.300 *Expenditures in restaurants, cafes, and hotels*

08.310 *Restaurants and cafes*

08.320 *Hotels and similar lodging places*

08.500[12] *Financial and other services n.e.s.*[r] (service charges for life insurance and for insurance against civil responsibility for injuries to other persons or other persons' property not arising from the operation of personal transport equipment; actual charges for bank services; fees and service charges for brokerage, investment counseling, household finance company loans and services of similar financial institutions; charges for money orders and other financial services provided by the post office; fees to tax consultants; administrative charges of private pension schemes. Fees for legal services and to employment agencies; dealers' margins on purchases from pawnbrokers; duplicating, blueprinting, photostating, addressing, mailing, and stenographic services; payments for copies of birth, death, and marriage certificates; charges for newspaper notices and advertisements; fees to house agents, etc. Welfare services.[ae])

08.900[13] *Net Expenditures of Residents Abroad*

1 *Gross Capital Formation*

Construction (10.000 through 13.000)

10.000 *Residential buildings* (Completed buildings consisting wholly or primarily of dwellings, excluding the value of the land before improvement, if this can be separately estimated; major alterations and improvements in residential buildings; and transfer and similar costs in respect of purchase of existing residential buildings. Includes the cost of external and internal painting of new buildings and of all permanent fixtures such as furnaces, fixed stoves, and central-heating, air-conditioning, and water-supply installations, as well as all equipment customarily installed before dwellings are occupied. Hotels, motels, and similar buildings operated on a purely transient basis are considered as nonresidential.)

10.100 *One- and two-dwelling buildings* (detached, twin, and row houses, including prefabricated units)

10.200 *Multidwelling buildings* (apartment buildings with three or more units)

11.000 *Nonresidential buildings* (Completed buildings and structures wholly or primarily for industrial or commercial use; major alterations and improvements in nonresidential buildings; and transfer and similar costs in respect of purchase of existing nonresidential buildings.

---

[10] In the summary binary tables, these categories are combined as Education.

[11] In the summary binary tables, these categories appear as Personal Care.

[12] In the summary binary tables, these categories appear as Miscellaneous Services.

[13] In the detailed multilateral tables, this category appears as Miscellaneous Services. In the summary binary tables, it is included in total consumption only.

Includes the construction of factories, warehouses, office buildings, stores, restaurants, hotels, farm buildings such as stables and barns, and buildings for religious, educational, recreational, and similar purposes; and the fixtures and nonmovable equipment that are an integral part of these structures.)

11.100 *Hotels and other nonhousekeeping units* (including dormitories)

11.200 *Industrial buildings* (factories, mines, and special buildings for utility industries such as power, communications, and transportation)

11.300 *Commercial buildings* (stores, banks, warehouses, and garages)

11.400 *Office buildings*

11.500 *Educational buildings* (including day nurseries, laboratories, libraries, and museums)

11.600 *Hospital and institutional buildings*

11.700 *Agricultural buildings* (barns and storage facilities)

11.800 *Other buildings* (including buildings for cultural, religious, sports, and social purposes)

12.000 *Other construction* (Completed new construction and major alterations and renewals of nonmilitary projects such as the permanent ways of railroads; roads, streets, sewers; bridges, viaducts, subways, and tunnels; harbors, piers, and other harbor facilities; car-parking facilities; airports; pipelines, oil wells, and mineshafts; canals and waterways; water-power projects, dams and dikes that are not part of irrigation and flood-control projects; aqueducts; drainage and sanitation projects; athletic fields; electric-transmission lines, gas mains and pipes, telephone and telegraph lines, etc. Includes the cost of raising the surface of future building sites, leveling the sites, and laying out the necessary streets and sewers, but excludes groundwork within the building line, when a start is made on the actual construction, which should be included in residential or nonresidential buildings, as the case may be. Includes as well transfer and similar costs in respect of purchase of existing assets of this type.)

12.100 *Roads, streets, and highways* (including road bridges and tunnels)

12.200 *Transport (other than road) and utility lines* (railroad ways; lines for telephone and power; pipes for gas, water, and sewer systems; airplane runways; canals; harbor facilities)

12.300 *Other construction* (including dams for power; petroleum and gas well drilling and exploration)

13.000[14] *Land improvement and plantation and orchard developments*[s] (All land reclamation and land clearance, irrespective of whether it represents an addition to total land availability or not; irrigation and flood-control projects and dams and dikes that are part of these projects; forest clearance and afforestation; and transfer costs in connection with transactions in land, mineral and concessions, forests, fishing and concessions, and the like. Includes also planting and cultivation, until they yield products, of new orchards, rubber planta-

tions, and other new holdings of fruit-bearing and sap-bearing plants that require more than a year to become productive.)

Producers' Durables[t] (14.000 through 17.000)

14.000 *Transport equipment* [384]

14.100[15] *Railway vehicles* [3842] (locomotives of any type or gauge, and railway and tramway cars for freight and passenger service; specialized parts for locomotive, railroad, and tramway cars [3710, 3829, 3819])

14.110 *Locomotives*

14.120 *Other*

14.200[15] *Passenger cars* [3843] (complete passenger automobiles, commercial cars, taxis; specialized passenger automobile parts [3560] and accessories such as engines, brakes, clutches, axles, gears, transmissions, wheels, and frames)

14.300[15] *Trucks, buses, and trailers* [3843] (complete buses, trucks, and truck trailers, universal carriers, special-purpose motor vehicles [ambulances, fire trucks; trailer and pickup coaches; vehicle-drawn caravans; motorized sleighs]; specialized motor-vehicle parts and accessories, except automobile [3560], such as engines, brakes, clutches, axles, gears, transmissions, wheels, and frames)

14.400[15] *Aircraft* [3845] (airplanes, gliders, aircraft, and parts such as engines, propellers, pontoons, and undercarriages; space vehicles and specialized parts [3560])

14.500[15] *Ships and boats* [3841] (ships, barges, lighters, and boats, except rubber boats, specialized marine engine and ship parts [3560]; the conversion, alteration, and breaking up of ships [6100])

14.600[15] *Other transport equipment* [3844, 3849] (motorcycles, scooters, bicycles, tricycles, pedicabs, and specialized parts such as motors, saddles, seat posts, frames, gears, and handlebars [3844]; transport equipment not elsewhere classified, such as animal-drawn wagons, carts, and sleighs, hand-drawn pushcarts, wheelbarrows, and baby carriages [3849])

15.000 *Nonelectrical machinery and equipment* [382]

15.100[16] *Engines and turbines* [3821] (steam and gas engines and steam, gas, and hydraulic turbines; and gas, diesel, and other internal-combustion engines. Complete steam, gas, and hydraulic turbine-generator sets are classified as electrical industrial machinery and apparatus in category 16.100. Turbines or engines for a given type of transport equipment are classified in the appropriate transport-equipment category.)

15.200[16] *Agricultural machinery* [3822] (machinery and equipment for use in the preparation and maintenance of the soil, in planting and harvesting of the crop, in preparing crops for market on the farm, or in dairy farming and livestock raising; for use in performing other farm operations and processes such

---

[14]In the summary binary tables, this category is included with Other Construction.

[15]In the summary binary tables, these categories are combined as Transport Equipment.

[16]In the summary binary tables, these categories are combined as Non-Electrical Machinery.

as planting, seeding, fertilizing, cultivating, harvesting: for example, ploughs, harrows, stalk cutters, milking machines, farm tractors, etc.)

15.210 *Tractors*

15.220 *Other*

15.300[16] *Office machines* [3825] (office machines and equipment, such as calculating machines, adding machines, accounting machines; punch-card–system machines and equipment; digital and analog computers and associated electronic data-processing equipment and accessories; cash registers; typewriters; weighing machines except scientific apparatus for laboratories; duplicating machines except photocopying machines; etc.)

15.400[16] *Metalworking machinery* [3823] (metalworking machinery such as lathes and machines for boring, drilling, milling, grinding, shearing, and shaping; drop forges and other forging machines; rolling mills, presses, and drawing machines; extruding, melting, and nonelectrical machines; and machine tools, dies, and jigs, including accessories for metalworking machines.)

15.500[16] *Construction, mining, and oil-field machinery* [3824] (cement-making and other heavy machinery and equipment used by construction industries; oil-refining machinery and equipment and heavy machinery and equipment used by mining industries.)

15.600[16] *Special industry machinery, n.e.s.* [3824, 3823] (special industrial machinery and equipment except metalworking machinery: for example, machinery used in the food, textile, paper, printing, chemical, and woodworking industries.)

15.700[16] *General industry machinery* [3829] (machinery and equipment, except electrical machinery, not elsewhere classified, such as pumps, air and gas compressors; blowers, air conditioning and ventilating machinery; fire sprinklers; refrigerators and equipment; mechanical power-transmission equipment; lifting and hoisting machinery, cranes, elevators, moving stairways, industrial trucks, tractors, trailers, and stackers; sewing machines; small arms and accessories, heavy ordnance and artillery; industrial process furnaces and ovens. Included are general-purpose parts of machinery such as ball and roller bearings, piston rings, valves; parts and accessories on a job or order basis.)

15.800[16] *Service industry machinery* [3829] (automatic merchandising machines; washing, laundry, dry-cleaning, and pressing machines; cooking ranges and ovens; etc.)

16.000[17] *Electrical machinery and appliances* [383, 385]

16.100[17] *Electrical transmission, distribution, and industrial apparatus* [3831] (electric motors; generators and complete turbine-generator and engine-generator sets; transformers; switchgear and switchboard apparatus; rectifiers; other electrical transmission and distribution equipment; electrical industrial-control devices such as motor starters and controllers, electronic timing and positioning devices, electromagnetic clutches and brakes; electrical welding apparatus; etc.)

16.200[17] *Communications equipment* [3832] (radio and television receiving sets, sound reproducing and recording equipment, including public address systems, phonographs, dictating machines, and tape recorders; phonograph records and prerecorded magnetic tapes; wire and wireless telephone and telegraph equipment; radio and television transmitting, signalling, and detection equipment and apparatus; radar equipment and installations; parts and supplies specifically classified in this group; semiconductor and related sensitive semiconductor devices; fixed and variable electronic capacitors and condensers; radiographic, fluoroscopic, and other X-ray apparatus and tubes)

16.300[17] *Other electrical equipment* [3839] (other electrical apparatus, accessories, and supplies not elsewhere classified, such as insulated wires and cables; storage and primary batteries, wet and dry; electric lamps and tubes; fixtures and lamp sockets and receptacles; snap switches, conductor connectors, and other current-carrying wiring devices; conduits and fittings; electrical insulators and insulation materials, except porcelain and glass insulators)

16.400[17] *Instruments* [3851, 3852, 3853] (laboratory and scientific instruments and measuring and controlling equipment not elsewhere classified; cyclatrons, betatrons, and other accelerators; surgical, medical, and dental equipment, instruments and supplies and orthopedic and prosthetic appliances [3851]; optical instruments and lenses, ophthalmic goods, photographic and photocopying equipment and supplies. Included are optical instruments for scientific and medical use [3852]; clocks and watches of all kinds; clock and watch parts and cases; and mechanisms for timing devices [3853].)

17.000 *Other durable furnishings and equipment*

17.100[18] *Furnitures and fixtures* [3320, 3812, 3851, 3901, 3902, 3909] (equipment, furnishings and furniture used by businesses, governments, offices, hotels, boardinghouses, restaurants, hospitals, research institutions, schools, and other services)

17.200[18] *Miscellaneous durable goods* [3813, 3819, 3811] (all durable goods, n.e.s., such as containers, tanks, and nonelectrical hand tools)

18.000 *Increase in stocks*

18.100[19] *Commodity stocks* (increase in value of materials and supplies, work in progress, and finished products and goods in the possession of industries; excludes standing timber and crops, but includes logs and harvested crops; excludes partially completed construction works.)

18.200[19] *Livestock, including breeding stock, dairy cattle and the like*[k] (livestock raised for slaughter; all chicken and other fowl; value of additions to, less disposals of, breeding stocks, draught animals, dairy cattle, sheep, llamas, etc., raised for wool clipping)

---

[18]In the summary binary tables, these categories are combined as Other Durable Equipment.

[19]In the summary binary tables, these categories are included in Capital Formation.

[17]In the summary binary tables, these categories are combined as Electrical Machinery.

19.000[19] *Exports less imports of goods and services* (merchandise exports, f.o.b. [free-on-board] and imports, c.i.f. [cost, insurance, and freight] include all transactions [sales and purchases] between the residents of a country and the rest of the world in commodities; include new and used ships and aircraft, though they may not cross the customs frontier of the country, and also electricity, gas, and water. Exclude such items as goods in direct transit through the country, goods not owned by residents for purposes of storage and transshipment only, tourists' and travelers' effects, and goods for exhibition or study, samples that are returnable or of no commercial value, returnable containers and animals for racing or breeding. Data are net of the value of returned goods and in-transit losses. Include freight, passenger, and other transport and communication services; insurance services.)

2   *Public Final Consumption Expenditure (PFC)*[u]

20.000   *Compensation of employees*

  20.100[20]   *Compensation of employees having first level of education*[v]

  20.200[20]   *Compensation of employees having second level of education*[v]

    20.210   *Compensation of "blue-collar" employees*[w]

    20.220   *Compensation of "white-collar" employees*[x]

  20.300[20]   *Compensation of employees having third level of education*[v]

21.000   *Expenditure on commodities*

[a]CEP (Final consumption expenditure of the Population) is identical with "Household Final Consumption Expenditure" as defined by the SNA except for the following points:

  [aa]CEP *includes* certain expenditures on medical and other health services not included in Household Final Consumption Expenditure by the SNA. The expenditures to be included are defined in terms of SNA Tables 5.3 and 5.4 (SNA, pp. 87–89), as follows:

    [aaa]CEP *includes* government expenditures on Hospitals and clinics and Individual health services (items 4.2 and 4.3 in the SNA classification of the purposes of government—SNA Table 5.3). All expenditures of government on these items, which according to the SNA would be recorded as parts of "Government Final Consumption Expenditure," should be included in CEP.

    [aab]CEP *includes* expenditures of nonprofit bodies serving households—SNA Table 5.4. All expenditures of such nonprofit bodies on these items, which according to the SNA would be recorded as parts of "Final Consumption Expenditure of Nonprofit Institutions Serving Households," should be included in CEP.

  [ab]CEP *includes* certain expenditures on schools and other educational facilities not included in Household Final Consumption Expenditure by the SNA. The expenditures to be included are defined in terms of SNA Tables 5.3 and 5.4, as follows:

    [aba]CEP *includes* government expenditures on Schools, universities and other educational facilities and Subsidiary services (items 3.2 and 3.3 in SNA Table 5.3). The inclusion applies to all expenditures of government on these items, which according to the SNA would be recorded as parts of "Government Final Consumption Expenditure."

[20]In the summary binary tables, these categories are combined as Compensation of Government Employees.

    [abb]CEP *includes* expenditures of private nonprofit bodies on education (item 2 in SNA Table 5.4). The inclusion affects all expenditures of nonprofit bodies on this item, which according to the SNA would be recorded as parts of "Final Consumption Expenditure of Nonprofit Institutions Serving Households."

  [ac]CEP *includes* current expenditures of government for provision, assistance, or support of housing (for example, government expenditures to meet current costs of dwellings). Insofar as such expenditures of government constitute part of the compensation of employees in the government sector as income in kind, they are already included in household consumption expenditure (and therefore in CEP); and hence the inclusion of this item does not require additional rearrangement between household and government expenditures. However, government expenditure for provision, assistance, or support of housing *other* than that included in the compensation of employees of the government sector should be *included* in CEP and excluded from public final consumption expenditure.

  [ad]CEP *includes* certain expenditures on recreational and related cultural services not included in household final consumption expenditure by the SNA. The expenditures to be *included* are the following:

    [ada]Expenditures on recreational and related cultural services and religion and services n.e.c. (items 7.1 and 7.2 in SNA Table 5.3), treated as part of Final Government Consumption Expenditure in the SNA.

    [adb]Expenditures on recreational and related cultural services and religious organizations (items 5 and 6 in SNA Table 5.4), treated as part of Final Consumption Expenditure of Nonprofit Institutions Serving Households in the SNA.

  [ae]CEP *includes* expenditures on welfare services by government and by nonprofit institutions serving households. The expenditures to be *included* are those described in item 5.2 of SNA Table 5.3 and item 4 of SNA Table 5.4.

[b]Includes government expenditures for housing, as described in note ([ac]), above.

[c]Includes certain expenditures of government and of nonprofit institutions serving households; see note ([aa]), above.

[d]Includes certain expenditures of government and of private nonprofit bodies on educational, recreational and cultural services; see notes ([ab]) and ([ad]), above.

[e]Includes expenditures of government and of nonprofit institutions serving households on welfare services; see note ([ae]), above.

[f]"Gross Capital Formation" is identical with "Gross Capital Formation" as defined by the United Nations *System of National Accounts* (1968) except that it includes Exports Less Imports of Goods and Services.

[g]For the definition of the scope of this category, see item 1 in Table 6.3 of the SNA (p. 114).

[h]For the definition of the scope of this category, see item 2 in Table 6.3 of the SNA (p. 114).

[i]For the definition of the scope of this category, see item 3 in Table 6.3 of the SNA (p. 114).

[j]For the definition of the scope of this category, see item 4 in Table 6.3 of the SNA (p. 114).

[k]Includes breeding stocks, draught animals, dairy cattle, and the like, though these are in the SNA as part of Gross Fixed Capital Formation rather than as stocks.

[l]In the SNA, custom tailoring and hire of clothing are included in the category "clothing other than footwear."

[m]Expenditures on indoor repair and upkeep are included in gross rents in the SNA.

[n]In the SNA, each subcategory of "Furniture, Furnishings, Household Equipment and Operation" includes a separate item for repair. The present classification combines all repairs within category 04. into a single subcategory.

[o]In the SNA, repairs are treated as a separate category rather than being added to each breakdown.

[p]Stationery is placed with miscellaneous goods in the SNA.

[q]Includes SNA categories "goods for personal care," "jewelry, watches, rings and precious stones," and "other personal goods."

[r]Membership dues in professional associations, included in this category by the SNA, here are classified with Government. Also, the SNA separates financial services from other services, and both of them are included here.

[s]SNA separates "land improvement" and "plantation, orchard, and vineyard development."

[t]Bracketed numbers following categories refer to codes of the *International Standard Industrial Classification*, United Nations (1968). Descriptions, taken over with little or no modification, include some consumers durables that should be excluded, insofar as they are purchased by the consumer. The ISIC codes are used solely to indicate the types of products included in each ICP category. Products used for current repairs rather than for additions or replacements to the stock of capital are excluded, in accordance with the rules of the SNA (see SNA paragraph 6:23).

[u]"Public Final Consumption Expenditure" (PFC) is identical with "Government Final Consumption Expenditure," as defined by the SNA, except for the following points:

[ua]PFC *includes*, in addition to the expenditures of government (that is, central government, state and local government, social security agencies, and the like) certain expenditures of private nonprofit institutions serving households. The purposes for which expenditures are included are:

[uaa]Research and scientific institutes (item 1 in SNA Table 5.4)

[uab]Professional, labor, and civic organizations (item 7 in SNA Table 5.4)

[ub]PFC *excludes* some expenditure classified as government final expenditure in the SNA. The excluded categories are:

[uba]PFC *excludes* expenditures for provision, assistance or support of housing (for example, government expenditures to meet current costs of dwellings) unless they are part of the compensation of employees in governments.

[ubb]Hospitals and clinics and individual health services (items 4.2 and 4.3 in the classification of the purposes of government, SNA Table 5.3). All expenditures of government on these items, which according to the SNA would be recorded as parts of "Government Final Consumption Expenditure," should be included in the final consumption expenditure of the population (CEP).

[ubc]PFC *excludes* expenditures on recreation and related cultural services and religion and services n.e.c. (items 7.1 and 7.2 in SNA Table 5.3). All expenditures of government on these items, which according to the SNA would be recorded as parts of "Government Final Consumption Expenditure," should be included in CEP.

[ubd]Schools, universities, and other educational facilities and subsidiary services (items 3.2 and 3.3 in SNA Table 5.3). All expenditures of government on these items, which according to the SNA would be recorded as parts of "Government Final Consumption Expenditures," should be included in CEP.

[ube]PFC *excludes* expenditures on welfare services (item 5.2 in SNA Table 5.3). All expenditures of government on this item, which according to the SNA would be recorded as parts of "Government Final Consumption Expenditures," should be included in CEP.

[v]The general definitions of the first, second, and third levels of education—as suggested by UNESCO—are as follows:

[va]The first level of education consists of schools such as elementary and primary schools "whose main function is to provide basic instruction in tools of learning."

[vb]The second level of education consists of schools such as middle, secondary, high, and vocational schools "which provide general or specialized instruction, or both, based upon at least four years previous instruction at the first level."

[vc]The third level of education consists of schools such as universities and higher professional schools, "which require, as a minimum condition of admission, completion of ten or more years of previous instruction at the first and second level or equivalent."

For the purposes of the present reporting, the three educational levels should be approximated in the following way: (1) first level, 7 to 9 years of completed education or less; (2) third level, more than 12 years of completed education; and (3) second level, years of completed education above the first and under the third level. In case of lack of adequate data, the educational qualifications usually required for a given grade in government employment should be used for subdividing government employment (and the related PFC expenditures) according to the categories requested.

[w]Government employees at the second level of education whose occupations fall within the following ISCO (*International Standard Classification of Occupations*, ILO, 1968) major groups can be considered as "blue-collar" employees:

Major group no.	*Title*
7/8/9	Production and related workers, transport equipment operators, and laborers
5	Service workers
6	Agricultural, animal husbandry, and forestry workers, fishermen and hunters
10	Workers not classifiable by occupation

[x]Government employees at the second level of education whose occupations fall within the following ISCO major groups can be considered as "white-collar" employees:

Major group no.	*Title*
3	Clerical and related workers
2	Administrative and managerial workers
0/1	Professional, technical, and related workers
4	Sales workers

Chapter 4

Methods of the binary comparisons

The data described in Chapter 3 are the materials from which we constructed first binary and then multilateral comparisons of prices and quantities. In this chapter, we deal with the binary comparisons; the multilateral comparisons are described in Chapter 5. In addition, we anticipate some of the final results of the binary comparisons, which are described in Chapter 13, in order to show how alternative methods would have affected the overall measure of relative per capita GDP.

Three kinds of data were available for each of the ten countries:

1. There were expenditures in domestic currencies for approximately 150 detailed categories. There were some empty boxes—that is, zeros—but for the most part, data were provided for each category by each of the ten countries. Expenditures for the categories added up to GDP.
2. For each category, there was a sample of prices that in almost all cases provided at least one price ratio with the United States and sometimes as many as a dozen or more. The items for which prices were compared with the United States, however, were not always the same items for all countries.
3. For categories that lent themselves to direct comparisons, there were quantity data measured in physical units.

We start with a set of binary comparisons in which each of the other nine countries is compared with the United States as the base country. At a second stage, we present comparisons between other pairs of countries.

A. The Desired Properties

The methods chosen for the binary comparisons should be judged on the basis of several considerations: characteristicity, the country-reversal test, and the factor-reversal test.

- *Characteristicity.*[1] Each binary comparison should be optimal for that pair of countries. This requires that the comparison between each pair should be based on the best sample of representative items that can be obtained for that pair so that the prices will be most directly comparable, and that the weights used in the comparison be based solely on spending patterns of the countries. In a quantity comparison, for example, the relative evaluation of different goods or services used in aggregating the quantities (that is, the price weights) should be as close as possible to the relative evaluations in the individual countries.
- *Country-reversal test.* In addition, a set of consistency conditions should be satisfied. One type of desired consistency is that, in a given binary comparison, it should not matter which country is used as the denominator country. Adapting the language of index number theory, the "country-reversal" test should be satisfied:[2] that is, if $I_{j/k}$ represents the price or quantity index for two countries, j and k, with the base country in the denominator, then $I_{j/k} \cdot I_{k/j}$ should equal 1. (It is assumed, of course, that each index is computed independently.)
- *Factor-reversal test.* Another consistency requirement is that the product of the price and quantity comparisons should equal the expenditure ratio: that is, the factor-reversal test should be satisfied. In a trivial sense, this test is satisfied whenever a direct price (quantity) index is joined to an indirect quantity (price) index, because the latter is obtained by dividing the former into the expenditure ratio. For the test

[1]The term was suggested by L. Drechsler in a thoughtful paper dealing with the desired properties of international comparisons, among other things. See his "Weighting of Index Numbers in Multilateral International Comparisons," *Review of Income and Wealth* (March 1973), pp. 17–34.

[2]This is the time-reversal test as modified to allow for country comparisons rather than temporal ones. I. Fisher, *The Making of Index Numbers* (Boston: Houghton Mifflin, 1922), Chap. 13.

to be satisfied meaningfully, both the price and quantity indexes must be computed independently.

Each of these criteria has much to commend it. The first hardly needs further comment. The consistency criteria are important because it is highly desirable to produce, if possible, a single set of unambiguous estimates. In many applications, the utility of the results would be greatly diminished if, for example, it were necessary to provide two estimates of the comparison between the countries depending upon which was taken as the denominator country in the ratio between them.

B. Averaging within Detailed Categories

The first step in making the binary comparisons was to aggregate the data within each detailed category. Because the expenditures were not available below the detailed category level, the first aggregation task consisted of averaging the price relatives or occasionally the quantity ratios relating to different specifications.

The basic method of averaging when more than one price ratio was available for a detailed category was to use a simple, or unweighted, geometric mean of the price relatives. That is, for category i,

$$\left(\frac{\rho_j}{\rho_n}\right)_i = \left[\prod_{\alpha=1}^{A} \left(\frac{\rho_{\alpha j}}{\rho_{\alpha n}}\right)\right]^{1/A},$$

where (ρ_j/ρ_n) is the average relative price or purchasing power parity (PPP) of the jth country relative to the nth country, $\rho_{\alpha j}$ is the price of the αth item in the jth country (stated in the jth country's currency), $\rho_{\alpha n}$ is the price of the αth good in the numeraire country (which in the present study is the United States, the last country alphabetically among the ten), and A is the number of items within the category priced in both the jth and n^{th} countries.

A geometric mean was preferred to an arithmetic one because the former meets the country-reversal test, whereas the latter does not. The use of a simple rather than a weighted geometric mean represents a departure from widespread practice and, therefore, merits careful consideration. Most of the rest of this section is given over to this question.

The use of a simple mean, or "equal weighting," could be justified easily if the within-category dispersion of price ratios were small. In that case, the results of weighted and simple averages of price relatives would not be different. It would be pleasant to be able to report that this was the case in the binary comparisons presented in this volume. In truth, however, it was not uncommon to find, for different specifications within a detailed category, that the highest price ratio was two or three times the lowest one.

A simple average can distort the comparison in cases in which two or more specifications are of significantly different importance in the expenditures of the countries being compared. This is particularly true if one item is quite inexpensive relative to another in one country, and the opposite price relationship exists in the other partner country.

Nevertheless, chief reliance was placed on unweighted averages rather than on "item-weighted" averages, in which expenditure weights are assigned to the price relative for each item for which prices are compared within the category. The compelling reason for this procedure was that the data required for weighting usually were lacking. In some categories, greater effort might have uncovered the required data; in others, not.

Note that item weighting requires a knowledge of the final expenditures on each specific item, not just on each detailed commodity category. It calls, for example, for expenditure data on dresses, skirts, jackets, blouses, sweaters, and so forth, rather than merely for women's outer clothing. Data in this degree of detail simply are not available in many countries. In most developing countries, the estimate of final expenditure by households is derived as a residual from gross domestic product after public consumption expenditures (government) and capital formation are estimated directly. Because they do not build up the consumption total from data on individual categories, it is already a major task in these countries to estimate final expenditures for the more than 100 categories of consumption expenditures used in the ICP; data rarely are provided by the countries in this fine detail. Even where the underlying data are available, they usually are not processed and published in a way that matches the national accounts concepts. The United States, for example, publishes personal consumption expenditures subclassified in about 75 categories. One of the more important aggregates, "clothing and accessories, other than footwear," is broken down into three categories: women's and children's, men's and boys', and standard clothing issued to military personnel. The corresponding category in the ICP is subdivided into eight detailed categories.

Basically two kinds of source information exist for the detailed breakdown of consumption expenditures. One consists of household expenditures surveys, which vary considerably in the degree of detail in which they report expenditures. Rarely do they go down to the level of the individual item. "Women's outer clothing," for example, is more frequently to be found than its individual components, "dresses," "skirts," "coats," or the like. The other basic source of information consists of statistics of production, shipments, or sales obtained from surveys or censuses of manufacturers. These materials usually have more product detail than do the family expenditure surveys, but too often they stop short of the item level. Even where they do provide information about individual items, further knowledge is required to estimate consumption expenditures. Exports must be subtracted from and imports added to domestic manufacturing production; and shipments or sales intended for direct household use must be separated from those going for intermediate products. For example, to assign an expenditure weight to zippers, an item priced for the ICP in a number of countries as part of the "other clothing" category (ICP 02.150),[3] one would have to know the total domestic absorption (production plus imports minus exports), the division of the domestic absorption of zippers between households, on the one hand, and industry (for dresses and the like), on the other hand, as well as the trade and transport margins. Of course, such estimates of final consumption expenditures reflecting these considerations often are made for national accounts and input–output purposes, but rarely at such a detailed commodity level.

If all the necessary information were available, item-weighted averages undoubtedly would be preferable to unweighted ones in producing binary comparisons. In the real world, however, some of the requisite data will not be available, and it will be necessary to introduce into the weighting scheme arbitrary elements that reduce the advantages of item weighting. The reason is that, even if we could get the necessary expenditure data in sufficient detail, not all of the major items in a category are priced, and the problem arises of imputing the weights of the omitted items to those which are included. In the women's outerwear category, for example, the Japan–United States comparison is based upon a cotton blouse, a skirt, a street dress, and a raincoat. These items account for about one-half of the U.S. outerwear expenditures total for women and girls 18 and over, with dresses alone making up 36 percent.[4] In the method used in the ICP, the weights for the missing items—consisting chiefly of coats, suits, slacks, and sweaters—are assigned equally to the four included items. Weighting, in its ideal form, would assign the weights for the missing items to the included items on the basis of similar price relationships. But we do not know what these similarities are: we do not know, for example, whether the Japan–U.S. price ratio for sweaters is more like the one for a dress than like the ones for a skirt or blouse or raincoat. Under item weighting, in this illustration we would assign over 70 percent

of the weights for sweaters and the other missing items to the Japan-U.S. price relative for dresses. It is not at all clear that this is superior to the strategy of assuming that the price relatives we have—four, in this case—represent a random sample of all of those in the category, in which case our procedure of equal weighting may be used.

An intermediate solution would allow each item to receive its own weight plus an equal share of the weight of the excluded items.[5] Considering the impossibility of getting expenditure data in some cases and the added labor involved where it is possible, however, we decided against any general attempt at importance weighting.

Because our rejection of item weighting is purely pragmatic and not a matter of principle, we made a serious effort to review the categories in which substantial dispersion of price ratios occurs. We looked for cases in which some systematic element appeared to be making some kinds of items within a category relatively inexpensive in one country and relatively expensive in the other. Where this seemed to be the case, we made a special effort to obtain weights despite the difficulties involved.

The result is that we have resorted to weighting in the case of the following categories in the consumption sector: (1) rents, in which international differences exist in the price ratios related to the age and facilities of dwelling units (see Chapter 9); (2) potatoes, in which category the price ratios for yams differ substantially from those for potatoes (see Chapter 6); (3) passenger cars, in which category U.S. models become progressively cheaper as size and horsepower rise (see Chapter 8); (4) local transport, in which category price relatives for buses and taxis were quite different (see Chapter 6); and (5) purchased meals, in which category price relatives for food and beverages varied widely (see Chapter 6). In some of these cases, it was possible to obtain data for weighting from all or most countries, although even in these instances it cannot be claimed that weights could be assigned in a manner free from arbitrary judgment. In other cases, we used similar weights for all countries based on information available for a few countries. Some illustrations of the difference in results between item weighting and equal weighting are given for EEC countries in the next section.

The methods outlined up to this point were used in the case of most detailed categories to estimate category purchasing-power parities (PPPs), relative to the United States, for each of the nine other countries studied by

---

[3] For more detailed descriptions of these categories, as well as their contexts, refer to the Appendix to Chapter 3.

[4] U.S. Bureau of Labor Statistics, *Consumer Expenditure and Income*, BLS report 237–238, supplement 3, part B. (Washington: Government Printing Office, July 1964). According to the 1967 *Census of Manufactures*, the four items accounted for about two-thirds of manufactured shipments of women's outerwear in the United States in 1967, with street dresses alone making up nearly one-half of the total.

[5] The smaller the fraction of expenditures represented by the particular commodities for which prices are obtained, the less the advantage of the weighting. Although every effort has been made to select important expenditure items (see Chapter 3), there are some detailed categories, particularly catch-all classifications such as "other clothing" (ICP 02.150), in which the included items are apt to represent a small fraction of total expenditures.

the ICP. The PPP then was divided into the expenditure ratio to derive the quantity ratio to obtain the corresponding quantity index.

In a few cases, notably in medical care and education, direct quantity indexes also were computed on the basis of physical quantities. In a number of these, the direct quantity indexes were retained and indirect PPPs, those derived from the division of the quantity indexes into the expenditure ratios, were used in place of the direct price indexes. We did this because, for various reasons, more credence could be placed in the direct quantity index than in the direct price index. Thus, we maintained the consistency between the product of the price and quantity indexes, on the one hand, and the expenditure ratio, on the other, by adjusting one of the former, rather than the expenditure ratio.[6]

The PPPs and quantity indexes for the detailed categories are presented in Appendix Tables 13.1 to 13.14 in Chapter 13. It should be stressed that these data are worksheet data underlying our estimates for the more aggregated categories in Tables 13.1 to 13.14. The data for the detailed categories are subject to errors of observation and sampling with respect to expenditures, prices, and quantities. We cannot fully assess the magnitude of these errors, but we know them to be large in some cases.

The PPPs are subject mainly to sampling errors, but the quantity indexes, obtained by dividing the PPPs into the expenditure ratios, are subject also to some rather obvious errors in the expenditure ratios. For example, substantial differences exist among the countries in their estimates of their distribution of footwear expenditures among men, women, and children. Some of this may reflect true differences in spending patterns, but we suspect a large part arises from country-to-country differences in the allocation of the footwear total to these categories. Incomparabilities in expenditure data are likely to be particularly great for residual categories such as "other household appliances" (ICP 04.360) and "other services" (ICP 08.400), because it is unlikely that national income accountants in different countries assigned difficult-to-classify expenditures to these categories in identical ways. (The incomparabilities in the expenditure data, incidentally, lend support to our decision not to try to break down expenditures to the item level.)

The reader should understand why we make available the worksheet data of the Appendix tables of Chapter 13 when they do not meet the usual standards of publication. We do not believe that they can stand on their own as reliable estimates of price and quantity relationships. We do believe, however, that the numbers are adequate as inputs to an aggregation process. We describe and present the results of our own preferred aggregation method in the next section, but we make available the Appendix tables for the use of researchers who wish to pursue an alternative aggregation procedure.

Before describing our own methods of aggregation, it is worth pointing out two reasons why considerably more confidence can be placed in our aggregate results than in the detailed-category data. First, the aggregation of the category PPPs increases the number of price ratios averaged together to give any particular aggregate PPP estimate and thereby reduces the sampling error. Second, the errors in the expenditure ratios are negatively correlated, so consolidation of the detailed categories tends to reduce the errors in the (indirect) quantity ratio. If the German-U.S. expenditure ratio for children's shoes is too high because of an error in either country's expenditure estimate, it is likely that the expenditure ratio for one of the other footwear categories will be too low because of an offsetting error in the expenditure data. Consequently the indirect quantity ratios will be biased in opposite directions and the error in the quantity ratio for footwear as a whole will be reduced.

C. Aggregation

The averaging process within detailed categories left us with PPPs and quantity indexes for each of the nine other countries relative to the United States for each of about 150 detailed categories.

We used these materials to produce two kinds of binary comparisons. One was a straightforward comparison of each of the nine other countries with the United States. We call these "original-country comparisons" because they involve no data other than those of the two countries in the binary comparison. (A more natural term to describe these comparisons would be "direct," but we have already used this adjective to refer to price [or quantity] comparisons based on a sample of items in contrast to those "indirect" ones derived by dividing the quantity [or PPP] index into the expenditure ratio.) The other kind of binary comparisons, via "a bridge country," is discussed in the next section.

Standard index number formulas were used to compute the original-country comparisons; to obtain the PPP for GDP or other desired aggregate, weighted arithmetic means of price relatives were employed. Thus, the PPPs for the detailed categories were aggregated first using U.S. expenditure weights and then the partner country's "own" expenditure weights. The formulas for the U.S.-and own-weighted indexes are

$$\sum_{i=1}^{m} \left(\frac{\rho_j}{\rho_n}\right)_i \cdot w_{in} \quad \text{and} \quad \frac{1}{\sum_{i=1}^{m} \left(\frac{\rho_n}{\rho_j}\right)_i \cdot w_{ij}},$$

[6]See page 20.

where index i runs over the categories, n is the subscript for the United States (the numeraire country), and j is the subscript of the partner country. The weights are:

$$w_{in} = \frac{e_{in}}{\sum\limits_{i=1}^{m} e_{in}} \quad \text{and} \quad w_{ij} = \frac{e_{ij}}{\sum\limits_{i=1}^{m} e_{ij}} \quad ,$$

where e is per capita expenditure in national currency. The same formulas were used in those few cases in which weights were used within a detailed category.[7]

We also present the "ideal," or Fisher, index, the geometric mean of the own-weighted and U.S.-weighted indexes. Although this index is not easy to justify in theoretical terms, it is a widely used compromise between the index reflecting one partner's consumption pattern and the index reflecting that of the other.[8]

Despite an effort to obtain expenditures and price comparisons for each detailed category for each country, expenditures and/or prices were missing in some cases. In a few instances, the category turned out to be relatively unimportant in all or most countries, and the category was consolidated with another. A miscellaneous cereal category, for example, was merged with meal and flour of wheat, barley, and other cereals.

It was obviously undesirable, however, to merge categories wherever there was missing information. Thus, we reached the aggregation stage with some categories for which expenditure or prices were unavailable in one or a few countries. If price comparisons were missing, the PPP for some other category was selected to represent the missing information. These "imputations" have been mentioned in some of the product chapters (for example, in Chapter 10 dealing with producers' durables).

Missing expenditure data could signify either nil expenditures or simply the unavailability of an estimate. In the former case, no price comparison was available for the category. The problem then posed was how to treat the U.S. expenditure. The solution was simply to include it in the lowest level of aggregation of categories that included the zero expenditure category. For example, in the India–U.S. comparison, India reported a zero expenditure for washing appliances (ICP 04.320); the U.S. expenditure for this category was included in major household appliances (ICP 04.300) for the purpose of aggregating to obtain PPPs for furnishings and, subsequently, for total consumption. The effect of this treatment was, of course, to impute the PPPs of other major appliances, such as refrigerators (04.310), to the U.S. expenditure on washing appliances.

In other cases, the zero expenditure was thought to represent missing information rather than nil expenditures (for example, there was no separate expenditure for lard for the EEC countries). In such instances, a price comparison usually was available. No special problem arises here in using the U.S. expenditure weight to obtain the U.S.-weighted PPP. For the PPP employing the weights of the other country, the U.S. expenditure was transferred to that category which was thought to contain the expenditure of the other country on the category for which it reported a zero (U.S. lard expenditures were transferred to fresh pork in the comparisons with the EEC countries). The available price ratios, if any, also were transferred to the selected category (fresh pork in the example), and a geometric mean was calculated of all the price ratios in the newly enlarged category.

The original-country binary comparisons produced by the methods described above are summarized in Tables 13.17 to 13.22 and are shown in more detail in Tables 13.1 to 13.14.

D. Bridge-Country Binary Comparisons

The advantage of the original-country comparisons is that they represent the best comparison that can be made for each pair of countries taken alone; they have the maximal possible degree of characteristicity. One might conceive of preparing such comparisons for each pair of countries, but, as noted earlier, the number of binary pairs quickly becomes large; even for the ten countries in the first phase of the ICP, there are forty-five possible pairs. The task of obtaining prices for enough matching specifications for all possible pairs would be formidable.

Beyond the problem of numbers, original-country binary comparisons will not yield a transitive system of comparisons. Country j may be shown to have a GDP 15 percent above that of Country k and Country l only 5 percent above that of Country k, but the original-country binary comparison between Countries j and l could conceivably show j to have a smaller GDP than country l.

Such inconsistencies would be avoided if in all the binary comparisons with the United States, an identical list of items and an identical set of weights were used. The disadvantage of this approach is that such a universal list of goods would exclude many goods that were important in many individual countries. Although a way might be found to represent the total GDP of each country through the goods in the list, there would be some pairs of countries that had more goods in common than those on the universal list; for these pairs, the universal list would provide an inferior comparison to

---

[7] These formulas were used in lieu of that given on page 47. For the categories in which weights were used, see page 48.

[8] See Fisher's reasons for preferring this over near alternatives: Fisher, *The Making*, p. 221.

Table 4.1. Bridge-Country Binary Comparisons of Gross Domestic Product, 1970

	Numerator country								
Base country	Kenya	India	Colombia	Hungary	Italy	Japan	U.K.	Germany (F.R.)	France
Part A. Bridging at the level of GDP									
1. India	96.7								
2. Colombia	38.3	39.6							
3. Hungary	14.8	15.3	38.7						
4. Italy	12.3	12.8	32.2	83.3					
5. Japan	9.7	10.0	25.2	65.2	78.4				
6. United Kingdom	9.4	9.8	24.6	63.7	76.5	97.6			
7. Germany (F.R.)	8.0	8.3	20.9	54.1	64.9	82.9	84.9		
8. France	7.9	8.2	20.7	53.4	64.2	81.9	83.9	98.8	
9. (United States)†	5.9	6.1	15.4	39.8	47.8	61.0	62.5	73.6	74.5
Part B. Bridging at the detailed category level									
10. India	89.0								
11. Colombia	34.6	39.0							
12. Hungary	13.2	15.2	40.5						
13. Italy	11.9	12.4	31.7	82.2					
14. Japan	9.2	9.7	25.9	64.8	84.2				
15. United Kingdom	8.8	9.4	24.9	64.8	77.3	95.3			
16. Germany (F.R.)	7.7	8.4	20.6	51.0	64.9	79.8	83.7		
17. France	7.3	7.6	19.4	50.6	63.0	77.2	80.7	98.1	

†Line 9 is obtained from the original-country comparisons with the United States.

that which could be made on the basis of a more comprehensive list of common goods. The use of an identical set of weights also would distort the comparison between individual pairs of countries, particularly if one country's own weights were close to those used, whereas the other country's own weights deviated substantially from them. These disadvantages of a universal list may be small for relatively homogeneous groups of countries, but for any worldwide comparisons, a universal list is bound to provide too small a set of items. Furthermore, the things that are available everywhere conceivably may be important nowhere.

Another alternative is simply to ignore the possibility that an original-country comparison for j and l will produce a different answer from that derived by each country's comparison with Country k. In the context of our study, we could compute the relationship between every pair of countries simply on the basis of the nine original-country comparisons with the United States. These binary comparisons, made by way of another country, are referred to as "bridge-country" binary comparisons.

Bridge-country binary comparisons are presented in Table 4.1. The starting point, the original-country binary comparisons, are shown on line 9 for 1970. These figures represent the Fisher per capita quantity indexes, which are presented in greater detail in Chapter 13. The countries are listed from top to bottom and from left to right according to the size of the Fisher indexes on line 9. We defer a discussion of these original-country binary results to Chapter 13; our concern here is solely methodological. We draw upon them to illuminate the methods of binary comparisons between pairs of countries other

than those for which original-country comparisons have been made.

In Part A of the table, the bridging has been carried out at the level of GDP. All the numbers on lines 1 to 8 have been derived from line 9. For example, the percentage of the per capita GDP of Italy relative to that of Japan, 78.4, is calculated simply by dividing the original-country binary percentage of Italy relative to the United States, 47.8, by the corresponding figure for Japan, 61.0. The Japan–Italy GDP relationship is, of course, the reciprocal (127.5) of that for Italy–Japan.

Notice that the result of this method of bridging is to produce a unique cardinal scaling of countries with respect to their GDP. The figures in any column bear a fixed relationship to the figures in any other column, and an analogous point applies to the lines. Transitivity has been achieved, but it is a superficial kind of transitivity: the result simply of taking account only of comparisons relying upon the United States as a bridge country and of ignoring the alternative estimates that would be produced by using any other country as the bridge or by making original-country comparisons.

The United States was taken as the bridge country only because it was easier as a practical matter to start the system of comparisons on a U.S. data base. The central staff of the ICP was located in the United States; there was a wide variety of readily available price and quantity data for matching with other countries; and the official price agency in the United States was able to extend more aid in the price comparisons than were the comparable agencies of other potential base countries.

The basic objection to the bridge-country method remains, however, whatever the country selected as a bridge. The objection is that the use of any bridge country interposes its sample of goods and its price weights, neither of which is necessarily characteristic of either of the countries in a binary comparison. The comparison of Kenya and India, for example, by way of the United States or of the United Kingdom may exclude many goods the two countries have in common but that are not found in the bridge country. In addition, the bridge country's pattern of final expenditure may be particularly inappropriate for these countries.

The influence of the bridge country can be reduced but not eliminated by bridging, not as in Part A of Table 4.1 at the aggregate level, but at the level of the detailed categories.[9] For each pair of countries, the PPP is derived from each country's PPP relative to the bridge country. In the context of the ICP, where the United States is the bridge country, the $PPP_{j/k}$ for category i for countries j and k is:

$$\left(\frac{\rho_j}{\rho_k}\right)_i = \left(\frac{\rho_j}{\rho_n}\right)_i \div \left(\frac{\rho_j}{\rho_n}\right)_i ,$$

where ρ stands for prices and n for the bridge country, the United States. The PPPs thus obtained for the individual detailed categories may be aggregated first with j's weights and then with k's weights, and an ideal index finally computed. The results of such a procedure are shown in Part B of Table 4.1.

Bridging at the detailed-category level limits the influence of the bridge country to effects within detailed categories; the bridge country has no impact upon the weights used to aggregate the detailed categories. The within-category effects can be either relatively indirect, as in the case in which representative goods are included in the j/n and k/n comparisons, which are irrelevant to the j/k comparison; or more explicit, as in cases in which within-category weights are used, with the result that the bridge country's weights affect the j/k comparisons.

The use of simple means within categories further reduces the influence of the bridge country, because it obviates the need to use the bridge country's weights. The influence of the bridge country (n) still is not entirely eliminated, however, because items that are important in it play a role in the j/k, k/l, and so on comparisons, even though such items might not have been chosen for original-country comparisons between j and k, k and l, and so on.

When the results of bridging at the detailed level are compared with the results of bridging at the level of GDP, the differences for particular pairs of countries range from -7 to $+12$ percent, with large differences

[9]See E. Krzeczkowska, "On the International Comparison of Consumption Level Carried Out by the Polish Central Statistical Office," *Review of Income and Wealth* (December, 1967), pp. 353–366.

being particularly marked in comparisons involving Kenya.

Linking at the detailed category level improves the characteristicity of the comparisons, but the facade of transitivity afforded by bridging at the GDP level is lost. For example, the Italy-Japan relationship in line 14 is shown to be 84.2, whereas that inferred from the Italy-France and Japan-France relationships on line 17 is 81.6 (that is, $63.0 \div 77.2 = 81.6$).

Using the data gathered by the EEC, we were able to estimate original-country binary comparisons for the three EEC member countries. The results are presented below and compared with the results obtained by bridging by way of the United States at the detailed-category level:

	Germany (F.R.)-France	Italy-France	Italy-Germany (F.R.)
Original-country comparisons			
Numerator country weights	98.2	62.1	63.0
Denominator country weights	102.3	65.3	66.5
Ideal index	100.2	63.7	64.7
Bridge-country comparisons			
Ideal index	101.9	63.0	64.9

In these cases, the bridge-country method came close to the original-country results.

The original-country comparisons reported in the previous paragraph were carried out using ICP methods, including the computation of PPPs for most categories by unweighted geometric means. Because the EEC Statistical Office used item weighting in its work, we had the opportunity to calculate the difference between item-weighted results and the results produced by our procedure of equal weighting for the items within categories. The item weights available for consumption enabled us to examine ninety-seven ICP categories accounting for 97 or 98 percent of total consumption in the three countries. The ratios of the PPPs derived from equal weighting within categories to those derived from item weighting for total included consumption and the major subaggregates (using ideal indexes) are as follows:

Consumption	PPPs based on equal weighting as % of PPPs based on item weighting		
	Germany (F.R.)-France	Italy-France	Italy-Germany (F.R.)
Food, beverages, tobacco	100.0	102.2	102.2
Clothing & footwear	96.4	100.3	102.7
Gross rent & fuel	101.7	103.8	101.5
House furnishings & operations	100.0	102.4	101.1
Medical care	101.6	104.0	98.5
Transportation & communications	101.0	99.4	99.4
Recreation & education	104.2	106.5	100.1
Other	100.0	104.3	108.5
	101.6	102.9	105.6

The largest difference, for recreation and education in the Italy–Federal Republic of Germany comparison, was 8.5 percent. All in all, however, the two methods give similar results.

Of course, greater differences were found in the detailed categories. The distribution of the ratios is as follows:

Ratio, equal to item weighted	Germany (F.R.)-France	Italy-France	Italy-Germany (F.R.)
> 1.10	3	9	8
1.05–1.099	11	10	8
1.01–1.049	19	24	26
1.00	37	30	27
.95–.999	13	16	16
.90–.949	9	6	9
< .90	5	2	3
Total	97	97	97

In general, the overall results tend to be close, but, even though more than 70 percent of the ratios in each comparison fall within ± 5 percent of 1.00, some large deviations exist for individual categories. Some of the differ-ences in excess of 10 percent, including the largest one of 54 percent, were found in the alcoholic beverage category. This is a sector for which good weights are likely to be available in most countries, and the item-weighted results probably are better than the equal-weighted results. (In retrospect, we feel it would have been better to incorporate weights for alcoholic bever-ages.) On the other hand, big differences occurred also in categories such as women's clothing, in which case it is doubtful, for reasons given above,[10] that item weighting improves the situation.

The methods we have been considering in this chapter, those involving binary comparisons or compari-sons based on a single bridge country, cannot achieve genuine transitivity, whether item weighting is or is not used. The methods required to produce transitivity are described in Chapter 5.

[10] See page 48.

Chapter 5

Methods of the multilateral comparisons

The binary comparisons discussed in the preceding chapter suffer from the disadvantage that they are not efficient in the sense that they fail to make use of all the relevant price information available in arriving at particular comparisons, and they depend upon the choice of base, or bridge, country. From the standpoint of a comparison involving a single pair of countries, this may not matter. But when a system of international comparisons, one involving many countries at once, is the objective, the lack of efficiency and dependence upon the choice of base country are important deficiencies. This chapter discusses ways of achieving efficiency and base-country invariance and explains the procedure we prefer.

A. The Desired Properties

In some respects, the desired properties we seek in the comparisons are similar to those we wanted in the binary comparisons. Specifically, our concerns about characteristicity and the satisfying of the factor reversal test are unchanged. In other respects, however, the properties we want are altered or new ones are added when many countries are to be compared jointly rather than merely in pairs. The multilateral methods ultimately used should produce indexes which have the following properties:

- *Base-country invariance.* Symmetry with respect to the countries should be preserved so that in the final comparisons, it makes no difference which country is chosen as the base. The country selected as the base should serve as no more than a numeraire. This is a generalization of the country-reversal test.
- *Equality of treatment of countries.* Individual countries of the ICP set should be treated in such a way that a lack of representativeness of the ICP set of countries relative to the world as a whole should not unduly influence the final comparisons. This property

will be discussed in connection with the discussion of "supercountries" in Section E, below.

- *Transitivity.* Each index sought, price or quantity, should be a number on a continuous scale such that pairwise comparisons between the indexes of members of any group of countries will be transitive in the sense that $I_{j/k} = I_{j/l} \div I_{k/l}$. This property, Fisher's "circular test," is relevant only to relationships between more than two countries.
- *Additive consistency.* Quantities stated in value terms are to be estimated for each category so that (1) the values for any category will be directly comparable between countries, and (2) the values for any country will be directly comparable between categories. The latter requirement is necessary because a country's quantity at any level of aggregation is to be obtained as the sum of the quantities of all the categories comprising that aggregate. If the quantities, measured in physical units, were known for all countries and all categories, the quantity numbers would meet (1), above. Such quantity numbers would not meet (2), however, because they could not be added together meaningfully across categories for a particular country to get the country's aggregate quantity. (No special reference to "additive consistency" was necessary in the discussion of binary comparisons in Chapter 4 because the procedures used there automatically gave estimates possessing this property.)
- *Statistical efficiency.* Because the underlying data collected by the ICP are subject to sampling errors, the multilateral methods used should give quantity and price indexes that are relatively insensitive to these underlying sampling errors. (In formal statistical terms: the aggregation method should give estimates of relative quantities and prices that have minimum variance.) Statistical efficiency plays a role in binary as well as multilateral comparisons; but where the methodological choices in the binary case were limited, it did not warrant serious consideration.

In everything that follows, we will insist that our indexes possess base-country invariance and additive consistency, and that they pass the factor-reversal and circular tests. These are the properties most important for a system of comparisons that can be used readily by the scholar and man of affairs who does not wish to make a detailed study of index-number problems before using the comparisons. Characteristicity and statistical efficiency will be sought, but not at the cost of failing to satisfy the other criteria.

It should be clear that the properties are not derived explicitly from economic theory. In fact, economic theory indicates that all desirable properties cannot be possessed by any single set of indexes. Stricter requirements—for example, Slutsky conditions—would flow from the standard theory of consumer behavior, but we have chosen not to attempt to impose such requirements on our data. Economic theory in its present form provides limited guidance on aggregation procedures across individual households, business firms, and governmental units and gives virtually none across diverse geographical regions of countries at different seasons of the year.[1]

The ICP accepts as fundamental the notion that, in a basic way, prices faced by purchasers reflect preferences and, therefore, should be helpful in making commensurable different goods and services. Even if the theory did point to a specific index number formula, however, it must be remembered that the prices gathered for the ICP can give no more than a reasonable approximation of the *average* of prices faced by purchasers within a country. It would, indeed, be making a strong assumption to require in the estimation process that the country quantities be related to the country prices in as restrictive a way as the theory of consumer behavior and investment theory would imply. One of the first investigations of the ICP empirical estimates surely should focus precisely on how closely, given relative prices and GDP, countries' quantity compositions conform to what is implied by the theory of consumer behavior. Chapter 15 represents a first, quick attempt to do this.

As in the case of the binary comparisons, two stages in making multilateral comparisons may be distinguished: (1) combining item data at the detailed category level to obtain price (quantity) indexes for each category; and (2) averaging in a suitable way the price (quantity) indexes for the different categories to obtain price (quantity) indexes at various levels of aggregation.

These stages will be discussed in turn, the first in Sections B and C, below, and the second in Sections D and E. The results of applying the various methods of these sections are presented in Section F, and estimates of the precision of the results appear in Section G.

B. Estimating PPPs at the Detailed-Category Level (Frequency-Weighted CPD)

One possible way of handling the data at the detailed-category level in order to derive multilateral comparisons would be simply to use the results of the binary comparisons. The different aggregation methods described below could be applied to the binary PPPs of the detailed categories (that is, those which are set out in the Appendix tables to Chapter 13). These binary results, however, possess neither the transitivity nor base-country invariance properties and, therefore, are not ideal raw materials for multilateral comparisons. If we are to have multilateral comparisons characterized by transitivity and base-country invariance, at each stage we should use methods that produce estimates with these properties. In this section, a procedure we call the Country–Product–Dummy (CPD) method is developed: when applied at the detailed-category level, it gives us the kind of numbers we want. In the following section, we extend the use of CPD in a special way to handle some data deficiencies that remain at the category level. We postpone a discussion of the problem of aggregating the detailed category results until the fourth and fifth sections.

For now, we concentrate exclusively on the problem of estimating the country purchasing-power parities for a detailed category. The data input will be a collection of entries in the price tableau P (5.1).

	Item (α)	\multicolumn{4}{c}{Country (j)}
		1	2	$\dots$	n
	1	ρ_{11}	ρ_{12}	$\dots$	ρ_{1n}
	2	ρ_{21}	ρ_{22}	$\dots$	ρ_{2n}
(5.1) P:	$\vdots$	$\vdots$	$\vdots$	$\vdots$	$\vdots$
	A	ρ_{A1}	ρ_{A2}	$\dots$	ρ_{An}

where $\rho_{\alpha j}$, the price of the αth commodity in the jth country, is expressed in the units of the jth country's national currency. (Example: If $A = 9$ and $N = 10$, ρ_{38} represents the price of the third commodity, out of nine commodities in the category, in the eighth country of the set of ten countries; the price is stated in the currency unit of the eighth country.) For ease in dis-

---

[1] In special cases, if a person is prepared to assume a common utility function of a sufficiently simple functional form, he may be able to find the exact price or quantity index of the theory of consumer behavior. For example, if all individuals in all countries are assumed to have identical utility functions of the Cobb-Douglas form and all individuals of each country simultaneously face the same prices, it is easy enough to work out the appropriate aggregation procedure for consumption. In fact, it turns out to involve the Walsh index, described below. The implied unitary elastic demand curves of this index, however, make the Cobb-Douglas form much too special.

course, we will speak interchangeably of commodities, items, and specifications in referring to the rows of P.

In the second section of Chapter 3, the process of selecting and pricing individual items was discussed in detail. It was noted in particular that the sets of items priced in the various countries were not all identical.[2] This means that the data input for estimating most category PPPs is a P tableau with missing entries. Coping with these holes in making binary comparisons is an easy enough matter: in comparing any two countries, where only the two columns of P corresponding to the countries are relevant, any row containing a hole in either or both columns is ignored. The geometric mean is computed simply for the ratios of "included" items in the columns. The discussion of weighting—or, rather, of nonweighting—in computing the geometric means will not be repeated here.[3] In this chapter's multilateral work, as in the binary case, price-ratio averaging is done without weighting at the detailed category level—with only a few exceptions. The effects of ignoring weights in a binary comparison were described in Chapter 4.[4]

Category PPPs that are geometric means based upon included entries only ($GM_{j/k}$, where the jth and k^{th} countries are being compared) may be satisfactory for particular pairwise comparisons (though, even here, considerations of statistical efficiency are important), but their fatal flaw is that they do not possess the property of transitivity. If P contains holes, in general it will not be true[5] that $GM_{j/k} = GM_{j/l} \div GM_{k/l}$.

Transitivity is essential, so some accommodation must be made. One possibility, a modified binary method based upon the use of a bridge country, already has been discussed in Chapter 4. We shall see presently that our CPD method is another way of satisfying the transitivity requirement.

The bridge-country method has the advantage of being easy to implement: a base or bridge country is selected and all price indexes are computed from the binary comparisons of the individual countries with the bridge country—that is, binary comparisons in the form of geometric means of "included price ratios." Let the bridge country be the one numbered n. $GM_{j/n}$ is the geometric mean of included price ratios for the jth country relative to the bridge country. Two nonbridge countries, j and k, are compared not by their direct geometric mean, $GM_{j/k}$, but rather by the result of the calculation $I_{j/k}^n = GM_{j/n} \div GM_{k/n}$. The direct geometric mean derived from the two original countries will *not*, in general, be the same as $I_{j/k}^n$ if there are holes in the jth and k^{th} columns of P, but in the bridge-country method any such discrepancy is ignored. Thus, the bridge-country method of treating a P tableau containing holes gives price indexes possessing the transitivity property, but only in an artificial sense.

Its arbitrary way of achieving transitivity makes the bridge-country method a target for criticism on at least two counts. First, the method gives indexes that are not invariant under a change of bridge country. If there are holes in P, and this is the empirical case of interest, then $I_{j/k}^n$ normally will be different computationally for each possible bridge country (other than the jth and k^{th} countries).[6]

Second, the bridge-country method is not statistically efficient, because it fails to make use of all of the information contained in P. To show this, we review why the bridge-country method itself is an improvement in an international sense over original-country binary comparisons. The basic logic underlying the use of the bridge-country method, when appropriately generalized, leads to the Country-Product–Dummy method.

---

[2] See page 31.

[3] See pages 47–49.

[4] See pages 52–53.

[5] Suppose the price of the hth good is missing for the lth country. Then

$$I_{j/k} = \left[\frac{\rho_{1j}}{\rho_{1k}} \cdot \ldots \cdot \frac{\rho_{Aj}}{\rho_{Ak}}\right]^{1/A},$$

$$I_{j/l} = \left[\frac{\rho_{1j}}{\rho_{1l}} \cdot \ldots \cdot \frac{\rho_{hj}}{\rho_{hl}} \left(\cdot \ldots \cdot \frac{\rho_{Aj}}{\rho_{Al}}\right)\right]^{\frac{1}{A-1}},$$

and

$$I_{k/l} = \left[\frac{\rho_{1k}}{\rho_{1l}} \cdot \ldots \cdot \frac{\rho_{hk}}{\rho_{hl}} \left(\cdot \ldots \cdot \frac{\rho_{Ak}}{\rho_{Al}}\right)\right]^{\frac{1}{A-1}}$$

(The backward parentheses bracket a ratio that is *not* in the price tableau and, therefore, is not in the product.)

It follows that

$$I_{j/l} \div I_{k/l} = \frac{\left[\frac{\rho_{1j}}{\rho_{1l}} \cdot \ldots \cdot \frac{\rho_{hj}}{\rho_{hl}} \left(\cdot \ldots \cdot \frac{\rho_{Aj}}{\rho_{Al}}\right)\right]^{\frac{1}{A-1}}}{\left[\frac{\rho_{1k}}{\rho_{1l}} \cdot \ldots \cdot \frac{\rho_{hk}}{\rho_{hl}} \left(\cdot \ldots \cdot \frac{\rho_{Ak}}{\rho_{Al}}\right)\right]^{\frac{1}{A-1}}}$$

$$= \left[\frac{\rho_{1j}}{\rho_{1k}} \cdot \ldots \cdot \frac{\rho_{hj}}{\rho_{hk}} \left(\cdot \ldots \cdot \frac{\rho_{Aj}}{\rho_{Ak}}\right)\right]^{\frac{1}{A-1}}.$$

But this latter expression is not quite equal to $I_{j/k}$, because it is the geometric mean of the price ratios of all the items of the category except the hth one.

[6] Under appropriate random sampling assumptions, the bridge-country method will give estimators of relative price levels that are "consistent" as that term is used in statistical estimation theory. For any fixed sample size, however, the method does not define unique estimators. There will be as many distinct consistent estimators as there are countries to be compared less one.

To illustrate the role of a bridge country and its connection with the CPD method, let us imagine three alternative situations with respect to the available price information for a detailed category. We have a set of items from which we can calculate France–United States ratios and a completely different set from which we can calculate Japan–United States price comparisons. Because there is no overlap between the items priced in France and Japan, clearly the only possible way of comparing the two countries is by seeing how they each compare with the United States. If, for example, the geometric mean of price ratios of the Japan–United States set was 400 yen per dollar and that of the France–United States set was 3.5 francs per dollar, the best estimate of the purchasing power parity of the yen in terms of francs would be 400/3.5 = 114.3 yen per franc. In this case, "increased efficiency" is not the natural term to use in describing the motivation for resorting to the bridge-country method in comparing France and Japan. Its use is a matter of necessity.

Now let us suppose a second situation: there are, say, nine items in the Japan–United States set and ten in the France–United States set, of which two are found in both sets. Two Japan–France price ratios can be calculated, and from these an original-country comparison can be made. Such a comparison is based on only two observations, however, and it ignores seven "pieces" of information contained in the available Japan–United States price ratios and eight pieces in the available France–United States price ratios. On the other hand, the bridge-country method would bring to bear these fifteen additional pieces of information in the estimation process.

So far, the bridge-country method appears better. Pushing the example farther, however, will illustrate its shortcomings. If, in addition to the nine-item and ten-item sets, there was one additional item for which both a Japanese and a French price were available but not a U.S. one, the Japan–France original-country comparison would be based upon three price ratios. Again, the bridge-country comparison would be based upon the 15 price ratios and, therefore, apparently would be the method to choose. But here the bridge-country method actually would ignore one of the Japan–France price ratios. As we will see, the CPD method uses both kinds of information—the original-country and bridge-country price ratios—and more.

The "more" consists of information derived from the use of other bridge countries. If it is sensible to infer relative Japan–France prices by using the United States as a bridge country, as outlined two paragraphs above, the logic applies with equal force to the use of other countries as bridges. This brings us to our third situation. Suppose we have, as before, the set of nine Japan–United States prices and the set of ten France–United States prices (including the two prices common to both sets), but now we have, in addition, a set of nine Japan–

United Kingdom prices and a set of ten France–United Kingdom prices, all of which correspond exactly to the sets involving the United States. If we are going to use a bridge-country approach, we certainly should not ignore this information and similar data from other possible bridge countries. Furthermore if, as is more likely, the elements in the other bridge-country sets varied from one bridge country to another, the relevance of the added data would be enhanced; in fact, the CPD method meets the criterion in this case of being base (or bridge) country invariant.

The reader should be reminded that, at the category level where no quantity weights are used, gains from introducing a bridge country—or doing anything more than simply comparing countries directly—can result only if there are holes in P. If P is complete, no additional information about the Japan–France comparison can be obtained from prices in other countries.

Clearly, the distinction between binary and multilateral comparisons turns on the nature of the data used in comparing any particular pair of countries. An original-country binary comparison draws upon data relating only to the two countries. The bridge-country method is a half-way step toward a multilateral comparison in that it draws on the data of the two countries in addition to the data of the bridge country. A multilateral comparison, on the other hand, even when only two countries are being considered, draws upon the data of *all* countries.

The CPD method is a multilateral one that takes advantage of all the information of the P tableau in estimating each of the price indexes. Because the CPD method has been described more fully elsewhere,[7] we present only a bare-bones stochastic formulation of the estimating problem and then go directly to a description of the multilateral regression procedure implied by the stochastic formulation.

For the purposes of most of what follows, it will be assumed that conceptually an indefinitely large number of items exist in each category, and that A represents only the actual number of observations in a sample that has been generated by the following model.

Pairs of prices in any row of P are assumed to be related to each other in the manner indicated in equation (5.2):

$$(5.2) \qquad \frac{\rho_{\alpha j}}{\rho_{\alpha k}} = \frac{\rho_j}{\rho_k} \cdot w_\alpha^{jk}$$

ρ_j/ρ_k is PPP, with respect to the category in question, of Country j's currency to that of Country k; and w_α^{jk} is a random variable that is lognormally distributed[8] with

---

[7] Robert Summers, "International Comparisons With Incomplete Data," *Review of Income and Wealth* (March 1973), pp. 1–16.

[8] A lognormally distributed random variable is one for which the natural logarithm of the variable is distributed normally. The parameters of the lognormal distribution are the mean and variance of the distribution of logs.

parameters 0 and σ^2. The assumption that the w_α^{jk}s are distributed lognormally is a typical one in situations wherein multiplicative relationships are assumed. The assumption that the variance of w_α^{jk}, σ^2, needs neither subscripts nor superscripts is a strong one, however; it asserts that the dispersion of the distribution of price ratios is the same for all pairs of countries and categories. Clearly, such an assumption can be defended only on the grounds of expediency; the available data are insufficient in quantity to allow a more realistic distinction to be made empirically between country pairs. Fortunately, violation of this assumption would not cause the estimates to be biased on that account alone. More important, it is assumed that the w_α^{jk}s for different goods are independent. This is the sense in which random sampling is assumed, and this assumption must be complied with.

Equation (5.2) and the associated specification of the stochastic properties of w_α^{jk} imply a complicated likelihood function. Fortunately, however, it can be shown that the maximum-likelihood estimators of the PPPs, ρ_j/ρ_k, can be obtained using a straightforward multiple-regression approach.

The history of price index construction has been shaped by the fact that what is interesting about price levels—for time-to-time or, place-to-place comparisons—is the level of one set of prices *relative* to another. As a consequence, price *ratios* have been the natural element of observation. The fact that price ratios are units-invariant seemed to add additional weight to the feeling that the price ratio or some function thereof should be the basic dependent variable. It is possible, however, with no loss of generality either of a statistical or economic character, to devise a multiple regression equation that draws upon individual $\rho_{\alpha j}$'s from the P tableau. This is actually an advantage, because then all countries are treated symmetrically.

Equation (5.3), the linear regression equation that forms the keystone of CPD, involves two sets of dummy variables $\{X_{\alpha j}, Y_{\alpha j}\}\ j = 1, \ldots, (n-1); \alpha = 1, \ldots, A.$ (n: number of countries; A: number of items).

$$(5.3) \quad ln\ \rho_{\alpha j} = \beta_1\ X_{\alpha 1} + \ldots + \beta_{n-1}\ X_{\alpha, n-1}$$

$$+ \gamma_1\ Y_{1j} + \ldots + \gamma_A\ Y_{Aj} + v_\alpha^j,$$

where $ln\ \rho_{\alpha j}$ is the natural logarithm of $\rho_{\alpha j}$, $X_{\alpha j'} = 1$ if $j' = j$ and 0 otherwise; $Y_{\alpha' j} = 1$ if $\alpha' = \alpha$ and 0 otherwise; and v_α^j is a normally distributed variable with mean zero and variance σ^2.

The coefficient of the $X_{\alpha j}$ dummy, β_j, in equation (5.3) is to be interpreted as the natural log of the PPP of Country j's currency relative to the base country, chosen here to be the nth country. If the regression coefficient estimates are denoted $\hat{\beta}_j$, then $\hat{\beta}_j$ is an estimate of the natural logarithm of the category PPP (that is, of ρ_j/ρ_n). On the assumption of lognormality of the original dis-

turbance, $e^{\hat{\beta}_j}$ will be the maximum likelihood estimate of ρ_j/ρ_n, but the expected value of $e^{\hat{\beta}_j}$ is not ρ_j/ρ_n. Similarly, $e^{\hat{\beta}_j - \hat{\beta}_k}$ is an estimate of ρ_j/ρ_k. Clearly $e^{\hat{\beta}_j - \hat{\beta}_k}$ equals both $1/e^{\hat{\beta}_k - \hat{\beta}_j}$ and $e^{\hat{\beta}_j - \hat{\beta}_l}/e^{\hat{\beta}_k - \hat{\beta}_l}$. Therefore, the estimates of relative price levels are both base invariant and circular.

Incidentally, observe that the assumption of lognormality of the underlying disturbance term, w_α^{jk}, in equation (5.2) (or, equivalently, that v_α^j in equation [5.3] is normal) is not essential; without that assumption, one can still rely on the optimal properties flowing from the Gauss-Markov theorem on Least Squares. That is, the $\hat{\beta}_j$s will remain both unbiased and, if the number of items in the category is not too small, approximately normally distributed.

The coefficients of the $Y_{\alpha j}$ dummies have no significance for country price-level comparisons, though conceivably they may be useful in an analysis of the average relative values that purchasers in all n countries put on the individual items within the category.[9]

A possible disadvantage of this generalized bridge-country method is that a country for which there are many price observations within the given category will have more influence upon the regression coefficients than a country for which there are few price observations. Because in many of the categories of our data set there are more prices for the United States and other advanced countries than for any other individual country, this is a problem to be reckoned with. Our response to this consideration was to weight each price observation for each country proportional to the reciprocal of the number of price observations for the country. Thus, in the Fresh Vegetables example, (see Table 5.1), below, each of the eleven Colombian observations receives a relative weight of 0.909; each of the twelve French observations, a relative weight of 0.833; and so on.[10] Hence, each country's observations in their totality received equal weight. The consequence of using the frequency-weighted version of CPD rather than the unweighted one is discussed below.[11]

---

[9] If, for example, the units of the items are standardized for an attribute—say, caloric content in the case of a fuel category or nutritional content in the case of a food category—so that a unit of each item contains the same quantity of the attribute, then $(\gamma_1 - \gamma_2)$ is directly relevant to the question of how attractive Item 1 is compared with Item 2 as a way of securing a standard unit of the attribute. Specifically, if $\gamma_7 - \gamma_3 = .21$, then the cost of obtaining a unit of the attribute through the purchase of the seventh item would be 23 percent ($e^{.21} = 1.23$) greater than if it were obtained through the purchase of the third item. Because a change in the units of an item will lead only to a change in the Y coefficient associated with the item, the price-level estimates for the various countries will be invariant under a change in units.

[10] Actually, these weights were blown up by the ratio of the number of observations to the number of countries (by 105/10 in this category) so that the sum of the weights would equal the number of observations. This was done to avoid bias in the standard errors.

[11] See page 62.

In a few cases in which it seemed crucial to weight the items within a category,[12] we used what we refer to as the "double-weighted CPD." Double weighting within categories was confined to house rents (ICP 03.110), automobiles (ICP 06.110), and restaurant food (ICP 08.310). The main use of double-weighted CPD, however, was to obtain PPPs for some categories for which no items at all had been priced in a particular country. This application of CPD is described in section C.[13]

Before passing on to the Fresh Vegetables empirical example, the precision of the price level estimates and the notion of randomness should be discussed. First, the regression procedure delivers estimates of the standard errors of the regression coefficient estimates. These, of course, provide a basis for computing confidence intervals for the true regression coefficients.[14] Because the category PPPs are simply the exponentials of the regression coefficients, to go on to compute confidence intervals for the price-level ratios themselves is an easy matter. Specifically,

$$(5.4)\quad \text{Prob}\left\{e^{\hat{\beta}_j - t_\pi\, \hat{\sigma}_{\beta_j}} < \frac{\rho_j}{\rho_n} < e^{\hat{\beta}_j + t_\pi\, \hat{\sigma}_{\beta_j}}\right\} = \pi \; ,$$

where t_π is an appropriate entry from a Student's t distribution table and $\hat{\sigma}_{\beta_j}$ is an estimate of the standard error of $\hat{\beta}_j$. (One qualification: Equation [5.4] holds strictly only if the disturbance term of equation [5.3] is normal. If it is not, the Student's t distribution is not the correct source for t_π. If the number of degrees of freedom of the regression is large, however—that is, the number of prices actually present in the P tableau minus the number of parameters estimated in the regression, $A+(n-1)$, is not too small—then the expression within the brace of equation [5.4] is likely to be an acceptable approximation to a "true" confidence interval.)

Second, the notion of random sampling needs amplification. In regression analysis, it is the disturbances that must be distributed randomly, not the independent variables. Thus, it is not necessary that the holes in P be distributed randomly, provided that the systematic pattern of the holes—with respect to countries and items—does not lead to a systematic pattern among the disturbances. The fact that countries at different stages of development may not consume identical goods and services within a category may give rise to a nonrandom pattern of holes, but this does not necessarily introduce any bias in the regression coefficient estimates. The only concern about the pattern of the holes is that it must not lead to a singular variance–covariance matrix for the independent variables. (Singularity could occur if, to give one example, the set of goods in a detailed category and the set of countries each can be divided into two subsets such that no member of the first goods subset is priced in the first country subset, and no member of the second goods subset is priced in the second country subset. Intuitively, this means simply that country price levels cannot be compared unless some overlap exists in the list of goods that have been priced in the two countries.) To summarize: the random sampling requirement is simply that the price of an item in a country should

[12] See pages 48–49.

[13] See pages 63–65.

[14] It should be noted that the inevitable assumption that the variance of v_α^j does not depend upon either α or j has implications for these standard errors. Loosely speaking, all of the individual standard errors as computed will be more nearly equal than if the assumption could be relaxed. In the extreme case of a P tableau with no holes, the assumption will lead to identical standard errors for all country-dummy coefficients. See pages 57–58.

Table 5.1. Prices of Fresh Vegetables, Ten Countries, 1970 (prices per kilogram)

Item	Colombia (P)	France (Fr)	Germany, F.R. (DM)	Hungary (Ft)	India (Re)	Italy (L)	Japan (¥)	Kenya (Sh)	U.K. (£)	U.S. ($)
1. Artichokes	—	2.75	3.26	—	—	646	—	—	—	2.22
2. Beets	3.90	—	—	—	—	—	—	—	.07	.42
3. Brussels sprouts	—	2.35	1.69	—	—	485	—	—	—	1.89
4. Cabbage	1.41	.98	.55	2.9	.91	157	75.4	.47	.08	.32
5. Cauliflower	5.33	1.90	1.13	—	1.27	195	156.6	2.58	.17	.63
6. Carrots	2.10	.93	.86	3.2	.75	172	115.1	2.58	.07	.39
7. Celery, pascal	4.49	—	—	—	—	—	—	—	—	.44
8. Cucumbers	—	—	—	4.7	.87	—	173.3	—	—	.61
9. Eggplant	—	—	—	—	.72	—	—	—	—	.59
10. Escarole	—	1.82	.98	—	—	212	—	—	—	1.16
11. Green peppers	17.40	2.62	2.32	8.7	—	186	195.4	—	—	.67
12. Kunde greens	—	—	—	—	.56	—	—	.79	—	.53
13. Lettuce	4.82	3.23	2.27	9.3	—	239	218.1	.62	—	1.95
14. Mushrooms	—	7.90	5.60	—	—	790	—	—	.54	.35
15. Onions, yellow	5.59	1.18	.86	4.8	.67	.27	98.6	.77	.13	.88
16. Radishes	—	—	—	—	.55	—	—	—	—	.12
17. Red cabbage	—	1.27	.56	—	—	—	—	—	—	1.24
18. Spinach	4.71	—	—	—	—	—	133.8	—	—	—
19. Tomatoes	5.79	2.55	1.85	6.7	1.21	226	160.9	1.19	.31	.92
20. Yellow squash	2.29	—	—	1.5	—	—	—	—	—	.66

Note: — = Price not available

$$(5.5) \quad \ln \rho_{\alpha j} = 1.9623\, X_{\alpha 1} + .9234\, X_{\alpha 2} + .5711\, X_{\alpha 3} + 2.0209\, X_{\alpha 4} + .3450\, X_{\alpha 5} + 5.6774\, X_{\alpha 6} + 5.3201\, X_{\alpha 7}$$
$$(.1700) \qquad (.1717) \qquad (.1717) \qquad (.1726) \qquad (.1727) \qquad (.1724) \qquad (.1714)$$

$$+ .5658\, X_{\alpha 8} - 1.5641\, X_{\alpha 9} + .5556\, Y_{1j} - .8904\, Y_{2j} - .2257\, Y_{3j} - 1.0174\, Y_{4j} - .1828\, Y_{5j}$$
$$(.1733) \qquad (.1738) \qquad (.2396) \quad (.2487) \quad (.2396) \qquad (.1659) \qquad (.1710)$$

$$- .6661\, Y_{6j} - .5886\, Y_{7j} - .3931\, Y_{8j} - .6266\, Y_{9j} - .4095\, Y_{10j} + .1357\, Y_{11j} - .7778\, Y_{12j}$$
$$(.1659) \qquad (.3242) \qquad (.2196) \qquad (.3093) \qquad (.2695) \qquad (.1883) \qquad (.2433)$$

$$- .2061\, Y_{13j} + .999\, Y_{14j} - .6616\, Y_{15j} - .6808\, Y_{16j} - 1.2005\, Y_{17j} - .2873\, Y_{18j} - .0971\, Y_{19j}$$
$$(.1784) \qquad (.2110) \qquad (.1659) \qquad (.3093) \qquad (.2726) \qquad (.2579) \qquad (.1659)$$

$$- 1.2171\, Y_{20j}$$
$$(.2536)$$

$\overline{R}^2 = .97$ Standard error of estimate = .375

depart from an amount defined by the country's category PPP and by the specific item only by an amount that stochastically does not depend upon either the country or the item.

This discussion of the CDP method ends with the observation that the most commonly used technique in empirical economies, regression analysis, has been harnessed to do category PPP estimating with only a minimum of complications in transforming price data into a regression format. In the limiting case, when there are no missing observations in the price tableau, it can be shown easily that the regression procedure amounts to no more than the computation of a set of geometric means. Because this is what a person normally would compute to estimate relative price levels if he did not introduce stochastic considerations into his framework of analysis—that is, using the original-country method or the bridge-country method—it is reassuring to see that the regression method is consistent with ordinary practice when a full information price tableau is available. Furthermore, the weighting procedure grafted onto CPD[15] gives results identical to those given by the unweighted CPD procedure if there are no holes in P. (Note, though, that the estimation of precision is always important, so casting the problem in stochastic terms is useful even in the case of complete data.)

To illustrate these ideas, regressions based upon equation (5.3) are presented for the Fresh Vegetable price tableau given in Table 5.1. The regression result for the ten countries and twenty items are given in equation (5.5). The numbers in parentheses are the standard errors of the coefficients directly above them. The Xs refer to countries, with the second subscript keyed to the countries as arrayed in Table 5.1, and the Ys to the vegetables with the first subscript keyed to the list in Table 5.1. When the coefficients of the Xs are exponentiated, the PPPs are obtained. For example, $X_{\alpha 7}$

refers to Japan. The natural antilog of its coefficient is 204.5, and this PPP is entered in the first line of Table 5.2. $\overline{R}^2$ is the coefficient of determination adjusted for degree of freedom.[16]

In this and the five following paragraphs, the discussion centers on a detailed example of the Fresh Vegetables category. This category was selected because we had many price observations for it, and because it was expected that price relatives would vary widely from item to item. The frequency-weighted CPD results for Fresh Vegetables in line 1 of Table 5.2 are based on 105 price observations for twenty different vegetables in the ten countries. We investigate the sensitivity of the results to exactly what items and which countries are represented in the data. Our conclusions come from a set of regressions carried out with various omissions of lines and columns of Table 5.1. The results may be summarized as follows:

1. Regressions based upon all ten countries but with the deletion of a few randomly chosen items give PPPs that can vary by as much as 15 or 20 percent (see lines 1–4 and 13 of Table 5.2). When the number of items is halved in a random way, even more substantial changes can occur (see lines 5 and 14). This underscores the sampling variability underlying the PPPs (binary as well as multilateral) for individual categories, as well as our strictures[17] about the reliability of price and quantity comparisons for the detailed categories.

2. Regressions based upon all twenty items but upon smaller subsets of countries generally do not reveal as much variability in the PPPs (see lines 6–9 and 15).

---

[15]See page 58.

[16]If all the prices in Table 5.1 were converted to U.S. dollars at the prevailing exchange rates, the regression would give the same PPPs and standard errors. The $\overline{R}^2$ in that case, however, is smaller (.78). This is to be expected if the exchange rates are correlated with the Fresh Vegetables PPPs.

[17]See page 49.

Table 5.2. Purchasing-Power Parities Relative to the U.S. Dollar, as Estimated Using the Frequency-Weighted Country-Product-Dummy, Unweighted Country-Product-Dummy, and Original-Country Methods: Fresh Vegetables, 1970

Items, Table 5.1	Countries	Colombia (P) (1)	France (Fr) (2)	Germany, F.R. (DM) (3)	Hungary (Ft) (4)	India (Re) (5)	Italy (L) (6)	Japan (¥) (7)	Kenya (Sh) (8)	U.K. (£) (9)	U.S. ($) (10)	N
						(currency units per U.S. dollar)						
Part A. Country-Product-Dummy Method, Frequency-Weighted												
1. All 20	All	7.108	2.516	1.768	7.530	1.410	291.9	204.5	1.757	.2092	1.000	105
2. All but #20	All	7.387	2.649	1.859	8.460	1.485	306.9	215.6	1.857	.2200‡	1.000	102
3. All but #19, #20	All	7.480	2.616	1.834	8.670	1.515	311.9	221.8	1.971	.2004	1.000	92
4. All but #18, #19, #20	All	7.925‡	2.721‡	1.907‡	9.030‡	1.568‡	324.4‡	236.9‡	2.057‡	.2092	1.000	89
5. All but #11-20	All	6.032	2.199	1.588	7.710	1.740	353.8	238.3	2.979	.1854	1.000	51
6. All 20	All but Hungary	7.034	2.594	1.823	—	1.432	301.2	209.5	1.821	.2134	1.000	97
7. All 20	All but Colombia, India, and Kenya	—	2.655§	1.866§	7.786	—	308.4§	212.3	—	.2314§	1.000	78
8. All but #20	All but Colombia, France, Germany (F.R.), and Italy	—	—	—	7.335§	1.307§	—	193.0§	1.651§	.2010	1.000	59
9. All but #10†	All but France, Germany (F.R.), and Italy	6.942§	—	—	7.407	1.371	—	199.0	1.745	.2073	1.000	70
Part B. Country-Product-Dummy Method, Unweighted												
10. All 20	All 10	7.127	2.616	1.841	7.560	1.418	300.6	208.4	1.800	.2167	1.000	105
Part C. Original-Country Method, All Items, All Countries												
11. All 20	All 10	7.350	3.005	2.163	8.010	1.425	324.4	229.7	2.057	.2538	1.000	
12. Number of price ratios ($\rho_{\alpha j}/\rho_{\alpha,\text{U.S.}}$)		11	11	11	8	9	10	9	7	7	—	

Addendum

13. Maximum percentage deviation of frequency-weighted CPD estimates in lines 2–4 from line 1‡

	Colombia	France	Germany	Hungary	India	Italy	Japan	Kenya	U.K.
13.	11.5	8.1	7.9	19.9	11.2	11.1	15.8	17.1	5.2

14. Percentage deviation of frequency-weighted CPD estimates in line 5 from line 1

	Colombia	France	Germany	Hungary	India	Italy	Japan	Kenya	U.K.
14.	17.8	14.4	11.3	2.4	23.4	21.2	16.5	70.0	12.8

15. Maximum percentage deviation of frequency-weighted CPD estimates in lines 6–9 from line 1§

	Colombia	France	Germany	Hungary	India	Italy	Japan	Kenya	U.K.
15.	2.1	6.4	6.6	2.3	2.8	6.2	4.1	3.6	11.1

16. Percentage deviation of unweighted CPD estimates (line 10) from frequency-weighted CPD estimates (line 1)

	Colombia	France	Germany	Hungary	India	Italy	Japan	Kenya	U.K.
16.	0.3	4.0	4.1	0.4	0.7	3.0	1.9	2.4	3.6

17. Percentage deviation of original-country estimates (line 11) from frequency-weighted CPD estimates (line 1)

	Colombia	France	Germany	Hungary	India	Italy	Japan	Kenya	U.K.
17.	3.4	19.4	22.3	6.4	1.1	11.1	12.3	17.1	21.3

†Prices for item #10 were available only for France, the Federal Republic of Germany, and Italy.
‡The line entry in lines 2 to 4 deviating most from the line 1 entry is marked by a double dagger.
§The line entry in lines 6 to 9 deviating most from the line 1 entry is marked by a section symbol.

Line 10 of Table 5.2 shows the estimates of the Fresh Vegetables PPPs obtained from unweighted CPD. The entries on line 16 indicate that it makes little difference whether frequency weighting is used in dealing with Fresh Vegetables. This conclusion is generalized beyond Fresh Vegetables in the fifth paragraph below.

In line 11 of Table 5.2, we give PPP estimates using the original-country binary method. Line 12 gives the number of price ratios that entered into the original-country geometric means. (Note that with twenty items represented in the Fresh Vegetable category, the number of ratios could be as high as twenty.) The percentage deviations in line 17 show that the frequency-weighted CPD estimates differ from the original-country estimates by amounts ranging from 1 to 22 percent. In the Fresh Vegetables category, the CPD estimates are all larger than the original-country estimates. We shall see below that over a large number of categories, frequency-weighted CPD estimates are slightly larger on the average, but the differences are small.

Confidence intervals at the 0.95 probability level for the relative price levels are given in Table 5.3. The first set of lower and upper limits are CPD ones based upon the regression estimates of equation (5.5) and the confidence interval formula given by equation (5.4). The second set of limits are original-country results based upon the geometric means appearing in line 10 of Table 5.2 and the variance of the natural logarithms of the $\rho_{\alpha j}/\rho_{\alpha,10}$ price ratios. Note that the confidence intervals derived from the original-country method are less likely

Table 5.3. .95 Confidence Intervals for Estimates of Relative Price Levels Based on the Frequency-Weighted Country-Product-Dummy Method and on the Original-Country Method: Fresh Vegetables, 1970

	Country-product dummy[†]		Original-country[‡]	
	Lower limit (1)	Upper limit (2)	Lower limit (3)	Upper limit (4)
Colombia–United States	5.27	9.99	5.18	10.43
France–United States	1.79	3.55	1.98	4.55
Germany (F.R.)–United States	1.26	2.49	1.58	2.95
Hungary–United States	5.34	10.65	4.86	13.23
India–United States	.998	1.995	.998	2.048
Italy–United States	207.	412.	253.	416.
Japan–United States	145.	288.	170.	311.
Kenya–United States	1.24	2.49	1.09	3.87
United Kingdom–United States	.148	.296	.196	.329

[†]Derived from parameter estimates of equation (5.5) (10 countries, 20 items).

[‡]Based upon all "available price ratios." Lower limit $= e^{\bar{r} + t_{.95}\hat{\sigma}_r/\sqrt{N-1}}$, upper limit $= e^{\bar{r} + t_{.95}\hat{\sigma}_r/\sqrt{N-1}}$,

where $\bar{r} = \frac{1}{N} \Sigma \ln\left[\frac{\rho_{\alpha j}}{\rho_{\alpha,10}}\right]$, $\hat{\sigma}_r^2 = \frac{1}{N} \Sigma \left[\ln\left(\frac{\rho_{\alpha j}}{\rho_{\alpha,10}}\right) - \bar{r}\right]^2$,

$t_{.95}$ is the appropriate entry from the Student's t table, and N is the number of available price ratios.

to be robust with respect to (that is, be more sensitive to) the assumption of lognormality than those derived from the regression.

It was expected that, at least on the average, confidence intervals obtained by the original-country method would be wider than the corresponding intervals of the frequency-weighted CPDs. The efficiency arguments underlying this were (1) the regression approach, taking full advantage of circularity, uses the data more efficiently, and (2) the small numbers of price ratios on which the geometric means are based lead to relatively large t values in the confidence interval formula. The confidence intervals using both methods are distressingly large (even the frequency-weighted CPD regression estimates twenty-nine parameters on the basis of only 105 observations), but the greater efficiency of CPD does peek through. In five cases, there is a distinct difference between the widths of the confidence intervals, and in four of these the CPD interval is the narrower one. In two cases, the differences are small, with the CPD interval and the original-country interval each being smaller in one case. In the two remaining cases, the differences were negligible.

The inferences we drew from Table 5.2 all were based on comparisons involving the United States. We made similar comparisons for non-U.S. pairs of countries and found similar relationships.

The consequences of using frequency-weighted CPD, unweighted CPD, and the original-country binary method have been compared in considerable detail for a single category, Fresh Vegetables. Now we generalize our conclusions by applying the three methods to each of 129 categories to which the CPD methods are relevant.[18] Tables 5.4 and 5.5 summarize the results, giving for each country a frequency distribution of the ratio of two different kinds of estimates of each category's PPP. In Table 5.4, the ratio of the unweighted CPD estimate to the frequency-weighted CPD one is examined. The heavy concentration of the frequencies at or near unity indicates that, on the average, the two estimating procedures give practically the same results. Table 5.4 and the evidence presented below,[19] indicate that it makes almost no difference to our final international comparisons which is used. In view of this similarity, the principle of Occam's razor suggests that unweighted CPD should be used. Though it makes virtually no difference, we have opted nevertheless for frequency-weighted CPD on the basis of the logic set out above ensuring that no country will unduly influence the results.

Table 5.5 gives equivalent frequency distributions for comparing frequency-weighted CPD estimates with original-country estimates. Again, there is a concentration of ratios around unity. More than 40 percent of all ratios are within 5 percent of 1.00, and more than 70 percent are within 15 percent. The means are not as close to unity and standard deviations as close to zero as in the comparison of unweighted CPD with frequency-weighted CPD. The mean of the ratios tends to be greater than unity (only one being below), but in just three cases are they more than 2 percent.

[18]See page 65.

[19]See the following page.

Table 5.4. Comparison of Country-Product-Dummy Method with Frequency-Weighted Country-Product-Dummy Method for 129 Categories, Including Prices Estimated by Double-Weighted Country-Product-Dummy Method, 1970

Ratio of CPD to FCPD estimate of PPP†	Purchasing-power-parity estimates Frequency									
	Colombia	France	Germany, F.R.	Hungary	India	Italy	Japan	Kenya	U.K.	Total
.6000 to .6999	0	0	0	0	0	0	0	1	0	1
.7000 to .7999	0	0	0	0	0	0	0	0	0	0
.8000 to .8999	4	2	2	3	0	2	0	2	1	16
.9000 to .9999	30	38	36	34	30	38	29	38	28	301
1.0000	52	54	54	58	53	54	55	51	53	484
1.0001 to 1.0999	39	31	33	32	42	32	44	36	45	334
1.1000 to 1.1999	3	4	4	2	3	3	1	0	2	22
1.2000 to 1.2999	1	0	0	0	1	0	0	1	0	3
Mean	1.0032	0.9995	1.0002	1.0014	1.0087	0.9988	1.0035	0.9954	1.0018	
Standard deviation	0.0458	0.0413	0.0409	0.0350	0.0379	0.0399	0.0284	0.0523	0.0322	
Number	129	129	129	129	129	129	129	129	129	1161

†CPD estimate: PPPs with the United States the base obtained from unweighted CPD. FCPD estimate: PPPs with the United States the base obtained from frequency-weighted CPD.

When the confidence intervals of the binary PPPs are compared with those of the PPPs produced by the frequency-weighted CPD, the expectations expressed in the fourth paragraph above are clearly borne out. The binary confidence intervals are larger than those of the frequency-weighted CPDs in over two-thirds of the cases; for individual countries, they are larger in as few as 57 percent and as many as 83 percent of the cases.

Before leaving the description of our use of frequency-weighted CPD, it should be mentioned that, for reasons associated with the mechanics of handling large quantities of data in two locations, the CPD regressions for the 24 durables categories were carried out on price data in a slightly different format from the one used with the other 105. Only non-U.S. prices entered the regressions, and each country's price for an item was the ratio of its actual price to the U.S. price for the same item. Thus, the dependent variable in the CPD regressions was the natural logarithm of $\rho_{\alpha j}/\rho_{\alpha, US}$, and the independent variables did not include item dummies. This alternative can, lead to slightly different regression estimates, but it need not; in any case, the estimates based upon this alternative format also will be unbiased.

C. Filling Holes in the Matrix of PPPs for the Categories (Double-Weighted CPD)

Thus far, we have discussed the use of frequency-weighted CPDs to obtain transitive PPPs from an incomplete matrix of prices for a detailed category. The CPD method at this level overcomes the handicap of missing prices within a given category. CPD has been applied also at a second stage—namely, to deal with situations in which no items have been priced for a particular country for an entire category. In the binary comparisons, problems posed by missing prices for entire categories were met by imputing prices from other categories or by reassigning expenditures.[20] For example, we had no price observations for the category Other Fuels (ICP 03.240) in the case of Colombia. In the binary comparison, we assumed that the Colombia–U.S. price relatives for the three other detailed fuel categories—Electricity (ICP 03.210), Gas (ICP 03.220), and Liquid Fuels (ICP 03.230)—could be averaged to represent the missing Colombia–U.S. PPP.

The second-stage CPD method provides a less arbitrary imputation that, though still ad hoc, is useful for multilateral comparisons. The matrix we are confronted with here is like the P matrix set out earlier,[21] except that the row entries refer to detailed categories instead of items. The holes in the matrix occur not because a particular specification within a detailed category was left unpriced in a given country, but because no specification at all was priced in that category in the country. We use this new matrix—call it R—to estimate PPPs for categories for which no pricing was done in a given country. We do this by inference from the relationships among the PPPs in the remainder of R.

The application of the CPD method to this task would be quite straightforward were it not for the fact that we have some important additional information about the R matrix that we did not have about the earlier matrix. Because the R matrix refers to detailed categories, we have expenditure information associated with each price entry. We know the relative importance of each. With few exceptions apart from automobiles and residential housing, we did not have this information for the items in the P matrices.

[20] See page 50.
[21] See page 55.

Table 5.5. Comparison of Original-Country Method with Frequency-Weighted Country-Product-Dummy Method for 129 Categories, Including Prices Estimated by Double-Weighted Country-Product-Dummy Method, 1970

Ratio of binary to FCPD estimate of PPP†	Purchasing-power-parity estimates Frequency									
	Colombia	France	Germany, F.R.	Hungary	India	Italy	Japan	Kenya	U.K.	Total
0 to .3499	1	0	0	0	1	2	0	0	1	5
.3500 to .4499	0	0	0	0	1	0	0	0	1	1
.4500 to .5499	4	0	0	0	0	0	0	1	0	6
.5500 to .6499	6	3	5	3	3	2	0	4	3	29
.6500 to .7499	3	6	5	4	3	4	1	2	1	29
.7500 to .8499	6	11	8	7	3	9	8	13	7	72
.8500 to .9499	19	24	23	18	20	25	15	20	17	181
.9500 to 1.0499	54	53	56	51	50	52	60	48	61	485
1.0500 to 1.1499	17	13	7	19	20	15	24	17	22	154
1.1500 to 1.2499	10	8	14	11	19	9	8	16	8	103
1.2500 to 1.3499	5	4	5	7	3	5	7	5	3	44
1.3500 to 1.4499	2	2	1	5	1	1	2	0	3	17
1.4500 to 1.5499	1	0	1	0	2	0	0	1	0	5
1.5500 to 1.6499	1	3	2	0	1	1	2	0	2	12
1.6500 and above	0	2	2	4	2	4	2	2	0	18
Mean	0.9860	1.0089	1.0162	1.0493	1.0638	1.0191	1.0454	1.0068	1.0058	
Standard deviation	0.1982	0.2256	0.2275	0.2251	0.4420	0.2453	0.1619	0.1947	0.1832	
Number	129	129	129	129	129	129	129	129	129	1161

†Binary estimate: Original-country PPPs with the United States as the base country. FCPD: PPPs obtained from frequency-weighted CPD, with the United States the base country.

Clearly, we should make use of the knowledge of the relative importance of the various cells in the R matrix to allow entries for the more important cells to have a proportionately greater impact in the CPD regressions. There are two possible ways of assessing the relative importance of the cells: one is by columns, the other, by lines. In the former, the importance of each cell is assessed relative to the other cells (for different categories) of the same country. The appropriate weight here (w_1) is the proportion of the country's expenditure for the category to which the cell refers. Line importance is assessed relative to the other cells (for different countries) referring to the same category. The desired weight (w_2) is obtained by taking the proportion of the quantity in each cell to the total quantity for the line (that is, the "world" quantity).

We resolved the question of which of these weights to use by using them both—hence, the term "double-weighted CPD." Specifically, the weight for each cell is the product of w_1 and w_2 normalized by the sum of the products of the two weights in all the cells.

As far as the number of columns is concerned, the size of the R matrix is fixed by the number of countries. With respect to the number of lines, there is room for choice. We can form the R matrix by including all the other 151 lines along with the line corresponding to a category for which a PPP is missing.[22] Alternatively, we

can include only a selected few lines that are closely related to the problem row in our classification system. The issue is whether missing PPPs can be estimated best from the PPP relation inherent in all 152 categories or from PPP relationships of closely related categories. We have opted for the latter way of constituting the R matrices. Missing PPPs for categories have been estimated by applying the double-weighted CPD method to R matrices consisting of the category for which a PPP is missing and the other categories that, together with the given category, constitute the lowest aggregation level in our summary tables (see Tables 14.1 to 14.5).

The total R matrix consisted of 1,520 PPPs in 152 categories (with all 1's in the U.S. column). For reasons to be explained shortly, CPD was used in only 129 of the categories. Of the 1,290 cells for these 129 categories, 89 PPPs in 38 different categories were missing. These holes were filled on the basis of eighteen separate regressions using the double-weighted CPD method. For example, there were seven PPPs missing out of the sixty meat cells in the R matrix (six detailed meat categories times ten countries). The seven were obtained as follows:

[22]In the multilateral comparisons, the number of categories is 152, one less than in the binary comparisons. Net Expenditures of Residents Abroad (ICP 08.900) has been consolidated into "Other Services" (ICP 08.400). It will be noted that the line number of this category (110) simply has been omitted so that

all the subsequent line numbers in the multilateral appendix tables correspond to those in the binary appendix tables. See page 70.

It should be mentioned also that the actual Geary-Khamis computations and the other aggregations were carried out with government purchases of commodities subdivided into 13 categories. The expenditure breakdowns were too rough to warrant publication of the results. It was thought simpler to describe our calculations in terms of the number of categories presented in our tables. See page 163.

1. A double-weighted CPD was applied to the elements of the six-line, ten-column R matrix for meat;
2. Each appropriate country dummy and category dummy (directly analogous to item dummies in the previous CPD discussion) was set equal to 1 and all other dummies were set equal to zero; and then,
3. The right side of the regression equation was evaluated for these dummy values.

The rationale for our choice of six meat lines for R is illustrated by considering the missing Japan–U.S. PPP for lamb (ICP 1.112). This PPP, we felt, could be estimated better from the price relationships for various categories of meats in the ten countries than from either (1) some arbitrary selection of another price relationship, perhaps the Japan–U.S. PPP for beef (ICP 1.111); or (2) price relationships for a wider set of goods (that is, from an R matrix including nonmeat as well as meat categories). In principle, of course, the R matrix selected should comprise lines representing categories sharing the production characteristics of the category with the missing price, rather than consumption characteristics.

Reference has already been made several times to the fact that CPD methods were applied to 129 categories, but before moving on to the use made of these PPPs for aggregation purposes, we should explain how the PPPs for the remaining 23 categories were obtained. In 8, only a single item was priced (for example, eggs); in 6, indirect price and direct quantity comparisons were chosen;[23] for 8, imputations were made directly rather than by means of CPD methods; and in one, Exports Minus Imports, the exchange rate was used.

In the categories in which there was only one item, the use of CPD was possible but trivial. No confidence intervals could be estimated, however, in these degenerate cases.

The categories for which imputations were made directly were those for which there was reason to believe that the missing price relationships could be approximated better from a selected category than from the more generalized approach represented by the double-weighted CPD. For example, the PPPs for the expenditures of educational institutions on Books and Supplies (ICP 07.431) were taken to be the same as the PPPs for household purchases of Books, Papers, and Magazines (ICP 07.310). This was preferred over a mechanical application of the double-weighted CPD method in which the missing PPPs (for ICP 07.431) would have been inferred from the PPPs for other educational categories, such as teachers' salaries (ICP 07.411 and 07.412) and Expenditures on Physical Facilities (ICP 07.420).

Among the other categories for which imputations were made, two may be singled out for special comment. The PPPs for the Increase in Stocks (ICP 18.000) were taken simply from the original-country binary calcula-

tions.[24] The PPPs for Government Purchases of Commodities (ICP 21.000) were obtained by including thirteen separate subcategories of government purchases in the aggregation procedures described in Section D below. Only the PPPs for total government purchases actually are presented in our final tables (see Chapter 14) because less confidence could be placed in those subdivisions of expenditures. The PPPs for the individual subcategories were the same as those used in the binary comparisons; they were imputed from the PPPs estimated for other categories.[25]

By these means, PPPs for 152 detailed categories were obtained. A corresponding set of quantity indexes also was obtained. In 146 categories, the PPPs were estimated directly and the quantity indexes derived by the division of the PPPs into the expenditure ratios. In the other six categories, quantity indexes were estimated directly and the PPPs derived by division into the expenditure ratio. These, then, are the PPPs and the quantity indexes that are the inputs for the multilateral aggregations described in Sections D and E.

D. Alternative Aggregation Methods

We now are at the second stage of the estimating procedures outlined earlier.[26] Having suitably combined item price data at the category level, we take up the problem of how to combine the various category PPPs and quantity indexes to estimate (1) relative GDPs and their components, and (2) PPPs at the level of both GDP and their components.

FOUR ALTERNATIVE AGGREGATION METHODS

Four multilateral methods are considered in detail: (1) Walsh, (2) EKS, (3) Van Yzeren, and (4) Geary-Khamis. Each method goes beyond the binary procedures of Chapter 4 by drawing upon price and quantity data of all countries simultaneously in aggregating up from the category level. They all are base country invariant, have the transitivity property, and can be adapted to a form that gives additive consistency. The EKS method meets the factor-reversal test. The Geary-Khamis method also satisfies the test at the GDP level. Only in a purely definitional sense (that is, by deriving either the PPPs or the quantity index indirectly) can the Walsh and Van Yzeren methods and the Geary-Khamis subaggregates be said also to meet the test.

The ignoring of quantity weights in averaging item prices to get category relative prices cannot be repeated when aggregating upward from the category level. The index-number problem of economics calls for an answer to this sort of question: "With what weights should the

[23]See pages 19–20.

[24]See page 159.
[25]See page 164.
[26]See page 55.

various category PPPs be combined to get a single PPP for GDP (or some subaggregate) so as to reflect in a satisfactory way the importance of each category to the group of countries as a whole?"

Alternatively, the question may be set in these quantity index terms: "How can the quantity indexes for the various individual categories be combined so that a correct cardinal quantum index is obtained for GDP (or some subaggregate)?"

Economic theory gives no explicit procedure for answering these questions in the sense of providing a specific computing algorithm. Each of the four multilateral methods, however, involves a computing formula that can be used to answer one or the other of these questions. In Chapter 15, we engage in some preliminary demand analysis of the international comparisons generated using the methodology of this chapter. Without attempting to anticipate the Chapter 15 materials here, we wish to acknowledge that, in principle, the economic framework used in the demand analysis should be consistent with the methods of the present chapter. If, for example, a particular utility function is assumed to be common to all countries in the demand analysis, it might be expected that our aggregation method would stem from that utility function, or at least be consistent with it. It will be seen that, in fact, we have proceeded in a much looser fashion. We have selected the Geary-Khamis method for computing our final PPPs and quantity indexes, but each method will be discussed here and computational results for the various methods will be described in Section F.

Average weight methods. The overall quantum index may be obtained for each country by deflating its GDP, expressed in domestic currency units, by a PPP arrived at by an appropriate averaging process—either geometric or arithmetic—of individual category PPPs. The distinguishing feature of "average-weight" methods is not that they are concerned directly with this averaging process; rather, they are directed at the method of arriving at the weights that are used in the process. The weights assigned to each category's PPPs are obtained by assessing the average importance of the category, relative to all other categories, across all of the countries, measured either by quantity[27] or expenditure averages. A number of different average-weights methods have been employed experimentally in the ICP computation work, but results are reported only for the Walsh Price Index.

Walsh method. The distinguishing feature of the Walsh method is that expenditures are used as weights. In the version of the Walsh index used in the ICP, expenditures were averaged arithmetically.[28] The formula is given by equation (5.6):

$$(5.6) \quad \text{PPP}_j = \prod_{i=1}^{m} P_{ij}^{v_i} \; ; \; v_i = \frac{1}{n} \sum_{j=1}^{n} \left[e_{ij} / \sum_{i=1}^{m} e_{ij} \right]$$

where m is the number of detailed categories, n is the number of countries, and e is the expenditures. Because the negative correlation between prices and quantities within a country is basically what lies behind the index number problem, it seems plausible that expenditures may be more suitable than quantities, in the Walsh method, in weighting the category PPPs. A modified form of the Walsh index is just right if all demand curves are of unitary elasticity.[29]

EKS method.[30] As indicated in the discussion of binary methods, in comparing two countries' outputs at any level of aggregation, we should like to make different items commensurable by using price weights that are closely relevant to the two countries. (To spell out further: the index using one country's weights unfortunately neglects the other country's consumption pattern; on the other hand, the index using the second country's weights unfortunately neglects the first country's consumption pattern; average-price weights do not specifically represent the patterns of either country, but rather reflect a compromise pattern.) Although it may be hard to decide just what consumption pattern to refer to in obtaining price weights, most economists would agree that those of a third country markedly different from the first two should not be considered. It may be impossible to decide on theoretical grounds whether to use American prices or Japanese prices in comparing the outputs of the United States and Japan, but almost everyone would consider either set of prices superior to the set of prices prevailing in, say, Colombia—except, of course, Colombians.

---

[27] Average quantity weights were used in the comparisons made by the Economic Commission for Latin America. See U.N. Economic Commission for Latin America, *A Measurement of Price Levels and the Purchasing Power of Currencies in Latin America, 1960-62,* Document E/CN. 12/653 (New York: United Nations, 1963). See also S. N. Braithwaite, "Real Income Levels in Latin America," *Review of Income and Wealth,* (June 1968), pp. 113-82. The ICP could not apply the average quantity weight method because it requires prices and quantities at the category levels not available to us. The prices we have at the detailed category level are *relative* prices (PPPs relative to the dollar).

[28] Correa M. Walsh, *The Measurement of General Exchange Values* (New York: Macmillan, 1910). The ICP did not use the geometric-average weighting procedure because it assigns a negligible weight to a category for which even one country has a tiny expenditure.

[29] Richard Ruggles has argued cogently for average-expenditure weights because they allow for price elasticity. Also, in "Price Indexes and International Price Comparisons" (in *Ten Economic Studies in the Tradition of Irving Fisher* [New York: John Wiley, 1967], p. 200), he develops other arguments for average-expenditure weights.

[30] Named for its three independent discoverers, Elteto, Koves, and Szulc. The original publications describing these methods are not in English, but see L. Dreschler, "Weighting of Index Numbers in International Comparisons," *Review of Income and Wealth* (March 1973), pp. 17-34. This method has been used in some international comparison work by the socialist countries of Eastern Europe.

The EKS method calls for the computation of circular quantity indexes with the property that the full collection of them—that is, the estimate of Country j's output relative to Country k's for all j and k—should deviate "minimally" (in an appropriate logarithmic least-squares sense) from what would be obtained if Fisher ideal indexes were used. This underlying principle of quadratic minimization leads to a formula for execution:

$$(5.7) \qquad \text{EKS}_{jk} = \left[F_{jk}^2 \cdot \prod_{\substack{l=1 \\ l \neq j,k}}^{n} \frac{F_{jl}}{F_{kl}} \right]^{\frac{1}{n}},$$

where F_{jk} is the Fisher quantity index for Country j relative to Country k. (It should be remembered that the Fisher indexes are not circular, and this is one important reason for going beyond them to EKS.)

The EKS method is a multilateral method because a comparison of any two countries makes use of prices in all other countries.[31] Certainly, this method gives results in accord with one's intuition. It is to be expected that any sensible method of comparing the outputs of two countries will lean heavily on an original-country binary comparison between the two. But a direct comparison of each of the countries with a third (and fourth, fifth, and so on) country tells something additional about how two countries compare. Suppose one knows that, as measured by the Fisher index, the first country's output is twice that of the third country, and the second country's output is only half again as much as that of the third. These two fragments of information suggest that the first country's output is in the neighborhood of 1.33 ($2 \div 1.5$) times as great as that of the second. Now, if those bridge-country comparisons (Country 1/Country 3 and Country 2/Country 3) were known along with the original-country Fisher index, say 1.20, for the two countries, how should 1.20 and 1.33 be combined to get a single estimate?

The EKS method calls for a weighted geometric mean of the two numbers, with the original-country comparison getting a weight of 2 and the bridge-country comparisons each getting a weight of 1. (The EKS method, as outlined, ignores the implications of some countries being larger or more important than others. If such a consideration were deemed important, it would be appropriate to take it into account in the least-squares function. The natural way of introducing the importance factor into that function would lead to a formula in which the index is a weighted geometric mean such as the EKS formula above but with weights different from $[2, 1, \ldots, 1]$.)

The Van Yzeren method(s).[32] The Van Yzeren approach, like the Walsh procedure, was designed to measure the purchasing power of various countries' currency. These PPPs could then be used as deflators to obtain quantum indexes. Like the EKS method, it builds up multilateral comparisons out of binary ones. The criterion for combining the binary indexes, however, is based upon Van Yzeren's concept of a complicated set of common market baskets. Thus, it avoids the quite special and arbitrary quadratic minimization principle. (But in the limiting case of two countries, both EKS and Van Yzeren reduce to the Fisher index.) Essentially, the method calls for pricing the goods and services of each of a number of countries in each of the other countries. A set of purchasing-power indexes is computed on the basis of minimizing what Van Yzeren calls a "discordance function," which is "a yardstick for the degree to which the currency ratios are adapted to the price and quantity patterns of the different countries."

Van Yzeren has devised three different methods, each of which can be used with or without weighting, but only his preferred, so-called "balanced," method will be described here. Consider a world consisting of four countries, A, B, C, and D, which have as their national currencies A-francs, B-francs, C-francs, and D-francs. Our problem of finding relative purchasing powers amounts to seeking a set of "exchange rates" (what we call PPPs), r_{BA}, r_{CA}, and r_{DA}, which will tell how many B-francs, C-francs, and D-francs will be received in exchange for one A-franc. The conditions to be imposed upon r_{BA}, r_{CA}, and r_{DA} involve costs incurred by four men, one from each country, buying a basket in the proportions of his own country's basket in each of the other countries. Essentially, r_{BA}, r_{CA}, and r_{DA} should be such that the total cost of buying three standardized baskets (one of the B-basket type, another of the C-basket type, and a third of the D-basket type) in A with A-francs is equal to the total cost of three standardized A-baskets, one each bought in B, C, and D. Here, payments are made in the currencies of those three countries, the currencies having been obtained by exchanging A-francs at r_{BA}, r_{CA}, and r_{DA} rates. Similarly, the total cost of buying an A-basket, a C-basket, and a D-basket in B with B-francs must be equal to the total cost of three B-baskets bought in A, C, and D. These two conditions on r_{BA}, r_{CA}, and r_{DA}, plus the analogous one involving purchases in C,

---

[31] In principle, at least, the EKS method also could have been used to average item prices to arrive at category PPPs. It may be conjectured that countries with similar quantity structures within categories will exhibit similar pricing patterns. That is, the same items will be priced or will be left unpriced. If this were so, original-country price indexes would be most "characteristic" (in the sense set out early in Chapter 4). Therefore, EKS comparisons might be regarded as a good compromise between conflicting desires for characteristicity and efficiency (via bridge-countries). It is easy to show, however, that the EKS method applied to a P matrix with holes does not necessarily give circular PPPs. As a consequence, the EKS method as a way of obtaining category PPPs was rejected almost at the outset.

[32] J. van Yzeren, "Three Methods of Comparing the Purchasing Power of Currencies," Netherlands Central Bureau of Statistics, *Statistical Studies* (December 1956), pp. 3–34. This method was used by the European Coal and Steel Community.

together define a set of three equations that the three PPPs must satisfy. (The fourth analogous equation is not independent of the other three, so it may be ignored because of its redundancy.)

Solving the set of equations is a simple matter, even though it is not a linear system, because a convenient algorithm has been provided by Van Yzeren. The equation system will not be reproduced here. Suffice to say, the coefficients appearing in it will be indexes in which each country's market basket is valued at each country's prices. Once we have the r_{BA}, r_{CA}, and r_{DA}, it is an easy matter to deflate the national outputs valued in their local currencies to get relative quantum indexes for the four countries.

The Geary-Khamis method. If each country's price for a particular good or service were adjusted for the known purchasing power of the country's currency, it would be easy to find a (weighted) average "international price," denoted π_i, for the good or service. Similarly, if the international price were known for each good or service, it would be a simple matter to compute for each country the average (weighted) deviation of its prices from the international prices and thereby obtain the corresponding purchasing power, denoted PPP_j, of its currency. That is to say, using the prices and quantities for all countries and all goods and services, p_{ij} and q_{ij}, one can obtain all the π_i's if all the PPP_js are known; and the PPP_js can be obtained if all the π_is are known. Geary has suggested the use of a system of homogeneous linear equations that would make it possible to find the π_is and PPP_js simultaneously.[33] Subsequently, Khamis demonstrated that the equation system can indeed be depended upon to give nonnegative π_i's and PPP_js and, in a number of ways he amplified the method.[34]

GDP then can be found for each country in either of two ways: either (1) by valuing the category quantities at the calculated international prices (the π_i's) and aggregating across all 152 categories; or (2) by deflating each country's GDP expressed in domestic currency units, by its calculated purchasing power parity (PPP_j). The two procedures give the same amount.

[33] R. G. Geary, "A Note on Comparisons of Exchange Rates and Purchasing Power Between Countries," *Journal of the Royal Statistical Society* 21 (1958), pp. 97–99. The essence of the Geary system was suggested also by Smith and Jablon, as reported in D. Brady and A. Hurwitz, "Measuring Comparative Purchasing Power," in *Studies in Income and Wealth* (Princeton, N.J.: Princeton University Press, 1957), p. 307. An iterative method that converges to the Geary-Khamis PPPs is described there.

[34] S. H. Khamis, "Some Problems Relating to International Comparability and Fluctuating of Production Volume Indicators," *Bulletin of International Statistical Institute* 42 (1967), pp. 213–320; "Properties and Conditions for the Existence of a New Type of Index Number," *Sankhya* 32, (1970), pp. 81–98; "A New System of Index Numbers for National and International Purposes," *Journal of the Royal Statistical Society* 135 (1972) pp. 96–121. The Geary-Khamis method has been used at the Food and Agriculture Organization and the Indian Statistical Institute.

The Geary-Khamis equation system is as follows:

$$(5.8) \qquad \pi_i = \sum_{j=1}^{n} \frac{p_{ij}}{PPP_j} \left[\frac{q_{ij}}{\sum_{j=1}^{n} q_{ij}} \right] \quad i = 1, \ldots, m,$$

$$(5.9) \qquad PPP_j = \frac{\sum_{i=1}^{m} p_{ij} q_{ij}}{\sum_{i=1}^{m} \pi_i q_{ij}} \quad j = 1, \ldots, n,$$

where n is the number of countries and m is the number of detailed categories. Note the economic interpretations of the two subsystems: equation (5.8) says that the international price of the ith category is the quantity-weighted average of the purchasing-power–adjusted prices of the ith category in the n countries; and equation (5.9) says that the purchasing power of a country's currency is equal to the ratio of the cost of its total bill of goods at national prices to the cost at international prices.[35]

Though the system as written consists of $(n + m)$ equations in $(n + m)$ unknowns, one is redundant. After suitable manipulation, the sum over i of equation (5.8) can be shown to be equal to the sum over j of equation (5.9)[36]—and the system is homogeneous. By dropping one equation and setting $PPP_n = 1$, and then rearranging terms, equations (5.8) and (5.9) become:

[35] The original Geary conception can be restated easily in terms of weighted geometric averages instead of weighted arithmetic ones. (See D. S. Prasada Rao, *Contributions to Methodology of Construction of Consistent Index Numbers* [unpublished dissertation, Indian Statistical Institute, Calcutta, 1972]). This alternative version does not provide the additivity which is so useful in disaggregation.

[36] Multiply both sides of equation (5.8) by $\sum_{j=1}^{n} q_{ij}$ and transpose the right-hand side to the left to obtain:

$$(5.8') \quad (\sum_{j=1}^{n} q_{ij}) \pi_i - \sum_{j=1}^{n} p_{ij} q_{ij} \cdot \frac{1}{PPP_j} = 0 \quad i = 1, \cdots, m.$$

Similarly, multiply both sides of equation (5.9) by $\sum_{i=1}^{m} \pi_i q_{ij}/PPP_j$ and transpose the right-hand side to the left to obtain:

$$(5.9') \quad \sum_{i=1}^{} q_{ij} \pi_i - \sum_{i=1}^{m} p_{ij} \cdot \frac{1}{PPP_j} = 0 \quad j = 1, \ldots, n.$$

Now sum equation (5.8') over i from 1 to m to get

$$\sum_{i=1}^{m} \sum_{j=1}^{n} q_{ij} \pi_i - \sum_{i=1}^{m} \sum_{j=1}^{n} p_{ij} q_{ij} \cdot \frac{1}{PPP_j} = 0.$$

This is exactly what is obtained if equation (5.9') is summed over j from 1 to n. Therefore, one equation is redundant.

Note that equation (5.10) in the text is the system given by (5.8') and (5.9') except that the last equation ($i=n$) of (5.9') has been dropped and PPP_n has been set equal to 1.

$$Q_1\pi_1 \qquad -e_{11}\frac{1}{PPP_1} -e_{12}\frac{1}{PPP_2} -\cdots -e_{1,n-1}\frac{1}{PPP_{n-1}} = e_{1n}$$

$$Q_2\pi_2 \qquad -e_{21}\frac{1}{PPP_1} -e_{22}\frac{1}{PPP_2} -\cdots -e_{2,n-1}\frac{1}{PPP_{n-1}} = e_{2n}$$

$$\vdots \qquad\qquad \vdots \qquad\qquad \vdots \qquad\qquad \vdots \qquad\qquad \vdots$$

$$Q_m\pi_m -e_{m1}\frac{1}{PPP_1} -e_{m2}\frac{1}{PPP_2} -\cdots -e_{m,n-1}\frac{1}{PPP_{n-1}} = e_{m,n}$$

(5.10)

$$q_{11}\pi_1 + q_{21}\pi_2 + \cdots + q_{m1}\pi_m - e_1\frac{1}{PPP_1} = 0$$

$$q_{12}\pi_1 + q_{22}\pi_2 + \cdots + q_{m2}\pi_m \qquad\quad - e_2\frac{1}{PPP_2} = 0$$

$$\vdots \qquad\qquad \vdots \qquad\qquad \vdots \qquad\qquad\qquad \vdots$$

$$q_{1,n-1}\pi_1 + q_{2,n-1}\pi_2 + \cdots + q_{m,n-1}\pi_m \qquad\quad - e_{n-1}\frac{1}{PPP_{n-1}} = 0,$$

where Q_i is the total quantity for all countries of the ith category; q_{ij} is the quantity of the ith category consumed in the jth country, e_j is the value of the total expenditure of the jth country in its own domestic prices; and e_{ij} is the expenditure of the jth country on the ith category in its own currency. Notice that the system is no longer homogeneous because everything is now standardized on the nth country.

The special structure of the $(m + n - 1)$ equation system in as many unknowns given by equation (5.10) requires comment. In the ICP application of Geary-Khamis, m is equal to 152 and n is equal to 10, so the system is quite large.[37] Fortunately, the presence of many strategically located zero coefficients in the system, 23,033 out of a total of 26,082, makes easy what otherwise would be a formidable computing exercise. Though modern high-speed computers make possible if awkward the solution of a system of 161 linear equations, the problem of round-off error would be a matter of serious concern in such a large system. Equation (5.10) can be rewritten, however, so that the matrix of left-hand–side coefficients will consist of two diagonal submatrices along the diagonal. By taking advantage of an elementary theorem about the inverse of partitioned matrices, it is possible to solve the 161-equation system with dispatch by engaging in computations no more complicated than various matrix multiplications and the inversion of a nine-by-nine matrix. Furthermore, the location of the zeros makes the round-off problem quite manageable if double-precision arithmetic is used.

As inputs, the Geary-Khamis method requires prices and physical quantities for the sets of goods and services to be covered. The ICP's data base, after the raw item prices were refined into category PPPs, comprised (1) a set of 152 prices for each of nine countries, denominated in national currency units and expressed relative to the U.S. dollar; and (2) a set of 152 expenditures for each of the ten countries, again denominated in national currency units. Our inputs into Geary-Khamis, then, are not quite those originally envisioned by Geary. We use the category PPPs as prices and a set of "notional" quantities, each obtained as the ratio of expenditure to PPP (the latter derived from a frequency-weighted CPD, or, in the twenty-three instances described above[38] by other methods). If the international prices and purchasing power parities obtained using ICP inputs are denoted $\bar{\pi}_i$ and $\overline{PPP}_j$ then their values are determined by the conditions of equations (5.11) and (5.12)

$$(5.11) \qquad \bar{\pi}_i = \sum_{j=1}^{n} \frac{P_{ij}}{\overline{PPP}_j} \left[\frac{Q_{ij}}{\sum\limits_{j=1}^{n} Q_{ij}} \right]$$

$$(5.12) \qquad \overline{PPP}_j = \frac{\sum\limits_{i=1}^{m} P_{ij} Q_{ij}}{\sum\limits_{i=1}^{m} \bar{\pi}_i Q_{ij}} \,,$$

where $P_{ij} = p_{ij}/p_{i,US}$ and $Q_{ij} = \dfrac{pp_{ij} \cdot q_{ij}}{p_{ij}/p_{i,US}} = q_{ij}p_{i,US}$. It is easy to show that $\bar{\pi}_i = \pi_i/p_{i,US}$ and $PPP_j = PPP_j$. Thus, the ICP's PPP_j is indeed correct. The fact that the ICP international price for each category $(\bar{\pi}_i)$ deviates from

---

[37]The system was even larger, because 164 categories actually were used in the computations. See the latter part of footnote 22.

[38]See page 65.

the Geary concept (π_i) by a factor equal to the U.S. price for that category would appear to be a source of concern. We use international prices, however, only as a basis for valuing ICP notional quantities. They never are used alone, but rather have application only in connection with terms of the form $\overline{\pi}_i Q_{ij}$. Because this product is equal to $(\pi_i/p_{i,\ US}) \cdot (q_{ij}p_{i,\ US}) = \pi_i q_{ij}$, the ICP real quantity values coming from Geary-Khamis are correct even though the quantity input was notional rather than physical.

The Geary-Khamis method can be applied at any level of aggregation. We have chosen to apply the method to all 152 categories of GDP, but, alternatively, we could have operated at the level of the major sectors Consumption, Capital Formation, and Government or even at lower levels. The ICP groups all 152 categories together at once because of the special character of the additivity feature of Geary-Khamis quantity indexes. The general approach to finding the quantity indexes for the major sectors, and indeed for subsectors within the major sectors, was foreshadowed in the previous paragraph. The procedure is explained in Chapter 14, and the indexes are presented in Table 14.4. It is sufficient here to observe that a country's quantity index for a grouping of categories is obtained by (1) valuing the country's quantities for each of the categories using the international prices obtained from the 152 category grouping; (2) valuing the U.S. quantities in the grouping in the same way; and (3) computing the ratio of the first value to the second. It should be recognized that, in general, the quantity index obtained this way will not be identical to the quantity index obtained by applying Geary-Khamis to the categories of the grouping alone. In Section F, below,[39] we show that in fact this distinction is unimportant empirically.

THE CHOICE OF GEARY-KHAMIS

We chose Geary-Khamis over the other estimating methods primarily because it is based upon the assumption that is implicit in the question asked whenever international comparisons are made: it assumes that there is a unique price level for each country, and that this can be measured in terms of the weighted average deviation of its prices from average international prices. Looked at from another standpoint, it defines international prices in a straightforward and appropriate manner. It is, in turn, the availability of these international prices that enables us to achieve additivity conjointly with transitivity. Finally, the method makes it possible to pick a base country that will be no more than a numeraire country. That is, the method is base country invariant. In having this clear economic rationale, it compares favorably with the EKS method, which, as noted above, transforms Fisher indexes into transitive indexes so as to minimize the squared deviations of the

new indexes from the original ones. Although Fisher indexes have wide acceptance and the EKS indexes exhibit a high degree of characteristicity,[40] the procedure still must be regarded as rather mechanical relative to the Geary-Khamis approach. The Van Yzeren method's complicated interpretation puts it at a substantial disadvantage relative to Geary-Khamis.

The Walsh index is perhaps the most attractive of the alternatives to Geary-Khamis. Expenditure weights have the advantage of implying price elasticities of unity, which probably is more realistic than the zero elasticities implied by quantity weights. (Of course, demand theorists would find the Cobb-Douglas form of the utility function implied by the Walsh index to be unsatisfactory.) This advantage of building some elasticity in the demand functions is offset by the attractiveness of the Geary-Khamis conception of a world price system with country and commodity influences accounting for observed prices, and its being amenable to aggregations over less than full GDP. (Incidentally, it is possible to estimate international prices using the Walsh method by introducing Walsh PPPs into equation [5.8]. The real GDPs of each country valued at these international prices, however, would not be equal to the real GDPs found by deflating domestic GDPs by the Walsh PPPs.)

PROBLEM CATEGORIES

In using the Geary-Khamis technique, as well as other methods, categories that sometimes have negative expenditures—namely, Net Expenditures of Residents Abroad (ICP 08.900), Increase in Stocks (ICP 18.000), and Exports Minus Imports (ICP 19.000)—need special treatment. In Walsh, for example, it makes no sense to apply a negative expenditure weight to the PPP for a category where expenditures are negative. In the Geary-Khamis method, the presence of negative expenditures implies negative quantities. In addition to having no easy interpretation, negative quantities can lead to meaningless results—as, for example, a negative international price for a category. (Khamis's demonstration that the Geary system will not give negative international prices assumed only positive quantities.)

The category Net Expenditures of Residents Abroad is reported by only three of the ten countries, and comparisons would afford little analytical interest. Therefore, it was consolidated with Other Services (ICP 08.400).

The Increase in Stocks happened to be positive for all ten countries, and this category, therefore, could be treated like all the others. Otherwise, special treatment along the lines accorded to Exports Minus Imports, as described below, would have been required.

The first step in the procedure for dealing with the category Exports Minus Imports, for which four countries had negative signs in 1970, was to exclude it from

---

[39] See pages 76–77.

[40] See L. Drechsler, "Weighting of Index Numbers."

the initial Geary-Khamis calculations. When the nominal U.S. quantities for all the other categories were valued at international prices, they added up to U.S. GDP less the foreign balance (that is, to GDP less Exports Minus Imports). We then performed a special calculation, described in the next paragraph, for the foreign balance to obtain its value in international dollars. The results appear in Appendix Table 14.5 (line 148). They were added to the figures for the other categories in the same table (which were derived by Geary-Khamis formulas) to form the totals for capital formation and GDP in Table 14.5. The relative quantities (that is, U.S. = 100) for capital formation and GDP in Table 14.4 embody these relationships. The PPPs for these two aggregates, reported in Summary Table 14.3, were derived from the ratio of each aggregate in national currency (Table 14.1) to the corresponding aggregate in international dollars (Table 14.5).

The starting point for the estimation of the international price for the foreign balance was to take for each country the ratio of its exchange rate to its PPP, as estimated from the initial Geary-Khamis calculation for GDP excluding the foreign balance. The exchange rate (national currency units per U.S. dollar) was a natural way to view the national price of the foreign balance. A glance at the Geary formulas[41] will indicate that it was quite in the spirit of the calculations for the other categories to divide these national prices by the PPPs. The next issue was how to weight these ratios to obtain an average international price. For the other categories, the weights used in calculating average international prices were the category quantities. Because that was not feasible here, the weights were based on the relative importance of the supercountry which each of the ten countries represented (see next section). The prices being averaged, it will be noted, correspond to the exchange rate deviation index (that is, the exchange rate divided by the PPP).

In view of the relationship between the exchange rate deviation index and the level of per capita GDP noted in Chapter 13,[42] the expedient of using supercountry importance weights does not seem particularly disadvantageous. Because this estimate of the average international price turns out to be greater than unity, however, the valuation of the U.S. foreign balance at the international price makes it larger than the original U.S. dollar figure. When it is added to the other U.S. categories (those derived through Geary-Khamis), valued at international prices, the U.S. total GDP thus exceeds the original dollar figure for U.S. GDP. Because as a matter of convenience we wished to retain the original U.S. GDP total, all international prices were scaled downward so that the sum of GDP of the United States at international prices equaled U.S. GDP at U.S. prices. This adjustment does not affect the relation of the GDP of other countries to the U.S. at international prices, because the aggregates and subaggregates for all countries are adjusted in the same proportion.

E. From Representative Countries to "Supercountries"

An essential aspect of the Geary-Khamis method is that the international price of any category is equal to the weighted average of the individual country prices for that category after the country prices have each been made commensurate by division by the various country overall PPPs. But the weight for any country is its share of the "worldwide" quantity of the category good or service. If the ICP countries are not properly representative of the countries of the world, our international prices (and, therefore, our estimates of per capita GDP in international dollars for each country) will depend upon which countries are, fortuitously, in the ICP set. In fact, the ten ICP countries are far from representative (as will be made evident shortly), so some method must devised to take account of this complication. We must decide how to derive from the prices of the ten included countries a set of average international prices that will reflect the average price structure prevailing in the world as a whole. Our basic procedure is to weight the price structure of each of the ten countries in accordance with the degree to which each is likely to be representative of the price structures of the countries that are not included in the ICP set.

The computing formulas for the Fisher, Walsh, EKS, and Van Yzeren indexes, by the way, do not depend upon the relative sizes of the ICP countries or the degree of their unrepresentativeness. That is not to say, however, that the results of these methods for each given country will not depend on which other countries are included.

In considering the representativeness of the ten ICP countries—or the lack thereof—one is struck immediately by the fact that, on average, the ICP countries are distinctly more affluent than the world as a whole. In 1970 the total GDP of the developed market economies was US$2,083,200 millions, whereas that of the developing market economies was US$386,600 millions, a ratio of 5.4 to 1.[43] In the case of the ICP countries, the total GDP of the six developed market economies was US$1,738,750 millions, as opposed to US$61,841 millions for the three developing market economies (see Table 1.1), a ratio of 28.1 to one. (Because these GDP figures are based upon exchange rate conversions, they overstate the real differences between developed and

[41] See page 68.
[42] See page 170.
[43] U.N. Statistical Office, *U.N. Yearbook of National Accounts, 1971*, Vol. 3 (New York: U.N.).

developing countries.[44] This consideration, however, is equally relevant to both the world and the ICP countries.) In the ICP set, the developing countries clearly are underrepresented. Similarly, the geographic distribution of the ICP set is far from random, with Western Europe overrepresented and Africa, Asia, and Latin America underrepresented.

To achieve a proper balance, a weighting procedure was adopted in which a "supercountry" was constituted with reference to each of our ten ICP countries. That is, ten synthetic supercountries, one for each ICP country, were established, each representing the weight of a group of countries on the basis of income, as well as some other criteria such as geography. The ICP country belonging to a supercountry is called the "representative" country of that supercountry. The ten supercountries account for all 189 countries of the world listed in the *World Bank Atlas, 1972*.[45] Each supercountry is assumed to have the same price and expenditure structure as the countries it represents, but its total GDP is assumed to equal the sum of the 1970 GDPs of the class of countries making up that supercountry.

In the foregoing description of the Geary-Khamis procedure, the unit of analysis was a country. In fact, we apply the procedure to supercountries. The synthetic nature of the country units does not necessitate any special provision in the computing, but the output of Geary-Khamis then will be the international prices and purchasing-power parities of the ten supercountries. We return soon[46] to a description of how we apply the supercountry PPP_is and π_is to the representative countries to make comparisons among the representative countries.

The assumption that the price and expenditure structures of the supercountries match the structures of the corresponding representative countries, along with the weighting procedure that determines total supercountry GDPs, define our inputs for Geary-Khamis. The category prices for each supercountry are merely the category PPPs of its representative country.[47] Again, each cate-

gory quantity is a notional quantity, but now it is equal to the product of the supercountry's GDP times the proportion of the GDP of its representative country that was spent on the category, all divided by the representative country's category PPP. In effect, we have scaled all of the ICP countries' notional quantities up or down relatively to take account of the degree to which each country type is overrepresented or underrepresented in the ICP set.

It remains to indicate the basis for allocating the countries of the world to the various supercountries in order to arrive at the scaling factors. We have, in fact, partitioned the 189-country list in a number of ways, and, as will be demonstrated below,[48] have found the results relatively insensitive to minor changes in the assignments.

In our preferred partitioning, the 189 countries are arrayed by 1970 per capita GNP, as reported in the *World Bank Atlas*, and then divided into three tiers. (To facilitate exposition, the GNP figures from the *Atlas* henceforth are referred to simply as "GDP," because the ICP works with the GDP concept. The difference between the two aggregates will be trivial for present purposes, particularly because they are summed over a number of countries.) The 17 most affluent countries were placed in the first tier, the next 32 countries in the array were placed in the second tier, and the 140 least affluent were placed in the third tier. Specifically, the split was made so that all of the upper-tier countries had per capita GDPs above US$2,500, all of the lower-tier countries had per capita GDPs below US$1,000, and all of the middle-tier countries had per capita GDPs between US$1,000 and US$2,500. The total GDP of each tier was summed and then divided evenly among the ICP countries assigned to the tier. The United States, the Federal Republic of Germany, and France were in the upper tier; the United Kingdom, Japan, Italy, and Hungary were in the middle tier; and Colombia, Kenya, and India were in the lower tier. The total GDP of each tier and of each supercountry were as follows:

Upper tier	US$millions	Middle tier	US$millions	Lower tier	US$millions
Total GDP	1,545,930	Total GDP	1,141,800	Total GDP	548,250
Supercountry GDP:		Supercountry GDP:		Supercountry GDP:	
United States	515,310	United Kingdom	285,450	Colombia	182,750
Germany, F.R.	515,310	Japan	285,450	Kenya	182,750
France	515,310	Italy	285,450	India	182,750
		Hungary	285,450		

---

[44] See page 5.

[45] International Bank for Reconstruction and Development, *World Bank Atlas: Population, Per Capita Product and Growth Rates* (Washington: IBRD, 1972). The Atlas includes estimates

for some developing countries that do not report to the United Nations.

[46] See the following page.

[47] See page 65.

[48] See the following page.

Two other partitionings were examined. In the first of these, six tiers were defined. The ICP countries were assigned to the tiers as follows: Tier 1, the United States; Tier 2, the Federal Republic of Germany and France; Tier 3, the United Kingdom and Japan; Tier 4, Italy and Hungary; Tier 5, Colombia; Tier 6, Kenya and India. The first five countries in the *World Bank Atlas* (those with per capita GDP above US$3,500) with a total GDP of US$1,090 billion were put in the first tier, and the GNP of the U.S. supercountry was set at the entire $1,090 billion. The next two countries (those with per capita GDP between US$2,500 and US$3,500) with a total GDP of US$456 billion constituted the second tier; and the GDPs of the German (F.R.) and French supercountries were each set at US$228 billion. The other four supercountries were treated in the same manner.

In the second of the alternatives, the partitioning was based primarily upon the geographical regions of the ICP countries. In addition, however, political affiliations or trade relationships were taken into account. All of Latin America was assigned to the Colombian supercountry; all of the developing countries of Asia (and Oceania) and Africa were assigned to the Indian and Kenyan supercountries, respectively; the Commonwealth countries and some other related areas were assigned to the United Kingdom; the Socialist countries were assigned to Hungary (except that the Peoples' Republic of China was grouped with India); and so on.

Before examining the consequences of these alternative ways of assigning the countries of the world to the ten ICP countries, a reminder about the purpose of applying Geary-Khamis to the supercountries is in order. The PPPs obtained from applying Geary-Khamis to the ten supercountries could be used to find the relative size of a supercountry's GDP compared with that of the United States supercountry, which fact is not without interest. But, the more important application—and, indeed, the point of the entire procedure—is to value the GDPs of the representative countries. In the Geary-Khamis method, the weights (total GDPs) of the supercountries directly affect the importance of the individual countries in determining the international prices (see equation [5.8]). Of course, the weights affect the PPPs as well, but only indirectly insofar as they are critical in determining the international prices (see equation [5.9]). It should be emphasized, however, that it is the notional quantities of the representative countries and not the notional quantities of the supercountries that are valued at the international prices. International prices derived through the use of supercountries are preferred because they bring us closer to a price structure like the one that would be obtained if all the countries of the world—or a representative sample of countries—were included in the ICP.

As stated earlier, the three-tier weighting system is the one preferred by the ICP. It combines a correction for unrepresentativeness with simplicity. A more complicated classification such as the one based on six tiers increases the number of cases in which arbitrary decisions must be made about the assignment of countries to one tier or another. In any case, the three classification schemes examined provide some basis for gauging the extent of the differences produced by alternative ways of constituting the supercountries. The following table compares estimates of relative per capita GDP using alternative weighting systems. Columns 1 and 2 show the percentage deviations between the results of the three-tier partition and both the six-tier and geography partitions.

Percentage Difference of Each Weighting Method from the Three-Tier Results

	Six tiers	"Geography"	Unweighted	Unweighted per capita
	(1)	(2)	(3)	(4)
Colombia	1.9	3.1	17.5	9.4
France	3.8	4.3	3.9	.2
Germany, F.R.	2.7	3.6	2.8	-.1
Hungary	4.8	2.5	11.2	4.5
India	4.2	2.9	22.5	12.7
Italy	4.2	3.9	7.3	2.8
Japan	2.8	4.2	6.5	1.8
Kenya	6.3	5.3	26.3	17.6
United Kingdom	3.0	2.0	6.8	2.7

The maximum difference between per capita GDP as estimated by the three-tier partition and either the six-tier or the geography partition is only 6.3 percent.

Another basis for judging the three-tier results is through a Geary-Khamis calculation in which no special supercountry weighting is used. That is, the notional quantities for each country are the actual ones for each country. The difference between these and the three-tier results, shown in column 3, is substantial enough to justify the ICP concern with weighting. Specifically, reliance on the price structures of only the ten ICP countries to derive the average international prices would bias the results for lower-income countries sharply upwards. This is the result of what is often termed the "Gerschenkron effect," to be discussed presently.

Still another weighting scheme of possible interest involves representative countries instead of supercountries, but where GDPs are represented in per capita terms. Such a scheme would reduce the impact of differences in population, and in this sense it would treat the countries as more nearly equal. The entries in column 4 show that per capita weights produce results similar to those in column 3, though in every case they are closer to the three-tier supercountry results.

Geary-Khamis is a multilateral method that must be recalculated every time a new country is added to the system of comparisons. If our supercountries were ideally constituted, however, the average international prices would reflect the average world price structure, and they would not change even if recomputed with new countries added. Therefore, the same prices could be used to value the quantities of the new countries. Furthermore, the addition of new countries to the ICP comparisons would not significantly affect the relative GDP standings of the presently included countries—provided, of course, that the same reference year was retained.

The practical question, therefore, is: "To what extent would our international prices change with the addition of new countries?" Until data for additional countries are fully available, the only way a judgment can be made is by dropping some countries and recomputing the international prices.

An experiment was performed in which international prices were computed using the Geary-Khamis supercountry approach applied to the 1970 prices and expenditures for six of the ten countries (Hungary, India, Japan, Kenya, the United Kingdom, and the United States). Two sets of comparisons were then made:

1. The standings of the six countries relative to the United States based upon the six-country data were compared with the standings based upon the ten-country data; and
2. The standings of the other four countries (Colombia, France, the Federal Republic of Germany, and Italy) relative to the United States as calculated from the six-country international prices were compared with the standings based upon the ten-country international prices.

The motivation for picking this particular set of six countries stemmed from the fact that necessarily we had singled out these countries already for our 1967 comparisons on grounds of availability of data. The experiment was flawed because the category PPPs used in calculating the six-country international prices for 1970 were obtained using CPD applied to all ten countries rather than to the six alone. Nevertheless, the table giving the results of this experiment is illuminating:

Percentage Difference of Results Based on
Six Country Prices from Those Based on
Ten Country Prices

	International Prices Based on	
	US$2,500 Cutoff	US$3,500 Cutoff
	(1)	(2)
Kenya	7.0	3.5
India	5.6	2.8
Hungary	6.5	3.7
United Kingdom	4.0	2.2
Japan	7.5	5.0

The percentage difference in per capita GDP relative to the United States is shown for the five countries (other than the United States) using two variants of the six-country application. In the variant reported in column 1, the weights assigned to the supercountry tiers corresponded exactly to those of the first partitioning described above:[49] that is, a per capita GDP of US$2,500 was the line of division for assignment of countries to the middle and upper tiers. The differences in column 1 are between 4 and 7.5 percent, with the six-country comparisons always larger.

It is not difficult to understand why this method produces higher per capita GDPs for the five countries relative to the United States than does the corresponding method based on ten-country data. Because the same per capita GDP limits were used to define the tiers, the deletion of France and the Federal Republic of Germany leaves the entire weight of the top tier to the United States. Thus, the U.S. price structure has a great influence upon the international prices, and the nearer-U.S. price structure pushes up the quantity indexes. This is the consequence of the well-known tendency, often referred to as the "Gerschenkron effect," for the valuation of a country's quantities to be high when a price structure much different from its own is the basis for the valuation. U.S. prices for domestic services, for example, are high relative to Indian prices and—as one would expect from demand theory—U.S. quantities relatively low (compared to other India–United States quantity ratios). Thus, when U.S. prices are used to value Indian quantities, much higher values result for Indian domestic servies than when Indian prices or prices taken from a price structure closer to that of India are used.

This consideration suggests that if the weight assigned to the U.S. supercountry in the six-country calculation were reduced, the column 1 differences would be reduced. This has been done by expanding the middle tier to cover a per capita GNP range of US$1,000 to US$3,500; in effect, the weights of the missing France and Federal Republic of Germany are shifted from the top to the middle tier. The results shown in column 2, as expected, are closer to the ten-country figures. We have used this alternative way of defining supercountries in the 1967 calculations of Chapter 14 on the grounds that they will produce international prices closer to the world average and also increase the comparability of the 1967 and 1970 results.

The second part of the experiment relating to the effects of the addition of countries used the six-country international prices to compute the relative per capita GDPs of the other four countries—France, the Federal Republic of Germany, Italy, and Colombia. The results were 5.5 to 9 percent higher than the results of the ten-country, three-tier results with the US$2,500 cut-off and 5 to 6 percent higher with the US$3,500 cut-off.

In general, the results are encouraging with respect to future ICP work; they suggest that the quantity indexes for the present ICP countries will not change greatly when new countries are added and a new set of international prices based on old and new countries is used to value the quantities of the old countries.

[49] See page 72.

Before going on to a discussion of the results of using different aggregation methods such as Walsh, EKS, and Van Yzeren, two implications of the supercountry weighting system should be made clear. First, although all the representative countries within a tier have equal weight, affluent nations having larger notional quantities will have more influence in the determination of international prices than poor countries.

Second, the supercountry weighting system has the merit of yielding results that are independent of the degree of political integration or subdivision of the countries. Changes in political organization—including the integration of separate countries into a single new one as well as the subdivision of a large country into smaller components, both processes having been witnessed in recent years—should not change the estimate of aggregate real GDP for the region in which the changes have occurred. The aggregate real GDP of the United States relative to the rest of the world, for example, should be the same whether the United States consists of a single political entity or of 50 separate national states. To take another illustration, the aggregate GDP of the nine countries that have made up the European Economic Community since January 1973 should be the same relative to the United States and other countries whether they are considered as separate countries or as a single aggregate. The supercountry weighting systems, like others that use total GDP to derive the quantity weights for averaging prices, satisfy this condition, but the use of per capita GDP as the basis for quantity weights produces indexes that are not invariant to the degree of political integration.

F. Comparison of Different Aggregation Methods

The results of our preferred method—Geary-Khamis applied to three tiers of supercountries—are set out in Chapter 14. Here, we compare results of our preferred method for GDP as a whole with the results of the other aggregation methods we have discussed. In Tables 5.6 and 5.7, GDP per capita and PPP at the GDP level, both expressed relative to the United States, appear as estimated by each of four multilateral methods, using the three-tier weighting system (lines 1, 2, 3, and 4). In addition to displaying these various estimates, the tables also give the estimates (line 6) derived by the original-country method, which is the basis of Chapters 4 and 13, and the Fisher ideal index (line 5), derived from the same data that were used as inputs for the multilateral methods reported in lines 1 to 4. To put these estimates into perspective, official exchange rates and GDP estimates derived from the exchange rates also are incorporated in the tables (line 7).

In Table 5.6, it will be observed that the Fisher ideal indexes of line 5 tend to be close to the corresponding original-country binary indexes of line 6. This is to be expected because both are aggregated in the same way from the category PPPs and quantity indexes to get GDP, though they were derived from slightly different category data. The original-country method involves category PPPs for two countries based upon only the item prices of the two countries, whereas the Fisher method of line 5 operates on category PPPs that were

Table 5.6. Per Capita Quantity Indexes for Gross Domestic Product, 1970, Ten Countries Estimated by Alternative Methods

(U.S.=100)

Method[†]	Colombia	France	Germany, F.R.	Hungary	India	Italy	Japan	Kenya	U.K.	U.S.
1. Geary-Khamis	15.9	75.0	74.7	40.3	7.1	45.8	61.5	5.7	60.3	100.0
2. Walsh	14.5	75.3	72.4	40.7	6.2	47.1	60.9	5.1	63.3	100.0
3. EKS	15.1	77.3	74.4	40.7	6.2	48.4	62.6	5.6	63.8	100.0
4. Van Yzeren	15.1	77.6	74.4	40.8	6.2	48.4	62.7	5.7	64.0	100.0
5. Fisher ideal	15.0	73.5	73.5	40.2	6.3	47.7	63.6	6.0	64.0	100.0
6. Original-country binary (Fisher)[‡]	15.4	74.5	73.6	39.8	6.1	47.8	61.0	5.9	62.5	100.0
7. Exchange rate basis[§]	6.85	60.4	64.2	21.6	2.04	35.4	41.7	3.0	49.6	100.0
Range of (1), (2), (3), (4)										
A. Low	14.5	75.0	72.4	40.3	6.2	45.8	60.9	5.1	60.3	100.0
B. High	15.9	77.6	74.7	40.8	7.1	48.4	62.7	5.7	64.0	100.0
C. High/Low	1.10	1.03	1.03	1.01	1.15	1.06	1.03	1.12	1.06	1.00
Geary-Khamis as % of										
D. Exchange rate basis[¶]	232	124	116	187	348	129	147	190	122	100.0
E. Original-country binary (Fisher)	103	101	101	101	116	96	101	97	96	100.0
F. Nearest alternative among (2), (3), (4)	105	100	100	99	115	97	101	100	95	100.0

[†]See text. The methods of lines 1–5 are applied to category PPPs obtained by CPD and the like. The category PPPs used in the method of line 6 are obtained strictly by the original-country method described in Chapter 4.
[‡]From Table 13.1 to 13.9.
[§]Each country's GDP in domestic currency converted to US$ by the prevailing exchange rates.
[¶]This is the same as the exchange-rate–deviation index multiplied by 100, discussed in Chapters 1, 13, and 14.

Table 5.7. Purchasing-Power Parities for Gross Domestic Product, 1970,
Ten Countries Estimated by Alternative Methods

(U.S.=1.000)

Method†	Colombia (P)	France (Fr)	Germany, F.R. (DM)	Hungary (Ft)	India (Re)	Italy (L)	Japan (¥)	Kenya (Sh)	U.K. (£)	U.S. ($)
1. Geary-Khamis	8.01	4.48	3.14	16.07	2.16	483	244	3.74	.308	1.000
2. Walsh	8.76	4.46	3.24	15.92	2.46	470	247	4.17	.291	1.000
3. EKS	8.42	4.35	3.16	15.93	2.47	457	240	3.80	.291	1.000
4. Van Yzeren	8.41	4.33	3.16	15.90	2.47	457	239	3.79	.291	1.000
5. Fisher ideal	8.47	4.56	3.19	16.13	2.44	464	236	3.57	.291	1.000
6. Original-country binary (Fisher)‡	8.2	4.51	3.19	16.3	2.53	463	246	3.64	.298	1.000
7. Exchange rate§	18.56	5.554	3.66	30.0	7.50	625.0	360.0	7.143	.4167	1.000
Range of (1), (2), (3), (4)										
A. Low	7.96	4.33	3.14	15.90	2.16	457	240	3.76	.291	1.000
B. High	8.76	4.51	3.24	16.10	2.47	484	247	4.17	.308	1.000
C. High/Low	1.10	1.03	1.03	1.01	1.14	1.06	1.03	1.12	1.05	1.000
Geary-Khamis as % of										
D. Exchange rate	43	81	86	54	29	77	68	52	74	100
E. Original-country binary (Fisher)‡	98	99	98	99	85	104	99	103	103	100
F. Nearest alternative among (2), (3), (4)	95	100	99	101	8	106	102	99	106	100

†See text. The methods of lines 1–5 are applied to category PPPs obtained by CPD and the like. The category PPPs used in the method of line 6 are obtained strictly by the original-country method described in Chapter 4.
‡From Table 13.19.
§From Table 1.1.

obtained by CPD. We see, then, that the differences between the original-country and the multilateral comparisons are not to be explained by differences in the treatment of the item data within detailed categories.

The differences among Geary-Khamis, Walsh, EKS, and Van Yzeren range from 2 to 15 percent (line C), with the largest differences arising for India, Kenya, and Colombia. Of the nine country comparisons, Geary-Khamis gave the highest estimate of per capita GDP in four instances and the lowest in four. Only in the case of India was Geary-Khamis more than 6 percent away from its nearest alternative (line F).

The Geary-Khamis results were within 4 percent of the original-country estimates except for India, for which they were 16 percent higher. Reasons for this difference are suggested in Chapter 14.[50]

The discrepancy between the exchange-rate–derived indexes of GDP per capita and the multilateral indexes of real GDP per capita is striking and far overshadows the differences among the multilateral methods. Clearly, the exchange-rate–deviation index as based on the Geary-Khamis results (line D) would not be changed much if another multilateral method were used.

Table 5.7 presents purchasing-power parities as estimated by the various methods just reviewed. No discussion is necessary for this table; it is simply the mirror image of Table 5.6.

Comparative results can be given also for other methodological alternatives discussed in the preceding sections of this chapter. The preferred results in line 1 of Table 5.6 are based on frequency-weighted CPDs. We now make good on a promise given in Section B[51] to show that frequency-weighted CPD and unweighted CPD give similar Geary-Khamis results. The differences between relative per capita GDP calculated using the two sets of category PPPs are less than 0.6 percent for the nine countries other than the United States. The differences are much smaller than the differences indicated by lines E and F in Table 5.6.

Another decision we made was to apply Geary-Khamis to all 164 categories[52] at once rather than sector by sector bases[53] (that is, to consumption, capital formation, and government, each in turn). Here, we document our assertion[54] that the two methods give virtually the same result. The following table compares our preferred results for consumption, capital formation, and government to results based on a separate application of Geary-Khamis to each of the three major subaggregates:

[50] See pages 231, 241.

[51] See page 62.
[52] With respect to the difference from the usual reference to 152 categories, see the latter part of footnote 22.
[53] See page 70.
[54] See page 70.

Per Capita Quantity Indexes

(U.S.=100)

	Consumption		Capital Formation		Government	
			Derived from Geary-Khamis applied to			
	All categories	Consumption only	All categories	Capital Formation only	All categories	Government only
No. of categories	164	109	164	38	164	17
Colombia	16.8	16.8	18.0	17.6	7.2	7.5
France	67.9	67.9	123.5	123.2	38.2	38.1
Germany, F.R.	61.2	61.1	134.8	123.8	55.9	55.4
Hungary	38.3	38.5	56.9	55.0	25.4	26.4
India	7.6	7.5	5.3	5.2	7.3	7.6
Italy	46.0	46.0	60.5	60.2	21.3	21.5
Japan	48.3	48.4	123.6	122.3	38.1	37.3
Kenya	5.8	5.8	4.7	4.6	6.7	7.3
United Kingdom	62.2	62.2	68.1	68.2	37.4	38.2

The differences are virtually zero for consumption and are quite small in the other two sectors also. The largest difference, 9 percent, is for the Kenya–United States government index.

G. Measures of Imprecision

Line 1 of Table 5.6 presents our best estimate of GDP per capita relative to the United States for each of the countries of the ICP set. The inevitable question to be asked of such numbers is: "How accurate are they?" The conventional rules governing significant figures would suggest that, in presenting them to three digits, we believe they are correct to that number of digits. We have of course, no such exaggerated confidence in the precision of our results. As is noted several times in this book, there are three sources of error, arising, respectively, from errors in the expenditure data, errors in the prices, and the use of improper aggregation methods.

With respect to the magnitude of errors arising from the expenditure data, we have no basis for quantitative assessment. Incomparabilities undoubtedly affect the classification of expenditures into the detailed categories, especially miscellaneous categories,[55] but such classification errors tend to be offsetting. What we do not know and find difficult to judge is the extent to which our relative per capita GDPs in international dollars for different countries may be affected differentially by (1) incorrect aggregate GDP totals in national currencies and (2) improper allocation of GDP to the detailed categories.

Something can be said, however, about the other two sources of imprecision. In considering errors in the prices, we focus on an aspect of the category PPPs that were developed from item prices at the subcategory level using the CPD method. Great care was taken to ensure that the item prices were accurate both when they were collected originally in the various countries and during the processing of them by the ICP. But even if all the individual item prices were exactly correct, the fact that they are regarded as sample observations means that the category PPPs based upon them will be subject to error. This source of error can be quantified—for the 128 categories[56] examined here—because a by-product of each category CPD regression is an estimate of the variance-covariance matrix of the estimated coefficients of the country dummies.

The nine relative per capita GDP estimates—call them g_j—are related in a complicated way to the category PPPs and the corresponding set of expenditures. In principle, the sampling variances of the g_js can be found analytically if one knows the relationship and the joint density function of the category PPPs. In this case, the Geary-Khamis method is a relationship too awkward to handle analytically in connection with the lognormal PPPs. However, a numerical method is available to get estimates of the desired variances and covariances of the g_js.

Distribution sampling, or "Monte Carlo," can be used in the following way: From the set of 128 CPD regressions, we know the sampling properties of all the 1,152 category PPPs (128·9). Therefore, we can perturbate the PPPs in accordance with their sampling properties to get a new set of PPPs, to which we apply Geary-Khamis in order to get a new set of g_js. This process can be repeated T times, to get T different sets of g_js. If T is sufficiently large, the calculated variance of each g_j will be an adequate estimate of the sampling variance of g_j.

An abbreviated description of the perturbation process will suffice here. A replication is calculated by initially generating 1,152 pseudo-random normal deviates, all with means equal to the logs of the estimated PPPs

---

[55] See page 49.

[56] In all, there are 129 CPD categories, but variances and covariances were available for only 128 categories when the computation described in this section was done.

Table 5.8. Confidence Interval Estimates for Geary-Khamis Quantity Indexes and Precision Intervals

	Colombia	France	Germany, F.R.	Hungary	India	Italy	Japan	Kenya	U.K.
1. g_j: 128 categories†	.163	.813	.760	.430	.0697	.501	.608	.0578	.644
2. Mean g_j based upon 299 replications	.164	.813	.765	.432	.0696	.505	.617	.0582	.649
3. Standard deviation of g_j based upon 299 replications	.004	.022	.021	.012	.0027	.014	.019	.0028	.017
4. possible deviation of g_j at .95 level (in %)	4.81	5.30	5.42	5.47	7.59	5.48	6.13	9.50	5.17
5. g_j 152 categories	.159	.750	.747	.403	.071	.458	.615	.057	.603
6. confidence interval limits at .95 level:									
lower limit	.151	.710	.707	.381	.066	.433	.577	.052	.572
upper limit	.167	.790	.787	.425	.076	.483	.653	.062	.634
7. Precision interval‡ limits at .95 level:									
lower limit	.138	.704	.688	.380	.058	.433	.575	.048	.572
upper limit	.168	.832	.788	.434	.076	.514	.667	.062	.673
8. Possible deviation taking into account aggregation (in %)	9.4	8.5	6.7	6.7	12.7	8.8	7.5	12.3	8.4

†g_j: Per capita GDP of the jth country relative to the United States (U.S.=100)

‡Precision interval: Lower limit=minimum (lower limits of .95 confidence intervals derived from the Geary-Khamis, Walsh, EKS, and Van Yzeren methods). Upper limit=maximum (upper limits of .95 confidence intervals derived from the Geary-Khamis, Walsh, EKS, and Van Yzeren methods).

and variances and covariances equal to the estimated variances and covariances of the estimated PPPs. That is, we let the 1,152 PPPs obtained from the regression coefficients define the location parameters and let the 664,128 variances and covariances of the coefficients (most of the latter being zero because of independence between regressions) define the dispersion parameters of the log normal price world with which we are concerned. When exponentiated, these pseudo-random normal deviates are treated as category PPPs.

To each replication of the PPPs, we apply the Geary-Khamis method, always using the same expenditure set, to get nine g_js. These T replications give us a basis for estimating the sampling variability (and covariances, also, though we have not bothered with them) of the g_js. Specifically, we computed 299 replications. The mean and standard deviation of the 299 element samples for the nine g_js are given in lines 2 and 3 of Table 5.8. (Incidentally, the entries of line 1 differ, but not much, from the entries of line 1 in Table 5.6—repeated in line 4—because all of the catergories of GDP are not covered in the Monte Carlo calculations.)

The quantity indexes (line 2) are close to the quantity indexes produced by our standard application of Geary-Khamis to the same 128 categories (line 1). This need not be so, because the Geary-Khamis method does not constitute a linear transformation of the PPPs; therefore, what differences appear there need not be merely the result of sampling variability. Indeed, the standard errors of the mean are so small (equal to the entries of line 3 divided by the square root of 299) that the differences are statistically significant in seven out of nine cases.

The sampling variability of the g_j estimates relative to the "true" value (that is, the amount of dispersion one can expect around g_j) is given in line 3. If these estimates are expressed relative to the elements of line 1 and then multiplied by 1.96, as in line 4, they give rough idea of the percentage variation to which g_j is subject at the .95 confidence level. But note that the g_js in question are the ones derived from 128 categories. If we assume the same percentage error carries over at least approximately to the 152-category case, we can obtain rough estimates of the confidence intervals for the main results of the ICP—that is, for Geary-Khamis applied to 152 categories. These key Geary-Khamis estimates are repeated in line 5 from Table 5.6. Our crude estimates of the .95 confidence interval limits of the g_js for 152 categories appear in line 6. The range of inaccuracy is around 5 percent for six countries and runs a little over 9 percent for one. This amounts to between 2 and 4 percentage points for six of the countries, and is less than 1 percentage point for the other three.

A minor point should be made about the variance-covariance matrices of country-dummy coefficients for categories in which there were holes that were filled by double-weighted CPD. The variances for the hole-filled PPPs and their associated covariances were set at zero, even though non-zero estimates could have been found if the Monte Carlo exercise had warranted a substantial effort. The variance could have been derived easily from the variance–covariance matrix of the double-weighted CPD regression. The covariances would have been a difficult matter, however, so neither the variances nor covariances were introduced into the Monte Carlo exercise for hole-filled PPPs. In such cases, a row and a column of that category's variance–covariance matrix would consist of zeros.) This resulted in less variance in the g_js than otherwise would have been the case.

Because of (1) these hole-filled PPPs, (2) the possible measurement errors in the item prices, and (3) the possibility that the 128 categories to which CPD was applied were not fully representative of all 152 categories, we must emphasize that the confidence intervals appearing in line 5 should be regarded as a floor to the uncertainty associated with prices.

In addition to the price effects just discussed, we have attempted a broader quantification to cover the cumulative effect of uncertainty arising from the choice of aggregation method. (Unfortunately, we must leave unassessed the possible consequences of expenditure uncertainties.) Table 5.6 showed that each country's g_j varied from one aggregation method to another (lines 1 to 4). In no case did the results of a particular method differ from the average for all methods by more than 11 percent (for India), and generally the differences were 3 or 4 percent or less. Although there is no assurance that any one of these methods is correct, the fact that they give results that are fairly close together even though they are dissimilar in their construction leads us to think that the uncertainty associated with the choice of aggregation methods is probably small. There is no clear way of quantifying this uncertainty, but line 7 of Table 5.8 offers a set of intervals that simultaneously take into account this uncertainty and the kind of price uncertainty discussed in previous paragraphs. The Monte Carlo replications that have been described involved the Geary-Khamis method, but similar replications were computed for the Walsh, EKS, and Van Yzeren methods. In every case, the sampling variability of g_j for these methods was close to the variability of the Geary-Khamis estimates. We have constructed for each country a synthetic inter-val defined as follows: the lower limit is the lowest of the lower confidence interval limits obtained for any of the four methods, and the upper limit is the largest of the four upper confidence interval limits. Of course, the nine new "precision intervals" (presented in line 7) are not confidence intervals in any technical sense, but they do convey a feeling for how accurate our g_js are. The entries on line 8, half the width of the precision intervals, can be interpreted in the same way as the entries in line 4—except that the term "at .95 level" no longer has a probability meaning, but rather must rest on an intuitive interpretation. The uncertainty band is in the 6 to 9 percent range for seven of the countries and the 12 or 13 percent range for the other two (Kenya and India).

This section has been devoted to an attempt to appraise the accuracy of our estimates of relative per capita GDP for the countries of the ICP set. Because the Geary-Khamis estimates of relative PPPs are inversely proportional to the relative per capita GDPs, the confidence intervals for the PPPs will have a width, stated in percentage terms, that is about the same size as the entries in lines 4 and 8 of Table 5.8.

Two final points may put into perspective our guesses about the accuracy of the estimates. First, we hesitate to offer a judgment about the accuracy of estimates of sub-aggregates because we have not explored this area. Second, we have estimated .95 confidence intervals for no better reason than that this is what is commonly done by statisticians. The "correct" level of confidence to use depends upon the cost to the investigator of being wrong, but normally the statistician sets this consideration aside and falls back on the (.05 hypothesis test, .95 confidence interval) rule of thumb because he does not know his own loss function. If the ICP had used .90 confidence intervals, each of the entries in line 4 and 8 of Table 5.8 would be one-sixth less; for .80 confidence intervals, the entries would have been one-third less; and for .99 confidence intervals, the entries would have been 40 percent more.

A detailed presentation of the results of our use of CPD and the Geary-Khamis methods, at a number of levels of aggregation, can be found in Chapter 14.

Chapter 6

Comparing consumer-goods prices

The price comparisons for consumers goods reported upon in this chapter were based upon traditional methods utilized in most countries for time-to-time comparisons.

The basic steps in making these comparisons were, first, to select an appropriate sample of items and, second, to ensure that in the actual gathering of prices for these items, identical or equivalent qualities were priced in different countries. The general principles underlying the approach to the sampling and matching problems have been outlined in Chapter 3 and only their application to consumer-goods pricing need be discussed in this chapter. Price collection in individual countries also is described briefly.

Consumers goods for which price comparisons were made by other methods include (1) automobiles and other consumers durables, in Chapter 8, (2) rents, in Chapter 9, and (3) education and health services, in Chapter 7. For the first two, regression methods were employed; for education and health services, for which units of output are difficult to define and therefore to price, the price comparisons for a number of the categories were derived from direct quantity comparisons of labor inputs.

A. General Procedures

OBTAINING THE SAMPLE OF MATCHING COMMODITIES

The design of the sample of prices for the traditional type of comparison began with the establishment of a minimum number of specifications to be sought for each detailed category in the consumption sector. As stated earlier, these target numbers were based initially on the relative importance of the categories in the GDPs of five or six countries. Subsequently, they were modified in the light of the expected degree of dispersion of price relatives within the categories. In the consumption

sector, the overall target number of specifications for price comparisons made by traditional methods was nearly 250, of which 67 were in the food categories (see Table 6.1).

The first step in identifying a list of specifications was to draw upon the written specifications prepared by the U.S. Bureau of Labor Statistics (BLS) for use in the U.S. Consumer Price Index (CPI) and for its other retail price work. An effort was made, of course, to select from the BLS list of specifications those which were likely to be found in other countries. In many cases, a number of variants of a specification were included so as to enhance the likelihood that each country would find a suitable one in the BLS list. In the case of a portable electric heater, for example, one variant referred to a 1,320-watt heater, another to one consuming 1,650 watts, and a third to a heater that could be run at either of these wattages.

When each of the other nine countries checked the initial U.S. list to determine which specifications were also common in its markets, it invariably found that a significant number of specifications could be matched. In a number of cases, identical or equivalent specifications actually were being priced for purposes of maintaining time-to-time indexes in the other countries. In other instances, an item identical with, or equivalent to, the BLS specification was not priced but was known to exist in acceptable quantities in the country's markets.

Each other country also was invited to suggest modified or substitute specifications for each detailed category to the extent necessary to provide good coverage of a particular category, especially if items important in that country's expenditures in the category were not on the original list.

There were many cases in which matching products could be found easily, even though they would not have been selected independently in one of the particular countries. In the case of drugs and medical preparations, for example, only a few of the original U.S. specifica-

Table 6.1 Number of Consumer-Goods Specifications in Sample, Included Countries, 1970

	Number of detailed categories	Total number	Target number	Number priced									
				Col	Fra	Ger (FR)	Hun	Ind	Ita	Jap	Ken	U.K.	U.S.
01. Food	40	283	67	89	114	113	86	106	111	99	63	103	244
02. Clothing and, footwear	15	158	50	56	40	40	87	59	38	62	41	79	139
03. Gross rent,† fuel and power	5	33	7	7	18	18	10	10	18	10	12	11	26
04. Furniture and furnishings	16	178	37	37	47	47	50	51	45	50	32	60	161
05. Medical care	8	81	23	18	16	17	33	14	17	36	19	26	79
06. Transport‡ and communication	12	42	21	24	21	21	18	20	21	24	18	26	36
07. Recreation and education	10	125	22	28	54	53	27	40	54	36	27	30	110
08. Other goods and services	7	91	16	20	27	28	41	38	28	29	20	28	75
Total	113	991	243	279	337	337	352	338	332	346	232	363	870

†Although ICP 03. includes rents as well as fuel and power, the rent component has been handled separately, and no accounting is given here of the number of rent specifications; see Chapter 9.

‡Excludes passenger cars (ICP 06.110); see Chapter 8.

tions were widely used in India, but preparations that were important in Indian practice were also commonly used in the United States, even though they were not on the original U.S. list. These included iron salts (for anemia), sulphonomides (for dysentery and other bacterial infections and topically for trachoma), antituberculosis drugs, digitalis, insulin, and antimalarial drugs.

Milk provides an illustration of the opposite situation; that is, the most common Indian specification, for buffalo milk, could not be found in the United States, but cow's milk, accounting for nearly one-half of total Indian consumption, was sufficiently common in India to warrant basing the price comparison on this kind of specification.

In a rough and approximate way, these procedures could be considered as embodying the criterion of concentrated selection described in Chapter 3. The very fact that the specifications were included in the BLS list suggests that they were important items in their categories— or, at the minimum, widely available ones. The addition of specifications by other countries in effect was applying the criterion from the standpoint of those countries.

The response of other countries resulted in substantial alterations of the original sample chosen from the BLS specifications. Of the original list of about 350 BLS specifications, nearly 300 could be matched in one or more of the other countries. About 700 additional specifications were added, however, to round out the sample in accordance with the criteria set out in Chapter 3. The great bulk of these were selected in the course of developing binary comparisons with the United States, but some were developed by the European Economic Community (EEC) for comparisons among its member

countries, and a few were selected with reference to the India-Japan comparison. About 100 additions were made to the BLS list by Hungary and the EEC and nearly 200 by Japan, these being countries among the other nine for which samples were chosen earliest.

Once a specification was added to round out the sample for one country, it was included in the list of specifications submitted to other countries for which the work of choosing commodity samples came later.

B. Price Collection in Individual Countries

The main burden of price collection in the individual countries fell upon the central statistical offices or other official price-collection agencies. The ICP staff, for the most part, was concerned with coordinating the selection of the appropriate number of specifications in each category and with ensuring that qualities were matched and that national average prices were gathered. The central staff's work in achieving these objectives varied widely from one country to another.

COLOMBIA

In Colombia, prices were gathered by the National Department of Statistical Administration (DANE) in seven cities and adjoining rural areas: Bogota, Baranquilla, Cali, Medellin, Pasto, Manizalez, and Bucaramanga. These seven areas provided broad coverage of the geographic regions of the country, including its diverse climatic and topographical zones. The number of rural prices was limited, however, and their geographical distribution, adjacent to the cities, did not produce an optimal sampling frame. Given these circumstances, we decided simply to average the rural and urban prices in each of the seven sets of data and to combine the seven in a national average. Expenditure weights, based on the region represented by each city and its adjacent rural area, were used to compute the national average prices. These weights were from a family expenditure study of 3,000 urban and 500 rural families. The identification of the items to be priced was agreed upon in the course of an exchange of experts between Colombia and the United States.

FRANCE, GERMANY, AND ITALY

The prices for the three Common Market countries were gathered in the course of a survey organized by the Statistical Office of the EEC. The survey, carried out in November 1970, was an expanded version of a long series of consumer-goods price comparisons, the first of which was conducted in the early 1950s. Over the years, a common list of specifications was developed for all of the member countries, although for some products there were variations to permit the pricing of the local brand or trademark. For the November 1970 survey, the sample of items priced was adjusted to include a number of ICP specifications, and, as noted earlier, a number of EEC specifications were incorporated into the ICP list. This was aided by an exchange of experts.

In the Federal Republic of Germany and Italy, prices were gathered in ten different towns, five large and five small. In each town, two department stores, two supermarkets, and two specialized shops were priced. In principle, therefore, sixty observations were obtained in each country for each item. In the case of France, the sample was divided into three geographic groupings: (1) Paris; (2) Lyon, Marseilles, Bordeaux, and Rennes; and (3) small towns. Weights of three, three, and four were assigned to these categories, respectively. More than six French prices were obtained for each item. The specifications and the nature of the sample were determined jointly with the statistical directors of all six EEC countries; the actual price collection was carried out by the statistical offices of the individual countries.

HUNGARY

All prices in Hungary were supplied by the Central Statistical Office (CSO). In 1967, the prices were fixed and were a matter of record. An exchange of experts with the United States helped to identify matching qualities of goods. In 1970, energy and basic foods, such as bread and milk, were still fixed in price. Among the other prices, some were free to fluctuate within minimal and maximal limits, and others were completely free. For most 1970 prices, therefore, the Hungarian CSO relied largely upon the standard kind of price-gathering system.

INDIA

Indian prices were supplied by that country's Central Statistical Organization (CSO),[1] which drew upon other statistical agencies as well as upon its own resources. There was also an exchange of experts, each with some familiarity with the other country's market as well as with his own.

Prices and the content of consumption varied more widely between cities and rural areas and from one region to another in India than in most of the other countries. This problem was resolved by estimating national average prices for India in successive stages, taking account of different price levels in metropolitan India (defined to include Bombay, Calcutta, Delhi, and Madras), urban India (nonmetropolitan cities), and rural India.

Specifically, national average prices for each detailed category were estimated from the following formula:

$$P_n = \frac{w_m P_m + \left(w_u P_m \cdot \dfrac{P_u}{P_m}\right) + \left(w_r \cdot P_m \cdot \dfrac{P_u}{P_m} \cdot \dfrac{P_r}{P_u}\right)}{w_m + w_u + w_r},$$

where P = price, n = national average, m = metropolitan (Bombay, Calcutta, Delhi and Madras), u = urban other than metropolitan, r = rural, and w = weights proportional to total expenditure. A completely symmetric treatment of the three different population densities would call for simpler expressions for the last two parenthetical expressions in the numerator on the right. However, the substantial differences in the nature and quality of the items commonly purchased within each detailed category in the rural and urban sectors necessitated the use of urban-metropolitan and rural-urban ratios based upon different sets of specifications.

The specifications used in the urban-metropolitan comparisons were selected to match U.S. goods. The CSO obtained prices both from existing sources and from special surveys. The former included National Sample Survey (NSS) prices from the nonmanual employees consumer price index and Labor Bureau prices from the industrial worker price index. The special surveys were made both by the CSO staff and by the NSS.

The rural-urban prices were taken from those gathered for the consumer price index for agricultural workers and industrial workers and from the consumer price index for nonmanual employees. In addition, prices were specially gathered through the NSS in one urban area and two rural areas in each of the eighteen states. The comparisons were made separately for each

---

[1] The work on the ICP in India benefited from the helpful advice of an advisory working group established by the CSO.

of the states because it was believed that the qualities of goods available differed less within states than across India as a whole; this method, therefore, made it easier to assure pricing of comparable qualities in rural and urban areas.

JAPAN

Japanese consumer prices for the ICP were provided by the Bureau of Statistics of the Office of the Prime Minister.[2]

The prices were obtained from three existing price surveys and from a special survey. Prices for nearly 200 specifications were taken (1) from the monthly retail price survey covering 170 cities, towns, and villages, which is the basis for the consumer price index; (2) from the National Survey of Retail Prices carried out in 770 cities, towns, and villages in November 1967; and (3) from the monthly department store survey conducted in Tokyo on the price of new products and imported items. The special price survey was carried out in department stores, supermarkets, and other retail outlets in Tokyo during 1970. The Tokyo prices obtained from the department store survey, and the special price survey were adjusted to national averages on the basis of the National Survey of Retail Prices for 1970. By using the most closely related indexes derived from the retail price surveys, prices obtained for 1967 were extrapolated forward to 1970, and prices referring to 1970 were extrapolated backward to 1967.

KENYA

In Kenya, the Statistical Department collected prices regularly only in Nairobi at the time of our reference dates. To obtain national average prices for ICP purposes, special urban and rural price surveys were conducted by the Statistical Department, with the aid of outside experts provided by the Economic Commission for Africa and the ICP.

In the urban sector, additional prices were gathered in several markets in Nairobi, and representative pricing was done in Mombasa and Kisumu to round out the urban sample. (Nairobi and Mombasa account for over three-quarters of the urban population, and with Kisumu they provide representation of each of the three major geographical and ethnic regions of the country.)

Rural prices were collected in thirteen villages chosen to include areas dominated by each of the eight major tribal groups. Because of the cost involved, no effort was made to obtain prices from the Northeastern provinces, inhabited for the most part by nomadic peoples with no

permanent markets and accounting for only about 3 percent of the total population of Kenya. Rural prices were collected for a total of forty-five items, including twenty-one food items, thirteen clothing items, and eleven household products. In markets where bargaining is customary, the purpose of the inquiry was explained to sellers in the local language so actual transaction prices could be obtained.[3]

UNITED KINGDOM

Prices in the United Kingdom were obtained through the Statistics Division of the Department of Employment. The specifications to be priced were chosen in collaboration with a U.S. expert. A substantial number of prices, particularly for foods, were obtained directly from records of prices maintained for the cost of living index. Fortunately, the regional variation within the United Kingdom of the other prices needed by the ICP is relatively small, so reliance could be placed on central office price lists of large chains and on prices observed in Watford, central London, and two or three other places. Some mail-order–catalog prices also were used.

UNITED STATES

Because initially the United States was taken as the base country in starting this system of consumer-goods prices, an unusually large number of prices was required. National average prices were estimated for nearly 900 specifications of consumer goods.

Nearly three-fourths of the prices were obtained from the U.S. Bureau of Labor Statistics. But only about one-third of the BLS prices, nearly one-half of which were foods, were provided directly in the form of national averages.[4] The others generally were based on prices for a limited number of cities; either only one (usually Philadelphia, New York, or Chicago) or a group of as many as five cities (usually including Chicago, Detroit, Los Angeles, New York, and Philadelphia). The number of observations typically ran from eight to ten per item in each city, but it was sometimes less when quality variations were considered. A substantial number of these prices (approximately 200) especially those pertaining to five cities, were taken from prices collected for the Consumer Price Index (CPI). Others (more than 200) were especially collected for the ICP; the latter usually were for one or two of the following cities: Chicago, New York, or Philadelphia. The balance of the BLS prices were obtained from the agency's miscellaneous records and sources; more than a score were estimated from BLS wholesale prices.

---

[2] See the report by Sadanori Nagayama, *Comparison of Levels of Living in Real Terms in Japan and the U.S.* (Tokyo: Japan Society for the Promotion of Science, March 1971). This volume is the report of a committee headed by Professor Yuzo Yamada, which was set up to carry on the Japanese side of the work with the ICP.

[3] For a further description of the price collection in Kenya, see G. Donald Wood, Jr., "Problems of Comparison in Africa with Special Regard to Kenya," *Review of Income and Wealth* (March 1973), pp. 105–16.

[4] A number of the national average prices came from the Bureau of Labor Statistics *City Workers Family Budget* Bulletin No. 1570–3 (Washington: Government Printing Office, 1966).

Two adjustments to the BLS prices usually were necessary. The first was to convert the city prices to national average prices. Fortunately, in the course of preparing standard budgets for city workers, the BLS had done pricing work that made it possible to compare the price level for each type of good in individual cities with the national average price level. Such place-to-place comparisons of clothing costs, for example, existed for a four-person family, separating the purchases made on behalf of the husband, the wife, a boy, and a girl, as well as expenditures on other clothing materials and services in each of thirty-nine metropolitan areas for the spring of 1969.[5] For most categories, the budget quantities were identical in all cities. For clothing and certain other categories, however, particularly fuel, the cost comparisons were based on different quantities to allow for climatic differences. The BLS kindly supplied the ICP with data giving the quantity adjustments for climatic conditions, and thus it was possible to estimate the pure price differences for each city relative to the national average.

When more than one city was used to estimate the national average price, a different answer usually was produced by each city's prices. We estimated the national average price by computing a weighted average of the individual prices, where the weights were the number of price observations in each city. (In principle, the number of obervations was proportional to the appropriate city weight.)

To check on the prices obtained from these procedures, an alternative set of calculations was made based on an earlier version of the city workers' standard budgets, referring to 1966 average prices. These 1966 relationships between city and national average prices were used as a basis for getting national average prices from our 1970 city prices. These estimates of national average prices for 208 items well matched the corresponding prices derived from the 1969 budgets. On the average, they were 1.6 percent lower, but the coefficient of determination, r^2, between the two sets of prices was 0.966.

A second adjustment that had to be made to BLS prices in many cases was to add sales taxes, which were excluded from the prices provided to the ICP. The national average price was estimated from a city price by the following formula:

$$C_x (1 + T) \frac{N_T}{C_T} = N_T,$$

where C_x = city price exclusive of sales tax, C_T = city price inclusive of sales tax, N_T = national price inclusive of sales tax, and T = sales tax. (The comparisons between city and national average prices in the standard budgets mentioned above were inclusive of sales taxes, and thus they provided ratios N_T/C_T.) In some cases, the prices provided to the ICP were national average prices (rather than prices for individual cities) exclusive of tax, and an average sales tax, taking account of the varying rates and coverages in different states and localities, had to be estimated. This was true, for example, of some drugs and medicines; 1 percent was added to the 1970 prices of prescription drugs and 3 percent to the prices of non-prescription medicines to allow for national average sales taxes on these items. In 1970, forty-five of the fifty states and a number of cities had sales taxes, the total rate of which varied between 2 percent and 7 percent.[6]

Somewhat over one-fourth of the prices were obtained directly by the ICP, over one-half of these from the city of Philadelphia, and most of the remainder from catalogs or through a mail survey of large food chains in the United States. In general, these represented items relatively simple to price, an effort having been made to leave the pricing of more difficult items to the BLS. Some prices were taken from the U.S. Department of Agriculture price materials and from the U.N. survey of retail prices in New York City.

Although the retail price work of the BLS focuses on clerical workers and wage earners residing in urban places, the BLS prices can be regarded as conforming substantially to national average prices. Well under 10 percent of retail sales occur outside of the urban areas and standard metropolitan statistical areas covered by the CPI sampling frame.[7] Because they have automobiles, most nonurban families in the United States make the bulk of their purchases in urban areas or in suburban shopping centers that are part of the CPI sample. The rural population also relies heavily on mail-order purchases, some of which enter the BLS sample, and in any case are not thought to be different from other urban prices. Thus, although the U.S. population does not live entirely in urban areas, the prices relevant to national average prices are substantially urban prices as collected for the CPI.

[5] Bureau of Labor Statistics, *Three Budgets for an Urban Family of Four Persons—Final Spring 1969 Cost Estimate* (Washington: Government Printing Office, December 1970). The intermediate budget was used for our calculations; the results would have been substantially the same if the budget for the low standard or the one for the high standard had been used.

[6] John F. Due, *State & Local Sales Taxation* (Chicago: Public Administration Service, 1971).

[7] This statement is based on data in the 1963 Census of Business (*Retail Trade Summary Statistics* Part I (Washington: Government Printing Office, 1966), pp. 135–38). Actually $26 billion out of a total of $244 billion of retail sales were accounted for by places of less than 2,500 population. About $5 billion of this, however, included purchases of farm equipment, building materials, and lumber, which are not included in consumption. Another $9 billion was spent in gasoline stations and restaurants or in car dealers' establishments.

C. Special Problems in Particular Consumer-Goods Categories

BREAD AND CEREALS (01.100)[8]

Rice (01.101). The relative importance of rice in consumption patterns varies widely with differences in income levels and with food consumption habits. Among the ten countries included in the present round of comparisons, rice was clearly most important in India, where it accounted for about 20 percent of household expenditures and more than 60 percent of total expenditures on bread and cereals. Rice also is a staple in Japan, where it accounted for seven percent of total consumption expenditures and more than 70 percent of total expenditures on bread and cereals. It is a common product in all the other countries, of course, and plays an important role in the bread and cereal expenditures of Italy (nearly 25 percent) and Kenya (more than 12 percent).

Rice comes in a large number of varieties and qualities. The varieties of rice commonly are classified according to the size and shape of the grain. In the Indian classification, for example, long rice (referred to in India as "fine") is three times as long as it is wide and is small in size. The medium variety has a 2.5 to 3 length-to-width ratio, and the short-grain variety (known in India as "bowled" or "coarse") has a length to breadth ratio of less than 2.5. For the most part, the price of rice varies positively with the length-breadth ratio. In Japan, however, the glutinous short-grain Japonica variety is preferred, and no market exists for long-grain rice. In India, all the varieties of rice are found, with long-grain rice making up about 10 percent of the crop, the medium variety about 30 percent, and short-grain rice the remaining 60 percent. In other countries, long-grain rice commands a price premium, varying from 10 to 40 percent over that of short-grain rice, with the Indian premium falling in the upper part of the range.

Within each major varietal category of rice there are a number of variants. India has a bewildering variety of kinds, many confined to particular regions of the country. To aid in ensuring proper comparability of the varieties of rice that were priced in India, the United States, Japan, and other countries, samples of six varieties of rice—three from the United States, one from Japan, and two from India as controls—were sent, with the help of the National Sample Survey, to seven Indian centers for matching with local varieties. The samples also were sent to the Food Corporation of India and the Central Rice Research Institute at Cuttack. (The latter did the matching by a scientific classification based on

length-breadth ratio.) U.S. and Indian rice samples also were taken to Japan. One important identification problem that the samples helped to resolve related to so-called parboiled rice, which is common in several countries including the United States, where it is marketed under a brand name.

The other major factor affecting rice prices is the quality of the grain. This factor involves moisture content, percentage of damaged or broken kernels, odors (particularly those which are commercially objectionable, such as mustiness), color, presence of insects and other foreign matter, the percentage of rices of mixed types, and the quality of milling. According to a U.S. Department of Agriculture study,[9] Japanese rice was, in general, close in quality to U.S. rice, but Indian rice was a lower-grade product. This was mainly because of the presence of foreign matter and the percentage of broken grains, which averaged to 27 percent for raw milled rice and 15 percent for parboiled (*selah*) rice. The main grade of Indian rice was not found on the U.S. market, but it was thought that it would sell at a discount of 10 to 20 percent below the standard U.S. grade. It has been assumed that the grades of rice in the other countries in the study are similar to that of the United States and Japan, and a discount of 15 percent has been applied to the Indian price to allow for the difference in quality.

The proper method of comparing Japanese rice prices with those of the United States and other countries was discussed at some length with Japanese colleagues. The Japanese considered the difference between short-grain and long-grain rice as a matter of taste and not of quality. In their view, if long-grain rice were marketed in Japan, it would not command any premium price over that of short-grain rice. The appropriate method of price comparisons, therefore, was to disregard the difference between the two kinds of rice and to compare the average price of rice in Japan with the average price of rice in other countries. We accepted this view, although for computational convenience we made the adjustment to the Japanese data (rather than to the data of each other country) simply by treating the Japanese price for short-grain rice as the price of long-grain rice also. This is one of the instances of what was referred to in Chapter 3 as "taste-equivalence" matching.

We considered subdividing rice into two subcategories, because of its great importance in Indian consumption and because of the small proportion of long-grain rice in the Indian total. This proved unnecessary, however, because the relationship of Indian rice prices to those of other countries was similar for the two subcategories under consideration.

[8] The parenthesized numbers refer to the ICP classification. See the Appendix to Chapter 3.

[9] USDA Economic Research Services, "Analysis of Selected Varieties and Grades of Rice Moving in World Trade in Terms of Official U.S. Rice Standards" *Rice Situation* Marketing Research Report No. 460 (Washington: Government Printing Office, March 1969).

Meal and flour (01.102). The India–United States comparison for wheat flour was another example of matching by taste equivalence. In the United States, an enriched processed white flour is the common product and sells at less per kilo than whole wheat flour. In India, either wheat grain is purchased and taken to a mill for grinding or ground whole wheat is purchased. The exception, though becoming less and less an exception, is purchase of a white bleached flour. The result is that in India, unlike the situation in the United States, brown flour is cheaper than white flour.

Another problem with the wheat flour comparison was to choose the appropriate grade of Indian wheat to which to add grinding charges for comparison with U.S. white flour. What is called in India "American" wheat—which is the best the United States has to offer and which is marketed throughout the world—is not preferred in India because it makes rather poor *chapaties,* the standard bread of North India.[10]

Although U.S. wheat sells for a discount relative to the medium Indian wheat, its general quality, in terms of foreign matter, moist kernels, and similar characteristics, is higher. A direct price comparison was made between the Indian wheat (plus grinding charges) and U.S. white flour; it was considered that the preferable cooking qualities of the Indian product and its higher internal price seemed to balance the outside view of the higher quality of the U.S. product.

Among products in the flour and meal category, maize flour, which was particularly important in Kenya and Colombia, posed some matching problems. The main difficulties were that countries use different terms and grind maize differently; also, they sometimes add wheat flour. Samples were helpful in clearing up these matters, though in general the price variation of different kinds of maize flour was small.

Macaroni, spaghetti, noodles, and like products (01.106). A different kind of matching difficulty was posed by Japanese noodles. These are made from hard wheat flour and contain all of the starch from the wheat kernel. They are dull white to gray in color and rather brittle. Spaghetti, the nearest western product, is made from enriched semolina or farina and contains the gluten part of the hard wheat kernel and little starch. Products made from semolina or farina are yellowish, somewhat translucent, and hard but fairly pliable. Thus, Japanese

noodles are not physically identical with noodles in the United States or pasta in Italy. They are, however, roughly similar in appearance and serve the same function, and hence we treated them as equivalent products on grounds of similarity in use.

Other cereals (01.107). Sorghum is grown in India (where it is known as *jowar*) both as a food crop and for fodder, whereas in the United States and most other countries in the study it was not consumed directly by households but was used, if at all, for fodder or in brewing. A U.S. retail price was estimated from the wholesale sorghum price on the basis of the spread between the wholesale wheat price and the retail price for wheat flour.

MEAT (01.110)

It was possible to compare meats for most countries for common cuts such as veal cutlets, sirloin steak, and the like. In some instances, however, differences exist in the ways in which the animals are butchered for retail distribution. In addition, beef sometimes is sold, as in Japan, by the quality of the animal without much regard to the particular cut. In the latter circumstances, for each quality of animal, we compared the weighted average retail price for which the total carcass was sold.

Unlike a number of other foods, meat appeared to vary significantly in average quality from country to country. Countries with high incomes tended to have highly developed animal husbandry industries catering to a taste for fine meat, whereas countries with lower incomes and lower meat consumption tended to have a lower average quality of meat. Fortunately, grading standards for meat are well developed in countries in which meat is important; these provided a basis for selecting the appropriate quality level for price comparisons with other countries.

FISH (01.120)

In the case of fish, some consideration was given to the possibility of comparing the average price of fish in each country regardless of the type of fish consumed. This would have been an attractive way of proceeding had it been true that each country simply consumed whatever kind of fish were available to it without any special effort to search out varieties regarded as more palatable. But this is a doubtful assumption in any case, and it certainly is no more warranted for a country such as Japan, in which fish is an important source of protein, than a corresponding assumption about the consumption of meat would be for the United States or Western Europe. Accordingly, fish price comparisons were based on identical species, the scientific names proving to be the saving element in an otherwise bewildering variation from one country to another in the common names for identical species of fish. Diagrammatic pictures of the fish on the specifications also proved helpful.

---

[10] In this connection, an interesting problem arose with the impact of the "green revolution" on Indian wheat prices. Mexican wheat, which is somewhat like American wheat, is the wheat variety with high yields. A local and lower-yielding Punjab wheat, which makes better *chapaties,* is the variety of wheat in the price index. As the green revolution hit the Indian Punjab, local wheat acreage declined with the introduction of Mexican wheat; consequently, the price of local wheat rose, and the consumer price index for wheat rose as Indians enjoyed the largest increases in domestic wheat production ever experienced. This phenomenon did not affect the particular wheat used for the ICP comparisons.

MILK, CHEESE, AND EGGS (01.130)

We tried to base price comparisons for cheese on domestic products, seeking, of course, to find types of cheese common to several countries. One reason for this procedure was that an imported cheese—say, a European cheese in the United States—may be expensive because of both cost of shipment and consumption by only a small percentage of the population. Another factor is that the quality of the exported product may differ from that commonly consumed in the country of origin. A brie in France, for example, may not be equivalent to one that is exported to the United States.

OILS AND FATS (01.140)

The most common type of oil purchased in the United States is so-called salad oil, which is a combination of various kinds of oils, usually soybean, corn, peanut (groundnut), and cottonseed oils. A 100 percent soybean salad oil also is available and sells at the same price as the combination salad oil. Oils commonly consumed in other countries, such as those derived from safflower, cottonseed, corn, rape or mustard, groundnut, and cocoanut, either are not available in U.S. food stores or are sold in small quantities. We have estimated, therefore, the U.S. retail prices for such oils from the relationships of their wholesale prices to the wholesale price of soybean oil. For example, no pure rape oil is sold in the United States at the retail level, except in such a specialty shop as an East Indian grocery, where it would be relatively expensive. The same is true of safflower oil and sunflower oil, the latter being the predominant oil used in Hungary.

FRESH FRUITS AND VEGETABLES (01.150)

Quantities of particular fruits and vegetables consumed tend to be highly price elastic. This presents serious problems for the ICP, because the growing of particular fruits and vegetables often is highly specialized to particular parts of the world. As a consequence, apples are cheap in Europe and Japan and expensive in Kenya and India, whereas the opposite is true for oranges and bananas.

Seasonality can cause problems, too. The price of fruit we want is the annual average price. Notice the following possible anomaly: strawberries may be cheaper every month of the year in the United States than in the United Kingdom, but because of a larger relative volume of U.S. purchases in months in which they are expensive in both countries, the U.S. annual average price may be higher than that of the United Kingdom.

Vegetable prices exhibit similar problems, though in less dramatic form. Perhaps there are enough universal varieties of vegetables—tomatoes and onions might suffice—that a valid comparison could be obtained by restricting the varieties compared. On this point more research is needed.

Our method of dealing with these problems has been to seek as large a sample across countries as possible. Thus, an item was eligible for inclusion as long as it was marketed in a sufficiently substantial volume that its price determination was not greatly influenced by factors that were different from those affecting other fruits and vegetables. For example, apples, grown mainly in Himachal Pradesh and Kashmir, meet the test in India.

Of course, a number of other fruits and vegetables were excluded because they were unique products, at least for the present group of countries. For example, the *chiku* (a fruit that if not allowed to ripen produces chicle for chewing gum and known as *sapadilla* in Spanish-speaking countries), the guava, the breadfruit or jackfruit, and the lichee fruit, all common in India, have not been included. Perhaps such fruits will be added to the ICP list at such time as new countries are brought into the project.

The fresh fruits and vegetables category also contains a case of matching on a taste-equivalence basis. In the United States, mandarin oranges command premium prices relative to other oranges, but the reverse is true in Japan. A direct price comparison was made between the cheaper of the two variants in each country.

FRUITS AND VEGETABLES OTHER THAN FRESH (01.160)

Considerable variation existed in the names and availabilities of dried peas and beans, and samples were essential to establish comparability. The final list included red kidney beans, lima beans, pinto beans, chick peas (also known as garbanzos and *channa*), black-eyed peas, green and red gram, and other varieties. Many of these were not known abroad by their U.S. name, and we encountered no nomenclature that seemed to be in international use. Because these items are quite important in countries such as India, several varieties were matched.

POTATOES AND TUBERS (01.170)

The importance of root vegetables differs widely among countries. We planned at first to include potatoes with other vegetables, but it quickly became necessary to separate potatoes. Then, as data came in, it became clear that even potatoes and tubers could not always be treated as a single category. In Kenya, yams are far more important than potatoes, which are common but relatively expensive. Potatoes and yams have quite different price relatives as between Kenya and the United States. Because the expenditure ratios also are different—being larger where prices are cheaper—it was decided to deviate from the usual practice of taking an unweighted geometric mean of the price relatives; instead, potatoes and yams were weighted separately in the Kenya-United States comparisons.

The problem posed for the multilateral comparisons was that yam prices were not available for the other countries. Because, as was described in Chapter 5, each detailed category is treated as a single product in these comparisons, the simplest procedure would have been to base Kenyan relative prices on potatoes alone. This procedure, however, would not have reflected adequately the substantial consumption of yams and would have produced a lower relative real quantity for the category than seemed warranted. Therefore, we linked the Kenyan price for the category to the prices of the other countries through the United States, using for the Kenya–United States price the Fisher index based on both potatoes and yams.

ALCOHOLIC BEVERAGES (01.320)

The principle problem in matching alcoholic beverages is that people tend to drink domestic beers, wines, and liquor rather than imported beverages largely because they are cheaper. The domestic product sometimes varies in type from one country to another. For example, no equivalent of U.S. bourbon or rye is widely distributed in the United Kingdom.

There are, however, branded wines and liquors and, to a more limited degree, beers that enjoy an international reputation and that can be found in the markets of most countries. The fact that they are usually more expensive than the local product is not surprising in view of shipping costs and import duties. A famous brand of U.K. sherry, for example, which the United Kingdom imports, bottles, and exports to the United States, entails shipping costs and import duties, each of which exceeds the value of the barreled wine.

In the sherry example, the alternative exists of matching the U.K. sherry against an equivalent sherry imported into the United States in barrels and bottled domestically. This was the course we followed.

Fortunately, however, matching need not depend entirely on locally bottled beverages having a common provenance. The EEC includes countries that take seriously the differences in wines, and in their wine price comparisons they match ordinary table wines indigenous to each country. To a considerable degree, our compromises have been in the same spirit.

Thus, we matched locally produced table wines and gins, generally seeking a medium quality by Western European standards. This solution also was applied to beer. Relative to the sherries of Portugal, the table wines of France, and the whiskies of the United Kingdom, there appears to be no universal beer. Most countries were quite willing to take a light beer of national origin with alcoholic content of 3 to 5 percent as an internationally comparable item. In addition, ale or heavy beers were priced in a few countries, and some European beers were priced in the United States.

For their internal comparisons, the EEC countries priced a standard Scotch whiskey and a good cognac, the latter being defined as one imported by the United States. (The U.S. price was about $10.00 for four-fifths of a quart in 1970). Both were priced in the United States as well. If there was a bias in other items selected, it was in the direction of heavy reliance on domestic products, and therefore the inclusion of imported Scotch and cognac served somewhat to balance the sample.

TOBACCO (01.400)

Comparability in cigarettes is clouded by the fact that, in some cases, tastes appear to have adapted themselves to local or at least readily available types of tobacco. In Hungary, for example, Bulgarian cigarettes long have been preferred; and, although the opposite relationship prevails on world markets, cigarettes made of Virginia tobacco would sell at a discount relative to those made in Bulgaria of Turkish tobaccos. Because Hungary and other countries as well indicated that their national preferences for tobacco did not match international tobacco price relationships, no effort was made to insist upon comparability of type of tobacco.

In the U.S. market, most cigarettes sell at roughly the same price. This is because the production and transportation cost components of the price are very low. Based on Census of Manufactures data, the tobacco, filter, wrapper, and transportation costs averaged 5.1 cents for a package of twenty in 1967, when the retail price was 36 cents a package. Because marketing costs and taxes, about the same for all brands, are so much larger than production costs, U.S. cigarettes generally have sold at common prices.[11]

In Japan as well little variation existed in price, explained by the dominance of a single brand. In other countries in which advertising is less important, however, there are sometimes substantial differentials in price. In India, for example, cigarettes in a price range from about Rs0.70 to Rs2.40 per package of twenty for a large-selling, loosely packed nonfilter as compared with a closely packed filter cigarette.[12] In addition, other volume nonfilter cigarettes sell for prices of Rs1.00 to Rs2.40 per package. Our procedure was to use an average of the three principal grades of nonfilter cigarettes in India for comparison with other countries. A similar averaging was performed for other countries, keeping filter and nonfilter cigarettes separate.

---

[11] It is true that, because of duties, imported cigarettes do sell for more in the United States, but they are such a small part of the U.S. market that they have been ignored.

[12] Left out of the discussion are *beedies,* a product widely smoked in both rural and urban areas, which sells for about Rs0.20 to Rs0.50 per package of 25. It would be difficult to match this product in other countries; *beedies* have been used for the internal price comparisons within India, however, though prices are nearly uniform throughout.

MATERIALS FOR CLOTHING (02.110)

The purchase of materials to make up clothing at home or by a tailor is more important in poor than in wealthy countries. Types of material vary in significant ways from one country to another. In India or Kenya, 100 percent cottons are important because they are inexpensive to purchase and easy to maintain where laundry services are cheap. Cotton blends are relatively cheaper in some industrialized countries such as Japan and the United States. Heavy woolens—say, 400 grams per square meter—are more common in Europe, and especially Hungary, in which central heating is less available than in the United States. Silks are more commonly available in India, Japan, and Italy than other countries. High-thread-count fabrics—say, 150 by 150 per square centimeter—are well known in countries such as Hungary and India. In the wealthier countries, however, as a consequence of blends, bonded fabrics, and special finishes, these high-thread-count fabrics are less important and also less known by retailers. In fact, a major problem with pricing textiles in the United States—and in other countries as well—is that the retailers do not know the technical characteristics of fabrics, particularly weight and thread count, so one cannot ask at a store simply for the price of 40-by-40-count cotton.

A set of cloth samples was developed to aid the identification of common fabrics. The initial set of samples, supplied by the U.S. Bureau of Labor Statistics, comprised mainly fabrics used in ready-made clothing priced for the CPI, but it included as well some materials priced as fabrics. Other countries sent samples: woolens from Hungary, India, Japan, and the United Kingdom; cottons from India and Japan; and silk from India.

The samples were shown to cloth manufacturers and distributors in a number of the countries, and their aid was obtained in matching and pricing. Examinations of the samples by these experts revealed the unavailability of some fabrics in particular countries and/or, in a number of cases, the inherent difficulty of matching fabrics. Fortunately, a number of common fabrics such as wool flannel, cotton and cotton blend broadcloth, lining silk, and nylon and rayon chiffon are available in most countries and provide an adequate basis for comparison.

In the United States for example, several major textile mills and textile jobbers in New York City were able to estimate prices for some of the sample materials of the other countries. One by-product of this consultation with U.S. industry personnel was the conclusion that factors like thread count and weight still loom large in price formation in the U.S. market, even if the technical knowledge is not widely had either by retailers or by consumers.

Several special fabrics are important in the consumption patterns of Kenya and India. Cloth for dashikis is used commonly in Kenya, and this kind of cotton print fortunately is widely available in the United States, so these prices could be compared easily.

A more difficult problem was posed by sari and *dhoti* cloth in India. Sari cloth may be cotton, silk, or any one of a number of synthetics; in India, when it is without a border, it does not sell as a sari at any different price per square meter than it would as material. Therefore, a comparison was sought for a common sari material. Silk was ruled out, and pure synthetic saris seemed inappropriate; synthetics often have a scarcity price in India because both domestic production and imports are limited. This left cotton saris, a heterogeneous group ranging from working saris at perhaps Rs3 per square meter, through office-girl saris at Rs5, to fine cotton saris at Rs8 to Rs12. The closest match in material is what is known in the United Kingdom and the United States as cotton voile, which also varies greatly as to quality. In the end, we matched a cotton voile in the United States with an office sari in India.

Another case of matching on the basis of equivalence in use relates to the Indian *dhoti*. This garment is worn in various styles, but basically it is a six-meter piece of cloth wrapped around the lower part of a man's body. A variation in South India and Ceylon is the *lungi*, a shorter piece of cloth wrapped at Bermuda short length. The *dhoti* can be of fine cotton material, but that which usually enters into price indexes is a fairly loosely woven cotton with a thread count of, say, 50 by 50 per square centimeter. This particular kind of cloth is not available at retail in the United States, nor for that matter are a number of the other common materials. U.S. industry experts, however, were able to make an estimate based on wholesale prices for the type priced in the Indian index.

In these textile comparisons, several factors have simply been ignored. For example, in the United States, a no-iron or "permanent press" finish on a fabric is important to a household that has a clothes dryer; however, without the use of a clothes dryer, a "permanent press" finish has no advantage over a wash-and-wear finish that is now international. Because in Europe and most of the rest of the world, clothes dryers are not common, we have simply ignored the "permanent press" finish on U.S. items: for example, a U.S. "permanent press" shirt was equated with any nonshrinkable finish in other countries. This procedure would be less defensible if "permanent press" finishes commanded a price differential over other finishes in the United States, but they do not. In fact, because "permanent press" finish is close to a wash-and-wear finish in the United States, which is little different in price from a Sanforized finish, the factor of finish frequently was ignored as a quality distinction.[13]

---

[13]Cotton grey cloth, which will retail at 70 cents per square meter before shrinkage and finishing, costs about 2 cents to Sanforize and little more to give a wash-and-wear finish. The finish is such a small part of the markup over mill price in the U.S. market that differences in finish can be ignored safely.

In the markets of the more affluent countries, the quality of materials in ready-made products may have little weight in determining price differences. Therefore, when we matched ready-made clothes, we often have weighted tailoring specifications more heavily as a guide to comparability than the identity of the fabric.

FOOTWEAR (02.210)

Typical shoe quality varies greatly between countries, and substantial quality variation exists as well within countries. The BLS specifications are quite explicit, and exchanges of pricing experts and samples between countries proved useful. In addition, the ICP consulted with a company that is the world's largest manufacturer and that sells its shoes all over the world, either under its own name or through such national distribution channels as large mail-order houses. The company's Indian office was helpful in matching Indian shoes with U.S. models. The same company is important in Kenya also, and their shoes were used for comparisons involving that country.

Reliance on the prices of this company was reviewed carefully with Indian colleagues. It was recognized that the company's shoes are regarded as a prestige item in India and are not typical of mass consumption. Further, the matching Indian item for an ICP specification for a man's shoe was the best in the Indian manufacturer's line; it was a shoe selling for Rs50, wheras the most commonly purchased shoe was about Rs20.[14] (The U.S. shoe matching the ICP specification was priced at $15.) The question was whether we should include the specification in the India–United States comparison in spite of its relatively high quality in terms of the Indian market.

Although it could not be claimed that the Rs50 shoe was representative in itself of Indian footwear expenditures, two considerations led us to include the item. For one thing, there was no way to match the Rs20-grade shoe in the United States. This was not, however, a sufficient reason. In addition, we needed to be convinced that the India–United States price ratio given by the item would fairly represent shoe price relationships for the two countries. The shoe industry in India is competitive, and upon inquiry, the difference in the Indian market between the Rs20 and the Rs50 shoes appeared to be due to more and better materials and workmanship and not to any special factors affecting the production or marketing of the two items, such as economies or diseconomies of scale or a price premium based on snob appeal. Therefore, we felt warranted in including the Rs50 shoe as an item to be considered representative of the price structure for the footwear category.

[14]Still more typical is the leather and rubber sandal selling for Rs10 or less. This item, included in the comparisons, was matched with a similar rubber-thonged sandal in the United States.

FURNITURE (04.000)

For several reasons, furniture is one of the most difficult categories in the comparison. In India, Japan, and, to a lesser extent, in other low-income or crowded countries, the amount of furniture that can be purchased, the amount that can be used in the available floor area, or both, is limited. In Japan, of course, floor area still is measured in *tatamis*, which is a mat approximating the space requirements of a person—3 by 6 feet. In general, the Japanese prefer to use their living space in a way that does not lend itself to beds, sofas, heavy chairs, and the like. In India, the situation is similar, and the common rope bed, or *charpoy*, often used for sleeping usually is stored upright or on the roof during the day. In contrast, a significant portion of expenditures in several of the ICP countries is for quite heavy and space-consuming furniture, in which area quality variations are substantial. For example, in the United States a basic livingroom piece such as a sofa may cost anywhere from $80 to more than $480 for a piece that seats three persons; this price range results from differences in materials and workmanship, as well as from styling.

Another difficulty with furniture is the material. In Japan, it is less expensive to make a kitchen or diningroom table of any type of wood base, including plywood or pressed wood with a plastic- or Formica-type finish, than to make a solid wood or hardwood veneer table. Further, in India, a metal desk would be much more expensive than wood, but not so in Japan. Woods also will differ by country, rosewood being more common in Europe, walnut more usual in the United States, and teak quite common in Asia. In India, a common material for a table is solid teak, which would be expensive in other countries.

Marketing of furniture is also quite different among the ICP countries. The household purchaser is close to the craftsman in India or Kenya but far removed in the U.S. In consequence, it is easy to get a price quotation of a piece of furniture in the United States because the outlet probably owns the piece and has limits within which it can quote prices and continue in business. In India, the quotations on furniture items for price indexes come from the craftsman, not necessarily for items available in the workshop (capital and space are too small for much inventory) but for items he would make. This presented a significant limitation on special price collection for the ICP, because investigators had little check on the accuracy of the estimates from different furniture shops, especially because the investigators themselves customarily would not own or deal much in furniture. Fortunately, cooperatives existed in Bombay and Delhi that carry a fair inventory of furniture, and considerable reliance had to be placed on quotations from these sources.

Another difficulty is the distinction involving styling and quality. A feature such as the joining of furniture by dovetail joints rather than flush attachment often commands a substantial premium in the U.S. market, but not in other countries. In practice, we tried to take account of such differences, which often meant that the best furniture in some countries was equated with medium-quality furniture in the United States. Even with such adjustments, of course, furniture is relatively expensive in the United States.

Because of these problems, special care was required for the furniture price comparison. For example, a particular sofa and chair set in Japan was identified as comparable with a BLS item in the United States by a visiting expert from the BLS; the Japanese then obtained brochures for these items, as well as upholstery samples. These carefully defined specifications then were used in India. Unfortunately, it was not possible to take such care with each furniture item. It is generally agreed that in this area, far more effort in identifying appropriate items for comparison appears to be warranted in the future.

HOUSEHOLD APPLIANCES (04.300)

Often the matching of appliances proved difficult because older and simpler models disappear rapidly in wealthy countries and, therefore, are unavailable for comparison with such items still common in poor countries. Matching often was attempted with simple products. For example, kerosene stoves are common in India and have had a wide use in Japan and the United States at various times. In Japan, however, the only kerosene stove available in 1970 was a specialty item for camping that was quite expensive, so no comparison was attempted. In the United States, the kerosene stove is also a camping item, but its more extensive use made it sufficiently common to justify including a U.S. price for it.

To take another example, in Hungary, the usual washing machine is a wringer style rather than the semiautomatic or automatic model that spins clothes dry. Several manufacturers still make wringer washers in the United States, so it seemed appropriate to use these models for the Hungary comparison, especially because they still must compete with spin-dry models in the U.S. market.

TRANSPORTATION AND COMMUNICATION (06.000)

Although quantity comparisons had been contemplated for the Transporation and Communication category, it was decided finally to rely on price comparisons. The possibility of quantity comparisons seemed attractive because within most of these detailed categories there tends to be one major type of homogeneous service for which quantity data are readily available. In local transport the number of passengers can be obtained, and for long distance transport the number of passenger kilometers. For communications, the number of letters and the number of telephones or telephone messages usually are reported in standard statistical

sources. The difficulty, however, is that most of these services are used by businesses as well as households. Therefore, without precise information on the way in which the national accountants have estimated the division of these expenditures between personal consumption and business use, it is difficult to place great reliance on the quantity ratios.

A complicating factor in the case of local transport and long distance transport by rail and bus is the existence in many countries of variegated fare structures, in which reduced fares are given to special groups in the population, such as students and the aged. In addition, for long-distance transport there often are special fares, such as those for excursions, that vary in importance from one country to another. The most appropriate resolution of this problem would be to obtain the average fare paid by all groups of passengers for a given distance on a local journey and for a given number of kilometers on a long-distance journey. With respect to local transport, we lacked the data to make this possible, and therefore we had to use price comparisons based on standard fares.

Another problem was that within the local transport category the price ratios varied widely for taxi and bus (or streetcar) fares. In Italy, for example, the PPP for taxis was almost four times that for bus fares, whereas for the United Kingdom it was only 1.2 times. Because of these great differences, we decided to apply rough weights in combining the PPPs for taxis and buses; the weights were based on the scattered expenditure data we could obtain for the United States, the Common Market countries, and India.

In the case of long-distance rail transport, it was possible to obtain both the number of passenger kilometers and passenger revenues for a number of the countries. Price comparisons for this category were based, therefore, on the average fare per kilometer in each country. Class II travel in France and air-conditioned Class III travel in India were equated to coach travel in the United States. For the other countries, the average revenue per kilometer was available only for all classes of travel combined, and comparisons were made in these terms. The extent of first-class travel, however, was small (around 5 percent) in all the countries for which we had data, and the error because of different composition of travel with respect to class seems likely to be small.

In the communications sector, price comparisons for the postal service were based on the cost of first-class mail; those for telephones and telegraph were based on the geometric average of PPPs for three telephone specifications—calls from public telephones and from home telephones and long-distance calls—and one telegraph specification.

RECREATION AND ENTERTAINMENT (07.000)

Recreational goods include a number of products that are marketed throughout the world under brand names or trademarks. We took advantage of this by including in the items to be compared certain German (F.R.), Japanese, and U.S. cameras, giving in each instance the model number and main features. The same was true for certain toys (including a matchbox-size car, a toy electric locomotive, and building blocks) and for a board game.

For other recreational and cultural activities, including religious activities, price comparisons were based both on output and inputs. In the former category were such things as the developing and printing of film and lessons in sewing, driving, or foreign language. The latter category, used as proxies for the wide variety of miscellaneous services in the category, included comparisons of the annual salaries of a television camera operator, a radio announcer, and a journalist. These occupations are involved in the production of radio and television services included in the category, although the persons in the occupations are paid in different countries variously from government funds, advertising revenues, or license fees. For the countries for which separate expenditures for religious activities were available, a PPP for religious expenditure was derived from the PPPs for teachers' salaries (representing personnel expenditures) and for indoor repair and upkeep and fuels (representing physical facilities).

SERVICES OF BARBER
AND BEAUTY SHOPS (08.100)

Even so simple a service as the cutting of men's hair posed a number of difficulties for the price comparisons. In India, many barbers ply their trade on the sidewalks; having no overhead costs, they ask for their haircuts and cold-water shaves a low price relative to those charged by shops. We used the sidewalk prices for the internal Indian comparisons (rural-urban and urban-metropolitan), but the comparisons with the United States were based on prices in shops. The internal comparisons indicate that shop prices in an Indian village would be less than in metropolitan areas because barbers earn less in a village; they also enable us to make the appropriate adjustment to metropolitan shop prices to obtain the national average.

A different problem for price comparisons in this category arose in Japan because of the practice of treating a shave, a haircut, and a shampoo as a single item. In Japan, a haircut seldom is the sole service provided; when it is, there is relatively little reduction from the price for the package of services. (A haircut alone is about 75 percent of the price of a shave, shampoo, and haircut.) In the United States, a haircut, a shampoo, and a shave represent separate transactions, each with its own price. A haircut, by far the most frequent service rendered in barber shops, usually costs less than half of the combined cost of the three services. Lacking a better solution, we compromised by using the geometric mean of the ratio of the Japan–United States haircut price and

the Japan–United States haircut, shampoo, and shave price. This was a price adjustment matching in which we were able to make the adjustment in terms of the prices of both countries (see Chapter 3).

RESTAURANTS AND CAFES (08.310)

We have made restaurant price comparisons in the standard way by comparing prices of the same items in similar outlets.[15] Most countries collect prices of away-from-home food, but comparability, except for snack items such as a cup of coffee or a soft drink, is limited. This is mainly because price relatives are calculated at the level of the individual restaurant for time-to-time price indexes. Thus, there is no necessary comparability between meals between outlets of a city or country.

It was easier to establish comparable meals between countries than to establish comparability of outlets. A set of entree items, sandwich items, and snack items was developed for all countries: although the menu is very much U.S. in name, latitude of interpretation was encouraged. For example, a chicken curry in India was equated with the same item in Japan, though the spices are different. In fact, almost all chicken preparations involving the same pieces of chicken were treated as substitutes. The number of items compared between countries usually was more than ten, and sometimes as large as thirty, so the error because of coverage of items should not be large.

Portion sizes also were collected for the United States, and adjustments for portion size proved possible and desirable for several entree items in comparisons of the United States with Hungary, Japan, and the United Kingdom.

Obviously, great differences exist in restaurant prices within countries, determined both by quality of food and service and by location. Some of this variability was eliminated by excluding restaurants with live entertainment (except such solo performers as an organist) and those associated with large hotels, even though the latter include international chains that offered matching items,

---

[15] Several indirect approaches also were considered, but participating countries did not regard them with favor. An example of an indirect method is to assume that the ratio of the quantity of food (QF) to nonfood services (QN) in the restaurants of the first country is the same as in the restaurants of the second country, whose quantities of food and nonfood are denoted by Qf and Qn respectively. Symbolically, the basic assumption is $\frac{QN}{QF} = \frac{Qn}{Qf}$. We may derive a quantity and price ratio for nonfood services as follows. From other parts of the study, we know the ratio $\frac{Pf}{PF}$, this being the ratio of the food prices in the two countries. For the quantity of restaurant foods, we can then derive the ratio $\frac{Qf}{QF}$, because we know the ratio of food expenditures in restaurants in both countries, namely, $\frac{P_f Q_f}{P_F Q_F}$. Because $\frac{Qn}{QN} = \frac{Qf}{QF}$, we can estimate $\frac{Pn}{PN}$ (the price ratio for nonfood expenditures in restaurants) by dividing $\frac{P_n Q_n}{P_N Q_N}$ by $\frac{Qn}{QN}$.

but at unusually high prices, in India, Japan, and Kenya. This still left a wide range of restaurants in all countries. In the case of India, except for hill areas, the sample was confined to restaurants with air conditioning, a criterion used to promote comparability with other countries in the physical aspects of the restaurant. In the case of Colombia, visiting Colombian experts identified outlets in Bogota comparable to those in the U.S. sample. Members of the ICP staff identified sample outlets in Kenya and the United Kingdom, while Hungarian experts chose their sample outlets after discussion in the United States. The possibility of error because of lack of comparability in outlets remains substantial.

Because price relationships varied widely for foods and beverages, the price relatives were weighted. We assigned a weight of 60 percent to food items, 20 percent to nonalcoholic beverages, and 20 percent to alcoholic beverages. These weights were chosen after the inspection of the available expenditure data for five countries.

HOTELS AND SIMILAR LODGING PLACES (08.320)

The hotel price comparisons are based on specifications designed to describe medium-quality accommodations using European standards. It was necessary to price a room with a private bath as well as one without bath. The latter, more usual in Europe, is not common in the United States or in this quality of hotel in India or Kenya.

For the comparisons of the EEC countries with the United States, the EEC prices, reported for rooms without bath, were multiplied by 1.66 to place them on a room-with-bath basis. The adjustment factor was based on rates for rooms with and without baths in comparable hotels as reported by two guidebooks that give extensive coverage of Europe.

The U.S. price for the ICP specification was based on prices reported by two guidebooks, each of which covered ten U.S. cities, some by both books. An unweighted average of the prices in each city was computed, and the prices for the cities then were combined with the aid of population weights to derive a national average price. From each guidebook, we selected the level of accommodation that appeared to match most closely the ICP specification; in one case, we had to choose among five categories, in the other among three. The average prices calculated from the two guidebooks were close, differing only by a few pennies.

One issue that had to be resolved was the treatment of tipping. In Japan, there is a service charge and no tipping. In Europe, India, and Kenya, hotels frequently levy service charges, but tipping often is expected for services whether or not a service charge is included in the bill. In the United States and the United Kingdom, usually there is no service charge, and tipping is expected for individual services and sometimes for total services; the total tip, however, does not necessarily amount to more than in countries in which a service charge is levied. Thus, it seems that if tipping is ignored, but the service charge is included, the only country in which the direction of the error is clear is Japan. Therefore, we have added a service charge of 15 percent to the basic rate in all the countries except Japan, for which only 10 percent has been added.

Because of the great difficulty of controlling quality in the international price comparisons for hotels, we checked the results obtained through the ICP work against price comparisons based on data in a worldwide travel guide issued by an international airline. We computed national average price for accommodations described in the guide as "modest" and "budget" by a method similar to that described above for getting average U.S. prices.

In many cases, the price relationships were similar to those derived from the ICP work. There were three important differences. First, the French prices based upon the airline guide were 10 to 20 percent higher than German (F.R.) prices, though the ICP data obtained from the EEC Statistical Office indicated that French prices were about one-third lower than the German (F.R.). Because the prices gathered by the Statistical Office could be presumed to be more widely applicable than those gathered by the airline, we retained them.

Second, the airline guide suggested a higher relative price for hotels in Colombia and Kenya than did the ICP results. Here again, we opted for the latter on the grounds that the airline was likely to have in mind the needs of international travelers rather than both domestic and foreign patrons.

Third, and more surprising, the airline source suggested a lower relative price for Indian hotels than the one we obtained directly. The Indian data were based on rates on more than thirty hotels, excluding the very top ones catering to high-income persons. The specification of a hotel with bath, however, was expensive by Indian standards, even though most of the hotels included were widely used by Indian clientel as well as by foreign tourists. Nevertheless, it was felt that the resulting price was high, and a price based on the ratio suggested by the airline travel guide was used.

Chapter 7

The role of quantity comparisons

For medical care and education, both price and quantity comparisons were attempted. These sectors are singled out for separate treatment because much greater reliance was placed on direct quantity comparisons. For most other sectors such as food, clothing, and construction, primary reliance was placed on price comparisons: that is, direct price comparisons were used in the aggregation to get PPPs for consumption and for GDP, and the corresponding indirect quantity indexes were used for the quantity aggregations. For many of the detailed categories in medical care and education, however, the direct quantity indexes and the indirect price comparisons were employed for aggregation purposes.

A. Medical Care

For the commodity components of medical care, including drugs (05.110), medical supplies (05.120), and therapeutic equipment (05.220), no special theoretical problems arose, so price comparisons were made along the lines described in Chapter 6. On the data-gathering level, however, it is doubtful that the objective of obtaining full-cost prices was achieved fully in some countries in which the state pays part or all of the costs. Failure in these instances distorted the purchasing power parities (PPPs). Because the expenditure estimates were on the same valuation basis as the prices, however, the correct quantity ratios nonetheless were obtained when the PPPs were divided into the expenditure ratios. For drugs, the sample of items for which prices were compared generally included from ten to a score of items, but the samples were much less satisfactory for the other two categories, and the possibility of errors was correspondingly greater.

For the service categories of medical care—including physicians' services (05.310), dentists' services (05.320), the services of other professional personnel such as nurses (05.330), and hospital services (05.400)—both

direct price and direct quantity comparisons were made. It is with these categories that the remainder of this section is concerned. Starting with professional services, we use these categories as a vehicle for setting out the general problems and methods relating to the categories in which both direct price and direct quantity comparisons could be made.

To obtain data for price comparisons, specifications for a visit to a physician, an appendectomy, a heart attack treated in a hospital, a tonsillectomy, and several other medical and dental services were circulated among the countries. Matching prices were obtained in most countries only for house calls, office visits, hospital-bed–days, and the filling of a cavity. For Hungary, Japan, and the United Kingdom, the price for these services was less than the factor cost of the service because of various programs to make medical care widely available at little or no cost to the patient. In Kenya, on the other hand, prices were obtained from only a few practitioners, and were probably above average prices.

A further difficulty with price comparisons based on specific services is the quality problem. The great differences among countries in the length of the training of the average physician and in the quality of medical education generally create a presumption that differences also must exist in the average quality of services rendered. Even the most common medical services, such as a visit to a physician, therefore are difficult to standardize for purposes of price comparisons.

An alternative basis for pricing services is to take the annual average earnings of the professionals. This does not avoid the quality problem referred to above, but it does have two advantages. First, it results in price comparisons that, in a sense, are more comprehensive than those based on a limited number of specific services. Second, national average compensation for professionals, at least for some countries, may be estimated with less error and with greater coverage of both private and government expenditures than estimates of national average prices for specific services. Even if it were assumed that there are no international differences in the quality of the practitioners, however, price comparisons based on annual compensation would be valid only if it could be assumed also that the productivity of each group of professionals (doctors, dentists, and so on) was the same in each country or if the differences in productivity were known and corrections were made for them.

The assumption of equal productivity is the simplest to make, though there is little evidence that it is correct. For example, dentists may see more patients per day by the use of extra offices and chairs, assigning tasks to assistants, sending out certain operations such as casting to specialized firms, and the use of high-speed equipment. According to one estimate for the United States, the real output per active dentist rose about 44 percent between 1953 and 1963. This was accomplished in part by an increased number of patient visits per dentist,[1] with a 4 percent increase in work hours playing a small role. It is doubtful that common levels of dental technology prevail in all the ICP countries. If, as the above illustration for dentists suggests, wealthier countries with higher real wages may have higher real output per professional, a comparison of salaries would make the relative price of services appear unduly inexpensive in low-income countries relative to high-income countries.

The problem of comparing the productivity of physicians is greater still, for the medical field has no simple and widely dispensed service, such as filling a cavity, that might conceivably serve as a quantity indicator. The office visit may come the closest, but as already noted, the qualifications of the practitioner may vary widely from country to country. Furthermore, even the time spent by the physician per office visit is different, especially as between private and publicly supplied services. One of the most striking differences is found between private practitioners in the United States and health center doctors in India. With 1.56 doctors per 1,000 persons in the United States and an average of 4.5 annual visits per person to physicians, there are roughly 2,885 visits per physician per year.[2] Taking 150 full working days devoted fully to visits as typical (excluding hospital visits), a U.S. doctor may average 20 visits in a full day, perhaps more if allowance is made for specialists. But however much we inflate the U.S. figure, it could never approach that of health center doctors in India, of whom 90 percent (in a Johns Hopkins survey) had less than five minutes per patient and one-third, between 30 and 60 seconds.[3] The Indian medical center

doctor is the first to say—and loudly—that he does not get enough time per patient. But is his two minutes per patient to be equated minute for minute with the U.S. visits, which may average 20 minutes? It might be argued that two minutes for rural Indian patients with obvious needs represent, in terms of contribution to welfare (and productivity?), the equal of a 20-minute visit to a U.S. physician by relatively healthy patients.[4]

If reliance is placed on direct comparisons either of prices of services or of annual earnings, quantity comparisons can be made indirectly by dividing the PPPs into the expenditure ratio. The alternative is to make direct quantity comparisons of the number of services or of the numbers of professional personnel. The number of services can be used in the case of hospitals, where a bed or bed-day can be identified as a quantity unit, but for the services of physicians, dentists, and other medical personnel, no unit is feasible other than such time units of input as man-years.

All the problems of quality and productivity mentioned earlier in connection with direct price comparisons are encountered as well in making direct quantity comparisons. As a practical necessity, we have assumed that the quality of each specified service (office visit, hospital-bed–day) and of each type of professional (doctor, dentist) is the same from one country to another, except for a crude adjustment for the amount of capital used in the provision of health care.[5] We know that this assumption is not warranted, but it would take a special effort, backed up by considerable financial and technical resources, to calibrate the differences. Further improvements of a modest nature are possible without such a large investment of resources, and it is hoped that they can be undertaken in the future development of the ICP. For example, the data on the value of the capital used in medical care may be improved, and rough quality adjustments for medical personnel may be based on length of education and training.

The quantity data come from sources that are completely independent of the price data. Because the product of the price and quantity ratios should yield the expenditure ratios, an opportunity exists to check the consistency of the two approaches. When, as is all too often the case, the product of the two direct ratios does

[1] Rashi Fein, *The Doctor Shortage: An Economic Diagnosis* (Washington: Brookings Institution, 1967) p. 120.

[2] Fein, *The Doctor Shortage*, pp. 68, 174.

[3] H. S. Takulia, Carl E. Taylor, S. Prakash Sangal, and Joseph D. Alter, *The Health Center Doctor in India* (Baltimore: The Johns Hopkins Press, 1967).

[4] It may be of interest to note that the average fee of a doctor in India for an office visit in 1969 was Rs4.26, as compared with a fee of Rs20.0 paid by the U.N. employees in India. U.N. Statistical Office, *Retail Price Comparisons for International Salary Determination* (New York: United Nations, 1971.) The difference probable reflects in part the longer visits of more affluent patients to physicians having more equipment and facilities than their counterparts charging lower fees. This situation within India probably is analogous to the difference between physicians in India and the United States. It may also be mentioned that the earlier reference to the large number of patients seen by the Indian Health Center doctor does not carry over to private physicians in India; the latter, who constitute the largest group, probably see fewer patients than U.S. doctors.

[5] See pages 97–98.

not equal the original expenditure ratio, we are confronted with a problem.

One possible course is to accept all three ratios, even though they are inconsistent. We reject this possibility because, for the study as a whole, we want to present final results in which this consistency test is met. If in most categories it were possible to produce direct quantity and direct price comparisons, it might be worthwhile to aggregate each separately in order to show the best possible estimate of the overall PPP and also the best possible estimate of the GDP quantity ratio. In fact, there are not many such categories, and independent estimates of PPPs and of the quantity ratios would add still another set of results—these not much different from others—to a study already surfeited with alternative answers.

If we opt for consistency, we have to choose two of the ratios and derive the third from them, rather than accept the independent estimate of it. As a practical matter, we have little choice but to include the expenditure ratio as one of the two that we accept. Each country's expenditures must add up to its GDP, and we cannot alter its expenditure in any one category without changing its expenditures in another category by an offsetting amount. The total GDP is not sacrosanct, but usually it is estimated by alternative approaches; thus, it seems wiser to accept the total as correct, even though one of the breakdowns looks suspicious.

The decisions (1) to maintain consistency and (2) to retain the expenditure ratio require that a choice be made between the direct price ratio and the indirect quantity ratio, on the one hand, and the direct quantity ratio and indirect price ratio, on the other hand.

One consideration governing this choice is the decision to give priority to obtaining the best possible quantity ratios wherever a conflict exists between accurate quantity and accurate price ratios. This is based on the view that the more important analytical and policy uses of the measures we are producing involve the quantity rather than the price ratios. The direct price ratios, however, are presented in this chapter; if anyone wishes to do so, they may be aggregated to form better estimates of the overall PPP than those we offer.

A second consideration in the choice between the use of the direct price versus the direct quantity ratios is the relative availability and trustworthiness of the data. Generally, in the health and education sectors, reliable information on quantities is more readily available than equally good information on national average prices. In the United States, for example, it is possible to place more confidence in the data on the total number of teachers at each educational level than it is on the national average salary of teachers. Salaries are different in private and public schools; each private school and each locality operating a public school system generally establishes its own salary scales. Earnings figures also are

difficult to obtain in some countries in which private practitioners are important in the provision of medical care. Resort might be had to comparisons of earnings for certain subgroups of professionals who are salaried in all countries, such as public health officers. In some countries such as the United States, however, a public health officer earns less than the average physician, whereas in India and other countries, he earns more. Furthermore, the salaries of public doctors are total earnings in some countries, whereas in others these salaries may be augmented by earnings from private practice.

The results of the alternative approaches to price and quantity comparisons that we have been discussing are set out for physicians' services in Table 7.1. The price comparisons on the simplest basis—the price of an office visit—are shown in column 2a. In most of the cases, a house call was the only additional service for which comparative prices were available, but in three cases there also were comparative prices of three to five other services. In one of these cases, Hungary–United States, the price index drops from 26 percent of the U.S. price to 12 percent (column 2b). For four comparisons, annual earnings data also were available:

	(U.S.=100)
Colombia	12
India	5
Japan	16
United Kingdom	34

The earnings ratio is different from the price ratios for services in all four cases, radically so in the case of Colombia. All in all, the price data offer a slender reed upon which to base our comparisons; few services are priced, and the addition of others or the use of earnings sometimes changes the results substantially.

This conclusion points to the use of quantity indicators. The number of physicians per capita is the basis of the direct quantity ratios in column 4a. These figures are not corrected, as they should be, for differences in average hours of work, let alone for differences in quality. An attempt was made to limit the data to physicians engaged in providing services to patients, but this proved not to be feasible.

The use of the number of personnel has the disadvantage of measuring only one component of the service rendered, although an important one. Each physician in a wealthy country is apt to be able to work with equipment and facilities that enhance the value of his services to his patients relative to the equipment and facilities available to the physician in a poor country.

Differences in the availability of equipment can have such a large impact on the quality of the services rendered by the professional staff that it seemed important to make some allowances for this factor, even though they had to be very crude. Therefore, we have introduced an extremely rough correction to the quan-

Table 7.1. Direct and Indirect Price and Quantity Comparisons, Physicians' Services (ICP 05.310), 1970

(U.S. = 100)

Country	Expenditure ratio† (1)	Price index Direct‡ (2) (a)§	Price index Direct‡ (2) (b)¶	Price index Indirect (3)=(1)÷(4b)	Quantity index Direct (4) (a)#	Quantity index Direct (4) (b)††	Quantity index Indirect (5)=(1)÷(2) (a)	Quantity index Indirect (5)=(1)÷(2) (b)	Derived expenditure ratio (6) (a)=(2a)×(4b)	Derived expenditure ratio (6) (b)=(2b)×(4b)
Colombia	7.6	66	68	30	29	26	12	11	19.1	19.7
France	105.3	48	46	128	85	82	219	229	40.8	39.1
Germany, F.R.	112.5	40	43	100	118	113	281	262	47.2	50.7
Hungary	7.6	26	12	7	122	112	29	63	31.7	14.6
India	0.34	10		3	13	11	3		1.3	
Italy	49.5	57	27	68	79	73	87	183	45.0	21.3
Japan	9.1	19	11	14	70	66	48	83	13.3	7.7
Kenya	1.5	38	37	21	8	7	4	4	3.0	3.0
United Kingdom	28.6	40	41	43	71	67	72	70	28.4	29.1

†Expenditures converted to dollars at the official exchange rate (column 3 of Table 1.1) and expressed as percentage of the U.S. expenditure, which was $47.38.

‡Price converted to dollars at official exchange rate (column 3 of Table 1.1) and expressed as percentage of U.S. price.

§Price ratio for office visit.

¶Average of ratios for house call and office visits except as follows: Hungary, house call, office visit, hernia, tonsillectomy, and obstetrical service; Japan, office visit, house call, office visit to pediatrican, hernia operation, tonsillectomy; Colombia, office visit, obstetrical service, appendectomy. In these three comparisons the average price ratio for office visits and house calls was averaged with the average price ratio for the other services, no weights being used other than those implicit in the averaging procedure.

#Figures are based on the number of physicians per capita in 1970, except for India (1969–70), Colombia (1969), Italy (1968), and France (1968); in these cases, the U.S. quantities refer also to the corresponding year.

††The physicians' quantity ratios have been adjusted downward to allow for capital in medicine, as discussed in the text (pp. 97–98).

tity ratios to allow for the amount of capital used in the provision of health care.[6]

We had estimates of capital used in providing medical care only for two countries, Hungary and the United States. For the former, the 1970 per capita estimate was Ft2,148.9 for the latter, $219.74.[7] Drawing upon the PPPs for construction and producers durable goods estimated below (Table 13.4), we find that the overall PPP in 1970 was Ft22.3 per dollar (ideal index). Dividing this into the ratio of the per capita capital stocks (2148.9/219.74), a real Hungary–United States quantity ratio for per capita medical capital of 43.9 percent is obtained.

This quantity ratio applies to all components of medical care taken together. The global ratio already is crude, and still more arbitrariness would have had to be introduced to make separate estimates for the capital quantity ratio for the four components of medical services: physicians, dentists, nurses, and hospitals. We propose, therefore, to work out the impact of allowing

for the use of capital equipment for these four components taken together.

To do this, we must anticipate somewhat and make use of the Hungary–United States quantity ratios not only for physicians but also for the other three components. When the quantity ratios are based solely on service inputs (numbers of professionals for physicians, dentists, and nurses, and the number of bed-days for hospitals), the ideal index comes to 95.1.

To include both the service and capital inputs, we combine the capital index of 43.9 and the service index of 95.1 with weights of 1 for capital and 6 for labor services. (The weights are based on the ratio of labor income to income from nonresidential structures and equipment in the United States and eight European countries.[8]) The result is an overall quantity index of 87.8. The adjustment on account of capital is 8 percent (87.8 ÷ 95.1 = 0.92). We apply this adjustment to the Hungary–United States quantity indexes based on service inputs (column 4a) for each of the four components to derive the quantity index based on both service and capital inputs (column 4b). In the case of physicians' services, for example, the Hungary–United States quantity ratio based on the numbers of physicians per capita is 122, but taking account of capital inputs, it is 112.

---

[6] The case for adjustments for capital inputs is perhaps less clear in connection with bed-days for hospital services because to a large degree these already reflect physical capital. The comfort provided, however, as well as the quality of medical care, depend on the amount of capital per bed.

[7] The estimate for Hungary was provided by the Hungarian Central Statistical Office. The estimate for the United States is based on an estimated capital stock of $8.9 billion for profit-seeking entities providing health care and hospital assets of $36,159 million. The former figure was estimated with the aid of Jack G. Faucett Associates of Chevy Chase, Md.; the latter figure was taken from "Hospital Statistics," *Journal of the American Hospital Association* 45 (August 1, 1971), p. 463.

[8] Compare E. Denison, *Why Growth Rates Differ* (Washington: Brookings Institution, 1967), p. 38. Denison's 1960–62 figures were used, although it would make little difference if his figures for other dates were used.

In the absence of capital estimates for the other countries, we have used the 8 percent adjustment for Hungary as a benchmark for making adjustments for the other countries based on preliminary estimates of the per capita GDPs relative to Hungary and the United States. The assumption was that the relative enhancement of physicians' services attributable to the provision of capital was related to per capita GDP level. Thus, for Italy, which has a per capita GDP only slightly higher than that of Hungary, the adjustment also was 8 percent. The adjustments for France and the Federal Republic of Germany, with about three-fourths of the U.S. per capita GDP, were 4 percent; for Japan and the United Kingdom, with nearly two-thirds of the U.S. GDP, 5 percent; and for the poorer countries, 10 percent for Colombia and 14 percent for India and Kenya.

If the direct price and direct quantity ratios for physicians' services were both correct, their product (shown in column 6) would equal the expenditure ratio (column 1). Only for Italy, Japan, and the United Kingdom is this condition met for the direct quantity comparison and at least one of the direct price comparisons. For the other countries, no more than two of the three ratios—price, quantity, or expenditure—can be correct. In some instances, as in the cases of France and the Federal Republic of Germany, the expenditure data seem doubtful; no plausible margins of error assigned to the underlying prices or quantities will alter either the price ratio (column 2) or the quantity ratio (column 4b) sufficiently to account for the extent of the shortfall in the derived expenditure ratio (column 6) relative to the original expenditure ratio (column 1). Nevertheless, for reasons given above, we accept the expenditure ratios and use them together with the direct quantity comparisons to derive the indirect PPPs in column 3. These may be compared with the direct PPPs (column 2), or the analogous comparison may be made between the direct quantity indexes (column 4b) and the indirect ones (column 5). For most of the countries, the answers are quite different, but it is difficult to see how the data on the number of physicians can be as likely to be in error as the price ratios or the expenditure ratios.

The comparisons for dental services and services of nurses and other professional personnel, shown in Tables 7.2 and 7.3, involve similar problems. The latter group of personnel is more heterogeneous than doctors or dentists, and the mix of skills probably varies widely from one country to another. Part of the problem for this category is that expenditures for nurses should in principle be separated from hospital expenditures, but in practice this breakdown has not been easy for some countries to provide.

The other major portion of medical expenditures is on hospitals, excluding professional personnel. In Table 7.4, direct per capita quantity ratios based on the number of beds (column 4a) and on the number of bed-days (column 4b) are shown. From the standpoint of measuring the flow of services to consumers, the latter seems more appropriate; in the seven instances in which both measures are available, the latter is larger in five cases, ranging from 69 to 142 percent of the former.

Even wider differences result when the quantity ratios are derived from the price ratios. These indirect quantity ratios (column 5) are substantially lower than the direct ones, being one-half or less in four out of the five cases in which they are available. The direction of the difference is explicable in terms of the quality difference that the direct price comparison tries to control

Table 7.2. Direct and Indirect Price and Quantity Comparisons, Dentists' Services (ICP 05.320), 1970

(U.S. = 100)

Country	Expenditure ratio†	Price index		Quantity index			Derived expenditure ratio
		Direct‡	Indirect	Direct		Indirect	
	(1)	(2)	(3)=(1)÷(4b)	(4)		(5)=(1)÷(2)	(6)=(2) × (4b)
				(a)§	(b)¶		
Colombia	3.6	40	33	17	15	12	6.8
France	199.6	50	266	78	75	399	39.0
Germany, F.R.	142.9	129	146	102	98	111	131.6
Hungary	2.0	24	5	47	43	8	11.3
India	0.01	49	6	2	2	0.02	1.0
Italy	74.9	72	79	103	95	104	74.2
Japan	6.7	18	10	73	69	37	13.2
Kenya	0.4	35	45	1	1	1	0.4
United Kingdom	31.5	35	66	50	48	90	17.5

†Expenditures converted to dollars at the official exchange rate (column 3 of Table 1.1) and expressed as percentage of the U.S. expenditure, which is $13.88.
‡Price for filling converted to dollars at official exchange rate (column 3 of Table 1.1) and expressed as percentage of U.S. price.
§Number of dentists for 1970, except 1969 (Colombia) and 1967 (United Kingdom, France, India, and Italy), where comparisons have been made with the United States for the appropriate year.
¶The dentists' quantity ratios have been adjusted downward to allow for capital in medicine, as discussed in the text (pp. 97–98).

Table 7.3. Direct and Indirect Price and Quantity Comparisons, Services of Nurses and Related Personnel (ICP 05.330)

(U.S. = 100)

Country	Expenditure ratio[†] (1)	Price index Direct[‡] (2)	Price index Indirect (3)=(1)÷(4b)	Quantity index Direct (4) (a)[§]	(b)[¶]	Quantity index Indirect (5)=(1)÷(2)	Derived expenditure ratio (6)=(2) × (4b)
Colombia	0.3	19	1.6	7	6	1	1.1
France	6.9		11	68	65		
Germany, F.R.	14.5		19	79	76		
Hungary	4.6		6	80	74		
India	0.3		6	6	5		
Italy	3.3		10	37	34		
Japan	4.6	34	9	57	54	14	19.4
Kenya	0.9		6	18	16		
United Kingdom	27.7	44	27	107	102	63	47.1

[†]Expenditures converted to dollars at the official exchange rate (column 3 of Table 1.1) and expressed as percentage of the U.S. expenditure, which is $82.89.
[‡]Based on nurses' salaries. Price converted to dollars at official exchange rate (column 3 of Table 1.1) and expressed as percentage of U.S. price.
[§]Based on figures for number of nurses, midwives, practical nurses, and auxilliary nurses per capita relative to the United States. Figures refer to 1970.
[¶]The nurse quantity ratios have been adjusted downward to allow for capital in medicine, as discussed in the text (pp. 97–98).

Table 7.4. Direct and Indirect Price and Quantity Comparisons for Hospital Services (ICP 05.410), 1970

(U.S. = 100)

Country	Expenditure ratio[†] (1)	Price index Direct[‡] (2)	Price index Indirect (3)=(1)÷(4b) (a)	(b)	Quantity index Direct (4) (a)[§]	(b)[¶]	Quantity index Indirect (5)=(1)÷(2)	Derived expenditure ratio (6) (a)=(2) × (4a)	(b)=(2) × (4b)
Colombia	1.5	14	6	8	26	18	11	4.2	3.3
France	5.8		10	7	57	81			
Germany, F.R.	10.2	38	8	7	129	140	27	50.9	55.1
Hungary	12.6		15	13	86	96			
India	0.2	4	3		7		5	0.3	
Italy	8.0	27	7	7	114	116	30	33.5	31.9
Japan	12.4	10	9	9	141	131	124	14.8	13.1
Kenya	2.1		14		15				
United Kingdom	25.5	39	26	22	97	115	65	39.8	24.8

[†]Expenditures converted to dollars at the official exchange rate (column 3 of Table 1.1) and expressed as percentage of the U.S. expenditure, which is $117.82.
[‡]Price converted to dollars at official exchange rate (column 3 of Table 1.1) and expressed as percentage of U.S. price.
[§]Number of beds per capita in 1968 relative to the United States, except Colombia, Kenya, and India figures, which are for 1967, and have been compared with U.S. 1967 figures.
[¶]Number of bed-days per capita in 1968 relative to the United States, except for Colombia and Japan, where the comparisons are for 1967 and 1966, respectively. The bed-day ratios have been adjusted downward to allow for capital in medicine, as discussed in the text (pp. 97–98). Figures are for total beds, except France, which excludes mental hospitals; the latter were excluded from total U.S. beds to obtain the France–United States ratio.

and that the direct quantity comparison ignores in this case. Large variations exist in the provision of hospital facilities in different countries.[9] In some countries, a member of the family may stay with the patient, per-haps cooking and serving the food for the patient; in others, meals are prepared and served by the hospital staff and included in the per diem price of the stay. The size of the room, the degree of privacy, and the quality

[9]Brian Abel-Smith, as part of his studies of international health, examined data on the cost of hospital-bed–days in several countries, but the United States was the only ICP coun-try included. See his *An International Study of Health Expenditure,* Public Health Papers No. 32 (Geneva: World Health Organization, 1967).

of the facilities and furnishings also vary; on the latter point, for example, private baths, telephones, and television are provided in some rooms in high-income countries. The type of hospital also affects the kind and quantity of services provided with a room; general hospitals are much more expensive than long-term hospitals, and the mix varies considerably between countries.

We would have preferred to use the direct price ratios, which have the advantage that, in principle, they reflect the quality differences between hospital rooms within the countries and thus yield a (indirect) quantity comparison for a comparable facility. Two reasons, however, led us to rely instead on the direct quantity comparisons in terms of bed-days. First, we did not have the data to make satisfactory price comparisons between the United States and three of the other nine countries. Second, in two or three of the remaining cases (the Federal Republic of Germany, Italy, and, to a lesser degree, the United Kingdom) the indirect quantity ratio (column 5) derived from the direct price ratio deviated so much from the direct (bed-day) quantity ratio as to make its plausibility questionable. In these instances, it seemed likely that the expenditure data were at fault, because the probable margins of error in neither the price nor quantity ratios could have been large enough to account for the fact that their product (column 6) is so far off from the expenditure ratio (column 1). Following the rule we have explained above,[10] we nevertheless retain the expenditure ratios and use the direct quantity (column 4b) and indirect price (column 3) ratios. For Kenya and India, for which no data on bed-days were available, we have used the number of beds as the quantity indicator (column 4a), which is equivalent to assuming the same utilization rate per bed as in the United States.

B. Education

As in the case of health care, some educational inputs were handled by means of direct price comparisons. These included expenditures related to physical facilities (ICP 07.420) and other expenditures of educational institutions (ICP 07.430). But for the greater part of educational expenditures, which refer to personnel (ICP 07.410), reliance has been placed on comparisons of the numbers of persons engaged in providing the services. We have made an effort, however, to produce direct price comparisons as well as direct quantity comparisons, even though it is the latter we finally use.

The simplest approach to this task was to compare the number of teachers per capita at each level of education. Following UNESCO definitions, teaching personnel have been divided into three levels of education: primary schools (first seven to nine years of education), secondary schools (years following the primary years up to and

including the twelfth year of education), and colleges and universities. Another category comprises administrative, clerical, and service personnel.

Upon further examination of the data on primary and secondary education, it appeared that if the education of the teacher is held constant, there was little difference in the salary of teachers at the first two levels. For example, in analysis of the data on 1,500 teachers from all parts of the United States, it was found that, holding constant the education of a teacher, secondary teachers earned less than 5 percent more than primary teachers.[11] Salaries rose by 8.4 percent for each year of additional schooling, holding other factors constant. In the United Kingdom, the salary scales for primary and secondary teachers are the same.[12]

In Kenya and India, large salary differences between secondary and primary teachers were reported—in 1967, £880 versus £216 in Kenya, and Rs2584 versus Rs1464 in India. But upon examination of these data, it was clear that large differences existed also in the education of teachers; in Kenya, the primary teacher averaged only nine years of education, the secondary school teacher, fifteen years. In India, only 14 percent of the primary teachers in 1965 had education beyond the high school level, whereas 91 percent of the secondary teachers had advanced education.

In what follows, we have assumed that for teachers of a given level of education, salaries in primary and secondary schools are the same. We have defined a "standard teacher" in all countries as one who has completed two years of study at the college or university level and have compared salaries between countries for such a teacher. We did not have the data necessary to estimate accurately the national average salary for a standard teacher in every country, and in some cases we had to resort to a considerable degree of approximation.[13]

---

[10] See pages 95–96.

[11] The analysis of U.S. teachers' salaries was made on the data underlying the National Education Association's *American Public School Survey of 1965–66* (Washington: National Education Association, 1967). The difference between primary and secondary salaries was not a result of secondary teachers having more experience, because this variable also was held constant.

[12] See, for example, Department of Education and Science, *Scales of Salaries for Teachers in Primary and Secondary Schools, England and Wales 1969* (London: Her Majesty's Stationery Office, 1969).

[13] For the United States, the estimated salary of a standard teacher was $8,110 in 1970. This was based on the analysis of the National Education Survey mentioned in footnote 9, above.

The reported salary of a secondary teacher in India in 1970 was Rs3040 and for primary teachers, Rs1781. The average years of education for secondary teachers was reported as fourteen years, so the salary of Rs3040 is taken as an estimate of a teacher with two years of college education. The ratios of teachers with different qualifications are from Ministry of Education, *Second All-India Educational Survey 1967* (New Delhi: Government of India, 1967), p. 66, and refer to 1965.

For Kenya, we simply interpolated the salary of teachers of fourteen years on the basis of their salaries for nine and fifteen years of education. This yields a salary of £800 for 1967 and £987 for 1970.

Table 7.5. Direct and Indirect Price and Quantity Comparisons for Primary and Secondary Education (ICP 07.411), 1970

(U.S. = 100)

Country	Expenditure ratio† (1)	Price index Direct‡ (2)	Indirect (3) Teachers (a) = (1)÷(4a)	Indirect (3) Pupils (b) = (1)÷(4b)	Quantity index Direct§ (4) Teachers (a)	Quantity index Direct§ (4) Pupils (b)	Indirect (5) = (1)÷(2) Teachers	Derived expenditure ratio (6) Teachers (a) = (2)×(4a)	Derived expenditure ratio (6) Pupils (b) = (2)×(4b)
Colombia	4.1	15.5	7.2	7.7	57.0	59.3	26.5	8.8	9.2
France	60.1	44.7	77.2	64.3	77.8	93.5	134.5	34.8	41.8
Germany, F.R.	50.0	63.9	69.4	77.4	72.0	64.6	78.2	46.0	41.3
Hungary	9.2	12.7	12.6	15.6	73.0	59.0	72.4	9.3	7.5
India	0.8	2.3	0.9	1.4	86.6	58.4	34.8	43.7	29.5
Italy	37.0	42.7	42.7	63.4	86.6	58.4	86.6	37.0	25.0
Japan	18.1	36.4	25.6	26.4	70.7	68.6	49.7	25.7	25.0
Kenya	3.0	34.1	10.6	5.2	28.3	58.1	8.8	9.7	19.8
United Kingdom	30.8	64.1	45.9	47.8	67.1	64.5	48.0	43.0	41.3

†Expenditures converted to dollars at the official exchange rate (column 3 of Table 1.1) and expressed as percentage of the U.S. expenditure, which is $185.05.

‡Based on salaries for teachers with two years of college education, salaries converted to dollars at official exchange rate (column 3 of Table 1.1) and expressed as percentage of U.S. salary. Sources for salary data are described in the text.

§Pupil and teacher data refer to 1969 and are from UNESCO *Statistical Yearbook, 1971.*

The price ratios based on the salary estimates for a standard teacher are given in column 2 of Table 7.5, and the indirect quantity ratios they yield are shown in column 5. Because the price comparisons are derived with the aid of a good deal of rough estimation, it seems preferable to rely upon the direct quantity comparisons. Such reliance upon the raw quantity data, however, would assume that the average quality of teachers is the same in all countries. We know that large differences exist in the education of teachers in Colombia, India, and Kenya, as compared with the other countries. Therefore, a basis had to be found for making quality adjustments for these countries.

Because the data for India seem fairly reliable, and because of the rather special situation in Kenya, where foreign nationals with higher salaries teach in secondary schools, we have taken India as a base for the adjustment. In India, the average salary of a primary teacher was Rs1781 in 1970, and the probable years of schooling was between 12 and 13.[14] For the United States and other countries, except Colombia and Kenya, the average education of teachers appears higher. For example, compared to a U.S. average of 15.2 years of education for all primary and secondary teachers, India was 13.3 years,[15] which we believe warrants an adjustment of the Indian quantity figures in column 4a.

We would have preferred to use the Indian price data to make this adjustment, but it was felt that the regres-

For France, secondary teachers range across the civil service grades 243 to 451, and we have taken the grade of 390 as an estimate for a four-year teacher, that grade referring to a sanitary engineer. A two-year teacher in France was assumed to be the grade of inferior schoolmaster. The former grade of civil servant received total earnings of Fr20,148, whereas the average earnings of teachers in secondary education was Fr23,018.

For the Federal Republic of Germany, data were not available to find teacher grades in any simple way. We took the ratio of the average German secondary salary (DM18,959) to the salary of sanitary engineers, yielding an estimate of DM21,309 for secondary teachers with four years of college, and used the above ratio for two- and four-year teachers for France (20,148/23,018 = .875) to estimate the German teacher with two years of education at DM18,965.

For Italy the same type of adjustment was made as described for the Federal Republic of Germany, the average secondary salary being L2,560,560 and the estimated salary for teachers with two years of college being L2,561,400, all for 1970.

For the United Kingdom, *Statistics of Education, 1967* (vol. 4, *Teachers,* p. 69) gives the average salary of graduates in primary or secondary education as £2,494; we made similar adjustments to the scale of nongraduates, who we assumed had two years of college, to estimate the salary for two years of college at £2,165 in 1970.

For Japan, the average salary for primary and secondary teachers was supplied as ¥918,943 for a teacher with an average of 14.7 years of education. The salary scale for Japanese teachers suggests that between two and four years of college, salary goes up 11.4 percent per year of education. This ratio has been applied to estimate for a teacher with two years of college education a salary of ¥814,482 for 1967, which was adjusted on the basis of government salaries to ¥1,062,360 for 1970.

For Hungary, primary teachers with fourteen years of education earned Ft30,800.

For Colombia, we took the average secondary salary of P23,400 to be that for a teacher with two years of education.

[14]As mentioned earlier, the *Second All-India Educational Study 1967,* reported only 14 percent of the primary teachers as having education beyond high school in 1965. Even if this percentage had doubled in 1970 and, say, 30 percent of the teachers had two years of college, the average years of education of primary teachers would be 12.6 years, and the average for both primary and secondary (taking the latter as all having two years of college) teachers would be 13.3 years.

[15]For estimate of Indian figure, see footnote 14.

sion analysis of teacher salaries we were able to make for the United States isolated the influence of teacher education in a way that could not be done with the Indian data available to us. Therefore, we applied the estimate of 8.4 percent more salary per additional year of schooling[16] to adjust the Indian quantity data to a standard level. The adjusted quantity estimate for India in column 4 of Table 7.5 is thus 8.4 x (15.2 - 13.3) = 16 percent less than actual. Although we did not have a basis for estimating the average years of education of teachers in Colombia, we have assumed that it would be the same as India, and we also adjusted their quantity by 16 percent. For Kenya, however, the average years of education for all primary and secondary teachers in 1967 was between nine and ten years. Application of the 8.4 percent adjustment factor thus would result in a near halving of the Kenyan quantity (the difference in education levels of approximately 5.5 years times 8.4). This seemed extreme, particularly because nine to ten years of teacher education is beyond the U.S. sample range from which the adjustment factor was derived. It was clear, however, that Kenya warranted a larger adjustment than India and Colombia, and therefore we reduced the Kenyan quantity ratio in column 4a by one-third.

Another reason for combining primary and secondary education is that the breakdown of pupils, teachers, and expenditures is not uniform across the countries, the end of primary education being anywhere from four to eight years. It would be possible to adjust the number of students to reflect a common definition of primary education, say grades 1 to 8, but this is not so easily done for expenditures on teachers. Because little difference exists in salaries between primary and secondary teachers of the same educational level, little disadvantage accrues from combining the two levels of education.

With respect to the category of administrative, clerical, and service personnel, several countries had rather large expenditures, equal to those for secondary education. Because the data for independent price or quantity comparisons for this category generally were lacking, it was assumed that the quantities of these personnel were proportional in each country to teaching personnel. Thus, the expenditures for this category were included with expenditures for teachers in primary and secondary education in column 1 of Table 7.5, and the price and quantity ratios in the table may be regarded as inclusive of these ancillary personnel.

As a matter of information, Table 7.5 also provides quantity indicators based on the number of pupils (column 4b). When the number of pupils rather than the number of teachers is used to form the quantity ratios, the relative quantities rise for Colombia, France, India, and Kenya. As incomes go up across countries, a rise occurs in both the affluence to support smaller classes and the cost of those smaller classes; the impact of

affluence can be expected to reduce class size (the income effect), and the influence of the higher price of teachers in the wealthier countries can be expected to increase class size (the substitution effect). Thus, the substantially lower incomes of Colombia, Kenya, and India seem to explain their relatively larger quantity of students compared to teachers. (Some of the differences result from the fact that the teacher ratio has been reduced by the quality adjustment, but the pupil-based quantity ratios for Kenya and India would be higher than the teacher-based quantity ratio without the quality adjustment.) Because the income and substitution effects are working in opposite directions, however, it is not surprising to find that, in at least one of the higher income countries, France, the quantity ratio based on pupils also is larger.

For grades 1 to 12 in general, Italy had smaller class sizes than Hungary, the Federal Republic of Germany, Japan, and the United States, in which the averages were about twenty-four students per teacher in 1967.[17] In Colombia, France, India, and Kenya, class sizes were closer to thirty per teacher.

The underlying assumption in our use of the teacher-based quantity ratios is that the productivity of a teacher with the same training is the same whether he is teaching a class of twenty-five or fifty. In this connection, it should be borne in mind that it is not solely the amount of learning that our quantity ratios should reflect but the total services rendered by teachers, including personal attention to pupils that may add to their well-being in ways other than learning. If it were assumed that a teacher of fifty produced more output than a teacher of twenty-four, some combination of pupil- and teacher-based quantity ratios would be appropriate.

It may be mentioned that quantity ratios based on pupils may be less reliable than those based on teachers because pupils are overcounted in some countries. This sometimes occurs when school administrators are motivated to register as many students as possible because the allocation of funds to local schools from central or state sources is on the basis of registered students rather than attendance. Measuring the number of teachers is also difficult because of the frequent use of part-time personnel in some countries such as Colombia.

The ratios of the reported expenditures in column 1 of Table 7.5 may be compared with the expenditure ratios in column 6 obtained by taking the product of the per capita quantity ratios and the price ratios. With the exception of France, the Federal Republic of Germany, and Hungary, the product of the price and quantity ratios yields higher expenditure ratios than those in column 1. In accordance with our general rule, we accept the expenditure figures in column 1, and as be-

---

[16] See page 100.

[17] Data have been taken from UNESCO *Statistical Yearbook* (Paris: UNESCO, 1971).

Table 7.6. Direct and Indirect Price and Quantity Comparisons for Third-Level Education (ICP 07.412)

(U.S. = 100)

Country	Expenditure ratio† (1)	Price index Direct‡ (2)	Price index Indirect (3)=(1)÷(4) Teachers (a)	Students (b)	Quantity Direct§ (4) Teachers (a)	Students (b)	Quantity Indirect (5)=(1)÷(2)	Derived expenditure ratio (6) Teachers (a) = (2) × (4a)	Students (b) = (2) × (4b)
Colombia	5.5	25.1	11.8	18.3	16.0	10.4	7.5	4.0	2.6
France	46.8	32.9	241.8	148.9	19.4	31.5	142.6	6.4	10.4
Germany, F.R.	52.7	41.7	206.7	281.8	25.5	18.7	126.3	10.6	7.8
Hungary	5.0	11.4	17.7	38.2	28.3	13.1	43.9	3.2	1.5
India	0.6	5.2	7.0	3.8	8.6	15.8	11.6	0.4	0.8
Italy	23.1	32.2	94.3	78.0	24.5	29.6	71.6	7.9	9.5
Japan	17.1	24.6	38.3	41.8	44.7	40.9	69.5	11.0	10.1
Kenya	0.9	38.9	75.0	69.0	1.2	1.3	2.3	0.5	0.5
United Kingdom	32.6	45.7	67.2	291.1	48.5	11.2	71.4	22.2	5.1

†Expenditures converted to dollars at the official exchange rate (column 3 of Table 1.1) and expressed as percentage of the U.S. expenditure, $35.19.
‡Based on teachers' salaries, salaries converted to dollars at official exchange rate (column 3 of Table 1.1), and expressed as percentage of U.S. salary. Sources for salary data are described in the text.
§Pupil and teacher data refer to 1969 and are from UNESCO *Statistical Yearbook, 1971.*

tween the combination of the direct price and indirect quantity ratios and the combination of indirect price and direct quantity ratios, we have already indicated that we opt for the latter. Therefore, the figures in columns 3a and 4a represent our final results.

We do make use, however, of the direct price comparisons (column 2) for certain other categories such as welfare services, in which salaries of primary and secondary teachers could be taken as representative of the level of salaries for occupations involving related educational and other qualifications.

Table 7.6 shows that most of the same problems exist for higher education as for primary and secondary education. The expenditures for France and the Federal Republic of Germany yield high derived price and quantity ratios, suggesting they may be too large. Large differences exist in student and teacher quantities, particularly for the United Kingdom, with its high teacher-student ratio. Again, we have chosen to work with teachers instead of pupils as the quantity indicator and

have used columns 3a and 4a as our preferred results for purposes of aggregation to obtain PPPs and quantity comparisons for consumption and GDP.

In education as in health, it can be expected that physical facilities will be better in a wealthy than in a poor country. More space per pupil and more comfortable or attractive facilities do not necessarily betoken more learning, but nevertheless they should be included as added product even if they represent only higher consumption in the form of a more pleasant environment for learning. In principle, therefore, the quantity indicators for education should be amplified to include measures of educational plant and equipment in each country. Because of the difficulty of obtaining the required data, however, we did not adjust the quantity ratios for capital inputs as we did in connection with health care. This reflects the judgment—perhaps mistaken—that international differences in capital inputs have a greater impact on differences in the delivery of health services than on the delivery of educational services.

Chapter 8

Matching qualities by regression methods

Regression methods were used to make international price comparisons for rents and for a number of producers and consumer goods. Their most extensive use was in connection with rents, to which the next chapter is devoted, and with automobiles, dealt with in this chapter.

The following section on methodological issues can be brief in view of the growing body of literature dealing with the multivariate analysis of price differences between two situations.[1]

A. Methodological Issues

Regression analysis provides a convenient method of international price comparison for complex products that are differentiated by their producers.[2] Each of these products may be regarded as a cluster of characteristics (for example, weight, horsepower, engine displacement, and so on), and each model produced by a given firm is apt to be unique in the sense that no other model has exactly the same combination of characteristics in the same proportions. The traditional method of price comparison—that is, the matching of identical or equivalent models in different countries—is easy to apply to such products only when a given model of a given producer commonly is consumed in the two or more countries for which prices are being compared. In many situations, identical brands and models are found in different countries, as, for example, the many kinds of producers' durables in Latin American countries and the United States. In other instances, however, overlap is only limited or nonexistent.

Where there are no identical models, the traditional method of price comparison involves matching pairs of models (one from each country) as closely as possible and making ad hoc adjustments in the price of one of the models to take account of the differences in characteristics. For example, in the Japanese–U.S. price comparison, if we wish to avoid basing the entire result on Japanese cars imported into the United States, the problem posed by the need to match cars from the two countries may be illustrated in terms of one of the closest matchings that was available:

	Japanese (Model C)[3]	U.S. (Model V)[3]
Horsepower (SAE)	115	115
Displacement (cu. in.)	137	170
RPM	5200	4400
Weight (lbs.)	2767	2836
Length (in.)	184	188
Width (in.)	67	70
Price ($)	2788	2337

The rated horsepower of the two cars was the same, but the U.S. car had a larger engine and a larger, heavier body. Should the U.S. price be adjusted downward by 24 percent on the basis of the larger displacement or by 2 to 4 percent on the basis of weight, length, or width? By some intermediate amount?

In Chapter 3, we described some of the methods by which we have tried to cope with these problems of matching qualities of goods in different countries. In Chapter 10, we describe a method we worked out for the rough interpolation of prices in just such a case as is posed in the preceding paragraph.

Such methods have the great advantage of requiring less comprehensive data than regression methods, but necessarily they are based on arbitrary assumptions

---

[1] See, for example, Z. Griliches, ed., *Price Indexes and Quality Change* (Cambridge: Harvard University Press, 1971).

[2] Compare I. Kravis and R. Lipsey, *Price Competitiveness in World Trade* (New York: Columbia University Press for the National Bureau of Economic Research, 1971), Chap. 5.

[3] Actual models found in each country.

about the relative importance of the key price-determining variables.

The advantage of the regression method is that it avoids the arbitrary and ad hoc character of such a rough interpolation. The price in each country can be expressed as a function of these several characteristics at the same time. The assumption underlying the use of a regression equation to estimate price is that the differences in prices for various models of a given product at a moment in time in a given market are accounted for by differences in the mix of the characteristics. The identity and relative importance of these characteristics can be uncovered by a systematic statistical investigation in which a search is conducted for those which best explain the observed variation in prices. Once the preferred equation is selected for the given country, it can be used to estimate the price for a car that matches a car found in the market of another country.

ALTERNATIVE WAYS OF DEFINING THE PRODUCT

One of the problems in using regression methods for international price comparisons is how to define the product for comparative purposes. The choices are (1) to define it in terms of identical price-determining characteristics for all countries (the "universal" definition); (2) to have identical variables for pairs of countries in binary comparisons (the "binary" definition); or (3) to select these variables in a separate and independent way for each country (the "national" definition).

Universal product definition. In a neat and tidy world with technological knowledge the same everywhere, the same price-explaining elements would be found in each market for a given product (though as indicated below, some of these elements might be of negligible importance in some countries). This happy set of circumstances would enable us to include identical characteristics for each country as the independent variables in the regressions in which price was the dependent variable. The coefficients of the independent variables, which can be interpreted as marginal prices for the characteristics, might differ, of course, from one country to another. Indeed, they could be expected to differ, because relative prices of the factors of production differ between countries and because a different mix of factors may be required to produce an increment of a particular characteristic in the various countries. A larger automobile, for example, may require mainly more metal, whereas an automobile with greater gasoline economy may require more skilled labor. If materials are relatively inexpensive and labor relatively expensive in the United States, one would expect the coefficient of weight to be smaller, and the coefficient of gasoline economy (if we could measure gasoline economy satisfactorily) would be higher than, say, in Europe. It is conceivable, though not likely, that factor prices and substitution possibilities

could produce zero or near zero prices for some characteristics in some countries. By and large, however, in a perfect world the variables contributing to the explanation of price would be the same in all countries.

The universal approach has the advantage that the product is defined unequivocally as a given cluster of characteristics, and that all of these characteristics are priced in each country. Because a unique price can be obtained for any given cluster for each country, then of course the universal approach also will produce intercountry comparisons that meet the circularity test (that is, $I_{j/l} \div I_{k/l} = I_{j/k}$).[4] These advantages are sufficiently attractive that imposing an identical list of variables upon the countries is worth considering, even though the statistical evidence leaves the choice of variables somewhat arbitrary. In the automobiles case, for example, we might decide—after examination of the correlations involving different combinations of variables in each of the countries—that weight, displacement, and pressure represented the best compromise combination of variables, and we would therefore use these three for all the countries. The disadvantage is that many or most of the price estimates and hence the intercountry comparisons will be subject to larger errors than they would be if the choice of the variables were tailored to each country individually. Thus, a strong statistical case exists against the universal definition, however attractive it is on conceptual grounds.

Binary product definition. A less sweeping constraint and one that would reduce the apparent errors of price estimates for the individual countries involves the selection of the cluster of independent variables solely on the basis of the data for each pair of countries. For the United Kingdom-United States comparison, for example, the selected characteristics might turn out to be weight and horsepower, whereas for a Japan-United States comparison, the characteristics might turn out to be weight, displacement, and pressure. In one sense, this binary approach corresponds to our treatment of the selection of specifications in the ICP where we are relying on the traditional method of price comparison: it is similar in that we are allowing the cluster of characteristics to differ from one pair of countries to another.

Although the binary approach reduces errors (in the standard error sense) arising from the misspecification of independent variables, it has the disadvantage of giving price ratios that fail the circularity test. Because the price for each country will be estimated from an equation that may differ according to the particular partner country with which it is compared, there is no necessity for the binary comparisons to be mutually consistent.

National product definition. A third possible approach is to specify independently the explanatory vari-

---

[4]Where I is a price index, and j, k, and l are countries. See Chapter 2.

ables for each country. A search is made in each market for the characteristics that best explain the variation of prices in the market of that nation. In the case of automobiles, for example, this may prove to be weight and horsepower in one country, length and displacement in the second country, and still other combinations of variables in other countries. The rationale of this approach is that we, as general economists, do not have the technical knowledge required really to understand the connection between prices and various independent variables and the relations among those independent variables. In view of this lack of knowledge, it is better simply to allow the data to determine which variables will be used, even though the variables selected may turn out to differ from one country to another. Price comparisons then can be made by estimating the price of a given model of the product (a Volkswagen 1600, a Fiat 850, or whatever) from each country's equation, even though the price, in the automobile illustration, may be based on the weight and horsepower of the selected model in one country, on length and displacement in another country, and on still different combinations of variables in other countries. Because in each country only one price will be estimated for each model, the circularity test is met.[5] The national definition has the additional merit of simplicity and ease of application, particularly in relation to the binary approach, and we have opted for it.

POOLING VERSUS SEPARATE REGRESSIONS FOR EACH COUNTRY

The national definition lends itself to computing separate regressions for each country, but it is not necessarily inconsistent with pooling data for several different countries.

The disadvantage of separate equations is that the coefficients of some of the variables may be estimated less reliably than would be the case if the data were pooled. If, for example, all U.K. cars are produced within a narrow range of displacements, the estimate of the coefficient for displacement based on U.K. data will be subject to substantial sampling error and therefore may turn out to be statistically insignificant. This should not be interpreted, however, as meaning that displacement is to be ignored in estimating the relative price of U.K. cars, especially if there is reason to believe that displacement is positively correlated with price and other independent variables (as, for example, if such a relationship is revealed in data in countries where cars with greater variability in displacement are produced). In such instances, a coefficient that is not statistically significant is to be construed as a reflection of poor resolving power

of the data rather than as an indication that displacement plays no role in determining price. Omitting displacement may lead to a biased price estimate.

An alternative is to rely on what has been called flexible pooling.[6] In this method, the data of two or more countries are used in a single regression, but one country is taken as the base country and dummy variables are inserted for the other(s) in connection with the intercept term and each independent variable. When the regression is run with the full set of these dummies, the results are substantially equivalent to running a separate regression for each country. The coefficients for the base country, the same as those obtained in a regression based upon that country's data alone, will be the coefficients of the basic variables (that is, those not involving dummy terms). If, for a given country, each dummy coefficient is added to the corresponding base-country coefficient, the result will be the coefficient that would be obtained from a regression based on the data of the second country alone.

When the coefficient of a dummy variable is not statistically significant, however, the implication is that the marginal price of that characteristic is the same in both countries included in the regression. Where that is the case, we are justified in dropping the dummy term for that characteristic from the equation. Thus, in flexible pooling, we pool the data of the two countries completely with respect to independent variables that turn out to have coefficients that are not significantly different in the two countries, but we retain dummy variables for those characteristics which the data show to be different in price in the two countries.

The attractiveness of the flexible-pooling procedure diminishes as we move from binary comparisons to those involving many countries. The reason is that the need to insert dummy variables for more than one country quickly increases the number of possible combinations of the basic variables with the dummy variables. As a practical matter, it is probably is desirable to work with binary pairs even if—keeping with the universal approach—it is desired to keep the basic variables always the same from one binary pair to another. It cannot be claimed that complete transitivity really will be achieved when the work is carried on with pairs of countries, because the dummy variables retained for a given country may well be different from those which would be retained were all the countries included in the regression at the same time. But it becomes extremely cumbersome, to say the least, to include as many as eight or ten countries at once, and it is doubtful that much would be gained by working with groups of three or four. Therefore, we have worked with separate equations for each country.

[5] This is true, however, only with respect to the countries for which the same set of models is priced. See the following section on the choice of representative models.

[6] See I. Kravis and R. Lipsey, *Price Competitiveness*.

THE CHOICE OF REPRESENTATIVE MODELS

Whatever the approach used, the relative prices estimated for any pair of countries generally will differ according to the characteristics of the model of the product that is selected for pricing. The way in which relative prices are affected by the values of the characteristics depends, of course, upon the mathematical form employed. When, as in the regressions employed below, the dependent variable is in log form, the countries being compared must have identical independent variables with identical coefficients for these variables if the results are not to depend upon the particular model selected for pricing. Because, in fact, the coefficients often differ substantially even when identical variables are used, the choice of the model to be compared can have a large impact on the outcome. In the case of automobiles, for example, large, powerful cars are relatively inexpensive in the United States and expensive in France, whereas the opposite is true for small, low-horsepower cars; that is, the coefficient for horsepower in an equation for French cars will be much larger than the comparable coefficient in an equation for U.S. cars. Thus, a price comparison based on the specifications of a standard size U.S. car will make French prices much higher than U.S. prices, whereas a comparison based on the specifications of a small, low-horsepower car will make French prices much lower than U.S. prices.

In principle, this problem should be met by applying the guidelines for the selection of representative items used elsewhere in the ICP for price comparisons of the traditional type (see Chapter 3, Section B). In general, the population of overlapping specifications should be sampled. In choosing the sample, an effort should be made to avoid items that are used infrequently in any of the countries and, consequently, are relatively high in price; and, instead, to select the items so as to match at least roughly the relative importance of expenditures of the classes of items found in the overlapping range. In the latter connection, if the relative importance differs from one country to another, each country's weights will have to be used in turn.

The implementation problems that arise in connection with binary comparisons are particularly great when the overlapping models available for a pair of countries are limited in number and, in one or both of the countries, are produced on a smaller-than-typical scale of production. The scale factor is important because, in the case of the durable goods to which we are applying regression analysis, it can be expected to have a significant influence upon price. Imports as well may involve a scale factor in terms of distribution costs within the importing country, although production-lot sizes in the country of manufacture may be the more important influence on price.

The case of no overlapping production. The problem of implementation is most difficult when there are no overlaps in consumption between pairs of countries. In the case of automobiles, for example, overlaps were found between the U.S. and French markets only if imported cars were included in the U.S. regression. Because our price comparisons are based on the final expenditure approach, imported products should be included. In some cases, however, even imports will not save the day. In India, for example, none of the three automobiles on its market was over 50 horsepower, and even imported cars in the U.S. market had higher horsepower ranges than this.

Two methods are available to deal with such cases in binary comparisons. One is to extrapolate the regression equation for one or both countries so as to estimate prices in the overlapping range. The disadvantage of this approach is that in the absence of any observations in this range, one's confidence in the extrapolations necessarily is limited.

The second solution is to compare the two countries through the medium of a third country that has some models falling within the range of each of the other two. In the automobiles case, for example, England has substantial production across a wide range of automobiles, and it could be used for the India–United States comparison. The disadvantage of this method is that its results will depend critically on which particular bridge country is used.

The case of overlapping models. There may be some cases in which the models found in the overlapping range can be regarded as representative of the whole range of models in each country. In the more usual situations, however, the models in the overlapping range are purchased infrequently in one or both of the countries and consequently may be relatively high in price. Several methods may be used to avoid the distortions from possibly atypical prices:

First, the size of output may be added as an independent variable in the equation for each country. The inclusion of this variable would make it possible to identify the effect of scale upon the prices. It would be appropriate, however, to estimate for each country the prices for the selected specifications within the overlapping range at the average scale of output typical for that country rather than at the scale associated with the particular specification. This method has the advantage of including all the observations; if those in the overlapping range are high in price because of low scale of output, this will not affect the results more than it should. The price estimate we make will be for the typical scale of output for the country, the latter being influenced, of course, by the number of models produced in small volume. A feature of this method is that it treats variety as a cost-increasing factor. Though this may be a disadvantage within a broad framework of welfare comparisons, it is consistent with our disregard of the benefits of variety elsewhere in our comparisons.[7]

---

[7] See Chapter 2, Section C.

A more compelling practical disadvantage of this approach is that often it will be difficult to ascertain what the scale of output is for a particular model. This is particularly true when, as in the case of automobiles, different models often share a commonality of design and parts.

Second, if it is not feasible to obtain a measure of scale of production, the comparisons may be based on the extrapolation of results derived from the main range of observations. This method meets the problem posed by the high prices of the infrequently consumed models in the overlapping range by excluding the observations in that range altogether. The extrapolation of the equation into that range then can be justified on the ground that if the country really produced such models on its typical scale, its costs and prices probably would lie along the line predicted by the equation. The disadvantage, here again, is that there is no experience that can be used to back up this expectation. It is possible, of course, that relationships in other countries may support the hypothesis that the functional relationship between price and the independent variables will continue into the range in which extrapolation may be more warranted. Even so, this method has the further disadvantage that, for purposes of price comparison, it does not capture that part of the country's output which is low in volume and high in cost and price. Ideally, this portion of the country's output should be included with its appropriate weight; the comparison will be biased if it is left out altogether, just as it will be biased if the comparison is too heavily influenced by it or based entirely upon it.

Third, weighted equations may be fitted to all observations in each country. Relative to the preceding method, this has the advantage of getting the high-priced, low production models into the regression without allowing them to influence it as much as they would without weighting. Weighted regressions also have advantages with respect to the models found within the middle ranges of a country's models. In principle, we would like to obtain the relationship between price and such independent variables as horsepower and weight based on a random sample of sales of each model in the market. The unweighted regressions considered in the first two methods weight each model equally, regardless of its volume of sales. In a market in perfect long-run equilibrium, this method could be expected to yield the proper relationship between price and the independent variables. Actually, however, the situation we observe may be one in which some prices are unduly high relative to their equilibrium levels and others unduly low, and we have no way of identifying these. Because we are interested in obtaining some sort of average price for a particular specification, it seems worthwhile to try to obtain a sample that reflects the structure of the market, and this implies weighting the observations in proportion to their sales. Sales data, incidentally, are more readily available than are reasonably reliable data on scale.

THE PROCEDURES ADOPTED

The national product definition and its concomitant of running a separate regression for each country were chosen because of their ease and simplicity. Were pooled regressions less awkward, the balance might have weighed in favor of a universal product definition. As already noted, however, even with national product definitions and separate regressions for each country, price comparisons between pairs of countries still will be estimated on the basis of the specifications of selected models that are held constant across all countries.

The preferred way to cope with the sensitivity of the results to the selection of these models would be to use a weighted regression fitted to all observations in the country and to include the volume of output of each model as an independent variable. Then it would be possible to estimate the price of any model within the range of observation of a given country that was found also in the market of another country. The price of each such model would be estimated on the assumption that it was produced on the scale that was typical for the given country. Because of the difficulty of finding a satisfactory scale variable, however, the weighted regressions used in the ICP only infrequently include a scale variable, and even in these cases it is doubtful that it catches the scale effects very fully.

Finally, mention should be made of cases in which the number of models or the information available is too limited for the use of regressions in one or more countries, though adequate data are available in others. In some of these instances, the actual prices for the few models available in the one country have been compared with estimated prices for models with the same characteristics derived from regression equations in the other country (or countries). In the case of automobiles, for example, the relatively few models available in the Indian and Kenyan markets were priced in the United States by means of the U.S. regression equation. A similar method has been used for a number of producers' durable goods for which regression equations were estimated for the United States but not for other countries.

B. The Automobile Price Comparisons

THE DATA

Retail list prices of all automobiles having any significant volume of sales were obtained for seven countries—France, the Federal Republic of Germany, Hungary, Italy, Japan, the United Kingdom, and the United States—for the reference year 1969. The prices were converted into U.S. dollars at exchange rates prevailing in June 1969.[8] In most instances, the data on prices and on

---

[8] The results were adjusted to 1967 and 1970 on the basis of indexes or prices in each country. The number of units of domestic currency equivalent to a dollar, taken from the U.N.

the physical characteristics of cars–including displacement, horsepower, RPM, weight, length, width, and number of cylinders–were obtained from trade journals or from the statistical offices of the cooperating countries. The latter also are the main source of data on the number of new registrations for each model. The prices include excise taxes, but special transportation charges such as those added to list prices in the United States were not included. The prices refer to cars with standard equipment. The major difference that came to our attention with respect to standard equipment was that radios, treated as an optional, extra-charge item in other countries, were included in the list price as standard equipment in the United States and Japan. An effort was made to include every domestic and imported model that was sold in any significant volume (1 percent of total sales) in each country. This criterion produced a number of models in each country, ranging from eleven in Hungary to eighty in the United States. Sports cars, station wagons, and luxury versions of models available in standard form were not included.

THE REGRESSION

For reasons described in the previous section, it was decided to work with weighted regressions. This was accomplished by replicating some of the observations so that the number of observations included in the regression of each model was roughly proportionate to the importance of that model in new-car registrations within the country concerned.[9]

A number of different regression forms were tried for each country. The inverse semilog form, in which logarithmic price is the dependent variable and the independent variables are in arithmetic form, was chosen partly because it performed as well as, or better than, other mathematical forms, and partly because a form in which the dependent variable is expressed as a logarithm has the advantage of minimizing the squares of percentage deviations rather than the squares of absolute deviations.[10] Because many of the U.S. models were hardtops (models in which the roofs were not supported by exterior columns immediately behind the front doors), and because these were known to be more costly than other

models, a dummy variable for hardtop models was included in all the equations in which U.S. data were involved.[11] In addition to the variables enumerated earlier (horsepower, weight, length, and the like), mean effective pressure[12] also was used in some regressions as an independent variable.

It quickly became clear that the relationships between price and the independent variables differed significantly from one country to another, and there was little point in trying to pool the data for different countries with respect to some or all of the variables. For this as well as for reasons discussed in the earlier section on methodology, the results that are discussed are confined to separate country equations.

Only a few of the equations that were estimated are reported upon here. The criteria for selecting sets of independent variables for each equation were as follows:

1. Each coefficient should have a sign that is consistent with expectations;
2. Each coefficient should be equal to, or larger than, its standard error; and
3. Subject to the foregoing conditions, the included variables should give the highest $\bar{R}^2$.

When these criteria were used to select the best equation for each country separately, the results were those shown in Table 8.1.

THE CHOICE OF MODELS FOR PRICING

Once the equations were selected, the next task was to choose the representative models for which prices were to be compared. For this purpose, a cross-classification was prepared of all the models in the sample with respect to weight and horsepower. Tables 8.2 and 8.3 show the resulting distributions, the first giving the original numbers in the sample, the second, the number inclusive of the duplications necessary to obtain the proper weighting. Ten cells were selected from the matrix of cells in these tables; the selected cells, heavily outlined in the two tables, were distributed over the various horsepower and weight categories to provide representatives of the entire overlapping range of weight and horsepower models consumed in the various countries. The smallest cars ranged from 26 to 50 horsepower and were below 1,401 pounds in weight; the largest were from 176 to 225 horsepower and from 2,901 to 3,200 pounds in weight. Although the United States produced many cars that were larger and more powerful than those in this range, including them was not worthwhile

---

Statistical Office, *Monthly Bulletin of Statistics* (New York: United Nations, December 1969), except for Hungary, were as follows: Colombia, 17.38 pesos; France, 4.969 francs; Federal Republic of Germany, 4.003 Deutschmarks; Hungary, 30.0 forints; India, 7.550 rupees; Italy, 626.5 lira; Japan, 359.0 yen; Kenya, 7.143 shillings; United Kingdom, 0.4182 pounds.

[9] The *t*-ratios as computed using standard regression procedures were adjusted by the factor $\sqrt{\frac{n-k}{N-k}}$ where n is the number of unduplicated observations, N the number including duplications, and k the number of coefficients including the constant.

[10] That is, a larger absolute error is acceptable in estimating the price of an expensive automobile than the price of an inexpensive one. See I. Kravis and R. Lipsey, *Price Competitiveness*, p. 109.

[11] The dummy variable was included in the regressions with the value of 1 for hardtops and with the value of 0 for other models. The coefficient of the dummy variable therefore indicated the amount that was added to the price because of the hardtop feature.

[12] This was computed by the formula: Mean effective pressure $= \dfrac{\text{Horsepower} \cdot \text{number of cycles}}{\text{Displacement} \cdot \text{RPM}} \cdot 198{,}000.$

Table 8.1. Automobile Regression Equations for Seven Countries

Independent variables†	France	Germany, F.R.	Hungary	Italy	Japan	United Kingdom	United States
Displacement (in.³)	0.0021421 (2.6)	—	0.0027178 (2.5)	0.0040272 (11.4)	0.0028278 (6.6)	—	0.0001146 (2.3)
Horsepower (SAE)	0.0023059 (3.3)	0.0017957 (5.6)				0.0018168 (4.3)	
RPM	0.0000126 (1.2)	0.0000328 (3.2)	0.0001330 (3.2)	0.0000703 (7.5)	0.0000502 (4.1)		0.0000224 (3.9)
Weight (lbs.)	—	0.0001388 (5.0)			0.0001088 (4.6)	0.0001225 (4.3)	0.0000779 (11.4)
Length (in.)	0.0008595 (1.2)	0.0011878 (2.3)	0.0021885 (1.1)				
Width (in.)	—	—	—	0.0030460 (1.6)	—	—	—
Mean effective pressure	—	—	—	0.0016553	—	—	
Registration (units)	—	−0.0000178 (−1.9)	—	−0.0000347 (−6.9)	—	−0.0000372 (−1.3)	0.0014620 (6.2)
Hardtop	—	—	—	—	—	—	0.02593 (5.5)
Constant	2.75697 (30.7)	2.46300 (32.8)	2.23381 (7.0)	2.15414 (23.1)	2.49165 (29.4)	2.93217 (78.6)	2.85047 (69.6)
Sample size	83	100	50	50	92	89	83
Number of observations (unduplicated)	38	59	11	22	28	55	80
R²	0.925	0.962	0.866	0.991	0.977	0.838	0.940
S.E. of estimate	0.030	0.030	0.044	0.014	0.015	0.043	0.018
Arithmetic mean price	1734.0	1748.0	2434.0	1280.0	1753.0	2042.0	2865.0
Log mean price	3.224	3.215	3.370	3.081	3.233	3.296	3.451
Error as % of arithmetic mean price	6.8%	6.4%	9.9%	3.1%	3.3%	9.7%	4.0%

Note: t-ratios in parentheses adjusted by factor $\sqrt{\dfrac{n-k}{N-K}}$

†Dependent variable: common log of price in US$.

Table 8.2. Distribution of Samples of Automobiles (Unduplicated) by Weight and Horsepower

Legend: F - France; G - Germany, F.R.; H - Hungary; I - Italy; J - Japan; UK - United Kingdom; US - United States. Underlined figures in each cell denote totals.

Horsepower \ Wt.	Below 1,401 (1)	1,401–1,700 (2)	1,701–2,000 (3)	2,001–2,300 (4)	2,301–2,600 (5)	2,601–2,900 (6)	2,901–3,200 (7)	3,201–3,500 (8)	Above 3,500 (9)	Total
1 Below 26	H-1, F-2, G-3, I-4 _(10)_									10
2 26–50	H-1, UK-6, F-5, G-4, I-3 _(19)_	H-2, UK-3, F-6, G-4, I-3 _(18)_	H-2, UK-2, F-3, G-4 _(11)_							48
3 51–75		US-2, F-3, J-12, G-8, UK-3, I-4 _(32)_	J-2, F-6, H-1, G-9, UK-12, I-2 _(32)_	US-1, F-4, H-2, G-4, UK-3, I-1 _(15)_	UK-1 _(1)_					80
4 76–100			UK-5 _(5)_	US-1, F-3, J-9, G-4, H-1, I-4, UK-4 _(26)_	UK-1, F-2, G-4 _(7)_	US-1, UK-3, F-1 _(5)_	H-1 _(1)_			44
5 101–125			US-1, UK-1 _(2)_	J-3, UK-1, F-1, G-4 _(9)_	UK-2, G-3 _(5)_	US-3, J-2, UK-4, F-1 _(10)_	G-2 _(2)_			28
6 126–175					UK-1, F-1, G-2, I-1 _(5)_	US-1, UK-1 _(2)_	US-8, G-2 _(10)_	US-5, G-1 _(6)_	US-8 _(8)_	31
7 176–225							US-3, UK-1, G-1 _(5)_	US-4, G-1 _(5)_	US-4 _(4)_	14
8 Above 225							US-1 _(1)_	US-4 _(4)_	US-33 _(33)_	38
Total	29	50	50	50	18	17	19	15	45	293

Table 8.3. Distribution of Samples of Automobiles (with Duplications) by Weight and Horsepower

Legend:
F - France; G - Germany, F.R.; H - Hungary; I - Italy; J - Japan; UK - United Kingdom; US - United States. Underlined figures in each cell denote totals.

Horsepower	Below 1,401 (1)	1,401–1,700 (2)	1,701–2,000 (3)	2,001–2,300 (4)	2,301–2,600 (5)	2,601–2,900 (6)	2,901–3,200 (7)	3,201–3,500 (8)	Above 3,500 (9)	Total
1 Below 26	H- 1, F- 3, G- 4 [23], I- 15									23
2 26–50	H- 11, UK- 8, F- 21 [53], G- 7, I- 6	H- 12, UK- 4, F- 9 [39], G- 8, I- 6	H- 5, UK- 2, F- 4 [27], G- 16							119
3 51–75		US- 2 F- 5, J- 40 G- 9, UK- 9 I- 9 [74]	J- 2 F-19, H- 9 G-17, UK- 26 I- 4 [77]	US- 4 F-11, H- 8 G- 7, UK- 6 I- 4 [40]	UK- 1 [1]					192
4 76–100			UK- 12 [12]	US- 1 F- 3, J- 32 G- 5, H- 1 I- 5, UK- 4 [51]	UK- 1, F- 3 [10], G- 6	US- 1, UK- 4 [7], F- 2	H- 3 [3]			83
5 101–125			US- 1, UK- 1 [2]	J- 9, UK- 1 [17], F- 1, G- 6	UK- 2, G- 4 [6]	US- 3, J- 9, UK- 4 [17], F- 1	G- 5 [5]			47
6 126–175					UK- 1, F- 1, G- 2 [5], I- 1	US- 1, UK- 1 [2]	US- 8, G- 2 [10]	US- 5, UK- 1 [6]	US- 8 [8]	31
7 176–225							US- 3, UK- 1 [5], G- 1	US- 4, G- 1 [5]	US- 4 [4]	14
8 Above 225							US- 1 [1]	US- 4 [4]	US- 33 [33]	38
Total	76	113	118	108	22	26	24	15	45	547

because virtually no overlapping observations were available for other countries. For each of the ten cells, a particular car falling within the cell was selected to represent it. An effort was made to select cars from the production of different countries, preferably those which were used in other countries as well. The result of this is shown in the list of cars included in Table 8.4. This table also shows the prices of each car as estimated from each country's best equation. Prices followed by the symbol (§) represent those estimated for cars that were beyond the range of sample observations in the country. The Japanese sample, for example, does not have any car under 51 or over 125 horsepower, and therefore the prices for the first two models in the list and for the last three had to be estimated by extrapolating the Japanese regression beyond the range of observation of the Japanese sample. Prices for models followed by the symbol (¶) lie outside the middle 90 percent of the country's (duplicated) sample.

ORIGINAL-COUNTRY BINARY PRICE COMPARISONS

Some alternative sets of results of the international price comparisons are presented in the upper half of Table 8.5. The first three columns show simple geometric means of prices relative to the United States based on different selections of the models to be included in the comparisons. The first column shows the results when all ten cars are included. The next column shows the results of including in each comparison with the United States only those which were common to the pair of countries.[13] The indexes for the Federal Republic of Germany and the United Kingdom are higher than when all cars were included because, in the overlapping comparisons, the small cars, which are relatively expensive in the United States, are excluded. The indexes for the other countries are lower because of the exclusion of very large cars that turn out to be very expensive when the regressions are extrapolated to estimate them.

The comparisons in the third column also are based on overlapping models but exclude those at the extreme (5 percent on each end) of the country's distribution.[14] The deletion of some of these models has a marked effect in some instances, most notably in the United Kingdom.

The next two columns of the table show weighted arithmetic mean price relatives for the overlapping observations when they are weighted first with U.S. expenditure weights and then with the other countries' weights.

[13] That is, the models followed by (§) in Table 8.4 were excluded. An alternative to the exclusion of these items would have been to weight them (and other items) inversely to the standard error of forecast.

[14] Models followed by either (§) or (¶) in Table 8.4 were excluded.

Table 8.4. Estimated Automobile Prices by Country and Model, 1969 (US $)

Cell†	Model	France	Germany, F.R.	Hungary	Italy	Japan	United Kingdom	United States‡
2,1	Renault R4-40V	1,281	1,061	1,991	988	1,017§	1,398	1,602§
2,2	Fiat 850 Berlina	1,373	1,125	1,962	1,105	1,065§	1,501	1,769§
2,3	Volkswagen 1300	1,714	1,369	2,544	1,338	1,371	1,718	1,740§
3,2	Escort 1100 DX 2D	1,695	1,405	3,097	1,438	1,367	1,667	1,798¶
3,3	Opel Kadett LS 45 PS	1,728	1,484	3,304	1,468	1,397	1,706	1,840¶
3,4	Peugeot 404 Berlina	2,063	1,833	3,544	1,665	1,765	2,106	1,982
4,4	Corona MkII 1600 DX 4D	2,463	1,990	3,970	2,068	1,882	2,247	2,123
5,5	Vauxhall Victor 2000 4D	3,028¶	2,340	5,265§	2,593¶	2,402§	2,509¶	2,112
6,6	American 6	5,288§	2,581¶	5,575§	4,807§	3,940§	3,098¶	2,004
7,7	Chevy II Nova V8	12,479§	4,296¶	12,405§	12,164§	8,665§	4,751¶	2,249

†First figure applies to row number and second figure to column number in Tables 8.2 and 8.3.
‡These prices have been adjusted from those estimated from the regression to allow for discounts from listed prices received by consumers. The adjustments were 10.7 percent for the last two cars in the list and 5.4 percent for the others. They are based on a Federal Trade Commission analysis of approximately 10,000 invoices for the model year 1969. (Memorandum by Steven R. Nelson dated September 10, 1969, entitled "Public Hearing Relating to Price Advertising of New Automobiles.")
§Outside of country's range of observations.
¶Outside of middle 90 percent of country's observations.

The geometric mean of these two indexes (Fisher's "ideal" index) is shown in the following column. As is to be expected, the U.S. weights tend to result in higher price relatives for other countries than any other form of computation.

The U.S. and other individual-country-weighted indexes (columns 4 and 5) are the results that are easiest to relate to the underlying economic theory of demand. In each index, prices are compared for the mix of automobiles in the consumption pattern of one of the countries. But the need to confine the comparison to overlapping models introduces an arbitrary element into the assignment of weights. In the case of the United States, for example, the largest car of the ten, the Chevy Nova, was assigned 62 percent of the U.S. weights in the comparison with the United Kingdom, because it seemed preferable to assign the weights of the larger cars to this one rather than to distribute them in part to still smaller models. Nevertheless, given the great differences in the types of automobiles purchased, these results represent the best price comparisons we can make between each country and the United States.

If a single answer is desired, the Fisher index is to be preferred at least marginally over unweighted indexes in columns 1 to 3 because it provides an explicit compromise between the indexes corresponding to each country's weights. Among the three unweighted indexes, the last one (column 3) is superior to the others because it is not affected by high prices associated with atypically small volume. It would be felicitous if the results of the Fisher index (column 6) and the simple geometric mean of overlapping models excluding extreme values (column 3) were in close agreement. The difference between them, however, is 30 percent for the United Kingdom–United States comparison and nearly 25 percent for the Germany (F.R.)–United States comparison.

BRIDGE-COUNTRY COMPARISONS

One way to compare the prices for pairs of countries other than pairs involving the United States is by using the United States as the bridge country. For example, the Fisher indexes for France–United States and Germany (F.R.)–United States, 119 and 123, respectively, imply a France–Germany (F.R.) price index of 97 (119 ÷ 123 = 97). The France–United States and Germany (F.R.)–United States Fisher indexes, however, like all the indexes in Table 8.5, are based on a set of cars that varies from one row of the table to another depending upon the overlap of models of each country, with the United States as the base country. Because the United States has missing observations for the three small cars, and most of the other countries have missing observations for at least two of the big cars, none of the indexes in columns 2 to 6 is based on more than seven cars, and some are based on as few as two. This means that although the index numbers under discussion may provide reasonable alternative estimates of each country's relation with the United States, it would be unwise to try to draw inferences about the relationships between pairs of countries other than the United States.

But the United States, which in most categories of goods has a broad range of varieties and thus provides a good market in which to find matching products for almost all other countries, clearly does not serve this function nearly as well when it comes to automobiles. Both the Federal Republic of Germany and the United Kingdom have all ten observations and, consequently, represent better base countries than does the United States.

Accordingly, the United Kingdom has been used as the base country in the second bank of figures in Table 8.5. The differences between the column 3 and column 6 indexes are much reduced as compared with the earlier

Table 8.5. Binary Automobile Price Comparisons, Based on Prices Estimated from Each Country's "Best" Index, 1969

	Simple geometric mean of price relatives			Weighted mean for all overlapping cars		
	All cars	Overlapping cars		Base country weights	Other country weights	Fisher index
		All	Except extreme			
	(1)	(2)	(3)	(4)	(5)	(6)
	Part A. United States the base country					
France	130	109	110	140	101	119
Germany, F.R.	93	106	99	163	93	123
Hungary	195	179	183	186	177	181
Italy	109	92	90	120	85	101
Japan	102	88	96	111	89	99
United Kingdom	111	121	106	184	104	138
United States	100	100	100	100	100	100
	Part B. United Kingdom the base country					
France	118	101	99	106	100	103
Germany, F.R.	84	84	82	87	85	86
Hungary	173	162	162	177	158	168
Italy	99	83	80	89	80	84
Japan	92	85	83	86	86	86
United Kingdom	100	100	100	100	100	100
United States	90	83	94	96	54	72

set of figures; aside from the United States, they are all within 6 percent. The shift to the new base country does not affect the relationship between the United States and the United Kingdom (because the comparison is identical except that numerator and denominator are reversed), but for the other countries, the relationships do change in relation both to the United States and to each other. With respect to comparisons of each country with the United States, the first bank of figures must be regarded as superior; but with respect to comparisons between other pairs (for example, France-Germany [F.R.]), the figures in the second bank are better because they are based on more observations (four to ten). It can be seen that the index number spread is smaller, and that results of the various indexes are much more in accord with one another—except, of course, for the row representing the United States. The implicit Fisher index for France-Germany (F.R.) using the United Kingdom as the bridge country is 120 (103 ÷ 86 = 120).

No bridge country, of course, can produce a binary comparison that is optimal purely from the standpoint of the two countries involved; only a direct comparison based on the models that overlap for the two countries can do that. But even a full set of direct binary comparisons would not be fully satisfactory from the standpoint of the ICP. What is desired is circularity and independence of the choice of a bridge-country, which neither binary indexes nor the Fisher indexes based on a single country will yield. This is a general problem in the ICP that has been resolved for other product categories by the Country-Product-Dummy method (CPD).

MULTILATERAL COMPARISONS

The Country-Product-Dummy method as explained in Chapter 5 assumes that the prices observed for the various models in different countries are related systematically to the countries and to the models. In a tableau of prices such as that which would be found in Table 8.4 if the prices followed by (§) were deleted (they are really missing observations and were obtained by extrapolation), the price in any cell may be regarded as depending, in one part, on the intercountry difference in prices and, in the other part, on the intermodel difference in prices. Accordingly, the log of prices is taken as the dependent variable in a regression in which the independent variables consist of two sets of dummy variables: in one set, there is a dummy variable for each model car in the tableau; and in the other set, there is a dummy variable for each country other than the numeraire country. The coefficient of the dummy variable for each country (strictly speaking, it is the antilog of the coefficient) provides a direct estimate of the car prices in that country relative to prices of the numeraire country. It may illuminate the underlying method to point out that when the regression equation is fitted to a completely filled-in tableau, the antilog of each country coefficient will be equal to the simple geometric mean of the price ratios for the individual cars.

The results of the CPD method are presented in columns 1 and 2 of Table 8.6, the first based on the treatment of the cells outside of the range of observation of the country sample (prices in Table 8.4 followed by

Table 8.6. Multilateral Automobile Price Comparisons, 1969

	Unweighted CPD		Weighted CPD	
	55 observations†	46 observations‡	55 observations†	46 observations‡
	(1)	(2)	(3)	(4)
	Part A. United States the numeraire country			
France	123	117	167	127
Germany, F.R.	105	97	137	104
Hungary	199	191	278	212
Italy	100	95	139	106
Japan	97	95	134	102
United Kingdom	125	118	154	119
United States	100	100	100	100
	Part B. United Kingdom the numeraire country			
France	99	99	108	107
Germany, F.R.	84	83	89	87
Hungary	160	162	181	178
Italy	81	80	90	89
Japan	78	80	87	86
United Kingdom	100	100	100	100
United States	80	85	65	84

†Cells in Table 8.4 followed by (§), representing cells outside of range of sample observations, are not included in the regression.

‡Cells in Table 8.4, followed by (§) or (¶), representing cells not falling within middle 90 percent range of observations, are not included in the regression.

[§]) as missing observations or holes, and the second treating the cells outside of the middle 90 percent of the country sample (prices followed by [§] and [¶]) as holes. These indexes are most comparable, respectively, to the simple geometric mean for all overlapping cars and to the simple geometric mean for the overlapping cars excluding the extremes in Table 8.5. Because these indexes are unweighted, it is probably better to base them on the middle 90 percent range, and the column 2 version therefore would be preferred over column 1.

An advantage of the CPD method, which was compelling for product categories other than automobiles, is that it uses all the information in the available set of prices to gauge the price level relationship between each pair of countries. The weakness of the method, which becomes important in the automobile context, is that it is based on a kind of averaging of country-to-country price differences across models which assumes that no systematic element exists in the behavior of the price ratios for different models. In fact, the country-to-country price differences do vary in a systematic way with the characteristics of the models. For example, the France–United States price ratio rises from around 89 for the smallest car found in both countries to 110 for the largest.

This difficulty may be mitigated by the use of the double-weighted version of the CPD.[15] Each price in the tableau (Table 8.4) is weighted by the product of two importance factors—one based on the relative importance of each model in the expenditures of the country, the other based on the relative importance of a given model in each country compared with the "world" (that is, seven-country) total for that model.

The results of the double-weighted CPD method are shown in columns 3 and 4 of Table 8.6. The underlying prices once again are those of Table 8.4. In column 3, the fifteen prices for cars beyond the range of observations in a given country (that is, the entries followed by [§]) are excluded, whereas in column 4, all the models outside the middle 90 percent range of observations are excluded.

Weighting raises the indexes for all countries relative to the United States. This effect is particularly notable in the case of the results based on fifty-five observations; the use of weights in conjunction with the inclusion of extreme observations has a large impact. In accordance with the basic approach outlined in our discussion of sampling,[16] we accept the results based on forty-six observations that exclude models not widely consumed.

These results in columns 3 and 4 in Part A of Table 8.6 differ substantially in some instances from the Fisher indexes in column 6 of Part A of Table 8.5. The comparison of the weighted CPD indexes and the Fisher indexes, however, can be better made by taking the United Kingdom as the numeraire country. From the CPD standpoint, it does not matter which country is used as the numeraire. The figures in Part B of Table 8.6 do serve, however, to call attention to the fact that the difference between the weighted calculations based on forty-six observations and those based on fifty-five observations concern mainly the United States; aside from the United States, there is little difference be-

[15] See pages 63–65.

[16] See Chapter 3, especially page 31.

tween the figures in columns 3 and 4 when they are expressed relative to the United Kingdom. That is, the relationships among countries other than the United States are quite similar in columns 3 and 4—and this is true whatever country is taken as the numeraire.

From the standpoint of the Fisher indexes, however, the U.K.-based estimates are clearly superior to those based on the United States, because they are derived from a larger and more similar list of cars. With the United Kingdom as the base country, the weighted CPD results are, with the exception of United States, not much different from the Fisher results of Table 8.5.

PRICE COMPARISONS FOR NONREGRESSION COUNTRIES

For three countries—Colombia, India, and Kenya—information was gathered for only a few models. Actually, only three models are available in India on any scale. Because regressions were not feasible for these countries, the method adopted was to use the equations in Table 8.1 to estimate U.S. and U.K. prices for cars comparable to the Colombian, Indian, and Kenyan models. The results are set out in Table 8.7.

Unweighted geometric means of the price ratios for the three or four models have been taken. In the case of India, where the three included models account for the great bulk of Indian cars, the method is about as satisfactory as can be found. For the other countries, regression methods might have been used, but they would have required a greater data-collection effort. The results suggest, however, the advantages of using regression methods. For Kenya the ratios range from 6.9 to 10.2, a spread of 45 percent, and for Colombia the range is still

greater. Some other selection of three or four models for price comparison might produce very different averages. The regression approach has the merit of taking into account the entire range of models in the marketplace in estimating the price for any particular model.[17]

Because the small cars for which prices must be estimated for comparisons with Colombia, India, and Kenya are within the range of observations for the United Kingdom but not for the United States, the former provides a better bridge country. Therefore, although the average price ratios relative to the United States are used as the automobile entries in the binary comparison of each country with the United States, the price ratios relative to the United Kingdom are used for the multilateral comparisons.

CONCLUSION

The final indexes selected are set out in Table 8.8. For the regression countries, the U.S.-weighted and own-weighted indexes based on regression estimated prices (columns 4 and 5, Table 8.5) are used for the binary comparisons with the United States. The weighted CPD indexes based on forty-six observations are used for these countries to accomplish the multilateral comparisons.

For the nonregression countries, the indexes are simple geometric means relative to the United States for the binary comparisons and simple geometric means relative to the United Kingdom for the multilateral compari-

[17]The comparisons involving Kenya and Colombia could have been improved by weighting, but the data required for this purpose are hardly less troublesome to gather than the data required for regressions.

Table 8.7. Comparison of Prices of Passenger Cars in Colombia, India, and Kenya with Estimated Prices for Comparable Cars in the United States and the United Kingdom, 1969

	HP	Weight (lbs.)	Prices† Domestic market	Prices† Est. U.S.	Prices† Est. U.K.	Price ratios U.S.= 100	Price ratios U.K.= 100
Colombian cars						125	152
Renault 4	37.5	1,367	2,181	1,751	1,438	145	171
Simca 1000	49.5	1,576	2,748	1,901	1,609	173	191
Zastava	72	2,116	3,952	2,289	2,070	291	195
Dodge Dart Big 6	145	3,013	7,102	2,440	3,649		
Geometric mean						174	176
Indian cars						110	122
Herald Mark III Standard	40	1,929	2,090	1,903	1,717	130	140
Fiat 1100 Delight	43	1,896	2,410	1,852	1,721	126	118
Ambassador Mark III	50	2,563	2,553	2,025	2,164		
Geometric mean						122	126
Kenyan cars‡						109	119
Volkswagen 1200 Deluxe	41.5	1,675	1,916	1,762	1,604	115	117
Volkswagen 1500 Deluxe	53	1,918	2,110	1,840	1,805	90	105
Toyota Corolla 1200 4-door	73	1,611	1,875	2,073	1,785	132	134
Ford Cortina 1600 DX 4-door	76	1,973	2,690	2,031	2,015		
Geometric mean						110	118

†Converted to U.S. dollars at the following exchange rates per US$: Colombia, 17.38 pesos (principal selling rate); India, 7.550 rupees; Kenya, 7.143 shillings; U.K., 0.4182 pounds sterling.
‡The Kenyan prices represent list prices reduced by 7 percent to allow for discounts.

Table 8.8. Final Automobile Price Comparisons, 1969

(U.S. = 100)

	Binary comparisons			
	Simple geometric mean	Weighted arithmetic mean		Multilateral comparisons
		U.S. weights	Own weights	
	(1)	(2)	(3)	(4)
France	–	140	101	127
Germany, F.R.	–	163	93	104
Hungary	–	186	177	212
Italy	–	120	85	106
Japan	–	111	89	102
United Kingdom	–	184	104	119
United States	–	100	100	100
Colombia	174	–	–	209
India	122	–	–	150
Kenya	110	–	–	140

sons. In the latter case, the indexes are converted to a U.S. base using the United Kingdom as the bridge country. Relative automobile prices for these countries appear lower when the comparison is based on U.S. prices than when they are made by way of the United Kingdom. This is attributable to the fact that the models involved in the comparisons are mainly small cars, which tend to be relatively expensive in the United States. This, together with the fact that some of the U.S. prices must be estimated by extrapolation of the U.S. equation into a range for which there are no U.S. observations, may point to a preference for the use of the results obtained by way of the United Kingdom even for the binary comparisons of each country with the United States. In this view, the figures in column 4 may give a better indication of what the relative prices of cars might be in each of the last three countries, assuming that country and the United States produced the same type of car, each maintaining its 1969 scale and other conditions of production.

Chapter 9

Rent comparisons

A. Conceptual Problems

The comparison of the cost of housing services posed special difficulties for the International Comparison Project. For one thing, a substantial number of dwelling units are owner-occupied in most countries (see Table 9.1). Market prices for housing services are available only for rented dwellings, and our price comparisons for housing services are necessarily based on rent comparisons. In this respect we do not deviate from standard national accounts practice, in which the intertemporal estimation of price changes for housing services within individual countries also is based on changes in rents.

Even within this framework, however, price comparisons involved some problems rather different from those encountered for the general run of consumer commodities and services.

First, it was not possible to obtain price information from a relatively few key sellers, as could be done for most consumer goods. In most countries, a substantial fraction of rented units is let out by landlords who have only a few units to rent.

Second, a much greater dispersion of rents around the national average probably exists for each given type of dwelling than is the case for most other commodities and services. In some measure, this is the result of limited knowledge of the market on the part of amateur landlords and on the part of tenants, who tend to rent with little and infrequent market research. What is even more important in making the market imperfect from a national standpoint is the limited possibility of substitution between houses in different localities: housing markets are uniquely local markets.

Third, most countries have a great variety of dwellings with respect to type of structure, condition, size, facilities, and location or neighborhood. Taken in conjunction with the imperfection of markets, this range increases the need for rent comparisons based on as wide a variety of dwellings as possible.

Fourth, housing tends to be one of the categories in which the difference between high- and low-income countries is great. As a result, the degree of overlap in the types of housing between a very poor country and a very wealthy country is apt to be much smaller than is the case for most other commodities and services.

One consequence of these difficulties is that even if we were able to measure every rent-determining quality of a housing unit, we would be able to estimate the rent of any particular unit only with a considerable margin of error.

Actually, we cannot measure or even identify with certainty all of the important quality variables. Only those that are capable of objective description and measurement fall within our reach: for example, size (floor area or number of rooms) and facilities or amenities (the presence or absence of electricity, inside running water, flush toilet, and tub or shower).

Thus, our matching of dwellings in different countries is necessarily approximate. It is based on key quantitative (floor area) and qualitative (presence or absence of facilities) characteristics. Other important variables such as the general quality of the neighborhood, which often has a major impact on rents, could not be taken into account. But, with some major exceptions, which will be pointed out, the estimates do not involve large elements of judgment, and it is unlikely that other analysts relying also upon available indicators of housing quantity and quality would come to substantially different results. Furthermore, a substantial fraction of the variation in rents within a country, generally about 0.6 or better, can be explained by the variables with which we work.

The objective variables we want to use are not always readily available. One of those sometimes difficult to obtain in a satisfactory form relates to the size of dwelling units. For countries to use the number of rooms as the measure of size in their housing statistics is common. This is understandable, because it is easier for the occupant or interviewer to count rooms than to measure floor area. But the definition of rooms and their average size on any standard definition may vary widely from country to country. Therefore, whenever information on floor area was not available directly, it was necessary in each country to obtain some estimate of the floor area

Table 9.1. Indicators of Quantity of Housing, Eight Countries

	Colombia 1964	France 1968	Germany (F.R.) 1968	Hungary 1970	India 1960	Italy 1961	Japan 1968	U.K. 1966	U.S. 1970
Population (000)	17,485	49,655	60,842	10,295‡	434,885	50,625	98,275	53,789	203,185
Number of dwellings									
Total (000)	1,258	15,190	19,347	3,035	79,194	13,032	24,198	17,016	63,450
Per 100 persons	7.2	30.6	31.8	29.5	18.2	25.7	24.6	31.6	31.2
Percent owner occupied	61	43	34	63	85	46	60	48	63
Average floor area (sq. m.)									
Per dwelling	n.a.	52.4	62.3	43.9	27.1	54.4	62.5	84.5	95.6
Per person	n.a.	16.0	19.8	13.0	4.9	14.0	15.4	26.7	29.8
Percent of dwellings with:									
Flush toilet	42	52	86	33	2	–	17	98	96
Inside piped water	41	91	99	36	5	62	95	–	98

‡Figure for 1969.

Sources: Population, number of dwellings, and precentage owner-occupied, U.N. *Statistical Yearbook, 1972,* Table 203, Summary of Housing Condition.
Average floor area: *France, the Federal Republic of Germany, and Italy:* number of rooms per dwelling unit reported in the U.N. *Statistical Yearbook, 1972* multiplied by the average size of rooms in dwellings occupied by iron and steel workers reported in *Situation des Logements des Travailleurs C.E.C.A., Statistiques Sociales,* No. 2, 1961, Office Statistique des Communautés Européennes. *Hungary:* estimated from data provided by the Central Statistical Office. *India:* estimated from the distribution of dwellings by room size as given in the *Census of India,* 1961, 1, part IV (B), *Housing and Establishment Tables:* and from average floor area of dwellings of different room sizes reported for 1968–69 in the Quick Tabulation Schedule, National Sample Survey, 23rd Round, and specially provided to the ICP. *Japan:* from tables relating to the *1968 Census of Housing,* specially prepared for the ICP by the Bureau of Statistics. *United Kingdom:* based on 5.35 rooms per dwelling computed from U.N. *Statistical Yearbook, 1972,* and on estimated floor area for that number of rooms. The latter figure is derived from data on dwellings subject to registered rents provided by the Department of the Environment. *United States:* estimated floor area of a five-room unit, reported as the median size in the *1970 Census of Housing.* Percentage of dwellings with flush toilet and with inside piped water: from U.N. *Statistical Yearbook, 1972,* except for India, which is from the National Sample Survey, 15th Round.

associated on the average with dwellings having different numbers of rooms.

Another variable that is an important indicator of the quality of housing, at least in some countries, is the age of the dwelling unit. In the United States, higher-income families tend to occupy newer and more expensive quarters; older dwellings tend to rent for relatively diminished amounts, partly because they are sometimes allowed to deteriorate and are found in declining neighborhoods, partly because newness itself commands a premium. It is also possible that newer buildings contain other desirable features not measured by the variables we use to explain rents—for example, more efficient heating systems. Thus, as can be seen from Table 9.2, dwellings built in the 1960s rented in the United States for 20 percent more than dwellings with the same physical characteristics built in the 1950s. The age factor also seemed to be an important influence on rents in Japan and India, although for the latter, the figures refer to Bombay alone. In Europe, on the other hand, age seems to have a smaller impact on rents. In England, the premium on ten-years age difference was much larger in the Greater London area (17 percent) than elsewhere (9 percent), but in Japan the premium in urban areas (18 percent) was lower than that in rural areas (35 percent).

A variable that we know to affect rents but that we have not utilized is location. Rents in London, for example, are 1.5 times the rents elsewhere in England and

Wales for recently constructed (post-1939) dwellings. Rents in Budapest tend to be 1.5 to 2 times those in rural communities in Hungary for dwellings with equal physical characteristics. Similar premiums for rents in large urban centers are found in India, Japan, and the United States and doubtless would be revealed in the other countries were the data available.

It seems clear that the rent differences attributable to location within a country reflect quality differences from the standpoint of consumers: a dwelling in London, Budapest, or Manhattan is more valuable than one with the same physical characteristics in a rural area in the same country. In the ICP, however, these locational scarcity values are not being taken into account. We regard these differences as price differences and seek merely the average national price for selected types of dwellings (that is, ones with given physical specifications). This has the advantage of simplicity; it avoids the need to match places in different countries having equivalent scarcity values. (From a land-scarcity standpoint, what U.S. cities are matching to London? To Budapest?) More important, it is consistent with our treatment of farm and urban consumption in other sectors (the "a potato is a potato" approach set out in Chapter 2). Taking account of scarcity values would lead us to regard, as between two countries with identical housing stocks, the country with the more concentrated population as having a larger real quantity of housing.

Table 9.2. Relative Rents for Dwellings with Equal
Amenities Constructed in Different Periods

Decade beginning	France	Germany (F.R.)	India	Italy	Japan	U.K.	U.S.
1910	100	96	77	96		70	66
1920			81			} 89	75
1930			85				80
1940			90				89
1950	100	100	100	100	100	100	100
1960	111	111	124	92	120		120

Sources: France, the Federal Republic of Germany, and Italy:
Rents per square meter supplied through the Statistical Office of
the European Economic Community for units built before 1949,
in 1949–61, and in 1962–70. These were regarded as referring
to the 1910s, 1950s, and 1960s. There was one overlapping
specification for the first pair of dates and two for the second
pair. *India:* Based on the Bombay regression. *Japan:* Rough
estimates based on regression coefficients for rents of structures
built in 1956–60, 1961–65, and 1966–68, all compared with
rents in structures built before 1956. *United Kingdom:* Rough
estimates based on separate regressions for London and non–
London, weighted together with weights of 1 and 3, respectively.
The 1910 entry actually refers to "pre-1919," and the average
date of construction of this group of dwellings was probably well
before the 1910 decade. *U.S.:* Based on regression of BLS urban
rents. For further explanations, see the sections of the chapter
dealing with the individual countries.

B. The Data

The raw materials for the international comparison of
rents are rent surveys within the individual countries.
These surveys vary in character from special samples
taken for the ICP and comprising only a thousand or so
observations to complete censuses of housing from
which the relevant data could be drawn.

The materials from these sources generally were provided to the ICP in one of two forms. In the more traditional form, rents were provided for dwelling units cross-
classified according to a number of different characteristics, which varied widely in complexity and detail. In the
case of the Common Market countries, for example, the
Statistical Office of the European Economic Community
provided us with data for seven housing specifications
defined in terms of the date of construction and the
presence or absence of a flush toilet, a bath, and central
heating. At the other extreme, the Japanese data consisted of nearly 500 tables especially tabulated from the
1968 housing census, with cross-classifications of such
characteristics as location, type of structure, date of
construction, floor area, and facilities; rents and the
number of observations were provided for more than
10,000 cells, each of which represented a fairly narrow
specification with respect to the key characteristics
affecting rents. Hungary also supplied tables of this
character, not nearly so detailed, but well suited to the
purpose at hand.

The other form in which rent data were provided to
the ICP was punched cards or tapes that contained information about the rents and characteristics of individual
dwelling units. Data in this form, supplied by Colombia,
India, Kenya, and the United States, had the advantage
of providing much more flexibility in use than did the
data in the traditional form.[1] Regressions were run with
rent as the dependent variable and the characteristics of
the dwelling unit as the independent variables. With such
a regression, it is possible to estimate the rent for any
desired combination of dwelling characteristics, subject
to the constraint that values of the independent variables
falling outside of the range of observations in a country
may yield unreliable estimates.

Further details about the data for the individual
countries are given in connection with the description of
the binary comparisons. The U.S. data are described here
at some length, partly because each other country was
compared initially with the United States in the series of
binary comparisons, and partly because the U.S. data
provide a convenient means of describing our use of
regression methods.

Rental units accounted for 37 percent of U.S. occupied dwelling units in 1970. Rented urban units, upon
which our analysis of U.S. rents is based, made up about
29 percent of all dwellings. The median number of
rooms was 5.0 in all units, 5.6 in owner-occupied units,
and 4.0 in rented units. The corresponding estimates of
floor area in square meters were 95.6, 107.5, and 79.0,
respectively.[2]

The U.S. data consisted of a tape containing around
39,000 rental observations gathered over a six-month
period from September 1966 through February 1967 as
part of the U.S. Bureau of Labor Statistics (BLS) regular
rent-survey work for the Consumer Price Index.[3] Each
observation refers to the actual rent paid for a particular
dwelling unit in one of the six months in one of 58
urban areas throughout the United States.

The characteristics of the units in the BLS sample and
the rents associated with each are shown in Table 9.3.
The BLS data, which were based on a sampling frame
originally using 1960 census data, are compared in Table
9.4 with data from census sources for 1968 and 1970. In
general, there is good agreement between the two
sources of data. The differences observed are in the
direction that one would expect given the differences in reference dates and coverage. Thus, we will not
be far off the mark if we regard the BLS sample as

[1] In one instance, the United Kingdom, the country supplied
completed regressions rather than the original data.
[2] See Table 9.7
[3] For a description of the survey, see U.S. Bureau of Labor
Statistics, Bulletin 1517 *The Consumer Price Index: History and
Techniques* (Washington: Government Printing Office, 1967),
Chap. 6

Table 9.3. United States: Characteristics of Dwelling Units in BLS Urban
Rent Sample, September 1966–February 1967

	Number of observations	Percentage of sample†	Average monthly rent	Standard deviation
Total sample	39,107	100	$ 84.60	$ 44.42
Type of house	39,081	100		
Single detached	6,234	16.0	72.82	34.76
Single semidetached	2,549	6.5	69.82	30.20
Single attached	1,335	3.4	74.56	32.76
Multiple unit	28,606	73.2	89.16	47.19
Other	357	0.9	66.79	25.12
Condition	39,063	100		
Sound	34,134	87.4	88.54	45.33
Deteriorating	4,188	10.7	58.61	23.36
Dilapidated	741	1.9	49.63	28.54
Year built	38,689	100		
Pre-1920	14,513	37.5	64.78	28.24
1920-29	6,434	16.6	77.51	36.19
1930-39	3,485	9.0	77.58	33.37
1940-49	4,527	11.7	87.80	34.64
1950-54	2,881	7.4	99.90	39.49
1955-60	3,137	8.1	109.25	47.95
1961-66	3,712	9.6	142.69	60.08
Number of rooms	39,058	100		
One	1,338	3.4	73.37	33.30
Two	4,355	11.1	72.94	33.15
Three	11,512	29.5	82.23	39.33
Four	11,290	28.9	89.62	46.19
Five	6,506	16.7	87.77	46.48
Six	2,995	7.7	86.28	55.62
Seven	691	1.8	93.18	58.23
Eight or more	371	0.9	103.97	81.44
Number of private bathrooms	39,065	100		
None or shared	2,061	5.3	54.42	27.40
Flush toilet only	510	1.3	40.36	34.47
Half bath	651	1.7	53.12	36.63
One complete bath	34,194	87.5	83.86	36.83
One-and-a-half baths	850	2.2	130.75	65.36
Two baths or more	799	2.0	198.88	106.93
Heating equipment	39,021	100		
None	1,366	3.4	103.05	55.80
Central	25,464	65.3	91.94	46.48
Other installed	11,273	28.9	68.48	32.74
Other not installed	948	2.4	52.82	23.70
Included in rent				
Refrigerator	39,097	100		
Yes	20,208	51.7	100.02	50.97
No	18,889	48.3	68.16	28.77
Stove	39,098	100		
Yes	23,676	60.6	97.14	49.57
No	15,422	39.4	65.42	25.98
Electricity	39,096	100		
Yes	8,524	21.8	91.28	50.73
No	30,572	78.2	82.76	42.65
Heat	39,019	100		
Yes	19,447	49.8	94.15	48.97
No	19,572	50.2	74.97	37.41
Garage	39,078	100		
Yes	8,427	21.6	95.43	46.09
No	30,651	78.4	81.58	43.64

†For each characteristic, the number of observations providing information about that characteristic is taken as 100.

indicating the most common characteristics of U.S. renter-occupied urban housing. The 1970 census data in the table, showing the characteristics of all dwellings—urban and rural, as well as rental and owner-occupied—will be useful for weighting purposes.

The rents in Table 9.3 refer to the payments actually made by the tenants to landlords, whether or not equipment or services as well as housing space were covered by the payments. About one-fifth of these "contract" rental payments, for example, included garages, about

Table 9.4. United States: Characteristics of Dwellings

	Renter occupied		All dwellings†
	BLS urban sample 1966–67 (%)	Bureau of Census sample, urban & rural 1968 (%)	Census of Housing 1970 (%)
Number of rooms	100	100	100
one and two	14	11	5
three	30	24	11
four	29	31	21
five or more	27	34	63
Number of housing units in structure	100	100	100
one	27	31	68
two	16	19	9
three or four	15	13	5
five or more	42	37	15
Year built	100	100	100
1939 or earlier	63	58	41
1940–49	12	13	13
1950–59	14	12	21
1960 or later	11	17	25
Median rent	$75.55	$78	$89
Mean rent	$84.60		

†Renter and owner occupied.
Source: BLS data from special tabulation. (The median BLS rent is based on the geometric mean. See text.) Census sample data from U.S. Bureau of the Census, *Current Housing Reports*, Series H-111, No. 55 (July 1969), Tables 17 and 18. 1970 Census of Housing data from *Detailed Housing Characteristics*, Final Report HC (1)-B1, U.S. Summary (July 1972), Tables 30, 31, and 32.

one-half included heat, and well over one-half included the use of stoves and refrigerators supplied by the landlord. The data that are required for the ICP represent "space" rents: they should exclude all such payments for equipment and for service and should cover the use of dwelling space alone.

THE GENERAL APPROACH

The exclusion of these payments was achieved in the course of a multivariate analysis in which facilities and services other than space were taken as explanatory variables and rent as the dependent variable. At the same time, other key quantitative and qualitative characteristics of the dwelling units, such as the number of rooms, bathroom facilities, and age of the dwelling also were included as explanatory variables. With the inclusion of such added variables as regional location, population size of the community in which the dwelling was located, and structural characteristics of the dwelling unit, the number of independent variables examined increased to forty.

A number of equations were estimated, using alternative combinations of independent variables. Most of the coefficients obtained seemed plausible and, despite some multicollinearity, proved in general to be quite stable with alternative combinations of the independent variables. The large size of the sample used in the regressions, 38,349, helped make it possible to isolate the separate effects on rent of the various variables despite the high correlation between some of them.

THE PREFERRED EQUATION

The preferred equation is summarized in Table 9.5. The percentage of explained variation ($\overline{R}^2 = 0.64$) is not as high as we would like, of course, probably reflecting the omission from the data of important quality variables associated with neighborhood and structure that are difficult to measure. Our inability to control these variables is not unique to the regression technique, however, and in the same manner would limit traditional-type rent comparisons. All of the coefficients in the equation are more than twice their standard errors. The merit of the preferred equation is that its coefficients provide plausible estimates of the separate effects of the different variables.

The natural logarithm of rent was taken as a function of thirty-three independent variables, of which only the log of population was a continuous variable. The coefficient for population indicates that the log of monthly rent was .0519 higher, holding everything else constant, for each increase of 1 million in city size. This works out to a 5.3 percent increase in rent for every rise of 1 million in city size (that is, the antilog of .0519 is 1.053).

All the other variables are dummy variables taking on a value of 1 if a given observation was characterized by

Table 9.5. United States: Coefficients of Regression Equation for Urban Rents, September 1966–February 1967

Variable	Coefficient†	Standard error
Population (log of millions)	0.0519	.0010
Location variables‡		
North Central states	0.0674	.0040
Western states	0.0710	.0052
Southern states	−0.0134	.0049
Alaska	0.6273	.0116
Hawaii	0.3960	.0105
Inclusions in rental payment§		
Refrigerator	0.1448	.0054
Cooking stove	0.0707	.0053
Electricity	0.0304	.0043
Heat	0.1320	.0044
Garage	0.0996	.0037
Furniture	0.0245	.0044
Structural characteristics		
Central heating¶	0.1449	.0039
Multiple unit#	0.0449	.0040
Condition††		
Deteriorating	−0.0879	.0049
Dilapidated	−0.1627	.0107
Year built‡‡		
1920–29	0.0886	.0043
1930–39	0.1463	.0055
1940–49	0.2444	.0053
1950–54	0.3250	.0062
1955–60	0.4237	.0060
1961–66	0.5634	.0059
Number of rooms§§		
two	0.0850	.0088
three	0.2243	.0084
four	0.3440	.0086
five	0.4551	.0092
six	0.5121	.0101
seven	0.5887	.0139
eight or more	0.6648	.0174
Bathroom facilities¶¶		
One-half bath	0.0646	.0124
One complete bath	0.2270	.0062
One-and-one-half baths	0.4058	.0118
Two or more baths	0.6419	.0123
Intercept	3.2413	—
$\bar{R}^2$ = .64	SEE =	.2769
Mean of logs of rent:	4.3248	

Definitions:

Number of rooms: A room has four (permanent) walls to the ceiling; is finished; and is used regularly for living quarters. Other spaces not completely separated from an adjoining room and with less than four walls to the ceiling are counted as half rooms. Bathrooms are not counted as rooms.

Condition of dwelling unit: A sound house has no defects or only slight defects, which normally are corrected during the course of regular maintenance: whereas a deteriorating housing needs more repairs than would be provided in the course of regular maintenance. A dilapidated house does not provide safe and adequate shelter. Shacks, huts, or other structures with makeshift walls or roofs or with dirt floors are considered to represent inadequate construction.

Bathroom: A complete bathroom contains (1) a flush toilet, (2) a wash bowl, and (3) a bathtub and/or shower. A half-bathroom consists of any two of these three standard fixtures.

Multiunit structures: A structure containing two or more housing units.

†Natural logarithms.
‡Northeast the base.
§Exclusion from rent the base in each case.

the specified characteristic and 0 if it was not. In this method, a dummy variable is included for each of a given set of characteristics except one.[4] The coefficient of each dummy variable then indicates the amount by which the log of rent for that characteristic differs from the log of rent for the omitted characteristic. In the case of rooms, for example, the omitted, or "base," characteristic is a one-room dwelling unit, and the coefficient for each room size indicates the amount by which the log of rent for that number of rooms exceeds the log of rent for one-room units, holding everything else constant. The number of rooms could have been treated as a continuous variable, but this would have implied an equal log rent increase for each unit increase in the number of rooms. Our coefficients show the increase is not really uniform; from one to two rooms, for example, the log of rent rises by .0850 (equivalent to 8.9 percent), but a third room adds another .1393 to the log of rent, equivalent to 14.9 percent. Incidentally, the continuous rise in rents with room size indicated by these coefficients is in contrast to the more erratic movement of rents in Table 9.3, the difference being that in Table 9.3 each room size group contains a different mix of the other rent-influencing characteristics, whereas in Table 9.5, all other characteristics are held constant and only the difference in the number of rooms is allowed to influence the coefficients.

In a similar way, the coefficients for the bathroom facilities indicate the increases for each type of bathroom facility over the rent for units with no bathroom, a shared bathroom, or private bathroom containing a flush toilet only. The dummies for date of construction show the difference in the log of rent for dwellings constructed at various periods after 1920 and those built before 1920. The coefficient of the dummy for multiunit buildings shows the difference between log of rent for dwellings in structures containing two or more units and that of single-unit structures, whereas the coefficients of the dummies for deteriorating and dilapidated units estimate the average amounts by which the log of rent in such structures fell below the log of rent in sound structures. Population, which was based on 1960 census figures, varied from 4,000 to 10.7 million for the fifty-eight urban areas; the average for all the places was

[4]See D. B. Suits, "Use of Dummy Variables in Regression Equations," *Journal of the American Statistical Association* (December 1957), pp. 548–51.

¶No heat or heating other than central heating the base.
#Dwelling in single structure the base.
††Sound structure the base.
‡‡Pre-1920 the base.
§§One room the base.
¶¶No bathroom, shared bathroom, or private bathroom containing only a flush toilet the base.

2,177,000. The coefficients for the regional (South, West, and on on) dummies indicate the amount by which the log of rent differs, all other things held constant, from the log of rent in the base area, the Northeast—for which no dummy variable is included.

THE USE OF THE EQUATION TO ESTIMATE RENTS

The equation was used in the first instance to estimate the space rent for a standard dwelling; that is, one close to the average in size, facilities, and the like. It then was used to provide adjustment factors to modify this rent so that other specifications, as required for comparisons with other countries, could be matched.

By setting equal to zero the variables reflecting the service and equipment variables such as electricity and heating included in the rent, we obtained the space-rent estimates. We assumed that the dwelling unit was in an average size urban place (population 2,177,000), and we estimated the average rent in such a place over all regions of the United States. For the latter purpose, we calculated an average (weighted by population) of the regional coefficients. This calculation, including the Northeast, with its implicit zero coefficient, indicates that the average urban log rent in the United States as a whole was .0276 more than in the Northeast.

With respect to the characteristics as well, we selected for our standard dwelling those specifications which are the most common in the United States: a dwelling with a complete bathroom in a sound, centrally heated structure. Because the impact upon rents of the number of dwellings in the structure could not be judged clearly in different countries, we simply took the average U.S. mix of single- and multiple-unit dwellings in estimating the urban rent for our standard dwelling. Assuming further that the dwelling had three rooms and was in a structure built in the 1920s, the calculation of the monthly space rent in the period September 1966 to February 1967 is:

Log of rent

1. Standardization for city size and region

   City size (log of 2.177 × .0519)   .1130

   Region   .0276

2. Standardization for specification of dwelling unit

   Three rooms   .2243

   Private complete bathroom   .2270

   Built in 1920–29   .0886

   Mix of multi- and single-unit structures   .0312

   Central heating   .1449

3. Constant term   3.2413

Total   4.0979

Antilog: $60.21

One further adjustment is necessary before reaching the mean urban rent for our standard dwelling. The dollar rents obtained from our double log equation (by taking the antilogs of the estimated log rents) should be considered as estimates of the median rather than mean rents.[5] If the data available for another country being compared with the United States are in terms of median rents, the rents represented by the antilogs of the results produced by the equation will be appropriate. If, however, the other country's figures are means, the U.S. medians can be converted to means by applying an adjustment factor based on the relationship between the arithmetic and geometric means.[6] This factor turns out to be 1.04, and the mean standard urban rent thus becomes $62.62.[7]

RURAL RENTS

Both the median and mean rents estimated above apply to urban rents. We need a basis for adjusting them to national averages inclusive of rural rents. About 30 percent of U.S. housing units were in rural areas in 1960, most of them (24 out of the 30 percent) being rural nonfarm dwellings.[8] Unfortunately, little information exists about rural rents, and we had to base our estimates on tenuous evidence.

The 1960 census gives the following information about urban and rural nonfarm dwellings:

	Urban	Rural nonfarm[9]
Median number of rooms in renter-occupied dwellings	3.8	4.2
Flush toilet, exclusive use (%)	94.2	75.7
Median gross rent	$73.	$55.

[5] The reason is that if it is assumed, as seems plausible, that rents for any given type of dwelling (specified by particular values of our independent values) are lognormally distributed, the estimate produced by the equation is the mean value of the log of rent for that kind of dwelling. The antilog of the mean value of the log of rent (the geometric mean) corresponds to the median rent when the distribution is lognormal. See J. Aitchison and J. A. C. Brown, *The Lognormal Distribution* (Cambridge: Cambridge University Press, 1957), p. 9.

[6] The relationship is $A = Ge^{\frac{1}{2}\sigma^2}$, where, for our purposes, A is the arithmetic estimate, G the antilog of the log rent estimated from the equation, $e = 2.7128$, and σ is the standard error of estimate. As can be seem from Table 9.5, $\sigma = .2769$. Therefore, the log of the expression $e^{\frac{1}{2}\sigma^2}$ works out to .0383, and the antilog is 1.04.

[7] $1.04 \cdot 60.21 = 62.62$.

[8] See Table W, P. XLIII, Vol. I, Part I, U.S. Bureau of the Census, *U.S. Census of Population, 1960* (Washington: Government Printing Office, 1963). In urban areas, 42 percent of dwellings were renter occupied, in rural areas, 29 percent.

[9] *Ibid.* Our comparisons are confined to rural nonfarm dwellings because the census gave no rental data for farm dwellings.

Median gross rent, which includes the rent actually paid plus the costs of utilities (gas, electricity, and water) and fuel if these items were not included in the rent, was about 75 percent of the urban level in rural nonfarm areas. Although slightly larger, rural nonfarm dwellings were of lower quality in that they more often lacked such facilities as flush toilets, bathtubs, central heating, and the like. It is difficult to say, therefore, to what extent the difference in gross rents represents lower rural prices.

An attempt to throw additional light on this question was made by means of a special tabulation of data from a one-in-a-thousand sample of the 1960 census. We compared monthly contract rents[10] in urban and rural non-farm areas for dwellings of four different room sizes in sound, centrally heated structures. The results, shown in Table 9.6, indicate an average ratio, subject to considerable variability, of rural nonfarm rents to urban rents of 0.85. The number of observations is small, totaling only a little over 500 for rural nonfarm, but we have assumed that rural rents are 85 percent of urban rents for equivalent dwelling units.

The results of the 1970 Census of Housing were not fully available at the time of writing, and more current calculations of these relationships could not be made. Figures were available, however, indicating that 26 percent of U.S. housing units were in rural areas in 1970. Using the 1970 rural-urban proportions for the number of housing units and assuming that the 0.85 rural-urban rent ratio derived from the 1960 census figures was still applicable in 1970, the adjustment factor necessary to convert the urban rents produced by our regression is 0.96.[11] This brings the national mean rent for the standard dwelling to $60.12.[12] A final adjustment was made for rent subsidies: 0.4 percent for 1967 and 0.6 percent for 1970.[13]

This rent estimate for a standard dwelling unit was used as the basis for estimating, with the aid of the equation, rents for other specifications so as to match those available in other countries. Central heating, for ex-

ample, is not usual in a number of the ICP countries (Colombia, India, and Kenya). Where all other features of the standard specification were present, comparability was attained by deducting 0.1449 from the log of U.S. rent. This is equivalent to 15.6 percent (the antilog of 0.1449 is 1.156), and the adjustment may be made by multiplying the standard rent by 0.87 (the reciprocal of 1.156). Similar adjustments were made for differences from the standard in the size of the dwelling unit, bathroom facilities, and date of construction. The adjustment factors are summarized in convenient form in Table 9.7.

Data on floor area, estimated on the basis of the number of rooms, are included in the table because, as noted earlier, they provide a better basis for international comparisons than the number of rooms. The floor area associated with each room size was estimated on the basis of (1) Federal Housing Administration (FHA) data relating to one-family houses on which the FHA insured mortgages, (2) census data relating to size of new houses sold, and (3) data provided by a private construction-statistics company indicating the relative floor areas both of newly built apartments and of one- or two-family dwellings.

Following is an illustrative use of Table 9.7 to adjust the standard rent to obtain the estimated monthly urban rent in 1967 for a two-room dwelling in a sound, not centrally heated, structure with a half bathroom, built in 1960–66.

Standard rent[14]		$60.12
Adjustment for:		
Two rooms	× .87	
Construction in 1960–66	× 1.59	
Absence of central heating	× .87	
Half-bathroom	× .85	
1967 (calendar year)	× 1.011	
Subsidy	× 1.004	
Estimated mean rent		$62.43

C. The Binary Comparisons

Initially, a series of binary comparisons was made between the United States and each other country. The first step in this work was to examine the distribution of housing in each country according to the various characteristics such as floor area, plumbing facilities, and so forth, for which data were available. On this basis, a number of specifications for dwelling units were selected, an effort being made (along the lines suggested in Chapter 3) to obtain a good sampling of the range within which housing of the two countries overlapped.

[10]Contract rent, as noted above, refers to rent actually paid regardless of utilities and other services or equipment included or not included. Space rents, it has been estimated by the BLS, are about 81 percent of contract rents. This estimate, which was based on October 1966 worksheets for "City Workers Family Budgets," involved, first, the application of the percentage of families having each utility included in its rent to the average dollar cost of that utility for families that did not have it included in the rent. Second, the estimated average values of rent-included utilities were aggregated and deducted from contract rent to get space rent. The average ratio of space to contract rent came out to 0.8093.

[11]$(1.00 \cdot .76) + (.85 \cdot .24) = .96.$

[12]$62.62 \cdot .96 = 60.12.$

[13]The adjustments were based on the proportion of rent subsidies to household expenditures for housing space. The estimates of the subsidies were based on data provided by the Department of Housing and Urban Development. See notes to Table 1.1.

[14]Monthly rent for period September 1966 to February 1967 for three-room unit with one full private bathroom in sound, centrally heated structure built in 1920–29.

Table 9.6. Monthly Contract Rents, Urban and Rural Nonfarm Dwellings in Sound, Centrally Heated Structures, 1960

Number of rooms	Urban		Rural nonfarm		Rural nonfarm as % of urban
	Number of observations	Rent/ (δ)	Number of observations	Rent/ (δ)	
two	787	68.20 (26.56)	19	60.00 (42.61)	88
three	2,350	73.73 (29.40)	78	57.31 (21.86)	78
four	2,464	78.19 (31.53)	238	62.29 (26.44)	80
five	1,624	80.43 (31.31)	182	74.64 (34.33)	93

Source: Special tabulation of one-in-a-thousand sample of 1960 U.S. Census of Population and Housing.

As noted earlier, when a poor country is compared with a wealthy country, the overlapping housing is apt to be found near the bottom of the high-income country's housing distribution and near the top of the low-income country's distribution. Thus, it was more difficult in the case of housing than in most other categories to avoid basing price comparisons on specifications that were unusual in either country. The best we were able to do was to try to avoid including in the rent comparisons specifications that fell outside the middle 90 percent of each country's housing.

Once these specifications were chosen, rents were estimated for each country either from a regression or from cross-classification tables. The number of specifications used in the binary comparisons varied from four in the case of the Colombia–United States and Kenya–United States comparisons to eighteen for United Kingdom–United States. The rent relatives for the selected specifications were averaged in turn (1) without any weighting, (2) with U.S. weights, and (3) with the other country's weights; in addition, (4) a Fisher index was computed of the U.S.-weighted and other-country–weighted indexes.

COLOMBIA–UNITED STATES

The rents for Colombia consisted of about 1,500 observations of tenant-occupied dwellings drawn from a household survey conducted by the Departamento Administrativo Nacional de Estadística (DANE). The survey, which was carried out in July 1971, covered seven different cities and their surrounding rural areas. In addition to the rent, the information about each dwelling included location (city and region), type of dwelling (house, apartment, rooms, hut, improvised housing unit, or other), number of rooms, facilities (flush toilet, shower, electricity, kitchen, and the like), and things other than space provided with the dwelling (light, water, furnishings, and so on) and included in the rent.

As in the case of the U.S. data, a multivariate analysis of the data was carried out in which the natural log rent was the dependent variable and the characteristics of the dwellings were the independent variables. Each independent variable was expressed in dummy form, taking on a value of 1 if the dwelling unit had the specified characteristic and 0 if it did not. The equation selected as the basis for estimating rents is set out in Table 9.8. The more important variables omitted from this regression were data indicating whether unit had (1) a shared flush toilet, (2) a private shower, (3) a shared shower, (4) a system for waste disposal, (5) whether the kitchen was private or shared, and, finally, (6) whether light and water were included in the rent. Most of these variables were discarded because their coefficients turned out not to be significant, either because they were highly correlated with variables included in the selected equation or because the coefficients appeared implausible for other reasons. The presence of the shower, for example, was highly correlated with the presence of a toilet. Again, for both the shower and toilet, the coefficients for shared facilities were higher than those for private facilities—for reasons that could not be determined.

A major difficulty in using the results for international rent comparisons was that, in the sample survey, the size of the dwelling units was expressed in terms of number of rooms. It proved difficult to obtain any reliable information on the average size of rooms in rented dwellings. We had to use data on the average floor area and number of rooms in newly constructed dwellings to produce rough estimates of the floor areas associated with each number of rooms reported in the survey. DANE reported that the floor areas in two typical urban dwellings used in the calculation of the construction-cost index were 47.60 square meters for a three-room unit and 74.48 square meters for a six-room unit (the room counts excluded kitchens). We then estimated the areas for the four- and five-room units by simple interpolation.

Another missing ingredient for the international comparison is the average age of Colombian dwellings. Census data indicate a 51 percent increase in the number of residential buildings in Colombia between 1951 and 1964. This fact, together with construction statistics for

Table 9.7. United States: Adjustment Factors to Convert the Rent for a Standard Dwelling to Rents for Other Specifications and Dates

Reason for adjustment			Multiply standard rent by
Size of dwelling unit Number of rooms†	Average floor area‡		
	(sq. ft.)	(sq. m.)	
1	375	34.8	.80
2	600	55.8	.87
3	700	65.1	1.00
4	850	79.0	1.13
5	1,030	95.6	1.26
6	1,240	115.5	1.32
Absence of central heating†			.87
Bathroom facilities†			
No private bath or flush toilet only			.80
Half-bathroom			.85
Single structure			.97
Multiunit structure†			1.01
Date of construction			
Before 1920			.92
1920–29			1.00
1930–39			1.06
1940–49			1.17
1950–54			1.27
1955–60			1.40
1961–66			1.61
1950–59§			1.33
1960–66§			1.59
1960–69§			1.66
Date of reference¶			
1967			1.011
1968			1.035
1969			1.068
1970			1.112
Rent subsidies			
1967			1.004
1970			1.006

Note: The "standard" in the table title refers to the mean national rent for September 1966–February 1967 for a dwelling with three rooms, one full private bathroom, in a sound, centrally heated structure built in 1920-29.

†For definitions, see Table 9.5.

‡Floor area refers to the interior area of living space, including kitchens, bathrooms, closets, and hallways; excluded are attics and basements not used for living quarters, balconies, terraces, and garages. See text.

§Estimated from the date of construction coefficient in Table 9.3 with the aid of the equation $\log C = -2.4468 \div .0470\,T$, where C is the natural log of the desired coefficient and T is the midpoint of the period measured in years, taking 1924–25 as 1. ($\bar{r}^2 = .998$). The antilog of $\log C$ produces an interpolated or extrapolated coefficient similar to the date of construction coefficient in Table 9.3. The adjustment factor is the antilog of this coefficient.

The adjustment factor for 1950–59, for example, is calculated in the following steps: (1) T is set equal to 31; (2) $\log C$ is computed at -0.9898; (3) the antilog of $\log C$ is 0.3720; the estimated coefficient analogous to those in Table 9.3; and (4) the adjustment factor is the antilog of the difference between this coefficient and the coefficient of the base period (1920-29): that is, antilog $(.3720 - .0886) = 1.33$.

¶Computed from BLS rent index.

the period 1964-70 suggests that the median dwelling was built in the 1940s.

Comparisons of rents between Colombia and the United States were made for fully equipped (complete bath, private kitchen) dwellings of four sizes (see Table 9.9). The floor areas of these units were selected so as to provide a spread within the range of overlapping sizes found in the two countries. The smallest of these sizes, 47.6 square meters, is not much if at all above the fifth percentile from the bottom of the U.S. size distribution,

but we have ample observations (roughly 9 percent of the BLS sample).[15] Units with less than complete facilities had to be excluded because the Colombian equation permitted us to estimate rents for dwellings with a full bath or without any bath but not for units with a half bath, whereas in the United States, units without any bath fell outside of the middle 90 percent range of

[15]Estimated by interpolating the room frequencies in Table 9.3 with the aid of the room sizes in Table 9.7.

Table 9.8. Colombia: Coefficients of Regression Equation for Rents, 1970

Variable	Coefficient†	Standard Error
Intercept	4.6989	0.1288
House	0.2655	0.1450
Apartment	0.5323	0.1444
Two rooms	0.3087	0.0471
Three rooms	0.6858	0.0571
Four rooms	0.8648	0.0645
Five rooms	1.1475	0.0715
Six or more rooms	1.2827	0.0769
Private toilet	0.1509	0.1432
Liquid cooking fuel	0.0033	0.0633
Gas cooking fuel	0.6337	0.7163
Electric cooking fuel	0.4716	0.0732
Public electricity	0.4587	0.1245
Gas included in rent	0.2200	0.1253
Telephone included in rent	0.1960	0.1316
Furniture included in rent	0.0200	0.0787
Atlantic region	−0.6804	0.0612
Oriental region	−0.3786	0.0714
Central region	−0.7022	0.0495
Pacific region	−0.4994	0.0474
Sublet	0.2837	0.0916

$\overline{R}^2$ = .6290   Arithmetic mean rent = 599
SEE = .5956   Mean of logs of rent = 5.910

†Natural logarithrms.
Note: The coefficients for house and apartment indicate the log of the amounts by which the rents of such dwellings exceed those of dwellings consisting of rooms, huts, or improvised units with equal space and facilities. The number of rooms is exclusive of kitchens. Over 60 percent of the sample dwellings had private kitchens, and nearly 30 percent shared kitchens.

dwellings to which we wished to confine the project's price comparisons.

The Colombian rents estimated from the equation referred to July 1971; they were adjusted to the annual average for 1970 on the basis of the rent component of the Colombian consumer price index (417.0 in July 1971 and 370.7 in 1970). U.S. rents were estimated by adjusting the standard rents to conform to the required specifications by the methods set out in the preceding section.[16]

It can be seen from Table 9.9 that the purchasing-power parities (PPPs) varied from 9.5 to 13.4 pesos per dollar. The overall results may be set out as follows:

	Pesos per dollar
A. Simple geometric mean	11.5
Weighted arithmetic means:	
B. Colombian weights	10.9
C. U.S. weights	11.8
D. Fisher index	11.4
E. Exchange rate	18.56
	U.S. = 100
F. Price ratio (D÷E)	64

[16] See pages 124–125.

Table 9.9. Comparison of Rents in Colombia and the United States, 1970

Square meters	Colombia (pesos) (1)	United States ($) (2)	Peso/Dollar (3)
47.60	549	57.59	9.53
56.56	657	60.19	10.92
65.52	872	68.59	12.71
74.48	998	74.33	13.43

The first row (A) shows the unweighted geometric mean of the PPPs for the four specifications for which prices are given in Table 9.8. Next, average PPPs are calculated with Colombian weights, B, and then with U.S. weights, C. In row D, the geometric mean of these two weighting systems—the Fisher index—is shown. Row F gives the price ratio derived by dividing the PPP based on the Fisher index by the official exchange rates. The difficulty of assigning weights to individual specifications, alluded to in Chapter 4, is particularly serious in binary rent comparisons. The necessarily approximate character of these weights is discussed more fully in connection with the following EEC comparisons.

FRANCE, GERMANY, AND ITALY

The rent data for France, the Federal Republic of Germany, and Italy were provided by the Statistical Office of the European Economic Community. Like the other EEC materials used in the ICP, the data were gathered as part of the internal-purchasing-power and product comparisons carried out by the Common Market in close cooperation with the U.N. International Comparison Project. Rents were gathered for units with a floor area ranging from 40 to 80 square meters. For the internal Common Market country comparison, rents were reduced to a per square meter basis.

A cross-classification of the characteristics for which data were collected—namely, date of construction and the presence or absence of a flush toilet, bathtub, and central heating—gave a total of seven specifications. The specifications are indicated in columns 2 to 5 of Table 9.10, and the rents in the European countries in columns 6 to 8.

It has been assumed that the median date of construction for buildings "built before 1949" fell in the decade from 1910 to 1919. This is a guess based only on the fact that the U.S. median for this group was around 1920 and on the assumption that European buildings still in existence and having been built before 1949 are probably older than the corresponding U.S. buildings.

Of the seven EEC specifications, the one referring to a dwelling unit without any toilet, tub, or central heating was regarded as too unusual in the United States for pricing (less than 5 percent of the U.S. units fell in this category). The U.S. prices for the other six specifica-

Table 9.10. Rents in France, the Federal Republic of Germany, Italy, and the United States, 1970, for Dwellings with Specified Characteristics

	Specifications				Monthly rent			
Specifications #	Date of construction	Toilet	Bathtub	Central heating	France (Fr)	Germany, F.R. (DM)	Italy (L)	United States ($)
(1)	(2)	(3)	(4)	(5)	(6)	(7)	(8)	(9)
13	Before 1949	no	no	no	104	97	10,920	—
14	Before 1949	yes	no	no	140	115	17,820	40.70
15	Before 1949	yes	yes	no	196	139	17,160	47.89
19E	1949–61	yes	yes	no	194	145	17,760	73.35
29E	1949–61	yes	yes	yes	235	198	25,500	83.81
24E	1962–70	yes	yes	no	212	167	16,260	91.42
34E	1962–70	yes	yes	yes	266	213	23,520	105.08

tions, entered in column 9, were calculated by adjusting the standard rent[17] with the aid of the regression equation data in Table 9.7 in the manner described in a preceding section. U.S. rents were calculated for dwellings with a floor area of 60 square meters.

In Table 9.11, the rent data are used to calculate PPPs for all the binary pairs among the six countries. The PPPs for the three European countries relative to the United States all show the effects of the age factor referred to earlier (see columns 1 to 3). The premium on newness or the discount on aged dwellings is greater in the United States than it is in Europe. Therefore, as the eye travels down the column in the direction of newer dwellings, a tendency becomes apparent for fewer European currency units to be required to command $1.00 worth of rental service. Among the Common Market countries, newness makes much less difference in Italy than in France or the Federal Republic of Germany (see columns 4 to 6). Within each age group, however, there is a tendency for the European countries to be slightly more expensive relative to the United States for the specifications involving better facilities.

One of the difficulties is the need to assign weights for types of dwellings for which we have no prices to those for which we do. In the EEC–United States comparisons, the six specifications priced exclude several major groups of U.S. dwelling units. The most important of these consists of units built before 1949 having central heating and full bathrooms. It seems likely that this group constituted well over one-third of all U.S. dwelling units in 1970, including owner-occupied and rented and urban and rural.[18] If we assign their weight to one of the specifications for the period before 1949, it has to be allocated to units having no central heating. If, on the other hand, we allocate their weight to the correct category with respect to facilities, it has to be the wrong category as far as year of construction is con-

cerned. We took an average of one allocation giving primacy to the age of the dwelling unit and one giving primacy to heating. Our estimates of the U.S. weights were derived with the aid of a special cross-classification of the BLS rent sample, which was then adjusted by using 1970 census data as the control distribution for dwelling units with respect to their age and to their heating facilities.

Despite the weighting difficulties, the weighted average PPPs probably deserve more credence than the simple averages. If we base our conclusions on the Fisher indexes, Italian, French, and German (F.R.) rents were 49, 55 and 64 percent, respectively, of U.S. rents in 1970. Italian rents were about 30 percent below German (F.R.) rents and 15 to 20 percent below French rents. There is relatively little variability around these averages in the PPPs for individual specifications, and the spread between the numerator- and denominator-weighted average PPPs is small.

HUNGARY–UNITED STATES

The data on rents in Hungary were provided by the Hungarian Central Statistical Office in the form of a series of tables giving the average monthly rents in 1967 for various categories of state-owned dwellings. The rents included both payments made by tenants and subsidies allocated by the state to communal management enterprises. Of the national average rent of 416 forints, only 80 forints was paid by tenants. The 1967 rents were still in effect during the calendar year 1970.

State-owned units included around 85 percent of all rented units and nearly one-forth of the total housing stock. About two-thirds of the privately owned dwelling units were room-and-kitchen flats without facilities, found mainly in rural villages.

The categories of state-owned dwellings for which rents were given were established in terms of location, size of dwelling, and facilities. Disregarding the classifications based on location for reasons given above,[19] we made use of the cross-classifications involving facilities

---

[17]See page 124.

[18]Dwellings with central heating and full bathrooms accounted for 46 percent of the BLS sample which refers to rented urban units in the latter part of 1966 and early 1967.

[19]See page 118.

Table 9.11. Comparison of Rents in France, the Federal Republic of Germany, Italy and the United States, 1970

Specification #	France/U.S. (Fr/$) (1)	Ger.(F.R.)–U.S. (DM/$) (2)	Italy–U.S. (L/$) (3)	France/Ger. (F.R.) (Fr/DM) (4)	Italy/Ger. (F.R.)(L/DM) (5)	Italy/France (L/Fr) (6)
		Part A. Purchasing-power parities for individual specifications				
13	—	—	—	1.06	112	104
14	3.44	2.82	437	1.21	114	126
15	4.10	2.90	358	1.40	122	87
19E	2.64	1.98	243	1.33	121	91
29E	2.80	2.37	304	1.18	128	108
24E	2.32	1.83	178	1.26	96	77
34E	2.53	2.03	224	1.24	109	87
		Part B. Average PPPs				
A. Unweighted geometric mean	2.51	2.29	277	1.24	119	96.2
Arithmetic means with weights of:						
B. Numerator country	2.94	2.29	311	1.22	125	100.6
C. Denominator country	3.12	2.43	300	1.27	122	97.8
D. Fisher index	3.03	2.36	305	1.24	123	99.2
E. Exchange rate	5.554	3.66	625	1.52	173	114.0
	(Rent in numerator country as % of rent in denominator country)					
F. Price ratio (D ÷ E)	54.6	64.4	48.8	81.7	71.3	87.0

Note: Lines A to D based on six specifications for comparisons involving the United States and on seven for other countries. Most intra-EEC results based on the six specifications used in the U.S. comparions were within 1 percent of those shown in the table; the maximal difference was 3 percent.

and room size. This yielded 24 specifications, of which 8 fell within the middle 90 percent range of the types of dwellings found both in Hungary and the United States.

The specifications of these dwellings and the Hungarian rents are shown in Table 9.12. The rents are taken directly from the information described above. U.S. rents once again were estimated by adjusting the standard rent[20] with the coefficients set out in Table 9.7.

In order to estimate the U.S. rent on a comparable basis, however, we had to form some estimate of the average age of Hungarian dwellings, about which information was lacking. On the basis of construction statistics and statistics on the housing stock, we have assumed the median date of construction to have fallen in the 1920s.[21] This corresponds to the median of the BLS sample of urban rental units, but it is 20 years earlier than the median for all U.S. dwellings—urban and rural,

owner occupied, and rented—occupied in 1968.[22] Our guess about the median age is unlikely to be off by more than a decade, which, if the data for the other European countries in Table 9.2 are any guide, would not make much difference in the Hungarian rent. U.S. rents for units built a decade earlier (the 1910s) were 8 percent less, and rents for those built a decade later (the 1930s) were 6 percent more than the rents for the dwellings built in the 1920s.

In Table 9.13, the forint/dollar purchasing powers are shown for each of the types of dwellings set out in the previous table. They vary from 7 to around 12 forints per dollar in a fairly regular pattern, rising from smaller to larger units and from units with few facilities to those with many. The simple geometric mean is 10.27 forints per dollar.

Once again, weighting posed difficulties. For neither country was it easy to develop a completely satisfactory weighting pattern for combining the PPPs in a way that took due account of the relative importance of the different types of dwelling units. In the case of Hungary, it was necessary to prorate the number of privately owned dwellings, which account for more than three-quarters of the total, to the various room size categories in accordance with the proportions for state-owned units with similar facilities. For the United States, dwellings with central heating but without complete facilities, which were not directly represented by our specifications, had to be allocated between the categories having heating with complete facilities (the only with-heating category included) and those without heating and less

[20] See pages 124–125.

[21] The basis for the assumption that the median construction date of Hungarian dwellings falls in the 1920s lies in a comparison of the number of newly constructed dwellings and the housing stock. From 1949 through 1967, 911,000 new dwellings were constructed in Hungary. (Hungarian Central Statistical Office, *Statistical Yearbook, 1970* [Budapest: Hungarian Central Statistical Office, 1972], p. 417 and Hungarian-language version of same for 1966, p. 310.) Assuming all of these units were still in existence in 1967, they accounted for 29.4 percent of the stock of 3,095,000 dwellings. The question is whether the proportion built in 1930–48 is greater or less than 20.6 percent. If at least 11,500 new dwellings per year had been built in the 1930–48 period, and if they were all still in existence in 1967, the proportion would be greater than 20.6 and the median would fall after 1930. The 1930–48 period, however, consisted largely of depression and war years, and our guess is that construction did not average as high as 11,500 per year. This rate would have been about 40 percent of the annual average rate for 1949–53, the earliest postwar years for which we have data.

[22] See Bureau of the Census, *Current Housing Reports, Housing Vacancies,* Series H-111, No. 55 (July 1969), Table 16.

Table 9.12. Hungary: Monthly Rents of State-owned Dwellings, 1967

Number of rooms	Size (sq. m.)	Without central heating		With central heating and full bath
		Half bath	Full bath	
2.5	48.1	313	480	583
3	63.6	313	545	702
3.5	78.6		686	847

Source: Central Statistical Office of Hungary, special tabulation for the ICP.

than complete facilities. Because the BLS sample referred only to urban dwellings, a distribution of all occupied U.S. dwellings for 1968, based on a census sample survey,[23] was taken as the control; and the BLS survey frequencies were used to distribute each room size to the different facilities categories.

The results of applying these distributions to calculate PPPs for rents are shown below.

	Forints per dollar	
	1967	1970
A. Simple geometric mean	10.27	9.31
Weighted arithmetic means:		
B. Hungarian weights	8.80	7.98
C. U.S. weights	11.98	10.86
D. Fisher index	10.27	9.31
E. Exchange rate	30	30
	U.S. = 100	
F. Price ratio (D÷E)	34.2	31.0

The 1970 rents simply were extrapolated from 1967 by the change in U.S. rents as measured by the BLS rent index, there having been no change in Hungarian rents during the time between 1967 and 1970. Thus, Hungarian rents were about one-third of U.S. rents when converted to a common currency by means of the exchange rate.

INDIA–UNITED STATES

As in the case of comparisons for other consumers goods and services, the problem of comparing Indian rents with those of the United States and other countries

[23]Bureau of the Census, *Current Housing Reports, Housing Vacancies,* Series H-111, No. 63, Pt. II, March 1971, p. 41.

turned largely on the great differences in quality within India. In India's great cities such as Delhi and Bombay, substantial numbers of dwellings are similar to those found in metropolitan centers throughout the world: that is, dwellings with amenities such as electricity and bathrooms with flush toilets and bathtubs or showers. There are also dwelling units in India that are very small, almost entirely without amenities, and simply constructed. These far outnumber the others because they characterize the rural sector in which more than 80 percent of the dwelling units are found (see Table 9.14).

Our method of meeting this great diversity of qualities and the incomparability of housing in rural India with that of other countries followed the same lines as our treatment of consumers goods in general. Prices for "metropolitan India" (defined as Bombay, Calcutta, Delhi, and Madras), in which qualities matching those in other countries could be found, were adjusted to national average prices on the basis of independent comparisons for metropolitan with "urban" India (defined as all urban places excluding the four metropolitan areas) and for urban with rural India.

Rural-urban and urban-metropolitan rent comparisons based on dwelling sizes. Published data on rural and urban rents made possible comparisons on the basis of type of construction and the number of rooms.[24] The difficulty with these data is that construction type was categorized only as *pucca* (good) or *kucha* (bad) on the basis of general criteria, which did not necessarily result in uniform evaluations in different parts of India. In addition, floor areas, a more reliable measure of size than rooms, were not provided.

[24]See, for example, *National Sample Survey,* 17th Round, Sept. 1961-July 1962, No. 150, Tables with Notes on Housing Conditions, Cabinet Secretariat, Government of India (New Delhi: Government of India Press, 1969).

Table 9.13. Hungarian–United States Rent Comparisons, 1967

				(forints per dollar)
Number of rooms	Size (sq. m.)	Without central heating		Central heating and full bath
		Half bath	Full bath	
2.5	48.1	8.26	10.77	11.37
3	63.6	7.08	10.48	11.74
3.5	78.6		11.43	12.28

Table 9.14. India: Number and Average Size of Households, Facilities, and Material of Structure for Urban and Rural Areas

	All India	All Urban	Metropolitan†	Urban†	Rural
Facilities					
Number of households (000)	83,553	14,842	2,001	12,841	68,711
Average size (persons per household)	5.2	5.1			5.2
Percentage of households having facilities for					
Piped water					
Inside	5.1	24.6			0.9
Outside	11.4	34.9			6.3
Bath	12.9	23.1			7.9
Toilet					
Flush	2.3	12.4			0.1
Other	10.4	41.6			3.7
Electricity	5.8	27.9			1.0
Material of structure					
Mud	50.6	21.5	10.2	23.2	56.9
Brick	23.7	56.1	70.6	53.9	16.7
Stone	11.9	11.6	0.8	13.2	12.0
Grass, leaves, reeds, or bamboo	11.3	6.0	4.2	6.3	12.5
Metal sheet	0.4	1.5	5.6	0.9	0.1
Cement, concrete	0.4	1.7	5.9	1.1	0.1
Total	100.0	100.0	100.0	100.0	100.0

Sources:
Facilities: Data on Housing Condition collected in National Sample Survey, 15th Round (July 1959–June 1960), draft report. Cabinet Secretariat (New Delhi: Government of India, 1970).
Material: Census of India 1961, Vol. I, Part IV(B)–Housing and Establishment Tables from the Office of the Registrar General of India. In computation, the relative weights were Delhi (.22), Madras (.16), Bombay (.32), and Calcutta (.30), with the four cities being .13 of urban India. These weights are based on the number of sample households underlying the census tables.
†"Metropolitan" comprises Bombay, Calcutta, Delhi, and Madras; "urban" comprises all other cities.

Fortunately, the Quick Tabulation Schedule of the 23rd Round (July 1968–June 1969) of the National Sample Survey (NSS) did contain a question asking both number of rooms and square meters for the rural and urban areas of each of the 15 states. The NSS did a tabulation of these results for the ICP, and these data provided a basis for comparing rural and urban rents, holding constant the size of dwellings. The data are limited in that they tell us nothing of such amenities as electricity, water, or plumbing nor about the type of structure. Further, few rural houses are rented (a total of 282 observations, or about 3 percent of households sampled in rural India, as opposed to 3,851 urban households, or about 45 percent of households sampled), so the nature of the sample is rather special. There is reason to suppose, however, that most rural renters will be people such as teachers, government officers, or other salaried individuals who probably rent better-than-average rural accommodations.[25] This means that the rural centers have a type of accommodation that more closely approximates the urban sample than would be

the case if the rented houses in rural areas were the average of rural houses.

The Central Statistical Organization (CSO) tabulated the monthly rural rents per square meter, as reported by the NSS, for different size dwellings (see Table 9.15). The average monthly rent per square meter was Rs .046 in rural areas, Rs0.80 in urban areas, and Rs1.77 in the four metropolitan cities. Though the rents are subject to wide sampling errors, especially for the rural sector, the premium on space in the more crowded areas is indicated clearly by the tendency for the ratio of urban to metropolitan rents and of rural to urban rents to fall as the size of the dwelling increases. Holding floor area constant, rural rents are from 77 to 37 percent of urban rents and urban rents from 67 to 38 percent of metropolitan rents. But these differences in rent per square meter between the areas reflect differences in facilities, as well as the space premium for urban and metropolitan areas.

Rural-urban comparisons with identical amenities. To compare rural rents with urban rents for dwellings with identical facilities, we utilized the rural rent data cited in Table 9.15 and urban rent data collected by the NSS for the middle-class consumer price index.

For each dwelling unit in the sample, the latter provided the 1969 rent, room size, floor area, and information about the presence or absence of various amenities.

[25] Money payments for haircuts and laundry were made mainly by such persons, who are residents of, but not native to, the village. This was reported by price collectors when they were asked how prices could be obtained in view of the prevalence of barter. It is inferred, and supported by prevailing opinion, that a similar situation applies where rents are paid.

Table 9.15. India: Monthly Rent per Square Meter, in Rupees, 1969

	Number of square meters in dwelling								
	Up to 5	5–10	10–15	15–20	20–30	30–40	40–50	Above 50	All
Rents:									
Rural	2.35	1.01	0.70	0.34	0.62	0.30	0.32	0.24	0.46
All urban	2.71	1.35	1.25	1.05	1.12	0.94	0.86	0.49	0.92
Urban	2.63	1.29	1.15	0.93	1.07	0.85	0.73	0.44	0.80
Metropolitan	3.03	1.54	1.69	1.75	1.45	1.65	1.93	1.48	1.97
Rent ratios:									
Rural-urban	.894	.783	.609	.366	.579	.353	.438	.545	.525
Urban-metropolitan	.868	.838	.680	.531	.738	.515	.378	.297	.452
Number of observations:									
Rural	8	64	62	55	41	25	9	18	282
All urban	202	877	834	607	606	295	138	292	3,851
Urban	165	681	669	521	519	261	122	274	3,212
Metropolitan	37	196	165	86	87	34	16	18	639

Source: National Sample Survey, 23rd Round (July 1968–June 1969), Quick Tabulation Schedule.
Note: For definitions of "metropolitan" and "urban," see Table 9.14.

There were 3,333 observations from 36 cities in the sample; 696 of them were from the four metropolitan cities.[26] Regression equations were estimated, with rent as the dependent variable and with independent variables consisting of living area and area per room and, in dummy form, the presence of a flush toilet system, electricity, water, and a veranda.[27] Furthermore, allowance was made for different rent levels in different cities by introducing intercept dummies. In the final equation, these coefficients were not retained in cases in which they were not significant at the 5 percent level. In the case of the four metropolitan cities, which we wished to distinguish from the others if the data warranted, we tested to determine whether they displayed a significant difference in the coefficients of the independent variables representing rent-determining factors from the corresponding coefficients of the other cities. The method was to fit equations with dummy slope coefficients for area, area per room, and the four amenities distinguishing the metropolitan cities from the others. Only the metropolitan slope coefficient for area proved to be statistically significant, and hence it is the only one retained in the equation finally selected. The equation is shown in Table 9.16.

In order to use the equation to estimate average rents for urban areas, account had to be taken of the different rent levels, indicated by these coefficients, in different cities. We combined these coefficients, using as weights the number of observations in the original sample.[28]

We used the equation to estimate an average urban rent for a dwelling corresponding to the average rural dwelling. This was a dwelling with 1.44 rooms and a floor area of 22.18 square meters (15.40 per room) and with the average proportion of facilities, shown in Table 9.11, for water (.009), electricity (.010), and flush toilet (.001). We set the proportion of verandas at 0.5. This is about the average for the middle-class sample, and it does not seem likely that rural areas have a smaller proportion of verandas than urban areas.

It turns out that the urban rent for a dwelling corresponding to the average rural dwelling is Rs0.75 per square meter. This result is a little surprising because it is not as much below the Rs0.80 figure for average urban rents in Table 9.15 as might have been expected. The average urban dwelling, however, is not so much better equipped as to make the result entirely implausible. Therefore, we take the rural-urban rent ratio as 0.61 (the rural rent of Rs0.46 per square meter from Table 9.15 divided by Rs0.75).

Urban-metropolitan rent comparisons. The same equation was used to estimate urban and metropolitan rents for dwellings with the average characteristics of urban dwellings. That is, the dwelling units were assumed to have, on the average, .246 piped water, .279 electricity, .124 flush toilets, and 0.5 verandas. In addition, it was assumed that the area per room was 5.88 square meters, the average for urban and metropolitan centers, and rents were estimated for six different size classes. The results are shown in Table 9.17.

[26]There was no systematic factor related to the exclusion of nine of the forty-five cities for which middle-class rent data are collected; the original schedules or the punch cards were not readily available for these cities when the work was organized.

[27]All of the equations were double log in form, so the dummy variables were additive in the logs. The colinearity between living area and number of rooms was reduced by taking area and area per room as the variables. The total explained variance, however, remains the same because, in logs, the variables are linear combinations of floor area and number of rooms.

[28]The city samples varied from 60 to 240 dwellings, with small centers such as Simla having 60, moderate centers such as Madurai having 90 dwellings, major centers such as Bangalore having 120, and Madras and Delhi having 180, Bombay and Calcutta 240.

Table 9.16. India: Rent Regression, Middle-Class Workers Sample, 1969

	Coefficient†	Standard error
Area	.748	.021
Area per room	−.443	.024
Veranda	.041	.009
Flush toilet	.122	.011
Electricity	.152	.011
Inside piped water	.090	.010
Area slope dummy for metropolitan	.113	.035
Constant	.789	.024
Intercept dummies for		
Average urban‡	−.096	—
Bombay	−.226	.050
Delhi	−.168	.047
Calcutta	−.067	.050
Madras	−.182	.048
$\overline{R}^2$ = 0.53	Mean of logs of rent: 1.484	
SEE = .232		

†In common logarithms.
‡Average for cities; see text.

In obtaining these estimates, the intercept coefficients for the various urban centers were averaged as they were for the rural-urban comparisons, but the intercept coefficients for the four metropolitan cities posed special problems. The difficulty is that reported rents in Bombay and Delhi do not correspond to average market rents. In Bombay, rents are controlled, and renters often make substantial additional payments to landlords every two or three years. (Bombay was said to be the only city in which such payments were common.) The Delhi rents are those actually paid by tenants, but for a substantial number of dwellings owned by the government of India and rented to government employees, the rents paid are below the market value. It was felt that if true market rents could be observed, rents in Bombay would be the highest, followed by rents in Delhi, Calcutta, and Madras. In these circumstances, we decided to take the Calcutta rents as the closest approximation to market rents that could be obtained for the metropolitan areas.

The urban-metropolitan rent ratios shown in Table 9.17 were averaged, using as weights the average of the urban and metropolitan sample distributions (Table 9.15). The final result is an urban-metropolitan ratio of 0.69.

Comparison of metropolitan India with the United States. For purposes of international comparisons, it seemed desirable to have information on more specifications of the dwelling unit than could be obtained from the data gathered in connection with the middle-class consumer price index. Accordingly, the CSO arranged for a special survey to be conducted by the NSS in Greater Bombay; it sampled heavily in areas that had a high proportion of large concrete apartment dwellings of the type of construction found in all the world's large cities. Nearly 1,500 usable observations were obtained in the survey, which was conducted over the period from July 1970 to June 1971. In addition to information on the floor area and the presence or absence of inside water, flush toilets, and electricity—all contained in the middle-class rent data—information was obtained on the average age of the dwelling, the main material of construction, and the presence or absence of a private bathroom.

This sample provided a unique link between rents and date of construction. Although age of structure was a variable tabulated for the middle-class cost of living survey in the early 1960s, it had not been collected in 1969. Bombay is a good choice from the standpoint of the age variable: it has had a population nearly 1 million for more than a century, so there is a large stock of older dwellings and room as well for newer dwellings on reclaimed land and in the northern and eastern suburbs. We already have noted that age of structure is important because newness itself may command a premium or new buildings may have more amenities, and rents may be higher in part because features are available that are not captured by other variables. Another factor, important in India, is that rent controls and lease rights tend to make rents less expensive for the same accommodation the longer the same tenant has occupied a given rental unit. Because tenants turn over slowly in India, old structures will have a higher proportion of tenants of long residence than new buildings and, hence, lower rents.[29] This phenomenon is not unusual in other countries, but it is pronounced in India.

[29] Two types of evidence from the middle-class rent sample support these propositions. First, the turnover of persons in the sample dwellings in 1961–69 was estimated by the NSS to be under 5 percent. Second, in the 1961 middle-class sample, there was a direct question asking how long the tenant had rented the accommodation. This variable was not available for all centers.

Table 9.17. India: Estimated Rents per Square Meter for Urban and Metropolitan Areas, Urban-Type Dwelling, 1969

Area	Square meters in dwelling α					
	5–10	10–15	15–20	20–30	30–40	40–50
			(rupees per square meter)			
Urban	1.70	1.49	1.37	1.25	1.15	1.08
Metropolitan†	2.28	2.13	2.03	1.93	1.84	1.77
Urban/Metropolitan	.75	.70	.68	.65	.62	.61

†Based on Calcutta; see text.

Table 9.18 gives the results of a regression equation in which Bombay rents were taken as the dependent variable and the various characteristics of the dwellings as independent variables. Among the latter, floor area and age were treated as continuous variables, and the others were incorporated by means of the dummy variable technique. A reasonably high proportion of the total variation in rents is explained, and the coefficients seem plausible.

For purposes of comparing metropolitan Indian rents with U.S. rents, we seek specifications of dwelling units that are common both in India and in the United States. This means that, with respect to size and facilities, we had to pick units that are near the upper limits of the Indian sample and near the lower limits of the U.S. sample. The comparative distribution of dwellings by size is shown in Table 9.19. By stretching a little our rule of avoiding observations outside of a country's middle 90 percent range, we may compare units with floor areas of 45 and 60 square meters. The 45-square meter size is probably a little below the fifth percentile from the bottom of the U.S. size distribution, but we have ample observations (11 percent of the BLS sample[30]). The 45-square meter size is well within the middle 90 percent range of all Indian housing but is near the top size for rental housing. For each of these sizes, we distinguish four different dates of construction. We compare Indian dwellings in concrete buildings having private bathrooms but without flush toilets to U.S. dwellings with a half bath. Thus, we compare rents for eight specifications. The specifications and the Bombay rents may be seen in Table 9.20.

Two adjustments are necessary to obtain national average rents from the Bombay rents. First, the Bombay rents have to be adjusted to the Calcutta level to represent our best judgment about the metropolitan average. The coefficients in Table 9.16 indicate that this requires a 44 percent increase in the Bombay rents.

The other adjustment is to correct the metropolitan rents to national averages. The formula, given in Chapter 6, is:

$$R_n = \left[R_m \cdot w_m \right] + \left[R_m \left(\frac{R_u}{R_m} \right) \cdot w_u \right] + \left[R_m \left(\frac{R_u}{R_m} \right) \left(\frac{R_r}{R_u} \right) \cdot w_r \right],$$

where R is rent, n national, m metropolitan, u urban, r rural, and w weights. We have estimated $\frac{R_u}{R_m}$ to be .69 and $\frac{R_r}{R_u}$ to be .61.[31] The weights, which are expressed as proportions so that their sum equals 1, are derived from the number of households in Table 9.14 and the rent data underlying Table 9.15. The formula indicates that national average rents are 53 percent of metropolitan rents. Taking account of this adjustment and of the Bombay-Calcutta adjustment, national average rents are 76 percent of the estimates yielded by the Bombay equation.

The resulting Indian national average rents are shown in column 2 of Table 9.20, together with the corresponding U.S. rents estimated from the U.S. regression equation. The averages for the eight purchasing-power equivalents are as follows:

	Rupees per dollar
A. Simple geometric mean	1.75
Weighted arithmetic means:	
B. India weight	1.72
C. U.S. weight	1.78
D. Fisher index	1.75
E. Official exchange rate	7.5
F. Price ratio (D÷E)	U.S. = 100 / 23.4

Because the percentage change in rents between 1967 and 1970 was identical in the two countries, these estimates apply to both years.

JAPAN–UNITED STATES

The data. The Japanese data were derived from special tabulations of the 1968 housing census in which separate tables were prepared for (1) privately owned rented dwelling units with exclusive facilities, (2) privately owned dwelling units sharing facilities, and (3)

Whenever it could be included in an equation estimating rent for individual centers, however, the coefficients were negative and significant, meaning that for the same amenities, rent would be less the longer one had rented the same accommodation.

[30]See footnote 15.

[31]w_m = .07; w_u = .25; and w_r = .68.

Table 9.18. India: Coefficients of Regression Equation for Bombay Rents, 1970–71

Independent variables	Coefficient†	Standard error
1. Space in sq. ft.	.5836	.0176
2. Age of building	−.1969	.0162
3. Concrete structure	.0789	.0132
4. Water in residence	.0544	.0144
5. Bathroom		
With tub	.1389	.0484
Without tub	.0679	.0248
6. Own flush toilet	.0837	.0256
7. Electricity		
Electricity and fan	.3071	.0275
Electricity	.0868	.0154
8. Intercept (nonconcrete constructions, new building, without water, bathroom, latrine or electricity in dwelling)	.1346	.0449

$\overline{R}^2 = .72$ Arithmetic mean rent: 28.78

SEE = .41   Mean of logs of rent: 1.240

†Common logarithms.

owner-occupied dwelling units. Only the first of these tabulations was used as a source of rental data for the comparisons. The relative importance, size, and average rents of these units may be compared with those in the other categories as follows:

	Number of dwellings (000)	Average floor area (sq. m.)	Average rent (yen)
All dwelling units	24,198		
Privately owned			
Rented			
Exclusive facilities	4,527	37.64	7,191
Shared facilities	2,000	17.51	5,479
Owner-occupied	14,594	85.36	—
Publicly owned	1,403	37.57	3,838
Issued	1,674	49.67	1,850

The tabulations for privately owned rented dwelling units with exclusive facilities included cross-classifications according to area (for example, rural versus urban), structural type (wooden detached house, wooden apartment) and water supply and bathroom installations. As a result of these cross-classifications, there were 240 tables, each of which provided data on the number of units, the floor area, and average rent for dwelling units further cross-classified by size (under 30 square meters, 30 to 50 square meters, and so on), and by date of construction (before 1955, 1956–60, and so on). Thus, privately owned rental dwelling units having exclusive facilities were cross-classified into 5,760 cells, each of which provided a fairly narrow specification with respect to the key characteristics affecting the rent of dwelling units.

Selection of the specifications. It was decided also to concentrate on a comparison of units that enjoyed private facilities, because shared facilities are rare in the United States. In the United States, units with no bathroom facilities were lumped with those sharing some facilities, and the combination of the two accounted for only nine percent of rented dwellings; the other 91 percent had at least one full bathroom (three fixtures including sink, flush toilet, and tub).[32]

In Japan, on the other hand, units with shared facilities made up about one-third of the privately owned rented dwellings, and even among those with exclusive

[32] U.S. Bureau of the Census, *1970 Census of Housing* (Washington: Government Printing Office, 1971).

Table 9.19. Comparative Distribution of Indian and U.S. Dwellings by Size

	India			United States		
No. of rooms	Area (M²)	All housing (%)	Rental housing (%)	Area (M²)	All housing (%)	Rental housing (%)
One	15.5	49.0	57.3	34.8	1.8	4.0
Two	31.1	26.4	28.3	55.8	3.5	7.5
Three	41.4	11.3	9.1	65.1	11.0	22.8
Four	42.7	5.9	3.6	70.0	20.8	30.1
Five plus	68.3	6.0	1.8	95.6	75.1	20.0
Six				115.5	20.1	10.1
Seven					9.5	3.3
Eight or more					8.2	2.2
Total	27.1	100.0	100.0	95.6	100.0	100.0

Sources:
India: Area and rental housing estimated from 1968-69 National Sample Survey; 23rd Round; all housing from *Census of India, 1961,* Vol. 1, Part IV (B), *Housing and Establishment Tables,* Table E-V.1. Office of Registrar General. (New Dehli: 1967).
United States: Area estimated (see text); all housing and rental housing, *1970 Census of Housing, Detailed Housing Characteristics,* U.S. Summary, Table 30.

Table 9.20. Comparison of Indian and U.S. Rents, 1970–71

	Monthly rents			
	India Bombay	National (Rs)	U.S. ($)	India–U.S. Rs/$
	(1)	(2)	(3)	(4) = (2) ÷ (3)
45 M^2				
1910s	192.34	70.18	37.17	1.89
1930s	100.88	76.67	44.78	1.71
1950s	119.26	90.64	56.19	1.61
1960s	148.08	112.54	70.12	1.60
60 M^2				
1910s	109.24	83.02	41.65	2.00
1930s	119.32	90.68	50.17	1.81
1950s	141.06	107.21	62.96	1.70
1960s	175.12	133.09	78.57	1.69

facilities, only 6.5 percent had both a flush toilet and a tub. Owner-occupied dwellings in Japan were only a little better equipped; about 8 percent had both flush toilet and tub. More than 80 percent of owner-occupied dwellings, however, and nearly 40 percent of rental units had tubs. Thus, it seemed warranted to take two overlapping specifications between Japanese and U.S. units with respect to bathroom facilities: one, in Japan, referring to a full bathroom and the other to a bathroom with no tub; and another, in the United States, to a bathroom with any two of the three fixtures.

The Japanese data were subdivided into four types of structures: wooden detached houses, wooden apartments, concrete apartments, and "others." It seemed likely that the concrete apartments were most similar to American dwelling units; 90 percent of them had flush toilets and two-thirds had both toilets and tubs. The mix of these structures between those made with reinforced concrete and those simply of fire-resistant concrete block is unknown. The latter approximate the structural qualities of most U.S. dwelling units that are built of brick, concrete block, or wood with insulation, lath, and plaster. The former are more substantial than the average U.S. dwelling, although some reinforced concrete structures are found in the United States as well. But taking account of the fact that concrete apartments in the Japanese setting, constituting only 2.5 percent of the privately owned rented units with exclusive facilities, represent luxury or semiluxury units that tend to be found in desirable locations, it is not unlikely that, on the average, they are of somewhat higher quality than the average U.S. rental unit with equal facilities. On the other hand, the wooden structures, which constitute over three-quarters of all privately owned Japanese rented dwellings with exclusive facilities, are clearly built less sturdily and with less insulation than the average U.S. structure.

In the U.S. data, the distinction is made between dwellings in multiple unit structures and various kinds of single units (detached, semidetached, and attached).

Other things being held constant, the rents for dwellings in multiple unit structures are about 4.5 percent higher than those for the others.

Because the Japanese concrete structures are probably above the overall U.S. average, a reasonable structural matching is to set rents for Japanese concrete units against rents for U.S. dwellings in multiple-unit structures. The disadvantage of this procedure is that it bases the comparison upon a small, high-quality segment of Japanese housing.

Thus, it was desirable to find a way to draw into the comparisons the wooden structures that are so important in Japanese housing, even though they cannot be matched in the United States. One method considered was to find a basis for adjusting the rents of these structures to represent rents for fireproof structures that would correspond more closely to the types found in the United States. We experimented with construction-cost data referring to 1958 for three types of structures—wooden buildings, simple fire-resistant structures (with concrete-block outer walls or comparable structure), and reinforced-concrete structures.[33] Japanese costs for the simple fire-resistant structures were about one-third more than for the wooden structures.[34] It seems likely, however, that the cost of fireproof structures fell relative to the cost of wooden structures in the period after 1958, particularly because the price of lumber rose sharply relative to the prices of other building materials. Therefore, a quality adjustment factor of 25 rather than 33 percent seemed more appropriate: that is, an increase of 25 percent was necessary to make the rents on Japanese dwellings in wooden structures comparable to the rents of U.S. dwellings other than those in multiple-unit structures. We made some preliminary calculations of PPPs based on such estimates of Japanese rents: for an urban dwelling of 55.8 square meters (600 square feet) with toilet and tub 1968 PPPs were 229 and 256 yen per dollar for buildings constructed in 1961–65 and in 1966–68, respectively. When Japanese concrete apartments were compared with U.S. dwellings in multiple-unit structures, the corresponding PPPs were 275 and 252 yen per dollar.

This adjustment factor, however, is subject to unsatisfactorily wide margins of error, and we finally adopted another approach to the estimation of Japanese rents based on the concrete apartment specification but taking into account the rents on wooden dwellings.

The method consisted of using the data for wooden dwellings to help determine the rent differentials for dwellings of different floor area, facilities, and dates of

[33] Housing Bureau, Ministry of Construction, *Housing in Japan, 1960* (Tokyo: Bureau of Statistics, 1961), p. 8.

[34] Estimated on the basis of midrange costs for dwellings with 35 square meters of floor area. The reinforced concrete dwellings were 25 percent more expensive than the simple fire-resistant structures.

Table 9.21. Japan: Coefficients of Regression Equation for Rents, 1968

Variable	Coefficient†	Standard error
Intercept‡	7.0582	.1132
Floor area (sq. m.)	.3016	.0249
Year built		
1956–60	.4924	.0450
1961–65	.5879	.0436
1966–68	.7039	.0454
Presence of		
Running water	.0177	.0471
Flush toilet	.4554	.0352
Tub	.2517	.0351
Concrete apartment	.2917	.0466

$\overline{R}^2$ = .76   Arithmetic mean rent = 9646 yen

SEE = .241   Mean of logs of rent = 9.034

†Natural logarithms.
‡Refers to wooden apartments or houses, built before 1956, and without running water, flush toilet, and tub.

construction. This was done by means of a regression based on 237 cells in the census tables, all relating to Japan as a whole. The observations were taken from twelve separate tables (four each) for wooden detached houses, wooden apartments, and concrete apartments. For each type of construction, the separate tables related to (1) dwellings without running water and (2) dwellings with running water with (a) a flush toilet, (b) a tub, and (c) both a toilet and a tub. In each of these twelve tables, average rents, average floor area, and number of dwellings were presented in a cross-classification for six floor-area categories (ranging from under 30 square meters to 150 square meters or greater) and for four periods of construction (1955 or before, 1956–60, 1961–65, and 1966–68). By using all the cells in the twelve tables that contained information for at least 100 dwellings, we obtained the 237 observations used in our regression work.

The dependent variable was the log of rent and the independent variables consisted of the log of floor area and dummy variables for (1) concrete apartments,[35] (2, 3, 4) three of the four age classes, and for the presence of (5) running water, (6) flush toilet, and (7) a bathtub. The equation is presented in Table 9.21.

This method may be compared with the most direct way of utilizing the Japanese census data, which is to take the rents for particular cells and to match them in each instance with U.S. rents for the same specification as that represented by the cell. The method we em-

ployed has the advantage of drawing upon more information to estimate the Japanese rent for each specification. Data about wooden and concrete apartments and apartments with and without toilet and tub are used to tell us what the difference in rent was for apartments of different sizes. Data relating to apartments with and without toilet and tub are used to tell us what the difference in rent was for wooden versus concrete apartments and so on.

We have indicated already that we would match Japanese concrete apartments with U.S. multiple-unit dwellings, in one series with full bath and in another series without a tub in Japan and with a half bath in the United States. It remains to choose the floor areas for which the matching will be done; the Japanese and U.S. rents can then be estimated from the regression equation for each country.

The distribution of Japanese dwelling units with respect to floor area is set out below for comparison with the U.S. distribution in Table 9.16:

Class limits (sq. m)	Mean (sq. m)	All housing† (%)	Rental housing (%)
Under 30	21.1	21.8	55.1
30–50	36.1	20.0	29.4
50–70	56.9	21.7	10.4
70–100	83.7	18.8	3.6
100–150	119.9	12.3	1.1
Over 150	197.1	5.4	0.3
Total		100.0	100.0

†Excludes publicly owned and issued housing, which accounts for about one-eighth of dwellings.

By stretching a little our rule of avoiding observations outside of a country's middle 90 percent range, we may compare units with floor areas of 45, 60, and 75 square meters. As already noted, we have ample observations for the 45-square-meter size, although it is probably a little below the fifth percentile from the bottom of the U.S. size distribution.[36] The 75-square-meter size is well within the middle 90 percent range of all Japanese housing but is near the top size for rental housing.

A final criterion used to increase the degree of comparability between Japanese and American units was the date of construction. The two more recent date-of-construction categories, 1961–65 and 1966–68, had certain advantages for the comparison: first, about half of Japanese privately owned rental dwelling units with exclusive facilities were built in these two periods; second, less than 0.1 percent of recently built units were in need of major repair and thus could be compared with "sound" units in the United States; and, third, there is some presumption that recently built units in Japan and the United States are more alike than are old units.

[35] When a separate dummy variable for wooden apartments was added, it indicated that rents for wooden apartments were about 4 percent lower than rents for wooden houses, holding size, facilities, and date of construction constant. The coefficient was less than twice its standard error, however, and the equation we selected for use in estimating rents does not contain this variable.

[36] See footnote 15, page 126.

Table 9.22. Comparison of Urban Rents, Japan and the United States, Selected Specifications, 1968

Variable	Japan (¥)	United States† ($)	Japan–United States (¥–$)
With flush toilet and bathtub			
1961–65			
45 square meters	18,730	69.85	
60 square meters	20,427	78.27	268.1
75 square meters	21,850	91.73	261.0
1966–68			238.2
45 square meters	21,015	78.47	
60 square meters	22,920	87.92	267.8
75 square meters	24,516	103.05	260.7
With flush toilet, no bathtub‡			237.9
1961–65			
45 square meters	14,516	59.37	
60 square meters	15,831	66.53	244.5
75 square meters	16,933	77.97	238.0
1966–68			217.2
45 square meters	16,288	66.70	
60 square meters	17,763	74.73	244.2
75 square meters	19,000	87.59	237.7
			216.9

Note: Apartments in concrete buildings in Japan; dwellings in multiunit buildings in the United States.
†Excludes U.S. subsidies, which added 0.4 percent to rents in 1967 and 0.6 percent in 1970.
‡Dwellings without tub in Japan and without one of three fixtures (sink, toilet, or tub) in the United States.

The comparisons. The result of these considerations was the selection of the twelve specifications of dwelling units, defined in terms of facilities, date of construction, and size. The specifications and the Japanese and U.S. rents for them are set out in Table 9.22. The estimation of U.S. rents for these specifications was based on the U.S. regression equation described earlier.

Average PPPs based on the twelve specifications are as follows:

	Yen per dollar		
		1968 extrapolated to	
	1968	1967	1970
A. Simple geometric mean	244	237	263
Weighted arithmetic means:			
B. Japanese weights	236	229	254
C. U.S. weights	243	237	262
D. Fisher index	240	233	258
E. Exchange rate	360	360	360
		U.S. = 100	
F. Price ratio (D÷E)	67	64.7	71.8

The 1968 figures have been extrapolated to the other years on the basis of the rent components of the consumer price index of each country. The 1967 and 1970 figures, unlike the 1968 data in Table 9.22, include the effects of U.S. rent subsidies, which added 0.4 and 0.7

percent, respectively, to the rents in the two years. Japanese rents were 65 percent of U.S. rents in 1967, 72 percent in 1970.

KENYA–UNITED STATES

The basic source of information on Kenyan rents was an expenditure survey of African households in Nairobi, Mombassa, and Kisumu conducted in mid-1970. A regression analysis was performed for 763 households reporting rental payments, following methods similar to those described in connection with the United States, Colombia, and India.

For a number of the characteristics of the dwelling units, answers to the questionnaire were consolidated; this left a maximum of twenty-six independent variables. In the equation adopted—see Table 9.23—twenty-two independent variables were used, including those indicating whether the landlord was an employer or public authority, as well as the characteristics of the dwelling relating to kitchen, plumbing, heating, and roofing and wall materials. The following variables were deleted because they did not produce significant coefficients and also, in one case (shared water pipe), yielded an untoward sign: (1) a house (rather than a flat), (2) a shared bathroom (or shower room), and (3) a shared inside water pipe or lack of water pipe (rather than a private inside water pipe). Owing to multicollinearity, the contribution to rent of these omitted variables could not be distinguished from that of the included variables. In any

Table 9.23. Kenya: Coefficients of Regression Equation for Urban Rents, 1970

Variable	Coefficient[†]	Standard error
Intercept	5.0661	0.1133
Employer-owned dwelling	−0.6838	0.0556
Government-owned dwelling	−0.4031	0.0642
Unit shared with another household	−0.1140	0.0438
Shared kitchen	−0.1172	0.0615
No kitchen	−0.2797	0.0663
Charcoal cooking fuel	−0.2503	0.0851
Firewood or paraffin cooking fuel	−0.1407	0.0927
Shared flush toilet	−0.0340	0.0703
No flush toilet or no toilet	−0.2003	0.0893
No electricity	−0.3904	0.0472
Walls other than stone, brick, or concrete	−0.4697	0.0644
Roof or iron	0.0650	0.0552
Roof of aluminum	−0.1001	0.0823
Roof other than tiles, iron, or aluminum	0.0342	0.0545
Two rooms	0.3159	0.0598
Three rooms	0.6269	0.0817
Four rooms	1.1018	0.1076
Five rooms	1.1012	0.1725
Six or more rooms	0.8922	0.2340
Unit located in Mombassa	−0.1905	0.0552
Unit located in Kisumu	−0.4101	0.0612

$\bar{R}^2 = 0.6266$

SEE = 0.5023

Arithmetic mean rent = 100.4

Mean of logs of rent = 4.250

[†]Natural logarithm.

case, the rent estimates did not differ much when these variables were included.

Rents were estimated from the selected equation for two-, three-, and four-room dwelling units of two types likely to be found in the United States. The characteristics of the units were a private house or flat having a private kitchen; running water; electricity in the dwelling; gas or electricity as cooking fuel; walls of stone, brick, or concrete; and a roof of tile. In addition, the unit could not be one that was shared or rented from an employer or from the government. Rents were estimated for (1) a unit meeting these requirements and having in addition a private toilet, and (2) for units having the given characteristics without the private toilet.

The rents in Kenyan shillings for these units in Nairobi were as follows:

	All facilities	No toilet
Two rooms	217	178
Three rooms	297	243
Four rooms	477	391

It can be seen from the regression equation that rents for identical facilities in Mombassa were 82.6 percent and rents in Kisumu 66.4 percent of those in Nairobi. In deriving national average urban rents, it was assumed that the level of Kisumu rents was representative of all excluded urban areas. Using population statistics from the 1969 census of weights, the rents of Nairobi, Mombassa, and Kisumu were averaged, assigning weights

of roughly 47, 23, and 30 percent, respectively. The result was that national average urban rents were estimated to be 86 percent of those of Nairobi.

Modern dwellings of the kind we have been considering are not found in rural Kenya. Rural housing consists of mud and wattle dwellings constructed by the family from local materials—mud and wood—obtained by family labor. Imputed rents on rural housing, which consist solely of owner-occupied units, are estimated for national-accounts purposes on the basis of the capital values of the units, which, in turn, are based on their imputed labor cost. To estimate the difference between imputed rents for mud-and-wattle dwellings in rural areas and such dwellings in urban areas is possible, therefore, on the basis of differences in labor rates and in location-scarcity values.

Some indication of rural-urban wage differences is given by the spread in minimum wages between Nairobi and one of the smallest towns, Naivasha: 175 versus 160 shillings per month, a difference of 8.6 percent. Other evidence is the difference in the housing allowance an employer had to pay in the same two cities if he did not provide an employee with housing: 35 versus 30 shillings per month, a difference of 14.3 percent.[37]   In view of these differences between urban areas, we have taken 20

[37]Both comparisons refer to July 1968 and are reported in Ministry of Economic Planning and Development, Statistical Division, *Statistical Abstract, 1969* (Nairobi: Statistical Division, 1969), p. 172.

percent as the urban-rural rent spread for equivalent types of dwelling units, thus making some allowance for location-scarcity values. Hence, taking into account that 10 percent of the population is urban and 90 percent rural, national average rents are around 70 percent of the Nairobi rents that were derived from the equation.[38] A final adjustment is needed such as the one required for the U.S. equation[39] to convert the rents derived from the double log equation from an estimate of median to mean rents. With a standard error of .5023, the adjustment factor comes to 1.14. Therefore, the Nairobi rents given in the previous text table must be multiplied by .80 to obtain our estimates of mean national rents.[40]

In addition to these urban averages, it was necessary to have some estimate of the floor area associated with each room size. The survey itself provided information only on the number of rooms (living rooms, dining rooms, and bedrooms) but not on floor area. Therefore, a means had to be found for estimating the floor areas associated with each number of rooms. This was done on the basis of about a score of different floor plans in *Homes for Kenya.*[41]

The average room sizes and the national urban average rents in Kenyan shillings estimated by the foregoing means[42] may be set out as follows:

| Number of rooms | All facilities | | Without flush toilet[43] | |
	Square feet	Rent	Square feet	Rent
Two	300	174	250	142
Three	450	238	400	194
Four	600	382	545	313

We need not again describe the source of the U.S. rent estimates, but can confine ourselves to a discussion of the problems of matching the specifications for which we estimated Kenyan rents.

In the end, it seemed inadvisable to attempt to estimate a U.S. rent for the smallest of the Kenyan specifications originally selected—that is, for the two-room Kenyan unit. Our estimated size for the two-room unit in Kenya, 300 square feet, was smaller than the smallest U.S. dwelling unit for which we could make any rent estimates. The smallest unit recorded in the U.S. statistics is a "one-room unit" in U.S. terms, and our estimated floor area for it is 375 square feet. But units this small accounted for only a little more than 3 percent of the BLS sample and only about 2 percent of all occupied

dwellings, urban and rural, rented and owner occupied, in the 1970 housing census.[44] Therefore, we confined the comparisons to the three- and four-room units.

Unfortunately, the Kenyan data do not include any information on date of construction. As already pointed out, the median construction date for the 1970 stock of U.S. dwellings fell in the early 1940s. We have assumed arbitrarily that the median for the Kenyan dwellings was in the mid–1930s. This may be too early, because the accumulation of durable housing units may be a relatively recent development in Kenya. If so, the error may offset that arising from what may be surmised to be the less substantial construction of Kenyan dwellings, even when all the features we can control are taken into account.

Table 9.24 shows the PPPs of Kenyan shillings to U.S. dollars for each of the four specifications. The PPPs vary between 4.54 and 7.08 shillings per dollar, with the smaller quarters being inexpensive in Kenya relative to the larger ones. Consequently, when weights are assigned to these four specifications based on the distribution of Kenyan and U.S. dwelling units, there is a large spread between the results produced by Kenyan weights and those produced by U.S. weights.

The results may be summarized as follows:

| | Kenyan shillings per dollar | |
	1967	1970
A. Simple geometric mean	6.28	5.70
Weighted arithmetic means:		
B. Kenyan weights	5.69	5.16
C. U.S. weights	7.67	6.95
D. Fisher index	6.60	5.98
E. Official exchange rate	7.143	7.143
	U.S. = 100	
F. Price ratio (D÷E)	92.4	83.7

The 1967 estimates were derived by applying an appropriate index to adjust each country's rents from 1970 to 1967.[45] Rents in Kenya on the average were around 8 percent less than those in the U.S. in 1967 and 16 percent less in 1970.

UNITED KINGDOM–UNITED STATES

The market for rental dwellings in the United Kingdom is stratified into a number of sectors between which

---

[38](.10 · .86) + (.90 · .86 · .80) = .705.

[39]See page 123.

[40].705 · 1.14 = .804.

[41]National Housing Corporation, *Homes for Kenya* (Nairobi: University Press of Africa, 1969).

[42]The Nairobi rents given on the preceding page have been multiplied by .80.

[43]It has been assumed that dwellings without flush toilets did not have separate bathrooms.

[44]U.S. Bureau of the Census, *1970 Census of Housing,* HC (1)-B1, Table 30.

[45]Between 1967 and 1970 rents in the United States increased by 11.2 percent according to the BLS rent index. For Kenya, no rent index is available. Rents were controlled, although small increases could occur in connection with new dwelling units. The change in the wage-earner consumer price index between December 1967 and December 1970 was 2.3 percent. It was assumed that rents increased by 1 percent.

Table 9.24. Comparison of Rents in Kenya and the United States, 1970

Dwelling and facilities	Kenya (Sh) (1)	U.S. ($) (2)	Sh/$ (3)
450-square-foot dwelling			
All facilities	238	50.85	4.68
No toilet	194	42.70	4.54
600-square-foot dwelling			
All facilities	382	53.96	7.08
No toilet	313	44.81	6.99

rents differ substantially. There is also a marked difference in rents between Greater London and the remainder of England and Wales. (Price comparisons for rents are based on data for England and Wales, but the expenditure data include Scotland and Northern Ireland as well.)

At the end of 1970, the most important sector of the market consisted of council houses, dwellings built and rented by local authorities, which accounted for less than one-half of the rented dwellings in London and about two-thirds of those in the rest of England and Wales. The next most important sector was the uncontrolled private sector, which provided about one-third of rental units in London and less than one-fifth of those in other parts of England and Wales. At the end of 1970, about one-eightth of these units were "registered." Registered rents are set by government authority upon application of either landlord or tenant, usually the former; such a rent is intended to be a fair rent that reflects market price excluding scarcity value. The remaining rental units, less than one-fifth of the London dwellings and about 15 percent of those outside of London, were rent controlled. The distribution of these types of units, in and out of London, are shown in Table 9.25.

Information relating rents to physical facilities was most readily available in connection with registered rents. A systematic sample of 517 registrations was selected from a 1970 total of around 29,000 registrations for analysis by the U.K. Department of the Environment (Statistics Housing). The department treated rents as the dependent variable in regressions in which the independent variables were number of rooms, state of repair, age of building, type of premise (flat, detached house, or whatever), location, and amenities (hot water, bath, and the like). The estimates for registered rents, shown in Table 9.26, are derived from two regressions, one for Greater London and the other for the remainder of England and Wales, selected by the department from among those it estimated. For pricing, we chose 18 various specifications of four-, five-, and six-room dwellings, each being a frequently encountered type of rental unit. These sizes are common as well in the United States.

The rent estimates refer to rents of registered dwellings, and our need is for average national rents, inclusive of rates (taxes paid by occupants) and subsidies.

The first step in converting the rents estimated from the regression to national average rents was to calculate a weighted average rent for the eighteen specifications. The average came to £18.4 per month.

This average for registered rents, exclusive of rates, compares with an estimated £17.2 per month for the national average rent, inclusive of subsidies and of imputations of owner-occupied dwellings.[46] This national average is suitable for our purposes in that it includes rates. It has the disadvantage, however, of including owner-occupied dwellings, which, on the average, are larger than rental units, and it spreads the subsidies that are paid on rental units over all dwellings. The national average rent figure we are seeking would be lower on the first count and higher on the second count—in the latter case, because the ICP includes both private and public payments for current housing costs. It turns out, however, that these two factors are almost precisely offsetting, and therefore we have retained this average figure.[47]

Having this national average in hand, the conversion of regression estimates in Table 9.26 was accomplished in two stages. First, the London and non–London figures were combined with weights of 1 and 3, respectively, reflecting the relative proportions of dwelling units.[48] Second, the resulting figures were adjusted by

[46] This estimate was based on rents and subsidies from national accounts data and on the number of occupied dwelling units reported in the General Register Office, *Sample Census 1966* (London: Her Majesty's Stationery Office, 1968), extrapolated in 1970 on the basis of the change in population.

[47] According to the Department of Employment and Productivity *Family Expenditure Survey*, Report for 1969 (London: Her Majesty's Stationery Office, 1970), p. 9, owner-occupied payments for housing were about 22 percent higher than payments made by renters of unfurnished dwellings. This difference, taken in conjunction with an average rent per dwelling unit derived from national accounts data when subsidies are excluded, suggests a difference of around £3 per month in the cost of owner-occupied and rented dwelling units. The subsidies on rented dwelling units average out to about the same amount.

[48] Based on data in General Register Office, *Sample Census 1966*, England and Wales, Housing Tables, Part I, Table 6.

Table 9.25. Estimated Number of Tenancies, England and Wales, April 1971

	Greater London	Other (000)	England & Wales
Council tenants	690	4,130	4,820
Private tenants	910	2,140	3,050
Controlled	300	1,000	1,300
Uncontrolled	610	1,140	1,750
Registered	(80)	(140)	(220)
Total	1,600	6,270	7,870

Source: U.K. Department of the Environment (Statistics Housing).

Table 9.26. Estimation of Registered Rents from Regression Equations, 1970

Part A: Coefficients of equations

	London	Other
	(£ per year)	
Intercept	91.6	125.4
Good state of repair	45.9	30.1
Number of rooms	46.2	18.3
Sole use of bath	73.2	39.6
Type of premise	−103.9†	−86.3†
Pre-1919	−102.7	−43.6
Post-1939	67.0	20.0‡

Part B: Estimated Rents §

	London		Other	
	Shared or no bath	Sole use of bath	Shared or no bath	Sole use of bath
		(£ per year)		
4 rooms (61.8 sq. m.)				
Pre-1919	115.7	188.9	98.8	138.4
1919–39	218.4	291.6	142.4	182.0
Post-1939	285.4	358.6	162.4	202.0
5 rooms (82.8 sq. m.)				
Pre-1919	161.9	235.1	117.1	156.7
1919–39	264.6	337.8	160.7	200.3
Post-1939	331.6	404.8	180.7	220.3
6 rooms (87.6 sq. m.)				
Pre-1919	208.1	281.3	135.4	175.0
1919–39	310.8	384.0	179.0	218.6
Post-1939	377.8	451.0	199.0	238.6

Source: Regressions from the U.K. Department of the Environment (Statistics Housing). The sample was taken from a total of 28,952 rent registrations. The Greater London regression was based on 190 observations and the regression for the rest of England and Wales on 327. The R²s were 0.48 and 0.57, respectively. The standard errors of estimate were 6.0 (mean rent of 302.7) and 7.7 (mean rent of 167.7). Each equation had a couple of other variables that were not used for present purposes (terrace houses and flats in converted houses in the London equation, and detached houses and a particular location in the other). All of the coefficients were larger than two times their standard errors.

†Represents average mix of flats and houses in Greater London (20–80 percent) and in the rest of England and Wales (6–94 percent). The effect of this treatment is to produce the average rent in each area for the existing mix. Coefficients for terrace houses in the regression equation were −129.9 and −91.8, respectively.
‡Not included in regression. Arbitrary estimate. Coefficient for this variable in a regression, including all England and Wales (rejected in favor of separate equations for London and non-London), was £26.
§Each rent is estimated by summing coefficients from the appropriate equation. For example, the London rent of a four-room dwelling with private bath and built before 1919 is the sum of the intercept (91.6) and the coefficients for good state of repair (45.9), number of rooms (4 × 46.2), private bath (73.2), and type of premise (−103.9), and pre–1919 construction (−102.7).

multiplying by the ratio 17.2/18.4 and dividing by 12 to obtain the monthly average. The results are entered in Table 9.27 for comparison with U.S. rents of similar dwelling units. It should be added that all the calculations refer to unfurnished accommodations.

Estimates of average floor area required for the comparisons with the United States were taken from a Department of the Environment analysis of the registered rent sample cross-classifying room size and floor area.

It can be seen from the table that the PPPs range from £0.2206 to £0.3204 per U.S. dollar. The simple geometric mean is £0.2737. Aside from the fact that more sterling consistently was required to match the purchasing power of a dollar over accommodations built in 1919–39 than was needed for dwellings constructed earlier or later, there is no marked systematic variation in the PPPs.

As in the other binary comparisons, we computed weighted rent PPPs even though the assignment of weights involved arbitrary elements. The resulting rent comparisons are as follows:

	Pounds sterling per dollar	
	1967	1970
A. Simple geometric mean	.2561	.2737
Weighted arithmetic means:		
B. United Kingdom weights	.2530	.2704
C. United States weights	.2544	.2719
D. Fisher index	.2542	.2716
E. Exchange rate	.3571	.4167
	U.S. = 100	
F. Price ratio (D÷E)	71	65

Table 9.27. Comparison of U.K. and U.S. Rents, Selected Specifications, 1970

Specifications	United Kingdom (£)	United States ($)	United Kingdom–United States (£/$)
4 rooms, private bath			
Pre-1919	11.76	45.50	.2584
1919–39	16.32	50.94	.3204
Post-1939	18.78	65.78	.2855
4 rooms, shared or no bath			
Pre-1919	8.03	36.40	.2206
1919–39	12.57	40.75	.3084
Post-1939	15.05	52.62	.2860
5 rooms, private bath			
Pre-1919	13.73	56.18	.2444
1919–39	18.28	62.90	.2906
Post-1939	20.75	81.20	.2556
5 rooms, shared or no bath			
Pre-1919	9.99	44.94	.2223
1919–39	14.55	50.31	.2892
Post-1939	17.02	64.97	.2619
6 rooms, private bath			
Pre-1919	15.70	58.09	.2703
1919–39	20.25	65.04	.3191
Post-1939	22.72	83.98	.2706
6 rooms, shared or no bath			
Pre-1919	11.96	46.47	.2574
1919–39	16.51	52.03	.3173
Post-1939	18.98	67.18	.2825

Sources: U.K. rents calculated from Table 9.26 and adjusted to national average (see text). U.S. rents from regression equation. See pp. 124–125.

The 1967 comparisons are derived from those for 1970 on the basis of the relative changes in the U.K. housing component of the general index of retail prices and the U.S. rent component of the consumer price index.

The spread between the U.K. and the U.S. weighted averages is small, reflecting both the relatively small dispersion of the PPPs and the similarity in the distribution of weights in the two countries. The PPPs (£ per $) rose slightly between 1967 and 1970, but because of the depreciation of sterling, the U.K.–U.S. price ratio (that is, relative rents in dollar terms) declined between the two dates.

D. The Multilateral Comparisons

The binary comparisons were based on specifications of dwelling units that were tailored to obtain overlapping specifications for the United States and each other country with which it was compared individually. Excluded were specifications that were common to other countries but were rare or not to be found in the United States. Thus, dwellings with 35 square meters of floor area (about equivalent to one-room units in the United States) or less, and dwellings without such facilities as running water and electricity, do not figure among the specifications upon which the binary comparisons are based, although they are quite important in India, Japan, and Kenya.

THE USE OF STANDARD SPECIFICATIONS

One way to remedy this defect is to make a series of binary comparisons involving each possible pair of countries, selecting specifications most suited to each pair in turn. That would be the way to get the best binary comparisons for each pair, but it would be quite arduous because it would involve 36 additional pairs of countries.

What has been done instead is to make multilateral rent comparisons on the basis of 34 standard specifications of dwelling units drawn up so as to cover the entire range of kinds of dwelling units found in the ten countries with respect to size, date of construction, and presence or absence of running water, flush toilet, a bathtub or shower, electricity, and central heating. These specifications and the rents estimated for them may be seen in Table 9.28. (The original list included 38 specifications, but 4 of them—numbers 32, 33, 35, and 36—were not used in the analysis because rents for them were not available in at least two countries).

In general, an effort was made to estimate a rent for every one of the multilateral specifications that fell within the middle 90 percent of the type of dwelling units found in the country. The problems encountered in accomplishing this varied somewhat from country to country.

ESTIMATING THE RENTS IN INDIVIDUAL COUNTRIES

For France, the Federal Republic of Germany, and Italy, the only data available were the rents for seven

Table 9.28. Multilateral Rents, 1970

	Size	Date	Facilities	Colombia (P)	France (Fr)	Germany (F.R.)(DM)	Hungary (Ft)	India (Rs)	Italy (L)	Japan (¥)	Kenya (Sh)	U.K. (£)	U.S. ($)
1	15	1930	None										
2	25	1930	None					10.64			31.8		
3	35	1930	None					14.34			41.0		
4	15	1930	Electricity only	112†				17.46			54.8		
5	25	1930	Electricity only					13.00			51.9		
6	35	1930	Electricity only	177†			192‡	17.51		3,679	67.0		
7	25	1950	Electricity only					21.32		4,073	89.5		
8	35	1950	Electricity only	217§				20.69		5,846			
9	25	1930	All except heat					25.18		6,467			
10	35	1930	All except heat	442†						10,182	163.4		
11	45	1930	All except heat	535†			408‡			11,270	206.3	23.99	
12	60	1930	All except heat	735†			463‡			12,156	280.8	12.73	51.48
13	60	1910	Electricity only				530‡			13,258	410.6	15.95	57.67
14	60	1910	Electricity, toilet only		104.4	96.6	266¶	53.19	10,920			8.03	
15	60	1910	All except heat		139.8	115.2	297¶	73.10	17,820			13.06	40.70
16	25	1950	All except heat		196.2	138.6	504¶		17,160			16.74	47.89
17	35	1950	All except heat	540§						16,163			
18	45	1950	All except heat	653§			449#			17,891		26.11	
19	60	1950	All except heat	899§	193.8	144.6	509#			19,299		13.85	64.59
20	75	1950	All except heat	1257§			583#			21,049		17.36	72.37
21	90	1950	All except heat				717#		17,760	22,515		21.57	84.82
22	35	1960	All except heat				833#			23,785		23.31	94.94
23	45	1960	All except heat							21,487			
24	60	1960	All except heat		212.4	166.8				23,180			80.62
25	75	1960	All except heat						16,260	25,281			90.33
26	90	1960	All except heat							27,042			105.87
27	35	1950	All including heat							28,567			118.50
28	45	1950	All including heat				568#						74.24
29	60	1950	All including heat				624#						83.19
30	75	1950	All including heat		234.6	198.0	741#		25,500				97.49
31	90	1950	All including heat				893#						
32	35	1960	All including heat				1024#						109.12
33	45	1960	All including heat										92.66
34	60	1960	All including heat		265.8	213.0							103.82
35	75	1960	All including heat						23,520				121.69
36	90	1960	All including heat										136.19
37	75	1930	All including heat				652‡			14,182		19.83	67.60
38	90	1930	All including heat				757‡			14,982		21.42	75.66

†Estimated rent for 1940s date of construction less 10 percent.
‡Probably 1920s, but no adjustment made.
§Estimated rent for 1940s date of construction plus 10 percent.
¶Estimated rent for 1910s date of construction less 5 percent.
#Estimated rent for 1950s date of construction plus 10 percent.

specifications selected by the Statistical Office of the Common Market for its own PPP comparisons. These specifications simply were included among the 38 standard ones. As noted earlier, we assumed that the pre-1949 dwellings had a median date of construction that fell in the 1910s. We assumed also that the other dates of construction given in the EEC specifications, 1949-61 and 1962-70, fell squarely in the nearest decades, the 1950s and the 1960s, respectively.

One quality of the dwelling units that we would have liked to have been able to measure more adequately related to the quality of construction. We had some information about construction materials of dwelling units in some countries, but in others it was missing. In any case, we could not assess fully those differences in comfort—for example, in protection from wind, rain, and sounds of neighbors—which were afforded by differences in construction; but we did make a rough divi-

sion of the multilateral specifications into three classes according to quality of construction. The standard quality that prevails on the average in Europe and the United States was taken for all the specifications beginning with number (9). All the countries had some dwellings that met these specifications, but in addition, some had important components of their housing stock that represented a simpler type of construction.

Japan, for example, had concrete apartments that were clearly similar in construction to those found in Europe and the United States, but it also had wooden detached houses and wooden apartments that were much less substantial. Kenya also had some dwellings in its towns and cities that matched the standard ones, but it had others, with aluminum roofs and mud and wattle walls, that clearly were of a lower quality.

Therefore, we set aside some specifications, generally small in size and with few facilities or none, and specified lower standards of construction for them. Specifications number (1) through (3) represent very simple types of construction. In the case of Kenya, these dwellings were assumed to have aluminum roofs rather than the standard tile roofs and walls other than the standard stone, brick, or concrete. An intermediate quality of construction was represented by specifications four through eight. In this category were assumed to fall the Japanese wooden detached houses and Kenyan dwellings with standard roofs but walls other than the standard stone, brick, and concrete.

In India, on the other hand, the comparable quality distinction appeared to be, on the one hand, between concrete structures and, on the other hand, those of brick, mud, or stone. When a dummy variable was added for structures of brick, there was no significant difference in the rent from that of mud and stone dwellings. The brick dwellings in the rent sample probably are closer to the quality of the mud and stone dwellings than to the brick dwellings of Western Europe and the United States. Although brick construction of the latter quality is found in India, it is much more likely to represent an owner-occupied bungalow than a rented dwelling. Accordingly, we took concrete dwellings for the standard quality and those of brick, mud, or stone for the specifications calling for simple construction. For the intermediate quality of construction, we took brick, mud, or stone dwellings with electricity; the jump in rent with the addition of electricity, holding all else constant, suggests that electricity is serving as a proxy for other aspects of quality. At the next stage upwards in quality, an electric fan plays a similar role, and we included it, as well as the specification of a concrete structure, for the standard quality of construction.

In Colombia, a rent estimate for the lower standard of construction was taken as referring to a dwelling other than a house or apartment: that is, to rented rooms, a hut, or an improvised shelter. As in the case of India, the addition of electricity alone was used as a proxy for quality to provide the jump to the intermediate standard of construction.

The main problem in estimating Hungarian rents for multilateral specifications was the dating problem discussed earlier,[49] where we gave our reasons for placing the median date of construction for Hungarian dwellings in the 1920s. For the multilateral specifications calling for construction in the 1930s, we made no adjustment for the small difference it probably would make in the rent—a course recommended by our uncertainty about whether the median may not actually fall in the 1930s anyway. We simply deducted 5 percent to obtain the estimates for the 1910s and added 10 percent to derive those for the 1950s, these percentages being rough guesses based on data for other European countries (see

Table 9.2). Rents were adjusted to the standard floor areas called for by the multilateral specifications by interpolation from data on rents for dwellings of different room sizes and on the average floor area associated with each room size.

For Kenya, the rent estimates for the multilateral specifications were derived in the same way as those for the binary specifications, except that interpolation was necessary to adjust rents for different room sizes to the desired floor areas.

In the case of Colombia, it was necessary both to estimate the average date of construction and to interpolate for floor areas. It seems reasonably clear that the average age of Colombian residences falls in the 1940s. We assumed, on the basis of the data in Table 9.2, that the rents would be 10 percent less for dwellings built in the 1930s and 10 percent more for those built in the 1950s. For the interpolations—and, in the case of the 35-square-meter size, the extrapolation—we used the (linear log) relationship between sizes as estimated for the binary comparison and the regression coefficients for dwellings with different numbers of rooms.

For the United Kingdom, national average rents were estimated for dwellings with two, three, four, five, and six rooms by the methods outlined in connection with the binary comparisons. These rents were used to estimate by interpolation the rents of the floor areas called for by the standard multilateral specifications. Adjustment factors for the dates of construction and the presence or absence of facilities were estimated, in some cases roughly, from the coefficients of the equations.

THE COMPARISONS

Once having assembled the rent estimates for the multilateral specifications, we were in a position to apply the Country-Product-Dummy method described in Chapter 5 to derive multilateral rent comparisons. These rent comparisons, unlike those derived in the binary comparisons, are transitive and base invariant.

We used the double-weighted form of the CPD method. The weights were a product of two sets of weights. The first was determined by the relative importance within each country of the dwelling units for which rents were available. That is, these weights were based upon the percentage distribution of the dwelling units in each column in Table 9.28. The second set of weights took account of the relative importance of each country in the "world" total of the dwellings for each specification. That is, these weights were based upon percentage distribution of the quantities of housing in each row of Table 9.28. The quantities were obtained by dividing the binary rent comparisons into the expenditures. The PPPs resulting from these calculations are shown in Table 9.29, column 3.

For convenience in comparing these rents with those of the binary comparisons, the ideal index calculated in

---

[49]See page 129.

Table 9.29. Comparisons of Rents and per Capita Housing Quantities, 1970

Country	Currency unit	Ratio of expenditures	Purchasing power parity		Quantity per capita		
					Direct	Indirect	
			Binary	Multilateral	Floor area	Binary	Multilateral
		(Currency units for $US)			(U.S. = 100)		
		(1)	(2)	(3)	(4)	(5)	(6)
Colombia	(Peso)	1.144	11.4	10.64	–	10	11
France	(Franc)	1.870	3.03	3.48	54	61	54
Germany (F.R.)	(Deutschmark)	1.540	2.36	2.69	66	65	57
Hungary	(Forint)	1.518	9.31	8.54	44	17	18
India	(Rupee)	.0506	1.75	1.66	16	2.9	3.0
Italy	(Lire)	149.5	305	348	47	49	43
Japan	(Yen)	97.30	258	242	52	31	40
Kenya	(Shilling)	.1399	5.98	4.96	–	2.4	2.8
United Kingdom	(Pound)	.1451	.2716	.255	90	53	57
United States	(Dollar)	1.00	1.00	1.00	100	100	100

Notes: Column (1): Ratio of rent expenditures (ICP 03.11) in columns (3) and (4), line 52, Appendix Tables 13.1 to 13.9. Imputed rents on owner-occupied dwellings are included, but expenditures on repair and upkeep are not. For quantity comparisons including the latter, see summary binary tables, 13.1 to 13.7, lines 52 to 53.
Column (2): Fisher indexes; see Section C, this chapter.
Column (3): Double-weighted CPD results; see Section D, this chapter.
Column (4): Floor area per person reported in Table 9.1. Not corrected for quality differences in housing. Reference dates are as much as 10 years apart.
Column (5): The binary PPP for rent (ideal index) in column (2) is divided into the expenditure ratio for rent. The PPPs and therefore the quantity ratios refer to comparable qualities of housing in the United States and each partner country.
Column (6): As in (5) except that the multilateral PPPs of column (3) are divided into the expenditure ratio.

the binary comparisons has been tabulated in column (2). It can be seen that the multilateral PPPs for Colombia, Hungary, India, Japan, and the United Kingdom are within ten percent of the binary estimates. The largest difference, 17 percent, is for Kenya. Here, more credence surely should be attached to the multilateral result that is based on ten observations for Kenya than to the binary comparison, for which it was possible to find only four overlapping Keyan-U.S. specifications—even with some straining of the 90 percent rule. Indeed, the Kenyan case illustrates the advantage of using a generalized bridge–country method such as the CPD. An examination of Table 9.28 will indicate that no single country provides a good bridge for all the other countries. The CPD method does not restrict us to specifications available in a single bridge country; thus more rent observations generally can be utilized for each country.

E. Summary of Rent and Quantity Comparisons for Housing, 1970

Table 9.29 also contains (indirect) quantity per capita ratios (columns 5 and 6) derived by dividing the PPPs into the ratio of expenditures. In addition, the direct quantity per capita ratios (column 4) derived from the estimated floor area figures in Table 9.1, are presented. The latter clearly are less appropriate quantity indicators than the indirect measures; not only are they subject to large errors as measures of floor area, but also they are deficient for our purposes because they do not contain any quality adjustment for amenities. We already have indicated our methodological reasons for preferring the multilateral rent estimates, and they carry over to a preference for the corresponding quantity estimates. Each reader will have to judge for himself whether the indirect quantity measures produced by the multilateral approach are likely, in fact, to be closer to the mark than those produced by the binary approach. The chief difference between the two sets of results is that the binary approach indicates that the Federal Republic of Germany and France enjoy a significant margin of superiority in the per capita quantity of housing services relative to the United Kingdom. The multilateral estimates—which by method of construction make such comparisons among countries other than the United States more warranted—suggest that there is little or no difference. The French and German results (like those for Italy) are sensitive to the weighting scheme because the price ratios vary substantially among the seven specifications (see Table 9.11).

Chapter 10

Comparing prices of producers' durables

This chapter deals with the overall experience of the International Comparison Project in connection with the comparison of producers' durables; it includes discussions on the following topics:

- The characteristics of the detailed expenditure categories
- The specifications, their origins, and the present sample
- The collection of data
- The types of comparisons performed
- Data processing and the adjustment of prices to purchasers' values

The only feasible way to approach international comparisons of real capital formation is through direct price comparisons from which the quantity comparisons can be derived with the aid of expenditure ratios (see Chapter 2, Section B). This method has been followed for producers' durables, covered in this chapter, and for construction, covered in the next. In both cases, the general principles followed in selecting the specifications and in matching qualities were those outlined in Chapter 3, and discussion is confined to matters that are unique to these sectors.

In many respects, the international comparison of producers' durable goods prices presented greater difficulties than the comparisons for consumer goods. In many countries, price statistics on producers' durables are virtually nonexistent; where they do exist, they are invariably weaker than those available in the consumer-goods area. The evaluation of differences in technical specifications is more difficult than in the case of relatively simple consumer goods. Ascertaining market prices for producers' goods presents many more problems than for items that are widely sold to a large number of consumers. In countries in which price statistics are relatively good in the area of producers' durables, prices rarely are published, as is the case for some consumer-goods prices. Indeed, the national statistical authorities usually obtain price and specification information on a voluntary basis, with the understanding that price and other data will not be identified or disclosed to outside users. As a result, in most instances statistical offices were able to provide less extensive assistance to the ICP in the comparison of producers' durable goods prices.

This forced the ICP staff to devote a great deal of time to learning about producers' durables. Statisticians as consumers are fairly well acquainted with the nature of a wide variety of consumer goods: they may not be able to grade oranges or gauge the number of threads per square inch in a coat, but they certainly know what each item is. In connection with producers' durables, it may be possible for a statistician to identify a grader and a scraper that, in most countries of the study, are fairly common items in the road-building sector (they are used outside and therefore are observable), but items such as a dobby loom, a warper creel, a Banbury mixer, or a flexitray are not likely to be so readily identified—or, for that matter, explained.

A. Choosing Specifications

The first task, as in the case of consumer goods, was to identify specifications that could be priced in different countries. A tentative list of specifications was drawn up with the help of the U.S. Bureau of Labor Statistics (BLS); it provided at least several specifications in each of the score or so detailed categories within the producers' durable-goods sector.

The specifications provided the product name and a brief technical description of the item, listing the measurements or other attributes for what were felt to be the price-important or -critical variables. We had attempted to determine, through research and discussions with industry experts, those variables which played a critical role in price determination and which, therefore, were important to a valid comparison of products between countries.

These specifications were intended as a starting point in developing the products to be priced for each binary comparison. Each partner country involved in a binary comparison with the United States was asked (1) to determine which specifications were appropriate to its expenditure pattern for producers' durables, (2) to suggest desirable modifications in these specifications, and (3) to offer supplementary or substitute specifications as necessary.

A revised, expanded, and more detailed set of specifications, with illustrations for most of the items, was prepared, incorporating the suggestions of the participating countries. The addition of an illustration to accompany the specification was intended to provide a visual interpretation of the item to be compared because, in some areas, there were sometimes difficulties associated with the interpretation of technical terms.

It was hoped that each participating country would provide prices for a minimal number of specifications included in the revised list. Countries were invited, of course, to offer their comments on the suitability of the specifications (as with the first list), but we hoped that out of the enlarged list of items a significant number could be priced in all countries. We found almost immediately that a list comprising mainly products identical across all of the countries in the study was even less possible than in the case of consumer goods.

One difficulty was that the physical size of an item chosen to typify U.S. goods often was too large for the other countries. For example, track-type tractors are usually sold in the over-90-horsepower range in the United States, whereas in other countries, smaller horsepower is more common. Furthermore, the average size in other countries, although consistently smaller than in the United States, tends to vary from country to country. Operationally, this meant that if track-type tractors were to be included in the comparison, the size supplied by partner countries had to be found in the United States. We tried, of course, to compare prices for as large a range of overlapping sizes as was available for a given type of machine in both the United States and the partner-country markets. Often, however, only one size (or a small-size range) was to be found in the other country's market.

In other respects as well, the U.S. variant of the item was not typical in the partner country. In the case of agricultural equipment and implements, for example, different types of soils, terrains, and crops determine the type of equipment purchased by the farmer. Often this meant that a particular type of harrow or plow would not be suitable as a representative item for a particular country. Only because the agricultural output, terrain, and soil are so diversified in the United States was it possible to accept, as items to be compared, almost all types of agricultural equipment.

Finally, some items simply are not to be found in some countries, are unimportant in terms of expenditures, or are extremely difficult to price because there is only one purchaser. Examples included textile machinery in Kenya, some types of service-industry machinery in India, aircraft in Hungary, and telephone-switching equipment in the EEC countries.

As already suggested, the basic way of minimizing these difficulties was to attempt to match with U.S. prices virtually all specifications offered by other countries. To have insisted upon a set of specifications that were common across all countries would have meant a very small number of comparisons: in fact, it would have made any significant comparison of producers' durables impossible.

The outcome was that a reasonably common list of general kinds of items were included in all the binary comparisons, but the particular variant of the items differed from one binary comparison to another. Thus, farm tractors are found in all of the comparisons, but the farm tractors in one comparison may be of 50 horsepower, for another, 75 horsepower, and for a third, 100 horsepower.

Altogether, a total of 1,000 variants of over 100 different producers' durable goods were included in the various binary comparisons. The types of items are listed by ICP detailed category in Appendix 1 at the end of this chapter. Not all items or identified variants of the same items appeared in each comparison, because either some were not available in each country or the expenditure on the item was insignificant.

B. The Collection of Data

For most of the countries in the study, the collection of prices and specifications was undertaken by the national statistical offices. The main exceptions were in the case of the Federal Republic of Germany, France, and Italy, for which the data collection was organized by the Statistical Office of the European Economic Community, and the United States, for which the data collection was undertaken by the ICP directly.

In the initial stages of the work, a list was drawn up of major U.S. suppliers covering all the ICP detailed producers' durable-goods categories. Data on specifications and list prices were requested from each firm. Care was taken to canvass suppliers in general rather than only domestic producers: in a number of cases, the products representative of U.S. expenditures are produced abroad. Over 300 manufacturers or other suppliers were contacted for information. The response on the part of the firms was extremely good, with informative replies received from roughly 90 percent.

At this stage, we had not requested information that was not generally in the public realm. That is, we limited our requests basically to information published by firms without restrictions as to dissemination.

Most U.S. companies make available current price sheets, either as information for potential buyers or as aids for their own sales representatives and/or distributors. These sheets "list the prices" (hence "list price" or "suggested list price") at the factory for the basic machine and for all additional equipment that may be added or that may replace (as an option) the basic equipment. For example, a price sheet for a truck with a gasoline engine may list as an option a diesel engine at additional cost. It may list also the additional cost for such items as nonstandard tires. Because a truck with many possible variations can be priced as may be required from comparison to comparison, these price sheets allow considerable flexibility in the approach to the comparison of producers' durables.

Furthermore, and of major importance, the price sheets helped the ICP staff to determine those components which were price important in relation to total cost. In other words, they assisted in defining the specification for the product so that when a comparison actually was performed, we could be reasonably sure that we had covered the major part of the cost—or at least not overlooked price-important components. During the initial collection, we acquired prices for over 50,000 items (including variations to basic items) from the 300 companies. Most of the prices collected were current (1969) prices. We requested current prices because this reduced the burden on the respondent, and for the United States, detailed price indexes are available for adjusting the prices to the reference periods of the ICP.

Most U.S. companies also supply detailed technical specifications of the products they sell (sometimes technical specifications appear on the same sheets as the prices). These "spec sheets" provide physical dimensions and performance or capacity data (usually under different conditions) for the products. The actual comparisons were made on the basis of the published technical descriptions that were collected, and the price data for components were used to build up an overall price that corresponded to the technical specification.

The ICP staff member in charge of the producers' durable-goods price comparisons visited some of the other countries to facilitate agreement on matching specifications, and experts on producers' durable goods from several of the other countries visited the United States. Specification sheets of the products commonly used in other countries were obtained whenever they were available.

To supplement the data originally collected, additional price and specification information was collected during later stages in the comparison. This supplementary collection was necessary because the United States was involved in the nine basic binary comparisons reported on herein, and thus U.S. prices had to be obtained to match all specifications received from partner countries (see Section A). The additional collection was relatively small in scale. It involved mainly the sending of foreign specifications to the major producers or suppliers in the United States for assistance in comparison. Usually the specifications that were sent to manufacturers and suppliers were for fairly complex types of procucts for which the ICP staff had not developed an expertise. In such cases, we found the assistance provided by industry experts to be substantial (see Section C on matching).

Information also was requested on the amount of discount that the producer offered final purchasers. This type of information usually is not available to the public, and less than half of the companies that replied to our request for data supplied a discount rate. We were able, however, to acquire a fairly good indication of the average discount to final purchasers for every ICP detailed category. Some products, of course, receive no discount from the producers' or distributors' list price, and others are discounted at different rates according to either the class of buyer or the size of shipment, or to both. Discounts were required, along with price indexes and other information (see Section D on data processing), in order to derive final users' prices from the list prices that were collected originally.

The producers' durable-goods prices gathered from the United States and other countries were collected under a pledge of confidentiality. In accordance with the advance understanding, no country has received the prices of any other country, and the prices have been used in a way that prevents the disclosure of the price of any individual firm.

C. Matching Techniques

The most difficult and time-consuming part of the producers'-durables segment of the study was the actual matching of the products for which prices were received from the countries. Virtually every product comparison raised some questions that had to be resolved through the collection of additional information, either from U.S. companies or from the country that supplied the price.

The main matching methods used were physical identity and quality equivalence. In certain cases estimation by using a single critical variable was used (see Chapter 3).

Only in cases where brand name and model number were the same in both countries could we be certain of physical identity. For many of the binary pairs, comparisons based on identical brand and model were made mainly for office machinery, agricultural tractors, and construction machinery.

Major kinds of office machinery are supplied on the world market by a relatively few manufacturers, and model numbers across countries are the same. Furthermore, there is little or no variation possible in the configuration (that is, the combination of specifications) of a given piece of office machinery (with the exception of computers) for a given model number. Thus, given the brand name and model number of a product, we were reasonably sure that a valid technical comparison was being made.

In the case of agricultural tractors as well, there is a relatively small number of worldwide producers. Although the model numbers are the same across countries, tractors are more complex in the sense that more variants can exist for a particular model than office machinery. For example, utility, row crop, and orchard tractors with the same model number can be found—but with a significant difference in price. Therefore, in this particular area and even though we were dealing with a relatively few brand names and model numbers, it was important to have as precise a description of the configuration as possible in order to make a valid comparison. Once they were adequately specified, however, no adjustments were deemed necessary for tractors. On the other hand, other agricultural equipment, though also produced by the tractor manufacturers, tends to vary in model number and basic type from region to region, and therefore it could not be compared on the basis of physical identity.

Neither are there many international producers of construction machinery and equipment: in fact, U.S. manufacturers and their licensees supply 85 to 90 percent of the world market (excluding Eastern European countries) for this type of equipment. In general, therefore, we were comparing a limited number of products, and the main problem, as for agricultural tractors, was simply one of adequate specification.

By far the most usual type of matching involved products produced by different firms. Overall, about three-quarters of all the comparisons fell into this category; in the case of Hungary, the percentage was much greater, and in Kenya and Colombia, it was much lower because of their high dependence on imports of producers' durables that could be compared on a brand-name basis.

Often it was possible to find nearly identical specifications despite production by different manufacturers. This occurred mainly in the case of such relatively simple types of machinery and equipment as electric motors, pumps, and compressors. In many cases, however, products were similar but not enough alike to be regarded as equivalent. Where large differences existed, of course, the products had to be dropped from the comparison.

Where the differences were not fundamental, various ways were used to estimate the price for an equivalent product. In a few cases, a specification in one country fell between two similar but not identical specifications in a second country. The application of the straddle method (see Chapter 3) in such cases permitted the comparison of the average price of the two specifications in the second country with the single price of the first country. The straddle method was advantageous, for example, in the comparison of flexitrays having slight differences in diameter but otherwise of the same quality characteristics.

Equivalence was established in a number of cases by averaging price comparisons obtained by matching the specification of one country with a number of similar specifications in the second country, each of the latter matching the former with respect to one price-determining influence. Assume, for example, that the price-important variables for an electric motor are (1) the horsepower (HP), (2) the revolutions per minute (RPM), and (3) the weight. Assume also that we have prices for one specification from Country A and for three specifications from the United States, as follows:

	Country A	U.S. 1	U.S. 2	U.S. 3
HP	25	25	26	24
RPM	1800	1750	1800	1850
Weight	50	48	52	50

None of the U.S. motors is much different from the Country A motor, but none is exactly the same. Each of the U.S. specifications has one element that matches the Country A specification: the first motor matches in horsepower; the second, in RPM; and the third, in weight. Three different price ratios can be formed with the Country A specification, each based on an exact match for one of the critical variables, with the other variables not being much different. An unweighted geometric mean of the three price ratios then may be formed to represent the comparison of the electric motor.

This method was extremely useful for utilizing price observations for nearly matching specifications. The possible drawbacks are that, first, equal weight is assigned to each price-determining characteristic on which models are aligned, although some may be more important than others; and second, the variables not used in each matching may bias the price comparison (for example, if a 90-horsepower luxury car were compared with a 90-horsepower compact).

But these potential disadvantages were minimized in our procedures. We usually did not apply the method where differences in key specifications were as large as 10 percent. In addition, we usually based the averaging on five to ten different characteristics and tried to avoid the bias referred to above by matching products with equal or offsetting values for the remaining characteristics that were not taken as the specifications to be matched in the particular case.

In the case of Hungary, however, some deviations occurred from the 10 percent rule. The weight of the machinery and equipment in relation to other variables tends to be higher in Hungary, even when the specifications are comparable to those of the United States and the other countries in other respects. We ignored the weight differences in these instances and concentrated on matching all other variables.

Specifications sometimes were matched on a one-to-one basis, and the price of one was adjusted to take account of the differences between them. Also, averaging occasionally was used when it was difficult to determine which of two specifications matched one in another country. In some cases the adjusted price could be estimated by the use of a single variable. For example, within certain technical limits, cotton-roving machines and spinning frames may be priced accurately according to the number of spindles, ovens by the square feet of heating surface, and cooling cabinets by cubic capacity.

In other instances, outside experts were relied upon to make quality adjustments. The outside experts whose aid was sought were involved almost routinely with the products on a day-to-day basis for complex specifications ranging from locomotives to transformers.

The guidance of the industry experts usually led us to use one of the matching methods described above, but in a few cases we relied directly upon their knowledge and judgment for quality adjustments. For example, in the comparison of locomotive prices, the experts' knowledge of the usual configuration of the locomotives that one of our countries purchased led us to adjust the U.S. price in order to account for features that usually would not be picked up in a technical specification. In another instance, because the quality of the output of a particular company differed from that of other competitors in a way that was well known in the industry but not apparent from the technical descriptions, expert judgement was used as the basis for adjusting prices for a quality difference.

On the other hand, it must be pointed out that, in some instances, industrial experts expressed skepticism at the validity of comparisons for producers' durables on the grounds that there were too many variables, both technical and nontechnical, that must be considered. In the area of machine tools, for example, an industry expert considered that one company's machines were unique and could not be compared meaningfully with machines of another manufacturer. In a strict sense he was correct: the technical specifications in all elements would not be exact matches, nor would the quality of the machines be precisely the same. In the market for machine tools, however, it is apparent that there are machines that do compete on the basis of their specifications and performance, and that a meaningful comparison of the prices for these alternative machines can be made.

The derivation of price ratio of producers' durables by means of regression methods described in Chapter 8 was applied to sixteen products, mainly to generate U.S.

prices for a variety of specifications. The products in the producers' durables sample studied by regression methods included railroad boxcars and hoppers; passenger cars and trucks; utility aircraft; diesel and gasoline engines; tractors, balers, and combines; compressors and pumps; forklift trucks; and electric motors.

The work included the preparation of descriptions (including key quantifiable characteristic variables) of the above producers' durables. For purposes of data collection, it was necessary to define the scope of the sample to be used for the regressions, as well as the individual variables for which data were required in the case of each item.

In connection with the scope of the sample, we tried to avoid the inclusion of very different kinds of models so as to keep the number of variables affecting price within easily manageable limits. For example, for purposes of the regression sample, a diesel engine was defined, to include all the equipment between "the fan and flywheel" that is necessary for the operation of the engine: engine, air cleaners (one stage), alternator, oil cooler; electric starter and generator; oil, fuel and jacket-water pumps; flywheel and housing; turbo charger and aftercooler, when standard; and the exhaust manifold. We specifically excluded two-stage air cleaners, specialized exhaust fittings, specialized governors, radiators or heat exchangers, and clutch or gear boxes. Diesel engines with these additional features could have been included and handled by intercept and slope dummies, of course; but, unless many observations were added to take account of these features, the regression only would have been complicated with no concomitant increase in the precision of the estimates of prices for particular specifications.

According to our experience with the United States, most of the information necessary to compile the samples is available from those brochures, catalogs, and price sheets which manufacturers normally would issue (see Section C) for marketing purposes; this information can be gathered from the major producing firms. Most often, those features which are included in the standard models and those which are offered as options differ from one firm to another. As a result, considerable time and care were required to prepare the data for regression analysis.

The result of these procedures was that the number of different kinds of producers' durable goods for which prices were matched in the binary comparisons with the United States ranged from 33 to 63, except for Japan, for which comparisons were available for only 18 different types. Comparisons usually were made for more than one specification of a good. A total of 41 specifications (of the 18 goods) were compared for Japan and the United States, more than 80 in the case of the comparisons involving the Common Market countries, and from more than 100 to 200 each in the comparisons of Colombia, Hungary, India, Kenya, and the United Kingdom with the United States. For each binary comparison, price ratios were unavailable for some detailed categories, and for aggregation purposes, the price relative for one or more other categories had to be assigned to the category for which price comparisons were missing. In the Hungary–United States comparison, for example, there were no price comparisons for aircraft (ICP 14.400), ships and boats (14.500), and other transport equipment (14.600), so for purposes of aggregation the geometric mean of the price relatives for locomotives (14.110), passenger cars (14.200), and trucks, buses, and trailers (14.300) was taken as the price relative for the missing categories. Sometimes, as in this instance, the missing information betokened small expenditures in the U.S. partner country, but this was not always the case. For most comparisons, imputations for missing price comparisons were necessary for less than half a dozen of the twenty-two producers' durable-goods detailed categories. The gaps were greatest for the Japan-United States comparison. The imputations are listed in part 2 of the Appendix to this chapter.

D. Data Processing

In the United States and in some of the other countries, price data were gathered on a current basis, and wholesale price indexes were used to adjust the prices to 1967 and 1970, our reference dates. The price data for the producers' durable-goods sectors generally are among the weakest price statistics, and it cannot be said that the extrapolating series used to adjust our prices to the required dates were always satisfactory.

The domestic indexes tend to be least satisfactory for commodities undergoing rapid technological change; these sometimes undergo large and sudden price movements. In one six-month period, for example, the U.S. price of one of the office machines in our sample was cut in half. A new, greater-capacity model had been introduced in the same price range, and consequently the stock of the old model was being unloaded at half price. This is not an isolated example: the office-machine category in particular has been marked by rapid change. During the few years we have been engaged in this study, we have seen the introduction, on a large scale, of electronic desk machines with transistorized circuits to replace electric desk machines; and, subsequently of electronic desk machines with integrated circuits to replace those with transistorized ones. It is difficult for ongoing wholesale price series to catch these kinds of changes, and in such cases we had to try to obtain prices for the reference period directly.

The adjustment of prices to purchasers' value (final users' prices) was left to the individual countries, except for the United States, for which the ICP staff adjusted the prices to the correct level and reference period, and for France, the Federal Republic of Germany, and Italy, for which that task was performed by the Statistical Office of the EEC.

In some cases the producers'-durables prices we obtained referred to final user prices and no adjustments were necessary. Often, however, the price data were on the basis of "factory FOB list price." Such prices do not include transport costs or retail taxes, which should be included for ICP purposes. On the other hand, they are not reduced, as is necessary for ICP use, for those discounts which, depending on industry practice and prevailing market conditions, may be offered to final users. In connection with U.S. farm machinery, for example, it was found recently that the price paid by the farmer, omitting retail taxes and transportation costs, was 14.5 percent below the suggested retail price.[1] Thus, where we had FOB list prices, adjustments had to be made for (1) transport costs, (2) retail taxes, where applicable, and (3) discounts from the list price given to final purchasers.

For the United States, the Office of Business Economics (OBE) input-output data were used to estimate transport costs and retail taxes. These data were available in value terms for entire categories of goods rather than for individual products, and it was necessary, therefore, to develop ratios that could be applied to the list prices we obtained for individual products.

Once the prices from the various countries were assembled and adjusted to the appropriate basis and dates, they were subjected to data-cleaning operations such as those described in connection with consumers goods in Chapter 5. A procedure such as that involved in COMPARE was used to scan the data; it involved the formation of price ratios for each pair of matched specifications in each binary comparison. The price ratios then were tabulated, each within its appropriate detailed expenditure category. Extreme price ratios stood out and led to a further in-house inquiry into the nature of the specifications being compared; to the staff's identification of the key price-determining characteristics of the product; and in many cases, to a request for additional and clarifying information from the individual countries themselves.

---

[1] The Royal Commission on Farm Machinery, *Special Report on Prices* (Ottawa: The Commission, 1969).

APPENDIX TO CHAPTER 10

1. Producers' Durable Goods for Which Price Comparisons Were Made

ICP category
14.000 Transport equipment
14.100 Railway vehicles
14.110 Locomotives
      Diesel electric
14.120 Other railway vehicles
      Boxcar
      Flatcar
14.200 Passenger car
14.300 Trucks, buses, and trailers
      Truck
14.400 Aircraft
      Commercial jetliner
      Utility aircraft
14.500 Ships and boats
      Ship
14.600 Other transport equipment
      Bicycle
      Motorcycle
15.000 Nonelectrical machinery
      and equipment
15.100 Engines and turbines
      Diesel engine
      Gasoline engine (large)
      Gasoline engine (small)
15.200 Agricultural machinery and
      equipment
15.210 Tractors
      Tractor
15.220 Other agricultural machinery
      and equipment
      Moldboard plow
      Rake
      Rotary cultivator
      Grain drill
      Manure spreader
      Baler
      Combine
      Disc plow
      Scarifier
      Disc harrow
15.300 Office machinery
      Electric typewriter
      Electronic calculator
      Copier
      Adding machine
      Manual typewriter
      Electric calculator
      Addressing machine
      Computer
      Accounting machine
15.400 Metalworking machinery and
      equipment

ICP category
      Drilling machine
      Milling machine (vertical)
      Milling machine (horizontal)
      Lathe
      Band saw
      Grinder
      Open back inclinable press
      Hacksawing machine
15.500 Construction and mining
      machinery
      Three-wheel roller
      Track-type tractor
      Dozer blade
      Wheel tractor scraper
      Power shovel (crawler)
      Hydraulic excavator (crawler)
      Wheel loader
      Motor grader
      Crawler loader
15.600 Special industry machinery
15.610 Special industry machinery
      other than chemical
      industry machinery
      Warper
      Knitting machine
      Wool-spinning frame
      Cotton-roving machine
      Loom
      Cotton-spinning frame
      Offset press
      Monotype keyboard
      Line casting machine
      Automatic platen press
      Roll mills
      Homogenizer
      Bread oven
      Combing machine
15.620 Chemical-industry machinery
15.700 General industry machinery
      Stationary compressor
      Portable compressor
      Pump
      Forklift truck (diesel)
      Forklift truck (electric)
      Forklift truck (gasoline)
15.800 Service-industry machinery
      Soft-drink vending machine
      Gasoline dispenser
      Freezer (food)
      Freezer (meat)
      Cooling cabinet

ICP category
16.000 Electrical machinery and
      appliances
16.100 Electrical transmission and
      distribution
      Motor (open drip proof)
      Motor (enclosed)
      Motor (explosion proof)
      Transformer (10/12 kv)
      Transformer (20/24 kv)
      Transformer (30/40.5 kv)
      Transformer (current)
      Transformer (potential)
      Welding equipment
      Diesel generator set
16.200 Communication equipment
      Telephone
      Telex
      Electron tube
      X-ray
      TV receiver (black and
      white, closed circuit)
      TV camera (portable)
16.300 Other electrical equipment
      Incandescent lamp
      Fluorescent lamp
      Flush tumbler switch
      Auto battery
      Cable for telephone
      Coaxial cable for TV
16.400 Instruments
      Watt-hour meter
      Voltmeter
      Ammeter
      Digital voltmeter
      Line recorder
      Centrifuge
      Oscilloscope
      Photocopier
17.000 Other durable furnishings
      and equipment
17.100 Furniture and fixtures
      Desk
      File cabinet
      Storage cabinet
      Medical furniture
      Fixed armchair
      Shelves
      High cupboard
17.200 Other durable goods
      Oil drum
      Steamboiler (building)

2. Imputations for Missing Price Comparisons in Producers' Durable-goods Categories

Country	Missing category	Category used for binary comparisons†
Colombia	14.120	Index of 14.110
	14.500	All other 14
France	14.400	All other 14
	15.1	All other 15
Germany, (F.R.)	14.300, 14.500	All other 14
	15.100	All other 15
Hungary	14.400, 14.500	All other 14
India	14.400, 14.500	All other 14
	16.200	All other 16
	17.200	Index of 17.100
Italy	14.300, 14.500	All other 14
	15.100	All other 15
Japan	14.100, 14.300, 14.400, 14.500, 14.600	Index of 14.200
	15.100, 15.200, 15.300, 15.800	All other 15
	16.100, 16.200	All other 16
	17.000	All other producers' durables
Kenya	14.400, 14.500	All other 14
United Kingdom	14.100, 14.300, 14.400, 14.500	All other 14
	15.800	All other 15
	16.100	All other 16
	17.200	Index of 17.100

†For multilateral imputations, see discussion in Section C of Chapter 5.

Chapter 11

Comparing the prices of construction

A. The General Approach

Construction costs can be compared internationally in a number of different ways, each of which has its advantages and disadvantages.

In a sense, the most direct method is to compare the costs for complete construction projects. This is much in the spirit of the other price comparisons we have made in the consumption and producers' durable-goods sectors, for which we selected a representative sample of specifications for each detailed category and tried to price matching versions of the specification in each country. The advantage of this "complete-project" approach is that it provides a direct estimate of the price comparison we are really seeking: namely, of construction final products purchased by private and public transactors in each country. The difficulties of the approach are, first, that of identifying specifications of construction projects that are common in every detail to the countries being compared, and second, of finding a means of obtaining cost estimates or prices for these specifications in each country.

An approach that played a large role in earlier comparisons[1] is one based on price comparisons for component units of work that go into construction, such as laying a certain number of bricks or pouring a certain amount of concrete. The great advantage of this "component-unit-of-work" approach over the complete-project method is that the specifications are simpler to prepare, easier to understand, and more readily priced in different countries. Even where the method of doing a particular unit of work is different from country to country, as in earth excavation, it usually is simpler to cope with the necessary adjustments than when an entire construction project is being considered. But this approach also has significant limitations. First, to cover a large part of the total cost of most construction projects with such simple operations is difficult. Second, the approach excludes a possibly significant aspect of productivity, namely, the efficiency with which various operations are combined to produce the whole. This is an important deficiency from the standpoint of international comparisons, one that is avoided by the complete-project approach.

Regression methods, used in connection with durable goods and rents,[2] also could be applied in principle to construction. In the case of residential buildings, for example, prices of individual units constructed in each country could be related to such physical characteristics as size, number of stories, and number of bathrooms. This method currently is being used in the United States as a means of measuring time-to-time changes in construction costs.[3] This is an attractive approach that may become feasible in the future, but the possibility of obtaining sufficient data in each country to relate the price of each construction project with key physical characteristics, even on a sample basis, seemed small.

Another possible way of comparing construction costs in different countries is to base the comparison on bills of inputs of materials and hours of work.[4] It is difficult, however, to see what advantages this approach has for our purposes over that based on the cost or price comparison for completed construction projects. If the bundle of inputs is used to define the quality of a construction project and therefore is held constant from one country to another, the implicit assumption becomes

---

[1] See M. Gilbert and I. Kravis, *An International Comparison of National Products and the Purchasing Power of Currencies* (Paris: Organization for European Economic Cooperation, 1954), p. 193.

[2] See Chapters 8 and 9.

[3] U.S. Department of Commerce, Bureau of the Census, "Housing Starts," *Construction Reports* (Washington: Government Printing Office, 1968), c20-69-5.

[4] Compare Douglas C. Dacey, "A Price and Productivity Index for a Nonhomogeneous Product," *Journal of the American Statistical Association* (June 1964), pp. 469–80.

that the productivity with which materials and labor are applied is identical in different countries; the price comparison in this case becomes one between weighted bundles of inputs. If, on the other hand, what is held constant is the quality of the final product, and the bundle of inputs required to produce that final product is allowed to vary from one country to another, we are really back to price comparisons based on completed construction units.

Thus, the practical choice boiled down to the complete-project approach versus the component-unit-of-work approach. The objections to the latter were sufficiently compelling to lead us to choose to work with entire construction projects. Our comparisons thus are based on the costs of specified building projects such as houses or factories and nonbuilding construction projects such as roads or dams as explained below.

The first problem was to identify specifications that represented common kinds of construction projects in different countries. It proved difficult to find published sources that were helpful on this point, and the initial selections were based on the opinions of persons familiar with conditions in a number of different countries. An effort also was made to provide a relatively large number of specifications so that each country would be able to find, in each of the fourteen detailed construction categories, at least some that were matched in its own construction activity. Countries were invited to suggest modifications or, if necessary, to provide supplementary specifications, bearing in mind the need to select specifications that could be found as well in other countries.

The specifications for buildings were drawn up initially from U.S. construction-cost manuals[5] with the aid of outside experts. Modifications and additions were suggested by Colombia, Hungary, Kenya, the United Kingdom, and the EEC Statistical Office. The specifications are abbreviated descriptions of buildings, usually less than a page in length (a point to which we will return).

The specifications for nonbuildings, initially provided by the Central Statistical Office (CSO) of Hungary, consist of worksheets that follow closely those supplied by the CSO. The worksheets, usually three or four pages in length, set out the main operations, tasks, or components involved in the project. They describe briefly the work to be performed in each operation—sometimes, as in the movement of earth, in quantitative terms—and call for a cost estimate for each item. The operations listed account for a large part, though not all, of the total cost of the project. Operations for which it is more

difficult to compare costs, for one reason or another, are not listed explicitly; rather, respondents are asked to provide cost estimates for the unenumerated balance of the project. As in the case of buildings, countries were requested to provide supplementary specifications, and some additions were made to the original list.

The outcome was a list of about 100 specifications, although the target number actually sought for price comparisons was less than half of this number (see Table 11.1). More than two-thirds of the specifications were for buildings (of these, about one-fourth were for residences and the rest were for other buildings) and the balance for highways, utility lines, dams, and the like.

The obvious obstacle to carrying out a scheme of pricing finished construction projects was the very great cost. The specifications and plans prepared for a builder by an architect might run 50 to 100 pages for a building and far more for some complicated nonbuilding construction projects. They would have been expensive to prepare and to have priced in the different countries, particularly because some require modification to meet local practices in particular countries. Even if the target number of projects had been limited to one for each of fourteen detailed categories, this would have involved a major effort that would have absorbed a substantial part, if not all, of the resources available for the ICP.

We met this problem by relying upon abbreviated descriptions of buildings, usually about a page in length, and on simplified descriptions of nonbuilding projects that indicated the major operations involved in them. Our strategy was to provide a broad description of a building or other construction project, but one detailed enough to ensure that any project meeting the description would be at least roughly comparable to any other one meeting it.

An important advantage of this approach is that the economical character of the estimates makes it more feasible to obtain costs for each of a large number of projects from alternative sources in each country.

It certainly is to be expected that cost comparisons from country to country will be more reliable if they are based upon a large number of different projects. One reason is that on any particular project, an unusual local material or local building practice may lead to an atypical cost comparison. It is desirable, too, to have estimates from alternative sources in each country in view of the unusual within-country variation of construction costs. Anyone who has ever examined bids for a particular project, even bids based on very detailed specifications, cannot help but be impressed with the large dispersion that characterizes construction pricing.

The ease with which the national statistical offices were able to obtain the cost data varied from one construction category to another and from country to country. Every government is itself a major final purchaser of construction. Knowledge of costs and prices for the kinds of construction financed by governments them-

[5] These manuals, designed for use by assessors, engineers, and architects, give detailed descriptions for a large variety of buildings and other forms of construction, with factors enabling the costs of a number of variants of each to be estimated. The ICP is grateful to the Chicago Real Estate Board for permission to use specifications from the *Chicago Building Cost Manual* and to the American Appraisal Company for permission to use specifications from the *Boeckh Building Valuation Manual.*

Table 11.1. Number of Construction Specifications

ICP Code	Expenditure category	Number of specifications	
		Total	Minimum desired
10.000	Residential buildings	18	6
10.100	One- and two-dwelling buildings	9	3
10.200	Multidwelling buildings	9	3
11.000	Nonresidential buildings	56	19
11.100	Hotels and other nonhousekeeping units	8	3
11.200	Industrial buildings	8	3
11.300	Commercial buildings	11	3
11.400	Office buildings	6	2
11.500	Educational buildings	5	2
11.600	Hospital buildings	4	2
11.700	Agricultural buildings	11	3
11.800	Other buildings	3	2
12.000	Other construction	24	10
12.100	Roads, streets, and highways	5	3
12.200	Transport and utility lines	14	5
12.300	Other construction	5	2
13.000	Land improvement and plantation and orchard development	6	3
13.100	Land improvement	4	2
13.200	Plantation and orchard development	2	1
	Total	104	38

selves—highways, office buildings, and the like—is available within the government, and the national statistical offices had little difficulty obtaining the desired estimates for such projects.

In most of the included countries, however, much of the information required related to projects usually carried out in the private sector. Knowledge about such costs was not readily available to the statistical offices, so it was necessary to consult private sources.

The success of the complete-project approach to construction cost comparisons is greatly facilitated when in the various countries there are groups of men whose business it is to make such shortcut estimates of building costs. In the United States, a number of professionals, including architects, builders, and engineers, customarily make such estimates as part of their work. In addition, several companies that specialize in keeping track of construction costs do so in terms of specified types of buildings or construction projects. U.S. cost estimates were obtained from three such companies, several construction companies, a few government agencies, and several utility companies doing own-account construction. A Philadelphia architectural firm provided guidance, not only by giving the ICP some cost estimates, but also, and more important, by advising us on specifications and on matching problems as data came in from the various countries. U.S. prices were obtained for all specifications, usually from three or four sources.

In the United Kingdom, a well-established professional group, the quantity surveyors, specialize in making cost estimates. Estimates for virtually all specifications were provided by quantity surveyors in the Department of Environment.

In the Common Market countries, on the other hand, the Statistical Office of the EEC concentrated its resources upon obtaining a smaller number of carefully prepared estimates conforming to detailed specifications agreed upon among the countries. Most of the specifications selected for this work were chosen from the ICP list, and the few exceptions subsequently were added to the ICP list.

By resort to government sources, companies, architects, and engineers, the statistical offices of the other countries generally were able to provide the desired estimates. These data sometimes represented the realized costs for actual construction projects, particularly in Colombia and Hungary. In some of these cases, the project deviated from the specification, and ways had to be found to make appropriate cost adjustments. The following section covers these matching problems.

B. Matching Procedures

The price sought was the national average cost of each project to its purchaser. Thus, overhead and profit were included. It was recognized that bid prices for construction projects vary widely with the location, site conditions, and other factors, but respondents were asked to approximate realized costs for the average circumstances in their country.

To standardize the estimation of costs, certain rules were laid down. For buildings, cost estimates were to apply to substructures and superstructures only. The estimates were to exclude architectural and engineering fees, expenditure on site development, external works within the curtilage such as pavings, walks, and land-scaping, and movable furnishings and equipment unless specifically noted within the technical characteristics.

In some cases, estimators work in terms of costs per square meter. We found that, in preparing such estimates, different sources treated basement areas in different ways. We requested that per-square-meter estimates for the cost of buildings that include basements be obtained by dividing the total cost of the building including basement by the total floor area excluding the basement area.

In terms of the matching techniques listed in Chapter 3, the chief methods used in construction were equivalence in use and price adjustment.

In general, an effort was made to compare the prices of construction that was equivalent in the utility provided the purchaser. In the case of buildings, prices were compared for units that provided equivalent space and comfort, even though the materials and equipment used to achieve the given result might differ from one country to another. Thus, local materials or local construction methods that differed from those provided in the specification could be used in estimating costs, with the proviso that the overall quality of the end result was not to differ from that called for in the specification. Respondents were asked to describe any such changes.

In the case of nonbuilding projects, a similar principle was applied. Each respondent was invited to consider whether the relative quantities provided in the specification for each step of the project corresponded to those commonly employed in the country. If this was not the case, the quantities considered more typical were to be noted and estimates based on them provided.

A striking example of a substitution involving factors of production rather than merely materials was provided in Kenya. An architect reported using larger reinforced-concrete columns than were necessary to support the weight they had to carry; his purpose was to avoid the need for the skilled carpenters and supervisors who would have been required to make smaller columns with more accurately fixed steel and more careful shuttering. Relative to concrete, he observed, good carpenters and supervisors were at a premium in Kenya.[6]

Our experience suggests that the degree of similarity in the materials and methods used in construction in different parts of the world varies widely from one type of construction to another. The differences are great in the construction of individual residences, whereas the construction of apartment buildings and office buildings tends to be more alike.

In a number of cases, the cost estimates obtained from the individual countries referred to specifications

that deviated in some respects from those that have been provided. The deviations were sometimes small and unlikely to have any significant impact upon relative costs. In other instances, the differences could be taken care of by reducing costs to a per-square-meter basis. For example, EEC specification for an apartment building related to a structure one story higher than that of the ICP specification. Because the building was of steel frame and did not have load-bearing walls, our architectural consultant advised us that a direct comparison could be made on a per-square-meter basis.

In some cases, however, the deviations were of a size and character that clearly would affect the cost comparison. The basic procedure in these instances was to align the deviant estimate to the ICP specification by making appropriate adjustments in costs. It would have been preferable to make these cost adjustments on the basis of the prices in the country that offered the deviant specification. The information usually was not available to carry out this procedure, however, sometimes because the ICP specification called for a feature that was not prevalent in the country concerned, as, for example, central heating in India.

In most cases, therefore, adjustment factors based on U.S. data had to be used. The U.S. price for the ICP specification was raised or lowered as necessary to match the deviant specification provided by another country. The PPP ratio for the comparable specification then was computed by dividing the other country's price by the U.S. dollar price. This PPP ratio then was used to standardize the other country's cost estimate by multiplying it by the U.S. price estimate for the original ICP specification. For example, the Japanese supplied a cost estimate for a chimney that excluded two job steps called for in the ICP specification. The U.S. estimate was reduced to eliminate the cost of these two steps. The PPP ratio of the yen versus the dollar for the comparable chimney was 186.7. Using this ratio and the complete U.S. cost for the original ICP specification, we obtained a Japanese cost estimate for the complete ICP specification. The advantage of standardizing all prices to a common set of specifications was simply the ease of handling the data in subsequent operations, particularly those involved in the multilateral comparisons.

The establishment of equivalence for buildings and other construction projects was necessarily very rough. We certainly could not take account of the relative future flows of utilities from the projects (see the discussion of the comparison of prices for capital goods in Chapter 2, Section C). In some instances, we were aware of such differences but did not undertake to adjust for them because of the complex factors involved. For example, in the comparison of U.S. and European school buildings, it came to our attention that the United States tends to use unit or modular heating, whereas in Europe central-heating systems installed in basements are still

[6] See D. Wood, "Problems of Comparisons in Africa, with Special Regard to Kenya," *Review of Income and Wealth* (March 1973), p. 105–16.

being used. Costs are about the same, and we treated them as equivalent, even though the maintenance costs on modular heating are lower.

C. Data Processing

Once the cost data were assembled, they were subjected to data-cleaning operations, including the use of CLEANSER and COMPARE, described in Chapter 3, Section D.

We fell farther short of the target number of specifications in construction than in the other major sectors. The shortfalls affected only some of the countries, however; data for Hungary, Japan, the United Kingdom, and the United States were available for almost all the specifications. For France, the Federal Republic of Germany, and Italy, there were costs for only eleven building and eight nonbuilding specifications, for reasons given above. The other countries fell in intermediate positions: India and Colombia had good coverage of buildings and fair coverage of nonbuilding specifications, and Kenya had only fair coverage of buildings and good coverage of nonbuilding specifications.

The lack of complete data in the case of some countries left some detailed categories without PPP estimates. In these instances, we assigned PPPs from other categories as seemed most appropriate. In the case of the missing data for railways, for example, we applied the PPPs for roads to railways as well.

Before leaving the subject of capital formation, mention should be made of two other components—net change in stocks and exports minus imports. PPPs for stocks were estimated as the weighted average of the PPPs for all the commodity components of consumption (that is, excluding services) and producers' durables. Admittedly, this is a makeshift device, but the special effort involved in identifying the composition of stock changes did not seem warranted in view of the small importance of the category and the methodological difficulties that were likely to be encountered. For net exports, we used exchange rates as the PPPs.

Chapter 12

Comparison of government services

The comparisons of government services in the ICP were greatly dependent on the decisions taken regarding the allocation of final consumption expenditures to householders and to government. In Chapter 1, Section B, and Chapter 3, Section A, reference was made to the general considerations regarding the scope of the government sector. This chapter begins by providing more specific detail on this matter; it then discusses the questions of productivity differences and the classification of government employees into major categories to facilitate adjustments in this respect. The comparisons of selected government occupations is described next. Finally, the treatment of government expenditures on goods and services, as well as other questions, are dealt with.

A. The Scope of Government Services

As noted earlier, the services provided by the government sector as defined by the ICP consist primarily of general public services—general administration, external affairs, public order and safety, defense, and research. The general administration component includes the carrying out of such governmental functions as setting standards: for example, in connection with health and education, whose major expenses are included elsewhere.

In more specific terms, the concept employed by the ICP called "Public Final Consumption Expenditure" (PFC) is identical with "Government Final Consumption Expenditure" as defined by the U.N. *System of National Accounts* (SNA),[1] except for certain inclusions and exclusions. The inclusions are the expenditures of the following private nonprofit institutions serving households:

- Research and scientific institutes (item 1 in SNA Table 5.4)
- Professional and labor organizations and civic organizations (item 7 in SNA Table 5.4)

On the other hand, the Public Final Consumption Expenditure concept of the ICP excludes some expenditures classified as Government Final Consumption Expenditure in the SNA. The excluded categories were expenditures for:

- Provision, assistance, or support of housing (for example, governmental expenditures to meet current costs of dwellings) unless they were part of the compensation of employees in governments
- Hospitals and clinics and individual health services (items 4.2 and 4.3 in SNA Table 5.3)
- Recreation and related cultural services and religion and services n.e.s. (items 7.1 and 7.2 in SNA Table 5.3)
- Schools, universities, and other educational facilities and subsidiary services (items 3.2 and 3.3 in Table 5.3)
- Welfare services (item 5.2 in SNA Table 5.3)

All expenditures of government on these items were included in the ICP "Final Consumption Expenditure of the Population" (CEP). As set out more fully in Chapter 3, Section A, the purpose was to provide a basis for comparing personal consumption that was invariant to institutional differences in the way in which nations finance expenditures on health, education, and like areas. These expenditures are set out in detail in Chapter 13, Appendix Table 13.14.

From the point of view of the various levels of government (central, state, local) and in respect to the handling of social security administrations, the scope of government was identical with the concept of "general government" in the SNA. In the ICP, "government" included all departments, offices, organizations, and

---

[1] United Nations Statistical Office, *A System of National Accounts,* Studies in Methods, Series F, No. 2, Rev. 3 (New York: United Nations, 1968).

other bodies that were agencies or instruments of the central, state, or local public authorities. Also included were nonprofit institutions that, though not an integral part of a government, were wholly or mainly financed and controlled by the public authorities or primarily served government bodies.

The concept of government in the project extended also to all social security arrangements for large sections of the population established, controlled, or financed by a government and to government enterprises that mainly produce goods and services for government itself or primarily sell goods and services to the public on a small scale. Other government enterprises and public corporations were excluded.

Because the SNA is concerned primarily with international standardization of the national accounting practices within countries and is not specifically concerned with international comparisons of the type undertaken by the ICP, the subdivisions of the government services for the ICP needed further thought. The SNA makes no suggestion on comparing government output between countries, but it does comment upon measuring government output at constant costs within a country. These comments were relevant to the ICP because of the similarities between the two problems. "Perhaps the suitable, feasible procedure in most instances is to base the constant price estimates of final consumption expenditure on the sum of estimates of real intermediate consumption and real primary inputs, reduced by real sales of goods and services, if significant. When compiling indicators of real primary inputs it would be desirable to take into account the consumption of fixed capital and changes in the mix of the employees. . . . It is questionable whether reliable adjustments can be made for other factors contributing to labor productivity."[2]

For practical reasons, we decided not to attempt to make real comparisons of government sales. Instead, government sales were deducted from government expenditures in national currencies before comparisons were made. Government capital consumption was not treated separately but was included with government expenditures on commodities. In all other respects, we followed the spirit of the SNA.

With respect to final consumption expenditure of the population and to gross capital formation, the SNA provided specific guidelines for disaggregating the main expenditure categories. As noted earlier, we used these guidelines in determining the detailed expenditure categories. In most instances the only change made in the

SNA system was to divide its most detailed expenditure categories into additional subaggregates.

The SNA, however, does not give comparable guidelines for disaggregating public final consumption by type of commodity or service purchased. Among the supporting and supplementary tables recommended in the SNA are tables suggesting a subdivision of government final consumption according to cost composition and purpose. The cost elements separated are (1) compensation of employees, (2) consumption of fixed capital, (3) the consumption of goods and services, and (4) other net outlays. The classification by purpose shows nine sectors (education, health, defense, and so on).[3] The only additional SNA recommendation with a bearing on the classification of government purchases was the one quoted above, which recommends that capital consumption and the mix of employees be taken into account.

The significance of an appropriate classification of government expenditures for the comparison assumed added importance because at an early stage it became clear that the comparison of government outputs among countries was hardly feasible. As is well known, national accounts practice generally values the output of the government sector at the cost of providing government services, because of the difficulty in obtaining any other meaningful measure of the output of this sector. The measurement of government output in this manner meant that international comparisons for this sector unavoidably are input comparisons that serve as proxies for the output comparisons being sought.

For the ICP comparisons, we divided government expenditures into a number of expenditure categories. The two major categories are Compensation of Employees (ICP 20) and Expenditures on Commodities (ICP 21). Compensation of employees was subdivided further into a number of detailed expenditure categories. Expenditures on commodities were not subdivided further into detailed expenditure categories, but additional information was requested from the countries concerning the composition of this category.

B. Adjustments for Productivity Differences

Because it was decided to compare the measures for government services among the countries on the basis of inputs rather than outputs, one possible procedure was to perform quantity comparisons in terms of one major element of input, personnel. Such comparisons are facilitated by the fact that most countries have detailed statistics of government employment.

---

[2] *SNA*, p. 144. Some countries recently have attempted to adjust for changes in labor productivity arising from sources other than employee mix. See, for instance, H. Bartels, "National Product at Constant Prices in the Federal Republic of Germany," *Review of Income and Wealth* (December, 1968), pp. 387–402.

[3] See *SNA*, tables 4 (p. 170), 13 (p. 185), 21 (p. 195), and 22 (p. 197).

Obviously, any comparison of the quantity of labor between countries must involve, explicitly or implicitly, assumptions about the difference in labor productivity between countries. The simplest hypothesis would be that the productivity of government employees is the same everywhere; in which case, the quantity ratio would be determined by the number of government employees in each country.

Although to adjust for different labor productivity of government employees between countries is not possible in any exact sense, one measurable aspect of potential or expected differences in productivity may arise from different levels of education. Accordingly, we assumed not that the productivity of all government employees was the same internationally, but rather that the productivity of government employees having the same level of education was the same. Thus, the comparisons were made for three levels of education, as defined by UNESCO.[4] Employees having a second level of education were further subdivided into blue- and white-collar workers. The definitions are as follows:

- Education at the first level, as in elementary, or primary, school, provides basic instruction in the tools of learning.
- Education at the second level—as in middle, secondary, or high school, vocational school, or teacher-training school—is based upon at least four years of previous instruction at the first level; it provides general or specialized instruction or both.
- Education at the third level—as in a university, teachers' college, or higher professional school—requires, as a minimal condition of admission, the successful completion of education at the second level or evidence of the attainment of an equivalent level of knowledge.

Employees with a second-level education were allocated between blue- and white-collar workers on the basis of the International Standard Classification of Occupation (ISCO).[5] Thus, quantity (and price) comparisons were made for the following detailed categories of government employment:

1. Employees having first-level education (ICP 20.100)
2. Employees having second-level education: blue-collar workers (ICP 20.210)
3. Employees having second-level education: white-collar employees (ICP 20.220)
4. Employees having third-level education (ICP 20.300)

[4]*Recommendation Concerning the International Standardization of Educational Statistics* adopted by the General Conference of UNESCO at its Tenth Session (Paris, 1958).

[5]*International Standard Classification of Occupations,* rev. 1968 (Geneva: International Labor Organization, 1969).

This treatment means that in the ICP aggregation process, the within-country differences in productivity between the various types of employees are measured by the differences in their compensation.

A further modification that was considered and rejected is to assume that the level of productivity of government employees of a given degree of education differs internationally in the same way as productivity in the commodity-producing sectors. Because estimates of productivity per worker in the commodity-producing industries could be derived readily from the consumption and capital-goods sectors treated above, this is a feasible alternative. The correction could not be properly made, however, unless commodity productivity also was adjusted for education and for differences in capital equipment. In any case, it would be equally arbitrary to assume that the international differences in productivity in one economic sector are exactly the same as the differences in productivity in another sector.

C. Comparison of Compensation of Government Employees

As mentioned earlier, the category "Compensation of Employees" was one for which both direct quantity and direct price comparisons could be made. In most other instances, the quantity comparisons are indirect in that the quantity comparison is obtained by dividing the expenditure ratio by the price comparison. Indirect price comparisons in the government sector can be made by dividing the quantity comparisons into the appropriate expenditure ratios, but it was decided to make direct price comparisons instead.

For the sake of these price comparisons, twenty-two detailed job specifications were drawn up on the basis of the international classification of occupations. At least five specifications were provided for each detailed expenditure category. Insofar as possible, the jobs were selected so as to represent relatively standard occupations likely to be common in all governments and to involve similar qualifications and duties in all countries. The need for adequate coverage of each category was also a consideration.

The specific job categories selected were as follows:

For the category comprising employees with first-level education and including jobs requiring little education or training, the selections were watchman, messenger, charworker, laborer, and postman.

The blue-collar category consisted of jobs that require some training and more than the first level of education (but no more than twelve years of completed education) and that falls within the following ISCO major groups: production and related workers (7), transport equipment operators (8), and laborers (9); service workers (5); agriculture, animal husbandry and forestry workers, fishermen, and hunters (6); and workers not classified by occupation (10). The jobs selected for this group were those of a maintenance electrician, offset pressman, bulldozer operator, cabinetmaker, and telephone and telegraph installer.

The white-collar category included jobs that also require second level of education and some training and that fall within the following ISCO major groups: clerical and related workers (3); administrative and managerial workers (2); professional, technical, and related workers (0/1); and sales workers (4). The jobs compared in this category were stenographer, secretary, office cashier, card- and tape-punching machine operator, bookkeeping clerk, statistical clerk, and policeman.

The jobs requiring third level of education were sanitary engineer, accountant, public health physician, farming adviser, and surveyor general.

For each of these jobs, a detailed description was furnished to the countries. These job specifications were based on ISCO, with the exception of the specifications for the accountant and the director of personnel, which were based on U.S. government job descriptions.

Each country was asked to supply average annual compensation for employees of each job description. In some instances a country could not provide th̲ pensation for every one of the twenty-two specifica tions. In these cases the comparisons were made with fewer price ratios or other job specifications were substituted. Colombia, the United Kingdom, and the United States provided wages for all the twenty-two specifications requested; Kenya and Hungary furnished all but one. For the Federal Republic of Germany, France, and Italy, nine out of the twenty-two were obtained. In these countries government employees with a given level of education and a given number of years of experience are located at a certain point in the salary scale: consequently, it was considered of no benefit to make more comparisons with the same salary rates.

In all these comparisons, the price was the SNA concept of average compensation of employees. This includes all payments by resident producers of wages and salaries to their employees, in kind and in cash, and of contributions, paid or imputed, for their employees to social security, private pension, family allowance, casualty insurance, life insurance, and similar schemes.[6] The compensation refers to the work year in the country reporting the information; no attempt was made to adjust to standard work years to take account of annual differences in working hours.

D. Government Purchases of Commodities

In the case of the other major part of government spending—that is, for government expenditures on com-

modities—only price comparisons could be made. The simplest means of making price comparisons for government purchases of commodities would have been to classify all government purchases into the expenditure categories used by the ICP for the consumption expenditure of the population and for capital goods. This was not completely feasible even in principle, because some government purchases were for products that would be classified as intermediate rather than final products from the standpoint of consumers and purchasers on capital account. Furthermore, no data are available in any country giving this kind of subdivision of government purchases of commodities.

Indeed, breakdowns of such expenditures are generally available, if at all, only in connection with input-output tables. The classifications employed usually follow the International Standard Industrial Classification (ISIC)[7] or a national industrial classification usually closely related to it. In the ICP, therefore, each country was asked to provide the estimated breakdown of government expenditures on commodities for certain categories of goods based on ISIC classifications.

These groupings, referred to below as G categories, were as follows:

ICP
Code   Industry (ISIC Code)

G31   Food, beverages, and tobacco (ISIC Division 31)

G32   Textiles, wearing apparel, and leather (ISIC Division 32)

G33   Wood and wood products, including furniture (ISIC Division 33)

G34   Paper and paper products, printing, and publishing (ISIC Division 34)

G35   Chemicals and chemical, petroleum, coal, rubber, and plastic products (ISIC Division 35)

G36   Nonmetallic mineral products except products of petroleum and coal (ISIC Division 36)

G37   Basic metal products (ISIC Division 37)

G38   Fabricated metal products, machinery, and equipment (ISIC Division 38)

G39   Products of other manufacturing industries (ISIC Division 39)

G40   Electricity, gas, and water (ISIC Major Division 4)

G50   Construction (ISIC Major Division 5)

G70   Transport, storage, and communication (ISIC Major Division 7)

G80   All other (ISIC Major Division 0,1,2,6,8, and 9)

---

[6]*SNA*, p. 231, and p. 121, paragraphs 7.11–7.14.

[7]United Nations Statistical Office, *International Standard Industrial Classification of All Economic Activities*, Statistical Papers, Series M, No. 4, Rev. 2 (New York: United Nations, 1968).

The breakdown available from an earlier year, corresponding to the reference year for an input-output or other special study, often was applied to the expenditures for the ICP reference year. For some countries, special inquiries were required to obtain the desired distributions. In India, for example, the estimates were based in part on sample data from some states and localities. Even though accurate estimates of government expenditures on detailed commodities could not be obtained in some cases, it was believed that even rough weights for different types of expenditures would be better than equal weighting in calculating the purchasing-power parity (PPP) for this category.

The grouping of all ISIC categories into thirteen categories for the purpose of the ICP was done in large part on a conjectural basis, because little objective information was available. On the basis of the data available in the ICP now, it can be seen that in countries studied the bulk of expenditures are concentrated in two or three categories. In most countries, expenditures on fabricated metal products, machinery, and equipment (G38) and on the all other (G80) categories[8] account for more than 60 percent of total expenditures. Other categories such as textiles (G32) and wood products (G33) often account for less than 1 percent of expenditures. It seems clear that a grouping in which expenditures were more equally divided between the categories would be better for international comparisons, and work is currently under way to develop an improved classification for future comparisons.

The expenditure data provided half of the required information; the other part of the task was to find a means for making price comparisons for each of the thirteen categories. This was done by selecting, to the greatest extent possible, those PPPs from other parts of the study which could be regarded as representative of the ISIC industries in each of our G categories. An unweighted geometric mean was taken of the PPPs selected for each G category, and the expenditure weights then were used to aggregate the G categories to obtain the PPPs for government purchases of commodities. In a few cases, PPPs from other parts of the study were directly relevant. For example, it was obviously advantageous to apply the results obtained from the food, beverages, and tobacco category in consumption to the similar G category in government. Similarly the results obtained from the construction comparisons (ICP 10, 11, and 12) described in Chapter 9 were used for category G50.

E. Measurement Problems

Although many difficulties were encountered in obtaining the prices, quantities, and expenditures required

[8]Capital consumption of government was included in item G80.

for all the countries in order to make the comparisons outlined above, this discussion is confined to those which were general for most or all countries and to problems that have some bearing on the reliability and the accuracy of the estimates.

ESTIMATING EXPENDITURES

Relatively little difficulty was encountered in adjusting government expenditures as prepared for the country's own use to the expenditures required by the ICP. The major adjustment required involved the health, education, and investment sectors. These sectors usually are of particular interest to governments, and generally there is a great deal of supplementary information—though usually not organized and assembled precisely for ICP needs. This is true of the developing countries as well as the developed countries. To the extent that difficulties arose, they usually were concerned with the detailed categories rather than with the aggregates. In all cases, for example, good data were available for the estimate of government expenditures on personnel engaged in educational activities. In some cases, however, less satisfactory data had to be used to make the allocations between the various types of labor (that is, to the three educational levels and between the blue- and white-collar groups). In addition, the detailed government expenditures to be transferred to CEP had to be subtracted from the G groups by using assumptions that could not be verified empirically. For instance, it had to be assumed in some cases that expenditure on commodities of a particular sector (health, education, or the like) was distributed among the G categories in the same manner as total government expenditures on commodities.

ESTIMATING QUANTITIES OF LABOR

A number of difficulties were associated with obtaining an estimate of the total quantity of labor employed by the government sector. First, obtaining complete coverage was more difficult than expected. All countries had good statistics on central, or national, government employment, but countries have a hierarchy of governments, and employment data covering local governments were difficult to estimate in some instances. (To avoid confusion, the term "local government" is used to designate all forms and types of government below the level of the central government.) The problem of allocating the employment of local government to the four detailed categories was particularly serious. The difficulties sometimes were increased by the fact that the bulk of government expenditures on health and education are undertaken by local authorities in a number of countries.

Even at the level of central government, information on the educational level of the employees sometimes was not available, although the distribution of employees by type of job—manual laborer, skilled blue-collar, secretarial, professional, and so on—was available. Furthermore, a clear and well-known relation usually existed between type of job and educational level for a number of job classifications. Accordingly, estimates of employment by educational attainment were made in these cases by associating a particular job with a certain level of education.

Difficulties were created, however, by the fact that a number of countries have educational systems that do not mesh well with the UNESCO education classification used by the ICP. This sometimes led to a certain amount of ambiguity as to what educational level should be associated with a particular job. For instance, a number of countries have a final degree that falls about halfway between the first and second levels of the UNESCO classification. Employees with this kind of intermediate degree often are found in the same type job—say, secretarial—as those with a second-level education. The allocation of employees in jobs of this nature between the two detailed expenditure categories—the one for first-level education and the other for second-level education—often had to be based upon the expert knowledge of individuals in the countries.

Another problem was posed by part-time government employees. All levels of government usually hire some part-time employees, but the relative importance of such employment appears to increase at the lower levels of the government structure. Part-time employees who were enumerated as such were adjusted to full-time equivalent employees according to the work year appropriate to the country. We believe that most part-time employees of the government sector have been properly treated, but it is doubtful that all part-time employees have been counted correctly: a few may have been included as full-time employees, whereas others may not have been enumerated at all. The errors in the comparisons caused on this account, however, are thought not to be substantial. Consultants, incidentally, are not counted as part-time employees; they are self-employed, and government expenditures on their services are treated as government expenditures on goods and services.

ESTIMATING THE COMPENSATION OF LABOR

The problems associated with estimating the compensation of particular types of labor were relatively minor compared to those involved in estimating the quantities. Most central governments have a general grading system for employees and a set of detailed job descriptions for employees within each grade. For each grade and job specification it was possible to find the exact wage paid. One difficulty was that, from a practical standpoint, the ICP specifications often were not as detailed as the national job descriptions. In these cases, several national specifications, each with a different compensation level, often fell within a given ICP specifi-

cation. When this occurred, an average of the highest and lowest national compensation was taken as the price.

Because the job specifications used were chosen by the ICP, the specifications could be selected so as to minimize any ambiguity as to which expenditure category the job belonged to; an effort was made to avoid job specifications that could be filled by either someone with a first-level education or by someone with a second-level education.

As in the case of the quantity data, the major difficulty was securing price data related to local government employees. To derive the national average price for each job specification, it was necessary to obtain compensation for the same type of employee for whom the central government's compensation had been obtained. In some cases, the relationship between central government and state and local government compensation could be approximated only on the basis of partial information. Because the work was done by each national statistical office, it had the benefit of expert judgement in each case.

Compensation of military personnel was not compared. Because of the possibility that information about military expenditures and personnel would be regarded as sensitive information, it was decided from the start not to seek such data. Expenditures on military employees and the quantities were included with the corresponding entries for civilian employees in the appropriate ICP detailed categories. To the extent that the relative compensation levels of military and civilian employees differ from country to country, the failure to make comparisons of military salaries will introduce an error into the overall price and quantity comparisons for government employees. Even comparisons of military salaries, which might be a less sensitive matter, would not remove this difficulty altogether because information on military expenditures on personnel, on the quantity of military personnel, or on both would also be needed.

ESTIMATING PRICES OF COMMODITIES

If the general procedures used by the ICP in other categories of expenditure were employed for the government expenditure on commodities, then actual prices paid by the government for well-specified items in each category would have been collected. This procedure had so many practical difficulties associated with it that it could not be employed. As described above, price comparisons from other ICP categories were used instead. The insurmountable difficulty in obtaining prices actually paid by government is that most governments simply do not know the actual average price that they pay for individual items. The complex methods of purchasing used are such that it is not possible for the countries to calculate such prices without a great deal of special effort. In this particular case, the information available at the level of central government usually is no better than that at the local level.

In principle, therefore, the procedures we have used will yield the price ratio that would exist if the commodities purchased by the governments had been purchased by private transactors. It is often thought that the government pays prices for commodities different from those paid by private transactors, although there is no agreement as to whether prices paid by government are, on the average, higher or lower. One argument states that the government can obtain discounts and other favorable conditions of sale because it is a large purchaser, and because of its special position. The counter-argument is that the individual government purchasing agent has little incentive to save on prices, but that a considerable incentive exists for the seller to cultivate the purchasing agent. But whatever the difference in the price paid for a given commodity by the government and the price paid in the private sectors, the PPP calculated by relying on prices paid in the private sector will be

inaccurate only to the extent that the prices paid in the private sector relative to prices paid by the government differ in direction or magnitude between countries.

Some consideration was given to collecting an entirely new set of prices for comparing the government sector. The prices collected would be prices paid by private transactors, but the items to be priced would be selected according to the G categories rather than the categories used for the other parts of the comparison. Although this would be more feasible than the process of obtaining prices actually paid by governments for standard specifications, the burden placed on the national statistical offices still would be great and the feasible sample of items small. Given these limitations, it was felt that PPPs selected from the other ICP sectors, supplemented by a few new PPPs collected for intermediate goods, would provide a better measure of the relative price level of items purchased by the government sector than would a PPP based upon a much smaller number of prices from a specially designed sample of government transactions.

Part III

The results of the comparisons

Chapter 13

Results of the binary comparisons

The full results of the binary comparisons are presented in the summary tables of this chapter. Tables 13.1 to 13.9 present original-country binary comparisons between the United States and each of nine other countries for 1970.[1] Tables 13.10 to 13.14 show the same kind of comparisons for five of the nine countries for 1967. Per capita expenditures in national currencies, purchasing-power parities (PPPs), and per capita quantity ratios, with the United States as 100, are shown for more than thirty subdivisions of GDP and for various aggregations.

A. The Major Aggregates

For the major aggregates, the results are shown both in terms of ICP and SNA concepts, the latter as addendum items. The ICP concepts, it will be recalled from Chapter 3, enable us to compare "consumption" and "government," each defined with a standard product coverage in different countries. The SNA concepts, on the other hand, correspond approximately to the sense of household purchases and of public purchases, respectively. No addendum items are included for the SNA concepts for investment and GDP. The ICP concept of investment is identical with that of the SNA, and the ICP concept of GDP differs only by the addition of rent subsidies, which affect the GDP comparisons only marginally. The categories that have been transferred from SNA "government" to ICP "consumption" and the expenditures of each country for these categories are given in Table 13.15.

The summary tables contain three sets of PPPs. The first set is aggregated from the PPPs for 153 detailed categories with the use of U.S. expenditure weights. The second is aggregated from the same materials using the partner country's own weights. The third set is the

geometric mean of the first two (that is, the Fisher, or ideal, index).

There are also three sets of per capita quantity indexes, each based on the United States as 100. These indexes usually are derived by dividing the PPPs into the expenditure ratio on each row of the tables. ("Usually," because there are, as described in Chapter 7, some direct quantity comparisons.) As is well known in index-number work, the division of the expenditure ratio by U.S.-weighted PPPs yields "own"-weighted quantity indexes:

$$\frac{\Sigma p_{ij}q_{ij}}{\Sigma p_{in}q_{in}} \div \frac{\Sigma p_{ij}q_{in}}{\Sigma p_{in}q_{in}} = \frac{\Sigma p_{ij}q_{ij}}{\Sigma p_{ij}q_{in}},$$

where the ps are prices, qs are quantities, n refers to the United States and j to one of the nine other countries, and the summation runs over the is, which refer to the detailed categories. Similarly, division of the expenditure ratio by "own"-weighted PPPs yields U.S.-weighted quantity indexes.

The methods by which these results have been produced have been described in previous chapters: the aggregation methods appear in Chapter 4, and methods for the various product sectors in Chapters 6 to 12.

Corresponding to each of the fourteen summary binary tables is an appendix table giving price and quantity comparisons for the 153 detailed categories. It has been pointed out several times, but it bears repeating: these data are worksheet materials; they do not meet the ordinary standards of publication, but they are made available for the use of statisticians and economists who wish to aggregate the data in ways different from those which we have chosen.

The figures in the summary binary tables can be subjected to many kinds of analysis. In this chapter, we confine ourselves mainly to pointing out some of the major features of the results. In Chapter 15, some simple analytical uses of the data are illustrated.

[Text resumes on page 184.]

[1] In the case of India, the actual reference date is April 1970–March 1971.

Table 13.1. Summary Binary Table: Expenditures per Capita, Purchasing-Power Parities, and Quantity per Capita, Colombia–U.S., 1970

Category (1)	Line Number (2)	Per Capita Expenditure		Purchasing-Power Parities Peso/Dollar			Quantity per Capita (U.S. = 100)		
		Colombia (Peso) (3)	U.S. (Dollar) (4)	U.S. Weight (5)	Colombia Weight (6)	Ideal (7)	U.S. Weight (8)	Colombia Weight (9)	Ideal (10)
Consumption, ICP	1 to 110	4574.6	3271.73	11.5	6.0	8.3	23.3	12.2	16.8
Food, beverages, tobacco	1 to 39	1518.7	564.14	13.0	9.1	10.8	29.7	20.7	24.8
Food	1 to 33	1425.1	446.80	14.4	9.2	11.5	34.5	22.1	27.6
Bread and cereals	1 to 6	240.4	55.88	17.6	13.2	15.2	32.5	24.5	28.2
Meat	7 to 12	400.2	150.82	11.7	10.2	10.9	26.0	22.6	24.3
Fish	13 to 14	14.4	11.98	13.7	15.0	14.3	8.0	8.8	8.4
Milk, cheese, eggs	15 to 17	169.4	67.34	11.5	10.2	10.8	24.8	21.8	23.2
Oil and fats	18 to 20	88.5	16.13	18.1	17.6	17.8	31.2	30.3	30.8
Fruits and vegetables	21 to 26	332.9	98.42	19.6	6.0	10.8	56.7	17.2	31.3
Coffee, tea, cocoa	27 to 29	56.8	14.64	12.5	11.7	12.1	33.2	30.9	32.1
Spices and sweets, sugar	30 to 33	122.5	31.59	10.6	9.2	9.9	42.3	36.5	39.3
Beverages	34 to 37	64.3	62.21	11.2	11.5	11.3	9.0	9.2	9.1
Tobacco	38 to 39	29.3	55.12	3.6	3.7	3.7	14.3	14.6	14.5
Clothing and footwear	40 to 51	257.1	256.37	12.0	10.2	11.0	9.8	8.4	9.1
Clothing	40 to 47	205.0	214.57	12.9	11.5	12.2	8.3	7.4	7.8
Footwear	48 to 51	52.1	41.80	7.0	7.1	7.0	17.6	17.8	17.7
Gross rent, fuel	52 to 57	631.3	560.25	10.8	9.8	10.3	11.5	10.4	10.9
Gross rents	52 to 53	559.9	455.04	11.6	10.4	11.0	11.9	10.6	11.2
Fuel and power	54 to 57	71.4	105.21	7.2	7.1	7.1	9.6	9.4	9.5
House furnishings, operation	58 to 71	394.8	252.07	13.8	3.5	6.9	44.8	11.4	22.6
Furniture, appliances	58 to 66	204.6	151.97	18.1	13.2	15.4	10.2	7.5	8.7
Supplies and operation	67 to 71	190.2	100.10	7.3	2.0	3.8	97.4	26.0	50.3
Medical care	72 to 78	124.4	314.74	3.6	2.9	3.2	13.8	10.9	12.2
Transport and communication	79 to 91	535.6	446.09	20.5	6.2	11.3	19.4	5.9	10.7
Equipment costs	79 to 80	208.3	158.16	38.2	17.9	26.1	7.4	3.5	5.0
Operation costs	81 to 84	127.4	201.28	13.6	5.9	9.0	10.7	4.6	7.1
Purchased transport	85 to 89	175.1	30.68	5.5	4.0	4.7	143.7	102.9	121.6
Communication	90 to 91	24.8	55.97	3.2	2.8	3.0	16.0	13.8	14.8
Recreation and education	92 to 103	450.3	506.75	9.1	3.1	5.3	28.5	9.7	16.7
Recreation	92 to 98	211.3	241.44	15.3	7.6	10.8	11.6	5.7	8.1
Education	99 to 103	239.1	265.30	3.5	2.1	2.7	43.9	25.9	33.7
Other expenditure	104 to 110	662.4	347.63	6.5	5.6	6.1	33.9	29.3	31.5
Personal care	104 to 106	79.3	80.05	9.7	9.1	9.4	10.8	10.3	10.6
Miscellaneous services	107 to 109	583.0	267.58	5.6	5.3	5.5	40.7	39.1	39.9
Capital formation	111 to 148	1217.3	837.11	14.8	6.4	9.7	22.7	9.8	14.9
Construction	111 to 124	724.1	463.96	4.3	4.3	4.3	36.3	36.7	36.5
Residential	111 to 112	189.7	147.14	4.3	4.4	4.4	29.2	29.9	29.6
Non-residential	113 to 120	179.8	171.55	4.1	3.9	4.0	26.6	25.7	26.1
Construction other than buildings	121 to 124	354.6	145.27	4.4	4.4	4.4	55.1	55.3	55.2
Producers' durables	125 to 146	485.9	349.12	28.8	24.9	26.8	5.6	4.8	5.2
Transport equipment	125 to 131	154.1	105.85	31.2	31.3	31.3	4.6	4.7	4.7
Nonelectrical machinery	132 to 140	203.5	144.83	31.4	25.5	28.3	5.5	4.5	5.0
Electrical machinery	141 to 144	96.0	59.47	25.0	19.7	22.2	8.2	6.5	7.3
Other durables	145 to 146	32.3	38.97	18.4	18.5	18.4	4.5	4.5	4.5
Government	149 to 153	321.0	692.37	7.7	4.0	5.5	11.7	6.0	8.4
Compensation	149 to 152	200.5	354.32	3.3	3.1	3.2	18.2	17.3	17.7
Commodities	153 to 153	120.5	338.05	12.3	7.1	9.4	5.0	2.9	3.8
Gross domestic product	1 to 153	6112.8	4801.20	11.5	5.9	8.2	21.5	11.1	15.4
Aggregates									
ICP Concepts									
Consumption (CEP)	1 to 110	4574.6	3271.73	11.5	6.0	8.3	23.3	12.2	16.8
Capital formation (GCF)	111 to 148	1217.3	837.11	14.8	6.4	9.7	22.7	9.8	14.9
Government (PFC)	149 to 153	321.0	692.37	7.7	4.0	5.5	11.7	6.0	8.4
GDP	1 to 153	6112.8	4801.20	11.5	5.9	8.2	21.5	11.1	15.4
SNA Concepts									
Consumption (PFCE)	1 to 110	4429.3	3019.73	12.2	6.4	8.8	22.9	12.0	16.6
Capital formation (GCF)	111 to 148	1217.3	837.11	14.8	6.4	9.7	22.7	9.8	14.9
Government (GFCE)	1 to 153	466.3	944.37	6.4	3.1	4.4	16.1	7.7	11.1
GDP	1 to 153	6112.8	4798.59	11.5	5.9	8.2	21.5	11.1	15.4

Notes:
1. Line numbers refer to Appendix Table 13.1 and show the detailed categories that are included in each aggregation.
2. Above expenditures for lines 1 to 110 include both household and government expenditures. The latter are shown separately in Appendix Table 13.15. SNA consumption excludes these government expenditures.
3. Consumption aggregate (lines 1 to 110) includes net expenditure of residents abroad (line 110) not shown separately above. Similarly, capital formation aggregate (lines 111 to 148) includes increase in stocks (line 147) and net exports (line 148). See appendix table for these items.
4. Ideal or Fisher Index is the geometric mean of the indexes with weights of the United States and of Colombia.
5. Letters in parentheses are first letters of official terms. See Glossary.
6. Exchange rate: P18.56=US$1.00 (see Table 1.1).

Table 13.2. Summary Binary Table: Expenditures per Capita, Purchasing-Power Parities and Quantity per Capita, France–U.S., 1970

Category (1)	Line Number (2)	Per Capita Expenditure		Purchasing-Power Parities Franc/Dollar			Quantity per capita (U.S. = 100)		
		France (Franc) (3)	U.S. (Dollar) (4)	U.S. Weight (5)	France Weight (6)	Ideal (7)	U.S. Weight (8)	France Weight (9)	Ideal (10)
Consumption, ICP	1 to 110	10302.14	3271.73	5.20	4.11	4.62	76.7	60.5	68.1
Food, beverage, tobacco	1 to 39	2841.57	564.14	5.27	3.89	4.52	129.6	95.6	111.3
Food	1 to 33	2310.67	446.80	5.75	4.54	5.11	113.8	89.9	101.2
Bread and cereals	1 to 6	325.74	55.88	7.12	4.06	5.38	143.5	81.8	108.4
Meat	7 to 12	796.81	151.66	5.27	5.10	5.18	103.1	99.6	101.4
Fish	13 to 14	112.06	11.98	6.71	6.23	6.46	150.1	139.4	144.7
Milk, cheese, eggs	15 to 17	302.01	67.34	3.74	3.70	3.72	121.3	120.0	120.6
Oils and fats	18 to 20	155.76	15.30	4.78	5.47	5.12	186.2	212.8	199.1
Fruits and vegetables	21 to 26	427.37	98.42	5.64	3.59	4.50	120.8	76.9	96.4
Coffee, tea, cocoa	27 to 29	61.74	14.64	8.34	8.19	8.26	51.5	50.5	51.0
Spices and sweets, sugar	30 to 33	129.18	31.59	9.15	7.39	8.22	55.4	44.7	49.8
Beverages	34 to 37	384.65	62.21	3.21	2.13	2.61	290.5	192.4	236.4
Tobacco	38 to 39	146.25	55.12	3.67	3.50	3.58	75.8	72.3	74.0
Clothing and footwear	40 to 51	954.41	256.37	6.88	6.35	6.61	58.7	54.1	56.3
Clothing	40 to 47	804.36	214.57	7.24	6.71	6.97	55.9	51.8	53.8
Footwear	48 to 51	150.05	41.80	5.00	4.93	4.96	72.9	71.8	72.3
Gross rent, fuel	52 to 57	1266.70	560.25	3.96	3.46	3.70	65.4	57.0	61.1
Gross rents	52 to 53	966.62	455.04	3.13	2.98	3.05	71.2	68.0	69.6
Fuel and power	54 to 57	300.08	105.21	7.59	7.08	7.33	40.3	37.6	38.9
House furnishings, operation	58 to 71	722.70	252.07	5.76	5.26	5.51	54.5	49.8	52.1
Furniture, appliances	58 to 66	475.79	151.97	5.64	5.42	5.53	57.8	55.5	56.6
Supplies and operation	67 to 71	246.91	100.10	5.95	4.99	5.45	49.4	41.5	45.3
Medical care	72 to 78	912.97	314.74	2.60	2.65	2.62	109.4	111.8	110.6
Transport and communication	79 to 91	1030.45	446.09	7.83	5.35	6.47	43.2	29.5	35.7
Equipment	79 to 80	264.99	158.16	6.99	5.22	6.04	32.1	24.0	27.7
Operation costs	81 to 84	552.72	201.28	9.41	6.20	7.64	44.3	29.2	36.0
Purchased transport	85 to 89	161.45	30.68	4.79	3.83	4.28	137.6	109.9	123.0
Communication	90 to 91	51.28	55.97	6.20	4.89	5.51	18.8	14.8	16.6
Recreation and education	92 to 103	1477.49	506.75	5.31	4.59	4.94	63.5	54.9	59.0
Recreation	92 to 98	720.85	241.44	4.87	4.46	4.66	66.9	61.3	64.0
Education	99 to 103	756.64	265.30	5.71	4.73	5.20	60.3	49.9	54.9
Other expenditure	104 to 110	1095.97	347.63	4.27	4.14	4.21	76.1	73.9	75.0
Personal care	104 to 106	336.20	80.05	5.19	4.71	4.94	89.2	81.0	85.0
Miscellaneous services	107 to 109	759.77	267.58	3.99	3.94	3.97	72.1	71.1	71.6
Capital formation	111 to 148	4661.46	837.11	4.50	4.09	4.29	136.3	123.8	129.9
Construction	111 to 124	2403.30	463.96	3.80	3.49	3.64	148.3	136.3	142.2
Residential	111 to 112	1114.11	147.14	4.71	4.11	4.40	184.3	160.7	172.1
Nonresidential bldgs.	113 to 120	794.86	171.55	4.12	3.79	3.95	122.2	112.4	117.2
Construction exc. bldgs.	121 to 124	494.33	145.27	2.49	2.38	2.44	142.9	136.4	139.6
Producers' durables	125 to 146	1760.71	349.12	5.36	4.92	5.14	102.6	94.0	98.2
Transport equipment	125 to 131	382.76	105.85	5.53	5.50	5.52	65.7	65.4	65.6
Nonelectrical machinery	132 to 140	793.98	144.83	5.52	5.05	5.28	108.5	99.4	103.8
Electrical machinery	141 to 144	397.22	59.47	4.43	3.98	4.20	167.7	150.8	159.0
Other durables	145 to 146	186.76	38.97	5.79	5.88	5.83	81.5	82.8	82.2
Government	149 to 153	1153.95	692.37	4.32	4.12	4.22	40.5	38.6	39.5
Compensation	149 to 152	630.06	354.32	3.77	3.76	3.76	47.3	47.2	47.2
Commodities	153 to 153	523.89	338.05	4.90	4.65	4.77	33.3	31.6	32.5
Gross domestic product	1 to 153	16117.49	4801.20	4.95	4.10	4.51	81.8	67.8	74.5
Aggregates									
ICP Concepts									
Consumption (CEP)	1 to 110	10302.14	3271.73	5.20	4.11	4.62	76.7	60.5	68.1
Capital formation (GCF)	111 to 148	4661.46	837.11	4.50	4.09	4.29	136.3	123.8	129.9
Government (PFC)	149 to 153	1153.95	692.37	4.32	4.12	4.22	40.5	38.6	39.5
GDP	1 to 153	16117.49	4801.20	4.95	4.10	4.51	81.8	67.8	74.5
SNA Concepts									
Consumption (PFCE)	1 to 110	9497.08	3019.73	5.25	4.17	4.68	75.5	59.9	67.2
Capital formation (GCF)	111 to 148	4661.46	837.11	4.50	4.09	4.29	136.3	123.8	129.9
Government (GFCE)	1 to 153	1959.03	944.37	4.40	3.84	4.11	54.0	47.1	50.4
GDP	1 to 153	16112.98	4798.59	4.95	4.10	4.51	81.8	67.8	74.5

Notes:
1. Line numbers refer to Appendix Table 13.2 and show the detailed categories that are included in each aggregation.
2. Above expenditures for lines 1 to 110 include both household and government expenditures. The latter are shown separately in Appendix Table 13.15. Consumption, SNA excludes these government expenditures.
3. Consumption aggregate (lines 1 to 110) includes net expenditure of residents abroad (line 110) not shown separately above. Similarly capital formation aggregate (lines 111 to 148) includes increase in stocks (line 147) and net exports (line 148). See appendix table for these items.
4. Ideal or Fisher Index is the geometric mean of the indexes with weights of the United States and of France.
5. Letters in parentheses are first letters of official terms. See Glossary.
6. Exchange rate: Fr5.554=US$1.00.

Table 13.3. Summary Binary Table: Expenditures per Capita, Purchasing-Power Parities and Quantity per Capita, Federal Republic of Germany–U.S., 1970

Category (1)	Line Number (2)	Per Capita Expenditure		Purchasing-Power Parities D. Mark/Dollar			Quantity Per Capita (U.S. = 100)		
		Germany, F.R. (D Mark) (3)	U.S. (Dollar) (4)	U.S. Weight (5)	Germany, F.R. Weight (6)	Ideal (7)	U.S. Weight (8)	Germany, F.R. Weight (9)	Ideal (10)
Consumption, ICP	1 to 110	6641.94	3271.73	3.62	3.01	3.30	67.5	56.0	61.5
Food, beverage, tobacco	1 to 39	1590.79	564.14	4.03	3.59	3.81	78.5	69.9	74.1
Food	1 to 33	1265.25	446.80	4.25	3.81	4.02	74.4	66.7	70.4
Bread and cereals	1 to 6	227.49	55.88	4.54	3.32	3.88	122.7	89.6	104.9
Meat	7 to 12	335.24	151.66	3.88	3.83	3.86	57.7	57.0	57.3
Fish	13 to 14	19.97	11.98	4.01	4.44	4.22	37.6	41.6	39.5
Milk, cheese, eggs	15 to 17	144.01	67.34	2.79	2.88	2.83	74.3	76.7	75.5
Oils and fats	18 to 20	124.65	15.30	4.15	4.08	4.11	199.8	196.3	198.1
Fruits and vegetables	21 to 26	196.06	98.42	4.10	3.34	3.70	59.7	48.5	53.8
Coffee, tea, cocoa	27 to 29	99.23	14.64	10.43	10.05	10.24	67.4	65.0	66.2
Spices and sweets, sugar	30 to 33	118.60	31.59	6.34	5.22	5.75	72.0	59.3	65.3
Beverages	34 to 37	164.59	62.21	2.46	2.40	2.43	110.2	107.6	108.9
Tobacco	38 to 39	160.95	55.12	4.05	3.84	3.94	76.1	72.1	74.1
Clothing and footwear	40 to 51	691.57	256.37	4.07	3.86	3.96	70.0	66.2	68.1
Clothing	40 to 47	569.35	214.57	4.30	4.19	4.24	63.3	61.8	62.6
Footwear	48 to 51	122.22	41.80	2.94	2.81	2.88	104.0	99.5	101.7
Gross rent, fuel	52 to 57	947.96	560.25	2.90	2.60	2.75	65.1	58.3	61.6
Gross rents	52 to 53	715.59	455.04	2.43	2.29	2.36	68.5	64.8	66.6
Fuel and power	54 to 57	232.36	105.21	4.96	4.38	4.66	50.5	44.5	47.4
House furnishings, operation	58 to 71	611.72	252.07	3.84	3.38	3.60	71.8	63.2	67.4
Furniture, appliances	58 to 66	386.62	151.97	3.87	3.64	3.75	69.9	65.8	67.8
Supplies and operation	67 to 71	225.10	100.10	3.81	3.01	3.38	74.8	59.1	66.5
Medical care	72 to 78	614.95	314.74	1.63	1.64	1.64	119.1	119.8	119.5
Transport and communication	79 to 91	726.66	446.09	5.83	3.82	4.72	42.7	27.9	34.5
Equipment	79 to 80	184.53	158.16	6.15	3.72	4.79	31.3	19.0	24.4
Operation costs	81 to 84	363.04	201.28	6.58	5.16	5.83	34.9	27.4	30.9
Purchased transport	85 to 89	124.63	30.68	3.41	2.63	3.00	154.3	119.2	135.6
Communication	90 to 91	54.45	55.97	3.54	2.36	2.89	41.3	27.5	33.7
Recreation and education	92 to 103	994.87	506.75	3.25	3.03	3.14	64.8	60.4	62.6
Recreation	92 to 98	498.53	241.44	3.07	3.07	3.07	67.2	67.3	67.3
Education	99 to 103	496.33	265.30	3.42	2.99	3.19	62.6	54.8	58.6
Other expenditure	104 to 110	463.49	347.63	3.15	3.19	3.17	41.9	42.3	42.1
Personal care	104 to 106	171.84	80.05	3.48	3.04	3.25	70.6	61.6	66.0
Miscellaneous services	107 to 109	291.65	267.58	3.05	3.28	3.16	33.3	35.7	34.5
Capital formation	111 to 148	3425.48	837.11	3.20	2.74	2.96	149.5	127.9	138.3
Construction	111 to 124	1609.85	463.96	2.44	2.12	2.27	163.8	142.1	152.6
Residential	111 to 112	608.98	147.14	3.08	2.25	2.64	183.6	134.2	157.0
Nonresidential bldgs.	113 to 120	574.55	171.55	2.46	2.35	2.41	142.6	135.9	139.2
Construction exc. bldgs.	121 to 124	426.32	145.27	1.76	1.74	1.75	168.8	166.6	167.7
Producers' durables	125 to 146	1359.30	349.12	4.16	3.65	3.90	106.7	93.6	99.9
Transport equipment	125 to 131	310.72	105.85	4.82	4.86	4.84	60.4	61.0	60.7
Nonelectrical machinery	132 to 140	578.98	144.83	3.99	3.40	3.69	117.6	100.1	108.5
Electrical machinery	141 to 144	311.98	59.47	3.15	3.02	3.08	173.9	166.3	170.1
Other durables	145 to 146	157.62	38.97	4.53	4.53	4.53	89.4	89.3	89.3
Government	149 to 153	1204.83	692.37	3.18	3.03	3.10	57.5	54.7	56.1
Compensation	149 to 152	527.74	354.32	3.03	2.85	2.94	52.3	49.1	50.7
Commodities	153 to 153	677.09	338.05	3.34	3.18	3.26	63.0	60.0	61.4
Gross domestic product	1 to 153	11272.17	4801.20	3.49	2.92	3.19	80.3	67.3	73.6
Aggregates									
ICP Concepts									
Consumption (CEP)	1 to 110	6641.94	3271.73	3.62	3.01	3.30	67.5	56.0	61.5
Capital formation (GCF)	111 to 148	3425.48	837.11	3.20	2.74	2.96	149.5	127.9	138.3
Government (PFC)	149 to 153	1204.83	692.37	3.18	3.03	3.10	57.5	54.7	56.1
GDP	1 to 153	11272.17	4801.20	3.49	2.92	3.19	80.3	67.3	73.6
SNA Concepts									
Consumption (PFCE)	1 to 110	6050.57	3271.73	3.69	3.26	3.47	61.5	54.3	57.8
Capital formation (GCF)	111 to 148	3425.48	837.11	3.20	2.74	2.96	149.5	127.9	138.3
Government (GFCE)	149 to 153	1796.22	944.37	3.08	2.40	2.72	79.2	61.8	69.9
GDP	1 to 153	11263.87	4798.59	3.49	2.92	3.19	80.3	67.3	73.5

Notes:

1. Line numbers refer to Appendix Table 13.3. and show the detailed categories that are included in each aggregation.
2. Above expenditures for lines 1 to 110 include both household and government expenditures. The latter are shown separately in Appendix Table 13.15. Consumption, SNA excludes these government expenditures.
3. Consumption aggregate (lines 1 to 110) includes net expenditure of residents abroad (line 110) not shown separately above. Similarly capital formation aggregate (lines 111 to 148) includes increase in stocks (line 147) and net exports (line 148). See appendix table for these items.
4. Ideal or Fisher Index is the geometric mean of the indexes with weights of the United States and of the Federal Republic of Germany.
5. Letters in parentheses are first letters of official terms. See Glossary.
6. Exchange rate: DM3.66=US$1.00.

Table 13.4. Summary Binary Table: Expenditures per Capita, Purchasing-Power Parities and Quantity per Capita, Hungary–U.S., 1970

Category (1)	Line Number (2)	Per Capita Expenditure		Purchasing-Power Parities Forint/Dollar			Quantity Per Capita (U.S. = 100)		
		Hungary (Forint) (3)	U.S. (Dollar) (4)	U.S. Weight (5)	Hungary Weight (6)	Ideal (7)	U.S. Weight (8)	Hungary Weight (9)	Ideal (10)
Consumption, ICP	1 to 110	18800.1	3271.73	19.4	11.6	15.0	49.5	29.7	38.3
Food, beverage, tobacco	1 to 39	6686.6	564.14	27.0	17.4	21.7	68.1	43.9	54.7
Food	1 to 33	5693.1	446.80	30.1	18.5	23.6	69.0	42.4	54.1
Bread and cereals	1 to 6	742.6	55.88	13.7	8.4	10.7	158.3	97.0	123.9
Meat	7 to 12	1660.3	150.82	35.4	33.7	34.6	32.6	31.1	31.9
Fish	13 to 14	43.8	11.98	33.5	20.3	26.1	18.0	10.9	14.0
Milk, cheese, eggs	15 to 17	693.9	67.34	16.9	17.1	17.0	60.2	61.0	60.6
Oils and fats	18 to 20	561.9	16.13	28.5	35.5	31.8	98.2	122.2	109.6
Fruits and vegetables	21 to 26	998.4	98.42	30.5	12.5	19.5	81.3	33.2	52.0
Coffee, tea, cocoa	27 to 29	229.8	14.64	102.3	101.6	101.9	15.4	15.3	15.4
Spices and sweets, sugar	30 to 33	762.5	31.59	26.2	25.5	25.9	94.6	92.0	93.3
Beverages	34 to 37	702.0	62.21	20.9	17.1	18.9	66.1	53.9	59.7
Tobacco	38 to 39	291.5	55.12	9.1	8.4	8.8	62.9	57.9	60.3
Clothing and footwear	40 to 51	2175.7	256.37	23.8	21.8	22.8	38.9	35.7	37.2
Clothing	40 to 47	1738.8	214.57	25.0	23.0	24.0	35.2	32.4	33.8
Footwear	48 to 51	436.8	41.80	17.8	18.0	17.9	58.0	58.8	58.4
Gross rent, fuel	52 to 57	1434.4	560.25	14.2	8.7	11.1	29.5	18.1	23.1
Gross rents	52 to 53	835.3	455.04	10.7	7.6	9.0	24.1	17.2	20.3
Fuel and power	54 to 57	599.2	105.21	29.2	10.7	17.7	53.2	19.5	32.2
House furnishings, operation	58 to 71	1548.0	252.07	23.9	21.2	22.5	29.0	25.7	27.3
Furniture, appliances	58 to 66	930.4	151.97	26.4	24.2	25.3	25.3	23.2	24.2
Supplies and operation	67 to 71	617.6	100.10	20.1	17.9	19.0	34.5	30.7	32.5
Medical care	72 to 78	1092.9	314.74	3.9	3.9	3.9	89.6	90.0	89.8
Transport and communication	79 to 91	1100.7	446.09	30.3	15.1	21.4	16.3	8.1	11.5
Equipment	79 to 80	346.1	158.16	50.5	37.3	43.4	5.9	4.3	5.0
Operation costs	81 to 84	182.6	201.28	23.9	18.3	20.9	4.9	3.8	4.3
Purchased transport	85 to 89	504.2	30.68	12.8	11.4	12.1	144.3	128.5	136.2
Communication	90 to 91	67.8	55.97	5.9	7.2	6.5	16.7	20.6	18.6
Recreation and education	92 to 103	2087.5	506.75	13.6	6.1	9.1	67.8	30.4	45.4
Recreation	92 to 98	1093.0	241.44	20.4	6.1	11.1	74.3	22.2	40.6
Education	99 to 103	994.5	265.30	7.3	6.1	6.7	61.9	51.0	56.2
Other expenditure	104 to 110	2674.5	347.63	16.6	13.5	15.0	57.0	46.3	51.4
Personal care	104 to 106	432.3	80.05	19.4	10.1	14.0	53.5	27.8	38.6
Miscellaneous services	107 to 109	2242.2	267.58	15.8	14.4	15.1	58.1	53.2	55.6
Capital formation	111 to 148	9901.2	837.11	25.1	20.0	22.4	59.2	47.1	52.8
Construction	111 to 124	5800.0	463.96	16.4	16.3	16.4	76.5	76.3	76.4
Residential	111 to 112	1526.9	147.14	16.6	15.9	16.3	65.2	62.4	63.8
Nonresidential bldgs.	113 to 120	2442.8	171.55	16.8	19.5	18.1	73.2	84.8	78.8
Construction exc. bldgs.	121 to 124	1830.3	145.27	15.6	13.7	14.6	91.8	80.6	86.0
Producers' durables	125 to 146	3815.9	349.12	36.8	31.9	34.2	34.3	29.7	31.9
Transport equipment	125 to 131	939.2	105.85	44.8	35.7	40.0	24.8	19.8	22.2
Nonelectrical machinery	132 to 140	1988.7	144.83	36.2	34.4	35.3	39.9	37.9	38.9
Electrical machinery	141 to 144	407.7	50.47	22.6	22.9	22.8	29.9	30.3	30.1
Other durables	145 to 146	480.3	38.97	38.4	26.9	32.1	45.9	32.1	38.4
Government	149 to 153	2414.3	692.37	15.3	11.6	13.3	30.1	22.9	26.2
Compensation	149 to 152	624.4	354.32	5.5	5.2	5.4	33.6	32.2	32.9
Commodities	153 to 153	1789.9	338.05	25.5	20.0	22.6	26.5	20.8	23.5
Gross domestic product	1 to 153	31115.6	4801.19	19.8	13.4	16.3	48.4	32.8	39.8
Aggregates									
ICP Concepts									
Consumption (CEP)	1 to 110	18800.1	3271.73	19.4	11.6	15.0	49.5	29.7	38.3
Capital formation (GCF)	111 to 148	9901.2	837.11	25.1	20.0	22.4	59.2	47.1	52.8
Government (PFC)	149 to 153	2414.3	692.37	15.3	11.6	13.3	30.1	22.9	26.2
GDP	1 to 153	31115.6	4801.19	19.8	13.4	16.3	48.4	32.8	39.8
SNA Concepts									
Consumption (PFCE)	1 to 110	16341.6	3019.73	20.5	14.8	17.4	36.6	26.4	31.1
Capital formation (GCF)	111 to 148	9901.2	837.11	25.1	20.0	22.4	59.2	47.1	52.8
Government (GFCF)	1 to 153	4872.8	944.37	12.9	6.7	9.3	76.7	40.0	55.4
GDP	1 to 153	30772.9	4798.59	19.8	13.5	16.3	47.5	32.4	39.2

Notes:
1. Line numbers refer to Appendix Table 13.4 and show the detailed categories that are included in each aggregation.
2. Above expenditures for lines 1 to 110 include both household and government expenditures. The latter are shown separately in Appendix Table 13.15. Consumption, SNA excludes these government expenditures.
3. Consumption aggregate (lines 1 to 110) includes net expenditure of residents abroad (line 110) not shown separately above. Similarly capital formation aggregate (lines 111 to 148) includes increase in stocks (line 147) and net exports (line 148). See appendix table for these items.
4. Ideal or Fisher Index is the geometric mean of the indexes with weights of the United States and of Hungary.
5. Letters in parentheses are first letters of official terms. See Glossary.
6. Exchange rate: Ft30.=US$1.00.

Table 13.5. Summary Binary Table: Expenditures per Capita, Purchasing-Power Parities and Quantity per Capita, India–U.S., 1970

Category (1)	Line Number (2)	Per Capita Expenditure		Purchasing-Power Parities rupee/Dollar			Quantity Per Capita (U.S. = 100)		
		India (Rupee) (3)	U.S. (Dollar) (4)	U.S. Weight (5)	India Weight (6)	Ideal (7)	U.S. Weight (8)	India Weight (9)	Ideal (10)
Consumption, ICP	1 to 110	555.56	3271.73	3.79	2.04	2.78	8.3	4.5	6.1
Food, beverage, tobacco	1 to 39	365.11	564.14	5.48	3.54	4.40	18.3	11.8	14.7
Food	1 to 33	349.67	446.80	4.63	3.56	4.06	22.0	16.9	19.3
Bread and cereals	1 to 6	191.84	55.88	5.27	3.69	4.41	93.0	65.2	77.8
Meat	7 to 12	6.77	150.82	4.29	4.43	4.36	1.0	1.0	1.0
Fish	13 to 14	6.28	11.98	3.54	1.34	2.18	39.2	14.8	24.1
Milk, cheese, eggs	15 to 17	24.92	67.34	3.87	3.08	3.45	12.0	9.6	10.7
Oils and fats	18 to 20	37.57	16.13	5.63	5.09	5.35	45.8	41.3	43.5
Fruits and vegetables	21 to 26	37.99	98.42	4.05	2.96	3.46	13.0	9.5	11.2
Coffee, tea, cocoa	27 to 29	6.23	14.64	9.58	3.38	5.69	12.6	4.4	7.5
Spices and sweets, sugar	30 to 33	38.07	31.59	6.14	3.87	4.88	31.1	19.6	24.7
Beverages	34 to 37	2.50	62.21	9.69	11.39	10.51	0.4	0.4	0.4
Tobacco	38 to 39	12.94	55.12	7.67	2.68	4.53	8.8	3.1	5.2
Clothing and footwear	40 to 51	23.08	256.37	3.93	4.07	4.00	2.2	2.3	2.3
Clothing	40 to 47	21.06	214.57	4.00	4.13	4.06	2.4	2.5	2.4
Footwear	48 to 51	2.02	41.80	3.56	3.59	3.58	1.3	1.4	1.4
Gross rent, fuel	52 to 57	54.36	560.25	2.90	2.36	2.61	4.1	3.3	3.7
Gross rents	52 to 53	24.31	455.04	1.74	1.57	1.65	3.4	3.1	3.2
Fuel and power	54 to 57	30.06	105.21	7.91	3.97	5.60	7.2	3.6	5.1
House furnishings, operation	58 to 71	21.98	252.07	3.80	1.19	2.12	7.3	2.3	4.1
Furniture, appliances	58 to 66	7.13	151.97	4.54	2.35	3.27	2.0	1.0	1.4
Supplies and operation	67 to 71	14.85	100.10	2.67	0.96	1.60	15.5	5.6	9.3
Medical care	72 to 78	16.24	314.74	0.62	0.74	0.68	7.0	8.3	7.6
Transport and communication	79 to 91	31.61	446.09	7.06	1.96	3.71	3.6	1.0	1.9
Equipment	79 to 80	2.18	158.16	11.18	6.82	8.74	0.2	0.1	0.2
Operation costs	81 to 84	3.83	201.28	5.96	2.50	3.86	0.8	0.3	0.5
Purchased transport	85 to 89	23.73	30.68	3.66	1.84	2.59	42.1	21.1	29.8
Communication	90 to 91	1.87	55.97	1.20	1.34	1.27	2.5	2.8	2.6
Recreation and education	92 to 103	21.90	506.75	2.50	0.30	0.86	14.6	1.7	5.0
Recreation	92 to 98	6.49	241.44	4.19	2.18	3.03	1.2	0.6	0.9
Education	99 to 103	15.41	265.30	0.96	0.22	0.46	26.9	6.0	12.7
Other expenditure	104 to 110	21.29	347.63	2.71	2.12	2.40	2.9	2.3	2.6
Personal care	104 to 106	7.42	80.05	3.77	3.28	3.52	2.8	2.5	2.6
Miscellaneous services	107 to 109	13.87	267.58	2.39	1.78	2.06	2.9	2.2	2.5
Capital formation	111 to 148	122.40	837.11	3.97	2.10	2.89	7.0	3.7	5.1
Construction	111 to 124	72.26	463.96	1.63	1.50	1.56	10.4	9.6	10.0
Residential	111 to 112	28.11	147.14	1.57	1.60	1.58	12.0	12.2	12.1
Nonresidential bldgs.	113 to 120	13.14	171.55	1.87	1.75	1.81	4.4	4.1	4.2
Construction exc. bldgs.	121 to 124	31.01	145.27	1.40	1.35	1.37	15.8	15.3	15.6
Producers' durables	125 to 146	35.95	349.12	7.03	6.78	6.90	1.5	1.5	1.5
Transport equipment	125 to 131	10.89	105.85	8.62	8.15	8.38	1.3	1.2	1.2
Nonelectrical machinery	132 to 140	11.85	144.83	7.16	7.23	7.20	1.1	1.1	1.1
Electrical machinery	141 to 144	9.64	59.47	5.74	6.53	6.12	2.5	2.8	2.6
Other durables	145 to 146	3.57	38.97	4.18	4.18	4.18	2.2	2.2	2.2
Government	149 to 153	58.23	692.37	2.02	0.74	1.23	11.3	4.2	6.9
Compensation	149 to 152	33.60	354.32	0.74	0.51	0.61	18.8	12.8	15.5
Commodities	153 to 153	24.63	338.05	3.36	2.08	2.65	3.5	2.2	2.8
Gross domestic product	1 to 153	736.18	4801.20	3.57	1.80	2.53	8.5	4.3	6.1
Aggregates									
ICP Concepts									
Consumption (CEP)	1 to 110	555.56	3271.73	3.79	2.04	2.78	8.3	4.5	6.1
Capital formation (GCF)	111 to 148	122.40	837.11	3.97	2.10	2.89	7.0	3.7	5.1
Government (PFC)	149 to 153	58.23	692.37	2.02	0.74	1.23	11.3	4.2	6.9
GDP	1 to 153	736.18	4801.20	3.57	1.80	2.53	8.5	4.3	6.1
SNA Concepts									
Consumption (PFCE)	1 to 110	543.60	3019.73	4.04	2.48	3.17	7.2	4.5	5.7
Capital formation (GCF)	111 to 148	122.40	837.11	3.97	2.10	2.89	7.0	3.7	5.1
Government (GFCE)	149 to 153	70.19	944.37	1.70	0.53	0.95	14.0	4.4	7.8
GDP	1 to 153	736.18	4798.59	3.57	1.80	2.53	8.5	4.3	6.1

Notes:

1. Line numbers refer to Appendix Table 13.5 and show the detailed categories that are included in each aggregation.

2. Above expenditures for lines 1 to 110 include both household and government expenditures. The latter are shown separately in Appendix Table 13.15. Consumption, SNA excludes these government expenditures.

3. Consumption aggregate (lines 1 to 110) includes net expenditure of residents abroad (line 110) not shown separately above. Similarly capital formation aggregate (lines 111 to 148) includes increase in stocks (line 147) and net exports (line 148). See appendix table for these items.

4. Ideal or Fisher Index is the geometric mean of the indexes with weights of the United States and of India.

5. Letters in parentheses are first letters of official terms. See Glossary.

6. Exchange rate: Rs7.5=US$1.00.

Table 13.6. Summary Binary Table: Expenditures Per Capita, Purchasing-Power Parities and Quantity Per Capita, Italy–U.S., 1970

Category (1)	Line Number (2)	Per Capita Expenditure — Italy (Lira) (3)	Per Capita Expenditure — U.S. (Dollar) (4)	Purchasing-Power Parities Lira/Dollar — U.S. Weight (5)	Italy Weight (6)	Ideal (7)	Quantity Per Capita (U.S. = 100) — U.S. Weight (8)	Italy Weight (9)	Ideal (10)
Consumption, ICP	1 to 110	741489.	3271.73	540.	412.	472.	55.0	42.0	48.1
Food, beverage, tobacco	1 to 39	279879.	564.14	658.	498.	572.	99.7	75.4	86.7
Food	1 to 33	229742.	446.80	701.	521.	604.	98.7	73.3	85.1
Bread and cereals	1 to 6	31666.	55.88	645.	394.	504.	143.8	87.8	112.4
Meat	7 to 12	70795.	151.66	641.	614.	628.	76.0	72.8	74.4
Fish	13 to 14	8548.	11.98	741.	732.	737.	97.5	96.3	96.9
Milk, cheese, eggs	15 to 17	29000.	67.34	575.	592.	583.	72.8	75.0	73.9
Oils and fats	18 to 20	13883.	15.30	693.	647.	670.	140.2	131.0	135.5
Fruits and vegetables	21 to 26	53690.	98.42	653.	375.	495.	145.5	83.5	100.2
Coffee, tea, cocoa	27 to 29	6770.	14.64	1738.	1811.	1774.	25.5	26.6	26.1
Spices and sweets, sugar	30 to 33	15392.	31.59	1013.	952.	982.	51.2	48.1	49.6
Beverages	34 to 37	29823.	62.21	430.	347.	387.	138.1	111.4	124.0
Tobacco	38 to 39	20314.	55.12	570.	571.	570.	64.6	64.6	64.6
Clothing and footwear	40 to 51	61150.	256.37	623.	532.	576.	44.8	38.3	39.6
Clothing	40 to 47	50616.	214.57	651.	546.	596.	43.2	36.2	39.6
Footwear	48 to 51	10533.	41.80	481.	474.	478.	53.1	52.4	52.8
Gross rent, fuel	52 to 57	88443.	560.25	402.	362.	382.	43.6	39.3	41.4
Gross rents	52 to 53	66691.	455.04	296.	308.	302.	47.6	49.5	48.5
Fuel and power	54 to 57	21753.	105.21	857.	795.	826.	26.0	24.1	25.0
House furnishings, operation	58 to 71	38984.	252.07	555.	509.	531.	30.4	27.9	29.1
Furniture, appliances	58 to 66	21064.	151.97	554.	496.	524.	27.9	25.0	26.4
Supplies and operation	67 to 71	17920.	100.10	556.	525.	540.	34.1	32.2	33.1
Medical care	72 to 78	51666.	314.74	188.	191.	190.	85.9	87.2	86.6
Transport and communication	79 to 91	69492.	466.09	864.	476.	641.	32.7	18.0	24.3
Equipment	79 to 80	18057.	158.16	753.	555.	646.	20.6	15.2	17.7
Operation costs	81 to 84	31532.	201.28	1131.	591.	818.	26.5	13.9	19.2
Purchased transport	85 to 89	13542.	30.68	441.	294.	360.	150.1	100.2	122.6
Communication	90 to 91	6361.	55.97	449.	450.	450.	25.2	25.3	25.3
Recreation and education	92 to 103	92026.	506.75	459.	346.	399.	52.5	39.5	45.6
Recreation	92 to 98	39333.	241.44	553.	439.	492.	37.1	29.5	33.1
Education	99 to 103	52693.	265.30	375.	299.	334.	66.5	53.0	59.4
Other expenditure	104 to 110	59851.	347.63	514.	500.	507.	34.4	33.5	34.0
Personal care	104 to 106	19835.	80.05	611.	429.	512.	57.7	40.6	48.4
Miscellaneous services	107 to 109	40015.	267.58	485.	545.	514.	27.4	30.8	29.1
Capital formation	111 to 148	243302.	837.11	481.	424.	452.	68.5	60.5	64.4
Construction	111 to 124	142984.	463.96	342.	358.	350.	86.2	90.2	88.2
Residential	111 to 112	74760.	147.14	396.	390.	393.	130.4	128.2	129.3
Nonresidential bldgs.	113 to 120	44239.	171.55	368.	378.	373.	68.3	70.0	69.1
Construction exc. bldgs.	121 to 124	23985.	145.27	255.	264.	259.	62.5	64.8	63.7
Producers' durables	125 to 146	82724.	349.12	656.	572.	613.	41.4	36.1	38.7
Transport equipment	125 to 131	31803.	105.85	811.	795.	803.	37.8	37.1	37.4
Nonelectrical machinery	132 to 140	22962.	144.83	582.	488.	533.	32.5	27.3	29.8
Electrical machinery	141 to 144	17523.	59.47	508.	402.	452.	73.3	58.0	65.2
Other durables	145 to 146	10436.	38.97	739.	753.	746.	35.6	36.2	35.9
Government	149 to 153	77567.	692.37	458.	398.	427.	28.1	24.4	26.2
Compensation	149 to 152	47358.	354.32	407.	385.	395.	34.9	32.9	33.8
Commodities	153 to 153	30209.	338.05	512.	424.	466.	21.1	17.4	19.2
Gross domestic product	1 to 153	1062357.	4801.20	518.	414.	463.	53.5	42.7	47.8

Aggregates

Category	Line Number	Italy (Lira)	U.S. (Dollar)	PPP U.S. Weight	Italy Weight	Ideal	Qty U.S. Weight	Italy Weight	Ideal
ICP Concepts									
Consumption (CEP)	1 to 110	741489.	3271.73	540.	412.	472.	55.0	42.0	48.1
Capital formation (GCF)	111 to 148	243302.	837.11	481.	424.	452.	68.5	60.5	64.4
Government (PFC)	149 to 153	77567.	692.37	458.	398.	427.	28.1	24.4	26.2
GDP	1 to 153	1062357.	4801.20	518.	414.	463.	53.5	42.7	47.8
SNA Concepts									
Consumption (PFCE)	1 to 110	683983.	3019.73	559.	453.	503.	50.0	40.5	45.0
Capital formation (GCF)	111 to 148	243302.	837.11	481.	424.	452.	68.5	60.5	64.4
Government (GFCE)	1 to 153	135072.	944.37	420.	279.	342.	51.3	34.1	41.8
GDP	1 to 153	1062357.	4798.59	518.	414.	463.	53.5	42.7	47.8

Notes:

1. Line numbers refer to Appendix Table 13.6 and show the detailed categories that are included in each aggregation.

2. Above expenditures for lines 1 to 110 include both household and government expenditures. The latter are shown separately in Appendix Table 13.15. Consumption, SNA excludes these government expenditures.

3. Consumption aggregate (lines 1 to 110) includes net expenditure of residents abroad (line 110) not shown separately above. Similarly capital formation aggregate (lines 111 to 148) includes increase in stocks (line 147) and net exports (line 148). See appendix table for these items.

4. Ideal or Fisher Index is the geometric mean of the indexes with weights of the United States and of Italy.

5. Letters in parentheses are first letters of official terms. See Glossary.

6. Exchange rate: L625=US$1.00.

Table 13.7. Summary Binary Table: Expenditures Per Capita, Purchasing-Power Parities and Quantity Per Capita, Japan–U.S., 1970

Category (1)	Line Number (2)	Per Capita Expenditure		Purchasing-Power Parities Yen/Dollar			Quantity Per Capita (U.S. = 100)		
		Japan (Yen) (3)	U.S. (Dollar) (4)	U.S. Weight (5)	Japan Weight (6)	Ideal (7)	U.S. Weight (8)	Japan Weight (9)	Ideal (10)
Consumption, ICP	1 to 110	367718.	3271.73	282.	199.	237	56.4	39.9	47.4
Food, beverage, tobacco	1 to 39	120286.	564.14	390.	316.	351.	67.5	54.6	60.7
Food	1 to 33	97590.	446.80	424.	330.	374.	66.3	51.5	58.4
Bread and cereals	1 to 6	29245.	55.88	314.	365.	338.	143.6	166.9	154.8
Meat	7 to 12	10684.	150.82	507.	474.	490.	15.0	14.0	14.5
Fish	13 to 14	16854.	11.98	311.	320.	315.	440.1	451.7	445.9
Milk, cheese, eggs	15 to 17	8116.	67.34	359.	319.	338.	37.7	33.6	35.6
Oils and fats	18 to 20	1260.	16.13	411.	394.	402.	19.8	19.0	19.4
Fruits and vegetables	21 to 26	20905.	98.42	382.	308.	343.	68.9	55.7	61.9
Coffee, tea, cocoa	27 to 29	1633.	14.64	622.	291.	425.	38.4	17.9	26.2
Spices and sweets, sugar	30 to 33	8893.	31.59	457.	230.	324.	122.2	61.7	86.8
Beverages	34 to 37	17813.	62.21	310.	292.	301.	97.9	92.3	95.0
Tobacco	38 to 39	4884.	55.12	208.	208.	208.	42.6	42.6	42.6
Clothing and footwear	40 to 51	29886.	256.37	234.	252.	243.	46.3	49.8	48.0
Clothing	40 to 47	27538.	214.57	244.	260.	252.	49.3	52.5	50.9
Footwear	48 to 51	2347.	41.80	182.	182.	182.	30.9	30.9	30.9
Gross rent, fuel	52 to 57	53846.	560.25	328.	266.	295.	36.2	29.3	32.5
Gross rents	52 to 53	44541.	455.04	259.	250.	255.	39.1	37.8	38.4
Fuel and power	54 to 57	9304.	105.21	628.	378.	487.	23.4	14.1	18.1
House furnishings, operation	58 to 71	18252.	252.07	308.	280.	294.	25.8	23.5	24.6
Furniture, appliances	58 to 66	9859.	151.97	364.	363.	363.	17.9	17.8	17.9
Supplies and operation	67 to 71	8393.	100.10	224.	221.	223.	37.9	37.4	37.6
Medical care	72 to 78	26164.	314.74	54.	76.	64.	109.5	154.1	129.9
Transport and communication	79 to 91	24526.	446.09	413.	110.	214.	49.8	13.3	25.8
Equipment	79 to 80	3291.	158.16	419.	359.	388.	5.8	5.0	5.4
Operation costs	81 to 84	4686.	201.28	483.	447.	464.	5.2	4.8	5.0
Purchased transport	85 to 89	14560.	30.68	147.	74.	105.	637.9	322.0	453.2
Communication	90 to 91	1988.	55.97	291.	290.	290.	12.2	12.2	12.2
Recreation and education	92 to 103	49106.	506.75	203.	184.	193.	52.6	47.8	50.1
Recreation	92 to 98	29404.	241.44	266.	281.	273.	43.3	45.8	44.5
Education	99 to 103	19701.	265.30	145.	122.	133.	61.0	51.1	55.9
Other expenditure	104 to 110	44592.	347.63	192.	184.	188.	69.6	66.9	68.2
Personal care	104 to 106	10842.	80.05	211.	191.	201.	71.0	64.1	67.5
Miscellaneous services	107 to 109	33750.	267.58	186.	182.	184.	69.1	67.8	68.5
Capital formation	111 to 148	296272.	837.11	303.	280.	292.	126.4	116.6	121.4
Construction	111 to 112	145817.	463.96	277.	244.	260.	128.7	113.6	120.9
Residential	111 to 122	50509.	147.14	251.	248.	250.	138.2	137.0	137.6
Nonresidential bldgs.	113 to 120	41686.	171.55	354.	334.	344.	72.7	68.7	70.6
Construction exc. bldgs.	121 to 124	53623.	145.27	212.	199.	205.	185.2	174.4	179.7
Producers' durables	125 to 146	109899.	349.12	337.	324.	330.	97.1	93.4	95.2
Transport equipment	125 to 131	32342.	105.85	374.	374.	374.	81.6	81.6	81.6
Nonelectrical machinery	132 to 140	47328.	144.83	305.	288.	296.	113.5	107.2	110.3
Electrical machinery	141 to 144	22006.	59.47	362.	354.	358.	104.5	102.2	103.4
Other durables	145 to 146	8224.	38.97	316.	316.	316.	66.8	66.8	66.8
Government	149 to 153	56558.	692.37	208.	153.	179.	53.3	39.2	45.7
Compensation	149 to 152	40511.	354.32	168.	136.	151	84.3	68.0	75.7
Commodities	153 to 153	16047.	338.05	250.	228.	239.	20.8	19.0	19.9
Gross domestic product	1 to 153	720548.	4801.20	275.	220.	246.	68.1	54.6	61.0

Aggregates

ICP Concepts

Category	Line Number	Japan (Yen)	U.S. (Dollar)	U.S. Weight	Japan Weight	Ideal	U.S. Weight	Japan Weight	Ideal
Consumption (CEP)	1 to 110	367718.	3271.73	282.	199.	237.	56.4	39.9	47.4
Capital formation (GCF)	111 to 148	296272.	837.11	303.	280.	292.	126.4	116.6	121.4
Government (PFC)	149 to 153	56558.	692.37	208.	153.	179.	53.3	39.2	45.7
GDP	1 to 153	720548.	4801.20	275.	220.	246.	68.1	54.6	61.0

SNA Concepts

Category	Line Number	Japan (Yen)	U.S. (Dollar)	U.S. Weight	Japan Weight	Ideal	U.S. Weight	Japan Weight	Ideal
Consumption (PFCE)	1 to 110	345106.	3019.73	294.	214.	251.	53.4	38.9	45.5
Capital formation (GCF)	111 to 148	296272.	837.11	303.	280.	292.	126.4	116.6	121.4
Government (GFCE)	1 to 153	79170.	944.37	188.	131.	157.	63.8	44.6	53.3
GDP	1 to 153	719437.	4798.59	275.	220.	246.	68.1	54.6	61.0

Notes:

1. Line numbers refer to Appendix Table 13.7 and show the detailed categories that are included in each aggregation.
2. Above expenditures for lines 1 to 110 include both household and government expenditures. The latter are shown separately in Appendix Table 13.15. Consumption, SNA excludes these government expenditures.
3. Consumption Aggregate (lines 1 to 110) includes net expenditure of residents abroad (line 110) not shown separately above. Similarly capital formation aggregate (line 111 to 148) includes increase in stocks (line 147) and net exports (line 148). See appendix table for these items.
4. Ideal or Fisher Index is the geometric mean of the indexes with weights of the United States and of Japan.
5. Letters in parentheses are first letters of official terms. See Glossary.
6. Exchange rate: ¥360=US$1.00.

Table 13.8. Summary Binary Table: Expenditures Per Capita, Purchasing-Power Parities and Quantity Per Capita, Kenya–U.S., 1970

Category (1)	Line Number (2)	Per Capita Expenditure		Purchasing-Power Parities Shilling/Dollar			Quantity Per Capita (U.S. = 100)		
		Kenya (Shilling) (3)	U.S. (Dollar) (4)	U.S. Weight (5)	Kenya Weight (6)	Ideal (7)	U.S. Weight (8)	Kenya Weight (9)	Ideal (10)
Consumption, ICP	1 to 110	703.58	3271.73	5.50	2.70	3.85	8.0	3.9	5.6
Food, beverage, tobacco	1 to 39	343.80	564.14	6.06	3.65	4.70	16.7	10.0	15.5
Food	1 to 33	312.17	446.80	5.86	3.48	4.52	20.1	11.9	15.5
Bread and cereals	1 to 6	125.34	55.88	4.03	5.18	4.57	43.3	55.7	49.1
Meat	7 to 12	31.04	150.82	4.39	3.32	3.82	6.2	4.7	5.4
Fish	13 to 14	7.52	11.98	6.52	4.49	5.41	14.0	9.6	11.6
Milk, cheese, eggs	15 to 17	42.05	67.34	4.94	4.27	4.60	14.6	12.6	13.6
Oils and fats	18 to 20	11.39	16.13	7.54	6.09	6.78	11.6	9.4	10.4
Fruits and vegetables	21 to 26	68.10	98.42	5.28	1.82	3.10	37.9	13.1	22.3
Coffee, tea, cocoa	27 to 29	4.72	14.64	6.99	3.44	4.90	9.4	4.6	6.6
Spices and sweets, sugar	30 to 33	22.01	31.59	18.19	5.49	10.00	12.7	3.8	7.0
Beverages	34 to 37	22.11	62.21	9.11	9.10	9.11	3.9	3.9	3.9
Tobacco	38 to 39	9.53	55.12	4.31	4.34	4.32	4.0	4.0	4.0
Clothing and footwear	40 to 51	27.56	256.37	6.24	4.39	5.23	2.4	1.7	2.1
Clothing	40 to 47	22.48	214.57	7.04	5.47	6.20	1.9	1.5	1.7
Footwear	48 to 51	5.08	41.80	2.11	2.35	2.23	5.2	5.8	5.5
Gross rent, fuel	52 to 57	72.39	560.25	7.46	4.27	5.64	3.0	1.7	2.3
Gross rents	52 to 53	61.35	455.04	6.80	5.15	5.92	2.6	2.0	2.3
Fuel and power	54 to 57	11.04	105.21	10.32	2.18	4.75	4.8	1.0	2.2
House furnishings, operation	58 to 71	43.58	252.07	5.90	2.65	3.95	6.5	2.9	4.4
Furniture, appliances	58 to 66	13.02	151.97	7.23	5.35	6.22	1.6	1.2	1.4
Supplies and operation	67 to 71	30.56	100.10	3.87	2.18	2.91	14.0	7.9	10.5
Medical care	72 to 78	36.31	314.74	1.34	0.98	1.15	11.7	8.6	10.0
Transport and communciation	79 to 91	51.21	466.09	7.21	4.28	5.55	2.7	1.6	2.1
Equipment	79 to 80	11.26	158.16	10.04	6.94	8.35	1.0	0.7	0.9
Operation costs	81 to 84	6.37	201.28	6.36	3.25	4.55	1.0	0.5	0.7
Purchased transport	85 to 89	32.16	30.68	5.97	4.06	4.92	25.8	17.6	21.3
Communication	90 to 91	1.43	55.97	2.94	3.05	3.00	0.8	0.9	0.9
Recreation and education	92 to 103	82.78	506.75	4.51	1.31	2.43	12.4	3.6	6.7
Recreation	92 to 98	28.66	241.44	6.88	3.67	5.02	3.2	1.7	2.4
Education	99 to 103	54.12	265.30	2.36	0.98	1.52	20.8	8.7	13.4
Other expenditure	104 to 110	45.96	347.63	3.45	3.21	3.32	4.1	3.8	4.0
Personal care	104 to 106	5.70	80.05	5.93	5.93	5.93	1.2	1.2	1.2
Miscellaneous services	107 to 109	40.26	267.58	2.70	3.01	2.85	5.0	5.6	5.3
Capital formation	111 to 148	206.45	837.11	5.80	4.97	5.37	5.0	4.3	4.6
Construction	111 to 124	112.41	463.96	4.14	4.03	4.09	6.0	5.8	5.9
Residential	111 to 112	42.61	147.14	3.37	3.31	3.34	8.7	8.6	8.7
Nonresidential bldgs.	113 to 120	30.89	171.55	3.51	3.66	3.58	4.9	5.1	5.0
Construction exc. bldgs.	121 to 124	38.91	145.27	5.68	5.92	5.80	4.5	4.7	4.6
Producers' durables	125 to 146	87.99	349.12	7.97	7.45	7.71	3.4	3.2	3.3
Transport equipment	125 to 131	33.38	105.85	7.65	7.69	7.67	4.1	4.1	4.1
Nonelectrical machinery	132 to 140	37.66	144.83	8.38	7.70	8.03	3.4	3.1	3.2
Electrical machinery	141 to 144	9.61	59.47	8.70	6.74	7.66	2.4	1.9	2.1
Other durables	145 to 146	7.35	38.97	6.24	6.40	6.32	2.9	3.0	3.0
Government	149 to 153	117.42	692.37	3.80	1.07	2.01	15.9	4.5	8.4
Compensation	149 to 152	89.22	354.32	2.52	0.87	1.48	28.9	10.0	17.0
Commodities	153 to 153	28.21	338.05	5.15	3.67	4.35	2.3	1.6	1.9
Gross domestic product	1 to 153	1027.46	4801.20	5.30	2.50	3.64	8.6	4.0	5.9
Aggregates									
ICP Concepts									
Consumption (CEP)	1 to 110	703.58	3271.73	5.50	2.70	3.85	8.0	3.9	5.6
Capital formation (GCF)	111 to 148	206.45	837.11	5.80	4.97	5.37	5.0	4.3	4.6
Government (PFC)	149 to 153	117.42	692.37	3.80	1.07	2.01	15.9	4.5	8.4
GDP	1 to 153	1027.46	4801.20	5.30	2.50	3.64	8.6	4.0	5.9
SNA Concepts									
Consumption (PFCE)	1 to 110	653.32	3019.73	5.79	3.19	4.30	6.8	3.7	5.0
Capital formation (GCF)	111 to 148	206.45	837.11	5.80	4.97	5.37	5.0	4.3	4.6
Government (GFCE)	1 to 153	167.69	944.37	3.30	1.01	1.83	17.5	5.4	9.7
GDP	1 to 153	1027.46	4798.59	5.30	2.50	3.64	8.6	4.0	5.9

Notes:
1. Line numbers refer to Appendix Table 13.8 and show the detailed categories that are included in each aggregation.
2. Above expenditures for lines 1 to 110 include both household and government expenditures. The latter are shown separately in Appendix Table 13.15. Consumption, SNA excludes these government expenditures.
3. Consumption aggregate (lines 1 to 110) includes net expenditure of residents abroad (line 110) not shown separately above. Similarly capital formation aggregate (lines 111 to 148) includes increase in stocks (line 147) and net exports (line 148). See appendix table for these items.
4. Ideal or Fisher Index is the geometric mean of the indexes with weights of the United States and of Kenya.
5. Letters in parentheses are first letters of official terms. See Glossary.
6. Exchange rate: Sh7.143=US$1.00.

Table 13.9. Summary Binary Table: Expenditures Per Capita, Purchasing-Power Parities and Quantity Per Capita, U.K.–U.S., 1970

Category (1)	Line Number (2)	Per Capita Expenditure		Purchasing-Power Parities Pound/Dollar			Quantity Per Capita (U.S. = 100)		
		U.K. (Pound) (3)	U.S. (Dollar) (4)	U.S. Weight (5)	U.K. Weight (6)	Ideal (7)	U.S. Weight (8)	U.K. Weight (9)	Ideal (10)
Consumption, ICP	1 to 110	634.348	3271.73	0.335	0.277	0.305	70.0	57.9	63.6
Food, beverage, tobacco	1 to 39	182.429	564.14	0.372	0.360	0.366	89.9	86.9	88.4
Food	1 to 33	111.200	446.80	0.314	0.288	0.301	86.4	79.2	82.7
Bread and cereals	1 to 6	15.342	55.88	0.260	0.233	0.246	117.7	105.5	111.4
Meat	7 to 12	32.363	150.82	0.277	0.270	0.273	79.6	77.6	78.6
Fish	13 to 14	3.894	11.98	0.347	0.325	0.336	100.0	93.6	96.8
Milk, cheese, eggs	15 to 17	16.950	67.34	0.329	0.318	0.324	79.1	76.5	77.8
Oils and fats	18 to 20	4.930	16.13	0.362	0.265	0.310	115.5	84.3	98.7
Fruits and vegetables	21 to 26	20.325	98.42	0.340	0.314	0.326	65.8	60.8	63.3
Coffee, tea, cocoa	27 to 29	4.233	14.64	0.337	0.212	0.267	136.5	85.9	108.2
Spices and sweets, sugar	30 to 33	13.163	31.59	0.432	0.416	0.424	100.3	96.5	98.4
Beverages	34 to 37	40.526	62.21	0.500	0.525	0.513	124.0	130.2	127.1
Tobacco	38 to 39	30.702	55.12	0.695	0.696	0.695	80.1	80.2	80.1
Clothing and footwear	40 to 51	48.706	256.37	0.353	0.321	0.336	59.3	53.9	56.5
Clothing	40 to 47	39.883	214.57	0.379	0.360	0.369	51.7	49.0	50.3
Footwear	48 to 51	8.823	41.80	0.215	0.215	0.215	98.2	98.0	98.1
Gross rent, fuel	52 to 57	102.699	560.25	0.319	0.302	0.310	60.7	57.4	59.1
Gross rents	52 to 53	76.122	455.04	0.275	0.281	0.278	59.5	60.8	60.1
Fuel and power	54 to 57	26.577	105.21	0.508	0.381	0.440	66.2	49.7	57.4
House furnishings, operation	58 to 71	44.044	252.07	0.363	0.330	0.346	52.9	48.2	50.5
Furniture, appliances	58 to 66	24.023	151.97	0.407	0.376	0.391	42.1	38.8	40.4
Supplies and operation	67 to 71	20.022	100.10	0.295	0.289	0.292	69.3	67.8	68.6
Medical care	72 to 78	39.115	314.74	0.131	0.124	0.128	100.2	94.5	97.3
Transport and communication	79 to 91	71.960	446.09	0.500	0.315	0.397	51.3	32.3	40.7
Equipment	79 to 80	18.075	158.16	0.728	0.434	0.562	26.4	15.7	20.3
Operation costs	81 to 84	30.345	201.28	0.428	0.328	0.374	46.0	35.2	40.3
Purchased transport	85 to 89	17.843	30.68	0.347	0.266	0.304	218.8	167.6	191.5
Communication	90 to 91	5.698	55.97	0.198	0.209	0.203	48.8	51.5	50.1
Recreation and education	92 to 103	87.356	506.75	0.287	0.224	0.253	77.0	60.1	68.0
Recreation	92 to 98	47.456	241.44	0.347	0.224	0.279	87.7	56.6	70.4
Education	99 to 103	39.901	265.30	0.232	0.223	0.228	67.3	64.9	66.1
Other expenditure	104 to 110	58.386	347.63	0.305	0.261	0.282	64.2	55.1	59.5
Personal care	104 to 106	12.860	80.05	0.267	0.205	0.234	78.6	60.1	68.7
Miscellaneous services	107 to 109	45.527	267.58	0.316	0.284	0.299	60.0	53.9	56.8
Capital formation	111 to 148	177.481	837.11	0.330	0.302	0.316	70.2	64.3	67.2
Construction	111 to 124	81.123	463.96	0.251	0.248	0.250	70.4	69.5	70.0
Residential	111 to 112	27.005	147.14	0.193	0.193	0.193	95.2	95.0	95.1
Nonresidential bldgs.	113 to 120	36.329	171.55	0.320	0.324	0.322	65.3	66.1	65.7
Construction exc. bldgs.	121 to 124	17.789	145.27	0.229	0.239	0.234	51.2	53.5	52.3
Producers' durables	125 to 146	82.713	349.12	0.430	0.364	0.396	65.0	55.1	59.9
Transport equipment	125 to 131	18.182	105.85	0.648	0.624	0.636	27.5	26.5	27.0
Nonelectrical machinery	132 to 140	43.705	144.83	0.357	0.338	0.347	89.3	84.5	86.9
Electrical machinery	141 to 144	18.486	59.47	0.363	0.322	0.342	96.6	85.6	90.0
Other durables	145 to 146	2.340	38.97	0.210	0.210	0.210	28.6	28.6	28.6
Government	149 to 153	81.248	692.37	0.262	0.212	0.236	55.2	44.8	49.8
Compensation	149 to 152	50.581	354.32	0.212	0.178	0.194	80.3	67.4	73.6
Commodities	153 to 153	30.667	338.05	0.314	0.313	0.313	29.0	28.9	28.9
Gross domestic product	1 to 153	893.073	4801.20	0.324	0.274	0.298	67.9	57.5	62.5
Aggregates									
ICP Concepts									
Consumption (CEP)	1 to 110	634.348	3271.73	0.335	0.277	0.305	70.0	57.9	63.6
Capital formation (GCF)	111 to 148	177.481	837.11	0.330	0.302	0.316	70.2	64.3	67.2
Government (PFC)	149 to 153	81.248	692.37	0.262	0.212	0.236	55.2	44.8	49.8
GDP	1 to 153	893.073	4801.20	0.324	0.274	0.298	67.9	57.5	62.5
SNA Concepts									
Consumption (PFCE)	1 to 110	552.619	3019.73	0.346	0.312	0.328	58.7	52.9	55.7
Capital formation (GCF)	111 to 148	177.481	837.11	0.330	0.302	0.316	70.2	64.3	67.2
Government (GFCE)	1 to 153	162.979	944.37	0.247	0.181	0.211	95.3	70.0	81.7
GDP	1 to 153	887.643	4798.59	0.324	0.274	0.298	67.5	57.2	62.1

Notes:

1. Line numbers refer to Appendix Table 13.9 and show the detailed categories that are included in each aggregation.
2. Above expenditures for lines 1 to 110 include both household and government expenditures. The latter are shown separately in Appendix Table 13.15. Consumption, SNA excludes these government expenditures.
3. Consumption aggregate (lines 1 to 110) includes net expenditure of residents abroad (line 110) not shown separately above. Similarly capital formation aggregate (lines 111 to 148) includes increase in stocks (line 147) and net exports (line 148). See appendix table for these items.
4. Ideal or Fisher Index is the geometric mean of the indexes with weights of the United States and of the United Kingdom.
5. Letters in parentheses are first letters of official terms. See Glossary.
6. Exchange rate: £0.417=US$1.00.

Table 13.10. Summary Binary Table: Expenditures Per Capita, Purchasing-Power Parities and Quantity Per Capita, Hungary–U.S., 1967

Category (1)	Line Number (2)	Per Capita Expenditure		Purchasing-Power Parities Forint/Dollar			Quantity Per Capita (U.S. = 100)		
		Hungary (Forint) (3)	U.S. (Dollar) (4)	U.S. Weight (5)	Hungary Weight (6)	Ideal (7)	U.S. Weight (8)	Hungary Weight (9)	Ideal (10)
Consumption, ICP	1 to 110	15255.7	2646.63	22.0	12.1	16.3	47.6	26.2	35.3
Food, beverage, tobacco	1 to 39	5419.0	475.64	31.0	18.4	23.9	61.9	36.7	47.7
Food	1 to 33	4702.8	376.67	34.6	19.2	25.8	65.0	36.1	48.5
Bread and cereals	1 to 6	724.0	47.11	14.5	9.5	11.7	162.6	106.3	131.4
Meat	7 to 12	1291.1	127.15	41.8	39.9	40.9	25.5	24.3	24.9
Fish	13 to 14	36.4	10.10	34.2	20.9	26.8	17.2	10.5	13.5
Milk, cheese, eggs	15 to 17	594.0	56.77	20.5	19.3	19.9	54.2	51.0	52.6
Oils and fats	18 to 20	492.2	13.59	32.7	42.1	37.1	86.1	110.7	97.6
Fruits and vegetables	21 to 26	768.7	82.98	31.3	11.6	19.0	80.1	29.6	48.7
Coffee, tea, cocoa	27 to 29	147.6	12.34	133.5	119.9	126.5	10.0	9.0	9.5
Spices and sweets, sugar	30 to 33	648.8	26.64	30.9	26.9	28.8	90.6	78.9	84.6
Beverages	34 to 37	475.0	52.20	23.1	18.0	20.4	50.5	39.3	44.6
Tobacco	38 to 39	241.2	46.77	11.4	10.4	10.8	49.8	45.4	47.6
Clothing and footwear	40 to 51	1813.4	210.62	25.6	22.7	24.1	38.0	33.7	35.8
Clothing	40 to 47	1408.7	177.12	26.8	24.4	25.6	32.5	29.7	31.1
Footwear	48 to 51	404.7	33.51	19.0	18.1	18.6	66.6	63.6	65.1
Gross rent, fuel	52 to 57	1176.7	455.21	16.5	9.2	12.3	28.1	15.7	21.0
Gross rents	52 to 53	685.1	365.08	11.8	8.3	9.9	22.7	16.0	19.0
Fuel and power	54 to 57	491.5	90.13	35.5	10.9	19.7	50.0	15.4	27.7
House furnishings, operation	58 to 71	1203.5	217.32	25.8	22.0	23.8	25.2	21.5	23.3
Furniture, appliances	58 to 66	700.9	127.92	28.9	26.2	27.5	20.9	19.0	19.9
Supplies and operation	67 to 71	502.6	89.40	21.3	18.0	19.6	31.2	26.4	28.7
Medical care	72 to 78	846.7	229.55	4.3	4.3	4.3	86.3	85.5	85.9
Transport and communication	79 to 91	862.1	363.71	34.1	15.2	22.8	15.6	6.9	10.4
Equipment	79 to 80	195.3	136.10	55.3	36.9	45.2	3.9	2.6	3.2
Operation costs	81 to 84	140.6	158.74	27.0	16.3	21.0	5.4	3.3	4.2
Purchased transport	85 to 89	462.1	25.12	13.9	14.2	14.0	129.4	132.5	130.9
Communication	90 to 91	64.1	43.75	5.4	6.2	5.8	23.6	27.2	25.3
Recreation and education	92 to 103	1621.5	383.00	15.0	5.7	9.2	74.6	28.3	45.9
Recreation	92 to 98	854.7	193.94	22.1	6.4	11.9	69.3	19.9	37.1
Education	99 to 103	766.9	189.07	7.6	5.1	6.2	80.0	53.3	65.3
Other expenditure	104 to 110	2312.9	292.13	18.4	14.3	16.2	55.2	43.0	48.7
Personal care	104 to 106	324.9	69.85	22.1	9.8	14.7	47.3	21.1	31.6
Miscellaneous services	107 to 109	1988.1	222.27	17.2	15.5	16.4	57.7	51.9	54.7
Capital formation	111 to 148	7274.9	735.72	25.5	20.5	22.8	48.3	38.8	43.3
Construction	111 to 124	3687.0	391.17	16.4	15.9	16.1	59.4	57.4	58.4
Residential	111 to 112	936.8	122.30	15.7	15.1	15.4	50.6	48.6	49.6
Nonresidential bldgs.	113 to 120	1341.8	149.84	17.2	19.3	18.2	46.3	52.1	49.2
Construction exc. bldgs.	121 to 124	1408.4	119.03	16.2	13.9	15.0	84.9	73.0	78.8
Producers' durables	125 to 146	2688.3	306.51	37.1	32.3	34.6	27.1	23.6	25.3
Transport equipment	125 to 131	655.9	90.33	46.9	38.6	42.5	18.8	15.5	17.1
Nonelectrical machinery	132 to 140	1453.9	132.32	34.9	33.6	34.2	32.7	31.5	32.1
Electrical machinery	141 to 144	339.0	51.38	22.6	22.4	22.5	29.5	29.2	29.3
Other durables	145 to 146	239.5	32.48	41.7	30.8	35.9	23.9	17.7	20.6
Government	149 to 153	1629.8	601.60	17.9	12.3	14.9	22.0	15.1	18.2
Compensation	149 to 152	467.5	271.90	6.4	6.2	6.3	27.7	26.7	27.2
Commodities	153 to 153	1162.4	329.70	27.4	20.4	23.6	17.3	12.9	14.9
Gross domestic product	1 to 153	24160.3	3983.95	22.1	13.8	17.5	43.8	27.5	34.7
Aggregates									
ICP Concepts									
Consumption (CEP)	1 to 110	15255.7	2646.63	22.0	12.1	16.3	47.6	26.2	35.3
Capital formation (GCF)	111 to 148	7274.9	735.72	25.5	20.5	22.8	48.3	38.8	43.3
Government (PFC)	149 to 153	1629.8	601.60	17.9	12.3	14.9	22.0	15.1	18.2
GDP	1 to 153	24160.3	3983.95	22.1	13.8	17.5	43.8	27.5	34.7
SNA Concepts									
Consumption (PFCE)	1 to 110	13345.6	2466.88	23.2	15.5	18.9	34.9	23.4	28.6
Capital formation (GCF)	111 to 148	7274.9	735.72	25.5	20.5	22.8	48.3	38.8	43.3
Government (GFCE)	1 to 153	3539.9	781.35	15.3	6.7	10.1	67.8	29.6	44.8
GDP	1 to 153	23895.5	3982.53	22.1	13.9	17.5	43.1	27.2	34.2

Notes:

1. Line numbers refer to Appendix Table 13.10 and show the detailed categories that are included in each aggregation.
2. Above expenditures for lines 1 to 110 include both household and government expenditures. The latter are shown separately in Appendix Table 13.15. Consumption, SNA excludes these government expenditures.
3. Consumption aggregate (lines 1 to 110) includes net expenditure of residents abroad (line 110) not shown separately above. Similarly capital formation aggregate (lines 111 to 148) includes increase in stocks (line 147) and net exports (line 148). See appendix table for these items.
4. Ideal or Fisher Index is the geometric mean of the indexes with weights of the United States and of Hungary.
5. Letters in parentheses are first letters of official terms. See Glossary.
6. Exchange rate: Ft30=US$1.00.

Table 13.11. Summary Binary Table: Expenditures Per Capita, Purchasing-Power Parities and Quantity Per Capita, India–U.S., 1967

Category (1)	Line Number (2)	Per Capita Expenditure		Purchasing-Power Parities Rupee/Dollar			Quantity Per Capita (U.S. = 100)		
		India (Rupee) (3)	U.S. (Dollar) (4)	U.S. Weight (5)	India Weight (6)	Ideal (7)	U.S. Weight (8)	India Weight (9)	Ideal (10)
Consumption, ICP	1 to 110	502.55	2646.63	3.92	2.30	3.00	8.3	4.8	6.3
Food, beverage, tobacco	1 to 39	340.72	475.64	5.42	3.45	4.32	20.8	13.2	16.6
Food	1 to 33	327.32	376.67	4.68	3.47	4.03	25.0	18.6	21.6
Bread and cereals	1 to 6	188.87	47.11	5.65	3.82	4.64	105.0	71.0	86.3
Meat	7 to 12	6.22	127.15	4.38	4.50	4.44	1.1	1.1	1.1
Fish	13 to 14	4.91	10.10	3.71	1.47	2.33	33.1	13.1	20.8
Milk, cheese, eggs	15 to 17	21.85	56.77	3.82	3.08	3.43	12.5	10.1	11.2
Oils and fats	18 to 20	29.36	13.59	4.92	4.44	4.67	48.6	43.9	46.2
Fruits and vegetables	21 to 26	40.45	82.98	3.90	2.99	3.42	16.3	12.5	14.3
Coffee, tea, cocoa	27 to 29	4.80	12.34	10.27	2.94	5.49	13.2	3.8	7.1
Spices and sweets, sugar	30 to 33	30.87	26.64	6.28	2.77	4.17	41.8	18.5	27.8
Beverages	34 to 37	1.65	52.20	8.54	11.81	10.04	0.3	0.4	0.3
Tobacco	38 to 39	11.74	46.77	7.90	2.65	4.58	9.5	3.2	5.5
Clothing and footwear	40 to 51	24.88	210.62	4.07	4.23	4.15	2.8	2.9	2.8
Clothing	40 to 47	22.15	177.12	4.14	4.30	4.22	2.9	3.0	3.0
Footwear	48 to 51	2.73	33.51	3.72	3.73	3.73	2.2	2.2	2.2
Gross rent, fuel	52 to 57	45.40	455.21	2.88	2.51	2.69	4.0	3.5	3.7
Gross rents	52 to 53	20.56	365.08	1.74	1.58	1.66	3.6	3.2	3.4
Fuel and power	54 to 57	24.84	90.13	7.48	4.92	6.07	5.6	3.7	4.5
House furnishings, operation	58 to 71	18.41	217.32	3.76	1.33	2.23	6.4	2.3	3.8
Furniture, appliances	58 to 66	6.30	127.92	4.52	2.58	3.41	1.9	1.1	1.4
Supplies and operation	67 to 71	12.11	89.40	2.68	1.06	1.69	12.8	5.0	8.0
Medical care	72 to 78	12.48	229.55	0.68	0.75	0.72	7.3	7.9	7.6
Transport and communication	79 to 91	23.80	363.71	7.08	2.42	4.14	2.7	0.9	1.6
Equipment	79 to 80	1.88	136.10	11.04	6.90	8.73	0.2	0.1	0.2
Operation costs	81 to 84	2.51	158.74	5.82	2.83	4.06	0.6	0.3	0.4
Purchased transport	85 to 89	18.04	25.12	3.63	2.31	2.90	31.1	19.8	24.8
Communication	90 to 91	1.37	43.75	1.36	1.57	1.46	2.0	2.3	2.1
Recreation and education	92 to 103	17.46	383.00	2.67	0.37	0.99	12.4	1.7	4.6
Recreation	92 to 98	5.12	193.94	4.19	2.12	2.98	1.2	0.6	0.9
Education	99 to 103	12.34	189.07	1.12	0.27	0.55	23.9	5.8	11.8
Other expenditure	104 to 110	19.41	292.13	3.11	2.37	2.72	2.8	2.1	2.4
Personal care	104 to 106	6.59	69.85	3.87	3.43	3.64	2.8	2.4	2.6
Miscellaneous services	107 to 109	12.81	222.27	2.88	2.05	2.43	2.8	2.0	2.4
Capital formation	111 to 148	91.63	735.72	4.18	2.10	2.97	5.9	3.0	4.2
Construction	111 to 124	62.26	391.17	1.81	1.63	1.72	9.7	8.8	9.3
Residential	111 to 112	25.72	122.30	1.71	1.76	1.73	12.0	12.3	12.1
Nonresidential bldgs.	113 to 120	12.23	149.84	2.11	1.99	2.05	4.1	3.9	4.0
Construction exc. bldgs.	121 to 124	24.31	119.03	1.52	1.40	1.46	14.5	13.5	14.0
Producers' durables	125 to 146	34.36	306.51	7.13	6.32	6.71	1.8	1.6	1.7
Transport equipment	125 to 131	9.95	90.33	8.68	8.32	8.50	1.3	1.3	1.3
Nonelectrical machinery	132 to 140	12.03	132.32	7.18	6.56	6.86	1.4	1.3	1.3
Electrical machinery	141 to 144	6.72	51.38	6.30	6.83	6.56	1.9	2.1	2.0
Other durables	145 to 146	5.66	32.48	3.97	3.97	3.97	4.4	4.4	4.4
Government	149 to 153	46.56	601.60	2.32	0.81	1.37	9.6	3.3	5.7
Compensation	149 to 152	27.35	271.90	0.82	0.56	0.68	18.0	12.3	14.9
Commodities	153 to 153	19.21	329.70	3.56	2.25	2.83	2.6	1.6	2.1
Gross domestic product	1 to 153	640.73	3983.95	3.73	2.00	3.73	8.0	4.3	5.9
Aggregates									
ICP Concepts									
Consumption (CEP)	1 to 110	502.55	2646.63	3.92	2.30	3.00	8.3	4.8	6.3
Capital formation (GCF)	111 to 148	91.63	735.72	4.18	2.10	2.97	5.9	3.0	4.2
Government (PFC)	149 to 153	46.56	601.60	2.32	0.81	1.37	9.6	3.3	5.7
GDP	1 to 153	640.73	3983.95	3.73	2.00	2.73	8.0	4.3	5.9
SNA Concepts									
Consumption (PFCE)	1 to 110	493.00	2466.88	4.14	2.68	3.33	7.5	4.8	6.0
Capital formation (GCF)	111 to 148	91.63	735.72	4.18	2.10	2.97	5.9	3.0	4.2
Government (GFCE)	1 to 153	56.11	781.35	2.01	0.61	1.10	11.8	3.6	6.5
GDP	1 to 153	640.73	3982.53	3.73	2.00	2.73	8.0	4.3	5.9

Notes:
1. Line numbers refer to Appendix Table 13.11 and show the detailed categories that are included in each aggregation.
2. Above expenditures for lines 1 to 110 include both household and government expenditures. The latter are shown separately in Appendix Table 13.15. Consumption, SNA excludes these government expenditures.
3. Consumption aggregate (lines 1 to 110) includes net expenditure of residents abroad (line 110) not shown separately above. Similarly capital formation aggregate (lines 111 to 148) includes increase in stocks (line 147) and net exports (line 148). See appendix table for these items.
4. Ideal or Fisher Index is the geometric mean of the indexes with weights of the United States and of India.
5. Letters in parentheses are first letters of official terms. See Glossary.
6. Exchange rate: Rs7.5=US$1.00.

Table 13.12. Summary Binary Table: Expenditures Per Capita, Purchasing-Power Parities and Quantity Per Capita, Japan–U.S., 1967

Category (1)	Line Number (2)	Per Capita Expenditure		Purchasing-Power Parities Yen/Dollar			Quantity Per Capita (U.S. = 100)		
		Japan (Yen) (3)	U.S. (Dollar) (4)	U.S. Weight (5)	Japan Weight (6)	Ideal (7)	U.S. Weight (8)	Japan Weight (9)	Ideal (10)
Consumption, ICP	1 to 110	243092.	2646.63	278.	184.	227.	49.8	33.0	40.6
Food, beverage, tobacco	1 to 39	85991.	475.64	393.	300.	344.	60.2	45.9	52.6
Food	1 to 33	70921.	376.67	427.	311.	364.	60.6	44.1	51.7
Bread and cereals	1 to 6	24506.	47.11	280.	327.	303.	159.1	185.8	171.9
Meat	7 to 12	6957.	127.15	524.	469.	496.	11.7	10.4	11.0
Fish	13 to 14	10152.	10.10	277.	266.	271.	378.4	363.0	370.7
Milk, cheese, eggs	15 to 17	6245.	56.77	380.	332.	355.	33.1	28.9	30.9
Oils and fats	18 to 20	961.	13.59	425.	413.	419.	17.1	16.6	16.9
Fruits and vegetables	21 to 26	14308.	82.98	364.	286.	323.	60.3	47.4	53.4
Coffee, tea, cocoa	27 to 29	1113.	12.34	619.	250.	394.	36.0	14.6	22.9
Spices and sweets, sugar	30 to 33	6678.	26.64	487.	272.	364.	92.3	51.5	68.9
Beverages	34 to 37	11200.	52.20	318.	281.	299.	76.3	67.5	71.7
Tobacco	38 to 39	3870.	46.77	209.	209.	209.	39.5	39.5	39.5
Clothing and footwear	40 to 51	25977.	210.62	231.	221.	226.	55.7	53.3	54.5
Clothing	40 to 47	24460.	177.12	241.	227.	234.	60.9	57.3	59.1
Footwear	48 to 51	1517.	33.51	182.	160.	171.	28.3	24.9	26.5
Gross rent, fuel	52 to 57	35059.	455.21	322.	244.	280.	33.0	31.7	32.4
Gross rents	52 to 53	26790.	365.08	231.	222.	227.	25.2	13.3	18.3
Fuel and power	54 to 57	8268.	90.13	688.	363.	500.	29.8	27.8	28.8
House furnishings, operation	58 to 71	18894.	217.32	313.	291.	302.	33.0	31.7	32.4
Furniture, appliances	58 to 66	8932.	127.92	379.	364.	371.	19.2	18.4	18.8
Supplies and operation	67 to 71	9962.	89.40	220.	247.	233.	45.1	50.7	47.8
Medical care	72 to 78	16717.	229.55	57.	68.	62.	107.6	128.8	117.7
Transport and communication	79 to 91	8797.	363.71	432.	132.	239.	18.4	5.6	10.1
Equipment	79 to 80	1991.	136.10	455.	383.	418.	3.8	3.2	3.5
Operation costs	81 to 84	1026.	158.74	499.	476.	488.	1.4	1.3	1.3
Purchased transport	85 to 89	4253.	25.12	163.	79.	114.	214.2	103.7	149.1
Communication	90 to 91	1526.	43.75	272.	273.	272.	12.8	12.8	12.8
Recreation and education	92 to 103	25786.	383.00	178.	123.	148.	54.7	37.7	45.4
Recreation	92 to 98	19476.	193.94	260.	206.	231.	48.9	38.6	43.4
Education	99 to 103	6310.	189.07	94.	55.	72.	60.7	35.4	46.3
Other expenditure	104 to 110	25201.	292.13	140.	139.	139.	62.2	61.7	61.9
Personal care	104 to 106	9441.	69.85	210.	173.	191.	78.1	64.3	70.9
Miscellaneous services	107 to 109	15760.	222.27	118.	124.	121.	57.2	60.2	58.7
Capital formation	111 to 148	163237.	735.72	305.	274.	289.	80.9	72.8	76.8
Construction	111 to 124	81057.	391.17	285.	246.	265.	84.3	72.6	78.2
Residential	111 to 112	28169.	122.30	253.	252.	252.	91.4	91.1	91.2
Nonresidential bldgs.	113 to 120	23365.	149.84	364.	348.	356.	44.8	42.8	43.8
Construction exc. bldgs.	121 to 124	29522.	119.03	220.	196.	207.	126.8	112.8	119.6
Producers' durables	125 to 146	58256.	306.51	328.	307.	317.	61.9	58.0	59.9
Transport equipment	125 to 131	19663.	90.33	423.	423.	423.	51.5	51.5	51.5
Nonelectrical machinery	132 to 140	26461.	132.32	306.	287.	296.	69.8	65.4	67.5
Electrical machinery	141 to 144	9364.	51.38	221.	221.	221.	82.5	82.5	82.5
Other durables	145 to 146	2768.	32.48	322.	322.	322.	26.5	26.5	26.5
Government	149 to 153	29860.	601.60	202.	153.	175.	32.5	24.6	28.3
Compensation	149 to 152	21276.	271.90	156.	135.	145.	57.8	50.2	53.9
Commodities	153 to 153	8584.	329.70	239.	224.	231.	11.6	10.9	11.3
Gross domestic product	1 to 153	436188.	3983.95	272.	207.	237.	53.0	40.3	46.2
Aggregates									
ICP Concepts									
Consumption (CEP)	1 to 110	243092.	2646.63	278.	184.	227.	49.8	33.0	40.6
Capital formation (GCF)	111 to 148	163237.	735.72	305.	274.	289.	80.9	72.8	76.8
Government (PFC)	149 to 153	29860.	601.60	202.	153.	175.	32.5	24.6	28.3
GDP	1 to 153	436188.	3983.95	272.	207.	237.	53.0	40.3	46.2
SNA Concepts									
Consumption (PFCE)	1 to 110	234971.	2466.88	292.	201.	242.	47.5	32.6	39.4
Capital formation (GCF)	111 to 148	163237.	735.72	305.	274.	289.	80.9	72.8	76.8
Government (GFCE)	1 to 153	37981.	781.35	176.	111.	140.	43.9	27.6	34.8
GDP	1 to 153	435455.	3982.53	272.	207.	237.	52.9	40.3	46.1

Notes:
1. Line numbers refer to Appendix Table 13.12 and show the detailed categories that are included in each aggregation.
2. Above expenditures for lines 1 to 110 include both household and government expenditures. The latter are shown separately in Appendix Table 13.15. Consumption, SNA excludes these government expenditures.
3. Consumption aggregate (lines 1 to 110) includes net expenditure of residents abroad (line 110) not shown separately above. Similarly capital formation aggregate (lines 111 to 148) includes increase in stocks (line 147) and net exports (line 148). See appendix table for these items.
4. Ideal or Fisher Index is the geometric mean of the indexes with weights of the United States and of Japan.
5. Letters in parentheses are first letters of official terms. See Glossary.
6. Exchange rate: ¥360=US$1.00.

Table 13.13. Summary Binary Table: Expenditures Per Capita, Purchasing-Power Parities and Quantity Per Capita, Kenya–U.S., 1967

Category (1)	Line Number (2)	Per Capita Expenditure — Kenya (Shilling) (3)	Per Capita Expenditure — U.S. (Dollar) (4)	Purchasing-Power Parities Shilling/Dollar — U.S. Weight (5)	Kenya Weight (6)	Ideal (7)	Quantity Per Capita (U.S. = 100) — U.S. Weight (8)	Kenya Weight (9)	Ideal (10)
Consumption, ICP	1 to 110	626.79	2646.63	5.96	2.90	4.15	8.2	4.0	5.7
Food, beverage, tobacco	1 to 39	313.12	475.64	6.43	4.14	5.16	15.9	10.2	12.8
Food	1 to 33	278.99	376.67	6.12	3.94	4.91	18.8	12.1	15.1
Bread and cereals	1 to 6	99.77	47.11	4.07	5.29	4.64	40.0	52.0	45.6
Meat	7 to 12	38.51	127.15	4.77	3.70	4.20	8.2	6.3	7.2
Fish	13 to 14	8.58	10.10	7.39	5.24	6.22	16.2	11.5	13.6
Milk, cheese, eggs	15 to 17	39.17	56.77	5.29	4.56	4.91	15.1	13.0	14.0
Oils and fats	18 to 20	10.44	13.59	7.83	6.18	6.96	12.4	9.8	11.0
Fruits and vegetables	21 to 26	58.37	82.98	5.31	2.40	3.57	29.3	13.3	19.7
Coffee, tea, cocoa	27 to 29	6.10	12.34	6.97	3.43	4.88	14.4	7.1	10.1
Spices and sweets, sugar	30 to 33	18.05	26.64	18.79	5.18	9.86	13.1	3.6	6.9
Beverages	34 to 37	20.54	52.20	9.84	9.25	9.54	4.3	4.0	4.1
Tobacco	38 to 39	13.59	46.77	5.06	5.11	5.09	5.7	5.7	5.7
Clothing and footwear	40 to 51	20.05	210.62	6.91	4.52	5.58	2.1	1.4	1.7
Clothing	40 to 47	15.87	177.12	7.78	5.71	6.67	1.6	1.2	1.3
Footwear	48 to 51	4.17	33.51	2.26	2.52	2.39	4.9	5.5	5.2
Gross rent, fuel	52 to 57	64.91	455.21	8.07	5.15	6.45	2.8	1.8	2.2
Gross rents	52 to 53	55.61	365.08	7.50	5.68	6.52	2.7	2.0	2.3
Fuel and power	54 to 57	9.29	90.13	10.36	3.32	5.87	3.1	1.0	1.8
House furnishings, operation	58 to 71	36.42	217.32	5.91	2.54	3.87	6.6	2.8	4.3
Furniture, appliances	58 to 66	8.38	127.92	7.04	4.49	5.62	1.5	0.9	1.2
Supplies and operation	67 to 71	28.04	89.40	4.30	2.24	3.11	14.0	7.3	10.1
Medical care	72 to 78	25.62	229.55	1.38	1.00	1.17	11.2	8.1	9.5
Transport and communication	79 to 91	57.97	363.71	8.09	5.88	6.90	2.7	2.0	2.3
Equipment	79 to 80	10.38	136.10	11.21	7.71	9.30	1.0	0.7	0.8
Operation costs	81 to 84	16.13	158.74	6.97	5.82	6.37	1.7	1.5	1.6
Purchased transport	85 to 89	30.32	25.12	6.61	5.61	6.09	21.5	18.3	19.8
Communication	90 to 91	1.15	43.75	3.34	3.43	3.38	0.8	0.8	0.8
Recreation and education	92 to 103	65.90	383.00	4.65	1.07	2.23	16.1	3.7	7.7
Recreation	92 to 98	22.62	193.94	7.10	3.47	4.97	3.4	1.6	2.3
Education	99 to 103	43.28	189.07	2.13	0.78	1.29	29.2	10.8	17.7
Other expenditure	104 to 110	42.81	292.13	3.82	3.56	3.68	4.1	3.8	4.0
Personal care	104 to 106	4.04	69.85	6.19	5.65	5.91	1.0	0.9	1.0
Miscellaneous services	107 to 109	38.77	222.27	3.07	3.42	3.24	5.1	5.7	5.4
Capital formation	111 to 148	171.03	735.72	5.80	5.38	5.59	4.3	4.0	4.2
Construction	111 to 124	81.41	391.17	4.13	4.16	4.14	5.0	5.0	5.0
Residential	111 to 112	25.44	122.30	3.53	3.50	3.52	5.9	5.9	5.9
Nonresidential bldgs.	113 to 120	20.73	149.84	3.75	3.37	3.56	4.1	3.7	3.9
Construction exc. bldgs.	121 to 124	35.24	119.03	5.21	5.72	5.46	5.2	5.7	5.4
Producers' durables	125 to 146	84.18	306.51	7.91	7.60	7.75	3.6	3.5	3.5
Transport equipment	125 to 131	37.26	90.33	7.87	7.88	7.87	5.2	5.2	5.2
Nonelectrical machinery	132 to 140	32.35	132.32	7.89	7.57	7.73	3.2	3.1	3.2
Electrical machinery	141 to 144	8.25	51.38	8.74	7.17	7.91	2.2	1.8	2.0
Other durables	145 to 146	6.31	32.48	6.78	6.85	6.82	2.8	2.9	2.9
Government	148 to 153	88.95	601.60	4.25	1.16	2.22	12.7	3.5	6.7
Compensation	149 to 152	67.58	271.90	2.75	0.95	1.62	26.2	9.0	15.4
Commodities	153 to 153	21.37	329.70	5.48	3.99	4.68	1.6	1.2	1.4
Gross domestic product	1 to 153	886.77	3983.95	5.67	2.73	3.93	8.2	3.9	5.7
Aggregates									
ICP Concepts									
Consumption (CEP)	1 to 110	626.79	2646.63	5.96	2.90	4.15	8.2	4.0	5.7
Capital formation (GCF)	111 to 148	171.03	735.72	5.80	5.38	5.59	4.3	4.0	4.2
Government (PFC)	149 to 153	88.95	601.60	4.25	1.16	2.22	12.7	3.5	6.7
GDP	1 to 153	866.77	3983.95	5.67	2.73	3.93	8.2	3.9	5.7
SNA Concepts									
Consumption (PFCE)	1 to 110	590.44	2466.88	6.26	3.48	4.67	6.9	3.8	5.1
Capital formation (GCF)	111 to 148	171.03	735.72	5.80	5.38	5.59	4.3	4.0	4.2
Government (GFCE)	1 to 153	125.30	781.35	3.69	1.01	1.93	15.8	4.3	8.3
GDP	1 to 153	886.77	3982.53	5.67	2.73	3.93	8.2	3.9	5.7

Notes:

1. Line numbers refer to Appendix Table 13.13 and show the detailed categories that are included in each aggregation.

2. Above expenditures for lines 1 to 110 include both household and government expenditures. The latter are shown separately in Appendix Table 13.15. Consumption, SNA excludes these government expenditures.

3. Consumption aggregate (lines 1 to 110) includes net expenditure of residents abroad (line 110) not shown separately above. Similarly capital formation aggregate (lines 111 to 148) includes increase in stocks (line 147) and net exports (line 148). See appendix table for these items.

4. Ideal or Fisher Index is the geometric mean of the indexes with weights of the United States and of Kenya.

5. Letters in parentheses are first letters of official terms. See Glossary.

6. Exchange rate: Sh7.143=US$1.00.

Table 13.14. Summary Binary Table: Expenditures Per Capita, Purchasing-Power Parities and Quantity Per Capita, U.K.–U.S., 1967

Category (1)	Line Number (2)	Per Capita Expenditure		Purchasing-Power Parities Pound/Dollar			Quantity Per Capita (U.S. = 100)		
		U.K. (Pound) (3)	U.S. (Dollar) (4)	U.S. Weight (5)	U.K. Weight (6)	Ideal (7)	U.S. Weight (8)	U.K. Weight (9)	Ideal (10)
Consumption, ICP	1 to 110	517.973	2646.63	0.332	0.274	0.302	71.5	58.9	64.9
Food, beverage, tobacco	1 to 39	156.499	475.64	0.367	0.346	0.357	95.0	89.6	92.3
Food	1 to 33	97.420	376.67	0.302	0.276	0.289	93.8	85.5	89.6
Bread and cereals	1 to 6	13.500	47.11	0.236	0.215	0.225	133.6	121.3	127.3
Meat	7 to 12	27.798	127.15	0.263	0.259	0.261	84.5	83.0	83.8
Fish	13 to 14	3.556	10.10	0.334	0.319	0.326	110.6	105.4	108.0
Milk, cheese, eggs	15 to 17	14.788	56.77	0.317	0.308	0.313	84.5	82.1	83.3
Oils and fats	18 to 20	4.573	13.59	0.355	0.257	0.302	131.1	94.7	111.4
Fruits and vegetables	21 to 26	18.163	82.98	0.334	0.309	0.321	70.9	65.6	68.2
Coffee, tea, cocoa	27 to 29	3.647	12.34	0.364	0.207	0.274	143.1	81.3	107.9
Spices and sweets, sugar	30 to 33	11.395	26.64	0.409	0.388	0.398	110.3	104.6	107.4
Beverages	34 to 37	31.717	52.20	0.493	0.510	0.501	119.2	123.3	121.2
Tobacco	38 to 39	27.362	46.77	0.749	0.748	0.749	78.2	78.1	78.1
Clothing and footwear	40 to 51	41.134	210.62	0.375	0.338	0.356	57.7	52.1	54.9
Clothing	40 to 47	33.695	177.12	0.402	0.380	0.391	50.0	47.3	48.6
Footwear	48 to 51	7.439	33.51	0.227	0.225	0.226	98.6	97.8	98.2
Gross rent, fuel	52 to 57	81.362	455.21	0.300	0.281	0.291	63.6	59.5	61.5
Gross rents	52 to 53	59.497	365.08	0.258	0.266	0.262	61.3	63.2	62.3
Fuel and power	54 to 57	21.865	90.13	0.472	0.334	0.397	72.6	51.4	61.1
House furnishings, operation	58 to 71	37.687	217.32	0.351	0.323	0.337	53.8	49.4	51.5
Furniture, appliances	58 to 66	20.867	127.92	0.395	0.357	0.376	45.7	41.3	43.4
Supplies and operation	67 to 71	16.820	89.40	0.288	0.288	0.288	65.3	65.4	65.3
Medical care	72 to 78	29.014	229.55	0.131	0.125	0.128	101.0	96.4	98.7
Transport and communication	79 to 91	55.777	363.71	0.507	0.326	0.406	47.1	30.3	37.8
Equipment	79 to 80	14.661	136.10	0.742	0.435	0.568	24.8	14.5	19.0
Operation costs	81 to 84	21.556	158.74	0.412	0.316	0.361	43.0	33.0	37.6
Purchased transport	85 to 89	15.133	25.12	0.369	0.307	0.337	196.0	163.2	178.8
Communication	90 to 91	4.427	43.75	0.197	0.220	0.208	45.9	51.3	48.5
Recreation and education	92 to 103	67.553	383.00	0.266	0.211	0.237	83.5	66.4	74.5
Recreation	92 to 98	37.215	193.94	0.311	0.210	0.255	91.5	61.7	75.2
Education	99 to 103	30.338	189.07	0.219	0.213	0.216	75.2	73.3	74.2
Other expenditure	104 to 110	47.594	292.13	0.309	0.256	0.281	63.6	52.7	57.9
Personal care	104 to 106	10.742	69.85	0.241	0.198	0.219	77.6	63.7	70.3
Miscellaneous services	107 to 109	36.852	222.27	0.330	0.280	0.304	59.2	50.2	54.5
Capital formation	111 to 148	129.463	735.72	0.322	0.283	0.302	62.2	54.6	58.3
Construction	111 to 124	69.168	391.17	0.263	0.254	0.258	69.7	67.3	68.5
Residential	111 to 112	26.981	122.30	0.206	0.209	0.207	105.7	107.0	106.3
Nonresidential bldgs.	113 to 120	29.377	149.84	0.330	0.331	0.331	59.2	59.4	59.3
Construction exc. bldgs.	121 to 124	12.810	119.03	0.236	0.234	0.235	46.0	45.7	45.8
Producers' durables	125 to 146	64.723	306.51	0.394	0.328	0.359	64.5	53.6	58.8
Transport equipment	125 to 131	12.284	90.33	0.588	0.566	0.577	24.0	23.1	23.6
Nonelectrical machinery	132 to 140	35.165	132.32	0.341	0.310	0.325	85.8	78.0	81.8
Electrical machinery	141 to 144	15.242	51.38	0.312	0.292	0.302	101.6	95.2	98.4
Other durables	145 to 146	2.032	32.48	0.200	0.200	0.200	31.3	31.3	31.3
Government	149 to 153	73.033	601.60	0.271	0.231	0.250	52.5	44.8	48.5
Compensation	149 to 152	39.011	271.90	0.235	0.193	0.213	74.2	61.0	67.3
Commodities	153 to 153	34.022	329.70	0.301	0.298	0.299	34.6	34.3	34.5
Gross domestic product	1 to 153	720.465	3983.95	0.321	0.270	0.295	66.9	56.3	61.4
Aggregates									
ICP Concepts									
Consumption (CEP)	1 to 110	517.973	2646.63	0.332	0.274	0.302	71.5	58.9	64.9
Capital formation (GCF)	111 to 148	129.463	735.72	0.322	0.283	0.302	62.2	54.6	58.3
Government (PFC)	149 to 153	73.033	601.60	0.271	0.231	0.250	52.5	44.8	48.5
GDP	1 to 153	720.465	3983.95	0.321	0.270	0.295	66.9	56.3	61.4
SNA Concepts									
Consumption (PFCE)	1 to 110	458.006	2466.88	0.342	0.303	0.322	61.2	54.2	57.6
Capital formation (GCF)	111 to 148	129.463	735.72	0.322	0.283	0.302	62.2	54.6	58.3
Government (GFCE)	1 to 153	133.002	781.35	0.254	0.190	0.220	89.5	67.1	77.5
GDP	1 to 153	716.927	3982.53	0.321	0.270	0.295	66.6	56.0	61.1

Notes:
1. Line numbers refer to Appendix Table 13.14 and show the detailed categories that are included in each aggregation.
2. Above expenditures for lines 1 to 110 include both household and government expenditures. The latter are shown separately in Appendix Table 13.15. Consumption, SNA excludes these government expenditures.
3. Consumption aggregate (lines 1 to 110) includes net expenditure of residents abroad (line 110) not shown separately above. Similarly capital formation aggregate (lines 111 to 148) includes increase in stocks (line 147) and net exports (line 148). See appendix table for these items.
4. Ideal or Fisher Index is the geometric mean of the indexes with weights of the United States and of the United Kingdom.
5. Letters in parentheses are first letters of official terms. See Glossary.
6. Exchange rate: £0.357=US$1.00.

Before attempting to describe the main results of the comparisons, we present as a useful background Table 13.16, a summary breakdown of the expenditures of each of the ten countries. We do not stop now to describe the relationships depicted in this table, but will draw upon them as they become relevant to the illumination of the quantity and price comparisons.

The main results of the binary quantity comparisons are summarized in Table 13.17, which is composed of figures from Tables 13.1 to 13.14. Part A refers to 1970 and Part B to 1967. The countries are arrayed from left to right in order of ascending real GDP per capita, as measured by the ideal index (line 4).

The 1970 per capita GDP for the nine countries varies from 4 percent to 68 percent of that of the United States when valued in each country's own prices, and from 8.5 to 82 percent when valued in United States prices. Kenya and India have the lowest per capita GDP. Colombia's, although notably higher, is still low. Hungary and Italy are at the next level, followed by Japan and the United Kingdom. The Federal Republic of Germany and France, with almost identical indexes, are closest to the United States level of per capita GDP. Although this broad picture applies regardless of the basis of evaluation, the ordinal rankings of Kenya and India are different for the two sets of valuations.

The per capita quantity indexes for the major sub-aggregates—consumption, capital formation, and government—generally show a rather similar pattern. The main exception is the high level of per capita capital formation in Japan, France, and the Federal Republic of Germany. These are the only cases in the table in which the figures exceed 100—indicating, of course, that the per capita product is greater than that of the United States. The per capita capital formation figures for France and the Federal Republic of Germany contrast sharply with the corresponding figures that were estimated for 1950 in a predecessor study.[2] As was noted in Chapter 1, the per capita quantity indexes for these two countries were only 30 to 40 percent of that of the United States at the earlier date; in 1970, they exceeded the United States by 20 to 50 percent. This reflects in large part the high proportion of GDP that these countries devoted to investment in 1970 relative to the U.S. proportion; around 30 percent of French and German GDP went for capital expenditures, compared with 17 percent in the United States (see Table 13.16). In Japan, 1970 real per capita investment was substantially higher than in the United States, and Japan devoted a high proportion of its GDP—41 percent—to capital formation. The United Kingdom did not have high levels of investment. Instead, its consumption accounted for a high share of total

GDP; in real terms, U.K. per capita consumption was about the same as that of France and the Federal Republic of Germany, even though its total per capita GDP was smaller.

For seven of the nine countries, the government indexes computed on the ICP basis (lines 13 to 15) are smaller than those for consumption. The ICP does not provide a breakdown for defense expenditures, but it seems clear that higher U.S. expenditures of this type, accounting in 1970 for about one-third of government purchases of goods and services (SNA concept), contribute to this result. (Note that the smaller government indexes mean that real per capita government services relative to the United States are smaller than real per capita consumption relative to the United States.)

A convenient way to evaluate the differences between the results for the ICP and SNA concepts of consumption and government is to compare the two sets of indexes for government. The fact that the SNA government figures are uniformly larger than those of the ICP indicates that in most other countries expenditures for education, medical care, and the like are financed by government to a greater degree than is the case in the United States. Among categories, the differences tend to be largest for medical care (see Table 13.15), and among countries, the difference is most marked for Hungary, the United Kingdom, and Italy (Table 13.17).

Large differences exist even among subsets of countries that sometimes are treated as though they were homogeneous. For example, among the three developing countries, the per capita GDP of Colombia is approximately 2.5 times that of Kenya or India, and among the Common Market countries, the per capita GDPs of France and the Federal Republic of Germany are 1.5 times that of Italy.

Fewer comparisons are available for 1967. The most notable difference revealed by these data is the remarkable rise in the relative position of Japan between 1967 and 1970. Hungary also gained ground relative to the United States. The differences between the two years for the other countries were marginal.

As expected, the gap (line 3) between own-weighted and U.S.-weighted quantity indexes (lines 1 and 2, respectively) is inversely correlated with GDP per capita (see Figure 13.1). For lowest-income countries—Kenya, India, and Colombia—valuation at U.S. prices produces a quantity index about twice as great as valuation at own prices. For the highest-income countries, the gap is only about 20 percent.

The economic reasons for the gap are, of course, well understood, as frequent references in the literature to the "Gerschenkron effect" testify. The structure of each country's quantities adapts to its own price structure: expensive commodities are consumed in relatively small amounts, and cheap ones are consumed in relatively large amounts. Thus, the size of the index spread is likely to be a function of the degree of similarity be-

---

[2] M. Gilbert and I. Kravis, *An International Comparison of National Products and the Purchasing Power of Currencies* (Paris: Organization for European Economic Cooperation, 1954).

Figure 13.1. Index-Number Spread in Relation to Real Per Capita GDP

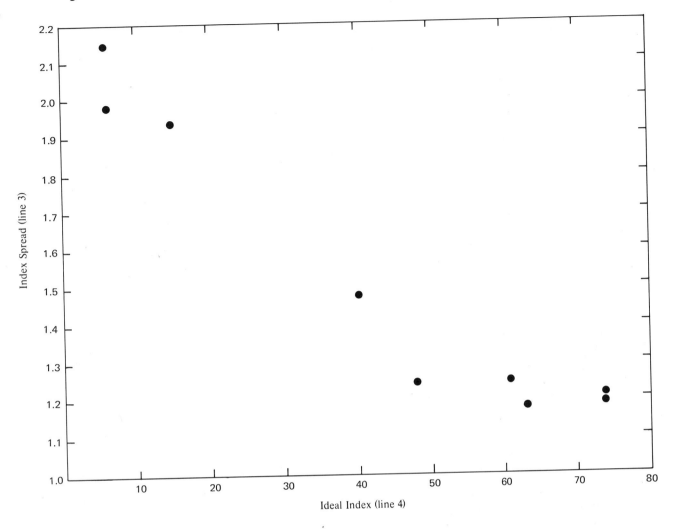

Source: Table 13.17

tween the price structure of the base country and that of the given country. It may be argued that, in turn, similarity in price structure is inversely associated with the size of the difference in real GDP per capita (see Chapter 15 for our findings on this point).

Among the countries included in the present study, labor-intensive commodities and services, for example, tend to be cheap in Kenya and India, both low GDP countries, so relatively large quantities are apt to be consumed. On the other hand, capital-intensive goods are likely to be expensive and therefore consumed in lesser quantities. In the United States, the opposite price and quantity relationships tend to prevail. Thus, when the quantities of a low-income country such as Kenya or India are valued at U.S. prices, the country's GDP is much larger relative to the U.S. GDP than when the country's own prices are used in the valuation.

The size of the index spread does not reflect merely economic factors, however. Its magnitude is also very much a function of the methods of aggregation. In the

ICP, unweighted price relatives within each of 153 categories were used to derive indirect quantity indexes (with a few exceptions in which direct quantity indexes were estimated). The two sets of prices, U.S. and "own," were applied to these relative quantities to obtain the aggregates for the binary comparisons summarized in Table 13.17. The index spread would have been different if we had applied the weights at a different level of aggregation: it would have been larger if we had applied weights at a more disaggregated level, smaller if we had applied them at a more aggregated level. Because the methods were the same for all fourteen comparisons, the index spread may legitimately be compared for different binary comparisons, as was done three paragraphs above. But comparisons of the spreads reported in Table 13.17 with those of the Gilbert-Kravis and other studies must take this source of difference into account.

To simplify the rest of our discussion, we work with the ideal index. The own-weighted and U.S.-weighted indexes have a clear economic rationale that the ideal

Table 13.15. Government Components of Final Consumption Expenditure of Population

		ICP category		Part A. Per Capita Expenditure, 1970									
				Colombia (Peso)	France (Franc)	Germany F.R. (D. Mark)	Hungary (Forint)	India (Rupee)	Italy (Lira)	Japan (Yen)	Kenya (Shilling)	U.K. (Pound)	U.S. (Dollar)
1	3	110G	Rents	0.0	4.51	8.30	342.7	0.0	0.	1111.	0.0	5.430	2.60
2	5	110G	Drugs, medical preparations	0.0	0.06	12.30	261.1	0.23	92.	783.	0.36	4.465	0.89
3	5	120G	Medical supplies	0.0	0.0	4.66	80.6	0.10	18.	793.	0.12	0.464	0.12
4	5	200G	Therapeutic equipment	0.0	0.75	5.21	0.0	0.13	73.	159.	0.00	1.268	0.21
5	5	310G	Physicians' services	9.5	33.09	29.25	101.4	0.42	1934.	944.	2.19	5.180	1.65
6	5	320G	Dentists' services	1.9	0.0	0.0	7.9	0.00	0.	203.	0.0	1.482	0.51
7	5	330G	Services, nurses, etc.	0.2	31.71	43.94	106.8	0.62	1734.	834.	2.97	9.466	14.76
8	5	410G	Hospitals	3.5	5.89	30.71	413.5	1.05	3831.	676.	8.40	12.395	15.77
9	7	210G	Public entertainment	0.0	0.0	0.0	126.3	0.09	0.	0.	0.13	3.054	7.95
10	7	230G	Other recreational cultural activities	0.0	0.0	0.0	46.9	0.11	0.	0.	0.0	0.0	0.0
11	7	411G	Teachers, 1st and 2nd	75.5	595.58	311.95	453.8	7.57	40463.	11144.	27.52	20.290	152.49
12	7	412G	Teachers, college	21.7	88.23	62.46	46.6	0.62	4798.	902.	1.36	3.179	19.87
13	7	420G	Educational physical facilities	12.1	34.39	58.75	237.8	0.37	2675.	2198.	3.81	5.358	19.19
14	7	431G	Educational books, supplies	2.2	5.30	2.75	24.7	0.22	457.	806.	1.57	1.947	4.58
15	7	432G	Other education expenditures	4.7	5.59	21.10	103.1	0.42	1431.	955.	1.83	3.644	4.87
16	8	400G	Other services	14.0	0.0	0.0	105.3	0.0	0.0	1103.	0.0	4.108	6.52

		ICP category		Part B. Per Capita Expenditure, 1967					
				Hungary (Forint)	India (Rupee)	Japan (Yen)	Kenya (Shilling)	U.K. (Pound)	U.S. (Dollar)
1	3	110G	Rents	264.9	0.0	732.	0.0	3.538	1.42
2	5	110G	Drugs, medical preparation	210.6	0.21	1665.	0.23	3.429	0.91
3	5	120G	Medical supplies	36.7	0.09	193.	0.09	0.345	0.12
4	5	200G	Therapeutic equipment	0.0	0.11	52.	0.00	0.962	0.13
5	5	310G	Physicians' services	93.2	0.33	302.	1.66	3.702	2.72
6	5	320G	Services of dentists	7.4	0.00	13.	0.0	1.052	0.28
7	5	330G	Services, nurses, etc.	97.9	0.49	254.	1.93	6.750	10.44
8	5	410G	Hospitals	317.0	0.86	600.	4.89	9.145	12.18
9	7	210G	Public entertainment	80.7	0.02	0.	0.12	2.214	5.58
10	7	230G	Other recreational, cultural activities	44.2	0.08	0.	0.0	0.0	0.0
11	7	411G	Teachers, 1st and 2nd	364.3	6.03	2628.	21.01	15.151	108.58
12	7	412G	Teachers, college	38.4	0.50	207.	1.00	2.377	11.33
13	7	420G	Educational, physical facilities	168.7	0.31	819.	2.87	4.137	15.20
14	7	431G	Educational books, supplies	17.2	0.18	300.	1.18	1.506	3.63
15	7	432G	Other education expenditures	83.0	0.36	356.	1.37	2.812	3.86
16	8	400G	Other services	85.7	0.0	0.	0.0	2.849	3.39

index lacks, but the convenience of a single number that is a compromise between the two is responsible for its widespread use and for our use here. (Actually, the multilateral indexes presented in the next chapter are to be preferred over the ideal index as single-number estimates of relative GDP per capita, but our task in this chapter is to summarize the results of the more familiar binary comparisons.) Little if anything that we have to say would be much altered if we worked with the two more basic sets of indexes: we would just have to say it in a more cumbersome way.

The first question to which we address ourselves is the difference between the relative per capita GDPs obtained by the ICP and those derived by the use of exchange rates. This is important because the major reason for this entire undertaking rests on the proposition that exchange rates are not the proper basis for making GDP commensurable.

Per capita comparisons of GDP that have been derived from exchange rates are entered on line 5 of

Table 13.17. The per capita GDP of Japan, for example, has been converted to dollars (by dividing its value in yen by 360), and taken as a percentage of the U.S. per capita GDP. The underlying data for these conversions—aggregate GDP, population, and exchange rates—may be found in Table 1.1. (The exchange rates are shown also in line 4 of Table 13.19.)

As a convenient means of indicating the difference between these exchange-rate-derived comparisons and the ICP results, an "exchange-rate-deviation index"[3] has been calculated and entered in line (6). The index is obtained by dividing the per capita GDP of each country relative to the United States, as measured by the ideal index, by the exchange-rate-derived comparisons. The exchange rate deviation index of 1.97 for Kenya, for

[3]Our use of this term is simply a matter of convenience; it is not intended to express any judgment about the appropriateness of the exchange rate. The "equilibrium" exchange rate is determined by more factors than simply the PPP for GDP. (See pages 9–10.

example, results from the division of the real per capita GDP of Kenya relative to the United States, 5.9 percent, by the exchange-rate–derived per capita GDP of Kenya relative to the United States, 3.0 percent. The exchange rate distortion index of nearly 2 reflects the fact that the real per capita GDP of Kenya relative to the United States is twice as high as would be inferred from exchange rates. (The own-weighted or U.S.-weighted quantity indexes also might have been used to calculate an exchange rate deviation index, but, as already noted, the use of the ideal index represents a useful compromise that serves the interests of brevity.)

Relative to the United States, the 1970 per capita GDPs of the other countries range from about 15 percent higher than that indicated by the exchange rate to three times greater. The differences tend to be larger for low-income countries, but factors other than income level are at work as well (see Figure 13.2). For example, among the industrialized market economies, the exchange-rate–deviation index is highest for Japan, though its per capita GDP is substantially greater than that of Italy; and among the developing countries, Kenya's index is lower than that of Colombia despite the fact that Kenya has a substantially lower per capita GDP.

The nature of the underlying structural relationship that may exist between the exchange-rate–deviation index and the level of real per capita GDP has attracted the attention of a number of investigators,[4] but it cannot be understood fully until more observations such as those we offer in this study have been accumulated. However, some a priori hypotheses about the identity of some of the other factors affecting this relationship receive some hints of support in the present set of results. As between two countries with equal per capita GDP, the one with closer trading ties with other countries may be expected to have a lower exchange-rate–deviation index than one whose economy is less influ-

---

[4]Gilbert and Kravis, *An International Comparison*, pp. 50–57; E. E. Hagen, "Comment," *Problems in the International Comparison of Economic Accounts*, Studies in Income and Wealth, Vol. XX (Princeton, N. J.: Princeton University Press, 1957), pp. 381–85; B. Balassa, "The Purchasing Power Parity Doctrine: A Reappraisal," *Journal of Political Economy* 72 (December 1964), pp. 584–96; C. Clague and V. Tanzi, "Human Capital, Natural Resources and the Purchasing Power Parity Doctine: Some Empirical Results," *Economia Internazionale* 25 (February 1972), pp. 3–18; and P. A. David, "Just how Misleading Are Official Exchange Rates?", *Economic Journal* 82 (September 1972), pp. 979–90.

Figure 13.2. Exchange-Rate Deviation Index in Relation to Real Per Capita GDP

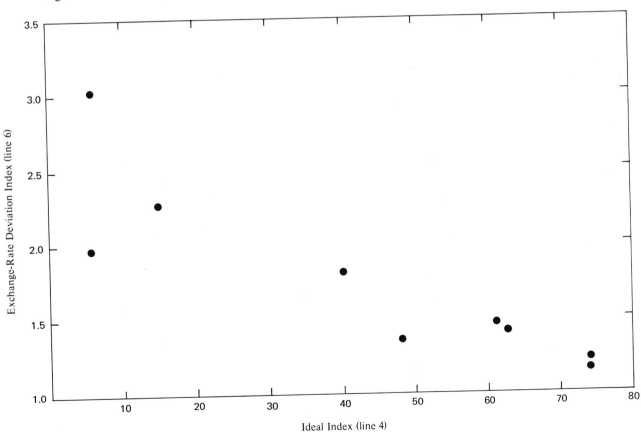

Source: Table 13.17

Table 13.16. Percentage Distribution of Expenditures on Gross Domestic Product, Ten Countries, 1970

	Kenya	India	Colombia	Hungary	Italy	Japan	U.K.	Germany, F.R.	France	U.S.
Consumption†	68.5	75.5	74.8	60.4	69.8	51.0	71.0	58.9	63.9	68.1
Food, beverages, tobacco	33.5	49.6	24.8	21.5	26.3	16.7	20.4	14.1	17.6	11.7
Clothing and footwear	2.7	3.1	4.2	7.0	5.8	4.1	5.5	6.1	5.9	5.3
Housing and household	11.3	10.4	16.8	9.6	12.0	10.0	16.4	13.8	12.3	16.9
Medical care	3.5	2.2	2.0	3.5	4.9	3.6	4.4	5.5	5.7	6.6
Education	5.3	2.1	3.9	3.2	5.0	2.7	4.5	4.4	4.7	5.5
Transport and communication	5.0	4.3	8.8	3.5	6.5	3.4	8.1	6.4	6.4	9.3
All other	7.3	3.8	14.3	12.1	9.3	10.3	11.9	8.5	11.3	12.3
Capital formation‡	20.1	16.6	19.9	31.8	22.9	41.1	19.9	30.4	28.9	17.4
Construction	10.9	7.8	11.8	18.6	13.5	20.2	9.1	14.3	14.9	9.7
Producers durables	8.6	4.9	7.9	12.3	7.8	15.3	9.3	12.1	10.9	7.3
Government	11.4	7.9	5.3	7.8	7.3	7.8	9.1	10.7	7.2	14.4
GDP	100.0	100.0	100.0	100.0	100.0	100.0	100.0	100.0	100.0	100.0

†Includes net expenditure of residents abroad.
‡Includes changes in stocks and net exports.

enced by world prices through trade. The relationships among our three less developed countries are consistent with this expectation. Exports plus imports as percentages of GDP for India, Colombia, and Kenya were 8.5, 20.9, and 39.1 percent, respectively, and the exchange-rate–deviation indexes were 3.05, 2.25, and 1.97, respectively.[5] Some support for the hypothesis is found also among the market economies; Japan's high index is matched by a relatively low trade proportion (19.3 percent), and the Federal Republic of Germany, with a lower index than France, has a higher trade proportion as well (34.2 percent, as against 28.2 percent for France). The United Kingdom, on the other hand, has both a higher exchange-rate–deviation index and a higher trade proportion (34.4 percent) than France and the Federal Republic of Germany.

The relationship between the exchange-rate–deviation index and the level of GDP also may be expected to alter at least for a time because of changes in exchange rates or, if exchange rates are left fixed, because of differential internal rates of inflation. For example, the shift in the exchange-rate–deviation index for the United Kingdom from 1.21 in 1967 to 1.40 in 1970 was influenced by changes in both of these factors, one working to increase the index, the other to reduce it. The change in the exchange rate from $2.80 per pound to $2.40 near the end of 1967 (a 16.7 percent rise in the sterling price of dollars) operated to diminish the dollar value of the U.K. GDP when converted at the exchange rate and thus to raise the exchange-rate–deviation index. At the same time, the internal rate of inflation between 1967 and 1970 was 17 percent in the United Kingdom and 6 percent in the United States, gauged by the change in each country's implicit price deflator for GDP. This factor, by raising the relative valuation placed on U.K. GDP when converted to dollars at a given exchange rate,

had the effect of lowering the exchange-rate–deviation index. If these two sets of influence were the only factors at work, a 5 percent increase in the index would have occurred instead of the 16 percent increase that did occur. We do not attempt to explain the difference, particularly because our main purpose is merely to call attention to the impact of exchange-rate changes and differential rates of inflation on exchange-rate–based comparisons of GDP.

B. Analysis of Subaggregates

So much for the broad picture in terms of GDP and its three main subaggregates. We turn now to the examination of further product detail on the composition of real GDP per capita. For this purpose, ideal indexes for some of the more important product categories have been taken from column 10 of Tables 13.1 to 13.9 and gathered in Table 13.18.

One notable feature of the table is the tendency for the per capita quantities relative to those of the United States to be larger for foods than for most other categories of consumption. For the lowest-income countries, Kenya and India, per capita food consumption is 16 and 19 percent, respectively, of the U.S. level whereas for consumption as a whole, the corresponding percentages are 5.6 and 6.1. At the other income extreme, French per capita food consumption is at practically the same level as that of the United States. All of the countries, it may be seen in Table 13.16, spend a higher proportion of GDP on food than does the United States. As Engel's law predicts, the proportion tends to be inversely related to income level: it is highest in India, in which food, beverages, and tobacco account for half of the expenditures.

Another consumption sector in which high quantity ratios are found is purchased transport services. These figures, which even exceed the food ratios, reflect the

[5]Trade figures from U.N. *Monthly Bulletin of Statistics* (August 1972); GDP figures from Table 1.1.

Table 13.17. Per Capita Quantity Indexes of Gross Product and Its Main Subdivisions (U.S. = 100)

Part A. 1970

	Kenya	India	Colombia	Hungary	Italy	Japan	United Kingdom	Germany, F.R.	France
GDP, ICP									
1. Own weights	4.0	4.3	11	33	43	55	58	67	68
2. U.S. weights	8.6	8.5	22	48	54	68	68	80	82
3. Index spread (line 2 ÷ line 1)†	2.15	1.98	1.94	1.48	1.25	1.25	1.18	1.19	1.21
4. Ideal index (√line 1 × line 2)	5.9	6.1	15	40	48	61	63	74	74
5. At exchange rates	3.0	2.0	6.9	22	35	42	45	64	60
6. Exchange-rate-deviation index (line 4 ÷ line 5)†	1.97	3.05	2.25	1.84	1.35	1.47	1.40	1.15	1.23
Consumption, ICP									
7. Own weights	3.9	4.5	12	30	42	40	58	56	60
8. U.S. weights	8.0	8.3	23	50	55	56	70	68	77
9. Ideal index	5.6	6.1	17	38	48	47	64	62	68
Capital formation									
10. Own weights	4.3	3.7	10	47	60	117	64	128	124
11. U.S. weights	5.0	7.0	23	59	68	126	70	150	136
12. Ideal index	4.6	5.1	15	53	64	121	67	138	130
Government, ICP									
13. Own weights	4.5	4.2	6	23	24	39	45	55	39
14. U.S. weights	15.9	11.3	12	30	28	53	55	58	41
15. Ideal index	8.4	6.9	8	26	26	46	50	56	40
Addendum									
Consumption, SNA									
16. Own weights	3.7	4.5	12	26	40	39	53	54	60
17. U.S. weights	6.8	7.2	23	37	50	53	59	62	76
18. Ideal index	5.0	5.7	17	31	45	46	56	58	67
Government, SNA									
19. Own weights	5.4	4.4	8	40	34	45	70	62	47
20. U.S. weights	17.5	14.0	16	77	51	64	96	79	54
21. Ideal index	9.7	7.8	11	55	42	53	82	70	50

Part B. 1967

	Kenya	India	Hungary	Japan	U.K.
GDP, ICP					
1. Own weights	3.9	4.3	28	40	56
2. U.S. weights	8.2	8.0	44	53	67
3. Index spread (line 2 ÷ line 1)	2.10	1.86	1.59	1.32	1.19
4. Ideal index (√line 1 × line 2)	5.7	5.9	35	46	61
5. At exchange rates	3.1	2.1	20	30	51
6. Exchange-rate-deviation index (line 4 ÷ line 5)	1.84	2.81	1.72	1.52	1.21
Consumption, ICP					
7. Own weights	4.0	4.8	26	33	59
8. U.S. weights	8.2	8.3	48	50	72
9. Ideal index	5.7	6.3	35	41	65
Capital formation					
10. Own weights	4.0	3.0	39	73	55
11. U.S. weights	4.3	5.9	48	81	62
12. Ideal index	4.2	4.2	43	77	58
Government, ICP					
13. Own weights	3.5	3.3	15	25	45
14. U.S. weights	12.7	9.6	22	32	52
15. Ideal index	6.7	5.7	18	28	48
Addendum					
Consumption, SNA					
16. Own weights	3.8	4.8	23	33	54
17. U.S. weights	6.9	7.5	35	48	61
18. Ideal index	5.1	6.0	29	39	58
Government, SNA					
19. Own weights	4.3	3.6	30	28	67
20. U.S. weights	15.8	11.8	68	44	90
21. Ideal index	8.3	6.5	45	35	78

†Lines 3 and 6 actually computed from Table 13.1 to 13.14 and from Table 1.1, in which one more digit usually was available.

relative decline of public transport in the United States and expansion in the use of the automobile. Medical care ratios also are high; in Japan, the Federal Republic of Germany, and France, per capita medical services exceed those of the United States.

Attention already has been called to the large ratios for capital formation. Table 13.18 indicates that as between the two major components of capital formation, the ratios are uniformly higher for construction than they are for producers' durables.

Table 13.18. Per Capita Quantities for Selected Summary Table Categories, Ideal Indexes, 1970

(U.S. = 100)

	Kenya	India	Colombia	Hungary	Italy	Japan	U.K.	Germany, F.R.	France
Consumption									
Food	15.5	19.3	27.6	54.1	85.1	58.4	82.7	70.4	101.2
Bread, cereals	49.1	77.8	28.2	123.9	112.4	154.8	111.4	104.9	108.4
Meat	5.4	1.0	24.3	31.9	74.4	14.5	78.6	57.3	101.4
Fish	11.6	24.1	8.4	14.0	96.9	445.9	96.8	39.5	144.7
Milk	13.6	10.7	23.2	60.6	73.9	35.6	77.8	75.5	120.6
Oils	10.4	43.5	30.8	109.6	135.5	19.4	98.7	198.1	199.1
Fruits, vegetables	22.3	11.2	31.3	52.0	110.2	61.9	63.3	53.8	96.4
Clothing, footwear	2.1	2.3	9.1	37.2	41.4	48.0	56.5	68.1	56.3
Clothing	1.7	2.4	7.8	33.8	39.6	50.9	50.3	62.6	53.8
Footwear	5.5	1.4	17.7	58.4	52.8	30.9	98.1	100.7	72.3
Gross rent, fuel	2.3	3.7	10.9	23.1	41.4	32.5	59.1	61.6	61.1
Gross rent	2.3	3.2	11.2	20.3	48.5	38.4	60.1	66.6	69.6
House furnishings, operations	4.4	4.1	22.6	27.3	29.1	24.6	50.5	67.4	52.1
Medical care	10.0	7.6	12.2	89.8	86.6	129.9	97.3	119.5	110.6
Transport & communication	2.1	1.9	10.7	11.5	24.3	25.8	40.7	34.5	35.7
Personal equipment	0.9	0.2	5.0	5.0	17.7	5.4	20.3	24.4	27.7
Public transport	21.3	29.8	121.6	136.2	122.6	453.2	191.5	135.6	123.0
Recreation and education	6.7	5.0	16.7	45.4	45.6	50.1	68.0	62.6	59.0
Recreation	2.4	0.9	8.1	40.6	33.1	44.5	70.4	67.3	64.0
Education	13.4	12.7	33.7	56.2	59.4	55.9	66.1	58.6	54.9
Capital Formation									
Construction	5.9	10.0	36.5	76.4	88.2	120.9	70.0	152.6	142.2
Producers' durables	3.3	1.5	5.2	31.9	38.7	95.2	59.9	99.9	98.2
Government									
Compensation of employees	17.0	15.5	17.7	32.9	33.8	75.7	73.6	50.7	47.2
Purchases of commodities	1.9	2.8	3.8	23.5	19.2	19.9	28.9	61.4	32.5

The points mentioned above are based on scanning Table 13.18 to see which rows have entries larger than the corresponding entries for per capita GDP in Table 13.17. This indicates the kinds of commodities that are relatively important in the composition of the final product in the nine countries compared with the composition in the United States. The table can be examined also by letting the eye travel across each row, comparing the successive columns. Because the countries are arrayed from left to right in order of increasing real per capita GDP, the tendency for the numbers on each row to rise is not surprising. More income means, for the most part, more of each category of product. For no commodity group, however, is the rise in per capita quantity with successively higher-income countries an uninterrupted one. Sometimes, these deviations from a smooth relationship with income levels can be explained easily as an adaptation to supply conditions, as in the case of Japanese fish or Italian vegetables. In such other cases as the relatively large European consumption of fats and oils, no such simple explanation comes to mind. (See Chapter 15 for a more explicit approach to demand analysis.)

We turn now from quantities to a similar examination of the data in Tables 13.1 to 13.14 for PPPs. First, Table 13.19 sets out the PPPs for GDP and its three major subaggregates. Following each aggregate or subaggregate, the PPPs are converted to price indexes, taking the United States as 100, by dividing them by the exchange rate (line 4).

Table 13.19 indicates that prices in 1970 varied from around 35 percent to nearly 90 percent of the U.S. level, judging on the basis of the ideal index (line 7). The tendency for internal prices to be lower relative to the exchange rate the poorer the country is the price aspect of our earlier finding that the exchange-rate–deviation index tends to be larger for poor countries. Because this and a number of other features of the price comparisons tend to be mirror images of the findings based on the quantity tables, our discussion of the PPPs and price levels can be brief.

Compared with consumption goods (line 13), capital goods (line 19) are relatively expensive in the lower-income countries and government services (line 25) relatively cheap, the latter because of low wages and the importance of the compensation of employees in this sector. In Italy, the Federal Republic of Germany, and France, on the other hand, the ratio of capital goods to consumer prices is lower than in the United States.

Further details about PPPs are set out in Table 13.20. Here again, it can be seen that prices of commodities and services that are labor intensive tend to be low in all countries relative to the United States, and among countries other than the United States, they tend to be lower in the low-income countries. Within consumption, medical services is the notable example,[6] and within capital

[6]The price indexes for medical services presented in Table 13.20 are based on the indirect price comparisons, but the direct price comparisons yield a similar result. See Chapter 7.

Table 13.19. Purchasing Power Parities and Relative Price Levels, GDP and Its Main Subdivisions

Part A. 1970

	Kenya (Shilling)	India (Rupee)	Colombia (Peso)	Hungary (Forint)	Italy (Lira)	Japan (Yen)	U.K. (Pound)	Germany, F.R. (D. Mark)	France (Franc)
GDP, ICP				Currency units per US$					
1. Own weights	2.50	1.80	5.9	13.4	414	220	.274	2.92	4.10
2. U.S. weights	5.30	3.57	11.5	19.8	518	275	.324	3.49	4.95
3. Ideal index	3.64	2.53	8.2	16.3	463	246	.298	3.19	4.51
4. Exchange rates	7.143	7.50	18.56	30.0	625	360	.4167	3.660	5.554
				Price indexes (U.S. = 100)					
5. Own weights	35	24	32	45	66	61	66	80	74
6. U.S. weights	74	48	62	66	83	76	78	95	89
7. Ideal index	51	34	44	54	74	68	72	87	81
Consumption, ICP				Currency units per US$					
8. Own weights	2.70	2.04	6.0	11.6	412	199	.277	3.01	4.11
9. U.S. weights	5.50	3.79	11.5	19.4	540	282	.335	3.62	5.20
10. Ideal index	3.85	2.78	8.3	15.0	472	237	.305	3.30	4.62
				Price indexes (U.S. = 100)					
11. Own weights	38	27	32	39	66	55	66	82	74
12. U.S. weights	77	51	62	65	86	78	80	99	94
13. Ideal index	54	37	45	50	76	66	73	90	83
Capital formation				Currency units per US$					
14. Own weights	4.97	2.10	6.4	20.0	424	280	.302	2.74	4.09
15. U.S. weights	5.80	3.97	14.8	25.1	481	303	.330	3.20	4.50
16. Ideal index	5.37	2.89	9.7	22.4	452	292	.316	2.96	4.29
				Price indexes (U.S. = 100)					
17. Own weights	70	28	34	67	68	78	72	75	74
18. U.S. weights	81	53	80	84	77	84	79	87	81
19. Ideal index	75	39	52	75	72	81	76	81	77
Government, ICP				Currency units per US$					
20. Own weights	1.07	0.74	4.0	11.6	398	153	.212	3.03	4.12
21. U.S. weights	3.80	2.02	7.7	15.3	458	208	.262	3.18	4.32
22. Ideal index	2.01	1.23	5.5	13.3	427	179	.236	3.10	4.22
				Price indexes (U.S. = 100)					
23. Own weights	15	10	22	39	64	42	51	83	74
24. U.S. weights	53	27	41	51	73	58	63	87	78
25. Ideal index	28	16	30	44	68	50	57	85	76

Part B. 1967

	Kenya	India	Hungary	Japan	U.K.		Kenya	India	Hungary	Japan	U.K.
GDP, ICP	Currency units per US$					Capital formation	Currency units per US$				
1. Own weights	2.73	2.00	13.8	207	.270	14. Own weights	5.38	2.10	20.5	274	.283
2. U.S. weights	5.67	3.73	22.1	272	.321	15. U.S. weights	5.80	4.18	25.5	305	.322
3. Ideal index	3.93	2.73	17.5	237	.295	16. Ideal index	5.59	2.97	22.8	289	.302
4. Exchange rate	7.143	7.5	30.0	360.0	.3571		Price indexes (U.S. = 100)				
	Price indexes (U.S. = 100)					17. Own weights	75	28	69	76	79
5. Own weights	38	27	46	58	76	18. U.S. weights	81	56	85	85	90
6. U.S. weights	79	50	74	76	90	19. Ideal index	78	40	76	80	85
7. Ideal index	55	36	58	66	83		Currency units per US$				
Consumption, ICP	Currency units per US$					Government, ICP					
8. Own weights	2.90	2.30	12.1	184	.274	20. Own weights	1.16	0.81	12.3	153	.231
9. U.S. weights	5.96	3.92	22.0	278	.332	21. U.S. weights	4.25	2.32	17.9	202	.271
10. Ideal index	4.15	3.00	16.3	227	.302	22. Ideal index	2.22	1.37	14.9	175	.250
	Price indexes (U.S. = 100)						Price indexes (U.S. = 100)				
11. Own weights	41	31	40	51	77	23. Own weights	16	11	41	42	65
12. U.S. weights	83	52	73	77	93	24. U.S. weights	59	31	60	56	76
13. Ideal index	58	40	54	63	85	25. Ideal index	31	18	50	49	70

Note: Price levels derived by dividing PPPs (i.e., the currency units per U.S. dollar) by the exchange rate.

Table 13.20. Price Indexes for Selected Summary Table Categories, Ideal Indexes, 1970

(U.S. = 100)

	Kenya	India	Colombia	Hungary	Italy	Japan	U.K.	Germany, F.R.	France
Consumption									
Food	63	54	62	79	97	104	72	110	92
Bread, cereals	64	59	82	36	81	94	59	106	97
Meat	53	58	59	115	100	136	66	105	93
Fish	76	29	77	87	118	88	81	115	116
Milk	64	46	58	57	93	94	78	77	67
Oils	95	71	96	106	107	112	74	112	92
Fruits, vegetables	43	46	58	65	79	95	78	101	81
Clothing & footwear	73	53	59	76	92	68	81	108	119
Clothing	87	54	66	80	95	70	89	116	125
Footwear	31	48	38	60	76	51	52	79	89
Gross rent, fuel	79	35	55	37	61	82	74	75	67
Gross rent	83	22	59	30	48	71	67	64	55
House furnishing, operation	55	28	37	75	85	82	83	98	99
Medical care	16	9	17	13	30	18	31	45	47
Transport & communication	78	49	61	71	103	59	95	129	116
Personal equipment	117	117	141	145	103	108	135	131	109
Public transport	69	35	25	40	58	29	73	82	77
Capital formation									
Construction	57	21	23	55	56	72	60	62	66
Producers' durables	108	92	144	114	98	92	95	107	93
Government									
Compensation employees	21	8	17	18	63	42	47	80	68
Purchases of commodities	61	35	51	75	75	66	75	89	86
Exchange rate	7.143	7.50	18.56	30.0	62.5	36.0	.4167	3.660	5.554

formation, the generalization applies to construction as compared with producers' durables. Producers' durables are the most nearly uniform in price in all countries, doubtless reflecting the large role that international trade plays in the markets for these goods.

We close this chapter with a brief description of our exploration—admittedly rather gross—of a few systematic relationships between the quantity ratios or PPPs of various subaggregates derived from categories classified in special ways.

1. How is GDP per capita related to the differences between the service aggregates and commodity aggregates?[7]

2. How is GDP per capita related to the difference between aggregates of categories of goods entering into international trade and aggregates of those unlikely to enter into international trade?[8]

3. How is GDP per capita related to the difference between aggregates of categories of goods and services which are valued by cost of labor inputs and aggregates valued by market prices of outputs?[9]

[7]The classification of categories into service and nonservice categories was suggested by M. Mukherjee, director of the Indian Statistical Institute, who thought it would be of particular analytic significance for the low-income countries.

[8]The second classification of the categories, into those traded and not traded, is suggested by the literature on PPPs. For example, Balassa (see footnote 4) suggested that the different price levels for traded and nontraded production played a significant role in explaining differences between exchange rates and PPPs (for example, exchange-rate deviations).

Tables 13.21 and 13.22 present the results of aggregating the categories by these three classification schemes. In each table, the countries are arranged from top to bottom in order of increasing per capita GDP. The first classification (columns 1 and 2) separates the service categories from the commodity categories. "Services" consist of categories in which expenditures are entirely on personnel (for example, domestic services, teachers, and government employees), repairs of various kinds (footwear, autos), rents, public transport and communication, public entertainment, and household services. We already have noted that service prices tend to be low in low-income countries, a tendency evident in the table. The PPPs for commodities (column 2) are about 5 times the PPPs for services (column 1) in the case of India, mostly in the range of 2.5 to 3 times for Kenya, Colombia, and Hungary, about 2 times for Japan, and less than 2 times for the United Kingdom, the Federal Republic of Germany, and France.

The relative quantities of services, shown in Part A of Table 13.22, rise with income level, but not as sharply or as consistently as commodities. The division of expenditures between services and commodities, set out in the

[9]The third classification is suggested by the work of Edward E. Denison, *Why Growth Rates Differ* (Washington: Brookings Institution, 1967). Our assumption of equal productivity for labor inputs relates to inputs with a given level of education. Also, there is a notable difference in our treatment of medical personnel in that an allowance has been made for differences in the input of capital.

Table 13.21. Relative Price Levels for Selected Classifications of Final Expenditures, 1970

| | Price indexes (U.S. = 100) | | | | | |
| | Services | Commodities | Traded goods | Nontraded goods | Equal productivity | Other |
	(1)	(2)	(3)	(4)	(5)	(6)
Kenya						
Own weights	18.2	58.1	58.5	22.3	11.8	54.9
U.S. weights	46.5	90.0	96.7	48.9	24.9	84.7
Fisher index	29.1	72.7	75.2	32.9	17.1	68.2
India						
Own weights	8.0	40.4	46.8	10.3	4.4	35.7
U.S. weights	16.1	66.3	74.4	17.3	6.1	56.3
Fisher index	11.3	51.7	59.1	13.3	5.2	44.9
Colombia						
Own weights	19.9	45.8	57.6	21.0	11.9	37.2
U.S. weights	29.6	81.4	91.6	28.6	13.5	72.2
Fisher index	24.2	60.9	72.7	24.2	12.4	51.7
Hungary						
Own weights	21.7	60.7	62.7	30.7	12.3	53.3
U.S. weights	27.3	89.0	95.0	33.0	14.3	77.0
Fisher index	24.3	73.3	77.3	31.7	13.3	64.0
Italy						
Own weights	47.7	77.3	84.0	50.4	39.2	72.8
U.S. weights	55.7	99.0	107.0	55.5	48.0	90.2
Fisher index	51.5	87.5	94.9	53.0	43.5	81.0
Japan						
Own weights	36.9	77.8	82.5	46.4	25.6	70.6
U.S. weights	49.1	92.5	95.3	55.0	30.3	86.1
Fisher index	42.8	85.0	88.6	50.6	27.8	78.1
U.K.						
Own weights	47.8	79.0	83.3	50.2	38.2	73.2
U.S. weights	54.7	91.2	97.0	55.9	43.9	84.7
Fisher index	51.1	85.0	89.8	52.8	40.8	78.7
Germany, F.R.						
Own weights	62.8	87.4	99.2	60.9	56.6	84.4
U.S. weights	75.4	107.1	114.5	73.5	70.2	100.5
Fisher index	68.9	96.7	106.6	66.9	63.1	92.1
France						
Own weights	63.7	78.1	83.4	63.4	64.1	75.4
U.S. weights	70.9	100.1	105.9	70.4	69.7	93.3
Fisher index	62.2	88.4	93.8	66.8	66.8	83.9

Table 13.22. Relative Quantities and Expenditures for Selected Classifications of Final Expenditures, 1970

| | Part A. Ideal Quantity Indexes (U.S. = 100) | | | | | |
| | Services | Commodities | Traded goods | Nontraded goods | Equal productivity | Other |
	(1)	(2)	(3)	(4)	(5)	(6)
Kenya	8.4	4.6	4.4	8.0	15.7	4.5
India	8.2	5.2	4.8	8.7	15.7	5.1
Colombia	25.4	11.9	9.7	27.5	23.9	14.8
Hungary	47.3	37.6	32.4	55.8	55.8	38.4
Italy	49.8	47.1	41.9	57.7	54.6	46.7
Japan	64.8	59.0	48.8	79.0	75.5	59.1
U.K.	72.7	57.7	56.1	72.2	76.3	60.3
Germany, F.R.	60.1	80.4	70.1	78.2	66.9	74.7
France	61.9	81.0	72.1	78.2	59.3	77.3
	Part B. Expenditure as Percent of GDP					
Kenya	30.4	69.6	58.7	41.3	15.6	84.4
India	17.0	83.0	73.2	26.8	7.0	93.0
Colombia	33.7	66.3	54.4	45.6	7.6	92.4
Hungary	19.9	80.1	61.5	38.5	6.0	94.0
Italy	27.1	72.9	59.5	40.5	11.7	88.3
Japan	24.7	75.3	55.0	45.0	8.8	91.2
U.K.	31.1	68.9	59.8	40.2	12.2	87.8
Germany, F.R.	24.0	76.0	61.7	38.3	11.4	88.6
France	25.7	74.3	59.4	40.6	11.4	88.6
U.S.	37.3	62.7	53.0	47.0	17.4	82.6

Figure 13.3. Exchange-Rate Deviation Index compared to Ratio of PPPs for Traded Goods to PPPs for Nontraded Goods

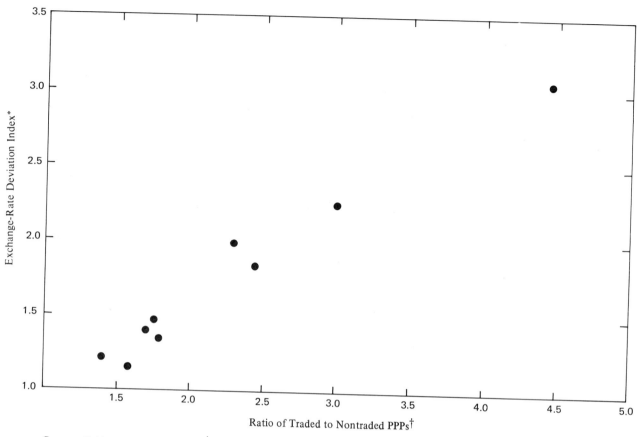

Sources: Tables 13.17* and 13.21†

lower part of the table, does not seem to vary systematically with per capita GDP. It is possible that the income and substitution effects are working in opposite directions. The rise in service prices associated with rising incomes restrains the increase in the quantity of services consumed.

The next two columns (3 and 4) in Tables 13.21 and 13.22 show price and quantity indexes for traded and nontraded goods. The latter are intended to refer to categories that are unlikely to enter into international trade; they consist of the service categories plus the construction categories. In view of the importance of the service categories in the total, it is not surprising that the price and quantity indexes do not behave much differently from those described earlier.

In Figure 13.3, the exchange-rate-deviation index is plotted against the ratio of the PPPs for traded goods to the PPPs for nontraded goods (using the Fisher index). As expected, the relationship is positive: India, for example, with a large difference between its overall PPP for GDP and the exchange rate, has a large difference as well between its PPP for traded goods and its PPP for nontraded goods.

The final distinction is between the categories that were compared on the basis of personnel inputs and all others. For categories compared on the basis of inputs, consisting of medical, educational, and government personnel, the assumption was made of equal productivity for equally educated personnel. As we would expect, the prices of these inputs are lower in low-income countries. The PPPs for all other categories (column 6) are 8 or 9 times as high as the PPPs for the "equal productivity" categories (column 5) in the case of India, 3 to 5 times as high for Kenya, Colombia, and Hungary, nearly 3 times as high for Japan, nearly 2 times as high for Italy and the United Kingdom, and about 1.5 times as high for the Federal Republic of Germany and France. Once again, we find that the increase in the relative quantities (for the "equal productivity" categories) is not continuous as income rises.

We have stretched the valid limits of the original-country binary comparisons to the extent that we have said things about the relationships not involving the United States. The multilateral comparisons in the next chapter provide a more appropriate basis for the analysis of such relationships.

APPENDIX TO CHAPTER 13

Detailed binary tables

Appendix Table 13.1. Expenditures per Capita, Purchasing-Power Parities, and Quantity per Capita for Detailed Categories, Colombia–U.S., 1970

Code	Category	Per capita expenditure Colombia (peso)	U.S. (dollar)	Purchasing-power parities peso/dollar	Quantity per capita (U.S.=100)	Line number
(1)	(2)	(3)	(4)	(5)	(6)	(7)
01.101	Rice	77.5	1.49	12.1	429.0	1
01.102	Meal, other cereals	63.9	6.49	17.2	57.1	2
01.103	Bread, rolls	46.4	17.96	11.8	21.8	3
01.104	Biscuits, cakes	16.7	19.79	22.9	3.7	4
01.105	Cereal preparations	16.8	8.32	20.8	9.7	5
01.106	Macaroni, spaghetti, related foods	19.1	1.84	7.4	141.4	6
01.111	Fresh beef, veal	286.9	69.83	10.1	40.9	7
01.112	Fresh lamb, mutton	4.7	2.83	3.1	53.1	8
01.113	Fresh pork	24.2	16.96	8.9	16.0	9
01.114	Fresh poultry	26.1	19.12	21.0	6.5	10
01.115	Other fresh meat	23.4	3.00	9.8	79.9	11
01.116	Frozen, salted meat	34.8	39.08	12.2	7.3	12
01.121	Fresh, frozen fish	5.2	8.15	11.6	5.5	13
01.122	Canned fish	9.2	3.83	18.1	13.2	14
01.131	Fresh milk	93.1	36.25	7.8	32.9	15
01.132	Milk products	35.1	16.79	14.6	14.3	16
01.133	Eggs, egg products	41.3	14.30	17.4	16.6	17
01.141	Butter	15.8	4.82	15.6	21.0	18
01.142	Margarine, edible oil	66.4	10.48	17.1	37.0	19
01.143	Lard, edible fat	6.3	0.83	44.6	17.0	20
01.151	Fresh fruits, tropical, subtropical	111.0	7.97	3.1	443.1	21
01.152	Other fresh fruits	4.9	12.13	22.8	1.8	22
01.153	Fresh vegetables	74.7	25.44	7.3	40.0	23
01.161	Fruit other than fresh	5.2	20.61	30.3	0.8	24
01.162	Vegetables other than fresh	68.2	20.78	34.6	9.5	25
01.170	Potatoes, manioc, other tubers	68.9	11.48	8.6	69.6	26
01.191	Coffee	33.4	11.64	11.4	25.1	27
01.192	Tea	0.8	2.16	18.9	1.9	28
01.193	Cocoa	22.7	0.83	11.9	227.6	29
01.180	Sugar	78.1	4.49	10.2	170.9	30
01.201	Jam, syrup, honey	9.2	4.99	13.4	13.8	31
01.202	Chocolate, ice cream	5.4	15.13	11.7	3.1	32
01.203	Salt, spices, sauces	29.8	6.98	6.6	65.0	33
01.310	Nonalcoholic beverages	10.4	13.13	9.4	8.4	34
01.321	Spirits	33.3	19.91	10.8	15.5	35
01.322	Wine, cider	11.7	4.25	35.4	7.7	36
01.323	Beer	8.9	24.92	8.3	4.3	37
01.410	Cigarettes	22.1	50.83	3.1	14.2	38
01.420	Other tobacco	7.3	4.29	10.5	16.2	39
02.110	Clothing materials	21.0	5.81	17.1	21.1	40
02.121	Men's clothing	73.9	49.80	10.1	14.7	41
02.122	Women's clothing	33.3	78.29	15.9	2.7	42
02.123	Boys', girls' clothing	22.5	23.88	11.5	8.2	43
02.131	Men's, boys' underwear	11.9	10.72	13.6	8.2	44
02.132	Women's, girls' underwear	20.6	28.86	12.2	5.8	45
02.150	Other clothing	15.2	12.94	10.1	11.6	46
02.160	Clothing rental, repair	6.6	4.28	5.6	27.9	47
02.211	Men's footwear	19.6	11.97	7.9	20.8	48
02.212	Women's footwear	15.5	15.77	6.4	15.4	49
02.213	Children's footwear	13.4	11.99	7.0	15.8	50
02.220	Footwear repairs	3.5	2.07	6.3	26.9	51
03.110	Gross rents	499.8	437.06	11.3	10.1	52
03.120	Indoor repair, upkeep	60.2	17.98	7.3	45.6	53
03.210	Electricity	35.2	48.39	7.2	10.1	54

Appendix Table 13.1. Continued

Code (1)	Category (2)	Per capita expenditure Colombia (peso) (3)	U.S. (dollar) (4)	Purchasing-power parities peso/dollar (5)	Quantity per capita (U.S.=100) (6)	Line number (7)
03.220	Gas	11.9	29.45	4.4	9.1	55
03.230	Liquid fuels	18.0	22.93	10.8	7.3	56
03.240	Other fuels, ice	6.3	4.44			57
04.110	Furniture, fixtures	103.7	52.56	11.0	18.0	58
04.120	Floor coverings	6.6	18.29			59
04.200	Household textiles, etc.	37.9	38.57	10.3	9.5	60
04.310	Refrigerators, etc.	7.9	14.79	31.9	1.7	61
04.320	Washing appliances	9.3	8.29	56.4	2.0	62
04.330	Cooking appliances	20.3	9.13	23.0	9.7	63
04.340	Heating appliances	4.3	4.44	20.8	4.7	64
04.350	Cleaning appliances	9.7	2.44	59.4	6.7	65
04.360	Other household appliances	4.9	3.47	54.2	2.6	66
04.400	Household utensils	13.9	20.13	10.2	6.8	67
04.510	Nondurable household goods	71.9	27.34	12.1	21.8	68
04.520	Domestic services	85.3	23.23	1.0	374.2	69
04.530	Household services	19.1	21.53	5.9	15.0	70
04.600	Household furnishing repairs		7.87			71
05.110	Drugs, medical preparations	32.7	38.26	14.7	5.8	72
05.120	Medical supplies		5.22			73
05.200	Therapeutic equipment	4.3	9.28	9.4	4.9	74
05.310	Physicians' services	41.7	47.38		26.2	75
05.320	Dentists' services	9.2	13.88		14.8	76
05.330	Services, nurses, other personnel	3.9	82.89		6.1	77
05.410	Hospitals, etc.	32.7	117.82		18.0	78
06.110	Personal cars	207.6	137.80	26.4	5.7	79
06.120	Other personal transport	0.7	20.36	30.9	0.1	80
06.210	Tires, tubes, accessories	22.9	27.50	16.7	5.0	81
06.220	Repair charges	40.6	37.82	5.1	20.9	82
06.230	Gasoline, oil, etc.	31.3	112.64	18.0	1.5	83
06.240	Parking, tolls, etc.	32.5	23.32			84
06.310	Local transport	59.5	12.41	2.3	204.2	85
06.321	Rail transport	31.5	0.73	3.7	1167.3	86
06.322	Bus transport	6.4	1.95	4.0	81.7	87
06.323	Air transport	77.8	11.92	9.0	72.3	88
06.330	Miscellaneous transport		3.67			89
06.410	Postal communication	2.1	7.49	7.1	3.9	90
06.420	Telephone, telegraph	22.7	48.49	2.6	17.9	91
07.110	Radio, TV, phonograph, etc.	53.1	40.62	29.0	4.5	92
07.120	Major durable recreation equipment	6.8	26.29	21.6	1.2	93
07.130	Other recreation equipment	14.9	39.81	24.5	1.5	94
07.210	Public entertainment	85.4	28.80	4.5	66.5	95
07.230	Other recreation, cultural events	16.6	57.68	6.3	4.6	96
07.310	Books, papers, magazines	32.1	37.14	10.0	8.6	97
07.320	Stationery	2.3	11.10	10.8	2.0	98
07.411	Teachers, 1st, 2nd	140.6	185.05		56.9	99
07.412	Teachers, college	36.0	35.19		16.0	100
07.420	Educational facilities	12.1	29.04			101
07.431	Educational supplies	19.5	7.54			102
07.432	Other education expenditures	30.8	8.48			103
08.100	Barber, beauty shops	14.6	19.91	4.3	17.2	104
08.210	Toilet articles	48.9	29.85	14.9	11.0	105
08.220	Other personal-care goods	15.9	30.29	8.0	6.6	106
08.310	Restaurants, cafes	253.9	140.16	6.3	28.6	107
08.320	Hotels, etc.	19.0	8.67	8.1	27.0	108
08.400	Other services	310.2	118.76			109
08.900	Expenditures of residents abroad		23.70			110
10.100	1- and 2-dwelling buildings	168.0	103.98	4.5	36.0	111
10.200	Multidwelling buildings	21.7	43.16	3.9	13.0	112
11.100	Hotels, etc.	5.6	6.69	3.8	22.2	113
11.200	Industrial buildings	57.3	36.17	6.5	24.5	114
11.300	Commercial buildings	18.0	25.28	4.2	17.0	115
11.400	Office buildings	36.1	32.68	2.8	39.9	116
11.500	Educational buildings	16.9	32.17	2.7	19.6	117
11.600	Hospital buildings	6.3	16.81			118
11.700	Agricultural buildings	33.1	3.36			119
11.800	Other buildings	6.5	18.38			120
12.100	Roads, highways	107.1	51.45	4.5	46.6	121
12.200	Transmission, utility lines	89.3	70.11	4.4	29.1	122
12.300	Other construction	62.4	13.57			123
13.000	Land improvement	95.9	10.14			124
14.110	Locomotives	0.1	1.16	16.5	0.7	125
14.120	Other	2.0	6.33			126
14.200	Passenger cars	42.2	34.27	35.0	3.5	127
14.300	Trucks, buses, trailers	60.0	44.01	31.6	4.3	128
14.400	Aircraft	19.3	14.40	28.1	4.8	129
14.500	Ships, boats	29.0	3.96			130

Appendix Table 13.1. Continued

Code (1)	Category (2)	Per capita expenditure Colombia (peso) (3)	U.S. (dollar) (4)	Purchasing-power parities peso/dollar (5)	Quantity per capita (U.S.=100) (6)	Line number (7)
14.600	Other transport	1.5	1.71	34.3	2.5	131
15.100	Engines and turbines	9.1	6.46	28.7	4.9	132
15.210	Tractors	8.8	8.24	19.5	5.4	133
15.220	Other agricultural machinery	12.1	11.81	32.7	3.1	134
15.300	Office machinery	12.1	32.00	45.8	0.8	135
15.400	Metalworking machinery	23.1	17.83	14.2	9.1	136
15.500	Construction, mining	32.4	16.37	31.6	6.3	137
15.600	Special industrial	44.6	15.33	22.7	12.8	138
15.700	General industrial	59.2	19.79	31.0	9.6	139
15.800	Service industrial	2.2	17.01	36.4	0.4	140
16.100	Electrical transmission	27.1	13.62	30.8	6.4	141
16.200	Communication equipment	17.7	25.45			142
16.300	Other electrical	33.3	3.88			143
16.400	Instruments	17.9	16.52			144
17.100	Furniture, fixtures	17.8	19.45	20.2	4.5	145
17.200	Other durable goods	14.5	19.52	16.7	4.4	146
18.000	Increase in stocks	106.7	16.60	14.0	45.9	147
19.000	Exports less imports	−99.4	7.42	18.6	−72.2	148
20.100	Blue-collar, unskilled	39.1	18.33	2.3	92.4	149
20.210	Blue-collar, skilled	8.7	94.41	3.0	3.1	150
20.220	White-collar	52.7	108.62	3.6	13.6	151
20.300	Professional	100.0	132.96	3.4	22.4	152
21.000	Government expenditure on commodities	120.5	338.05	9.4	3.8	153

Notes:
1. Above expenditures for lines 1 to 110 include both household and government expenditures. The latter are shown separately in Table 13.15.
2. Sugar (1 180) is intentionally out of order; the purpose is to facilitate aggregation.
3. The purchasing-power parities are direct except for the following: Purchasing-power parities are indirect and the quantity ratios are direct in lines 75,76,77,78,99, and 100. Blanks in columns (5) and (6) indicate no direct price or quantity comparisons were made. Where neither comparison was made, purchasing-power parities from other selected categories were imputed to these categories for aggregation purposes.
4. Exchange rate: P18.56=US$1.00 (see Table 1.1).

Appendix Table 13.2. Expenditures per Capita, Purchasing-Power Parities, and Quantity per Capita for Detailed Categories, France–U.S., 1970

Code (1)	Category (2)	Per capita expenditure France (franc) (3)	U.S. (dollar) (4)	Purchasing-power parities franc/dollar (5)	Quantity per capita (U.S.=100) (6)	Line number (7)
01.101	Rice	4.75	1.49	4.81	66.1	1
01.102	Meal, other cereals	13.29	6.49	6.98	29.3	2
01.103	Bread, rolls	150.05	17.96	2.47	337.8	3
01.104	Biscuits, cakes	138.67	19.79	11.36	61.7	4
01.105	Cereal preparations	1.89	8.32	8.28	2.7	5
01.106	Macaroni, spaghetti, related foods	17.09	1.84	4.08	228.2	6
01.111	Fresh beef, veal	300.10	69.83	4.48	96.0	7
01.112	Fresh lamb, mutton	24.70	2.83			8
01.113	Fresh pork	84.53	16.96	4.42	112.7	9
01.114	Fresh poultry	94.97	19.12	7.37	67.4	10
01.115	Other fresh meat	109.22	3.00	4.91	741.9	11
01.116	Frozen, salted meat	183.30	39.08	6.08	77.1	12
01.121	Fresh, frozen fish	77.87	8.15	5.42	176.3	13
01.122	Canned fish	34.19	3.83	9.45	94.5	14
01.131	Fresh milk	81.67	36.25	3.05	74.0	15
01.132	Milk products	166.20	16.79	3.69	268.4	16
01.133	Eggs, egg products	54.14	14.30	5.54	68.3	17
01.141	Butter	114.92	4.82	6.17	386.8	18
01.142	Margarine, edible oil	40.85	10.48	4.15	94.0	19
01.143	Lard, edible fat		0.83			20
01.151	Fresh fruits, tropical, subtropical	56.03	7.97	7.71	91.2	21
01.152	Other fresh fruits	94.97	12.13	2.95	265.6	22
01.153	Fresh vegetables	160.51	25.44	3.00	210.1	23
01.161	Fruit other than fresh	17.09	20.61	8.18	10.1	24
01.162	Vegetables other than fresh	52.23	20.78	8.83	28.5	25
01.170	Potatoes, manioc, other tubers	46.54	11.48	2.59	156.6	26
01.191	Coffee	52.23	11.64	8.90	50.4	27
01.192	Tea	2.86	2.16	6.49	20.4	28
01.193	Cocoa	6.66	0.83	5.40	147.7	29
01.180	Sugar	30.39	4.49	4.77	141.9	30

Appendix Table 13.2. Continued

Code (1)	Category (2)	Per capita expenditure France (franc) (3)	Per capita expenditure U.S. (dollar) (4)	Purchasing-power parities franc/dollar (5)	Quantity per capita (U.S.=100) (6)	Line number (7)
01.201	Jam, syrup, honey	15.20	4.99	4.67	65.2	31
01.202	Chocolate, ice cream	72.18	15.13	10.39	45.9	32
01.203	Salt, spices, sauces	11.40	6.98	12.47	13.1	33
01.310	Nonalcoholic beverages	33.24	13.13	3.25	77.8	34
01.321	Spirits	48.43	19.91	3.79	64.2	35
01.322	Wine, cider	279.23	4.25	1.86	3522.1	36
01.323	Beer	23.75	24.92	2.96	32.2	37
01.410	Cigarettes	125.35	50.83	3.78	65.3	38
01.420	Other tobacco	20.90	4.29	2.43	200.6	39
02.110	Clothing materials	34.15	5.81	6.54	89.8	40
02.121	Men's clothing	244.07	49.80	5.53	88.6	41
02.122	Women's clothing	188.04	78.29	8.93	26.9	42
02.123	Boys', girls' clothing	28.50	23.88	4.86	24.5	43
02.131	Men's, boys' underwear	76.93	10.72	6.95	103.3	44
02.132	Women's, girls' underwear	146.25	28.86	8.77	57.8	45
02.150	Other clothing	72.18	12.94	6.64	84.0	46
02.160	Clothing rental, repair	14.24	4.28	2.81	118.2	47
02.211	Men's footwear	46.54	11.97	5.71	68.1	48
02.212	Women's footwear	56.03	15.77	5.41	65.7	49
02.213	Children's footwear	37.05	11.99	3.76	82.2	50
02.220	Footwear repairs	10.44	2.07	5.00	100.8	51
03.110	Gross rents	817.51	437.06	3.03	61.8	52
03.120	Indoor repair, upkeep	149.11	17.98	3.26	254.7	53
03.210	Electricity	98.77	48.39	7.67	26.6	54
03.220	Gas	82.62	29.45	9.26	30.3	55
03.230	Liquid fuels	56.98	22.93	5.61	44.3	56
03.240	Other fuels, ice	61.72	4.44	5.93	234.4	57
04.110	Furniture, fixtures	208.94	52.56	4.48	88.7	58
04.120	Floor coverings	26.59	18.29	5.80	25.1	59
04.200	Household textiles, etc.	84.53	38.57	6.23	35.2	60
04.310	Refrigerators, etc.	26.59	14.79	4.86	37.0	61
04.320	Washing appliances	48.43	8.29	9.13	64.0	62
04.330	Cooking appliances	28.50	9.13	5.12	60.9	63
04.340	Heating appliances	20.90	4.44	7.75	60.7	64
04.350	Cleaning appliances	14.24	2.44	7.81	74.7	65
04.360	Other household appliances	17.09	3.47	7.90	62.5	66
04.400	Household utensils	82.62	20.13	3.81	107.8	67
04.510	Nondurable household goods	119.66	27.34	5.60	78.1	68
04.520	Domestic services		23.23			69
04.530	Household services	44.63	21.53	6.95	29.8	70
04.600	Household furnishing repairs		7.87			71
05.110	Drugs, medical preparations	382.82	38.26	2.77	361.6	72
05.120	Medical supplies	7.60	5.22	7.13	20.4	73
05.200	Therapeutic equipment	21.64	9.28	3.77	61.9	74
05.310	Physicians' services	277.16	47.38		82.0	75
05.320	Dentists' services	153.85	13.88		75.0	76
05.330	Services, nurses, other personnel	31.71	82.89		64.9	77
05.410	Hospitals, etc.	38.19	117.82		81.4	78
06.110	Personal cars	245.04	137.80	6.11	29.1	79
06.120	Other personal transport	19.95	20.36	5.63	17.4	80
06.210	Tires, tubes, accessories	81.67	27.50	6.38	46.6	81
06.220	Repair charges	174.75	37.82	8.92	51.8	82
06.230	Gasoline, oil, etc.	209.88	112.64	11.81	15.8	83
06.240	Parking, tolls, etc.	86.42	23.32	2.21	167.4	84
06.310	Local transport	60.78	12.41	3.40	144.1	85
06.321	Rail transport	45.38	0.73	3.22	1924.9	86
06.322	Bus transport	47.13	1.95	5.23	462.5	87
06.323	Air transport	8.17	11.92	6.62	10.4	88
06.330	Miscellaneous transport		3.67			89
06.410	Postal communication	21.84	7.49	3.62	80.7	90
06.420	Telephone, telegraph	29.44	48.49	6.60	9.2	91
07.110	Radio, TV, phonograph, etc.	134.87	40.62	8.70	38.2	92
07.120	Major durable recreation equipment	34.19	26.29	6.23	20.9	93
07.130	Other recreation equipment	180.44	39.81	6.03	75.2	94
07.210	Public entertainment	40.85	28.80	1.85	76.8	95
07.230	Other recreation, cultural events	58.89	57.68	3.02	33.9	96
07.310	Books, papers, magazines	173.80	37.14	4.07	114.8	97
07.320	Stationery	97.82	11.10	3.71	237.4	98
07.411	Teachers, 1st, 2nd	618.09	185.05		77.9	99
07.412	Teachers, college	91.56	35.19		19.4	100
07.420	Educational facilities	35.69	29.04			101
07.431	Educational supplies	5.49	7.54			102
07.432	Other education expenditures	5.81	8.48			103
08.100	Barber, beauty shops	73.13	19.91	2.62	140.2	104
08.210	Toilet articles	118.38	29.85	5.72	69.3	105
08.220	Other personal-care goods	144.69	30.29	6.35	75.3	106
08.310	Restaurants, cafes	520.44	140.16	4.49	82.7	107

Appendix Table 13.2. Continued

Code (1)	Category (2)	Per capita expenditure France (franc) (3)	U.S. (dollar) (4)	Purchasing power parities franc/dollar (5)	Quantity per capita (U.S.=100) (6)	Line number (7)
08.320	Hotels, etc.	207.99	8.67	3.03	793.0	108
08.400	Other services	31.33	118.76			109
08.900	Expenditures of residents abroad		23.70			110
10.100	1- and 2-dwelling buildings	362.38	103.98	5.11	68.2	111
10.200	Multidwelling buildings	751.73	43.16	3.76	463.8	112
11.100	Hotels, etc.	22.85	6.69	1.97	173.4	113
11.200	Industrial buildings	143.77	36.17	4.04	98.4	114
11.300	Commercial buildings	115.21	25.28	2.47	184.6	115
11.400	Office buildings	121.12	32.68	3.45	107.3	116
11.500	Educational buildings	129.98	32.17	6.45	62.6	117
11.600	Hospital buildings	43.33	16.81			118
11.700	Agricultural buildings	88.62	3.36	6.00	439.4	119
11.800	Other buildings	129.98	18.38			120
12.100	Roads, highways	128.01	51.45	2.45	101.7	121
12.200	Transmission, utility lines	331.65	70.11	2.37	199.9	122
12.300	Other construction	22.85	13.57	1.83	92.0	123
13.000	Land improvement	11.82	10.14	4.51	25.8	124
14.110	Locomotives	15.16	1.16	8.93	146.2	125
14.120	Other	23.48	6.33	9.22	40.2	126
14.200	Passenger cars	125.06	34.27	4.65	78.5	127
14.300	Trucks, buses, trailers	183.30	44.01			128
14.400	Aircraft	11.30	14.40	4.91	16.0	129
14.500	Ships, boats	23.16	3.96			130
14.600	Other transport	1.30	1.71	5.49	13.9	131
15.100	Engines and turbines	10.83	6.46			132
15.210	Tractors	55.95	8.24	4.89	138.8	133
15.220	Other agricultural machinery	94.53	11.81	5.39	148.6	134
15.300	Office machinery	121.77	32.00	5.54	68.7	135
15.400	Metalworking machinery	56.21	17.83	2.78	113.4	136
15.500	Construction, mining	160.53	16.37	7.88	124.5	137
15.600	Special industrial	186.86	15.33	4.79	254.5	138
15.700	General industrial	89.57	19.79	3.98	113.7	139
15.800	Service industrial	17.72	17.01	8.99	11.6	140
16.100	Electrical transmission	146.51	13.62	3.61	298.0	141
16.200	Communication equipment	100.28	25.45	5.46	72.2	142
16.300	Other electrical	28.34	3.88	3.60	202.6	143
16.400	Instruments	122.09	16.52	3.71	199.2	144
17.100	Furniture, fixtures	69.91	19.45	4.96	72.5	145
17.200	Other durable goods	116.85	19.52	6.61	90.6	146
18.000	Increase in stocks	464.67	16.60	5.26	532.1	147
19.000	Exports less imports	32.79	7.42	5.55	79.5	148
20.100	Blue-collar, unskilled	23.48	18.33	3.53	36.3	149
20.210	Blue-collar, skilled	139.24	94.41	3.09	47.7	150
20.220	White-collar	266.07	108.62	3.96	61.9	151
20.300	Professional	201.28	132.96	4.13	36.6	152
21.000	Government expenditure on commodities	523.89	338.05	4.77	32.5	153

Notes:
1. Above expenditures for lines 1 to 110 include both household and government expenditures. The latter are shown separately in Table 13.15.
2. Sugar (1 180) is intentionally out of order; the purpose is to facilitate aggregation.
3. The purchasing-power parities are direct except for the following: Purchasing-power parities are indirect and the quantity ratios are direct in lines 75,76,77,78,99, and 100. Blanks in columns 5 and 6 indicate no direct price or quantity comparisons were made. Where neither comparison was made purchasing-power parities from other selected categories were imputed to these categories for aggregation purposes.
4. Exchange rate: Fr5.554=US$1.00.

Appendix Table 13.3. Expenditures per Capita, Purchasing-Power Parities, and Quantity per Capita for Detailed Categories, Federal Republic of Germany–U.S., 1970

Code (1)	Category (2)	Per capita expenditure Germany (D. mark) (3)	U.S. (dollar) (4)	Purchasing power parities D. mark/dollar (5)	Quantity per capita (U.S.=100) (6)	Line number (7)
01.101	Rice	4.85	1.49	5.20	62.5	1
01.102	Meal, other cereals	40.53	6.49	5.51	113.4	2
01.103	Bread, rolls	117.99	17.96	2.45	267.6	3
01.104	Biscuits, cakes	49.01	19.79	6.17	40.1	4
01.105	Cereal preparations	2.41	8.32	4.56	6.4	5
01.106	Macaroni, spaghetti, related foods	12.69	1.84	3.38	204.9	6
01.111	Fresh beef, veal	69.59	69.83	3.20	31.1	7

Appendix Table 13.3. Continued

Code	Category	Per capita expenditure Germany (D. mark)	U.S. (dollar)	Purchasing-power parities D. mark/dollar	Quantity per capita (U.S.=100)	Line number
(1)	(2)	(3)	(4)	(5)	(6)	(7)
01.112	Fresh lamb, mutton		2.83			8
01.113	Fresh pork	96.82	16.96	3.38	168.8	9
01.114	Fresh poultry	18.76	19.12	5.85	16.8	10
01.115	Other fresh meat	5.44	3.00	3.68	49.3	11
01.116	Frozen, salted meat	144.62	39.08	4.38	84.5	12
01.121	Fresh, frozen fish	7.26	8.15	3.27	27.3	13
01.122	Canned fish	12.71	3.83	5.58	59.4	14
01.131	Fresh milk	52.04	36.25	2.28	62.8	15
01.132	Milk products	44.78	16.79	3.04	87.6	16
01.133	Eggs, egg products	47.19	14.30	3.76	87.8	17
01.141	Butter	80.48	4.82	4.01	417.0	18
01.142	Margarine, edible oil	44.17	10.48	4.22	100.0	19
01.143	Lard, edible fat		0.83			20
01.151	Fresh fruits, tropical, subtropical	24.20	7.97	5.03	60.4	21
01.152	Other fresh fruits	36.30	12.13	2.13	140.5	22
01.153	Fresh vegetables	37.52	25.44	2.16	68.2	23
01.161	Fruit other than fresh	23.00	20.61	4.88	22.9	24
01.162	Vegetables other than fresh	44.78	20.78	6.73	32.0	25
01.170	Potatoes, manioc, other tubers	30.25	11.48	3.71	71.1	26
01.191	Coffee	85.31	11.64	11.17	65.6	27
01.192	Tea	6.66	2.16	8.55	36.0	28
01.193	Cocoa	7.26	0.83	4.98	174.6	29
01.180	Sugar	41.76	4.49	4.54	204.9	30
01.201	Jam, syrup, honey	12.10	4.99	3.26	74.3	31
02.202	Chocolate, ice cream	61.11	15.13	6.47	62.4	32
02.203	Salt, spices, sauces	3.62	6.98	9.40	5.5	33
01.310	Nonalcoholic beverages	19.36	13.13	2.82	52.4	34
01.321	Spirits	44.78	19.91	2.52	89.1	35
01.322	Wine, cider	38.12	4.25	2.39	375.4	36
01.323	Beer	62.32	24.92	2.23	112.2	37
01.410	Cigarettes	145.21	50.83	4.21	67.8	38
01.420	Other tobacco	15.74	4.29	2.10	174.1	39
02.110	Clothing materials	27.83	5.81	3.97	120.6	40
02.121	Men's clothing	130.08	49.80	3.14	83.3	41
02.122	Women's clothing	148.24	78.29	4.67	40.5	42
02.123	Boys', girls' clothing	47.80	23.88	4.25	47.1	43
02.131	Men's, boys' underwear	44.17	10.72	5.62	73.3	44
02.132	Women's, girls' underwear	108.30	28.86	4.97	75.5	45
02.150	Other clothing	55.06	12.94	4.44	95.7	46
02.160	Clothing rental, repair	7.87	4.28	3.26	56.5	47
02.211	Men's footwear	24.20	11.97	3.52	57.5	48
02.212	Women's footwear	33.29	15.77	2.68	78.6	49
02.213	Children's footwear	39.32	11.99	2.77	118.4	50
02.220	Footwear repairs	25.42	2.07	2.55	482.2	51
03.110	Gross rents	673.24	437.06	2.36	65.3	52
03.120	Indoor repair, upkeep	42.35	17.98	2.38	99.1	53
03.210	Electricity	99.23	48.39	4.19	48.9	54
03.220	Gas	38.71	29.45	7.56	17.4	55
03.230	Liquid fuels	41.76	22.93	3.34	54.6	56
03.240	Other fuels, ice	52.65	4.44	4.47	265.0	57
04.110	Furniture, fixtures	158.53	52.56	2.86	105.6	58
04.120	Floor coverings	33.89	18.29	3.65	50.8	59
04.200	Household textiles, etc.	93.77	38.57	5.42	44.8	60
04.310	Refrigerators, etc.	14.53	14.79	2.65	37.1	61
04.320	Washing appliances	31.45	8.29	5.22	72.7	62
04.330	Cooking appliances	11.49	9.13	3.56	35.3	63
04.340	Heating appliances	12.10	4.44	3.97	68.6	64
04.350	Cleaning appliances	11.49	2.44	4.94	95.3	65
04.360	Other household appliances	19.36	3.47	4.86	115.0	66
04.400	Household utensils	88.95	20.13	2.41	183.1	67
04.510	Nondurable household goods	100.45	27.34	3.33	110.4	68
04.520	Domestic services		23.23			69
04.530	Household services	35.70	21.53	4.59	36.2	70
04.600	Household furnishing repairs		7.87			71
05.110	Drugs, medical preparations	189.56	38.26	3.35	147.8	72
05.120	Medical supplies	19.18	5.22	4.61	79.7	73
05.200	Therapeutic equipment	50.60	9.28	2.71	201.2	74
05.310	Physicians' services	195.04	47.38		113.0	75
05.320	Dentists' services	72.61	13.88		98.0	76
05.330	Services, nurses, other personnel	43.94	82.85		75.9	77
05.410	Hospitals, etc.	44.01	117.82		140.4	78
06.110	Personal cars	174.86	137.80	4.99	25.4	79
06.120	Other personal transport	9.67	20.36	3.04	15.6	80
06.210	Tires, tubes, accessories	43.57	27.50	4.99	31.8	81
06.220	Repair charges	87.74	37.82	6.42	36.1	82
06.230	Gasoline, oil, etc.	188.78	112.64	8.02	20.9	83
06.240	Parking, tolls, etc.	42.96	23.32	1.76	104.7	84
06.310	Local transport	30.86	12.41	2.56	97.2	85

Appendix Table 13.3. Continued

Code (1)	Category (2)	Per capita expenditure Germany (D. mark) (3)	U.S. (dollar) (4)	Purchasing-power parities D. mark/dollar (5)	Quantity per capita (U.S.=100) (6)	Line number (7)
06.321	Rail transport	63.47	0.73	2.62	3309.3	86
06.322	Bus transport	27.61	1.95	2.63	538.5	87
06.323	Air transport	2.69	11.92	4.73	4.8	88
06.330	Miscellaneous transport		3.67			89
06.410	Postal communication	34.50	7.49	1.94	238.0	90
06.420	Telephone, telegraph	19.96	48.49	3.78	10.9	91
07.110	Radio, TV, phonograph, etc.	54.45	40.62	4.01	33.5	92
07.120	Major durable recreation equipment	40.53	26.29	3.75	41.1	93
07.130	Other recreation equipment	196.63	39.81	4.09	120.9	94
07.210	Public entertainment	31.45	28.80	1.20	91.1	95
07.230	Other recreation, cultural events	61.72	57.68	2.19	48.8	96
07.310	Books, papers, magazines	83.49	37.14	3.30	68.1	97
07.320	Stationery	30.25	11.10	2.99	91.0	98
07.411	Teachers, 1st, 2nd	338.78	185.05		72.0	99
07.412	Teachers, college	67.83	35.19		25.5	100
07.420	Educational facilities	63.83	29.04			101
07.431	Educational supplies	2.98	7.54			102
07.432	Other education expenditures	22.91	8.48			103
08.100	Barber, beauty shops	45.98	19.91	1.81	127.4	104
08.210	Toilet articles	56.64	29.85	3.89	48.7	105
08.220	Other personal-care goods	69.23	30.29	4.18	54.7	106
08.310	Restaurants, cafes	178.48	140.16	3.63	35.1	107
08.320	Hotels, etc.	78.67	8.67	3.06	296.5	108
08.400	Other services	34.50	118.76			109
08.900	Expenditures of residents abroad		23.70			110
10.100	1- and 2-dwelling buildings	149.87	103.98	3.53	40.9	111
10.200	Multidwelling buildings	459.11	43.16	2.02	527.6	112
11.100	Hotels, etc.	23.61	6.69	1.39	253.5	113
11.200	Industrial buildings	218.08	36.17	2.44	247.5	114
11.300	Commercial buildings	65.59	25.28	1.65	156.8	115
11.400	Office buildings	81.98	32.68	2.03	123.6	116
11.500	Educational buildings	96.74	32.17	3.60	83.5	117
11.600	Hospital buildings	45.91	16.81	2.41	113.5	118
11.700	Agricultural buildings	32.79	3.36	4.35	224.1	119
11.800	Other buildings	9.84	18.38	2.41	22.2	120
12.100	Roads, highways	172.17	51.45	1.72	194.1	121
12.200	Transmission, utility lines	221.36	70.11	1.96	161.3	122
12.300	Other construction	24.60	13.57	0.89	203.2	123
13.000	Land improvement	8.20	10.14			124
14.110	Locomotives	2.05	1.16	4.95	35.6	125
14.120	Other	9.99	6.33	3.83	41.2	126
14.200	Passenger cars	104.46	34.27	5.61	54.3	127
14.300	Trucks, buses, trailers	113.24	44.01			128
14.400	Aircraft	23.50	14.40	3.35	48.7	129
14.500	Ships, boats	57.01	3.96			130
14.600	Other transport	0.48	1.71	4.11	6.8	131
15.100	Engines and turbines	5.66	6.46			132
15.210	Tractors	19.40	8.24	3.41	69.0	133
15.220	Other agricultural machinery	25.83	11.81	3.90	56.1	134
15.300	Office machinery	88.63	32.00	3.67	75.5	135
15.400	Metalworking machinery	67.93	17.83	2.66	143.2	136
15.500	Construction, mining	74.39	16.37	5.63	80.7	137
15.600	Special industrial	109.27	15.33	3.18	224.2	138
15.700	General industrial	168.20	19.79	2.99	284.3	139
15.800	Service industrial	19.68	17.01	6.80	17.0	140
16.100	Electrical transmission	102.79	13.62	2.83	266.8	141
16.200	Communication equipment	101.76	25.45	3.67	108.9	142
16.300	Other electrical	22.40	3.88	2.97	194.1	143
16.400	Instruments	85.03	16.52	2.67	192.8	144
17.100	Furniture, fixtures	78.74	19.45	4.39	92.2	145
17.200	Other durable goods	78.89	19.52	4.67	86.6	146
18.000	Increase in stocks	250.87	16.60	3.98	379.6	147
19.000	Exports less imports	205.45	7.42	3.66	756.2	148
20.100	Blue-collar, unskilled	34.20	18.33	3.01	61.9	149
20.210	Blue-collar, skilled	95.50	94.41	2.45	41.2	150
20.220	White-collar	333.60	108.62	2.85	107.7	151
20.230	Professional	64.44	132.96	3.60	13.5	152
21.000	Government expenditure on commodities	677.09	338.05	3.26	61.4	153

Notes:
1. Above expenditures for lines 1 to 110 include both household and government expenditures. The latter are shown separately in Table 13.15.
2. Sugar (1 180) is intentionally out of order; the purpose is to facilitate aggregation.
3. The purchasing-power parities are direct except for the following: Purchasing-power parities are indirect and the quantity ratios are direct in lines 75,76,77,78,99, and 100. Blanks in columns 5 and 6 indicate no direct price or quantity comparisons were made. Where neither comparison was made purchasing-power parities from other selected categories were imputed to these categories for aggregation purposes.
4. Exchange rate: DM3.66=US$1.00.

Appendix Table 13.4. Expenditures per Capita, Purchasing-Power Parities, and Quantity per Capita for Detailed Categories, Hungary–U.S., 1970

Code (1)	Category (2)	Per capita expenditure Hungary (forint) (3)	U.S. (dollar) (4)	Purchasing-power parities forint/dollar (5)	Quantity per capita (U.S.=100) (6)	Line number (7)
01.101	Rice	51.4	1.49	49.4	69.7	1
01.102	Meal, other cereals	179.8	6.49	19.3	143.4	2
01.103	Bread, rolls	301.0	17.96	5.4	312.8	3
01.104	Biscuits, cakes	96.7	19.79	20.0	24.5	4
01.105	Cereal preparations	81.1	8.32	16.5	107.4	5
01.106	Macaroni, spaghetti, related foods	32.5	1.84	40.4	2.9	6
01.111	Fresh beef, veal	81.9	69.83	13.0	46.4	7
01.112	Fresh lamb, mutton	17.1	2.83	45.7	92.1	8
01.113	Fresh pork	713.0	16.96	35.6	58.7	9
01.114	Fresh poultry	400.3	19.12	16.0	102.2	10
01.115	Other fresh meat	48.9	3.00	25.0	40.8	11
01.116	Frozen, salted meat	399.2	39.08	14.9	24.0	12
01.121	Fresh, frozen fish	29.1	8.15	73.1	5.2	13
01.122	Canned fish	14.6	3.83	11.9	63.0	14
01.131	Fresh milk	272.2	36.25	15.5	49.7	15
01.132	Milk products	129.4	16.79	31.1	65.7	16
01.133	Eggs, egg products	292.3	14.30	26.2	70.1	17
01.141	Butter	88.5	4.82	28.7	12.3	18
01.142	Margarine, edible oil	37.0	10.48	39.1	1339.2	19
01.143	Lard, edible fat	436.5	0.83	51.5	25.0	20
01.151	Fresh fruits, tropical, subtropical	102.8	7.97	11.6	230.2	21
01.152	Other fresh fruits	323.4	12.13	8.0	139.3	22
01.153	Fresh vegetables	283.8	25.44	63.9	4.0	23
01.161	Fruit other than fresh	52.1	20.61	36.7	7.3	24
01.162	Vegetables other than fresh	55.7	20.78	14.7	106.9	25
01.170	Potatoes, manioc, other tubers	180.6	11.48	115.7	15.4	26
01.191	Coffee	206.9	11.64	52.1	10.3	27
01.192	Tea	11.6	2.16	45.2	30.0	28
01.193	Cocoa	11.3	0.83	33.7	150.7	29
01.180	Sugar	228.0	4.49	18.6	6.6	30
01.201	Jam, syrup, honey	6.1	4.99	31.9	74.6	31
01.202	Chocolate, ice cream	359.4	15.13	14.7	165.0	32
01.203	Salt, spices, sauces	169.0	6.98	22.4	12.4	33
01.310	Nonalcoholic beverages	36.3	13.13	26.1	35.2	34
01.321	Spirits	183.1	19.91	14.2	593.1	35
01.322	Wine, cider	357.4	4.25	17.2	29.2	36
01.323	Beer	125.2	24.92	8.3	67.7	37
01.410	Cigarettes	287.1	50.83	18.6	5.6	38
01.420	Other tobacco	4.5	4.29	56.5	51.2	39
02.110	Clothing materials	168.1	5.81	23.7	35.5	40
02.121	Men's clothing	413.4	49.15	26.9	16.5	41
02.122	Women's clothing	318.1	71.81	21.6	43.5	42
02.123	Boys', girls' clothing	223.9	23.80	27.0	47.7	43
02.131	Men's, boys' underwear	138.0	10.72	24.7	19.7	44
02.132	Women's, girls' underwear	140.8	28.86	18.2	95.2	45
02.150	Other clothing	224.6	12.94	9.3	182.3	46
02.160	Clothing rental, repair	72.6	4.28	21.0	56.5	47
02.211	Men's footwear	141.9	11.97	20.3	59.1	48
02.212	Women's footwear	188.9	15.77	11.4	49.0	49
02.213	Children's footwear	67.3	11.99	16.9	110.8	50
02.220	Footwear repairs	38.7	2.07	9.3	16.3	51
03.110	Gross rents	663.5	437.06	6.5	147.1	52
03.120	Indoor repair, upkeep	171.7	17.98	30.3	11.0	53
03.210	Electricity	160.9	48.39	20.8	13.7	54
03.220	Gas	84.0	29.45	41.9	4.8	55
03.230	Liquid fuels	45.6	22.93	6.8	1024.7	56
03.240	Other fuels, ice	308.7	4.44	22.9	31.4	57
04.110	Furniture, fixtures	377.3	52.56	28.7	10.4	58
04.120	Floor coverings	54.7	18.29	24.6	22.6	59
04.200	Household textiles, etc.	214.0	38.57	44.0	13.9	60
04.310	Refrigerators, etc.	90.3	14.79	29.5	17.8	61
04.320	Washing appliances	43.6	8.29	14.3	60.8	62
04.330	Cooking appliances	79.7	9.13	34.9	25.3	63
04.340	Heating appliances	39.2	4.44	29.1	22.2	64
04.350	Cleaning appliances	15.8	2.44	24.4	18.8	65
04.360	Other household appliances	15.9	3.47	20.8	49.0	66
04.400	Household utensils	205.7	20.13	36.1	23.6	67
04.510	Nondurable household goods	232.9	27.34	9.3	17.1	68
04.520	Domestic services	36.7	23.23	14.9	7.6	69
04.530	Household services	24.4	21.53	9.4	159.6	70
04.600	Household furnishing repairs	117.9	7.87	10.7	80.5	71
05.110	Drugs, medical preparations	330.1	38.26	21.5	76.5	72
05.120	Medicial supplies	86.0	5.22			73
05.200	Therapeutic equipment		9.28			74

Appendix Table 13.4. Continued

Code (1)	Category (2)	Per capita expenditure Hungary (forint) (3)	U.S. (dollar) (4)	Purchasing-power parities forint/dollar (5)	Quantity per capita (U.S.=100) (6)	Line number (7)
05.310	Physicians' services	108.1	47.38		112.1	75
05.320	Dentists' services	8.4	13.88		43.0	76
05.330	Services, nurses, other personnel	113.9	82.89		73.7	77
05.410	Hospitals, etc.	446.4	117.82		96.2	78
06.110	Personal cars	254.4	137.80	53.6	3.4	79
06.120	Other personal transport	91.8	20.36	20.8	21.7	80
06.210	Tires, tubes, accessories	48.1	27.50	29.5	5.9	81
06.220	Repair charges	55.2	37.82	13.6	10.8	82
06.230	Gasoline, oil, etc.	72.0	112.64	30.1	2.1	83
06.240	Parking, tolls, etc.	7.3	23.32	3.9	8.0	84
06.310	Local transport	147.1	12.41	7.9	150.6	85
06.321	Rail transport	141.3	0.73	11.9	1619.5	86
06.322	Bus transport	162.6	1.95	15.0	556.7	87
06.323	Air transport	24.2	11.92			88
06.330	Miscellaneous transport	28.9	3.67	25.3	31.1	89
06.410	Postal communication	37.3	7.49	11.2	44.5	90
06.420	Telephone, telegraph	30.5	48.49	5.1	12.4	91
07.110	Radio, TV, phonograph, etc.	253.5	40.62	43.5	14.3	92
07.120	Major durable recreation equipment	9.7	26.29	19.3	1.9	93
07.130	Other recreation equipment	84.9	39.81	26.9	7.9	94
07.210	Public entertainment	236.5	28.80	3.1	265.0	95
07.230	Other recreation, cultural events	248.5	57.68	4.3	100.3	96
07.310	Books, papers, magazines	194.9	37.14	15.2	34.6	97
07.320	Stationery	65.1	11.10	52.5	11.2	98
07.411	Teachers, 1st, 2nd	510.4	185.05		72.8	99
07.412	Teachers, college	52.6	35.19		28.2	100
07.420	Educational facilities	272.8	29.04			101
07.431	Educational supplies	28.3	7.54			102
07.432	Other education expenditures	130.5	8.48			103
08.100	Barber, beauty shops	94.4	19.91	3.4	138.8	104
08.210	Toilet articles	135.1	29.85	14.4	31.4	105
08.220	Other personal-care goods	202.8	30.29	34.9	19.2	106
08.310	Restaurants, cafes	1726.8	140.16	17.9	68.8	107
08.320	Hotels, etc.	64.6	8.67	16.8	44.4	108
08.400	Other services	450.8	118.76			109
08.900	Expenditures of residents abroad		23.70			110
10.100	1- and 2-dwelling buildings	730.8	103.98	17.4	40.3	111
10.200	Multidwelling buildings	796.1	43.16	14.7	125.1	112
11.100	Hotels, etc.	106.6	6.69	17.0	93.6	113
11.200	Industrial buildings	1030.7	36.17	22.1	129.0	114
11.300	Commercial buildings	163.6	25.28	19.3	33.5	115
11.400	Office buildings	176.7	32.68	12.6	42.9	116
11.500	Educational buildings	140.6	32.17	14.6	29.9	117
11.600	Hospital buildings	49.1	16.81	12.1	24.1	118
11.700	Agricultural buildings	725.6	3.36	21.6	998.0	119
11.800	Other buildings	49.9	18.38	17.5	15.6	120
12.100	Roads, highways	287.1	51.45	19.3	28.9	121
12.200	Transmission, utility lines	926.7	70.11	14.6	90.7	122
12.300	Other construction	485.7	13.57	11.8	302.4	123
13.000	Land improvement	130.8	10.14	9.5	136.4	124
14.110	Locomotives	71.9	1.16	62.2	99.6	125
14.120	Other	149.8	6.33	42.5	55.6	126
14.200	Passenger cars	61.3	34.27	69.5	2.6	127
14.300	Trucks, buses, trailers	389.4	44.01	27.8	31.9	128
14.400	Aircraft	28.9	14.40			129
14.500	Ships, boats	16.0	3.96			130
14.600	Other transport	221.9	1.71	39.7	326.8	131
15.100	Engines and turbines	80.4	6.46	50.6	24.6	132
15.210	Tractors	124.8	8.24	30.7	49.3	133
15.220	Other agricultural machinery	184.1	11.81	24.9	62.7	134
15.300	Office machinery	119.6	32.00	45.1	8.3	135
15.400	Metalworking machinery	199.7	17.83	33.6	33.3	136
15.500	Construction, mining	210.1	16.37	31.7	40.5	137
15.600	Special industrial	777.6	15.33	36.0	140.8	138
15.700	General industrial	254.3	19.79	33.5	38.3	139
15.800	Service industrial	38.0	17.01	37.4	6.0	140
16.100	Electrical transmission	81.4	13.62	22.4	26.6	141
16.200	Communication equipment	110.5	25.45	21.2	20.5	142
16.300	Other electrical	21.3	3.88	27.1	20.2	143
16.400	Instruments	194.5	16.52	23.8	49.4	144
17.100	Furniture, fixtures	435.4	19.45	25.6	87.4	145
17.200	Other durable goods	44.9	19.52	51.2	4.5	146
18.000	Increase in stocks	1193.1	16.60	23.4	307.1	147
19.000	Exports less imports	−907.8	7.42	30.0	407.6	148

Appendix Table 13.4. Continued

Code (1)	Category (2)	Per capita expenditure Hungary (forint) (3)	U.S. (dollar) (4)	Purchasing-power parities forint/dollar (5)	Quantity per capita (U.S.=100) (6)	Line number (7)
20.100	Blue-collar, unskilled	220.4	18.33	4.7	258.5	149
20.210	Blue-collar, skilled	12.5	94.41	5.0	2.6	150
20.220	White-collar	205.5	108.62	5.4	34.9	151
20.300	Professional	186.0	132.96	5.9	23.5	152
21.000	Government expenditure on commodities	1789.9	338.05	22.6	23.5	153

Notes:

1. In other comparisons, lines 41–43 include leather clothing. In the Hungary–U.S. comparison, leather clothing has been treated as a separate category. The figures for columns 3 to 6 inclusive are:
2 140 Leather clothing   39.3   7.20   19.9   27.4

2. For purposes of the Hungary–U.S. comparison, special-industry machinery has been split into two categories: one for chemical-industry machinery and the other for all other. The purchasing-power parity shown above is the ideal index of the two. The purchasing-power parities for chemical machinery and for all others were 50.00 and 32.66 respectively. In the United States, 4.6 percent of special industry machinery expenditures were for chemical machinery; in Hungary, 35.0 percent.

3. Above expenditures for lines 1 to 110 include both household and government expenditures. The latter are shown separately in Table 13.15.

4. Sugar (1 180) is intentionally out of order: the purpose is to facilitate aggregation.

5. The purchasing-power parities are direct except for the following: Purchasing-power parities are indirect and the quantity ratios are direct in lines 75,76,77,78,99, and 100. Blanks in columns 5 and 6 indicate no direct price or quantity comparisons were made. Where neither comparison was made, purchasing-power parities from other selected categories were imputed to these categories for aggregation purposes.

6. Exchange rate: Ft30=US$1.00.

Appendix Table 13.5. Expenditures per Capita, Purchasing-Power Parities, and Quantity per Capita for Detailed Categories, India–U.S., 1970

Code (1)	Category (2)	Per capita expenditure India (rupee) (3)	U.S. (dollar) (4)	Purchasing-power parities rupee/dollar (5)	Quantity per capita (U.S.=100) (6)	Line number (7)
01.101	Rice	116.07	1.49	4.50	1726.8	1
01.102	Meal, other cereals	74.34	6.49	2.88	398.2	2
01.103	Bread, rolls	0.32	17.96	3.12	0.6	3
01.104	Biscuits, cakes	0.30	19.79	8.54	0.2	4
01.105	Cereal preparations	0.40	8.32	2.96	1.6	5
01.106	Macaroni, spaghetti, related foods	0.41	1.84	10.56	2.1	6
01.111	Fresh beef, veal	0.66	69.83	3.78	0.3	7
01.112	Fresh lamb, mutton	1.05	2.83	4.69	7.9	8
01.113	Fresh pork	0.20	16.96	1.86	0.6	9
01.114	Fresh poultry	1.66	19.12	7.64	1.1	10
01.115	Other fresh meat	3.19	3.00			11
01.116	Frozen, salted meat		39.08			12
01.121	Fresh, frozen fish	6.28	8.15	1.34	57.6	13
01.122	Canned fish		3.83			14
01.131	Fresh milk	20.95	36.25	2.88	20.1	15
01.132	Milk products	3.13	16.79	4.75	3.9	16
01.133	Eggs, egg products	0.84	14.30	5.35	1.1	17
01.141	Butter	17.55	4.82	4.00	91.2	18
01.142	Margarine, edible oil	20.02	10.48	6.69	28.6	19
01.143	Lard, edible fat		0.83			20
01.151	Fresh fruits, tropical, subtropical	3.97	7.97	2.95	16.9	21
01.152	Other fresh fruits	0.74	12.13	3.37	1.8	22
01.153	Fresh vegetables	10.03	25.44	1.43	27.6	23
01.161	Fruit other than fresh	0.28	20.61	6.02	0.2	24
01.162	Vegetables other than fresh	17.96	20.78	6.23	13.9	25
01.170	Potatoes, manioc, other tubers	5.01	11.48	3.81	11.5	26
01.191	Coffee	1.69	11.64	10.46	1.4	27
01.192	Tea	4.54	2.16	2.70	77.7	28
01.193	Cocoa		0.83			29
01.180	Sugar	18.98	4.49	7.37	57.4	30
01.201	Jam, syrup, honey	0.54	4.99	8.49	1.3	31
01.202	Chocolate, ice cream	1.52	15.13	6.71	1.5	32
01.203	Salt, spices, sauces	17.03	6.98	2.44	99.8	33
01.310	Nonalcoholic beverages	0.43	13.13	4.96	0.7	34
01.321	Spirits	0.15	19.91	10.34	0.1	35
01.322	Wine, cider	1.50	4.25	19.73	1.8	36
01.323	Beer	0.41	24.92	9.95	0.2	37
01.410	Cigarettes	1.20	50.83	8.11	0.3	38
01.420	Other tobacco	11.75	4.29	2.50	109.2	39
02.110	Clothing materials	8.50	5.81	7.02	20.8	40

Appendix Table 13.5. Continued

Code	Category	Per capita expenditure India (rupee)	U.S. (dollar)	Purchasing-power parities rupee/dollar	Quantity per capita (U.S.=100)	Line number
(1)	(2)	(3)	(4)	(5)	(6)	(7)
02.121	Men's clothing	4.66	49.80	3.24	2.9	41
02.122	Women's clothing	6.55	78.29	3.87	2.2	42
02.123	Boys', girls' clothing	0.68	23.88	2.39	1.2	43
02.131	Men's, boys' underwear	0.04	10.72	1.94	0.2	44
02.132	Women's, girls' underwear	0.04	28.86	5.88	0.0	45
02.150	Other clothing	0.02	12.94	7.72	0.0	46
02.160	Clothing rental, repair	0.55	4.28	1.25	10.3	47
02.211	Men's footwear	0.75	11.97	4.00	1.6	48
02.212	Women's footwear	0.75	15.77	4.02	1.2	49
02.213	Children's footwear	0.38	11.99	2.54	1.2	50
02.220	Footwear repairs	0.14	2.07	3.53	2.0	51
03.110	Gross rents	22.14	437.06	1.75	2.9	52
03.120	Indoor repair, upkeep	2.17	17.98	0.83	14.6	53
03.210	Electricity	1.15	48.39	6.98	0.3	54
03.220	Gas	0.04	29.45	6.15	0.0	55
03.230	Liquid fuels	5.29	22.93	13.00	1.8	56
03.240	Other fuels, ice	23.57	4.44	3.37	157.6	57
04.110	Furniture, fixtures	0.54	52.56	4.20	0.2	58
04.120	Floor coverings	1.99	18.29			59
04.200	Household textiles, etc.	3.83	38.57	1.82	5.5	60
04.310	Refrigerators, etc.	0.69	14.79	12.26	0.4	61
04.320	Washing appliances		8.29			62
04.330	Cooking appliances	0.01	9.13	6.11	0.0	63
04.340	Heating appliances	0.01	4.44	5.35	0.1	64
04.350	Cleaning appliances		2.44			65
04.360	Other household appliances	0.06	3.47	4.92	0.3	66
04.400	Household utensils	4.07	20.13	4.16	4.9	67
04.510	Nondurable household goods	3.91	27.34	5.40	2.6	68
04.520	Domestic services	2.22	23.23	0.24	39.6	69
04.530	Household services	3.50	21.53	1.10	14.7	70
04.600	Household furnishing repairs	1.16	7.87			71
05.110	Drugs, medical preparations	10.33	38.26	2.53	10.7	72
05.120	Medical supplies	0.96	5.22	2.40	7.6	73
05.200	Therapeutic equipment	0.24	9.28	1.44	1.8	74
05.310	Physicians' services	1.21	47.38		11.0	75
05.320	Dentists' services	0.01	13.88		1.0	76
05.330	Services, nurses, other personnel	1.79	82.89		4.8	77
05.410	Hospitals, etc.	1.71	117.82		6.8	78
06.110	Personal cars	0.99	137.80	9.47	0.1	79
06.120	Other personal transport	1.19	20.36	6.33	0.9	80
06.210	Tires, tubes, accessories	0.57	27.50	8.10	0.3	81
06.220	Repair charges	0.87	37.82	1.15	2.0	82
06.230	Gasoline, oil, etc.	1.57	112.64	7.95	0.2	83
06.240	Parking, tolls, etc.	0.81	23.32			84
06.310	Local transport	3.66	12.41	1.23	23.9	85
06.321	Rail transport	3.92	0.73	2.19	244.8	86
06.322	Bus transport	12.61	1.95	2.10	308.4	87
06.323	Air transport	0.08	11.92	7.17	0.1	88
06.330	Miscellaneous transport	3.46	3.67			89
06.410	Postal communication	0.84	7.49	1.88	6.0	90
06.420	Telephone, telegraph	1.03	48.49	1.09	1.9	91
07.110	Radio, TV, phonograph, etc.	1.10	40.62	7.89	0.3	92
07.120	Major durable recreation equipment	0.08	26.29			93
07.130	Other recreation equipment	0.15	39.81	5.57	0.1	94
07.210	Public entertainment	0.35	28.80	2.05	0.6	95
07.230	Other recreation, cultural events	1.55	57.68	1.34	2.0	96
07.310	Books, papers, magazines	2.53	37.14	2.68	2.5	97
07.320	Stationery	0.72	11.10	1.76	3.7	98
07.411	Teachers, 1st, 2nd	11.63	185.05		36.5	99
07.412	Teachers, college	1.58	35.19		8.6	100
07.420	Educational facilities	0.73	29.04			101
07.431	Educational supplies	0.65	7.54			102
07.432	Other education expenditures	0.82	8.48			103
08.100	Barber, beauty shops	1.16	19.91	1.31	4.5	104
08.210	Toilet articles	3.13	29.85	5.07	2.1	105
08.220	Other personal-care goods	3.13	30.29	4.11	2.5	106
08.310	Restaurants, cafes	5.14	140.16	3.65	1.0	107
08.320	Hotels, etc.	5.14	8.67	3.79	15.6	108
08.400	Other services	3.59	118.76			109
08.900	Expenditures of residents abroad		23.70			110
10.100	1- and 2-dwelling buildings	14.05	103.98	1.53	8.8	111
10.200	Multidwelling buildings	14.05	43.16	1.67	19.5	112
11.100	Hotels, etc.	0.51	6.69	1.64	4.7	113
11.200	Industrial buildings	1.17	36.17	2.57	1.3	114
11.300	Commercial buildings	3.13	25.28			115
11.400	Office buildings	1.30	32.68	1.55	2.6	116

Appendix Table 13.5. Continued

Code (1)	Category (2)	Per capita expenditure India (rupee) (3)	U.S. (dollar) (4)	Purchasing-power parities rupee/dollar (5)	Quantity per capita (U.S =100) (6)	Line number (7)
11.500	Educational buildings	0.79	32.17	1.72	1.4	117
11.600	Hospital buildings	0.50	16.81	1.35	2.2	118
11.700	Agricultural buildings	4.64	3.36			119
11.800	Other buildings	1.10	18.38			120
12.100	Roads, highways	3.84	51.45	1.62	4.6	121
12.200	Transmission, utility lines	11.11	70.11	1.24	12.8	122
12.300	Other construction	7.93	13.57	1.40	41.9	123
13.000	Land improvement	8.13	10.14	1.37	58.6	124
14.110	Locomotives	0.38	1.16	8.34	4.0	125
14.120	Other	0.85	6.33	6.79	2.0	126
14.200	Passenger cars	0.38	34.27	8.81	0.1	127
14.300	Trucks, buses, trailers	7.01	44.01	8.96	1.8	128
14.400	Aircraft	0.25	14.40			129
14.500	Ships, boats	0.76	3.96			130
14.600	Other transport	1.26	1.71			131
15.100	Engines and turbines	1.09	6.46	10.58	1.6	132
15.210	Tractors	0.62	8.24	5.15	1.5	133
15.220	Other agricultural machinery	0.12	11.81	6.88	0.1	134
15.300	Office machinery	0.19	32.00			135
15.400	Metalworking machinery	1.11	17.83	5.31	1.2	136
15.500	Construction	0.75	16.37	10.39	0.4	137
15.600	Special industrial	2.02	15.33	5.88	2.2	138
15.700	General industrial	5.53	19.79	8.04	3.5	139
15.800	Service industrial	0.42	17.01	7.63	0.3	140
16.100	Electrical transmission	4.28	13.62	8.24	3.8	141
16.200	Communication equipment	4.15	25.45			142
16.300	Other electrical	0.75	3.88			143
16.400	Instruments	0.46	16.52	3.07	0.9	144
17.100	Furniture, fixtures	0.13	19.45	4.18	0.2	145
17.200	Other durable goods	3.44	19.52			146
18.000	Increase in stocks	19.10	16.60	3.45	33.3	147
19.000	Exports less imports	-4.91	7.42	7.50	-8.8	148
20.100	Blue-collar, unskilled	11.38	18.33	0.33	185.4	149
20.210	Blue-collar, skilled	0.93	94.41	0.37	2.7	150
20.220	White-collar	12.79	108.62	0.56	21.2	151
20.300	Professional	8.50	132.96	1.20	5.3	152
21.000	Government expenditure on commodities	24.63	338.05	2.65	2.8	153

Notes:

1. Above expenditures for lines 1 to 110 include both household and government expenditures. The latter are shown separately in Table 13.15.

2. Sugar (1 180) is intentionally out of order; the purpose is to facilitate aggregation.

3. The purchasing-power parities are direct except for the following: Purchasing-power parities are indirect and the quantity ratios are direct in lines 75,76,77,78,99, and 100. Blanks in columns 5 and 6 indicate no direct price or quantity comparisons were made. Where neither comparison was made, purchasing-power parities from other selected categories were imputed to these categories for aggregation purposes.

4. Exchange rate: Rs7.500=US$1.00.

Appendix Table 13.6. Expenditures per Capita, Purchasing-Power Parities, and Quantity for Detailed Categories, Italy–U.S., 1970

Code (1)	Category (2)	Per capita expenditure Italy (lira) (3)	U.S. (dollar) (4)	Purchasing-power parities lira/dollar (5)	Quantity per capita (U.S.=100) (6)	Line number (7)
01.101	Rice	752.	1.49	590.	85.4	1
01.102	Meal, other cereals	1710.	6.49	875.	30.1	2
01.103	Bread, rolls	14911.	17.96	293.	283.7	3
01.104	Biscuits, cakes	5950.	19.79	704.	42.7	4
01.105	Cereal preparations	136.	8.32	1137.	1.4	5
01.106	Macaroni, spaghetti, related foods	8207.	1.84	467.	958.3	6
01.111	Fresh beef, veal	36458.	69.83	573.	91.1	7
01.112	Fresh lamb, mutton	1437.	2.83			8
01.113	Fresh pork	6088.	16.96	611.	58.7	9
01.114	Fresh poultry	9370.	19.12	935.	52.4	10
01.115	Other fresh meat	4242.	3.00	474.	298.5	11
01.116	Frozen, salted meat	13201.	39.08	641.	52.7	12
01.121	Fresh, frozen fish	5745.	8.15	677.	104.0	13
01.122	Canned fish	2803.	3.83	877.	83.5	14
01.131	Fresh milk	8139.	36.25	507.	44.3	15
01.132	Milk products	15047.	16.79	609.	147.3	16

Appendix Table 13.6. Continued

Code (1)	Category (2)	Per capita expenditure Italy (lira) (3)	U.S. (dollar) (4)	Purchasing-power parities lira/dollar (5)	Quantity per capita (U.S.=100) (6)	Line number (7)
01.133	Eggs, egg products	5814.	14.30	707.	57.5	17
01.141	Butter	3214.	4.82	904.	73.8	18
01.142	Margarine, edible oil	10669.	10.48	596.	170.8	19
01.143	Lard, edible fat		0.83			20
01.151	Fresh fruits, tropical, subtropical	7113.	7.97	870.	102.5	21
01.152	Other fresh fruits	12858.	12.13	272.	390.3	22
01.153	Fresh vegetables	24349.	25.44	324.	295.0	23
01.161	Fruit other than fresh	3693.	20.61	961.	18.7	24
01.162	Vegetables other than fresh	25.30	20.78	970.	12.5	25
01.170	Potatoes, manioc, other tubers	3147.	11.48	508.	54.0	26
01.191	Coffee	6291.	11.64	1902.	28.4	27
01.192	Tea	273.	2.16	1087.	11.6	28
01.193	Cocoa	205.	0.83	1145.	21.5	29
01.180	Sugar	5200.	4.49	887.	130.6	30
01.201	Jam, syrup, honey	1163.	4.99	527.	44.2	31
01.202	Chocolate, ice cream	5882.	15.13	1251.	31.1	32
01.203	Salt, spices, sauces	3147.	6.98	925.	48.7	33
01.310	Nonalcoholic beverages	3147.	13.13	609.	39.4	34
01.321	Spirits	4651.	19.91	366.	63.8	35
01.322	Wine, cider	19015.	4.25	314.	1426.7	36
01.323	Beer	3011.	24.92	408.	29.6	37
01.410	Cigarettes	19015.	50.83	572.	65.4	38
01.420	Other tobacco	1299.	4.29	549.	55.1	39
02.110	Clothing materials	5541.	5.81			40
02.121	Men's clothing	12107.	49.80	525.	46.3	41
02.122	Women's clothing	6293.	78.29	792.	10.2	42
02.123	Boys', girls' clothing	5060.	23.88	464.	45.7	43
02.131	Men's, boys' underwear	12381.	10.72	689.	167.6	44
02.132	Women's, girls' underwear	5473.	28.86	740.	25.6	45
02.150	Other clothing	1299.	12.94	586.	17.1	46
02.160	Clothing rental, repair	2462.	4.28	182.	316.7	47
02.211	Men's footwear	4719.	11.97	622.	63.4	48
02.212	Women's footwear	1915.	15.77	449.	27.0	49
02.213	Children's footwear	2803.	11.99	410.	57.0	50
02.220	Footwear repairs	1095.	2.07	311.	170.2	51
03.110	Gross rents	65324.	437.06	305.	48.9	52
03.120	Indoor repair, upkeep	1367.	17.98	207.	36.7	53
03.210	Electricity	9781.	48.39	752.	26.9	54
03.220	Gas	5609.	29.45	1224.	15.6	55
03.230	Liquid fuels	4515.	22.93	645.	30.5	56
03.240	Other fuels, ice	1848.	4.44	665.	62.6	57
04.110	Furniture, fixtures	9575.	52.56	415.	43.9	58
04.120	Floor coverings	890.	18.29	659.	7.4	59
04.200	Household textiles, etc.	4446.	38.57	714.	16.2	60
04.310	Refrigerators, etc.	958.	14.79	421.	15.4	61
04.320	Washing appliances	2257.	8.29	591.	46.0	62
04.330	Cooling appliances	1299.	9.13	355.	40.1	63
04.340	Heating appliances	752.	4.44	790.	21.4	64
04.350	Cleaning appliances	341.	2.44	926.	15.1	65
04.360	Other household appliances	547.	3.47	769.	20.5	66
04.400	Household utensils	3556.	20.13	332.	53.3	67
04.510	Nondurable household goods	5677.	27.34	686.	30.3	68
04.520	Domestic services		23.23			69
04.530	Household services	8687.	21.53	574.	70.3	70
04.600	Household furnishing repairs		7.87			71
05.110	Drugs, medical preparations	22393.	38.26	396.	147.7	72
05.120	Medical supplies	154.	5.22	309.	9.6	73
05.200	Therapeutic equipment	347.	9.28	588.	6.4	74
05.310	Physicians' services	14656.	47.38		73.0	75
05.320	Dentists' services	6499.	13.88		95.0	76
05.330	Services, nurses, other personnel	1734.	82.89		34.5	77
05.410	Hospitals, etc.	5884.	117.82		115.9	78
06.110	Personal cars	17235.	137.80	660.	18.9	79
06.120	Other personal transport	822.	20.36	539.	7.5	80
06.210	Tires, tubes, accessories	2394.	27.50	513.	17.0	81
06.220	Repair charges	6361.	37.82	654.	25.7	82
06.230	Gasoline, oil, etc.	18125.	112.64	1641.	9.8	83
06.240	Parking, tolls, etc.	4651.	23.32	167.	119.5	84
06.310	Local transport	6293.	12.41	296.	171.3	85
06.321	Rail transport	4205.	0.73	255.	2250.0	86
06.322	Bus transport	2651.	1.95	343.	396.5	87
06.323	Air transport	393.	11.92	662.	5.0	88
06.330	Miscellaneous transport		3.67			89
06.410	Postal communication	2462.	7.49	453.	72.6	90
06.420	Telephone, telegraph	3899.	48.49	449.	17.9	91
07.110	Radio, TV, phonograph, etc.	5335.	40.62	824.	15.9	92
07.120	Major durable recreation equipment	205.	26.29	697.	1.1	93

Appendix Table 13.6. Continued

Code (1)	Category (2)	Per capita expenditure Italy (lira) (3)	U.S. (dollar) (4)	Purchasing-power parities lira/dollar (5)	Quantity per capita (U.S.=100) (6)	Line number (7)
07.130	Other recreation equipment	6431.	39.81	643.	25.1	94
07.210	Public entertainment	11150.	28.80	287.	134.9	95
07.230	Other recreation, cultural events	3214.	57.68	422.	13.2	96
07.310	Books, papers, magazines	11150.	37.14	525.	57.2	97
07.320	Stationery	1848.	11.10	354.	47.0	98
07.411	Teachers, 1st, 2nd	42795.	185.05		86.6	99
07.412	Teachers, college	5073.	35.19		24.5	100
07.420	Educational facilities	2829.	29.04			101
07.431	Educational supplies	483.	7.54			102
07.432	Other education expenditures	1514.	8.48			103
08.100	Barber, beauty shops	7113.	19.91	247.	144.6	104
08.210	Toilet articles	5724.	29.85	732.	26.2	105
08.220	Other personal-care goods	6998.	30.29	730.	31.6	106
08.310	Restaurants, cafes	25993.	140.16	645.	28.7	107
08.320	Hotels, etc.	12243.	8.67	446.	316.4	108
08.400	Other services	1780.	118.76			109
08.900	Expenditures of residents abroad		23.70			110
10.100	1- and 2-dwelling buildings	56084.	103.98	441.	122.2	111
10.200	Multidwelling buildings	18676.	43.16	288.	150.1	112
11.100	Hotels, etc.	1831.	6.69	229.	119.7	113
11.200	Industrial buildings	1936.	36.17	413.	129.5	114
11.300	Commercial buildings	2747.	25.28	257.	42.3	115
11.400	Office buildings	7691.	32.68	327.	72.1	116
11.500	Educational buildings	3662.	32.17	460.	24.8	117
11.600	Hospital buildings	2563.	16.81			118
11.700	Agricultural buildings	4578.	3.36	542.	251.1	119
11.800	Other buildings	1831.	18.38			120
12.100	Roads, highways	9045.	51.45	232.	75.9	121
12.200	Transmission, utility lines	8752.	70.11	262.	47.7	122
12.300	Other construction	695.	13.57	83.	61.8	123
13.000	Land improvement	5493.	10.14	552.	98.1	124
14.110	Locomotives	750.	1.16	986.	65.5	125
14.120	Other	769.	6.33	1328.	9.1	126
14.200	Passenger cars	12285.	34.27	783.	45.8	127
14.300	Trucks, buses, trailers	12304.	44.01			128
14.400	Aircraft	2180.	14.40	660.	22.9	129
14.500	Ships, boats	2343.	3.96			130
14.600	Other transport	1172.	1.71	821.	83.6	131
15.100	Engines and turbines	732.	6.46			132
15.210	Tractors	1393.	8.24	557.	30.3	133
15.220	Other agricultural machinery	1831.	11.81	868.	17.9	134
15.300	Office machinery	2106.	32.00	669.	9.8	135
15.400	Metalworking machinery	3460.	17.83	300.	64.6	136
15.500	Construction, mining	2070.	16.37	842.	15.0	137
15.600	Special industrial	5090.	15.33	519.	64.0	138
15.700	General industrial	5365.	19.79	433.	62.6	139
15.800	Service industrial	916.	17.01	522.	10.3	140
16.100	Electrical transmission	8020.	13.62	401.	146.8	141
16.200	Communication equipment	3150.	25.45	591.	20.9	142
16.300	Other electrical	3460.	3.88	272.	327.6	143
16.400	Instruments	2893.	16.52	522.	33.5	144
17.100	Furniture, fixtures	3442.	19.45	693.	25.5	145
17.200	Other durable goods	6994.	19.52	786.	45.6	146
18.000	Increase in stocks	16586.	16.60	606.	164.8	147
19.000	Exports less imports	1009.	7.42	625.	21.8	148
20.100	Blue-collar, unskilled	13955.	18.33	378.	201.2	149
20.210	Blue-collar, skilled	6148.	94.41	341.	19.1	150
20.220	White-collar	23314.	108.62	387.	55.5	151
20.300	Professional	3941.	132.96	473.	6.3	152
21.000	Government expenditure on commodities	30209.	338.05	466.	19.2	153

Notes:

1. Above expenditures for lines 1 to 110 include both household and government expenditures. The latter are shown separately in Table 13.15.

2. Sugar (1 180) is intentionally out of order; the purpose is to facilitate aggregation.

3. The purchasing-power parities are direct except for the following: Purchasing-power parities are indirect and the quantity ratios are direct in lines 75,76,77,78,99, and 100. Blanks in columns 5 and 6 indicate no direct price or quantity comparisons were made. Where neither comparison was made purchasing-power parities from other selected categories were imputed to these categories for aggregation purposes.

4. Exchange rate: L625=US$1.00.

Appendix Table 13.7. Expenditures per Capita, Purchasing-Power Parities, and Quantity per Capita for Detailed Categories, Japan–U.S., 1970

Code (1)	Category (2)	Per capita expenditure Japan (yen) (3)	U.S. (dollar) (4)	Purchasing-power parities yen/dollar (5)	Quantity per capita (U.S.=100) (6)	Line number (7)
01.101	Rice	18447.	1.49	440.	2805.6	1
01.102	Meal, other cereals	300.	6.49	348.	13.3	2
01.103	Bread, rolls	1735.	17.96	187.	51.6	3
01.104	Biscuits, cakes	6722.	19.79	300.	113.2	4
01.105	Cereal preparations	182.	8.32	563.	3.9	5
01.106	Macaroni, spaghetti, related foods	1859.	1.84	340.	298.3	6
01.111	Fresh beef, veal	2402.	69.83	568.	6.1	7
01.112	Fresh lamb, mutton	42.	2.83			8
01.113	Fresh pork	3438.	16.96	447.	45.3	9
01.114	Fresh poultry	1720.	19.12	444.	20.3	10
01.115	Other fresh meat	639.	3.00			11
01.116	Frozen, salted meat	2442.	39.08	455.	13.7	12
01.121	Fresh, frozen fish	8615.	8.15	260.	407.1	13
01.122	Canned fish	8239.	3.83	422.	510.2	14
01.131	Fresh milk	3854.	36.25	375.	28.3	15
01.132	Milk products	856.	16.79	405.	12.6	16
01.133	Eggs, egg products	3405.	14.30	261.	91.1	17
01.141	Butter	186.	4.82	411.	9.4	18
01.142	Margarine, edible oil	1064.	10.48	389.	26.1	19
01.143	Lard, edible fat	11.	0.83	680.	1.9	20
01.151	Fresh fruits, tropical, subtropical	3530.	7.97	495.	89.4	21
01.152	Other fresh fruits	3648.	12.13	386.	78.0	22
01.153	Fresh vegetables	8321.	25.44	210.	155.8	23
01.161	Fruit other than fresh	796.	20.61	417.	9.3	24
01.162	Vegetables other than fresh	3558.	20.78	519.	33.0	25
01.170	Potatoes, manioc, other tubers	1051.	11.48	365.	25.1	26
01.191	Coffee	361.	11.64	709.	4.4	27
01.192	Tea	1114.	2.16	236.	218.2	28
01.193	Cocoa	159.	0.83			29
01.180	Sugar	987.	4.49	508.	43.3	30
01.201	Jam, syrup, honey	1538.	4.99	375.	82.2	31
01.202	Chocolate, ice cream	1431.	15.13	604.	15.7	32
01.203	Salt, spices, sauces	4937.	6.98	164.	432.3	33
01.310	Nonalcoholic beverages	2145.	13.13	353.	46.3	34
01.321	Spirits	1242.	19.91	263.	23.7	35
01.322	Wine, cider	9554.	4.25	269.	834.2	36
01.323	Beer	4871.	24.92	332.	58.8	37
01.410	Cigarettes	4876.	50.83	208.	46.1	38
01.420	Other tobacco	8.	4.29			39
02.110	Clothing materials	8873.	5.81	400.	382.0	40
02.121	Men's clothing	4747.	49.80	244.	39.1	41
02.122	Women's clothing	5659.	78.29	234.	30.9	42
02.123	Boys', girls' clothing	2192.	23.88	280.	32.8	43
02.131	Men's, boys' underwear	1719.	10.72	230.	69.7	44
02.132	Women's, girls' underwear	1425.	28.86	250.	19.8	45
02.150	Other clothing	1673.	12.94	218.	59.4	46
02.160	Clothing rental, repair	1250.	4.28			47
02.211	Men's footwear	869.	11.97	179.	40.6	48
02.212	Women's footwear	916.	15.77	211.	27.5	49
02.213	Children's footwear	501.	11.99	158.	26.4	50
02.220	Footwear repairs	62.	2.07	112.	26.6	51
03.110	Gross rents	42527.	437.06	258.	37.7	52
03.120	Indoor repair, upkeep	2014.	17.98	191.	58.7	53
03.210	Electricity	4300.	48.39	326.	27.2	54
03.220	Gas	2755.	29.45	1357.	6.9	55
03.230	Liquid fuels	889.	22.93	413.	9.4	56
03.240	Other fuels, ice	1360.	4.44	188.	162.6	57
04.110	Furniture, fixtures	2417.	52.56	335.	13.7	58
04.120	Floor coverings	935.	18.29	313.	16.3	59
04.200	Household textiles, etc.	988.	38.57	379.	6.8	60
04.310	Refrigerators, etc.	1927.	14.79	599.	21.8	61
04.320	Washing appliances	898.	8.29	225.	48.1	62
04.330	Cooking appliances	358.	9.13	259.	15.2	63
04.340	Heating appliances	972.	4.44	426.	51.4	64
04.350	Cleaning appliances	426.	2.44	426.	40.9	65
04.360	Other household appliances	938.	3.47	375.	72.2	66
04.400	Household utensils	2794.	20.13	204.	68.2	67
04.510	Nondurable household goods	2169.	27.34	340.	23.4	68
04.520	Domestic services	405.	23.23	136.	12.8	69
04.530	Household services	2814.	21.53	205.	63.8	70
04.600	Household furnishing repairs	211.	7.87			71
05.110	Drugs, medical preparations	8642.	38.26	155.	145.3	72
05.120	Medical supplies	8759.	5.22	191.	881.2	73
05.200	Therapeutic equipment	261.	9.28	69.	40.7	74

Appendix Table 13.7. Continued

Code (1)	Category (2)	Per capita expenditure Japan (yen) (3)	U.S. (dollar) (4)	Purchasing-power parities yen/dollar (5)	Quantity per capita (U.S.=100) (6)	Line number (7)
05.310	Physicians' services	1553.	47.38		66.0	75
05.320	Dentists' services	334.	13.88		68.9	76
05.330	Services, nurses, other personnel	1372.	82.89		54.0	77
05.410	Hospitals, etc.	5243.	117.82		130.6	78
06.110	Personal cars	2291.	137.80	373.	4.5	79
06.120	Other personal transport	1000.	20.36	436.	11.3	80
06.210	Tires, tubes, accessories	173.	27.50	304.	2.1	81
06.220	Repair charges	1108.	37.82	362.	8.1	82
06.230	Gasoline, oil, etc.	2314.	112.64	591.	3.5	83
06.240	Parking, tolls, etc.	1090.	23.32	370.	12.6	84
06.310	Local transport	9945.	12.41	63.	1276.1	85
06.321	Rail transport	3059.	0.73	117.	3583.9	86
06.322	Bus transport	818.	1.95	147.	285.7	87
06.323	Air transport	328.	11.92	253.	10.9	88
06.330	Miscellaneous transport	410.	3.67			89
06.410	Postal communication	254.	7.49	257.	13.2	90
06.420	Telephone, telegraph	1734.	48.49	296.	12.1	91
07.110	Radio, TV, phonograph, etc.	6169.	40.62	210.	72.4	92
07.120	Major durable recreation equipment	970.	26.29	211.	17.4	93
07.130	Other recreation equipment	4299.	39.81	269.	40.2	94
07.210	Public entertainment	10173.	28.80	408.	86.5	95
07.230	Other recreation, cultural events	2310.	57.68	181.	22.2	96
07.310	Books, papers, magazines	4566.	37.14	367.	33.5	97
07.320	Stationery	917.	11.10	261.	31.6	98
07.411	Teachers, 1st, 2nd	12083.	185.05		70.8	99
07.412	Teachers, college	2170.	35.19		44.8	100
07.420	Educational facilities	2632.	29.04			101
07.431	Educational supplies	877.	7.54			102
07.432	Other education exependitures	1939.	8.48			103
08.100	Barber, beauty shops	4165.	19.91	135.	154.4	104
08.210	Toilet articles	5260.	29.85	279.	63.0	105
08.220	Other personal-care goods	1417.	30.29	194.	24.1	106
08.310	Restaurants, cafes	13038.	140.16	214.	43.5	107
08.320	Hotels, etc.	5056.	8.67	267.	218.5	108
08.400	Other services	15656.	118.76			109
08.900	Expenditures of residents abroad	1064.	23.70			110
10.100	1- and 2-dwelling buildings	34424.	103.98	261.	126.7	111
10.200	Multidwelling buildings	16084.	43.16	225.	165.8	112
11.100	Hotels, etc.	2233.	6.69	272.	122.6	113
11.200	Industrial buildings	7091.	36.17	536.	36.6	114
11.300	Commercial buildings	7092.	25.28	446.	62.9	115
11.400	Office buildings	7845.	32.68	282.	85.0	116
11.500	Educational buildings	4918.	32.17	208.	73.6	117
11.600	Hospital buildings	1715.	16.81	180.	56.8	118
11.700	Agricultural buildings	1200.	3.36	622.	57.4	119
11.800	Other buildings	9592.	18.38	393.	132.8	120
12.100	Roads, highways	14244.	51.45	288.	96.0	121
12.200	Transmission, utility lines	16736.	70.11	167.	143.0	122
12.300	Other construction	22127.	13.57	191.	856.1	123
13.000	Land improvement	516.	10.14	160.	31.8	124
14.110	Locomotives	782.	1.16			125
14.120	Other	89.	6.33			126
14.200	Passenger cars	11408.	34.27	374.	88.9	127
14.300	Trucks, buses, trailers	14279.	44.01			128
14.400	Aircraft	364.	14.40			129
14.500	Ships, boats	3924.	3.96			130
14.600	Other transport	1497.	1.71			131
15.100	Engines and turbines	2070.	6.46			132
15.210	Tractors	410.	8.24			133
15.220	Other agricultural machinery	1916.	11.81			134
15.300	Office machinery	5508.	32.00			135
15.400	Metalworking machinery	7482.	17.83	427.	98.2	136
15.500	Construction, mining	4720.	16.37	302.	95.5	137
15.600	Special industrial	12427.	15.33	230.	351.9	138
15.700	General industrial	11744.	19.79	292.	203.0	139
15.800	Service industrial	1052.	17.01			140
16.100	Electrical transmission	7658.	13.62			141
16.200	Communication equipment	8000.	25.45			142
16.300	Other electrical	2203.	3.88			143
16.400	Instruments	4144.	16.52			144
17.100	Furniture, fixtures	5359.	19.45	316.	87.2	145
17.200	Other durable goods	2864.	19.52			146
18.000	Increase in stocks	31443.	16.60	326.	580.9	147
19.000	Exports less imports	9113.	7.42	360.	341.0	148
20.100	Blue-collar, unskilled	9844.	18.33	142.	377.6	149
20.210	Blue-collar, skilled	19445.	94.41	118.	174.2	150

Appendix Table 13.7. Continued

Code	Category	Per capita expenditure Japan (yen)	U.S. (dollar)	Purchasing-power parities yen/dollar	Quantity per capita (U.S.=100)	Line number
(1)	(2)	(3)	(4)	(5)	(6)	(7)
20.220	White-collar	4780.	108.62	124.	35.5	151
20.300	Professional	6441.	132.96	244.	19.9	152
21.000	Government expenditure on commodities	16047.	338.05	239.	19.9	153

Notes:
1. Above expenditures for lines 1 to 110 include both household and government expenditures. The latter are shown separately in Table 13.15.
2. Sugar (1 180) is intentionally out of order; the purpose is to facilitate aggregation.
3. The purchasing-power parities are direct except for the following: Purchasing-power parities are indirect and the quantity ratios are direct in lines 75,76,77,78,99, and 100. Blanks in columns 5 and 6 indicate no direct price or quantity comparisons were made. Where neither comparison was made, purchasing-power parities from other selected categories were imputed to these categories for aggregation purposes.
4. Exchange rate: ¥360=US$1.00.

Appendix Table 13.8. Expenditures per Capita, Purchasing-Power Parities, and Quantity per Capita for Detailed Categories, Kenya–U.S., 1970

Code	Category	Per capita expenditure Kenya (shilling)	U.S. (dollar)	Purchasing-power parities shilling/dollar	Quantity per capita (U.S.=100)	Line number
(1)	(2)	(3)	(4)	(5)	(6)	(7)
01.101	Rice	1.80	1.49	4.14	29.1	1
01.102	Meal, other cereals	115.79	6.49	5.74	310.9	2
01.103	Bread, rolls	4.76	17.96	3.05	8.7	3
01.104	Biscuits, cakes	2.02	19.79	1.06	9.7	4
01.105	Cereal preparations	0.83	8.32	10.22	1.0	5
01.106	Macaroni, spaghetti, related foods	0.15	1.84	11.42	0.7	6
01.111	Fresh beef, veal	22.43	69.83	3.14	10.2	7
01.112	Fresh lamb, mutton	2.74	2.83	2.76	35.1	8
01.113	Fresh pork	0.54	16.96	6.83	0.5	9
01.114	Fresh poultry	0.96	19.12	5.12	1.0	10
01.115	Other fresh meat	2.39	3.00			11
01.116	Frozen, salted meat	1.98	39.08	5.35	0.9	12
01.121	Fresh, frozen fish	6.54	8.15	4.11	19.5	13
01.122	Canned fish	0.99	3.83	11.63	2.2	14
01.131	Fresh milk	37.64	36.23	4.13	25.2	15
01.132	Milk products	4.07	16.79	6.11	4.0	16
01.133	Eggs, egg products	0.33	14.30	5.64	0.4	17
01.141	Butter	5.48	4.82	4.48	25.4	18
01.142	Margarine, edible oil	4.76	10.48	8.51	5.3	19
01.143	Lard, edible fat	1.15	0.83	13.09	10.5	20
01.151	Fresh fruits, tropical, subtropical	13.27	7.97	2.48	67.0	21
01.152	Other fresh fruits	0.32	12.13	15.77	0.2	22
01.153	Fresh vegetables	19.72	25.44	2.06	37.7	23
01.161	Fruit other than fresh	0.11	20.61	4.92	0.1	24
01.162	Vegetables other than fresh	3.61	20.78	5.90	2.9	25
01.170	Potatoes, manioc, other tubers	31.07	11.48	2.01	134.9	26
01.191	Coffee	0.96	11.64	7.63	1.1	27
01.192	Tea	3.49	2.16	2.88	56.1	28
01.193	Cocoa	0.26	0.83	8.70	3.6	29
01.180	Sugar	13.46	4.49	5.48	54.7	30
01.201	Jam, syrup, honey	2.69	4.99	3.49	15.4	31
01.202	Chocolate, ice cream	1.96	15.13	32.72	0.4	32
01.203	Salt, spices, sauces	3.90	6.98	5.40	10.4	33
01.310	Nonalcoholic beverages	5.86	13.13	14.68	3.0	34
01.321	Spirits	2.05	19.91	6.85	1.5	35
01.322	Wine, cider	0.47	4.25	7.79	1.4	36
01.323	Beer	13.73	24.92	8.22	6.7	37
01.410	Cigarettes	9.33	50.83	4.35	4.2	38
01.420	Other tobacco	0.20	4.29	3.82	1.2	39
02.110	Clothing materials	5.31	5.81	7.94	11.5	40
02.121	Men's clothing	7.92	49.80	4.66	3.4	41
02.122	Women's clothing	4.59	78.29	11.28	0.5	42
02.123	Boys', girls' clothing	2.36	23.88	2.80	3.5	43
02.131	Men's, boys' underwear	0.55	10.72	8.06	0.6	44
02.132	Women's, girls' underwear	0.47	28.86	4.17	0.4	45
02.150	Other clothing	0.66	12.94	4.73	1.1	46
02.160	Clothing rental, repair	0.62	4.28	3.56	4.0	47
02.211	Men's footwear	3.34	11.97	2.72	10.3	48
02.212	Women's footwear	0.83	15.77	1.80	2.9	49
02.213	Children's footwear	0.65	11.99	1.59	3.4	50

Appendix Table 13.8. Continued

Code (1)	Category (2)	Per capita expenditure Kenya (shilling) (3)	U.S. (dollar) (4)	Purchasing-power parities shilling/dollar (5)	Quantity per capita (U.S.=100) (6)	Line number (7)
02.220	Footwear repairs	0.27	2.07	4.01	3.2	51
03.110	Gross rents	61.15	437.06	5.99	2.3	52
03.120	Indoor repair, upkeep	0.20	17.98	3.15	0.4	53
03.210	Electricity	1.43	48.39	9.11	0.3	54
03.220	Gas	0.11	29.45	8.30	0.0	55
03.230	Liquid fuels	1.38	22.93	17.13	0.4	56
03.240	Other fuels, ice	8.12	4.44	1.69	108.2	57
04.110	Furniture, fixtures	6.00	52.56	3.77	3.0	58
04.120	Floor coverings	0.98	18.29	8.63	0.6	59
04.200	Household textiles, etc.	3.85	38.57	7.36	1.4	60
04.310	Refrigerators, etc.	0.59	14.79	8.93	0.4	61
04.320	Washing appliances	0.08	8.29			62
04.330	Cooking appliances	0.62	9.13	10.41	0.7	63
04.340	Heating appliances	0.56	4.44			64
04.350	Cleaning appliances	0.10	2.44			65
04.360	Other household appliances	0.24	3.47	16.48	0.4	66
04.400	Household utensils	6.79	20.13	3.25	10.4	67
04.510	Nondurable household goods	16.19	27.34	7.73	7.7	68
04.520	Domestic services	6.37	23.23	0.67	40.7	69
04.530	Household services	1.14	21.53	4.09	1.3	70
04.600	Household furnishing repairs	0.08	7.87	0.89	1.1	71
05.110	Drugs, medical preparations	7.06	38.26	3.31	5.6	72
05.120	Medical supplies	0.55	5.22	3.68	2.9	73
05.200	Therapeutic equipment	0.09	9.28	1.44	0.7	74
05.310	Physicians' services	5.05	47.38		7.0	75
05.320	Dentists' services	0.40	13.88		1.0	76
05.330	Services, nurses, other personnel	5.36	82.89			77
05.410	Hospitals, etc.	17.79	117.82		15.1	78
06.110	Personal cars	11.14	137.80	8.43	1.0	79
06.120	Other personal transport	0.11	20.36	8.61	0.1	80
06.210	Tires, tubes, accessories	2.18	27.50	10.76	0.7	81
06.220	Repair charges	2.18	37.82	1.77	3.3	82
06.230	Gasoline, oil, etc.	1.16	112.64	7.68	0.1	83
06.240	Parking, tolls, etc.	0.86	23.32			84
06.310	Local transport	2.24	12.41	1.93	9.4	85
06.321	Rail transport	1.40	0.73	3.16	60.5	86
06.322	Bus transport	13.24	1.95	2.67	254.9	87
06.323	Air transport	15.06	11.92	12.03	10.5	88
06.330	Miscellaneous transport	0.22	3.67			89
06.410	Postal communication	0.41	7.49	4.33	1.3	90
06.420	Telephone, telegraph	1.02	48.49	2.73	0.8	91
07.110	Radio, TV, phonograph, etc.	3.75	40.62	11.25	0.8	92
07.120	Major durable recreation equipment	5.43	26.29	10.06	2.1	93
07.130	Other recreation equipment	3.72	39.81	7.33	1.3	94
07.210	Public entertainment	5.61	28.80	1.35	14.4	95
07.230	Other recreation, cultural events	4.06	57.68	2.96	2.4	96
07.310	Books, papers, magazines	6.00	37.14	6.85	2.4	97
07.320	Stationery	0.09	11.10	16.16	0.0	98
07.411	Teachers, 1st, 2nd	40.04	185.05		28.6	99
07.412	Teachers, college	2.22	35.19		1.2	100
07.420	Educational facilities	5.72	29.04			101
07.431	Educational supplies	2.35	7.54			102
07.432	Other education expenditures	3.79	8.48			103
08.100	Barber, beauty shops	0.46	19.91	2.55	0.9	104
08.210	Toilet articles	2.62	29.85	8.65	1.0	105
08.220	Other personal-care goods	2.62	30.29	5.47	1.6	106
08.310	Restaurants, cafes	13.80	140.16	2.84	3.5	107
08.320	Hotels, etc.	14.48	8.67	4.01	41.7	108
08.400	Other services	11.97	118.76			109
08.900	Expenditures of residents abroad		23.70			110
10.100	1- and 2-dwelling buildings	37.06	103.98	3.27	10.9	111
10.200	Multidwelling buildings	5.56	43.16	3.61	3.6	112
11.100	Hotels, etc.	0.78	6.69	4.77	2.4	113
11.200	Industrial buildings	14.51	36.17	5.14	7.8	114
11.300	Commercial buildings	2.87	25.28	3.73	3.0	115
11.400	Office buildings	3.71	32.68	2.62	4.3	116
11.500	Educational buildings	3.64	32.17	2.52	4.5	117
11.600	Hospital buildings	3.71	16.81	3.01	7.4	118
11.700	Agricultural buildings	0.74	3.36	2.23	9.9	119
11.800	Other buildings	0.93	18.38			120
12.100	Roads, highways	11.60	51.45			121
12.200	Transmission, utility lines	8.76	70.11			122
12.300	Other construction	13.96	13.57	8.84	11.6	123
13.000	Land improvement	4.59	10.14	3.54	12.8	124
14.110	Locomotives	2.79	1.16	6.84	35.2	125
14.120	Other	4.95	6.33	9.46	8.3	126

Appendix Table 13.8. Continued

Code	Category	Per capita expenditure Kenya (shilling)	U.S. (dollar)	Purchasing-power parities shilling/dollar	Quantity per capita (U.S.=100)	Line number
(1)	(2)	(3)	(4)	(5)	(6)	(7)
14.200	Passenger cars	10.22	34.27	8.15	3.7	127
14.300	Trucks, buses, trailers	11.71	44.01	6.99	3.8	128
14.400	Aircraft	2.71	14.40			129
14.500	Ships, boats	0.46	3.96			130
14.600	Other transport	0.54	1.71	8.21	3.8	131
15.100	Engines and turbines	2.18	6.46	8.42	4.0	132
15.210	Tractors	2.40	8.24	6.82	4.3	133
15.220	Other agricultural machinery	3.39	11.81	9.56	3.0	134
15.300	Office machinery	1.87	32.00	9.85	0.6	135
15.400	Metalworking machinery	1.15	17.83	4.39	1.5	136
15.500	Construction, mining	4.75	16.37	9.29	3.1	137
15.600	Special industrial	10.20	15.33	6.60	10.1	138
15.700	General industrial	9.64	19.79	7.84	6.2	139
15.800	Service industrial	2.07	17.01	11.09	1.1	140
16.100	Electrical transmission	4.12	13.62	5.48	5.5	141
16.200	Communication equipment	2.93	25.45			142
16.300	Other electrical	1.12	3.88			143
16.400	Instruments	1.43	16.52	7.28	1.2	144
17.100	Furniture, fixtures	2.00	19.45	5.82	1.8	145
17.200	Other durable goods	5.35	19.52	6.65	4.1	146
18.000	Increase in stocks	23.83	16.60	5.51	26.0	147
19.000	Exports less imports	−17.78	7.42	7.14	−33.5	148
20.100	Blue-collar, unskilled	44.13	18.33	0.51	471.1	149
20.210	Blue-collar, skilled	3.12	94.41	1.18	2.8	150
20.220	White-collar	12.07	108.62	1.91	5.8	151
20.300	Professional	29.90	132.96	4.26	5.3	152
21.000	Government expenditure on commodities	28.21	338.05	4.35	1.9	153

Notes:
1. Above expenditures for lines 1 to 110 include both household and government expenditures. The latter are shown separately in Table 13.15.
2. Sugar (1 180) is intentionally out of order; the purpose is to facilitate aggregation.
3. The purchasing-power parities are direct except for the following: Purchasing-power parities are indirect and the quantity ratios are direct in lines 75,76,77,78,99, and 100. Blanks in columns 5 and 6 indicate no direct price or quantity comparisons were made. Where neither comparison was made purchasing-power parities from other selected categories were imputed to these categories for aggregation purposes.
4. In the Kenya–U.S. comparison, yams and potatoes were treated as separate categories, although for mechanical convenience they are printed above as a single category; the price ratio for potatoes was 3.350 and for yams, sweet potatoes, and cassava, 1.157. 75.0 percent of ICP 1 170 expenditure in Kenya was for yams and 9.1 percent in the United States.
5. Exchange rate: Sh7.143=US$1.00.

Appendix Table 13.9. Expenditures per Capita, Purchasing-Power Parities, and Quantity per Capita for Detailed Categories, U.K.–U.S., 1970

Code	Category	Per capita expenditure U.K. (pound)	U.S. (dollar)	Purchasing-power parities pound/dollar	Quantity per capita (U.S.=100)	Line number
(1)	(2)	(3)	(4)	(5)	(6)	(7)
01.101	Rice	0.107	1.49	0.390	18.4	1
01.102	Meal, other cereals	0.714	6.49	0.355	31.0	2
01.103	Bread, rolls		17.96	0.203	182.7	3
01.104	Biscuits, cakes	6.430	19.79	0.247	131.6	4
01.105	Cereal preparations	1.125	8.32	0.291	46.5	5
01.106	Macaroni, spaghetti, related foods	0.304	1.84	0.384	43.1	6
01.111	Fresh beef, veal	8.395	69.83	0.214	56.2	7
01.112	Fresh lamb, mutton	4.447	2.83	0.207	759.0	8
01.113	Fresh pork	2.018	16.96	0.347	34.3	9
01.114	Fresh poultry	2.876	19.12	0.351	42.8	10
01.115	Other fresh meat	1.268	3.00	0.324	130.6	11
01.116	Frozen, salted meat	13.360	39.08	0.323	105.8	12
01.121	Fresh, frozen fish	2.500	8.15	0.270	113.6	13
01.122	Canned fish	1.393	3.83	0.511	71.2	14
01.131	Fresh milk	9.180	36.25	0.361	70.2	15
01.132	Milk products	3.786	16.79	0.220	102.5	16
01.133	Eggs, egg products	3.983	14.30	0.376	74.1	17
01.141	Butter	3.161	4.82	0.217	302.4	18
01.142	Margarine, edible oil	1.179	10.48	0.421	26.7	19
01.143	Lard, edible fat	0.589	0.83	0.467	151.2	20
01.151	Fresh fruits, tropical, subtropical	1.840	7.97	0.447	51.6	21
01.152	Other fresh fruits	2.608	12.13	0.368	58.4	22

Appendix Table 13.9. Continued

Code (1)	Category (2)	Per capita expenditure U.K. (pound) (3)	U.S. (dollar) (4)	Purchasing-power parities pound/dollar (5)	Quantity per capita (U.S.=100) (6)	Line number (7)
01.153	Fresh vegetables	5.037	25.44	0.254	78.0	23
01.161	Fruit other than fresh	2.233	20.61	0.365	29.7	24
01.162	Vegetables other than fresh	3.983	20.78	0.407	47.1	25
01.170	Potatoes, manioc, other tubers	4.626	11.48	0.259	155.6	26
01.191	Coffee	1.161	11.64	0.369	27.0	27
01.192	Tea	2.965	2.16	0.180	761.9	28
01.193	Cocoa	0.107	0.83	0.293	43.8	29
01.180	Sugar	2.215	4.49	0.291	169.5	30
01.201	Jam, syrup, honey	1.143	4.99	0.189	121.1	31
01.202	Chocolate, ice cream	8.805	15.13	0.567	102.6	32
01.203	Salt, spices, sauces	1.000	6.98	0.403	35.6	33
01.310	Nonalcoholic beverages	2.947	13.13	0.395	56.8	34
01.321	Spirits	10.431	19.91	0.440	119.1	35
01.322	Wine, cider	4.930	4.25	0.690	168.1	36
01.323	Beer	22.219	24.92	0.572	155.9	37
01.410	Cigarettes	26.845	50.83	0.693	76.2	38
01.420	Other tobacco	3.858	4.29	0.714	125.8	39
02.110	Clothing materials	1.286	5.81	0.382	57.9	40
02.121	Men's clothing	7.573	49.80	0.317	48.0	41
02.122	Women's clothing	12.556	78.29	0.457	35.1	42
02.123	Boy's, girls' clothing	2.483	23.88	0.311	33.4	43
02.131	Men's, boys' underwear	4.019	10.72	0.497	75.4	44
02.132	Women's, girls' underwear	5.412	28.86	0.351	53.4	45
02.150	Other clothing	5.698	12.94	0.258	170.6	46
02.160	Clothing rental, repair	0.857	4.28	0.331	60.5	47
02.211	Men's footwear	2.590	11.97	0.208	104.0	48
02.212	Women's footwear	3.554	15.77	0.252	89.4	49
02.213	Children's footwear	1.929	11.99	0.174	92.5	50
02.220	Footwear repairs	0.750	2.07	0.220	164.8	51
03.110	Gross rents	63.423	437.06	0.271	53.5	52
03.120	Indoor repair, upkeep	12.699	17.98	0.356	198.4	53
03.210	Electricity	11.770	48.39	0.330	73.7	54
03.220	Gas	6.876	29.45	0.890	26.2	55
03.230	Liquid fuels	1.107	22.93			56
03.240	Other fuels, ice	6.823	4.44	0.287	535.3	57
04.110	Furniture, fixtures	6.162	52.56	0.494	23.7	58
04.120	Floor coverings	5.001	18.29	0.303	90.3	59
04.200	Household textiles, etc.	4.912	38.57	0.288	44.2	60
04.310	Refrigerators, etc.	1.429	14.79	0.438	22.1	61
04.320	Washing appliances	1.875	8.29	0.344	65.8	62
04.330	Cooking appliances	1.661	9.13	0.382	47.6	63
04.340	Heating appliances	1.554	4.44	0.556	62.9	64
04.350	Cleaning appliances	1.107	2.44	0.730	62.2	65
04.360	Other household appliances	0.321	3.47	0.643	14.4	66
04.400	Household utensils	6.716	20.13	0.351	95.0	67
04.510	Nondurable household goods	6.090	27.34	0.418	53.3	68
04.520	Domestic services	2.822	23.23	0.185	65.7	69
04.530	Household services	3.590	21.53	0.272	61.3	70
04.600	Household furnishing repairs	0.804	7.87	0.111	92.0	71
05.110	Drugs, medical preparations	6.555	38.26	0.164	104.5	72
05.120	Medical supplies	1.107	5.22	0.207	102.5	73
05.200	Therapeutic equipment	1.911	9.28	0.171	120.4	74
05.310	Physicians' services	5.644	47.38		66.9	75
05.320	Dentists' services	1.822	13.88		48.1	76
05.330	Services, nurses, other personnel	9.573	82.89		102.2	77
05.410	Hospitals, etc.	12.502	117.82		115.3	78
06.110	Personal cars	17.003	137.80	0.570	21.6	79
06.120	Other personal transport	1.072	20.36	0.522	10.1	80
06.210	Tires, tubes, accessories	4.465	27.50	0.240	67.7	81
06.220	Repair charges	4.215	37.82	0.172	64.8	82
06.230	Gasoline, oil, etc.	14.146	112.64	0.587	21.4	83
06.240	Parking, tolls, etc.	7.519	23.32	0.296	108.9	84
06.310	Local transport	9.609	12.41	0.214	361.9	85
06.321	Rail transport	2.518	0.73	0.283	1215.6	86
06.322	Bus transport	0.500	1.95	0.233	110.2	87
06.323	Air transport	3.394	11.92	0.393	72.4	88
01.101	Miscellaneous transport	1.822	3.67	0.720	68.9	89
06.410	Postal communication	1.947	7.49	0.268	97.0	90
06.420	Telephone, telegraph	3.751	48.49	0.187	41.4	91
07.110	Radio, TV, phonograph, etc.	3.215	40.62	0.576	13.7	92
07.120	Major durable recreation equipment	1.661	26.29	0.414	15.3	93
07.130	Other recreation equipment	11.002	39.81	0.437	63.2	94
07.210	Public entertainment	6.876	28.80	0.084	284.2	95
07.230	Other recreation, cultural events	14.485	57.68	0.355	70.8	96
07.310	Books, papers, magazines	8.269	37.14	0.166	134.1	97

Appendix Table 13.9. Continued

Code (1)	Category (2)	Per capita expenditure U.K. (pound) (3)	U.S. (dollar) (4)	Purchasing-power parities pound/dollar (5)	Quantity per capita (U.S.=100) (6)	Line number (7)
07.320	Stationery	1.947	11.10	0.339	51.7	98
07.411	Teachers, 1st, 2nd	23.719	185.05		67.1	99
07.412	Teachers, college	4.787	35.19		48.6	100
07.420	Educational facilities	5.590	29.04			101
07.431	Educational supplies	2.054	7.54			102
07.432	Other education expenditures	3.751	8.48			103
08.100	Barber, beauty shops	4.037	19.91	0.118	171.8	104
08.210	Toilet articles	4.251	29.85	0.366	38.9	105
08.220	Other personal-care goods	4.572	30.29	0.268	56.3	106
08.310	Restaurants, cafes	16.289	140.16	0.394	29.5	107
08.320	Hotels, etc.	10.413	8.67	0.285	421.5	108
08.400	Other services	18.825	118.76			109
08.900	Expenditures of residents abroad	−0.339	23.70	0.417	−3.4	110
10.100	1- and 2-dwelling buildings	18.414	103.98	0.183	96.8	111
10.200	Multidwelling buildings	8.591	43.16	0.218	91.3	112
11.100	Hotels, etc.	0.643	6.69	0.399	24.1	113
11.200	Industrial buildings	13.663	36.17	0.373	101.3	114
11.300	Commercial buildings	4.626	25.28	0.343	53.3	115
11.400	Office buildings	3.126	32.68	0.258	37.1	116
11.500	Educational buildings	6.055	32.17	0.308	61.1	117
11.600	Hospital buildings	2.983	16.81	0.242	73.3	118
11.700	Agricultural buildings	1.643	3.36	0.250	195.5	119
11.800	Other buildings	3.590	18.38	0.373	52.4	120
12.100	Roads, highways	8.216	51.45	0.243	65.7	121
12.200	Transmission, utility lines	4.858	70.11	0.185	37.5	122
12.300	Other construction	2.572	13.57	0.308	61.5	123
13.000	Land improvement	2.143	10.14	0.357	59.2	124
14.110	Locomotives	0.143	1.16			125
14.120	Other	0.232	6.33			126
14.200	Passenger cars	6.090	34.27	0.670	26.5	127
14.300	Trucks, buses, trailers	0.625	44.01			128
14.400	Aircraft	1.804	14.40			129
14.500	Ships, boats	5.698	3.96			130
14.600	Other transport	3.590	1.71			131
15.100	Engines and turbines	0.107	6.46	0.310	5.3	132
15.210	Tractors	0.929	8.24	0.320	35.2	133
15.220	Other agricultural machinery	1.375	11.81	0.390	29.9	134
15.300	Office machinery	3.108	32.00	0.410	23.7	135
15.400	Metalworking machinery	4.376	17.83	0.300	81.8	136
15.500	Construction, mining	4.590	16.37	0.370	75.8	137
15.600	Special industrial	7.591	15.33	0.370	133.8	138
15.700	General industrial	21.058	19.79	0.320	332.6	139
15.800	Service industrial	0.572	17.01			140
16.100	Electrical transmission	6.483	13.62			141
16.200	Communication equipment	8.502	25.45			142
16.300	Other electrical	1.786	3.88	0.150	306.5	143
16.400	Instruments	1.715	16.52	0.160	64.9	144
17.100	Furniture, fixtures	1.911	19.45	0.210	46.8	145
17.200	Other durable goods	0.429	19.52			146
18.000	Increase in stocks	6.626	16.60	0.381	104.7	147
19.000	Exports less imports	7.019	7.42	0.417	226.8	148
20.200	Blue-collar, unskilled	25.005	112.74	0.149	148.9	149
20.220	White-collar	17.575	108.62	0.201	80.5	151
20.300	Professional	8.002	132.96	0.274	22.0	152
21.000	Government expenditure on commodities	30.667	338.05	0.313	28.9	153

Notes:
1. Above expenditures for lines 1 to 110 include both household and government expenditures. The latter are shown separately in Table 13.15.
2. Sugar (1 180) is intentionally out of order; the purpose is to facilitate aggregation.
3. The purchasing-power parities are direct except for the following: Purchasing-power parities are indirect and the quantity ratios are direct in lines 75, 76, 77, 78, 99, and 100. Blanks in columns 5 and 6 indicate no direct price or quantity comparisons were made. Where neither comparison was made, purchasing-power parities from other selected categories were imputed to these categories for aggregation purposes.
4. Blue-collar workers (line 149) include both first- and second-level blue-collar workers. In other binary comparisons, these are found in lines 149 and 150, respectively.
5. Exchange rate: £0.417=US$1.00.

Appendix Table 13.10. Expenditures per Capita, Purchasing-Power Parities, and Quantity per Capita for Detailed Categories, Hungary–U.S., 1967

Code	Category	Per capita expenditure Hungary (forint)	U.S. (dollar)	Purchasing-power parities forint/dollar	Quantity per capita (U.S.=100)	Line number
(1)	(2)	(3)	(4)	(5)	(6)	(7)
01.101	Rice	48.9	1.26	50.8	76.6	1
01.102	Meal, other cereals	231.7	5.47	19.1	221.9	2
01.103	Bread, rolls	285.3	15.14	5.8	322.4	3
01.104	Biscuits, cakes	78.3	16.68	21.3	22.0	4
01.105	Cereal preparations	56.7	7.01			5
01.106	Macaroni, spaghetti, related foods	23.1	1.55	18.1	82.7	6
01.111	Fresh beef, veal	84.4	58.87	49.0	2.9	7
01.112	Fresh lamb, mutton	12.7	2.39	11.2	47.7	8
01.113	Fresh pork	583.4	14.30	51.7	78.9	9
01.114	Fresh poultry	315.2	16.12	41.7	46.9	10
01.115	Other fresh meat	20.0	2.53	18.1	43.7	11
01.116	Frozen, salted meat	275.4	32.94	28.8	29.0	12
01.121	Fresh, frozen fish	26.2	6.87	16.4	23.3	13
01.122	Canned fish	10.2	3.23	72.1	4.4	14
01.131	Fresh milk	269.3	30.56	13.2	66.6	15
01.132	Milk products	91.1	14.16	21.3	30.2	16
01.133	Eggs, egg products	233.6	12.05	38.1	50.9	17
01.141	Butter	83.3	4.06	36.1	56.8	18
01.142	Margarine, edible oil	27.1	8.83	30.2	10.2	19
01.143	Lard, edible fat	381.8	0.70	44.9	1214.9	20
01.151	Fresh fruits, tropical, subtropical	56.9	6.73	56.9	14.9	21
01.152	Other fresh fruits	296.2	10.23	13.5	214.0	22
01.153	Fresh vegetables	221.2	21.44	6.8	152.2	23
01.161	Fruit other than fresh	7.7	17.38	68.9	0.6	24
01.162	Vegetables other than fresh	2.7	17.52	32.4	0.5	25
01.170	Potatoes, manioc, other tubers	184.0	9.67	17.1	111.4	26
01.191	Coffee	125.3	9.81	153.2	8.3	27
01.192	Tea	10.9	1.82	59.0	10.1	28
01.193	Cocoa	11.5	0.70	50.0	32.7	29
01.180	Sugar	245.6	3.78	39.9	162.8	30
01.201	Jam, syrup, honey	70.9	4.21	20.3	82.9	31
01.202	Chocolate, ice cream	172.0	12.76	38.5	35.0	32
01.203	Salt, spices, sauces	160.4	5.89	16.0	170.0	33
01.310	Nonalcoholic beverages	22.9	11.07	26.9	7.7	34
01.321	Spirits	89.6	16.68	27.7	19.4	35
01.322	Wine, cider	281.4	3.56	15.7	503.2	36
01.323	Beer	81.1	20.39	18.8	20.7	37
01.410	Cigarettes	235.1	41.90	10.2	54.9	38
01.420	Other tobacco	6.1	4.97	21.2	5.9	39
02.110	Clothing materials	145.4	4.76	65.9	46.4	40
02.121	Men's clothing	328.8	41.31	25.6	31.0	41
02.122	Women's clothing	288.5	58.80	27.7	17.7	42
02.123	Boys', girls' clothing	165.5	19.68	23.6	35.6	43
02.131	Men's, boys' underwear	104.8	9.01	32.9	35.3	44
02.132	Women's, girls' underwear	106.8	23.63	27.8	16.3	45
02.150	Other clothing	169.9	10.70	20.4	78.0	46
02.160	Clothing rental, repair	72.1	3.29	9.1	239.9	47
02.211	Men's footwear	114.5	9.56	21.8	54.9	48
02.212	Women's footwear	176.4	12.59	22.3	62.7	49
02.213	Children's footwear	55.3	9.57	13.2	43.9	50
02.220	Footwear repairs	58.5	1.79	11.8	277.3	51
03.110	Gross rents	558.7	350.61	10.3	15.5	52
03.120	Indoor repair, upkeep	126.5	14.46	6.5	133.5	53
03.210	Electricity	123.4	37.73	35.5	9.2	54
03.220	Gas	45.8	25.67	22.0	8.1	55
03.230	Liquid fuels	15.3	22.40	56.4	1.2	56
03.240	Other fuels, ice	307.0	4.34	7.8	904.2	57
04.110	Furniture, fixtures	294.8	45.02	24.6	26.6	58
04.120	Floor coverings	35.0	15.29	26.8	8.5	59
04.200	Household textiles, etc.	166.9	31.17	29.9	17.9	60
04.310	Refrigerators, etc.	54.4	12.65	52.8	8.2	61
04.320	Washing appliances	39.2	7.09	25.9	21.4	62
04.330	Cooking appliances	61.7	7.82	16.1	49.2	63
04.340	Heating appliances	30.2	3.80	35.8	22.3	64
04.350	Cleaning appliances	12.7	2.09	29.1	21.0	65
04.360	Other household appliances	6.0	3.00	24.6	8.1	66
04.400	Household utensils	154.3	16.09	22.7	42.1	67
04.510	Nondurable household goods	192.6	23.81	41.5	19.5	68
04.520	Domestic services	27.4	22.53	7.8	15.6	69
04.530	Household services	31.9	20.35	15.5	10.1	70
04.600	Household furnishing repairs	96.4	6.61	8.8	165.3	71
05.110	Drugs, medical preparations	261.5	30.32	10.9	79.5	72
05.120	Medical supplies	42.1	4.13	24.1	42.3	73
05.200	Therapeutic equipment		8.10			74

Appendix Table 13.10. Continued

Code (1)	Category (2)	Per capita expenditure Hungary (forint) (3)	U.S. (dollar) (4)	Purchasing-power parities forint/dollar (5)	Quantity per capita (U.S.=100) (6)	Line number (7)
05.310	Physicians' services	97.1	38.71		111.5	75
05.320	Dentists' services	7.7	11.69		41.3	76
05.330	Services, nurses, other personnel	102.0	56.23		72.6	77
05.410	Hospitals, etc.	336.3	80.38		96.0	78
06.110	Personal cars	134.1	125.38	56.8	1.9	79
06.120	Other personal transport	61.2	10.71	21.3	26.8	80
06.210	Tires, tubes, accessories	39.2	19.37	33.4	6.1	81
06.220	Repair charges	36.0	29.57	12.9	9.4	82
06.230	Gasoline, oil, etc.	55.7	88.67	36.1	1.7	83
06.240	Parking, tolls, etc.	9.8	21.13	3.1	14.7	84
06.310	Local transport	137.0	11.15	9.4	130.0	85
06.321	Rail transport	146.8	1.04	15.0	942.2	86
06.322	Bus transport	137.0	1.80	22.5	338.0	87
06.323	Air transport	14.7	8.14			88
06.330	Miscellaneous transport	26.5	2.99	23.5	37.7	89
06.410	Postal communication	29.9	5.85	11.0	46.6	90
06.420	Telephone, telegraph	34.3	37.91	4.5	20.0	91
07.110	Radio, TV, phonograph, etc.	169.6	36.42	53.5	8.7	92
07.120	Major durable recreation equipment	8.2	19.68	18.7	2.2	93
07.130	Other recreation equipment	75.2	29.65	24.3	10.4	94
07.210	Public entertainment	171.9	23.84	3.2	222.1	95
07.230	Other recreation, cultural events	221.1	46.49	4.8	98.4	96
07.310	Books, papers, magazines	148.4	29.67	14.7	33.9	97
07.320	Stationery	60.3	8.18	52.4	14.1	98
07.411	Teachers, 1st, 2nd	407.1	133.01		97.8	99
07.412	Teachers, college	42.9	21.84		37.3	100
07.420	Educational facilities	191.2	22.12			101
07.431	Educational supplies	19.5	5.71			102
07.432	Other education expenditures	106.3	6.39			103
08.100	Barber, beauty shops	82.2	18.63	3.4	130.4	104
08.210	Toilet articles	97.0	24.44	20.1	19.8	105
08.220	Other personal-care goods	145.6	26.78	36.9	14.7	106
08.310	Restaurants, cafes	1624.4	116.93	19.2	72.4	107
08.320	Hotels, etc.	33.0	7.60	14.6	29.7	108
08.400	Other services	330.6	97.75			109
08.900	Expenditures of residents abroad		19.45			110
10.100	1- and 2-dwelling buildings	508.5	96.22	16.2	32.6	111
10.200	Multidwelling buildings	428.3	26.08	14.0	117.3	112
11.100	Hotels, etc.	82.9	6.17	16.4	82.1	113
11.200	Industrial buildings	676.7	35.22	22.4	85.9	114
11.300	Commercial buildings	82.7	18.74	18.9	23.3	115
11.400	Office buildings	84.6	23.03	12.6	29.2	116
11.500	Educational buildings	97.5	35.94	15.3	17.8	117
11.600	Hospital buildings	30.5	10.09	12.3	24.7	118
11.700	Agricultural buildings	250.1	3.18	20.8	378.0	119
11.800	Other buildings	36.8	17.47	17.4	12.1	120
12.100	Roads, highways	192.6	44.65	20.2	21.4	121
12.200	Transmission, utility lines	743.5	52.01	15.0	95.6	122
12.300	Other construction	277.6	10.67	12.7	204.8	123
13.000	Land improvement	194.8	11.70	9.7	170.8	124
14.110	Locomotives	82.3	1.31	65.5	96.0	125
14.120	Other	143.4	7.08	44.5	45.5	126
14.200	Passenger cars	29.6	30.68	68.0	1.4	127
14.300	Trucks, buses, trailers	214.4	29.14	27.8	26.5	128
14.400	Aircraft	12.3	16.72			129
14.500	Ships, boats	29.3	3.68			130
14.600	Other transport	144.6	1.72	42.4	198.6	131
15.100	Engines and turbines	70.8	5.04	53.6	26.2	132
15.210	Tractors	57.7	9.45	37.5	16.3	133
15.220	Other agricultural machinery	122.6	12.00	29.4	34.8	134
15.300	Office machinery	71.5	27.54	43.5	6.0	135
15.400	Metalworking machinery	225.3	18.98	28.4	41.9	136
15.500	Construction, mining	122.6	12.93	31.1	30.5	137
15.600	Special industrial	596.6	15.64	33.7	113.2	138
15.700	General industrial	147.5	16.17	33.7	27.0	139
15.800	Service industrial	39.2	14.57	32.2	8.3	140
16.100	Electrical transmission	116.3	12.37	20.0	46.9	141
16.200	Communication equipment	78.9	19.64	22.3	18.1	142
16.300	Other electrical	13.9	3.71	24.1	15.6	143
16.400	Instruments	130.0	15.66	24.8	33.5	144
17.100	Furniture, fixtures	204.0	16.93	28.6	42.1	145
17.200	Other durable goods	35.5	15.55	56.1	4.1	146
18.000	Increase in stocks	1373.4	34.50	24.6	161.8	147
19.000	Exports less imports	-473.7	3.54	30.0	-446.3	148

Appendix Table 13.10. Continued

Code (1)	Category (2)	Per capita expenditure Hungary (forint) (3)	U.S. (dollar) (4)	Purchasing-power parities forint/dollar (5)	Quantity per capita (U.S.=100) (6)	Line number (7)
20.100	Blue-collar, unskilled	165.2	13.82	5.6	215.3	149
20.210	Blue-collar, skilled	9.5	72.12	5.9	2.2	150
20.220	White-collar	153.7	82.97	6.4	29.0	151
20.300	Professional	139.1	102.98	7.0	19.3	152
21.000	Government expenditure on commodities	1162.4	329.70	23.6	14.9	153

Notes:

1. In other comparisons, lines 41–43 include leather clothing. In the Hungary–U.S. comparison, leather clothing has been treated as a separate category. The figures for columns 3 to 6 inclusive are:

2 140 Leather clothing 26.8 5.93 13.9 32.5

2. For purposes of the Hungary–U.S. comparison, special-industry machinery has been split into two categories, one for chemical-industry machinery and the other for all other. The purchasing-power parity shown above is the ideal index of the two. The purchasing-power parities for chemical machinery and for all other were 50.03 and 30.03, respectively. In the United States, 4.6 percent of special-industry machinery expenditures were for chemical machinery; in Hungary, 35.0 percent.

3. Above expenditures for lines 1 to 110 include both household and government expenditures. The latter are shown separately in Table 13.15.

4. Sugar (1 180) is intentionally out of order; the purpose is to facilitate aggregation.

5. The purchasing-power parities are direct except for the following: Purchasing-power parities are indirect and the quantity ratios are direct in lines 75,76,77,78,99, and 100. Blanks in columns 5 and 6 indicate no direct price or quantity comparisons were made. Where neither comparison was made, purchasing-power parities from other selected categories were imputed to these categories for aggregation purposes.

6. Exchange rate: Ft30=US$1.00.

Appendix Table 13.11. Expenditures per Capita, Purchasing-Power Parities, and Quantity per Capita for Detailed Categories, India–U.S., 1967

Code (1)	Category (2)	Per capita expenditure India (rupee) (3)	U.S. (dollar) (4)	Purchasing-power parities rupee/dollar (5)	Quantity per capita (U.S.=100) (6)	Line number (7)
01.101	Rice	111.45	1.26	4.79	1850.8	1
01.102	Meal, other cereals	76.18	5.47	2.94	474.1	2
01.103	Bread, rolls	0.30	15.14	3.46	0.6	3
01.104	Biscuits, cakes	0.35	16.68	8.99	0.2	4
01.105	Cereal preparations	0.29	7.01	3.36	1.2	5
01.106	Macaroni, spaghetti, related foods	0.29	1.55	11.76	1.6	6
01.111	Fresh beef, veal	0.54	58.87	3.94	0.2	7
01.112	Fresh lamb, mutton	0.98	2.39	4.81	8.5	8
01.113	Fresh pork	0.19	14.30	1.85	0.7	9
01.114	Fresh poultry	1.67	16.12	7.32	1.4	10
01.115	Other fresh meat	2.84	2.53			11
01.116	Frozen, salted meat		32.94			12
01.121	Fresh, frozen fish	4.91	6.87	1.47	48.6	13
01.122	Canned fish		3.23			14
01.131	Fresh milk	18.25	30.56	2.88	20.8	15
01.132	Milk products	2.82	14.16	4.68	4.3	16
01.133	Eggs, egg products	0.79	12.05	5.22	1.2	17
01.141	Butter	14.79	4.06	3.63	100.3	18
01.142	Margarine, edible oil	14.56	8.83	5.75	28.7	19
01.143	Lard, edible fat		0.70			20
01.151	Fresh fruits, tropical, subtropical	4.21	6.73	2.62	23.9	21
01.152	Other fresh fruits	0.64	10.23	2.97	2.1	22
01.153	Fresh vegetables	10.67	21.44	1.44	34.6	23
01.161	Fruit other than fresh	0.30	17.38	5.20	0.3	24
01.162	Vegetables other than fresh	19.39	17.52	6.65	16.7	25
01.170	Potatoes, manioc, other tubers	5.23	9.67	3.96	13.6	26
01.191	Coffee	0.80	9.81	11.34	0.7	27
01.192	Tea	4.00	1.82	2.56	85.8	28
01.193	Cocoa		0.70			29
01.180	Sugar	16.93	3.78	7.82	57.2	30
01.201	Jam, syrup, honey	0.33	4.21	7.37	1.1	31
01.202	Chocolate, ice cream	1.60	12.76	7.72	1.6	32
01.203	Salt, spices, sauces	12.01	5.89	1.38	148.2	33
01.310	Nonalcoholic beverages	0.16	11.07	5.26	0.3	34
01.321	Spirits	0.11	16.68	8.80	0.1	35
01.322	Wine, cider	1.08	3.56	17.64	1.7	36
01.323	Beer	0.30	20.89	8.51	0.2	37
01.410	Cigarettes	0.86	41.90	8.53	0.2	38
01.420	Other tobacco	10.88	4.87	2.52	88.9	39
02.110	Clothing materials	8.92	4.76	7.41	25.3	40

Appendix Table 13.11. Continued

Code (1)	Category (2)	Per capita expenditure India (rupee) (3)	U.S. (dollar) (4)	Purchasing-power parities rupee/dollar (5)	Quantity per capita (U.S.=100) (6)	Line number (7)
02.121	Men's clothing	4.89	41.85	3.29	3.6	41
02.122	Women's clothing	6.87	64.13	4.09	2.6	42
02.123	Boys', girls' clothing	0.72	19.74	2.44	1.5	43
02.131	Men's, boys' underwear	0.07	9.01	2.04	0.4	44
02.132	Women's, girls' underwear	0.06	23.63	5.97	0.0	45
02.150	Other clothing	0.03	10.70	8.01	0.0	46
02.160	Clothing rental, repair	0.60	3.29	1.37	13.4	47
02.211	Men's footwear	1.03	9.56	4.13	2.6	48
02.212	Women's footwear	1.03	12.59	4.28	1.9	49
02.213	Children's footwear	0.52	9.57	2.62	2.1	50
02.220	Footwear repairs	0.15	1.79	3.48	2.3	51
03.110	Gross rents	18.72	350.61	1.75	3.1	52
03.120	Indoor repair, upkeep	1.84	14.46	0.86	14.8	53
03.210	Electricity	0.85	37.73	6.95	0.3	54
03.220	Gas	0.03	25.67	4.27	0.0	55
03.230	Liquid fuels	4.61	22.40	12.65	1.6	56
03.240	Other fuels, ice	19.35	4.34	4.25	10.4	57
04.110	Furniture, fixtures	0.28	45.02	4.34	0.1	58
04.120	Floor coverings	1.83	15.29			59
04.200	Household textiles, etc.	3.52	31.17	2.07	5.4	60
04.310	Refrigerators, etc.	0.55	12.65	10.98	0.4	61
04.320	Washing appliances		7.09			62
04.330	Cooking appliances	0.01	7.82	5.64	0.0	63
04.340	Heating appliances	0.01	3.80	4.86	0.1	64
04.350	Cleaning appliances		2.09			65
04.360	Other household appliances	0.10	3.00	4.71	0.7	66
04.400	Household utensils	2.92	16.09	4.24	4.3	67
04.510	Nondurable household goods	3.41	23.81	5.70	2.5	68
04.520	Domestic services	2.00	22.53	0.31	29.0	69
04.530	Household services	2.77	20.35	1.15	11.8	70
04.600	Household furnishing repairs	1.02	6.61			71
05.110	Drugs, medical preparations	7.77	30.32	2.53	10.1	72
05.120	Medical supplies	0.73	4.13	2.71	6.5	73
05.200	Therapeutic equipment	0.21	8.10	1.53	1.7	74
05.310	Physicians' services	0.93	38.71		11.7	75
05.320	Dentists' services	0.00	11.69		1.8	76
05.330	Services, nurses, other personnel	1.38	56.23		5.0	77
05.410	Hospitals, etc.	1.46	80.38		7.0	78
06.110	Personal cars	0.94	125.38	9.09	0.1	79
06.120	Other personal transport	0.94	10.71	6.59	1.3	80
06.210	Tires, tubes, accessories	0.47	19.37	7.76	0.3	81
06.220	Repair charges	0.56	29.57	1.25	1.5	82
06.230	Gasoline, oil, etc.	0.98	88.67	7.83	0.1	83
06.240	Parking, tolls, etc.	0.50	21.13			84
06.310	Local transport	2.25	11.15	1.39	14.5	85
06.321	Rail transport	3.63	1.04	2.46	142.2	86
06.322	Bus transport	9.41	1.80	2.80	186.5	87
06.323	Air transport	0.06	8.14	7.65	0.1	88
06.330	Miscellaneous transport	2.69	2.99			89
06.410	Postal communication	0.64	5.85	3.00	3.7	90
06.420	Telephone, telegraph	0.73	37.91	1.11	1.7	91
07.110	Radio, TV, phonograph, etc.	0.85	36.42	7.42	0.3	92
07.120	Major durable recreation equipment	0.07	19.68			93
07.130	Other recreation equipment	0.12	29.65	5.66	0.1	94
07.210	Public entertainment	0.26	23.84	2.40	0.5	95
07.230	Other recreation, cultural events	1.50	46.49	1.32	2.4	96
07.310	Books, papers, magazines	1.81	29.67	2.97	2.1	97
07.320	Stationery	0.52	8.18	1.80	3.5	98
07.411	Teachers, 1st, 2nd	9.26	133.01		31.9	99
07.412	Teachers, college	1.26	21.84		9.9	100
07.420	Educational facilities	0.60	22.12			101
07.431	Educational supplies	0.54	5.71			102
07.432	Other education expenditures	0.68	6.39			103
08.100	Barber, beauty shops	1.02	18.63	1.36	4.0	104
08.210	Toilet articles	2.78	24.44	5.26	2.2	105
08.220	Other personal-care goods	2.79	26.78	4.33	2.4	106
08.310	Restaurants, cafes	4.83	116.93	4.35	0.9	107
08.320	Hotels, etc.	4.83	7.60	4.28	14.8	108
08.400	Other services	3.16	97.75			109
08.900	Expenditures of residents abroad		19.45			110
10.100	1- and 2-dwelling buildings	12.86	96.22	1.68	8.0	111
10.200	Multidwelling buildings	12.86	26.08	1.84	26.7	112
11.100	Hotels, etc.	0.42	6.17	1.81	3.8	113
11.200	Industrial buildings	1.11	35.22	2.82	1.1	114
11.300	Commercial buildings	2.96	18.74			115
11.400	Office buildings	1.21	23.03	1.71	3.1	116
11.500	Educational buildings	0.67	35.94	1.90	1.0	117

Appendix Table 13.11. Continued

Code (1)	Category (2)	Per capita expenditure India (rupee) (3)	U.S. (dollar) (4)	Purchasing-power parities rupee/dollar (5)	Quantity per capita (U.S.=100) (6)	Line number (7)
11.600	Hospital buildings	0.40	10.09	1.49	2.7	118
11.700	Agricultural buildings	4.43	3.18			119
11.800	Other buildings	1.02	17.47			120
12.100	Roads, highways	2.87	44.65	1.75	3.7	121
12.200	Transmission, utility lines	8.80	52.01	1.35	12.6	122
12.300	Other construction	4.79	10.67			123
13.000	Land improvement	7.86	11.70	1.37	49.0	124
14.110	Locomotives	0.64	1.31	9.15	5.4	125
14.120	Other	1.27	7.08	7.26	2.5	126
14.200	Passenger cars	0.41	30.68	8.91	0.1	127
14.300	Trucks, buses, trailers	5.84	29.14	9.03	2.2	128
14.400	Aircraft	0.35	16.72			129
14.500	Ships, boats	0.54	3.68			130
14.600	Other transport	0.91	1.72			131
15.100	Engines and turbines	0.96	5.04	11.44	1.7	132
15.210	Tractors	0.33	9.45	5.94	0.6	133
15.220	Other agricultural machinery	0.27	12.00	6.30	0.4	134
15.300	Office machinery	0.23	27.54			135
15.400	Metalworking machinery	1.93	18.98	5.64	1.8	136
15.500	Construction, mining	0.39	12.93	12.20	0.2	137
15.600	Special industrial	3.45	15.64	5.17	4.3	138
15.700	General industrial	3.93	16.17	7.76	3.1	139
15.800	Service industrial	0.53	14.57	8.07	0.5	140
16.100	Electrical transmission	3.07	12.37	8.96	2.8	141
16.200	Communication equipment	2.12	19.64			142
16.300	Other electrical	0.74	3.71			143
16.400	Instruments	0.79	15.66	3.51	1.4	144
17.100	Furniture, fixtures	0.16	16.93	3.97	0.2	145
17.200	Other durable goods	5.49	15.55			146
18.000	Increase in stocks	8.93	34.50	4.63	5.6	147
19.000	Exports less imports	-13.91	3.54	7.50	-52.4	148
20.100	Blue-collar, unskilled	9.26	13.82	0.36	184.0	149
20.210	Blue-collar, skilled	0.84	72.12	0.43	2.7	150
20.220	White-collar	9.71	82.97	0.61	19.2	151
20.300	Professional	7.54	102.98	1.32	5.5	152
21.000	Government expenditure on commodities	19.21	329.70	2.83	2.1	153

Notes:

1. Above expenditures for lines 1 to 110 include both household and government expenditures. The latter are shown separately in Table 13.15.

2. Sugar (1 180) is intentionally out of order; the purpose is to facilitate aggregation.

3. The purchasing-power parities are direct except for the following: Purchasing-power parities are indirect and the quantity ratios are direct in lines 75,76,77,78,99, and 100. Blanks in columns 5 and 6 indicate no direct price or quantity comparisons were made. Where neither comparison was made, purchasing-power parities from other selected categories were imputed to these categories for aggregation purposes.

4. Exchange rate: Rs7.5=US$1.00.

Appendix Table 13.12. Expenditures per Capita, Purchasing-Power Parities, and Quantity per Capita for Detailed Categories, Japan–U.S., 1967

Code (1)	Category (2)	Per capita expenditure Japan (yen) (3)	U.S. (dollar) (4)	Purchasing-power parities yen/dollar (5)	Quantity per capita (U.S.=100) (6)	Line number (7)
01.101	Rice	16702.	1.26	377.	3521.2	1
01.102	Meal, other cereals	360.	5.47	335.	19.6	2
01.103	Bread, rolls	1244.	15.14	169.	48.7	3
01.104	Biscuits, cakes	4671.	16.68	267.	105.0	4
01.105	Cereal preparations	102.	7.01	484.	3.0	5
01.106	Macaroni, spaghetti, related foods	1428.	1.55	320.	289.2	6
01.111	Fresh beef, veal	1599.	58.87	594.	4.6	7
01.112	Fresh lamb, mutton	25.	2.39			8
01.113	Fresh pork	2289.	14.30	402.	39.9	9
01.114	Fresh poultry	1077.	16.12	460.	14.5	10
01.115	Other fresh meat	447.	2.53			11
01.116	Frozen, salted meat	1519.	32.94	488.	9.5	12
01.121	Fresh, frozen fish	5837.	6.87	208.	407.7	13
01.122	Canned fish	4315.	3.23	423.	316.2	14
01.131	Fresh milk	2777.	30.56	384.	23.6	15
01.132	Milk products	587.	14.16	456.	9.1	16
01.133	Eggs, egg products	2882.	12.05	281.	85.2	17

Appendix Table 13.12. Continued

Code (1)	Category (2)	Per capita expenditure Japan (yen) (3)	U.S. (dollar) (4)	Purchasing-power parities yen/dollar (5)	Quantity per capita (U.S.=100) (6)	Line number (7)
01.141	Butter	169.	4.06	432.	9.6	18
01.142	Margarine, edible oil	784.	8.83	407.	21.8	19
01.143	Lard, edible fat	8.	0.70	613.	1.9	20
01.151	Fresh fruits, tropical, subtropical	2228.	6.73	511.	64.7	21
01.152	Other fresh fruits	2504.	10.23	309.	79.1	22
01.153	Fresh vegetables	5631.	21.44	196.	133.7	23
01.161	Fruit other than fresh	617.	17.38	431.	8.2	24
01.162	Vegetables other than fresh	2609.	17.52	464.	32.1	25
01.170	Potatoes, manioc, other tubers	719.	9.67	390.	19.0	26
01.191	Coffee	248.	9.81	715.	3.5	27
01.192	Tea	730.	1.82	195.	205.1	28
01.193	Cocoa	135.	0.70			29
01.180	Sugar	874.	3.78	500.	46.2	30
01.201	Jam, syrup, honey	795.	4.21	406.	46.5	31
01.202	Chocolate, ice cream	1095.	12.76	641.	13.4	32
01.203	Salt, spices, sauces	3914.	5.89	204.	325.7	33
01.310	Nonalcoholic beverages	896.	11.07	402.	20.2	34
01.321	Spirits	6874.	16.68	254.	161.9	35
01.322	Wine, cider	407.	3.56	292.	39.1	36
01.323	Beer	3023.	20.89	329.	44.0	37
01.410	Cigarettes	3855.	41.90	209.	44.0	38
01.420	Other tobacco	14.	4.87			39
02.110	Clothing materials	8375.	4.76	395.	444.8	40
02.121	Men's clothing	2743.	41.85	231.	28.4	41
02.122	Women's clothing	1600.	64.13	234.	10.7	42
02.123	Boys', girls' clothing	721.	19.74	292.	12.5	43
02.131	Men's, boys' underwear	3121.	9.01	236.	146.7	44
02.132	Women's, girls' underwear	2259.	23.63	230.	41.6	45
02.150	Other clothing	2434.	10.70	229.	99.3	46
02.160	Clothing rental, repair	3208.	3.29			47
02.211	Men's footwear	517.	9.56	182.	29.7	48
02.212	Women's footwear	513.	12.59	213.	19.1	49
02.213	Children's footwear	171.	9.57	155.	11.5	50
02.220	Footwear repairs	316.	1.79	101.	174.9	51
03.110	Gross rents	23043.	350.61	231.	28.5	52
03.120	Indoor repair, upkeep	3747.	14.46	187.	138.4	53
03.210	Electricity	3544.	37.73	334.	28.1	54
03.220	Gas	2187.	25.67	1483.	5.7	55
03.230	Liquid fuels	702.	22.40	470.	6.7	56
03.240	Other fuels, ice	1835.	4.34	200.	211.5	57
04.110	Furniture, fixtures	2964.	45.02	361.	18.2	58
04.120	Floor coverings	247.	15.29	274.	5.9	59
04.200	Household textiles, etc.	301.	31.17	402.	2.4	60
04.310	Refrigerators, etc.	1649.	12.65	656.	19.9	61
04.320	Washing appliances	747.	7.09	270.	39.0	62
04.330	Cooking appliances	795.	7.82	233.	43.6	63
04.340	Heating appliances	1013.	3.80	436.	61.2	64
04.350	Cleaning appliances	192.	2.09	369.	24.9	65
04.360	Other household appliances	1024.	3.00	327.	104.4	66
04.400	Household utensils	2458.	16.09	191.	80.0	67
04.510	Nondurable household goods	5354.	23.81	354.	63.5	68
04.520	Domestic services	333.	22.53	123.	12.0	69
04.530	Household services	188.	20.35	202.	4.6	70
04.600	Household furnishing repairs	1629.	6.61			71
05.110	Drugs, medical preparations	9340.	30.32	135.	228.2	72
05.120	Medical supplies	953.	4.13	179.	128.9	73
05.200	Therapeutic equipment	256.	8.10	70.	45.2	74
05.310	Physicians' services	1521.	38.71		66.0	75
05.320	Dentists' services	343.	11.69		66.3	76
05.330	Services, nurses, other personnel	1348.	56.23		54.0	77
05.410	Hospitals, etc.	2956.	80.38		130.8	78
06.110	Personal cars	1396.	125.38	409.	2.7	79
06.120	Other personal transport	596.	10.71	430.	12.9	80
06.210	Tires, tubes, accessories	35.	19.37	287.	0.6	81
06.220	Repair charges	178.	29.57	342.	1.8	82
06.230	Gasoline, oil, etc.	560.	88.67	617.	1.0	83
06.240	Parking, tolls, etc.	253.	21.13	418.	2.9	84
06.310	Local transport	2906.	11.15	65.	402.0	85
06.321	Rail transport	855.	1.04	136.	607.9	86
06.322	Bus transport	279.	1.80	216.	71.7	87
06.323	Air transport	79.	8.14	306.	3.2	88
06.330	Miscellaneous transport	134.	2.99			89
06.410	Postal communication	297.	5.85	330.	15.4	90
06.420	Telephone, telegraph	1230.	37.91	262.	12.4	91
07.110	Radio, TV, phonograph, etc.	3315.	36.42	222.	41.0	92
07.120	Major durable recreation equipment	1635.	19.68	182.	45.6	93
07.130	Other recreation equipment	1408.	29.65	270.	17.6	94

Appendix Table 13.12. Continued

Code (1)	Category (2)	Per capita expenditure Japan (yen) (3)	U.S. (dollar) (4)	Purchasing-power parities yen/dollar (5)	Quantity per capita (U.S.=100) (6)	Line number (7)
07.210	Public entertainment	453.	23.84	407.	4.7	95
07.230	Other recreation, cultural events	7529.	46.49	174.	93.1	96
07.310	Books, papers, magazines	4320.	29.67	343.	42.4	97
07.320	Stationery	815.	8.18	230.	43.2	98
07.411	Teachers, 1st, 2nd	2919.	133.01		73.6	99
07.412	Teachers, college	346.	21.84		37.9	100
07.420	Educational facilities	1276.	22.12			101
07.431	Educational supplies	375.	5.71			102
07.432	Other education expenditures	1393.	6.39			103
08.100	Barber, beauty shops	3984.	18.63	115.	185.3	104
08.210	Toilet articles	4414.	24.44	302.	59.7	105
08.220	Other personal-care goods	1042.	26.78	192.	20.3	106
08.310	Restaurants, cafes	7526.	116.93	102.	63.4	107
08.320	Hotels, etc.	2921.	7.60	305.	125.9	108
08.400	Other services	5313.	97.75		44.4	109
08.900	Expenditures of residents abroad	673.	19.45	306.	9.6	110
10.100	1- and 2-dwelling buildings	22005.	96.22	260.	88.0	111
10.200	Multidwelling buildings	6164.	26.08	227.	104.2	112
11.100	Hotels, etc.	918.	6.17	277.	53.7	113
11.200	Industrial buildings	6686.	35.22	550.	34.5	114
11.300	Commercial buildings	3967.	18.74	456.	46.4	115
11.400	Office buildings	4360.	23.03	287.	66.0	116
11.500	Educational buildings	2858.	35.94	210.	37.9	117
11.600	Hospital buildings	1053.	10.09	182.	57.3	118
11.700	Agricultural buildings	574.	3.18	612.	29.5	119
11.800	Other buildings	2949.	17.47	401.	42.1	120
12.100	Roads, highways	7393.	44.65	297.	55.8	121
12.200	Transmission, utility lines	12633.	52.01	171.	141.8	122
12.300	Other construction	5650.	10.67	196.	270.3	123
13.000	Land improvement	3847.	11.70	165.	199.9	124
14.110	Locomotives	121.	1.31			125
14.120	Other	749.	7.08			126
14.200	Passenger cars	4611.	30.68	423.	35.5	127
14.300	Trucks, buses, trailers	10755.	29.14			128
14.400	Aircraft	158.	16.72			129
14.500	Ships, boats	2599.	3.68			130
14.600	Other transport	670.	1.72			131
15.100	Engines and turbines	1198.	5.04			132
15.210	Tractors	518.	9.45			133
15.220	Other agricultural machinery	982.	12.00			134
15.300	Office machinery	1815.	27.54			135
15.400	Metalworking machinery	3649.	18.98	410.	46.9	136
15.500	Construction, mining	3611.	12.93	338.	82.6	137
15.600	Special industrial	8804.	15.64	252.	223.0	138
15.700	General industrial	3810.	16.17	242.	97.4	139
15.800	Service industrial	2074.	14.57			140
16.100	Electrical transmission	4306.	12.37			141
16.200	Communication equipment	4067.	19.64	221.	93.8	142
16.300	Other electrical	269.	3.71			143
16.400	Instruments	722.	15.66			144
17.100	Furniture, fixtures	1533.	16.93	322.	28.1	145
17.200	Other durable goods	1234.	15.55			146
18.000	Increase in stocks	22907.	34.50	313.	212.1	147
19.000	Exports less imports	1018.	3.54	360.	79.9	148
20.100	Blue-collar, unskilled	5164.	13.82	144.	259.2	149
20.210	Blue-collar, skilled	10217.	72.12	120.	118.4	150
20.220	White-collar	2519.	82.97	130.	23.4	151
20.300	Professional	3376.	102.98	204.	16.1	152
21.000	Government expenditure on commodities	8584.	329.70	231.	11.3	153

Notes:

1. Above expenditures for lines 1 to 110 include both household and government expenditures. The latter are shown separately in Table 13.15.

2. Sugar (1 180) is intentionally out of order; the purpose is to facilitate aggregation.

3. The purchasing-power parities are direct except for the following: Purchasing-power parities are indirect and the quantity ratios are direct in lines 75,76,77,78,99, and 100. Blanks in columns 5 and 6 indicate no direct price or quantity comparisons were made. Where neither comparison was made, purchasing-power parities from other selected categories were imputed to these categories for aggregation purposes.

4. Exchange rate: ¥360=US$1.00.

Appendix Table 13.13. Expenditures per Capita, Purchasing-Power Parities, and Quantity per Capita for Detailed Categories, Kenya–U.S., 1967

Code (1)	Category (2)	Per capita expenditure Kenya (shilling) (3)	U.S. (dollar) (4)	Purchasing-power parities shilling/dollar (5)	Quantity per capita (U.S.=100) (6)	Line number (7)
01.101	Rice	1.25	1.26	4.45	22.3	1
01.102	Meal, other cereals	90.96	5.47	6.00	277.3	2
01.103	Bread, rolls	4.75	15.14	3.07	10.2	3
01.104	Biscuits, cakes	1.89	16.68	1.07	10.6	4
01.105	Cereal preparations	0.77	7.01	9.99	1.1	5
01.106	Macroni, spaghetti, related foods	0.15	1.55	12.35	0.8	6
01.111	Fresh beef, veal	28.17	58.87	3.53	13.6	7
01.112	Fresh lamb, mutton	3.31	2.39	3.10	44.7	8
01.113	Fresh pork	0.66	14.30	7.55	0.6	9
01.114	Fresh poultry	1.39	16.12	5.27	1.6	10
01.115	Other fresh meat	2.73	2.53			11
01.116	Frozen, salted meat	2.26	32.94	5.68	1.2	12
01.121	Fresh, frozen fish	7.45	6.87	4.81	22.5	13
01.122	Canned fish	1.12	3.23	12.88	2.7	14
01.131	Fresh milk	34.72	30.56	4.40	25.8	15
01.132	Milk products	3.92	14.16	6.19	4.5	16
01.133	Eggs, egg products	0.53	12.05	6.51	0.7	17
01.141	Butter	5.05	4.06	4.49	27.7	18
01.142	Margarine, edible oil	4.34	8.83	8.83	5.6	19
01.143	Lard, edible fat	1.05	0.70	14.68	10.2	20
01.151	Fresh fruits, tropical, subtropical	12.41	6.73	2.54	72.6	21
01.152	Other fresh fruits	0.29	10.23	15.65	0.2	22
01.153	Fresh vegetables	18.38	21.44	2.20	38.8	23
01.161	Fruit other than fresh	0.08	17.38	4.89	0.1	24
01.162	Vegetables other than fresh	2.96	17.52	6.21	2.7	25
01.170	Potatoes, manioc, other tubers	24.32	9.67	2.29	109.6	26
01.191	Coffee	1.27	9.81	7.65	1.7	27
01.192	Tea	4.50	1.82	2.86	86.4	28
01.193	Cocoa	0.34	0.70	8.11	5.9	29
01.180	Sugar	6.91	3.78	5.79	31.6	30
01.201	Jam, syrup, honey	3.46	4.21	4.01	20.5	31
01.202	Chocolate, ice cream	2.52	12.76	34.44	0.6	32
01.203	Salt, spices, sauces	5.16	5.89	3.81	23.0	33
01.310	Nonalcoholic beverages	4.39	11.07	16.88	2.4	34
01.321	Spirits	2.07	16.68	7.17	1.7	35
01.322	Wine, cider	0.22	3.56	8.77	0.7	36
01.323	Beer	13.85	20.89	8.42	7.9	37
01.410	Cigarettes	13.35	41.90	5.13	6.2	38
01.420	Other tobacco	0.23	4.87	4.52	1.1	39
02.110	Clothing materials	2.59	4.76	8.91	6.1	40
02.121	Men's clothing	5.93	41.85	4.95	2.9	41
02.122	Women's clothing	3.49	64.13	12.87	0.4	42
02.123	Boys', girls' clothing	1.84	19.74	2.94	3.2	43
02.131	Men's, boys' underwear	0.52	9.01	8.76	0.7	44
02.132	Women's, girls' underwear	0.44	23.63	4.21	0.4	45
02.150	Other clothing	0.64	10.70	5.01	1.2	46
02.160	Clothing rental, repair	0.43	3.29	4.19	3.1	47
02.211	Men's footwear	2.74	9.56	2.89	9.9	48
02.212	Women's footwear	0.68	12.59	2.00	2.7	49
02.213	Children's footwear	0.53	9.57	1.72	3.2	50
02.220	Footwear repairs	0.22	1.79	3.67	3.4	51
03.110	Gross rents	55.43	350.61	6.61	2.4	52
03.120	Indoor repair, upkeep	0.18	14.46	3.35	0.4	53
03.210	Electricity	1.33	37.73	8.39	0.4	54
03.220	Gas	0.10	25.67	9.00	0.0	55
03.230	Liquid fuels	1.29	22.40	16.74	0.3	56
03.240	Other fuels, ice	6.58	4.34	2.58	58.8	57
04.110	Furniture, fixtures	3.91	45.02	2.87	3.0	58
04.120	Floor coverings	0.64	15.29	9.07	0.5	59
04.200	Household textiles, etc.	2.00	31.17	7.65	0.8	60
04.310	Refrigerators, etc.	0.49	12.65	9.45	0.4	61
04.320	Washing appliances	0.07	7.09			62
04.330	Cooking appliances	0.52	7.82	9.43	0.7	63
04.340	Heating appliances	0.47	3.80			64
04.350	Cleaning appliances	0.08	2.09			65
04.360	Other household appliances	0.20	3.00	17.15	0.4	66
04.400	Household utensils	5.68	16.09	3.50	10.1	67
04.510	Nondurable household goods	13.54	23.81	8.83	6.4	68
04.520	Domestic services	7.43	22.53	0.83	39.8	69
04.530	Household services	1.33	20.35	4.59	1.4	70
04.600	Household furnishing repairs	0.06	6.61	0.87	1.1	71
05.110	Drugs, medical preparations	5.19	30.32	3.20	5.3	72
05.120	Medical supplies	0.41	4.13	4.06	2.4	73
05.200	Therapeutic equipment	0.07	8.10	1.55	0.5	74

Appendix Table 13.13. Continued

Code (1)	Category (2)	Per capita expenditure Kenya (shilling) (3)	U.S. (dollar) (4)	Purchasing-power parities shilling/dollar (5)	Quantity per capita (U.S.=100) (6)	Line number (7)
05.310	Physicians' services	4.18	38.71		7.1	75
05.320	Dentists' services	0.29	11.69		1.0	76
05.330	Services, nurses, other personnel	3.73	56.23		16.0	77
05.410	Hospitals, etc.	11.75	80.38		15.1	78
06.110	Personal cars	10.22	125.38	9.35	0.9	79
06.120	Other personal transport	0.16	10.71	9.31	0.2	80
06.210	Tires, tubes, accessories	1.22	19.37	11.57	0.5	81
06.220	Repair charges	2.09	29.57	2.14	3.3	82
06.230	Gasoline, oil, etc.	11.93	88.67	8.48	1.6	83
06.240	Parking, tolls, etc.	0.89	21.13			84
06.310	Local transport	2.11	11.15	2.47	7.7	85
06.321	Rail transport	1.32	1.04	3.38	37.6	86
06.322	Bus transport	12.48	1.80	4.00	173.2	87
06.323	Air transport	14.20	8.14	14.55	12.0	88
06.330	Miscellaneous transport	0.21	2.99			89
06.410	Postal communication	0.33	5.85	6.00	0.9	90
06.420	Telephone, telegraph	0.82	37.91	2.92	0.7	91
07.110	Radio, TV, phonograph, etc.	2.25	36.42	11.00	0.6	92
07.120	Major durable recreation equipment	2.54	19.68	8.97	1.4	93
07.130	Other recreation equipment	1.74	29.65	7.77	0.8	94
07.210	Public entertainment	6.13	23.84	1.66	15.5	95
07.230	Other recreation, cultural events	4.45	46.49	3.21	3.0	96
07.310	Books, papers, magazines	5.42	29.67	8.02	2.3	97
07.320	Stationery	0.08	8.18	16.97	0.1	98
07.411	Teachers, 1st, 2nd	32.05	133.01		40.0	99
07.412	Teachers, college	1.72	21.84		2.5	100
07.420	Educational facilities	4.55	22.12			101
07.431	Educational supplies	1.87	5.71			102
07.432	Other education expenditures	3.09	6.39			103
08.100	Barber, beauty shops	0.70	18.63	2.85	1.3	104
08.210	Toilet articles	1.67	24.44	9.20	0.7	105
08.220	Other personal-care goods	1.67	26.78	5.78	1.1	106
08.310	Restaurants, cafes	12.49	116.93	3.36	3.2	107
08.320	Hotels, etc.	13.64	7.60	5.01	35.8	108
08.400	Other services	12.64	97.75			109
08.900	Expenditures of residents abroad		19.45			110
10.100	1- and 2-dwelling buildings	22.12	96.22	3.45	6.7	111
10.200	Multidwelling buildings	3.32	26.08	3.83	3.3	112
11.100	Hotels, etc.	0.67	6.17	5.07	2.1	113
11.200	Industrial buildings	5.28	35.22	5.42	2.8	114
11.300	Commercial buildings	2.74	18.74	3.97	3.7	115
11.400	Office buildings	2.39	23.03	2.78	3.7	116
11.500	Educational buildings	5.35	35.94	2.67	5.6	117
11.600	Hospital buildings	2.07	10.09	3.19	6.4	118
11.700	Agricultural buildings	1.33	3.18	2.35	17.9	119
11.800	Other buildings	0.89	17.47			120
12.100	Roads, highways	10.64	44.65			121
12.200	Transmission, utility lines	8.04	52.01	4.94	3.1	122
12.300	Other construction	12.81	10.67	9.35	12.8	123
13.000	Land improvement	3.75	11.70	3.74	8.6	124
14.110	Locomotives	3.12	1.31	7.32	32.6	125
14.120	Other	5.53	7.08	10.12	7.7	126
14.200	Passenger cars	11.41	30.68	7.86	4.7	127
14.300	Trucks, buses, trailers	13.07	29.14	7.32	6.1	128
14.400	Aircraft	3.02	16.72			129
14.500	Ships, boats	0.52	3.68			130
14.600	Other transport	0.60	1.72	8.54	4.1	131
15.100	Engines and turbines	1.87	5.04	9.05	4.1	132
15.210	Tractors	2.06	9.45	6.43	3.4	133
15.220	Other agricultural machinery	2.92	12.00	9.08	2.7	134
15.300	Office machinery	1.61	27.54	8.60	0.7	135
15.400	Metalworking machinery	0.99	18.98	4.42	1.2	136
15.500	Construction, mining	4.08	12.93	9.37	3.4	137
15.600	Special industrial	8.76	15.64	7.24	7.7	138
15.700	General industrial	8.28	16.17	6.86	7.5	139
15.800	Service industrial	1.78	14.57	11.19	1.1	140
16.100	Electrical transmission	3.54	12.37	5.74	5.0	141
16.200	Communication equipment	2.52	19.64			142
16.300	Other electrical	0.96	3.71			143
16.400	Instruments	1.23	15.66	7.59	1.0	144
17.100	Furniture, fixtures	1.72	16.93	6.66	1.5	145
17.200	Other durable goods	4.59	15.55	6.92	4.3	146
18.000	Increase in stocks	13.50	34.50	5.96	6.6	147
19.000	Exports less imports	−8.06	3.54	7.14	−31.9	148
20.100	Blue-collar, unskilled	33.43	13.82	0.56	434.9	149
20.210	Blue-collar, skilled	2.36	72.12	1.28	2.5	150

Appendix Table 13.13. Continued

Code (1)	Category (2)	Per capita expenditure Kenya (shilling) (3)	U.S. (dollar) (4)	Purchasing-power parities shilling/dollar (5)	Quantity per capita (U.S.=100) (6)	Line number (7)
20.220	White-collar	9.14	82.97	2.07	5.3	151
20.300	Professional	22.65	102.98	4.63	4.8	152
21.000	Government expenditure on commodities	21.37	329.70	4.68	1.4	153

Notes:

1. Above expenditures for lines 1 to 110 include both household and government expenditures. The latter are shown separately in Table 13.15.
2. Sugar (1 180) is intentionally out of order; the purpose is to facilitate aggregation.
3. The purchasing-power parities are direct except for the following: Purchasing-power parities are indirect and the quantity ratios are direct in lines 75,76,77,78,99, and 100. Blanks in columns 5 and 6 indicate no direct price or quantity comparisons were made. Where neither comparison was made, purchasing-power parities from other selected categories were imputed to these categories for aggregation purposes.
4. In the Kenya–U.S. comparison, yams and potatoes were treated as separate categories, although for mechanical convenience they are printed above as a single category. The price ratio for potatoes was 3.780 and for yams, sweet potatoes, and cassava, 1.462. 75.0 percent of ICP 1 170 expenditure in Kenya was for yams and 9.1 percent in the United States.
5. Exchange rate: Sh7.143=US$1.00.

Appendix Table 13.14. Expenditures per Capita, Purchasing-Power Parities, and Quantity per Capita for Detailed Categories, U.K.–U.S., 1967

Code (1)	Category (2)	Per capita expenditure U.K. (pound) (3)	U.S. (dollar) (4)	Purchasing-power parities pound/dollar (5)	Quantity per capita (U.S.=100) (6)	Line number (7)
01.101	Rice	0.091	1.26	0.347	20.8	1
01.102	Meal, other cereals	0.635	5.47	0.313	37.1	2
01.103	Bread, rolls	5.843	15.14	0.190	203.1	3
01.104	Biscuits, cakes	5.661	16.68	0.224	151.5	4
01.105	Cereal preparations	0.998	7.01	0.259	55.0	5
01.106	Macaroni, spaghetti, related foods	0.272	1.55	0.357	49.3	6
01.111	Fresh beef, veal	7.204	58.87	0.207	59.1	7
01.112	Fresh lamb, mutton	3.829	2.39	0.200	802.5	8
01.113	Fresh pork	1.742	14.30	0.331	36.8	9
01.114	Fresh poultry	2.468	16.12	0.315	48.6	10
01.115	Other fresh meat	1.089	2.53	0.304	141.8	11
01.116	Frozen, salted meat	11.468	32.94	0.311	111.9	12
01.121	Fresh, frozen fish	2.286	6.87	0.270	123.3	13
01.122	Canned fish	1.270	3.23	0.471	83.6	14
01.131	Fresh milk	8.020	30.56	0.349	75.2	15
01.132	Milk products	3.284	14.16	0.216	107.4	16
01.133	Eggs, egg products	3.484	12.05	0.356	81.2	17
01.141	Butter	2.921	4.06	0.208	345.8	18
01.142	Margarine, edible oil	1.107	8.83	0.411	30.5	19
01.143	Lard, edible fat	0.544	0.70	0.503	154.7	20
01.151	Fresh fruits, tropical, subtropical	1.742	6.73	0.433	59.8	21
01.152	Other fresh fruits	2.468	10.23	0.375	64.3	22
01.153	Fresh vegetables	4.373	21.44	0.245	83.2	23
01.161	Fruit other than fresh	2.105	17.38	0.373	32.5	24
01.162	Vegetables other than fresh	3.466	17.52	0.383	51.6	25
01.170	Potatoes, manioc, other tubers	4.010	9.67	0.256	161.9	26
01.191	Coffee	0.998	9.81	0.404	25.2	27
01.192	Tea	2.558	1.82	0.172	816.5	28
01.193	Cocoa	0.091	0.70	0.295	44.0	29
01.180	Sugar	1.923	3.78	0.252	201.7	30
01.201	Jam, syrup, honey	0.998	4.21	0.175	135.5	31
01.202	Chocolate, ice cream	7.657	12.76	0.555	108.1	32
01.203	Salt, spices, sauces	0.817	5.89	0.361	38.4	33
01.310	Nonalcoholic beverages	2.540	11.07	0.433	53.0	34
01.321	Spirits	8.056	16.68	0.418	115.5	35
01.322	Wine, cider	3.792	3.56	0.720	147.8	36
01.323	Beer	17.328	20.89	0.545	152.2	37
01.410	Cigarettes	23.860	41.90	0.753	75.6	38
01.420	Other tobacco	3.502	4.87	0.719	100.1	39
02.110	Clothing materials	1.089	4.76	0.426	53.7	40
02.121	Men's clothing	6.460	41.85	0.332	46.5	41
02.122	Women's clothing	10.524	64.13	0.495	33.2	42
02.123	Boys', girls' clothing	2.105	19.74	0.324	32.9	43
02.131	Men's, boys' underwear	3.448	9.01	0.527	72.6	44
02.132	Women's, girls' underwear	4.536	23.63	0.354	54.2	45

Appendix Table 13.14. Continued

Code (1)	Category (2)	Per capita expenditure U.K. (pound) (3)	U.S. (dollar) (4)	Purchasing-power parities pound/dollar (5)	Quantity per capita (U.S.=100) (6)	Line number (7)
02.150	Other clothing	4.808	10.70	0.277	162.2	46
02.160	Clothing rental, repair	0.726	3.29	0.347	63.6	47
02.211	Men's footwear	2.177	9.56	0.217	105.0	48
02.212	Women's footwear	2.994	12.59	0.271	87.8	49
02.213	Children's footwear	1.633	9.57	0.182	93.7	50
02.220	Footwear repairs	0.635	1.79	0.213	166.4	51
03.110	Gross rents	49.481	350.61	0.253	55.7	52
03.120	Indoor repair, upkeep	10.016	14.46	0.353	196.2	53
03.210	Electricity	9.417	37.73	0.298	83.8	54
03.220	Gas	4.681	25.67	0.825	22.1	55
03.230	Liquid fuels	1.089	22.40			56
03.240	Other fuels, ice	6.677	4.34	0.262	587.5	57
04.110	Furniture, fixtures	5.716	45.02	0.473	26.8	58
04.120	Floor coverings	4.627	15.29	0.256	118.2	59
04.200	Household textiles, etc.	3.992	31.17	0.319	40.1	60
04.310	Refrigerators, etc.	1.179	12.65	0.417	22.4	61
04.320	Washing appliances	1.542	7.09	0.333	65.4	62
04.330	Cooking appliances	1.361	7.82	0.336	51.8	63
04.340	Heating appliances	1.270	3.80	0.510	65.5	64
04.350	Cleaning appliances	0.907	2.09	0.678	64.1	65
04.360	Other household appliances	0.272	3.00	0.601	15.1	66
04.400	Household utensils	5.534	16.09	0.347	99.1	67
04.510	Nondurable household goods	5.353	23.81	0.407	55.2	68
04.520	Domestic services	2.450	22.53	0.198	54.9	69
04.530	Household services	2.849	20.35	0.259	54.0	70
04.600	Household furnishing repairs	0.635	6.61	0.108	89.0	71
05.110	Drugs, medical preparations	5.153	30.32	0.137	124.1	72
05.120	Medical supplies	0.889	4.13	0.200	107.6	73
05.200	Therapeutic equipment	1.506	8.10	0.174	106.9	74
05.310	Physicians' services	4.064	38.71		66.9	75
05.320	Dentists' services	1.325	11.69		45.9	76
05.330	Services, nurses, other personnel	6.841	56.23		102.2	77
05.410	Hospitals, etc.	9.236	80.38		114.9	78
06.110	Personal cars	13.790	125.38	0.574	19.1	79
06.120	Other personal transport	0.871	10.71	0.483	16.8	80
06.210	Tires, tubes, accessories	3.175	19.37	0.224	73.2	81
06.220	Repair charges	2.994	29.57	0.176	57.5	82
06.230	Gasoline, oil, etc.	10.034	88.67	0.563	20.1	83
06.240	Parking, tolls, etc.	5.353	21.13	0.279	90.8	84
06.310	Local transport	8.601	11.15	0.239	322.7	85
06.321	Rail transport	1.996	1.04	0.608	316.6	86
06.322	Bus transport	0.454	1.80	0.250	100.7	87
06.323	Air transport	2.450	8.14	0.420	71.7	88
06.330	Miscellaneous transport	1.633	2.99	0.705	77.4	89
06.410	Postal communciation	1.960	5.85	0.303	110.6	90
06.420	Telephone, telegraph	2.468	37.91	0.181	36.0	91
07.110	Radio, TV, phonograph, etc.	2.631	36.42	0.513	14.1	92
07.120	Major durable recreation equipment	1.270	19.68	0.308	21.0	93
07.130	Other recreation equipment	8.419	29.65	0.379	74.9	94
07.210	Public entertainment	5.316	23.84	0.085	262.3	95
07.230	Other recreation, cultural events	11.486	46.49	0.351	70.4	96
07.310	Books, papers, magazines	6.550	29.67	0.139	158.8	97
07.320	Stationery	1.542	8.18	0.307	61.4	98
07.411	Teachers, 1st, 2nd	17.873	133.01		72.6	99
07.412	Teachers, college	3.647	21.84		63.0	100
07.420	Educational facilities	4.318	22.12			101
07.431	Educational supplies	1.597	5.71			102
07.432	Other education expenditures	2.903	6.39			103
08.100	Barber, beauty shops	3.212	18.63	0.117	147.4	104
08.210	Toilet articles	3.629	24.44	0.328	45.3	105
08.220	Other personal-care goods	3.901	26.78	0.249	58.5	106
08.310	Restaurants, cafes	13.572	116.93	0.426	27.2	107
08.320	Hotels, etc.	8.691	7.60	0.282	405.3	108
08.400	Other services	14.588	97.75			109
08.900	Expenditures of residents abroad	1.361	19.45	0.357	19.6	110
10.100	1- and 2-dwelling buildings	18.399	96.22	0.199	96.1	111
10.200	Multidwelling buildings	8.583	26.08	0.233	141.2	112
11.100	Hotels, etc.	0.472	6.17	0.406	18.8	113
11.200	Industrial buildings	11.849	35.22	0.378	89.0	114
11.300	Commercial buildings	3.520	18.74	0.348	54.0	115
11.400	Office buildings	2.304	23.03	0.262	38.2	116
11.500	Educational buildings	5.135	35.94	0.312	45.8	117
11.600	Hospital buildings	2.268	10.09	0.246	91.4	118
11.700	Agricultural buildings	1.107	3.18	0.252	138.3	119
11.800	Other buildings	2.722	17.47	0.379	41.1	120
12.100	Roads, highways	4.772	44.65	0.242	44.2	121
12.200	Transmission, utility lines	4.627	52.01	0.187	47.6	122

Appendix Table 13.14. Continued

Code	Category	Per capita expenditure U.K. (pound)	U.S. (dollar)	Purchasing-power parities pound/dollar	Quantity per capita (U.S.=100)	Line number
(1)	(2)	(3)	(4)	(5)	(6)	(7)
12.300	Other construction	1.760	10.67	0.312	52.8	123
13.000	Land improvement	1.651	11.70	0.359	39.3	124
14.110	Locomotives	0.181	1.31			125
14.120	Other	0.272	7.08			126
14.200	Passenger cars	4.990	30.68	0.610	26.7	127
14.300	Trucks, buses, trailers	0.526	29.14			128
14.400	Aircraft	0.671	16.72			129
14.500	Ships, boats	2.685	3.68			130
14.600	Other transport	2.958	1.72			131
15.100	Engines and turbines	0.091	5.04	0.300	6.0	132
15.210	Tractors	0.744	9.45	0.320	24.6	133
15.220	Other agricultural machinery	1.107	12.00	0.360	25.6	134
15.300	Office machinery	2.486	27.54	0.410	22.0	135
15.400	Metalworking machinery	3.520	18.98	0.280	66.2	136
15.500	Construction, mining	3.702	12.93	0.360	79.5	137
15.600	Special industrial	6.097	15.64	0.360	108.3	138
15.700	General industrial	16.947	16.17	0.280	374.3	139
15.800	Service industrial	0.472	14.57			140
16.100	Electrical transmission	5.371	12.37			141
16.200	Communication equipment	7.022	19.64			142
16.300	Other electrical	1.470	3.71	0.140	282.7	143
16.400	Instruments	1.379	15.66	0.150	58.7	144
17.100	Furniture, fixtures	1.651	16.93	0.200	48.8	145
17.200	Other durable goods	0.381	15.55			146
18.000	Increase in stocks	3.956	34.50	0.361	31.8	147
19.000	Exports less imports	−8.383	3.54	0.357	−663.7	148
20.100	Blue-collar, unskilled	19.270	85.94	0.161	139.3	149
20.220	White-collar	13.591	82.97	0.218	75.1	151
20.300	Professional	6.151	102.98	0.311	19.2	152
21.000	Government expenditure on commodities	34.022	329.70	0.299	34.5	153

Notes:

1. Above expenditures for lines 1 to 110 include both household and government expenditures. The latter are shown separately in Table 13.15.

2. Sugar (1 180) is intentionally out of order; the purpose is to facilitate aggregation.

3. The purchasing-power parities are direct except for the following: Purchasing-power parities are indirect and the quantity ratios are direct in lines 75,76,77,78,99, and 100. Blanks in columns 5 and 6 indicate no direct price or quantity comparisons were made. Where neither comparison was made purchasing-power parities from other selected categories were imputed to these categories for aggregation purposes.

4. Blue-collar workers (line 149) include both first- and second-level blue-collar workers. In other binary comparisons, these are found in lines 149 and 150, respectively.

5. Exchange rate: £0.375=US$1.00.

Chapter 14

Results of the multilateral comparisons

The results of the multilateral comparisons for ten countries in 1970 are presented in this chapter. Per capita expenditures in national currencies are given in Table 14.1 and then repeated in terms of a percentage distribution in Table 14.2. In these tables and the ones to follow, GDP and 47 subaggregates are given. Three multilateral tables complete the 1970 descriptions: PPPs in Table 14.3, real per capita quantities relative to the United States in Table 14.4, and quantities in international prices in Table 14.5, all presented at the aggregate and disaggregate levels. Corresponding results for 1967 for six countries are presented in an equivalent set of tables—Tables 14.6 to 14.10. The discussion that follows will be addressed to the 1970 tables. By adding five to each table number and following the 1970 discussion, the reader should have no difficulty threading through the 1967 tables.

A. An Explanation of the Tables

Chapter 5 described the methods by which these comparisons have been made. The key steps in the methodology are (1) the production of transitive, base-invariant PPPs at the detailed category level through the Country-Product–Dummy method, and (2) aggregation by means of the Geary-Khamis formulas, which also incorporate transitive and base-invariant properties. The methods may be illuminated further by setting out the mechanical operations by which some of the tables are derived from others.

For this purpose, it is convenient to refer to the set of appendix tables, which are similar in content and numbering to the main tables except that they refer to 152 detailed categories[1] rather than to aggregations. Once

again, we remind the reader that these tables are to be regarded as worksheet materials rather than as publishable estimates of price and quantity relations.[2]

Tables 14.1 and 14.2 and the corresponding appendix tables, representing simply the expenditure data, are identical with the corresponding data in the summary binary tables, Tables 13.1 through 13.9, and in the detailed binary tables, Appendix Tables 13.1 through 13.9.

The starting point for the preparation of the other tables was the PPPs for the detailed categories. Most of these were obtained by means of the CPD method outlined in the preceding portions of Chapter 5.[3] The PPPs set out in Appendix Table 14.3 are expressed in terms of national currency units per U.S. dollar, but, as was brought out in the presentation of the method, the United States serves simply as a numeraire country in this procedure. The relative purchasing powers would be the same if another country had been chosen for this role.

Once the PPPs have been determined in this manner, the quantity comparisons are obtained by dividing the PPP for each category for each country into the corresponding expenditure ratio.[4] For example, the French quantity index for bread was obtained by dividing the ratio of French to U.S. expenditures on bread (150.05÷17.96=8.355) from Appendix Table 14.1 by the PPP for bread (2.65) from Appendix Table 14.3. The result (8.40÷2.65=3.15) is entered (multiplied by 100 to place it in percentage form) in Appendix Table 14.4.

---

[1] In the multilateral comparisons, the number of categories is 152, one less than in the binary comparisons. Expenditures of residents abroad (ICP 89.00) has been consolidated into "Other services" (ICP 84.00) for reasons explained on page 70. The

line number of this category (110) simply has been omitted so that all the subsequent line numbers in the multilateral appendix tables correspond to those in the binary appendix tables.

[2] See page 49.

[3] See page 65.

[4] For a given category: $\frac{p_F \, q_F}{p_{US} q_{US}} \div \frac{p_F}{p_{US}} = \frac{q_F}{q_{US}}$, where p represents price, q quantity, and the subscripts, France and the United States.

Each row of this table shows the real quantity for a detailed category as a percentage of the U.S. quantity.

The next step is to combine the PPPs and the quantity comparisons for these detailed categories into the desired levels of aggregation ("rice," "bread," and so on into "bread and cereals"; then "bread and cereals," "meat," and so on into "food"; and so on to "consumption" and "GDP").

The procedures used to produce the aggregations in Tables 14.3 and 14.4 are based on the Geary-Khamis method described in Chapter 5. As stated there, the essence of the Geary-Khamis method is that PPPs relative to a set of "international" prices are determined simultaneously with the international prices themselves by means of a system of linear equations. One set of equations defines the international price of the ith good or service as the quantity-weighted average of the purchasing-power–adjusted prices of the ith good in the M countries. A second set makes the purchasing power of a country's currency equal to the ratio of the cost of its output at prices in national currency to the cost at international prices. The supercountry weighting system used in connection with the Geary-Khamis procedure is described in Section E of Chapter 5.

The inputs for the estimation of the Geary-Khamis equations are the expenditures of Appendix Table 14.1 rescaled by the supercountry weights and the PPPs of Appendix Table 14.3. The qs are notional qs obtained by dividing the PPPs into expenditures for each detailed category in each country, the expenditures being denominated in each country's own national currency.[5] The quantity for French bread (56.6), for example, was obtained by dividing the French expenditure on bread (150.05 francs) from Appendix Table 14.1 by the PPP for bread (2.65) from Appendix Table 14.3. (These notional quantities are not shown in our tables because they represent only intermediate data.)

The solution of the equations yields an international price for each detailed category. This set of prices, which has been entered in the right-most column of Appendix Table 14.3, can be used to value each country's quantities. The international price of bread, for example, is 0.581. The quantities are the notional quantities described above. Thus, in the French bread illustration, the notional quantity 56.6 is multiplied by the international price of bread (0.581) to obtain the value of French bread consumption at international prices. This turns out to be 32.9 and is entered in Appendix Table 14.5.

Appendix Table 14.5 is in a form that enables us to aggregate real quantities simply by addition over whatever categories we choose. That is, the quantities for the

detailed categories have been made commensurable from row to row as well as from column to column by valuing them at international prices. This simple additivity is the key to the derivation of the summary tables, particularly Table 14.4 and, more indirectly, Table 14.3

Before turning to the summary tables in the main part of the chapter, we call attention to Appendix Table 14.4. The relationships along any row of this table are identical to those along the corresponding row of Appendix Table 14.5: that is, relative quantities among the different countries for any given category are the same in both tables. The figures are expressed with the United States = 100 in Appendix Table 14.4 to facilitate comparisons with the United States.

To explain the PPP and quantity comparisons in the summary tables, it is convenient to start with Table 14.5. The values in this table represent merely selected aggregations of the figures in the corresponding Appendix Table 14.5. The values are in terms of "international dollars" (I$), which have the same purchasing power over total GDP as a U.S. dollar (US$). For sub-aggregates and for the detailed categories, however, the purchasing power of an I$ differs from that of a US$ because it depends upon the structure of average international prices rather than upon the U.S. relative price structure.

Because the aggregations of Table 14.5 are summations at international prices of the quantities of a given set of goods consumed by the different countries, they may be recast in index number form. This has been done with the United States taken as 100 in Table 14.4. For example, U.K. expenditure on meat at international prices comes to I$133.8, whereas that of the United States is I$192.5 (Table 14.5). The ratio between the two is 0.695, which is entered in percentage form in Table 14.4.

The PPPs for the aggregated categories have been obtained by dividing the quantity ratios in Table 14.4 into expenditure ratios taken from Table 14.1. For example, when the United Kingdom–United States expenditure ratio for meat (32.363÷150.82) is divided by the quantity ratio (0.695), the result is a PPP of .309 pounds per dollar, which is entered in Table 14.3.

B. The Results of the Comparisons

The main results of the multilateral comparisons have been set out in Chapter 1. On a more detailed level, the multilateral comparisons show the same broad features about the quantity and price comparisons that emerged from the binary comparisons discussed in the last chapter. Within consumption, food and purchased transportation show high quantity ratios relative to the United States, particularly with respect to food in the poorer countries. Medical services per capita are high in the European countries and Japan. Within capital formation,

---

[5] For a given category: $\dfrac{p_F q_F}{PPP_{F/S}} = \dfrac{p_F q_F}{p_F/p_S} = q_F$, because $p_S = 1$. It may be noted that for purposes of the multilateral comparisons, each detailed category is treated as a single commodity with a price, quantity, and expenditure for each country.

Summary Multilateral Table 14.1 Per Capita Expenditures in National Currencies, 1970

	Line number	Colombia (peso)	France (franc)	Germany, F.R. (D. mark)	Hungary (forint)	India (rupee)
1 Consumption, ICP	1 to 109	4,574.6	10,302.16	6,641.95	18,800.1	555.56
2 Food, beverage, tobacco	1 to 39	1,518.7	2,841.57	1,590.79	6,686.6	365.11
3 Food	1 to 33	1,425.1	2,310.67	1,265.25	5,693.1	349.67
4 Bread & cereals	1 to 6	240.4	325.74	227.49	742.6	191.84
5 Meat	7 to 12	400.2	796.81	335.24	1,660.3	6.77
6 Fish	13 to 14	14.4	112.06	19.97	43.8	6.28
7 Milk, cheese, eggs	15 to 17	169.4	302.01	144.01	693.9	24.92
8 Oils & fats	18 to 20	88.5	155.76	124.76	561.9	37.57
9 Fruits & vegetables	21 to 26	332.9	427.37	196.06	998.4	37.99
10 Coffee, tea, cocoa	27 to 29	56.8	61.74	99.23	229.8	6.23
11 Spices & sweets, sugar	30 to 33	122.5	129.18	118.60	762.5	38.07
12 Beverages	34 to 37	64.3	384.65	164.59	702.0	2.50
13 Tobacco	38 to 39	29.3	146.25	160.95	291.5	12.94
14 Clothing & footwear	40 to 51	257.1	954.41	691.57	2,175.7	23.08
15 Clothing	40 to 47	205.0	804.36	569.35	1,738.8	21.06
16 Footwear	48 to 51	52.1	150.05	122.22	436.8	2.02
17 Gross rent, fuel	52 to 57	631.3	1,266.70	947.96	1,434.4	54.36
18 Gross rents	52 to 53	559.9	966.62	715.59	835.3	24.31
19 Fuel & power	54 to 57	71.4	300.08	232.36	599.2	30.06
20 House furnishings, operation	58 to 71	394.8	722.70	611.72	1,548.0	21.98
21 Furniture, appliances	58 to 66	204.6	475.79	386.62	930.4	7.13
22 Supplies & operation	67 to 71	190.2	246.91	225.10	617.6	14.85
23 Medical care	72 to 78	124.5	912.97	614.95	1,092.9	16.24
24 Transport & communications	79 to 91	535.6	1,030.45	726.66	1,100.7	31.61
25 Equipment	79 to 80	208.3	264.99	184.53	346.1	2.18
26 Operation costs	81 to 84	127.4	552.72	363.04	182.6	3.83
27 Purchased transport	85 to 89	175.1	161.45	124.63	504.2	23.73
28 Communication	90 to 91	24.8	51.28	54.45	67.8	1.87
29 Recreation & education	92 to 103	450.3	1,477.49	994.87	2,087.5	21.90
30 Recreation	92 to 98	211.3	720.85	498.53	1,093.0	6.49
31 Education	99 to 103	239.1	756.64	496.33	994.5	15.41
32 Other expenditure	104 to 109	662.4	1,095.97	463.49	2,674.5	21.29
33 Personal care	104 to 106	79.3	336.20	171.84	432.3	7.42
34 Miscellaneous services	107 to 109	583.0	759.77	291.65	2,242.2	13.87
35 Capital formation	111 to 148	1,217.3	4,661.46	3,425.48	9,901.2	122.40
36 Construction	111 to 124	724.1	2,403.30	1,609.85	5,800.0	72.26
37 Residential	111 to 112	189.7	1,114.11	608.98	1,526.9	28.11
38 Nonresidential bldgs.	113 to 120	179.8	794.86	574.55	2,442.8	13.14
39 Other construction	121 to 124	354.6	494.33	426.32	1,830.3	31.01
40 Producers' durables	125 to 146	485.9	1,760.71	1,359.30	3,815.9	35.95
41 Transport equipment	125 to 131	154.1	382.76	310.72	939.2	10.89
42 Nonelectrical machinery	132 to 140	203.5	793.98	578.98	1,988.7	11.85
43 Electrical machinery	141 to 144	96.0	397.22	311.98	407.7	9.64
44 Other durables	145 to 146	32.3	186.76	157.62	480.3	3.57
45 Government	149 to 153	321.0	1,153.95	1,204.83	2,414.3	58.23
46 Compensation	149 to 152	200.5	630.06	527.74	624.4	33.60
47 Commodities	153	120.5	523.89	677.09	1,789.9	24.63
48 Gross domestic product	1 to 153	6,112.9	16,117.48	11,272.15	31,115.6	736.18

Note: Line numbers refer to the Appendix Table 14.1 and show the detailed categories that are included in each aggregation.

Italy (lira)	Japan (yen)	Kenya (shilling)	U.K. (pound)	U.S. (dollar)
741,489.	367,719.	703.58	634.350	3,271.73
279,879.	120,286.	343.80	182.429	564.14
229,742.	97,590.	312.17	111.200	446.80
31,666.	29,245.	125.34	15.342	55.88
70,795.	10,684.	31.04	32.363	150.82
8,548.	16,854.	7.52	3.894	11.98
29,000.	8,116.	42.05	16.950	67.54
13,883.	1,260.	11.39	4.930	16.13
53,690.	20,905.	68.10	20.325	98.42
6,770.	1,633.	4.72	4.233	14.64
15,392.	8,893.	22.01	13.163	31.59
29,823.	17,813.	22.11	40.526	62.21
20,314.	4,884.	9.53	30.702	55.12
61,150.	29,886.	27.56	48.706	256.37
50,616.	27,538.	22.48	39.883	214.57
10,533.	2,347.	5.08	8.823	41.80
88,443.	53,846.	72.39	102.699	560.25
66,691.	44,541.	61.35	76.122	455.04
21,753.	9,304.	11.04	26.577	105.21
38,984.	18,252.	43.58	44.044	252.07
21,064.	9,859.	13.02	24.023	151.97
17,920.	8,393.	30.56	20.022	100.10
51,666.	26,164.	36.31	39.115	314.74
69,492.	24,526.	51.21	71.960	446.09
18,057.	3,291.	11.26	18.075	158.16
31,532.	4,686.	6.37	30.345	201.28
13,542.	14,560.	32.16	17.843	30.68
6,361.	1,988.	1.43	5.698	55.97
92,026.	49,106.	82.78	87.356	506.75
39,333.	29,404.	28.66	47.456	241.44
52,693.	19,701.	54.12	39.901	265.30
59,851.	45,655.	45.96	58.047	371.33
19,835.	10,842.	5.70	12.860	80.05
40,015.	34,814.	40.26	45.187	291.28
243,302.	296,272.	206.45	177.481	837.11
142,984.	145,817.	112.41	81.123	463.96
74.760.	50,509.	42.61	27.005	147.14
44,239.	41,686.	30.89	36.329	171.55
23,985.	53,623.	38.91	17.789	145.27
82,724.	109,899.	87.99	82.713	349.12
31,803.	32,342.	33.38	18.182	105.85
22,962.	47,328.	37.66	43.705	144.83
17,523.	22,006.	9.61	18.486	59.47
10,436.	8,224.	7.35	2.340	38.97
77,567.	56,558.	117.42	81.248	692.37
47,358.	40,511.	89.22	50.581	354.32
30,209.	16,047.	28.21	30.667	338.05
1,062,356.	720,548.	1,027.46	893.073	4,801.18

the other countries tend to have larger quantity indexes, relative to the United States, for construction than for producers' durables.

It is of interest to examine the differences as well as the similarities between the multilateral and binary comparisons, using Fisher indexes for the latter. We begin with a simple comparison of the estimates of per capita GDP relative to that of the United States:

	Binary comparison		Multilateral comparison		Ratio multilateral to binary percent
	Rank	%	Rank	%	
	(1)	(2)	(3)	(4)	(5)=(4)÷(2)
Kenya	1	5.9	1	5.7	0.97
India	2	6.1	2	7.1	1.16
Colombia	3	15.4	3	15.9	1.03
Hungary	4	39.8	4	40.3	1.01
Italy	5	47.8	5	45.8	0.96
U.K.	7	62.5	6	60.3	0.96
Japan	6	61.0	7	61.5	1.01
Germany, F.R.	8	73.6	8	74.7	1.01
France	9	74.5	9	75.0	1.01
U.S.	10	100.0	10	100.0	1.00

The overall differences are small except for India. The rankings of the United Kingdom and Japan change, but these countries are so close on either measure that not much significance can be attributed to a ranking of one ahead of the other. (See Section G of Chapter 5 for a discussion of the precision of our numerical comparisons.) But the extent to which the multilateral basis pushes up the relative GDP of India—the multilateral result is 16 percent higher than the binary result—indicates that the differences can be substantial. Therefore, the possible sources of the differences between the binary and multilateral methods are worth considering.

An examination of the details of the multilateral and binary comparisons (using the categories of Table 13.18) indicates that most of the large differences occur in the food categories. The largest difference between the two sets of results for India, for example, is for bread and cereals. In the binary comparison, the Indian per capita quantity is 77.8 percent of that of the U.S. (Table 13.5); in the multilateral, it is 153.5 (Table 14.4). This difference seems to be an extreme observation, but it is worth exploring because it reflects one of the major sources of the difference between the two approaches.

The binary approach values all quantities at own prices and U.S. prices in turn and then offers the geometric mean of the two results as a compromise answer. The multilateral approach values the quantities of each and every country at a single set of international prices. These prices are the average prices of all the included countries, with due account—by way of the super-country technique—of the extent to which each of the countries can be regarded as being representative of the excluded countries of the world.

[Text resumes on page 241.]

Summary Multilateral Table 14.2. Percentage Distribution of Expenditures in National Currencies, 1970

	Line number	Colombia	France	Germany, F.R.	Hungary	India	Italy	Japan	Kenya	U.K.	U.S.
1 Consumption, ICP	1 to 109	74.8	63.9	58.9	60.4	75.5	69.8	51.0	68.5	71.0	68.1
2 Food, beverage, tobacco	1 to 39	24.8	17.6	14.1	21.5	49.6	26.3	16.7	33.5	20.4	11.7
3 Food	1 to 33	23.3	14.3	11.2	18.3	47.5	21.6	13.5	30.4	12.5	9.3
4 Bread & cereals	1 to 6	3.9	2.0	2.0	2.4	26.1	3.0	4.1	12.2	1.7	1.2
5 Meat	7 to 12	6.5	4.9	3.0	5.3	0.9	6.7	1.5	3.0	3.6	3.1
6 Fish	13 to 14	0.2	0.7	0,2	0.1	0.9	0.8	2.3	0.7	0.4	0.2
7 Milk, cheese, eggs	15 to 17	2.8	1.9	1.3	2.2	3.4	2.7	1.1	4.1	1.9	1.4
8 Oils & fats	18 to 20	1.4	1.0	1.1	1.8	5.1	1.3	0.2	1.1	0.6	0.3
9 Fruits & vegetables	21 to 26	5.4	2.7	1.7	3.2	5.2	5.1	2.9	6.6	2.3	2.0
10 Coffee, tea, cocoa	27 to 29	0.9	0.4	0.9	0.7	0.8	0.6	0.2	0.5	0.5	0.3
11 Spices & sweets, sugar	30 to 33	2.0	0.8	1.1	2.5	5.2	1.4	1.2	2.1	1.5	0.7
12 Beverages	34 to 37	1.1	2.4	1.5	2.3	0.3	2.8	2.5	2.2	4.5	1.3
13 Tobacco	38 to 39	0.5	0.9	1.4	0.9	1.8	1.9	0.7	0.9	3.4	1.1
14 Clothing & footwear	40 to 51	4.2	5.9	6.1	7.0	3.1	5.8	4.1	2.7	5.5	5.3
15 Clothing	40 to 47	3.4	5.0	5.1	5.6	2.9	4.8	3.8	2.2	4.5	4.5
16 Footwear	48 to 51	0.9	0.9	1.1	1.4	0.3	1.0	0.3	0.5	1.0	0.9
17 Gross rent, fuel	52 to 57	10.3	7.9	8.4	4.6	7.4	8.3	7.5	7.0	11.5	11.7
18 Gross rents	52 to 53	9.2	6.0	6.3	2.7	3.3	6.3	6.2	6.0	8.5	9.5
19 Fuel & power	54 to 57	1.2	1.9	2.1	1.9	4.1	2.0	1.3	1.1	3.0	2.2
20 House furnishings, operation	58 to 71	6.5	4.5	5.4	5.0	3.0	3.7	2.5	4.2	4.9	5.3
21 Furniture, appliances	58 to 66	3.3	3.0	3.4	3.0	1.0	2.0	1.4	1.3	2.7	3.2
22 Supplies & operation	67 to 71	3.1	1.5	2.0	2.0	2.0	1.7	1.2	3.0	2.2	2.1
23 Medical care	72 to 78	2.0	5.7	5.5	3.5	2.2	4.9	3.6	3.5	4.4	6.6
24 Transport & communications	79 to 91	8.8	6.4	6.4	3.5	4.3	6.5	3.4	5.0	8.1	9.3
25 Equipment	79 to 80	3.4	1.6	1.6	1.1	0.3	1.7	0.5	1.1	2.0	3.3
26 Operation costs	81 to 84	2.1	3.4	3.2	0.6	0.5	3.0	0.7	0.6	3.4	4.2
27 Purchased transport	85 to 89	2.9	1.0	1.1	1.6	3.2	1.3	2.0	3.1	2.0	0.6
28 Communication	90 to 91	0.4	0.3	0.5	0.2	0.3	0.6	0.3	0.1	0.6	1.2
29 Recreation & education	92 to 103	7.4	9.2	8.8	6.7	3.0	8.7	6.8	8.1	9.8	10.6
30 Recreation	92 to 98	3.5	4.5	4.4	3.5	0.9	3.7	4.1	2.8	5.3	5.0
31 Education	99 to 103	3.9	4.7	4.4	3.2	2.1	5.0	2.7	5.3	4.5	5.5
32 Other expenditure	104 to 109	10.8	6.8	4.1	8.6	2.9	5.6	6.3	4.5	6.5	7.7
33 Personal care	104 to 106	1.3	2.1	1.5	1.4	1.0	1.9	1.5	0.6	1.4	1.7
34 Miscellaneous services	107 to 109	9.5	4.7	2.6	7.2	1.9	3.8	4.8	3.9	5.1	6.1
35 Capital formation	111 to 148	19.9	28.9	30.4	31.8	16.6	22.9	41.1	20.1	19.9	17.4
36 Construction	111 to 124	11.8	14.9	14.3	18.6	9.8	13.5	20.2	10.9	9.1	9.7
37 Residential	111 to 112	3.1	6.9	5.4	4.9	3.8	7.0	7.0	4.1	3.0	3.1
38 Nonresidential bldgs.	113 to 120	2.9	4.9	5.1	7.9	1.8	4.2	5.8	3.0	4.1	3.6
39 Other construction	121 to 124	5.8	3.1	3.8	5.9	4.2	2.3	7.4	3.8	2.0	3.0
40 Producers' durables	125 to 146	7.9	10.9	12.1	12.3	4.9	7.8	15.3	8.6	9.3	7.3
41 Transport equipment	125 to 131	2.5	2.4	2.8	3.0	1.5	3.0	4.5	3.2	2.0	2.2
42 Nonelectrical machinery	132 to 140	3.3	4.9	5.1	6.4	1.6	2.2	6.6	3.7	4.9	3.0
43 Electrical machinery	141 to 144	1.6	2.5	2.8	1.3	1.3	1.6	3.1	0.9	2.1	3.0
44 Other durables	145 to 146	0.5	1.2	1.4	1.5	0.5	1.0	1.1	0.7	0.3	1.2
45 Government	149 to 153	5.3	7.2	10.7	7.8	7.9	7.3	7.8	11.4	9.1	14.4
46 Compensation	149 to 152	3.3	3.9	4.7	2.0	4.6	4.5	5.6	8.7	5.7	7.4
47 Commodities	153	2.0	3.3	6.0	5.8	3.3	2.8	2.2	2.7	3.4	7.0
48 Gross domestic product	1 to 153	100.0	100.0	100.0	100.0	100.0	100.0	100.0	100.0	100.0	100.0

Note: Line numbers refer to the Appendix Table 14.2 and show the detailed categories that are included in each aggregation.

Summary Multilateral Table 14.3. Purchasing-Power Parities per U.S. Dollar, 1970

	Line number	Colombia (peso)	France (franc)	Germany, F.R. (D.mark)	Hungary (forint)	India (rupee)	Italy (lira)	Japan (yen)	Kenya (shilling)	U.K. (pound)	U.S. (dollar)
1 Consumption, ICP	1 to 109	8.3	4.64	3.32	15.0	2.24	493.	233.	3.68	0.312	1.00
2 Food, beverage, tobacco	1 to 39	9.5	4.78	3.78	20.0	3.08	622.	339.	4.29	0.369	1.00
3 Food	1 to 33	9.8	5.24	3.96	21.2	3.13	645.	343.	4.19	0.301	1.00
4 Bread & cereals	1 to 6	9.3	5.33	3.78	11.3	2.24	523.	238.	3.34	0.232	1.00
5 Meat	7 to 12	10.1	5.33	3.95	28.0	4.41	677.	430.	4.03	0.309	1.00
6 Fish	13 to 14	12.6	6.18	3.43	15.1	1.43	691.	326.	4.06	0.423	1.00
7 Milk, cheese, eggs	15 to 17	10.7	3.92	2.95	17.3	3.20	619.	288.	4.71	0.307	1.00
8 Oils & fats	18 to 20	14.9	6.15	4.61	30.0	5.73	649.	361.	6.35	0.286	1.00
9 Fruits & vegetables	21 to 26	8.5	4.94	3.94	18.5	3.43	571.	410.	3.44	0.315	1.00
10 Coffee, tea, cocoa	27 to 29	12.1	7.85	9.70	95.5	6.55	1657.	578.	6.59	0.373	1.00
11 Spices & sweets, sugar	30 to 33	8.7	6.24	4.36	24.9	4.55	786.	316.	5.10	0.333	1.00
12 Beverages	34 to 37	11.6	3.25	2.50	23.3	13.19	474.	381.	8.43	0.516	1.00
13 Tobacco	38 to 39	4.1	4.00	4.41	8.4	2.80	667.	211.	5.13	0.640	1.00
14 Clothing & footwear	40 to 51	11.1	6.69	4.07	23.9	3.48	577.	240.	4.64	0.334	1.00
15 Clothing	40 to 47	12.2	6.98	4.26	25.0	3.57	591.	251.	5.41	0.360	1.00
16 Footwear	48 to 51	7.3	5.19	3.09	18.3	3.26	494.	188.	2.46	0.227	1.00
17 Gross rent, fuel	52 to 57	10.6	3.86	2.86	9.5	2.19	367.	289.	4.68	0.331	1.00
18 Gross rents	52 to 53	10.8	3.16	2.43	8.1	1.32	290.	257.	4.92	0.277	1.00
19 Fuel & power	54 to 57	7.8	7.71	4.87	15.1	5.28	853.	414.	3.73	0.457	1.00
20 House furnishings, operation	58 to 71	9.0	4.91	3.21	21.5	1.83	493.	258.	4.76	0.342	1.00
21 Furniture, appliances	58 to 66	13.7	5.78	3.77	23.3	1.63	551.	308.	5.87	0.407	1.00
22 Supplies & operation	67 to 71	5.5	3.63	2.40	18.3	1.64	395.	191.	3.58	0.254	1.00
23 Medical care	72 to 78	3.0	2.06	1.53	4.4	0.69	181.	67.	1.37	0.133	1.00
24 Transport & communications	79 to 91	11.5	7.25	4.84	26.4	3.52	695.	240.	6.14	0.439	1.00
25 Equipment	79 to 80	37.5	6.23	4.23	46.2	8.76	643.	404.	10.39	0.519	1.00
26 Operation costs	81 to 84	9.9	8.62	6.01	21.5	3.34	852.	490.	3.87	0.397	1.00
27 Purchased transport	85 to 89	5.4	5.66	3.68	16.9	2.32	458.	127.	4.22	0.399	1.00
28 Communication	90 to 91	2.8	4.52	2.25	9.5	1.71	405.	200.	3.49	0.236	1.00
29 Recreation & education	92 to 103	5.5	5.39	3.31	8.4	0.61	523.	195.	2.53	0.253	1.00
30 Recreation	92 to 98	12.4	4.92	3.36	9.7	2.60	595.	249.	5.46	0.288	1.00
31 Education	99 to 103	2.9	6.59	3.37	7.2	0.34	523.	145.	1.51	0.220	1.00
32 Other expenditure	104 to 109	7.5	3.80	2.72	15.1	2.31	453.	169.	3.06	0.281	1.00
33 Personal care	104 to 106	11.1	5.84	3.85	12.6	3.74	591.	255.	4.91	0.269	1.00
34 Miscellaneous services	107 to 109	6.8	3.27	2.37	15.5	1.91	414.	150.	2.76	0.286	1.00
35 Capital formation	111 to 148	8.1	4.51	3.03	20.8	2.74	480.	286.	5.30	0.311	1.00
36 Construction	111 to 124	4.6	3.96	2.40	15.4	1.69	377.	249.	4.06	0.244	1.00
37 Residential	111 to 112	4.3	4.71	2.60	16.9	1.69	437.	254.	3.23	0.192	1.00
38 Nonresidential bldgs.	113 to 120	4.1	3.77	2.31	18.1	1.85	363.	328.	3.45	0.309	1.00
39 Other construction	121 to 124	4.8	3.19	2.32	11.6	1.54	293.	196.	7.70	0.257	1.00
40 Producers' durables	125 to 146	22.8	5.04	3.81	29.9	7.92	595.	329.	7.19	0.395	1.00
41 Transport equipment	125 to 131	21.9	4.86	4.67	29.2	7.96	739.	382.	7.16	0.572	1.00
42 Nonelectrical machinery	132 to 140	25.9	5.17	3.50	32.8	7.31	530.	291.	7.78	0.356	1.00
43 Electrical machinery	141 to 144	20.5	4.43	3.22	21.7	8.23	453.	327.	7.30	0.350	1.00
44 Other durables	145 to 146	17.7	5.44	4.21	29.1	8.40	679.	351.	6.07	0.252	1.00
45 Government	149 to 153	6.4	4.36	3.11	13.7	1.15	526.	215.	2.55	0.314	1.00
46 Compensation	149 to 152	4.9	3.88	3.38	6.8	0.67	532.	166.	1.79	0.285	1.00
47 Commodities	153	8.0	4.63	3.16	21.2	2.45	472.	254.	4.19	0.309	1.00
48 Gross domestic product	1 to 153	8.0	4.48	3.14	16.1	2.16	483.	244.	3.74	0.308	1.00

Note: Line numbers refer to the Appendix Table 14.4 and show the detailed categories that are included in each aggregation.

Summary Multilateral Table 14.4. Quantities per Capita with U.S.=100, 1970

	Line number	Colombia	France	Germany, F.R.	Hungary	India	Italy	Japan	Kenya	U.K.	U.S.
1 Consumption, ICP	1 to 109	16.8	67.9	61.2	38.3	7.6	46.0	48.3	5.8	62.2	100.0
2 Food, beverage, tobacco	1 to 39	28.4	105.4	74.6	59.2	21.0	79.8	62.9	14.2	87.5	100.0
3 Food	1 to 33	32.7	98.8	71.5	60.2	25.0	79.7	63.6	16.7	82.6	100.0
4 Bread & cereals	1 to 6	46.1	109.3	107.8	117.3	153.5	108.3	220.3	67.2	118.6	100.0
5 Meat	7 to 12	26.2	99.2	56.3	39.3	1.0	69.3	16.5	5.1	69.5	100.0
6 Fish	13 to 14	9.6	151.3	48.7	24.1	36.6	103.2	431.8	15.5	76.8	100.0
7 Milk, cheese, eggs	15 to 17	23.6	114.3	72.5	59.4	11.6	69.5	41.8	13.3	82.0	100.0
8 Oils & fats	18 to 20	36.8	157.0	167.8	116.0	40.6	132.7	21.6	11.1	106.9	100.0
9 Fruits & vegetables	21 to 26	39.8	87.9	50.5	54.9	11.3	95.6	51.9	20.1	65.6	100.0
10 Coffee, tea, cocoa	27 to 29	32.2	53.7	69.9	16.4	6.5	27.9	19.3	4.9	77.5	100.0
11 Spices & sweets, sugar	30 to 33	44.7	65.5	86.1	96.9	26.5	62.0	89.1	13.7	125.2	100.0
12 Beverages	34 to 37	8.9	190.2	106.0	48.4	0.3	101.1	75.2	4.2	126.2	100.0
13 Tobacco	38 to 39	12.9	66.3	66.3	62.9	8.4	55.2	42.0	3.4	67.0	100.0
14 Clothing & footwear	40 to 51	9.0	55.7	66.4	35.5	2.6	41.3	48.5	2.3	56.9	100.0
15 Clothing	40 to 47	7.8	53.7	62.3	32.4	2.7	39.9	51.2	1.9	51.7	100.0
16 Footwear	48 to 51	17.2	69.1	94.6	57.2	1.5	51.1	29.9	4.9	93.0	100.0
17 Gross rent, fuel	52 to 57	10.6	58.6	59.2	27.1	4.4	43.0	33.3	2.8	59.0	100.0
18 Gross rents	52 to 53	11.4	67.3	64.8	22.8	4.0	50.6	38.1	2.7	60.4	100.0
19 Fuel & power	54 to 57	8.7	37.0	45.4	37.8	5.4	24.2	21.3	2.8	55.3	100.0
20 House furnishings, operation	58 to 71	17.5	58.4	75.5	28.6	4.8	31.4	28.1	3.6	51.2	100.0
21 Furniture, appliances	58 to 66	9.9	54.1	67.5	26.3	2.9	25.2	21.0	1.5	38.9	100.0
22 Supplies & operation	67 to 71	34.6	68.0	93.6	33.6	9.0	45.3	43.9	8.5	78.8	100.0
23 Medical care	72 to 78	13.2	141.1	127.7	79.7	7.5	90.6	124.8	8.4	93.7	100.0
24 Transport & communications	79 to 91	10.5	31.8	33.7	9.3	2.0	22.4	22.9	1.9	36.7	100.0
25 Equipment	79 to 80	3.5	26.9	27.6	4.7	0.2	17.8	5.2	0.7	22.0	100.0
26 Operation costs	81 to 84	6.4	31.9	30.0	4.2	0.6	18.4	4.8	0.8	38.0	100.0
27 Purchased transport	85 to 89	106.1	93.0	110.3	97.4	33.3	96.3	374.3	24.8	145.9	100.0
28 Communication	90 to 91	15.7	20.3	43.3	12.8	2.0	28.1	17.8	0.7	43.2	100.0
29 Recreation & education	92 to 103	16.1	54.1	59.2	48.8	7.1	34.8	49.7	6.5	68.3	100.0
30 Recreation	92 to 98	7.1	60.7	61.5	46.6	1.0	27.4	48.8	2.2	68.3	100.0
31 Education	99 to 103	31.0	43.3	55.5	52.4	17.1	46.9	51.1	13.5	68.2	100.0
32 Other expenditure	104 to 109	23.8	77.7	45.9	47.8	2.5	35.6	72.5	4.0	55.7	100.0
33 Personal care	104 to 106	8.9	71.9	55.7	42.9	2.5	41.9	53.1	1.4	59.8	100.0
34 Miscellaneous services	107 to 109	29.3	79.8	42.2	49.7	2.5	33.2	79.8	5.0	54.2	100.0
35 Capital formation	111 to 148	18.0	123.5	134.8	56.9	5.3	60.5	123.6	4.7	68.1	100.0
36 Construction	111 to 124	33.9	130.9	144.5	81.4	9.2	81.8	126.3	6.0	71.6	100.0
37 Residential	111 to 112	29.9	160.8	159.3	61.5	11.3	116.4	135.0	9.0	95.6	100.0
38 Nonresidential bldgs.	113 to 120	25.3	122.9	144.8	78.8	4.1	71.0	74.1	5.2	68.6	100.0
39 Other construction	121 to 124	50.4	106.8	126.7	108.3	13.9	56.3	188.3	3.5	47.7	100.0
40 Producers' durables	125 to 146	6.1	100.0	102.1	36.5	1.3	39.8	95.7	3.5	60.0	100.0
41 Transport equipment	125 to 131	6.6	74.4	62.8	30.4	1.3	40.7	80.0	4.4	30.1	100.0
42 Nonelectrical machinery	132 to 140	5.4	106.1	114.2	41.9	1.1	29.9	112.3	3.3	84.7	100.0
43 Electrical machinery	141 to 144	7.9	150.6	162.9	31.7	2.0	65.0	113.1	2.2	88.8	100.0
44 Other durables	145 to 146	4.7	88.1	96.1	42.4	1.1	39.5	60.1	3.1	23.8	100.0
45 Government	149 to 153	7.2	38.2	55.9	25.4	7.3	21.3	38.1	6.7	37.4	100.0
46 Compensation	149 to 152	11.6	45.8	44.0	26.0	14.2	25.1	68.9	14.1	50.1	100.0
47 Commodities	153	4.5	33.5	63.4	25.0	3.0	18.9	18.7	2.0	29.4	100.0
48 Gross domestic product	1 to 153	15.9	75.0	74.7	40.3	7.1	45.8	61.5	5.7	60.3	100.0

Note: Line numbers refer to the Appendix Table 14.4 and show the detailed categories that are included in each aggregation.

Summary Multilateral Table 14.5. Quantities per Capita Valued at International Prices, 1970 (I$)

	Line number	Colombia	France	Germany, F.R.	Hungary	India	Italy	Japan	Kenya	U.K.	U.S.
1 Consumption, ICP	1 to 109	555.1	2,238.0	2,015.4	1,262.8	249.7	1,516.1	1,590.7	192.6	2,049.6	3,295.3
2 Food, beverage, tobacco	1 to 39	198.5	735.4	520.4	413.2	146.4	556.5	439.0	99.2	610.6	697.7
3 Food	1 to 33	184.1	556.6	402.7	339.3	141.0	449.1	358.5	94.1	465.4	563.5
4 Bread & cereals	1 to 6	25.7	60.9	60.1	65.4	85.5	60.3	122.7	37.4	66.1	55.7
5 Meat	7 to 12	50.5	190.9	108.4	75.7	2.0	133.4	31.7	9.8	133.8	192.5
6 Fish	13 to 14	1.3	20.0	6.4	3.2	4.8	13.6	57.0	2.0	10.1	13.2
7 Milk, cheese, eggs	15 to 17	18.3	88.6	56.2	46.0	9.0	53.9	32.4	10.3	63.5	77.5
8 Oils & fats	18 to 20	11.0	46.8	50.0	34.6	12.1	39.5	6.5	3.3	31.9	29.8
9 Fruits & vegetables	21 to 26	45.7	101.0	58.1	63.1	12.9	109.9	59.6	23.1	75.4	114.9
10 Coffee, tea, cocoa	27 to 29	10.4	17.3	22.6	5.3	2.1	9.0	6.2	1.6	25.0	32.3
11 Spices & sweets, sugar	30 to 33	21.3	31.2	41.0	46.1	12.6	29.5	42.4	6.5	59.6	47.6
12 Beverages	34 to 37	6.4	137.8	76.8	35.1	0.2	73.2	54.5	3.1	91.5	72.5
13 Tobacco	38 to 39	7.9	41.0	40.9	38.9	5.2	34.1	26.0	2.1	53.7	61.8
14 Clothing & footwear	40 to 51	29.2	180.6	215.3	115.3	8.4	134.0	157.4	7.5	184.5	324.4
15 Clothing	40 to 47	22.2	152.4	176.6	91.9	7.8	113.1	145.2	5.5	146.5	283.5
16 Footwear	48 to 51	7.0	28.3	38.7	23.4	0.6	20.9	12.2	2.0	38.0	40.9
17 Gross rent, fuel	52 to 57	56.7	313.3	316.6	144.8	23.7	229.9	177.9	14.8	230.3	381.2
18 Gross rents	52 to 53	43.3	256.6	247.1	86.8	15.4	192.7	145.2	10.5	230.3	381.2
19 Fuel & power	54 to 57	13.3	56.7	69.6	58.0	8.3	37.2	32.7	4.3	84.8	153.3
20 House furnishings, operation	58 to 71	47.2	157.7	204.0	77.1	12.9	84.7	75.9	9.8	138.2	270.0
21 Furniture, appliances	58 to 66	18.4	101.2	126.1	49.2	5.4	47.0	39.3	2.7	72.6	186.9
22 Supplies & operation	67 to 71	28.8	56.6	77.9	28.0	7.5	37.7	36.5	7.1	65.5	83.2
23 Medical care	72 to 78	17.4	185.8	168.1	105.0	9.8	119.2	164.2	11.1	123.3	131.6
24 Transport & communications	79 to 91	64.2	195.0	206.2	57.2	12.3	137.2	140.6	11.5	225.1	612.6
25 Equipment	79 to 80	8.9	68.2	70.0	12.0	0.4	45.0	13.1	1.7	55.9	53.7
26 Operation costs	81 to 84	18.5	91.8	86.6	12.2	1.6	53.0	13.7	2.4	109.5	288.2
27 Purchased transport	85 to 89	30.1	26.4	31.3	27.6	9.5	27.3	106.3	7.1	41.4	28.4
28 Communication	90 to 91	6.6	8.6	18.3	5.4	0.8	11.9	7.5	8.3	18.2	42.2
29 Recreation & education	92 to 103	63.2	212.5	232.7	191.6	27.9	136.5	195.1	25.4	268.1	392.8
30 Recreation	92 to 98	17.3	148.4	150.3	113.9	2.5	66.9	119.3	5.3	166.9	244.4
31 Education	99 to 103	46.0	64.2	82.4	77.7	25.4	69.6	75.8	20.1	101.2	148.3
32 Other expenditure	104 to 109	78.8	257.6	152.1	158.6	8.2	118.0	240.7	13.4	184.7	331.7
33 Personal care	104 to 106	8.0	64.9	50.2	38.7	2.2	37.8	47.9	1.3	53.9	90.2
34 Miscellaneous services	107 to 109	70.8	192.7	101.9	119.9	6.0	80.2	192.7	12.1	130.8	241.5
35 Capital formation	111 to 148	165.6	1,138.2	1,242.6	524.2	49.2	557.8	1,138.6	42.9	627.3	921.6
36 Construction	111 to 124	132.9	513.4	566.8	319.2	36.2	320.8	495.4	23.4	280.8	392.3
37 Residential	111 to 112	38.6	207.8	205.8	79.4	14.6	150.3	174.4	11.6	123.5	129.2
38 Nonresidential bldgs.	113 to 120	38.7	187.7	221.1	120.2	6.3	108.3	113.1	8.0	104.7	152.6
39 Other construction	121 to 124	55.7	118.0	139.9	119.6	15.3	62.2	207.9	3.8	52.7	110.4
40 Producers' durables	125 to 146	30.3	495.6	505.8	181.1	6.4	197.4	474.0	17.4	297.5	495.5
41 Transport equipment	125 to 131	11.1	124.1	104.8	50.6	2.2	67.8	133.5	7.3	50.1	166.8
42 Nonelectrical machinery	132 to 140	10.8	211.4	227.4	83.4	2.2	59.6	223.7	6.7	168.7	199.2
43 Electrical machinery	141 to 144	5.8	110.8	119.9	23.3	1.5	47.8	83.2	1.6	65.4	73.6
44 Other durables	145 to 146	2.6	49.2	53.7	23.7	0.6	22.1	33.6	1.7	13.3	55.9
45 Government	149 to 153	42.2	223.3	326.7	148.3	42.7	124.5	222.4	38.9	218.5	584.3
46 Compensation	149 to 152	26.1	103.3	99.2	58.6	32.0	56.7	155.4	31.7	113.0	225.5
47 Commodities	153	16.0	120.1	227.4	89.7	10.7	67.9	67.0	7.2	105.5	358.8
48 Gross domestic product	1 to 153	762.8	3,599.5	3,584.8	1,935.3	341.6	2,198.5	2,951.8	274.4	2,895.4	4,801.1

Note: Line numbers refer to the Appendix Table 14.5 and show the detailed categories that are included in each aggregation.

Summary Multilateral Table 14.6. Per Capita Expenditures in National Currencies, 1967

		Line number	Hungary (forint)	India (rupee)	Japan (yen)	Kenya (shilling)	U.K. (pound)	U.S. (dollar)
1	Consumption, ICP	1 to 109	15,255.7	502.55	243,092.	626.80	517.975	2,646.64
2	Food, beverage, tobacco	1 to 39	5,419.0	340.72	85,991	313.12	156.499	475.64
3	Food	1 to 33	4,702.8	327.32	70,921.	278.99	97.420	376.64
4	Bread & cereals	1 to 6	724.0	188.87	24,506.	99.77	13.500	47.11
5	Meat	7 to 12	1,291.1	6.22	6,957.	38.51	27.798	127.15
6	Fish	13 to 14	36.4	4.91	10,152.	8.58	3.556	10.10
7	Milk, cheese, eggs	15 to 17	594.0	21.85	6,245.	39.17	14.788	56.77
8	Oils & fats	18 to 20	492.2	29.36	961.	10.44	4.573	13.59
9	Fruits & vegetables	21 to 26	768.7	40.45	14,308.	58.37	18.163	82.98
10	Coffee, tea, cocoa	27 to 29	147.6	4.80	1,113.	6.10	3.647	12.34
11	Spices & sweets, sugar	30 to 33	648.8	30.87	6,678.	18.05	11.395	26.64
12	Beverages	34 to 37	475.0	1.65	11,200.	20.54	31.717	52.20
13	Tobacco	38 to 39	241.2	11.74	3,870.	13.59	27.362	46.77
14	Clothing & footwear	40 to 51	1,813.4	24.88	25,977.	20.05	41.134	210.62
15	Clothing	40 to 47	1,408.7	22.15	24,460.	15.87	33.695	177.12
16	Footwear	48 to 51	404.7	2.73	1,517.	4.17	7.439	33.51
17	Gross rent, fuel	52 to 57	1,176.7	45.40	35,059.	64.91	81.362	455.21
18	Gross rents	52 to 53	685.1	20.56	26,790.	55.61	59.497	365.08
19	Fuel & power	54 to 57	491.5	24.84	8,268.	9.29	21.865	90.13
20	House furnishings, operation	58 to 71	1,203.5	18.41	18,894.	36.42	37.687	217.32
21	Furniture, appliances	58 to 66	700.9	6.30	8,932.	8.38	20.867	127.92
22	Supplies & operation	67 to 71	502.6	12.11	9,962.	28.04	16.820	89.40
23	Medical care	72 to 78	846.7	12.48	16,717.	25.62	29.014	229.55
24	Transport & communications	79 to 91	862.1	23.80	8,797.	57.97	55.777	363.71
25	Equipment	79 to 80	195.3	1.88	1,991.	10.38	14.661	136.10
26	Operation costs	81 to 84	140.6	2.51	1,026.	16.13	21.556	158.74
27	Purchased transport	85 to 89	462.1	18.04	4,253.	30.32	15.133	25.12
28	Communication	90 to 91	64.1	1.37	1,526.	1.15	4.427	43.75
29	Recreation & education	92 to 103	1,621.5	17.46	25,786.	65.91	67.553	383.00
30	Recreation	92 to 98	854.7	5.12	19,476.	22.62	37.215	193.94
31	Education	99 to 103	766.9	12.34	6,310.	43.29	30.338	189.07
32	Other expenditure	104 to 109	2,312.9	19.41	25,874.	42.81	48.955	311.58
33	Personal care	104 to 106	324.9	6.59	9,441.	4.04	10.742	69.85
34	Miscellaneous services	107 to 109	1,988.1	12.81	16,434.	38.77	38.213	241.72
35	Capital formation	111 to 148	7,274.9	91.63	163,237.	171.03	129.463	735.72
36	Construction	111 to 124	3,687.0	62.26	81,057.	81.41	69.168	391.17
37	Residential	111 to 112	936.8	25.72	28,169.	25.44	26.981	122.30
38	Nonresidential bldgs.	113 to 120	1,341.8	12.23	23,365.	20.73	29.377	149.84
39	Other construction	121 to 124	1,408.4	24.31	29,522.	35.24	12.810	119.03
40	Producers' durables	125 to 146	2,688.3	34.36	58,256.	84.18	64.723	306.51
41	Transport equipment	125 to 131	655.9	9.95	19,663.	37.26	12.284	90.33
42	Nonelectrical machinery	132 to 140	1,453.9	12.03	26,461.	32.35	35.165	132.32
43	Electrical machinery	141 to 144	339.0	6.72	9,364.	8.25	15.242	51.38
44	Other durables	145 to 146	239.5	5.66	2,768.	6.31	2.032	32.48
45	Government	149 to 153	1,629.8	46.56	29,860.	88.95	73.033	601.59
46	Compensation	149 to 152	467.5	27.35	21,276.	67.58	39.011	271.90
47	Commodities	153	1,162.4	19.21	8.584.	21.37	34.022	329.70
48	Gross domestic product	1 to 153	24,160.3	640.73	436,188.	886.78	720.465	3,983.95

Note: Line numbers refer to the Appendix Table 14.6 and show the detailed categories that are included in each aggregation.

Summary Multilateral Table 14.7. Percentage Distribution of Expenditures in National Currencies, 1967

	Line number	Hun-gary	India	Japan	Kenya	U.K.	U.S.
1 Consumption, ICP	1 to 109	63.1	78.4	55.7	70.7	71.9	66.4
2 Food, beverage, tobacco	1 to 39	22.4	53.2	19.7	35.3	21.7	11.9
3 Food	1 to 33	19.5	51.1	16.3	31.5	13.5	9.5
4 Bread & cereals	1 to 6	3.0	29.5	5.6	11.3	1.9	1.2
5 Meat	7 to 12	5.3	1.0	1.6	4.3	3.9	3.2
6 Fish	13 to 14	0.2	0.8	2.3	1.0	0.5	0.3
7 Milk, cheese, eggs	15 to 17	2.5	3.4	1.4	4.4	2.1	1.4
8 Oils & fats	18 to 20	2.0	4.6	0.2	1.2	0.6	0.3
9 Fruits & vegetables	21 to 26	3.2	6.3	3.3	6.6	2.5	2.1
10 Coffee, tea, cocoa	27 to 29	0.6	0.7	0.3	0.7	0.5	0.3
11 Spices & sweets, sugar	30 to 33	2.7	4.8	1.5	2.0	1.6	0.7
12 Beverages	34 to 37	2.0	0.3	2.6	2.3	4.4	1.3
13 Tobacco	38 to 39	1.0	1.8	0.9	1.5	3.8	1.2
14 Clothing & footwear	40 to 51	7.5	3.9	6.0	2.3	5.7	5.3
15 Clothing	40 to 47	5.8	3.5	5.6	1.8	4.7	4.4
16 Footwear	48 to 51	1.7	0.4	0.3	0.5	1.0	0.8
17 Gross rent, fuel	52 to 57	4.9	7.1	8.0	7.3	11.3	11.4
18 Gross rents	52 to 53	2.8	3.2	6.1	6.3	8.3	9.2
19 Fuel & power	54 to 57	2.0	3.9	1.9	1.0	3.0	2.3
20 House furnishings, operation	58 to 71	5.0	2.9	4.3	4.1	5.2	5.5
21 Furniture, appliances	58 to 66	2.9	1.0	2.0	0.9	2.9	3.2
22 Supplies & operation	67 to 71	2.1	1.9	2.3	3.2	2.3	2.2
23 Medical care	72 to 78	3.5	1.9	3.8	2.9	4.0	5.8
24 Transport & communications	79 to 91	3.6	3.7	2.0	6.5	7.7	9.1
25 Equipment	79 to 80	0.8	0.3	0.5	1.2	2.0	3.4
26 Operation costs	81 to 84	0.6	0.4	0.2	1.8	3.0	4.0
27 Purchased transport	85 to 89	1.9	2.8	1.0	3.4	2.1	0.6
28 Communication	90 to 91	0.3	0.2	0.3	0.1	0.6	1.1
29 Recreation & education	92 to 103	6.7	2.7	5.9	7.4	9.4	9.6
30 Recreation	92 to 98	3.5	0.8	4.5	2.6	5.2	4.9
31 Education	99 to 103	3.2	1.9	1.4	4.9	4.2	4.7
32 Other expenditure	104 to 109	9.6	3.0	5.9	4.8	6.8	7.8
33 Personal care	104 to 106	1.3	1.0	2.2	0.5	1.5	1.8
34 Miscellaneous services	107 to 109	8.2	2.0	3.8	4.4	5.3	6.1
35 Capital formation	111 to 148	30.1	14.3	37.4	19.3	18.0	18.5
36 Construction	111 to 124	15.3	9.7	18.6	9.2	9.6	9.8
37 Residential	111 to 112	3.9	4.0	6.5	2.9	3.7	3.1
38 Nonresidential bldgs.	113 to 120	5.6	1.9	5.4	2.3	4.1	3.8
39 Other construction	121 to 124	5.8	3.8	6.8	4.0	1.8	3.0
40 Producers' durables	125 to 146	11.1	5.4	13.4	9.5	9.0	7.7
41 Transport equipment	125 to 131	2.7	1.6	4.5	4.2	.7	2.3
42 Nonelectrical machinery	132 to 140	6.0	1.9	6.1	3.6	+.9	3.3
43 Electrical machinery	141 to 144	1.4	1.0	2.1	0.9	2.1	1.3
44 Other durables	145 to 146	1.0	0.9	0.6	0.7	0.3	0.8
45 Government	149 to 153	6.7	7.3	6.8	10.0	10.1	15.1
46 Compensation	149 to 152	1.9	4.3	4.9	7.6	5.4	6.8
47 Commodities	153	4.8	3.0	2.0	2.4	4.7	8.3
48 Gross domestic product	1 to 153	100.0	100.0	100.0	100.0	100.0	100.0

Note: Line numbers refer to the Appendix Table 14.7 and show the detailed categories that are included in each aggregation.

Summary Multilateral Table 14.8. Purchasing-Power Parities per U.S. Dollar, 1967

	Line number	Hungary (forint)	India (rupee)	Japan (yen)	Kenya (shilling)	U.K. (pound)	U.S. (dollar)
1 Consumption, ICP	1 to 109	15.1	2.37	212.	3.81	0.294	1.00
2 Food, beverage, tobacco	1 to 39	20.6	3.24	309.	4.59	0.352	1.00
3 Food	1 to 33	21.6	3.19	315.	4.34	0.287	1.00
4 Bread & cereals	1 to 6	10.7	2.03	175.	2.97	0.220	1.00
5 Meat	7 to 12	29.6	4.38	375.	4.66	0.292	1.00
6 Fish	13 to 14	14.4	1.62	301.	5.70	0.397	1.00
7 Milk, cheese, eggs	15 to 17	19.8	3.36	296.	4.80	0.283	1.00
8 Oils & fats	18 to 20	32.8	5.05	393.	6.45	0.288	1.00
9 Fruits & vegetables	21 to 26	15.6	3.38	349.	3.19	0.287	1.00
10 Coffee, tea, cocoa	27 to 29	109.5	6.50	578.	6.96	0.394	1.00
11 Spices & sweets, sugar	30 to 33	29.8	3.89	426.	5.51	0.316	1.00
12 Beverages	34 to 37	20.8	11.84	330.	8.74	0.504	1.00
13 Tobacco	38 to 39	10.3	2.72	213.	6.06	0.683	1.00
14 Clothing & footwear	40 to 51	25.0	3.44	227.	4.74	0.342	1.00
15 Clothing	40 to 47	26.5	3.48	235.	5.79	0.370	1.00
16 Footwear	48 to 51	19.1	3.45	178.	2.48	0.235	1.00
17 Gross rent, fuel	52 to 57	10.3	2.48	278.	5.62	0.291	1.00
18 Gross rents	52 to 53	8.7	1.41	240.	5.45	0.259	1.00
19 Fuel & power	54 to 57	16.1	6.80	445.	5.45	0.421	1.00
20 House furnishings, operation	58 to 71	22.1	1.85	230.	4.40	0.332	1.00
21 Furniture, appliances	58 to 66	24.6	1.73	281.	6.92	0.425	1.00
22 Supplies & operation	67 to 71	18.5	1.71	177.	3.36	0.238	1.00
23 Medical care	72 to 78	4.8	0.72	59.	1.17	0.123	1.00
24 Transport & communications	79 to 91	21.7	3.02	209.	6.16	0.405	1.00
25 Equipment	79 to 80	42.2	7.87	421.	11.80	0.529	1.00
26 Operation costs	81 to 84	20.9	3.67	510.	6.07	0.351	1.00
27 Purchased transport	85 to 89	21.4	2.82	143.	5.40	0.458	1.00
28 Communication	90 to 91	6.8	1.68	211.	3.46	0.215	1.00
29 Recreation & education	92 to 103	8.3	0.88	153.	2.46	0.232	1.00
30 Recreation	92 to 98	9.5	2.65	228.	5.96	0.256	1.00
31 Education	99 to 103	6.8	0.49	76.	1.37	0.206	1.00
32 Other expenditure	104 to 109	13.2	2.41	157.	3.24	0.260	1.00
33 Personal care	104 to 106	13.4	3.79	238.	6.65	0.266	1.00
34 Miscellaneous services	107 to 109	12.8	2.02	132.	2.93	0.258	1.00
35 Capital formation	111 to 148	21.0	2.56	285.	5.48	0.303	1.00
36 Construction	111 to 124	16.1	1.82	268.	4.72	0.253	1.00
37 Residential	111 to 112	15.5	1.75	269.	3.47	0.203	1.00
38 Nonresidential bldgs.	113 to 120	18.3	1.89	360.	3.59	0.322	1.00
39 Other construction	121 to 124	14.3	1.69	205.	8.17	0.244	1.00
40 Producers' durables	125 to 146	29.5	5.58	302.	6.43	0.355	1.00
41 Transport equipment	125 to 131	35.2	4.67	369.	6.27	0.517	1.00
42 Nonelectrical machinery	132 to 140	29.3	6.50	268.	7.04	0.331	1.00
43 Electrical machinery	141 to 144	20.8	6.45	283.	6.71	0.296	1.00
44 Other durables	145 to 146	30.5	5.32	295.	6.48	0.263	1.00
45 Government	149 to 153	14.6	1.45	212.	2.84	0.314	1.00
46 Compensation	149 to 152	8.0	0.88	163.	1.97	0.311	1.00
47 Commodities	153	20.5	2.52	236.	4.38	0.295	1.00
48 Gross domestic product	1 to 153	16.1	2.31	227.	3.94	0.296	1.00

Note: Line numbers refer to the Appendix Table 14.8 and show the detailed categories that are included in each aggregation.

Summary Multilateral Table 14.9. Quantities per Capita with U.S.=100, 1967

	Line number	Hungary	India	Japan	Kenya	U.K.	U.S.
1 Consumption, ICP	1 to 109	38.3	8.0	43.3	6.2	66.6	100.0
2 Food, beverage, tobacco	1 to 39	55.2	22.1	58.5	14.3	93.6	100.0
3 Food	1 to 33	57.7	27.2	59.9	17.1	90.1	100.0
4 Bread & cereals	1 to 6	143.8	197.6	296.5	71.3	130.1	100.0
5 Meat	7 to 12	34.3	1.1	14.6	6.5	74.8	100.0
6 Fish	13 to 14	25.0	29.9	334.0	14.9	88.7	100.0
7 Milk, cheese, eggs	15 to 17	52.9	11.5	37.1	14.4	92.0	100.0
8 Oils & fats	18 to 20	110.6	42.7	18.0	11.9	116.8	100.0
9 Fruits & vegetables	21 to 26	59.3	14.4	49.5	22.0	76.1	100.0
10 Coffee, tea, cocoa	27 to 29	10.9	6.0	15.6	7.1	75.1	100.0
11 Spices & sweets, sugar	30 to 33	81.7	29.8	58.8	12.3	135.3	100.0
12 Beverages	34 to 37	43.8	0.3	64.9	4.5	120.4	100.0
13 Tobacco	38 to 39	50.0	9.2	38.8	4.8	85.7	100.0
14 Clothing & footwear	40 to 51	34.4	3.4	54.4	2.0	57.1	100.0
15 Clothing	40 to 47	30.1	3.6	58.9	1.5	51.4	100.0
16 Footwear	48 to 51	63.1	2.4	25.5	5.0	94.3	100.0
17 Gross rent, fuel	52 to 57	25.2	4.0	27.7	2.5	61.4	100.0
18 Gross rents	52 to 53	21.6	4.0	30.5	2.8	62.9	100.0
19 Fuel & power	54 to 57	33.9	4.1	20.6	1.9	57.7	100.0
20 House furnishings, operation	58 to 71	25.0	4.6	37.9	3.8	52.3	100.0
21 Furniture, appliances	58 to 66	22.2	2.9	24.9	0.9	38.4	100.0
22 Supplies & operation	67 to 71	30.4	7.9	63.0	9.3	79.1	100.0
23 Medical care	72 to 78	76.7	7.5	123.9	9.5	103.0	100.0
24 Transport & communications	79 to 91	10.9	2.2	11.6	2.6	37.9	100.0
25 Equipment	79 to 80	3.4	0.2	3.5	0.6	20.4	100.0
26 Operation costs	81 to 84	4.2	0.4	1.3	1.7	38.6	100.0
27 Purchased transport	85 to 89	86.0	25.5	118.6	22.4	131.4	100.0
28 Communication	90 to 91	21.6	1.9	16.5	0.8	47.1	100.0
29 Recreation & education	92 to 103	50.9	5.2	43.9	7.0	75.9	100.0
30 Recreation	92 to 98	46.6	1.0	44.0	2.0	74.9	100.0
31 Education	99 to 103	59.3	13.4	43.8	16.7	77.9	100.0
32 Other expenditure	104 to 109	56.2	2.6	52.8	4.2	60.4	100.0
33 Personal care	104 to 106	34.6	2.5	56.8	0.9	57.8	100.0
34 Miscellaneous services	107 to 109	64.0	2.6	51.4	5.5	61.3	100.0
35 Capital formation	111 to 148	47.1	4.9	78.0	4.2	58.1	100.0
36 Construction	111 to 124	58.6	8.7	77.4	4.4	70.0	100.0
37 Residential	111 to 112	49.3	12.0	85.7	6.0	108.7	100.0
38 Nonresidential bldgs.	113 to 120	48.9	4.3	43.3	3.9	61.0	100.0
39 Other construction	121 to 124	82.9	12.1	120.8	3.6	44.1	100.0
40 Producers' durables	125 to 146	29.7	2.0	63.0	4.3	59.5	100.0
41 Transport equipment	125 to 131	20.6	2.4	59.0	6.6	26.3	100.0
42 Nonelectrical machinery	132 to 140	37.5	1.4	74.5	3.5	80.3	100.0
43 Electrical machinery	141 to 144	31.7	2.0	64.4	2.4	100.1	100.0
44 Other durables	145 to 146	24.2	3.3	28.9	3.0	23.7	100.0
45 Government	149 to 153	18.6	5.3	23.4	5.2	38.7	100.0
46 Compensation	149 to 152	21.5	11.4	48.1	12.6	46.1	100.0
47 Commodities	153	17.2	2.3	11.0	1.5	35.0	100.0
48 Gross domestic product	1 to 153	37.6	7.0	48.3	5.6	61.0	100.0

Note: Line numbers refer to the Appendix Table 14.9 and show the detailed categories that are included in each aggregation.

Summary Multilateral Table 14.10. Quantities per Capita Valued at International Prices, 1967 (I$)

	Line number	Hungary	India	Japan	Kenya	U.K.	U.S.
1 Consumption, ICP	1 to 109	988.6	206.5	1,119.0	160.5	1,718.2	2,581.4
2 Food, beverage, tobacco	1 to 39	331.4	132.6	351.3	86.0	561.3	600.0
3 Food	1 to 33	270.0	127.2	279.9	79.9	421.3	467.6
4 Bread & cereals	1 to 6	55.6	76.4	114.7	27.6	50.3	38.7
5 Meat	7 to 12	56.9	1.9	24.2	10.8	123.9	165.7
6 Fish	13 to 14	2.8	3.4	37.6	1.7	10.0	11.3
7 Milk, cheese, eggs	15 to 17	36.1	7.8	25.4	9.8	62.9	68.3
8 Oils & fats	18 to 20	27.7	10.7	4.5	3.0	29.3	25.1
9 Fruits & vegetables	21 to 26	54.3	13.2	45.3	20.2	69.8	91.6
10 Coffee, tea, cocoa	27 to 29	2.8	1.5	4.0	1.8	19.4	25.8
11 Spices & sweets, sugar	30 to 33	33.6	12.3	24.2	5.1	55.7	41.2
12 Beverages	34 to 37	33.5	0.2	49.7	3.4	92.1	76.5
13 Tobacco	38 to 39	27.9	5.2	21.7	2.7	47.9	55.9
14 Clothing & footwear	40 to 51	87.0	8.7	137.6	5.1	144.3	252.7
15 Clothing	40 to 47	65.9	7.9	129.1	3.4	112.8	219.3
16 Footwear	48 to 51	21.1	0.8	8.5	1.7	31.5	33.4
17 Gross rent, fuel	52 to 57	114.0	18.2	125.5	11.5	278.3	453.4
18 Gross rents	52 to 53	69.6	12.9	98.5	9.0	202.7	322.4
19 Fuel & power	54 to 57	44.5	5.3	27.0	2.5	75.5	131.0
20 House furnishings, operation	58 to 71	57.7	10.6	87.3	8.8	120.5	230.5
21 Furniture, appliances	58 to 66	33.8	4.3	37.8	1.4	58.3	151.9
22 Supplies & operation	67 to 71	23.9	6.2	49.5	7.3	62.2	78.6
23 Medical care	72 to 78	70.1	6.9	113.2	8.7	94.2	91.4
24 Transport & communications	79 to 91	46.8	9.3	49.5	11.1	162.2	427.8
25 Equipment	79 to 80	6.2	0.3	6.4	1.2	37.3	183.3
26 Operation costs	81 to 84	7.6	0.8	2.3	3.0	69.6	180.2
27 Purchased transport	85 to 89	25.4	7.5	35.1	6.6	38.8	29.5
28 Communication	90 to 91	7.5	0.6	5.8	0.3	16.4	34.8
29 Recreation & education	92 to 103	131.5	13.4	113.5	18.0	196.2	258.3
30 Recreation	92 to 98	79.4	1.7	75.0	3.3	127.7	170.5
31 Education	99 to 103	52.1	11.7	38.5	14.7	68.4	87.8
32 Other expenditure	104 to 109	150.2	6.9	141.2	11.3	161.4	267.3
33 Personal care	104 to 106	24.7	1.8	40.5	0.6	41.2	71.3
34 Miscellaneous services	107 to 109	125.5	5.1	100.7	10.7	120.2	195.9
35 Capital formation	111 to 148	412.3	42.5	682.6	37.1	509.1	875.6
36 Construction	111 to 124	227.9	33.9	300.8	17.1	272.2	388.8
37 Residential	111 to 112	55.4	13.5	96.2	6.7	122.1	112.3
38 Nonresidential bldgs.	113 to 120	81.8	7.2	72.3	6.4	101.9	167.1
39 Other construction	121 to 124	90.8	13.2	132.8	4.0	48.3	109.5
40 Producers' durables	125 to 146	128.2	8.7	272.1	18.5	256.9	431.7
41 Transport equipment	125 to 131	29.1	3.3	83.1	9.3	37.0	140.8
42 Nonelectrical machinery	132 to 140	67.5	2.5	134.2	6.3	144.7	180.1
43 Electrical machinery	141 to 144	20.3	1.3	41.3	1.5	64.1	64.0
44 Other durables	145 to 146	11.3	1.5	13.5	1.4	11.1	46.8
45 Government	149 to 153	98.1	28.2	123.3	27.4	204.0	526.9
46 Compensation	149 to 152	37.7	20.1	84.5	22.2	81.0	175.7
47 Commodities	153	60.4	8.1	38.8	5.2	123.0	351.2
48 Gross domestic product	1 to 153	1,499.0	277.2	1,924.9	225.0	2,431.2	3,983.9

Note: Line numbers refer to the Appendix Table 14.10 and show the detailed categories that are included in each aggregation.

The bread and cereal case illustrates the factors at work. In low-income countries, cereal products loom large in total expenditures, and the quantity comparisons that are obtained are influenced significantly by the prices assigned to these products. In India, rice alone accounted for nearly 16 percent of 1970 GDP in national currency, and in Kenya, meal and flour accounted for 11 percent. Thus, the per capita quantity of GDP, of consumption of food, and, most of all, of bread and cereals (ICP 01.100), the food group that includes rice and meal and flour, is sensitive to the prices used to value the quantities of these grains and related products. The great difference between the multilateral and binary results in the case of India suggests a high international price of rice relative to the price of rice in the Indian and U.S. price structures. Of course, the sensitivity of the resulting quantity indexes to the prices used is greater when we focus upon a narrow category such as bread and cereals than it is for a broader aggregate such as food or consumption.

In order to show the role of price structure in producing the difference in the results, we start with the international price of rice, which Appendix Table 14.3 tells us is 2.00. The position of this price in the international price structure is established by other prices. We note that the average price of all 152 categories is 1.0 and, more particularly, that the average international price for the six detailed categories making up the bread and cereals group (of which rice is one) is 1.19. Thus, rice is 68 percent higher than the price of breads and cereals in general. (This calculation is very approximate because the bread and cereal prices were averaged without weighting.)

If our explanation is correct—that is, that the prices used to value quantities have pushed up the Indian multilateral bread and cereal quantity ratio—then the relative price of rice should be much less in the United States and still less in India. In order to examine the relative position of rice in the bread and cereal sector of the Indian and U.S. price structures, we first compute an average rupee price and an average dollar price for those specifications in each of the six categories for which both Indian and U.S. prices are available. Next, an overall average price for the six bread and cereal categories is computed by averaging the average prices for the six detailed categories. It turns out that rice in India is 41 percent of the Indian average, and rice in the United States, 52 percent of the U.S. average.

Thus, the relatively high international prices of rice in conjunction with relatively large Indian consumption of rice produces a high Indian/U.S. quantity ratio in the multilateral comparison. In the binary comparison, the lower U.S. relative price produces a lower ratio, and the Indian price structure, in which rice is cheaper still, yields the lowest ratio.

The relative price of rice in the United States thus is seen to be closer to the Indian than to the international relative price. The United States, as a producer and exporter of rice and only a moderate consumer, has a lower internal relative rice price than most of the other countries in the study. Japan, Germany, and Hungary have higher rice prices than the United States even when converted at the exchange rate; when account is taken of the fact that prices of most goods in all three of these countries are well below the level implied by the exchange rate, rice can be seen to be a relatively high-priced item in the price structures of those countries. Even in countries in which the price of rice converted to dollars by means of the exchange rate is not higher than the U.S. price, its price relative to other goods is often high.

The question arises whether the result produced by international prices or that produced by the ideal index is a better general purpose measure of relative GDP. It is natural to be inclined to use the binary results as a standard against which to assess the reasonableness of the multilateral results. One may ask, however, whether this does not depend mainly or even completely upon a natural tendency to rely on the familiar to assess the new. If we wish to measure the per capita GDP of India relative to that of 9 or 19 or 49 or any other number of countries, there is more logic in using average international prices to value the quantities of all the countries than there is in a procedure that allows U.S. prices, but no other outside country's prices, to help determine the GDP of India relative to Kenya. If rice is expensive in the world relative to the U.S. and Indian prices, that is the relevant input into the evaluation of Indian product relative to the world of other countries—and if rice were cheaper in the world than in India, in the United States, or in both, that would be the appropriate input.

Another way of examining the effect of valuing each country's quantities at international prices is to compare the distribution of its expenditures at such a valuation (that is, the percentage distribution of the international dollar figures in Table 14.5) with the distribution at its own prices (Table 14.2). A comparison along these lines was offered earlier for the three main subaggregates of GDP.[6] The comparison with respect to more disaggregated data is offered in Table 14.11.

Among the most interesting differences are those found within the capital formation sector. The proportion of GDP for which producers' durable goods accounted is much lower in India, Kenya, Colombia, and Hungary when international prices are used than when local prices are the basis of valuation: for India the percentage is only 1.9 at international prices and 4.9 at national prices. This, of course, is a reflection of the high price of these goods in the Indian price structure compared with the relative prices of such goods in the average price structure of the "world" (that is, the ten super-

[6] See pages 5–6.

Table 14.11. Comparison of Percentage Distribution of Expenditures at National and at International Prices, 1970

	Colombia		France		Germany, F.R.		Hungary		India	
	Nat'l.	Int'l.	Nat'l.	Int'l.	Nat'l.	Int'l.	Nat'l.	Int'l.	Nat'l.	Int'l.
Consumption	74.8	72.7	63.9	62.2	58.9	56.2	60.4	65.2	75.5	73.1
Food, beverage, tobacco	24.8	26.0	17.6	20.4	14.1	14.5	21.5	21.4	49.6	42.9
Food	23.3	24.1	14.3	15.5	11.2	11.2	18.3	17.5	47.5	41.3
Bread and cereals	3.9	3.4	2.0	1.7	2.0	1.7	2.4	3.4	26.1	25.0
Meat and fish	6.8	6.8	5.6	5.9	3.2	3.2	5.5	4.1	1.8	2.0
Milk, cheese, eggs	2.8	2.4	1.9	2.5	1.3	1.6	2.2	2.4	3.4	2.6
Oils and fats	1.4	1.4	1.0	1.3	1.1	1.4	1.8	1.8	5.1	3.5
Fruits and vegetables	5.4	6.0	2.7	2.8	1.7	1.6	3.2	3.3	5.2	3.8
Other foods	2.9	4.2	1.2	1.3	1.9	1.8	3.2	2.7	6.0	4.3
Beverages	1.1	0.8	2.4	3.8	1.5	2.1	2.3	1.8	0.3	0.1
Tobacco	0.5	1.0	0.9	1.1	1.4	1.1	0.9	2.0	1.8	1.5
Clothing and footwear	4.2	3.8	5.9	5.0	6.1	6.0	7.0	6.0	3.1	2.5
Gross rents, fuel	10.3	7.4	7.9	8.7	8.4	8.8	4.6	7.5	7.4	6.9
Gross rents	9.2	5.7	6.0	7.1	6.3	6.9	2.7	4.5	3.3	4.5
Fuel and power	1.2	1.7	1.9	1.6	2.1	1.9	1.9	3.0	4.1	2.4
House furnishings, operation	6.5	6.2	4.5	4.4	5.4	5.7	5.0	4.0	3.0	3.8
Medical care	2.0	2.3	5.7	5.2	5.5	4.7	3.5	5.4	2.2	2.9
Transport and communication	8.8	8.4	6.4	5.4	6.4	5.8	3.5	3.0	4.3	3.6
Personal transport	5.5	3.6	5.1	4.4	4.9	4.4	1.7	1.2	0.8	0.6
Purchased transport	2.9	3.9	1.0	0.7	1.1	0.9	1.6	1.4	3.2	2.8
Communication	0.4	0.9	0.3	0.2	0.5	0.5	0.2	0.3	0.3	0.2
Recreation and education	7.4	8.3	9.2	5.9	8.8	6.5	6.7	9.9	3.0	8.2
Recreation	3.5	2.3	4.5	4.1	4.4	4.2	3.5	5.9	0.9	0.7
Education	3.9	6.0	4.7	1.8	4.4	2.3	3.2	4.0	2.1	7.4
Other expenditure	10.8	10.3	6.8	7.2	4.1	4.2	8.6	8.2	2.9	2.4
Capital formation†	19.9	21.7	28.9	31.6	30.4	34.7	31.8	27.1	16.6	14.4
Construction	11.8	17.4	14.9	14.3	14.3	15.8	18.6	16.5	9.8	10.6
Producers' durables‡	7.9	4.0	10.9	13.8	12.1	14.1	12.3	9.4	4.9	1.9
Transport equipment	2.5	1.5	2.4	3.4	2.8	2.9	3.0	2.6	1.5	0.6
Machinery	4.9	2.2	7.4	9.0	7.9	9.7	7.7	5.5	2.9	1.1
Government	5.3	5.5	7.2	6.2	10.7	9.1	7.8	7.7	7.9	12.5
Gross domestic product	100.0	100.0	100.0	100.0	100.0	100.0	100.0	100.0	100.0	100.0

Source: Distribution at national prices from Table 14.2; distribution at international prices derived from Table 14.5.
†Includes net exports and increase in stocks.
‡Includes miscellaneous producers durables.

countries) as a whole. For construction, the relationship is less systematic; some low-income countries (Kenya and Hungary) also have high construction prices, but others (Colombia and India) have low ones. The result is that for capital formation as a whole, India, Kenya, and Hungary—but not Colombia—have lower GDP proportions at international than at national prices. There are also some notable differences in the consumption sector. U.S. medical care, for example, accounts for 2.7 percent of GDP at international prices versus 6.6 percent at U.S. prices.

It would be possible, of course, to extend further this verbal description of the multilateral results. Beyond the main features we have highlighted already, however, what is noteworthy will depend largely upon the interests of each reader. Therefore, we turn to Chapter 15, in which we apply some simple statistical techniques to the data.

	Italy		Japan		Kenya		United Kingdom		United States	
	Nat'l.	Int'l.	Nat'l.	Int'l.	Nat'l.	Int'l.	Nat'l.	Int'l.	Nat'l.	Int'l.
Consumption	69.8	69.0	51.0	53.9	68.5	70.2	71.0	70.8	68.1	68.6
Food, beverage, tobacco	26.3	25.3	16.7	14.9	33.5	36.2	20.4	21.1	11.7	14.5
Food	21.6	20.4	13.5	12.1	30.4	34.3	12.5	16.1	9.3	11.7
Bread and cereals	3.0	2.7	4.1	4.2	12.2	13.6	1.7	2.3	1.2	1.2
Meat and fish	7.5	6.7	3.8	3.0	3.8	4.3	4.1	5.0	3.4	4.3
Milk, cheese, eggs	2.7	2.5	1.1	1.1	4.1	3.8	1.9	2.2	1.4	1.6
Oils and fats	1.3	1.8	0.2	0.2	1.1	1.2	0.6	1.1	0.3	0.6
Fruits and vegetables	5.1	5.0	2.9	2.0	6.6	8.4	2.3	2.6	2.0	2.4
Other foods	2.1	1.8	1.5	1.6	2.6	3.0	1.9	2.9	1.0	1.7
Beverages	2.8	3.3	2.5	1.8	2.2	1.1	4.5	3.2	1.3	1.5
Tobacco	1.9	1.6	0.7	0.9	0.9	0.8	3.4	1.9	1.1	1.3
Clothing and footwear	5.8	6.1	4.1	5.3	2.7	2.7	5.5	6.4	5.3	6.8
Gross rents, fuel	8.3	10.5	7.5	6.0	7.0	5.4	11.5	10.9	11.7	11.1
Gross rents	6.3	8.8	6.2	4.9	6.0	3.8	8.5	8.0	9.5	7.9
Fuel and power	2.0	1.7	1.3	1.1	1.1	1.6	3.0	2.9	2.2	3.2
House furnishings, operation	3.7	3.9	2.5	2.6	4.2	3.6	4.9	4.8	5.3	5.6
Medical care	4.9	5.4	3.6	5.6	3.5	4.0	4.4	4.3	6.6	2.7
Transport and communication	6.5	6.2	3.4	4.8	5.0	4.2	8.1	7.8	7.3	12.8
Personal transport	4.7	4.5	1.1	0.9	1.7	1.5	5.4	5.7	7.5	11.3
Purchased transport	1.3	1.2	2.0	3.6	3.1	2.6	2.0	1.4	0.6	0.6
Communication	0.6	0.5	0.3	0.3	0.1	0.1	0.6	0.6	1.2	0.9
Recreation and education	8.7	6.2	6.8	6.6	8.1	9.3	9.8	9.3	10.6	8.2
Recreation	3.7	3.0	4.1	4.0	2.8	1.9	5.3	5.8	5.0	5.1
Education	5.0	3.2	2.7	2.6	5.3	7.3	4.5	3.5	5.5	3.1
Other expenditure	5.6	5.4	6.3	8.2	4.5	4.9	6.5	6.4	7.7	6.9
Capital Formation†	22.9	25.4	41.1	38.6	20.1	15.6	19.9	21.7	17.4	19.2
Construction	13.5	14.6	20.2	16.8	10.9	8.5	9.1	9.7	9.7	8.2
Producers' durables‡	7.8	9.0	15.3	16.1	8.6	6.3	9.3	10.3	7.3	10.3
Transport equipment	3.0	3.1	4.5	4.5	3.2	2.7	2.0	1.7	2.2	3.5
Machinery	3.8	4.9	9.6	10.4	4.6	3.0	7.0	8.1	4.3	5.7
Government	7.3	5.7	7.8	7.5	11.4	14.2	9.1	7.5	14.4	12.2
Gross domestic product	100.0	100.0	100.0	100.0	100.0	100.0	100.0	100.0	100.0	100.0

APPENDIX TO CHAPTER 14

Detailed multilateral tables

Appendix Table 14.1 Per Capita Expenditures in National Currencies, 1970

			Colombia (peso)	France (franc)	Germany, F.R. (D.mark)	Hungary (forint)	India (rupee)	Italy (lira)	Japan (yen)	Kenya (shilling)	U.K. (pound)	U.S. (dollar)
1	01.101	Rice	77.5	4.75	4.85	51.4	116.07	752.	18,447.	1.80	0.107	1.49
2	01.102	Meal, other cereals	63.9	13.29	40.53	179.8	74.34	1,710.	300.	115.79	0.714	6.49
3	01.103	Bread, rolls	46.4	150.05	117.99	301.0	0.32	14,911.	1,735.	4.76	6.662	17.96
4	01.104	Biscuits, cakes	16.7	138.67	49.01	96.7	0.30	5,950.	6,722.	2.02	6.430	19.79
5	01.105	Cereal preparations	16.8	1.89	2.41	81.1	0.40	136.	182.	0.83	1.125	8.32
6	01.106	Macaroni, spaghetti, related foods	19.1	17.09	12.69	32.5	0.41	8,207.	1,859.	0.15	0.304	1.84
7	01.111	Fresh beef, veal	286.9	300.10	69.59	81.9	0.66	36,458.	2,402.	22.43	8.395	69.83
8	01.112	Fresh lamb, mutton	4.7	24.70	0.0	17.1	1.05	1,437.	42.	2.74	4.447	2.83
9	01.113	Fresh pork	24.2	84.53	96.82	713.0	0.20	6,088.	3,438.	0.54	2.018	16.96
10	01.114	Fresh poultry	26.1	94.97	18.76	400.3	1.66	9,370.	1,720.	0.96	2.876	19.12
11	01.115	Other fresh meat	23.4	109.22	5.44	48.9	3.19	4,242.	639.	2.39	1.268	3.00
12	01.116	Frozen, salted meat	34.8	183.30	144.62	399.2	0.0	13,201.	2,442.	1.98	13.360	39.08
13	01.121	Fresh, frozen fish	5.2	77.87	7.26	29.1	6.28	5,745.	8,615.	6.54	2.500	8.15
14	01.122	Canned fish	9.2	34.19	12.71	14.6	0.0	2,803.	8,239.	0.99	1.393	3.83
15	01.131	Fresh milk	93.1	81.67	52.04	272.2	20.95	8,139.	3,854.	37.64	9.180	36.25
16	01.132	Milk products	35.1	166.20	44.78	129.4	3.13	15,047.	856.	4.07	3.786	16.79
17	01.133	Eggs, egg products	41.3	54.14	47.19	292.3	0.84	5,814.	3,405.	0.33	3.983	14.30
18	01.141	Butter	15.8	114.92	80.48	88.5	17.55	3,214.	186.	5.48	3.161	4.82
19	01.142	Margarine, edible oil	66.4	40.85	44.17	37.0	20.02	10,669.	1,064.	4.76	1.179	10.48
20	01.143	Lard, edible fat	6.3	0.0	0.0	436.5	0.0	0.	11.	1.15	0.589	0.83
21	01.151	Fresh fruits, tropical, subtropical	111.0	56.03	24.20	102.8	3.97	7,113.	3,530.	13.27	1.840	7.97
22	01.152	Other fresh fruits	4.9	94.97	36.30	323.4	0.74	12,858.	3,648.	0.32	2.608	12.13
23	01.153	Fresh vegetables	74.7	160.51	37.52	283.8	10.03	24,349.	8,321.	19.72	5.037	25.44
24	01.161	Fruit other than fresh	5.2	17.09	23.00	52.1	0.28	3,693.	796.	0.11	2.233	20.61
25	01.162	Vegetables other than fresh	68.2	52.23	44.78	55.7	17.96	2,530.	3,558.	3.61	3.983	20.78
26	01.170	Potatoes, manioc, other tubers	68.9	46.54	30.25	180.6	5.01	3,147.	1,051.	31.07	4.626	11.48
27	01.191	Coffee	33.4	52.23	85.31	206.9	1.69	6,291.	361.	0.96	1.161	11.64
28	01.192	Tea	0.8	2.86	6.66	11.6	4.54	273.	1,114.	3.49	2.965	2.16
29	01.193	Cocoa	22.7	6.66	7.26	11.3	0.0	205.	159.	0.26	0.107	0.83
30	01.180	Sugar	78.1	30.39	41.76	228.0	18.98	5,200.	987.	13.46	2.215	4.49
31	01.201	Jam, syrup, honey	9.2	15.20	12.10	6.1	0.54	1,163.	1,538.	2.69	1.143	4.99
32	01.202	Chocolate, ice cream	5.4	72.18	61.11	359.4	1.52	5,882.	1,431.	1.96	8.805	15.13
33	01.203	Salt, spices, sauces	29.8	11.40	3.62	169.0	17.03	3,147.	4,937.	3.90	1.000	6.98
34	01.310	Nonalcoholic beverages	10.4	33.24	19.36	36.3	0.43	3,147.	2,145.	5.86	2.947	13.13
35	01.321	Spirits	33.3	48.43	44.78	183.1	0.15	4,651.	1,242.	2.05	10.431	19.91
36	01.322	Wine, cider	11.7	279.23	38.12	357.4	1.50	19,015.	9,554.	0.47	4.930	4.25
37	01.323	Beer	8.9	23.75	62.32	125.2	0.41	3,011.	4,871.	13.73	22.219	24.92
38	01.410	Cigarettes	22.1	125.35	145.21	287.1	1.20	19,015.	4,876.	9.33	26.845	50.83
39	01.420	Other tobacco	7.3	20.90	15.74	4.5	11.75	1,299.	8.	0.20	3.858	4.29
40	02.110	Clothing materials	21.0	34.15	27.83	168.1	8.50	5,541.	8,873.	5.31	1.286	5.81
41	02.121	Men's clothing	73.9	244.07	130.08	417.0	4.66	12,107.	4,747.	7.92	7.573	49.80
42	02.122	Women's clothing	33.3	188.04	148.24	353.4	6.55	6,293.	5,659.	4.59	12.556	78.29
43	02.123	Boys', girls' clothing	22.5	28.50	47.80	224.3	0.68	5,060.	2,192.	2.36	2.483	23.88
44	02.131	Men's, boys' underwear	11.9	76.93	44.17	138.0	0.04	12,381.	1,719.	0.55	4.019	10.72
45	02.132	Women's, girls' underwear	20.6	146.25	108.30	140.8	0.04	5,473.	1,425.	0.47	5.412	28.86
46	02.150	Other clothing	15.2	72.18	55.06	224.6	0.02	1,299.	1,673.	0.66	5.698	12.94
47	02.160	Clothing rental, repair	6.6	14.24	7.87	72.6	0.55	2,462.	1,250.	0.62	0.857	4.28
48	02.211	Men's footwear	19.6	46.54	24.20	141.9	0.75	4,719.	869.	3.34	2.590	11.97
49	02.212	Women's footwear	15.5	56.03	33.29	188.9	0.75	1,915.	916.	0.83	3.554	15.77
50	02.213	Children's footwear	13.4	37.05	39.32	67.3	0.38	2,803.	501.	0.65	1.929	11.99
51	02.220	Footwear repairs	3.5	10.44	25.42	38.7	0.14	1,095.	62.	0.27	0.750	2.07
52	03.110	Gross rents	499.8	817.51	673.24	663.5	22.14	65,324.	42,527.	61.15	63.423	437.06
53	03.120	Indoor repair, upkeep	60.2	149.11	42.35	171.7	2.17	1,367.	2,014.	0.20	12.699	17.98
54	03.210	Electricity	35.2	98.77	99.23	160.9	1.15	9,781.	4,300.	1.43	11.770	48.39
55	03.220	Gas	11.9	82.62	38.71	84.0	0.04	5,609.	2,755.	0.11	6.876	29.45

Appendix Table 14.1. Continued

			Colombia (peso)	France (franc)	Germany, F.R. (D.mark)	Hungary (forint)	India (rupee)	Italy (lira)	Japan (yen)	Kenya (shilling)	U.K. (pound)	U.S. (dollar)
56	03.230	Liquid fuels	18.0	56.98	41.76	45.6	5.29	4,515.	889.	1.38	1.107	22.93
57	03.240	Other fuels, ice	6.3	61.72	52.65	308.7	23.57	1,848.	1,360.	8.12	6.823	4.44
58	04.110	Furniture, fixtures	103.7	208.94	158.53	377.3	0.54	9,575.	2,417.	6.00	6.162	52.56
59	04.120	Floor coverings	6.6	26.59	33.89	54.7	1.99	890.	935.	0.98	4.912	38.57
60	04.200	Household textiles, etc.	37.9	84.53	93.77	214.0	3.83	4,446.	988.	3.85	1.429	14.79
61	04.310	Refrigerators, etc.	7.9	26.59	14.53	90.3	0.69	958.	1,927.	0.59	1.875	8.29
62	04.320	Washing appliances	9.3	48.43	31.45	43.6	0.0	2,257.	898.	0.08	1.661	9.13
63	04.330	Cooking appliances	20.3	28.50	11.49	79.7	0.01	1,299.	358.	0.62	1.554	4.44
64	04.340	Heating appliances	4.3	20.90	12.10	39.2	0.01	752.	972.	0.56	1.107	2.44
65	04.350	Cleaning appliances	9.7	14.24	11.49	15.8	0.0	341.	426.	0.10	0.321	3.47
66	04.360	Other household appliances	4.9	17.09	19.36	15.9	0.06	547.	938.	0.24	6.716	20.13
67	04.400	Household utensils	13.9	82.62	88.95	205.7	4.07	3,556.	2,794.	6.79	6.090	27.34
68	04.510	Nondurable household goods	71.9	119.66	100.45	232.9	3.91	5,677.	2,169.	16.19	2.822	23.23
69	04.520	Domestic services	85.3	0.0	0.0	36.7	2.22	0.	405.	6.37	3.590	21.53
70	04.530	Household services	19.1	44.63	35.70	24.4	3.50	8,687.	2,814.	1.14	0.804	7.87
71	04.600	Household furnishing repairs	0.0	0.0	0.0	117.9	1.16	0.	211.	0.08	6.555	38.26
72	05.110	Drugs, medical preparations	32.7	382.82	189.56	330.1	10.33	22,393.	8,642.	7.06	1.107	5.22
73	05.120	Medical supplies	0.0	7.60	19.18	86.0	0.96	154.	8,759.	0.55	1.911	9.28
74	05.200	Therapeutic equipment	4.3	21.64	50.60	0.0	0.24	347.	261.	0.09	5.644	47.38
75	05.310	Physicians' services	41.7	277.16	195.04	108.1	1.21	14,656.	1,553.	5.05	1.822	13.88
76	05.320	Dentists' services	9.2	153.85	72.61	8.4	0.01	6,499.	334.	0.40	9.573	82.89
77	05.330	Services, nurses, other personnel	3.9	31.71	43.94	113.9	1.79	1,734.	1,372.	5.36	12.502	117.82
78	05.410	Hospitals, etc.	32.7	38.19	44.01	446.4	1.71	5,884.	5,243.	17.79	17.003	137.80
79	06.110	Personal cars	207.6	245.04	174.86	254.4	0.99	17,235.	2,291.	11.14	1.072	20.36
80	06.120	Other personal transport	0.7	19.95	9.67	91.8	1.19	822.	1,000.	0.11	4.465	27.50
81	06.210	Tires, tubes, accessories	22.9	81.67	43.57	48.1	0.57	2,394.	173.	2.18	4.215	37.82
82	06.220	Repair charges	40.6	174.75	87.74	55.2	0.87	6,361.	1,108.	2.18	14.146	112.64
83	06.230	Gasoline, oil, etc.	31.3	209.88	188.78	72.0	1.57	18,125.	2,314.	1.16	7.519	23.32
84	06.240	Parking, tolls, etc.	32.5	86.42	42.96	7.3	0.81	4,651.	1,090.	0.86	9.609	12.41
85	06.310	Local transport	59.5	60.78	30.86	147.1	3.66	6,293.	9,945.	2.24	2.518	0.73
86	06.321	Rail transport	31.5	45.38	63.47	141.3	3.92	4,205.	3,059.	1.40	0.500	1.95
87	06.322	Bus transport	6.4	47.13	27.61	162.6	12.61	2,651.	818.	13.24	3.394	11.92
88	06.323	Air transport	77.8	8.17	2.69	24.2	0.08	393.	328.	15.06	1.822	3.67
89	06.330	Miscellaneous transport	0.0	0.0	0.0	28.9	3.46	0.	410.	0.22	1.947	7.49
90	06.410	Postal communication	2.1	21.84	34.50	37.3	0.84	2,462.	254.	0.41	3.751	48.49
91	06.420	Telephone, telegraph	22.7	29.44	19.96	30.5	1.03	3,899.	1,734.	1.02	3.215	40.62
92	07.110	Radio, TV, phonograph, etc.	53.1	134.87	54.45	253.5	1.10	5,335.	6,169.	3.75	1.661	26.29
93	07.120	Major durable recreation equip.	6.8	34.19	40.53	9.7	0.08	205.	970.	5.43	11.002	39.81
94	07.130	Other recreation equipment	14.9	180.44	196.63	84.9	0.15	6,431.	4,299.	3.72	6.876	28.80
95	07.210	Public entertainment	85.4	40.85	31.45	236.5	0.35	11,150.	10,173.	5.61	14.485	57.68
96	07.230	Other recreation, cultural events	16.6	58.89	61.72	248.5	1.55	3,214.	2,310.	4.06	8.269	37.14
97	07.310	Books, papers, magazines	32.1	173.80	83.49	194.9	2.53	11,150.	4,566.	6.00	1.947	11.10
98	07.320	Stationery	2.3	97.82	30.25	65.1	0.72	1,848.	917.	0.09	23.719	185.05
99	07.411	Teachers, 1st, 2nd	140.6	618.09	338.78	510.4	11.63	42,795.	12,083.	40.04	4.787	35.19
100	07.412	Teachers, college	36.0	91.56	67.83	52.6	1.58	5,073.	2,170.	2.22	5.590	29.04
101	07.420	Educational facilities	12.1	35.69	63.83	272.8	0.73	2,829.	2,632.	5.72	2.054	7.54
102	07.431	Educational supplies	19.5	5.49	2.98	28.3	0.65	483.	877.	2.35	3.751	8.48
103	07.432	Other education expenditures	30.8	5.81	22.91	130.5	0.82	1,514.	1,939.	3.79	4.037	19.91
104	08.100	Barber, beauty shops	14.6	73.13	45.98	94.4	1.16	7,113.	4,165.	0.46	4.251	29.85
105	08.210	Toilet articles	48.9	118.38	56.64	135.1	3.13	5,724.	5,260.	2.62	4.572	30.29
106	08.220	Other personal-care goods	15.9	144.69	69.23	202.8	3.13	6,998.	1,417.	2.62	16.289	140.16
107	08.310	Restaurants, cafes	253.9	520.44	178.48	1726.8	5.14	25,993.	13,038.	13.80	10.413	8.67
108	08.320	Hotels, etc.	19.0	207.99	78.67	64.6	5.14	12,243.	5,056.	14.48	18.486	142.45
109	08.400	Other services	310.2	31.33	34.50	450.8	3.59	1,780.	16,720.	11.97	18.414	103.98
111	10.100	1- and 2-dwelling buildings	168.0	362.38	149.87	730.8	14.05	56,084.	34,424.	37.06	8.591	43.16
112	10.200	Multidwelling buildings	21.7	751.73	459.11	796.1	14.05	18,676.	16,084.	5.56	0.643	6.69
113	11.100	Hotels, etc.	5.6	22.85	23.61	106.6	0.51	1,831.	2,233.	0.78	13.663	36.17
114	11.200	Industrial buildings	57.3	143.77	218.08	1030.7	1.17	19,336.	7,091.	14.51	4.626	25.28
115	11.300	Commercial buildings	18.0	115.21	65.59	163.6	3.13	2,747.	7,092.	2.87	3.126	32.68
116	11.400	Office buildings	36.1	121.12	81.98	176.7	1.30	7,691.	7,845.	3.71	6.055	32.17
117	11.500	Educational buildings	16.9	129.98	96.74	140.6	0.79	3,662.	4,918.	3.64	2.983	16.81
118	11.600	Hospital buildings	6.3	43.33	45.91	49.1	0.50	2,563.	1,715.	3.71	1.643	3.36
119	11.700	Agricultural buildings	33.1	88.62	32.79	725.6	4.64	4,578.	1,200.	0.74	3.590	18.38
120	11.800	Other buildings	6.5	129.98	9.84	49.9	1.10	1,831.	9,592.	0.93	8.216	51.45
121	12.100	Roads, highways	107.1	128.01	172.17	287.1	3.84	9,045.	14,244.	11.60	4.858	70.11
122	12.200	Transmission, utility lines	89.3	331.65	221.36	926.7	11.11	8,752.	16,736.	8.76	2.572	13.57
123	12.300	Other construction	62.4	22.85	24.60	485.7	7.93	695.	22,127.	13.96	2.143	10.14
124	13.000	Land improvement	95.9	11.82	8.20	130.8	8.13	5,493.	516.	4.59	0.143	1.16
125	14.110	Locomotives	0.1	15.16	2.05	71.9	0.38	750.	782.	2.79	0.232	6.33
126	14.120	Other	2.0	23.48	9.99	149.8	0.85	769.	89.	4.95	6.090	34.27
127	14.200	Passenger cars	42.2	125.06	104.46	61.3	0.38	12,285.	11,408.	10.22	0.625	44.01
128	14.300	Trucks, buses, trailers	60.0	183.30	113.24	389.4	7.01	12,304.	14,279.	11.71	1.804	14.40
129	14.400	Aircraft	19.3	11.30	23.50	28.9	0.25	2,180.	364.	2.71	5.698	3.96
130	14.500	Ships, boats	29.0	23.16	57.01	16.0	0.76	2,343.	3,924.	0.46	3.590	1.71
131	14.600	Other transport	1.5	1.30	0.48	221.9	1.26	1,172.	1,497.	0.54	0.107	6.46
132	15.100	Engines and turbines	9.1	10.83	5.66	80.4	1.09	732.	2,070.	2.18		

Appendix Table 14.1. Continued

			Colombia (peso)	France (franc)	Germany, F.R. (D.mark)	Hungary (forint)	India (rupee)	Italy (lira)	Japan (yen)	Kenya (shilling)	U.K. (pound)	U.S. (dollar)
133	15.210	Tractors	8.8	55.95	19.40	124.8	0.62	1,393.	410.	2.40	0.929	8.24
134	15.220	Other agricultural machinery	12.1	94.53	25.83	184.1	0.12	1,831.	1,916.	3.39	1.375	11.81
135	15.300	Office machinery	12.1	121.77	88.63	119.6	0.19	2,106.	5,508.	1.87	3.108	32.00
136	15.400	Metalworking machinery	23.1	56.21	67.93	199.7	1.11	3,460.	7,482.	1.15	4.376	17.83
137	15.500	Construction, mining	32.4	160.53	74.39	210.1	0.75	2,070.	4,720.	4.75	4.590	16.37
138	15.600	Special industrial	44.6	186.86	109.27	777.6	2.02	5,090.	12,427.	10.20	7.591	15.33
139	15.700	General industrial	59.2	89.57	168.20	254.3	5.53	5,365.	11,744.	9.64	21.058	19.79
140	15.800	Service industrial	2.2	17.72	19.68	38.0	0.42	916.	1,052.	2.07	0.572	17.01
141	16.100	Electrical transmission	27.1	146.51	102.79	81.4	4.28	8,020.	7,658.	4.12	6.463	13.62
142	16.200	Communication equipment	17.7	100.28	101.76	110.5	4.15	3,150.	8,000.	2.93	8.502	25.45
143	16.300	Other electrical	33.3	28.34	22.40	21.3	0.75	3,460.	2,203.	1.12	1.786	3.88
144	16.400	Instruments	17.9	122.09	85.03	194.5	0.46	2,893.	4,144.	1.43	1.715	16.52
145	17.100	Furniture, fixtures	17.8	69.91	78.74	435.4	0.13	3,442.	5,359.	2.00	1.911	19.45
146	17.200	Other durable goods	14.5	116.85	78.89	44.9	3.44	6,994.	2,864.	5.35	0.429	19.52
147	18.000	Increase in stocks	106.7	464.67	250.87	1193.1	19.10	16,586.	31,443.	23.83	6.626	16.60
148	19.000	Exports less imports	-99.4	32.79	205.45	-907.8	-4.91	1,009.	9,113.	-17.78	7.019	7.42
149	20.100	Blue-collar, unskilled	39.1	23.48	34.20	220.4	11.38	13,955.	9,844.	44.13	22.254	18.33
150	20.210	Blue-collar, skilled	8.7	139.24	95.50	12.5	0.93	6,148.	19,445.	3.12	2.751	94.41
151	20.220	White-collar	52.7	266.07	333.60	205.5	12.79	23,314.	4,780.	12.07	17.575	108.62
152	20.300	Professional	100.0	201.28	64.44	186.0	8.50	3,941.	6,441.	29.90	8.002	132.96
153	21.000	Government expenditure commodities	120.5	523.89	677.09	1789.9	24.63	30,209.	16,047.	28.21	30.667	338.05

Note: The net expenditure of residents abroad, line 110 in the binary tables, has been consolidated with other services (line 109) in the multilateral comparisons. Thus, there are 152 categories in this table. See page 70.

Appendix Table 14.2. Percentage Distribution of Expenditures in National Currencies, 1970

			Colombia	France	Germany, F.R.	Hungary	India	Italy	Japan	Kenya	U.K.	U.S.
1	01.101	Rice	1.27	0.03	0.04	0.17	15.77	0.07	2.56	0.18	0.01	0.03
2	01.102	Meal, other cereals	1.05	0.08	0.36	0.58	10.10	0.16	0.04	11.27	0.08	0.14
3	01.103	Bread, rolls	0.76	0.93	1.05	0.97	0.04	1.40	0.24	0.46	0.75	0.37
4	01.104	Biscuits, cakes	0.27	0.86	0.43	0.31	0.04	0.56	0.93	0.20	0.72	0.41
5	01.105	Cereal preparations	0.27	0.01	0.02	0.26	0.05	0.01	0.03	0.08	0.13	0.17
6	01.106	Macaroni, spaghetti, related foods	0.31	0.11	0.11	0.10	0.06	0.77	0.26	0.01	0.03	0.04
7	01.111	Fresh beef, veal	4.69	1.86	0.62	0.26	0.09	3.43	0.33	2.18	0.94	1.45
8	01.112	Fresh lamb, mutton	0.08	0.15	0.0	0.06	0.14	0.14	0.01	0.27	0.50	0.06
9	01.113	Fresh pork	0.40	0.52	0.86	2.29	0.03	0.57	0.48	0.05	0.23	0.35
10	01.114	Fresh poultry	0.43	0.59	0.17	1.29	0.23	0.88	0.24	0.09	0.32	0.40
11	01.115	Other fresh meat	0.38	0.68	0.05	0.16	0.43	0.40	0.09	0.23	0.14	0.06
12	01.116	Frozen, salted meat	0.57	1.14	1.28	1.28	0.0	1.24	0.34	0.19	1.50	0.81
13	01.121	Fresh, frozen fish	0.08	0.48	0.06	0.09	0.85	0.54	1.20	0.64	0.28	0.17
14	01.122	Canned fish	0.15	0.21	0.11	0.05	0.0	0.26	1.14	0.10	0.16	0.08
15	01.131	Fresh milk	1.52	0.51	0.46	0.87	2.85	0.77	0.53	3.66	1.03	0.75
16	01.132	Milk products	0.57	1.03	0.40	0.42	0.43	1.42	0.12	0.40	0.42	0.35
17	01.133	Eggs, egg products	0.68	0.34	0.42	0.94	0.11	0.55	0.47	0.03	0.45	0.30
18	01.141	Butter	0.26	0.71	0.71	0.28	2.38	0.30	0.03	0.53	0.35	0.10
19	01.142	Margarine, edible oil	1.09	0.25	0.39	0.12	2.72	1.00	0.15	0.46	0.13	0.22
20	01.143	Lard, edible fat	0.10	0.0	0.0	1.40	0.0	0.0	0.00	0.11	0.07	0.02
21	01.151	Fresh fruits, tropical, subtropical	1.82	0.35	0.21	0.33	0.54	0.67	0.49	1.29	0.21	0.17
22	01.152	Other fresh fruits	0.08	0.59	0.32	1.04	0.10	1.21	0.51	0.03	0.29	0.25
23	01.153	Fresh vegetables	1.22	1.00	0.33	0.91	1.36	2.29	1.15	1.92	0.56	0.53
24	01.161	Fruit other than fresh	0.09	0.11	0.20	0.17	0.04	0.35	0.11	0.01	0.25	0.43
25	01.162	Vegetables other than fresh	1.11	0.32	0.40	0.18	2.44	0.24	0.49	0.35	0.25	0.43
26	01.170	Potatoes, manioc, other tubers	1.13	0.29	0.27	0.58	0.68	0.30	0.15	3.02	0.52	0.24
27	01.191	Coffee	0.55	0.32	0.76	0.66	0.23	0.59	0.05	0.09	0.13	0.24
28	01.192	Tea	0.01	0.02	0.06	0.04	0.62	0.03	0.15	0.34	0.33	0.05
29	01.193	Cocoa	0.37	0.04	0.06	0.04	0.0	0.02	0.02	0.03	0.01	0.02
30	01.180	Sugar	1.28	0.19	0.37	0.73	2.58	0.49	0.14	1.31	0.25	0.09
31	01.201	Jam, syrup, honey	0.15	0.09	0.11	0.02	0.07	0.11	0.21	0.26	0.13	0.10
32	01.202	Chocolate, ice cream	0.09	0.45	0.54	1.16	0.21	0.55	0.20	0.19	0.99	0.32
33	01.203	Salt, spices, sauces	0.49	0.07	0.03	0.54	2.31	0.30	0.69	0.38	0.11	0.15
34	01.310	Nonalcoholic beverages	0.17	0.21	0.17	0.12	0.06	0.30	0.30	0.57	0.33	0.27
35	01.321	Spirits	0.54	0.30	0.40	0.59	0.02	0.44	0.17	0.20	1.17	0.41
36	01.322	Wine, cider	0.19	1.73	0.34	1.15	0.20	1.79	1.33	0.05	0.55	0.09
37	01.323	Beer	0.15	0.15	0.55	0.40	0.06	0.28	0.68	1.34	2.49	0.52
38	01.410	Cigarettes	0.36	0.78	1.29	0.92	0.16	1.79	0.68	0.91	3.01	1.06

Appendix Table 14.2. Continued

			Colombia	France	Germany, F.R.	Hungary	India	Italy	Japan	Kenya	U.K.	U.S.
39	01.420	Other tobacco	0.12	0.13	0.14	0.01	1.60	0.12	0.00	0.02	0.43	0.09
40	02.110	Clothing materials	0.34	0.21	0.25	0.54	1.15	0.52	1.23	0.52	0.14	0.12
41	02.121	Men's clothing	1.21	1.51	1.15	1.34	0.63	1.14	0.66	0.77	0.85	1.04
42	02.122	Women's clothing	0.55	1.17	1.32	1.14	0.89	0.59	0.79	0.45	1.41	1.63
43	02.123	Boys', girls' clothing	0.37	0.18	0.42	0.72	0.09	0.48	0.30	0.23	0.28	0.50
44	02.131	Men's, boys' underwear	0.19	0.48	0.39	0.44	0.01	1.17	0.24	0.05	0.45	0.22
45	02.132	Women's, girls' underwear	0.34	0.91	0.96	0.45	0.01	0.52	0.20	0.05	0.61	0.60
46	02.150	Other clothing	0.25	0.45	0.49	0.72	0.00	0.12	0.23	0.06	0.64	0.27
47	02.160	Clothing rental, repair	0.11	0.09	0.07	0.23	0.08	0.23	0.17	0.06	0.10	0.09
48	02.211	Men's footwear	0.32	0.29	0.21	0.46	0.10	0.44	0.12	0.32	0.29	0.25
49	02.212	Women's footwear	0.25	0.35	0.30	0.61	0.10	0.18	0.13	0.08	0.40	0.33
50	02.213	Children's footwear	0.22	0.23	0.35	0.22	0.05	0.26	0.07	0.06	0.22	0.25
51	02.220	Footwear repairs	0.06	0.06	0.23	0.12	0.02	0.10	0.01	0.03	0.08	0.04
52	03.110	Gross rents	8.18	5.07	5.97	2.13	3.01	6.15	5.90	5.95	7.10	9.10
53	03.120	Indoor repair, upkeep	0.98	0.93	0.38	0.55	0.30	0.13	0.28	0.02	1.42	0.37
54	03.210	Electricity	0.58	0.61	0.88	0.52	0.16	0.92	0.60	0.14	1.32	1.01
55	03.220	Gas	0.20	0.51	0.34	0.27	0.01	0.53	0.38	0.01	0.77	0.61
56	03.230	Liquid fuels	0.29	0.35	0.37	0.15	0.72	0.43	0.12	0.13	0.12	0.48
57	03.240	Other fuels, ice	0.10	0.38	0.47	0.99	3.20	0.17	0.19	0.79	0.76	0.09
58	04.110	Furniture, fixtures	1.70	1.30	1.41	1.21	0.07	0.90	0.34	0.58	0.69	1.09
59	04.120	Floor coverings	0.11	0.16	0.30	0.18	0.27	0.08	0.13	0.10	0.56	0.38
60	04.200	Household textiles, etc.	0.62	0.52	0.83	0.69	0.52	0.42	0.14	0.37	0.55	0.80
61	04.310	Refrigerators, etc.	0.13	0.16	0.13	0.29	0.09	0.09	0.27	0.06	0.16	0.31
62	04.320	Washing appliances	0.15	0.30	0.28	0.14	0.0	0.21	0.12	0.01	0.21	0.17
63	04.330	Cooking appliances	0.33	0.18	0.10	0.26	0.00	0.12	0.05	0.06	0.19	0.19
64	04.340	Heating appliances	0.07	0.13	0.11	0.13	0.00	0.07	0.13	0.05	0.17	0.09
65	04.350	Cleaning appliances	0.16	0.09	0.10	0.05	0.0	0.03	0.06	0.01	0.12	0.05
66	04.360	Other household appliances	0.08	0.11	0.17	0.05	0.01	0.05	0.13	0.02	0.04	0.07
67	04.400	Household utensils	0.23	0.51	0.79	0.66	0.55	0.33	0.39	0.66	0.75	0.42
68	04.510	Nondurable household goods	1.18	0.74	0.89	0.75	0.53	0.53	0.30	1.58	0.68	0.57
69	04.520	Domestic services	1.40	0.0	0.0	0.12	0.30	0.0	0.06	0.62	0.32	0.48
70	04.530	Household services	0.31	0.28	0.32	0.08	0.48	0.82	0.39	0.11	0.40	0.45
71	04.600	Household furnishing repairs	0.0	0.0	0.0	0.38	0.16	0.0	0.03	0.01	0.09	0.16
72	05.110	Drugs, medical preparations	0.54	2.38	1.68	1.06	1.40	2.11	1.20	0.69	0.73	0.80
73	05.120	Medical supplies	0.0	0.05	0.17	0.28	0.13	0.01	1.22	0.05	0.12	0.11
74	05.200	Therapeutic equipment	0.07	0.13	0.45	0.0	0.03	0.03	0.04	0.01	0.21	0.19
75	05.310	Physicians' services	0.68	1.72	1.73	0.35	0.16	1.38	0.22	0.49	0.63	0.99
76	05.320	Dentists' services	0.15	0.95	0.64	0.03	0.00	0.61	0.05	0.04	0.20	0.29
77	05.330	Services, nurses, other personnel	0.06	0.20	0.39	0.37	0.24	0.16	0.19	0.52	1.07	1.73
78	05.410	Hospitals, etc.	0.54	0.24	0.39	1.43	0.23	0.55	0.73	1.73	1.40	2.45
79	06.110	Personal cars	3.40	1.52	1.55	0.82	0.13	1.62	0.32	1.08	1.90	2.87
80	06.120	Other personal transport	0.01	0.12	0.09	0.29	0.16	0.08	0.14	0.01	0.12	0.42
81	06.210	Tires, tubes, accessories	0.38	0.51	0.39	0.15	0.08	0.23	0.02	0.21	0.50	0.57
82	06.220	Repair charges	0.66	1.08	0.78	0.18	0.12	0.60	0.15	0.21	0.47	0.79
83	06.230	Gasoline, oil, etc.	0.51	1.30	1.67	0.23	0.21	1.71	0.32	0.11	1.58	2.35
84	06.240	Parking, tolls, etc.	0.53	0.54	0.38	0.02	0.11	0.44	0.15	0.08	0.84	0.49
85	06.310	Local transport	0.97	0.38	0.27	0.47	0.50	0.59	1.38	0.22	1.08	0.26
86	06.321	Rail transport	0.51	0.28	0.56	0.45	0.53	0.40	0.42	0.14	0.28	0.02
87	06.322	Bus transport	0.10	0.29	0.24	0.52	1.71	0.25	0.11	1.29	0.06	0.04
88	06.323	Air transport	1.27	0.05	0.02	0.08	0.01	0.04	0.05	1.47	0.38	0.25
89	06.330	Miscellaneous transport	0.0	0.0	0.0	0.09	0.47	0.0	0.06	0.02	0.20	0.08
90	06.410	Postal communication	0.03	0.14	0.31	0.12	0.11	0.23	0.04	0.04	0.22	0.16
91	06.420	Telephone, telegraph	0.37	0.18	0.18	0.10	0.14	0.37	0.24	0.10	0.42	1.01
92	07.110	Radio, TV, phonograph, etc.	0.87	0.84	0.48	0.81	0.15	0.50	0.86	0.37	0.36	0.85
93	07.120	Major durable recreation equip.	0.11	0.21	0.36	0.03	0.01	0.02	0.13	0.53	0.19	0.55
94	07.130	Other recreation equipment	0.24	1.12	1.74	0.27	0.02	0.61	0.60	0.36	1.23	0.83
95	07.210	Public entertainment	1.40	0.25	0.28	0.76	0.05	1.05	1.41	0.55	0.77	0.60
96	07.230	Other recreation, cultural events	0.27	0.37	0.55	0.80	0.21	0.30	0.32	0.40	1.62	1.20
97	07.310	Books, papers, magazines	0.52	1.08	0.74	0.63	0.34	1.05	0.63	0.58	0.93	0.77
98	07.320	Stationery	0.04	0.61	0.27	0.21	0.10	0.17	0.13	0.01	0.22	0.23
99	07.411	Teachers, 1st, 2nd	2.30	3.83	3.01	1.64	1.58	4.03	1.68	3.90	2.66	3.85
100	07.412	Teachers, college	0.59	0.57	0.60	0.17	0.21	0.48	0.30	0.22	0.54	0.73
101	07.420	Educational facilities	0.20	0.22	0.57	0.88	0.10	0.27	0.37	0.56	0.63	0.60
102	07.431	Educational supplies	0.32	0.03	0.03	0.09	0.09	0.05	0.12	0.23	0.23	0.16
103	07.432	Other education expenditures	0.50	0.04	0.20	0.42	0.11	0.14	0.27	0.37	0.42	0.18
104	08.100	Barber, beauty shops	0.24	0.45	0.41	0.30	0.16	0.67	0.58	0.04	0.45	0.41
105	08.210	Toilet articles	0.80	0.73	0.50	0.43	0.43	0.54	0.73	0.26	0.48	0.62
106	08.220	Other personal-care goods	0.26	0.90	0.61	0.65	0.43	0.66	0.20	0.26	0.51	0.63
107	08.310	Restaurants, cafes	4.15	3.23	1.58	5.55	0.70	2.45	1.81	1.34	1.82	2.92
108	08.320	Hotels, etc.	0.31	1.29	0.70	0.21	0.70	1.15	0.70	1.41	1.17	0.18
109	08.400	Other services	5.07	0.19	0.31	1.45	0.49	0.17	2.32	1.17	2.07	2.97
111	10.100	1- and 2-dwelling buildings	2.75	2.25	1.33	2.35	1.91	5.28	4.78	3.61	2.06	2.17
112	10.200	Multidwelling buildings	0.35	4.66	4.07	2.56	1.91	1.76	2.23	0.54	0.96	0.90
113	11.100	Hotels, etc.	0.09	0.14	0.21	0.34	0.07	0.17	0.31	0.08	0.07	0.14
114	11.200	Industrial buildings	0.94	0.89	1.93	3.31	0.16	1.82	0.98	1.41	1.53	0.75
115	11.300	Commercial buildings	0.29	0.71	0.58	0.53	0.43	0.26	0.98	0.28	0.52	0.53
116	11.400	Office buildings	0.59	0.75	0.73	0.57	0.18	0.72	1.09	0.36	0.35	0.68

Appendix Table 14.2. Continued

#	code		Colombia	France	Germany, F.R.	Hungary	India	Italy	Japan	Kenya	U.K.	U.S.
117	11.500	Educational buildings	0.28	0.81	0.86	0.45	0.11	0.34	0.68	0.35	0.68	0.67
118	11.600	Hospital buildings	0.10	0.27	0.41	0.16	0.07	0.24	0.24	0.36	0.33	0.35
119	11.700	Agricultural buildings	0.54	0.55	0.29	2.33	0.63	0.43	0.17	0.07	0.18	0.07
120	11.800	Other buildings	0.11	0.81	0.09	0.16	0.15	0.17	1.33	0.09	0.40	0.38
121	12.100	Roads, highways	1.75	0.79	1.53	0.92	0.52	0.85	1.98	1.13	0.92	1.07
122	12.200	Transmission, utility lines	1.46	2.06	1.96	2.98	1.51	0.82	2.32	0.85	0.54	1.46
123	12.300	Other construction	1.02	0.14	0.22	1.56	1.08	0.07	3.07	1.36	0.29	0.28
124	13.000	Land improvement	1.57	0.07	0.07	0.42	1.10	0.52	0.07	0.45	0.24	0.21
125	14.110	Locomotives	0.00	0.09	0.02	0.23	0.05	0.07	0.11	0.27	0.02	0.02
126	14.120	Other	0.03	0.15	0.09	0.48	0.11	0.07	0.01	0.48	0.03	0.13
127	14.200	Passenger cars	0.69	0.78	0.93	0.20	0.05	1.16	1.58	0.99	0.68	0.71
128	14.300	Trucks, buses, trailers	0.98	1.14	1.00	1.25	0.95	1.16	1.98	1.14	0.07	0.92
129	14.400	Aircraft	0.32	0.07	0.21	0.09	0.03	0.21	0.05	0.26	0.20	0.30
130	14.500	Ships, boats	0.47	0.14	0.51	0.05	0.10	0.22	0.54	0.04	0.64	0.08
131	14.600	Other transport	0.02	0.01	0.00	0.71	0.17	0.11	0.21	0.05	0.40	0.04
132	15.100	Engines and turbines	0.15	0.07	0.05	0.26	0.15	0.07	0.29	0.21	0.01	0.13
133	15.210	Tractors	0.14	0.35	0.17	0.40	0.08	0.13	0.06	0.23	0.10	0.13
134	15.220	Other agricultural machinery	0.20	0.59	0.23	0.59	0.02	0.17	0.27	0.33	0.15	0.2.
135	15.300	Office machinery	0.20	0.76	0.79	0.38	0.03	0.17	0.76	0.18	0.35	0.25
136	15.400	Metalworking machinery	0.38	0.35	0.60	0.64	0.15	0.20	1.04	0.11	0.49	0.67
137	15.500	Construction, mining	0.53	1.00	0.66	0.68	0.10	0.19	0.66	0.46	0.51	0.37
138	15.600	Special industrial	0.73	1.16	0.97	2.50	0.27	0.48	1.72	0.99	0.85	0.34
139	15.700	General industrial	0.97	0.56	1.49	0.82	0.75	0.50	1.63	0.94	2.36	0.32
140	15.800	Service industrial	0.04	0.11	0.17	0.12	0.06	0.09	0.15	0.20	0.06	0.41
141	16.100	Electrical transmission	0.44	0.91	0.91	0.26	0.58	0.75	1.06	0.40	0.73	0.28
142	16.200	Communication equipment	0.29	0.62	0.90	0.36	0.56	0.30	1.11	0.29	0.95	0.53
143	16.300	Other electrical	0.55	0.18	0.20	0.07	0.10	0.33	0.31	0.11	0.20	0.08
144	16.400	Instruments	0.29	0.76	0.75	0.62	0.06	0.27	0.58	0.14	0.19	0.34
145	17.100	Furniture, fixtures	0.29	0.43	0.70	1.40	0.02	0.32	0.74	0.19	0.21	0.41
146	17.200	Other durable goods	0.24	0.72	0.70	0.14	0.47	0.66	0.40	0.52	0.05	0.41
147	18.000	Increase in stocks	1.75	2.88	2.23	3.83	2.59	1.56	4.36	2.32	0.74	0.35
148	19.000	Exports less imports	1.63	0.20	1.82	2.92	0.67	0.09	1.26	1.73	0.79	0.15
149	20.100	Blue-collar, unskilled	0.64	0.15	0.30	0.71	1.55	1.31	1.37	4.29	2.49	0.38
150	20.210	Blue-collar, skilled	0.14	0.86	0.85	0.04	0.13	0.58	2.70	0.30	0.31	1.97
151	20.220	White-collar	0.86	1.65	2.96	0.66	1.74	2.19	0.66	1.17	1.97	2.26
152	20.300	Professional	1.64	1.25	0.57	0.60	1.15	0.37	0.89	2.91	0.90	2.77
153	21.000	Government expenditure on commodities	2.0	3.3	6.0	5.8	3.3	2.8	2.2	2.7	3.4	7.0

Note: The net expenditure of residents abroad, line 110 in the binary tables, has been consolidated with other services (line 109) in the multilateral comparisons. Thus, there are 152 categories in this table. See page 70.

Appendix Table 14.3. Purchasing-Power Parities per U.S. Dollar, Nine Countries, and International Prices, 1970

#	code		Colombia (peso)	France (franc)	Germany, F.R. (D.mark)	Hungary (forint)	India (rupee)	Italy (lira)	Japan (yen)	Kenya (shilling)	U.K. (pound)	International prices
1	01.101	Rice	12.0	4.80	5.20	49.7	4.50	589.	440.	4.16	0.390	2.00
2	01.102	Meal, other cereals	15.4	8.32	6.56	19.9	3.07	1,042.	311.	4.86	0.317	1.39
3	01.103	Bread, rolls	11.4	2.65	2.14	5.1	2.56	321.	178.	2.50	0.153	0.58
4	01.104	Biscuits, cakes	22.2	8.65	4.43	22.3	8.58	759.	314.	1.06	0.243	1.21
5	01.105	Cereal preparations	16.4	6.53	3.60	8.2	3.05	896.	352.	8.06	0.240	0.90
6	01.106	Macaroni, spaghetti, related foods	7.1	4.30	3.67	15.9	10.96	456.	352.†	11.85	0.384	1.05
7	01.111	Fresh beef, veal	8.7	4.97	4.16	40.4	2.48	651.	597.	3.41	0.241	1.10
8	01.112	Fresh lamb, mutton	4.3	4.42†	3.66	13.0	4.01	542.†	377.†	3.30	0.247	0.93
9	01.113	Fresh pork	8.9	5.02	3.84	45.7	2.11	696.	448.	6.01	0.347	1.60
10	01.114	Fresh poultry	18.0	6.31	5.01	30.5	6.55	801.	480.	4.39	0.351	1.61
11	01.115	Other fresh meat	9.8	4.92	3.68	16.0	4.39†	474.	410.†	3.19†	0.324	1.19
12	01.116	Frozen, salted meat	13.4	5.79	4.53	23.2		676.	438.	6.21	0.340	1.31
13	01.121	Fresh, frozen fish	11.7	4.99	3.18	8.5	1.06	648.	299.	2.79	0.387	0.81
14	01.122	Canned fish	17.4	8.07	4.77	62.4	7.93	749.	421.	12.64	0.490	1.71
15	01.131	Fresh milk	8.1	3.17	2.37	12.4	2.77	526.	375.	4.29	0.375	1.06
16	01.132	Milk products	14.3	3.86	3.30	15.4	5.06	643.	348.	5.17	0.186	1.09
17	01.133	Eggs, egg products	17.4	5.54	3.77	31.2	5.35	706.	261.	5.64	0.376	1.44
18	01.141	Butter	15.6	6.16	4.03	26.2	4.00	906.	410.	4.48	0.217	1.50
19	01.142	Margarine, edible oil	14.3	4.25	4.33	28.8	7.11	612.	364.	7.49	0.347	1.96
20	01.143	Lard, edible fat	40.4	8.36	5.53	39.1	7.50	1,069.	616.	11.85	0.423	2.41
21	01.151	Fresh fruits, tropical, subtropical	3.5	7.01	4.58	56.9	3.16	793.	548.	2.74	0.433	0.82
22	01.152	Other fresh fruits	22.6	2.92	2.12	11.2	3.43	270.	373.	14.77	0.370	0.74
23	01.153	Fresh vegetables	7.1	2.60	1.83	7.5	1.42	299.	203.	1.79	0.215	0.62
24	01.161	Fruit other than fresh	28.4	8.70	5.18	49.2	6.00	1,022.	337.	3.59	0.294	1.44

Appendix Table 14.3. Continued

			Colombia (peso)	France (franc)	Germany, F.R. (D.mark)	Hungary (forint)	India (rupee)	Italy (lira)	Japan (yen)	Kenya (shilling)	U.K. (pound)	International prices
25	01.162	Vegetables other than fresh	27.8	8.91	6.79	29.4	6.48	979.	505.	5.13	0.348	2.20
26	01.170	Potatoes, manioc, other tubers	6.7	2.01	2.88	11.4	2.95	394.	283.	2.02	0.201	0.69
27	01.191	Coffee	11.1	8.67	10.88	109.9	10.46	1,853.	709.	7.82	0.369	2.50
28	01.192	Tea	16.6	5.72	7.53	45.9	2.38	957.	236.	2.54	0.159	0.89
29	01.193	Cocoa	11.9	5.40	4.98	45.3	7.50	1,144.	312.†	8.70	0.293	1.49
30	01.180	Sugar	10.2	4.77	4.54	33.7	7.37	886.	508.	5.49	0.291	1.92
31	01.201	Jam, syrup, honey	14.3	4.75	3.31	17.9	8.20	536.	367.	3.37	0.193	1.13
32	01.202	Chocolate, ice cream	13.9	9.45	5.88	29.0	6.10	1,137.	512.	18.05	0.349	1.77
33	01.203	Salt, spices, sauces	5.4	5.99	4.51	14.7	2.23	444.	159.	5.22	0.343	0.93
34	01.310	Nonalcoholic beverages	9.4	3.00	2.87	24.4	5.41	517.	328.	12.59	0.345	1.18
35	01.321	Spirits	10.3	3.98	2.48	26.1	9.95	396.	266.	6.51	0.418	1.12
36	01.322	Wine, cider	60.0	1.93	2.03	15.3	18.49	304.	292.	13.21	0.896	0.70
37	01.323	Beer	8.3	2.96	2.23	17.2	9.97	408.	332.	8.21	0.571	1.27
38	01.410	Cigarettes	3.6	4.46	4.97	8.3	8.10	676.	211.	5.14	0.638	1.12
39	01.420	Other tobacco	7.4	2.47	2.14	17.1	2.63	559.	157.†	4.59	0.658	1.12
40	02.110	Clothing materials	13.2	8.39	5.24	57.7	7.27	747.	410.	7.71	0.380	2.09
41	02.121	Men's clothing	10.1	5.32	3.02	21.4	2.95	505.	243.	4.64	0.313	1.13
42	02.122	Women's clothing	17.2	9.81	5.00	26.8	3.30	859.	235.	9.46	0.441	1.46
43	02.123	Boys', girls' clothing	12.9	4.84	4.23	22.7	2.46	461.	268.	3.09	0.299	1.15
44	02.131	Men's, boys' underwear	12.7	6.16	4.98	26.8	1.78	611.	264.	8.85	0.432	1.36
45	02.132	Women's, girls' underwear	13.3	9.13	5.17	24.7	5.53	769.	255.	4.39	0.350	1.47
46	02.150	Other clothing	10.0	5.14	3.44	18.4	6.73	453.	191.	4.14	0.245	1.02
47	02.160	Clothing rental, repair	6.2	3.94	4.56	9.0	1.19	254.	112.†	3.02	0.320	0.65
48	02.211	Men's footwear	7.7	5.18	3.19	22.9	3.52	566.	195.	2.99	0.237	1.05
49	02.212	Women's footwear	6.9	5.84	2.90	19.5	3.40	484.	202.	1.73	0.242	1.01
50	02.213	Children's footwear	7.3	4.47	3.30	11.7	2.68	488.	177.	1.89	0.195	0.89
51	02.220	Footwear repairs	6.4	5.00	2.55	16.9	3.52	311.	112.	4.01	0.220	0.86
52	03.110	Gross rents	10.6	3.02	2.42	8.6	1.38	292.	261.	4.94	0.264	0.84
53	03.120	Indoor repair, upkeep	13.2	4.02	2.49	6.1	0.87	228.	184.	3.59	0.348	0.78
54	03.210	Electricity	7.3	7.76	4.24	31.8	7.39	761.	303.	9.34	0.823	1.29
55	03.220	Gas	6.1	9.76	7.91	15.9	7.22	1,359.	1,039.	11.33	0.413	1.69
56	03.230	Liquid fuels	10.8	5.61	3.34	41.9	12.97	644.	414.	17.14	0.292	1.61
57	03.240	Other fuels, ice	5.3†	5.85	4.38	6.9	2.89	739.	192.	1.86	0.530	0.91
58	04.110	Furniture, fixtures	10.5	4.67	2.77	19.1	3.19	469.	239.	3.71	0.303	1.07
59	04.120	Floor coverings	10.3†	6.22	3.91	28.7	0.49	706.	313.	8.71	0.269	0.73
60	04.200	Household textiles, etc.	11.2	6.66	5.69	28.0	2.39	744.	323.	8.11	0.531	1.34
61	04.310	Refrigerators, etc.	25.9	4.82	2.62	53.3	9.95	417.	599.	10.81	0.435	1.51
62	04.320	Washing appliances	64.2	9.14	5.22	29.5	7.50	591.	285.	12.14†	0.357	1.60
63	04.330	Cooking appliances	16.2	6.29	4.38	11.9	6.02	436.	211.	11.16	0.814	1.14
64	04.340	Heating appliances	36.6	10.78	5.52	43.7	4.99	1,099.	566.	14.35†	0.823	2.13
65	04.350	Cleaning appliances	65.1	7.57	4.79	32.8	7.50	897.	427.	13.26†	0.643	2.02
66	04.360	Other household appliances	45.1	7.90	4.86	24.4	4.09	769.	312.	13.71	0.376	1.59
67	04.400	Household utensils	7.8	4.03	2.70	23.2	3.98	369.	212.	3.59	0.278	1.30
68	04.510	Nondurable household goods	10.4	5.45	3.65	28.3	4.39	549.	266.	6.66	0.185	0.17
69	04.520	Domestic services	1.0	5.55	3.66	9.3	0.24	625.	136.	0.67	0.242	0.85
70	04.530	Household services	5.7	5.90	4.14	13.9	1.10	526.	219.	3.72	0.138	0.51
71	04.600	Household furnishing repairs	18.6	5.55	3.66	10.4	0.61†	625.	178.†	1.70	0.152	0.79
72	05.110	Drugs, medical preparations	18.5	2.76	3.35	11.5	2.44	396.	140.	3.55	0.211	0.86
73	05.120	Medical supplies	9.3	3.50	2.27	21.5	2.32	152.	194.	4.25	0.171	0.65
74	05.200	Therapeutic equipment	10.4	2.77	1.99	3.2	1.06	432.	69.	1.90	0.178	0.60
75	05.310	Physicians' services	3.4	7.13	3.65	2.0	0.23	424.	50.	2.86	0.273	1.17
76	05.320	Dentists' services	4.5	14.78	5.34	1.4	0.04	492.	35.	0.40	0.113	0.25
77	05.330	Services, nurses, other personnel	0.8	0.59	0.70	1.9	0.45	61.	31.	1.00	0.092	0.22
78	05.410	Hospitals, etc.	1.5	0.40	0.27	3.9	0.22	43.	34.	10.57	0.520	1.63
79	06.110	Personal cars	38.2	6.26	4.32	62.1	11.93	652.	363.	10.01	0.608	1.40
80	06.120	Other personal transport	35.9	6.54	3.53	24.1	6.33	626.	507.	9.77	0.216	1.13
81	06.210	Tires, tubes, accessories	17.9	5.30	4.15	14.6	7.36	436.	279.	1.36	0.164	0.95
82	06.220	Repair charges	4.5	7.51	4.29	18.1	1.10	487.	347.	7.31	0.587	1.82
83	06.230	Gasoline, oil, etc.	17.1	11.81	8.02	28.6	7.57	1,642.	590.	2.04	0.298	0.71
84	06.240	Parking, tolls, etc.	4.4†	3.06	2.43	5.4	1.34†	231.	273.	1.97	0.223	0.45
85	06.310	Local transport	2.7	3.91	2.95	9.0	1.42	338.	58.	3.15	0.283	0.69
86	06.321	Rail transport	3.7	3.22	2.62	11.9	2.19	255.	117.	2.66	0.233	0.87
87	06.322	Bus transport	4.0	5.23	2.63	15.0	2.10	343.	147.	11.98	0.417	1.46
88	06.323	Air transport	8.8	6.19	4.42	20.1†	7.22	619.	237.	2.26	0.720	0.86
89	06.330	Miscellaneous transport	6.3	4.52	2.79	25.3	1.61	340.	96.	4.96	0.308	0.87
90	06.410	Postal communication	7.1	4.15	2.22	12.8	1.97	519.	257.	3.16	0.217	0.74
91	06.420	Telephone, telegraph	2.6	5.47	3.13	7.8	1.69	372.	192.	10.51	0.560	1.61
92	07.110	Radio, TV, phonograph, etc.	24.8	10.45	4.81	37.9	7.12	991.	198.	11.57	0.444	1.28
93	07.120	Major durable recreation equip.	23.8	6.04	3.37	26.3	7.12†	621.	198.	7.25	0.408	1.30
94	07.130	Other recreation equipment	24.2	6.16	4.12	25.2	5.63	653.	266.	2.08	0.130	0.65
95	07.210	Public entertainment	6.8	2.98	1.68	4.8	2.34	459.	362.	2.53	0.251	0.50
96	07.230	Other recreation, cultural events	5.9	3.24	3.35	2.5	1.02	380.	153.	6.06	0.159	0.92
97	07.310	Books, papers, magazines	10.2	3.92	3.18	11.9	2.66	505.	332.	13.74	0.319	1.08
98	07.320	Stationery	10.1	4.49	3.62	44.6	1.55	429.	282.	0.76	0.191	0.33
99	07.411	Teachers, 1st, 2nd	1.3	4.29	2.54	3.8	0.17	267.	92.	5.36	0.280	0.88
100	07.412	Teachers, college	6.4	13.40	7.57	5.3	0.52	589.	138.	5.36	0.280	0.88

Appendix Table 14.3. Continued

			Colombia (peso)	France (franc)	Germany, F.R. (D.mark)	Hungary (forint)	India (rupee)	Italy (lira)	Japan (yen)	Kenya (shilling)	U.K. (pound)	International prices
101	07.420	Educational facilities	9.3	5.65	3.74	24.1	5.02	690.	356.	7.09	0.417	1.32
102	07.431	Educational supplies	10.7	3.94	3.20	11.1	2.70	507.	322.	5.81	0.154	0.95
103	07.432	Other education expenditures	12.7	5.39	4.08	23.2	3.53	595.	381.	4.97	0.330	1.33
104	08.100	Barber, beauty shops	4.8	2.97	2.05	3.4	1.33	280.	135.	2.89	0.133	0.53
105	08.210	Toilet articles	15.1	5.34	3.76	11.7	5.52	694.	307.	12.81	0.352	1.26
106	08.220	Other personal-care goods	9.4	8.39	4.95	28.9	4.09	692.	194.	3.76	0.279	1.39
107	08.310	Restaurants, cafes	10.5	3.93	2.90	19.7	3.15	520.	130.	2.56	0.387	1.00
108	08.320	Hotels, etc.	8.1	3.72	2.47	16.8	3.79	451.	267.	4.01	0.285	0.97
109	08.400	Other services	4.6	3.61	2.40	10.4	0.76	304.	148.	2.44	0.227	0.65
111	10.100	1- and 2-dwelling buildings	4.5	5.85	4.04	17.0	1.68	506.	256.	3.27	0.188	0.91
112	10.200	Multidwelling buildings	3.9	3.93	2.11	15.7	1.60	302.	247.	3.61	0.199	0.79
113	11.100	Hotels, etc.	3.8	1.97	1.39	16.8	1.70	229.	290.	4.86	0.399	0.69
114	11.200	Industrial buildings	6.4	4.04	2.44	24.5	2.31	413.	435.	4.48	0.379	1.06
115	11.300	Commercial buildings	4.3	2.47	1.65	19.6	1.64†	257.	426.	3.59	0.339	0.78
116	11.400	Office buildings	2.8	3.45	2.03	12.4	1.55	327.	284.	2.59	0.258	0.72
117	11.500	Educational buildings	2.8	6.45	3.60	14.1	1.72	460.	206.	2.63	0.306	0.94
118	11.600	Hospital buildings	3.6†	3.34†	2.06†	11.7	1.34	333.†	181.	3.19	0.242	0.74
119	11.700	Agricultural buildings	5.6†	6.00	4.35	21.8	2.51†	542.	765.	2.38	0.245	1.19
120	11.800	Other buildings	4.4†	4.10†	2.53†	21.4	1.99†	408.†	393.	4.04†	0.373	1.09
121	12.100	Roads, highways	4.3	2.95	1.99	17.0	1.61	244.	291.	8.95†	0.249	0.77
122	12.200	Transmission, utility lines	5.5	3.54	3.41	10.7	1.63†	409.	154.	7.05	0.209	0.78
123	12.300	Other construction	4.3	1.83	0.89	10.6	1.51	83.	188.	8.96	0.324	0.70
124	13.000	Land improvement	4.4	3.30	1.82	11.7	1.10	309.	149.	3.59	0.386	0.61
125	14.110	Locomotives	16.5	8.93	4.95	62.2	11.74†	986.	549†	6.84	0.800	2.35†
126	14.120	Other	13.6†	4.85†	4.50†	31.6†	6.80	739.†	384.†	9.46	0.560†	1.72
127	14.200	Passenger cars	35.0	4.65	5.61	69.5	8.81	783.	374.	8.15	0.670	1.59
128	14.300	Trucks, buses, trailers	31.6	4.93†	4.57†	27.8	9.01	751.†	390.†	6.99	0.569†	1.61
129	14.400	Aircraft	28.1	4.92	3.35	31.1†	8.11†	661.	379.†	6.76†	0.553†	1.46
130	14.500	Ships, boats	5.6†	3.83†	2.60†	16.9†	3.46†	405.†	267.†	5.49†	0.335†	0.92
131	14.600	Other transport	36.9	5.49	4.11	32.9†	8.57†	821.	401.†	7.59	0.584†	2.02
132	15.100	Engines and turbines	29.3	5.60†	3.45†	45.8	9.34	515.†	304.†	8.21	0.308	1.75
133	15.210	Tractors	19.5	4.89	3.41	30.7	5.14	557.	288.†	6.81	0.322	1.35
134	15.220	Other agricultural machinery	32.3	5.38	3.90	23.0	6.77	868.	301.†	9.56	0.378	1.38
135	15.300	Office machinery	44.0	5.57	3.68	45.1	6.31	670.	303.†	9.98	0.431	1.32
136	15.400	Metalworking machinery	13.9	3.04	2.74	29.0	5.32	327.	410.	4.48	0.283	1.11
137	15.500	Construction, mining	32.1	7.89	5.66	36.5	9.20†	881.	303.	9.92	0.357	1.73
138	15.600	Special industrial	21.8	4.89	3.38	34.3	5.83	521.	217.	6.64	0.366	1.34
139	15.700	General industrial	29.9	3.59	2.57	27.8	7.53	422.	292.	7.54	0.314	1.19
140	15.800	Service industrial	36.5	9.13	6.80	37.3	7.63	523.	302.†	11.09	0.363†	1.53
141	16.100	Electrical transmission	32.3	3.60	2.83	22.1	9.08	401.	260.†	5.44	0.310†	1.09
142	16.200	Communication equipment	23.7	5.46	3.66	15.8	9.08†	591.	347.†	11.93	0.540	1.43
143	16.300	Other electrical	11.1†	3.60	2.96	27.1	5.78†	272.	351.	4.89†	0.214	1.00
144	16.400	Instruments	24.9	4.23	2.89	25.6	3.38	577.	395.	7.28	0.164	1.12
145	17.100	Furniture, fixtures	18.3	4.24	3.71	23.9	6.30	568.	314.†	5.91	0.199	1.22
146	17.200	Other durable goods	16.7	6.61	4.67	51.2	9.68†	786.	370.†	6.65	0.442†	1.65
147	18.000	Increase in stocks	14.0	5.26	3.98	23.4	3.45	606.	326.	5.51	0.381	1.36
148	19.000	Exports less imports	18.6	5.55	3.66	30.0	7.50	625.	360.	7.14	0.417	1.50
149	20.100	Blue-collar, unskilled	2.3	3.23	2.75	4.4	0.34	346.	142.	0.48	0.153	0.23
150	20.210	Blue-collar, skilled	3.0	3.12	2.48	5.0	0.37	345.	118.	1.18	0.145	0.60
151	20.220	White-collar	3.6	4.00	2.89	5.3	0.38	391.	124.	1.91	0.201	0.51
152	20.300	Professional	6.4	4.03	3.56	5.9	1.21	492.	243.	4.26	0.274	0.83
153	21.000	Government expenditure on commodities	8.0	4.63	3.16	21.2	2.45	472.	254.	4.19	0.309	1.06

Note: The net expenditure of residents abroad, line 110 in the binary tables, has been consolidated with other services (line 109) in the multilateral comparisons. Thus there are 152 categories in this table. See page 70.

†The PPPs for these items where price and quantity data were missing have been estimated by applying the double-weighted CPD method and are considered less reliable than direct estimates. The corresponding quantity estimates in Table 14.5 share the same weakness.

Appendix Table 14.4. Quantities per Capita with U.S.=100, 1970

			Colombia	France	Germany, F.R.	Hungary	India	Italy	Japan	Kenya	U.K.	U.S.
1	01.101	Rice	432.0	66.2	62.4	69.2	1,727.2	85.5	2,805.5	29.0	18.4	100.0
2	01.102	Meal, other cereals	63.9	24.6	95.3	139.1	373.4	25.3	14.9	366.7	34.7	100.0
3	01.103	Bread, rolls	22.7	315.4	306.8	330.6	0.7	258.4	54.3	10.6	243.2	100.0
4	01.104	Biscuits, cakes	3.8	81.0	55.9	21.9	0.2	39.6	108.4	9.6	133.8	100.0
5	01.105	Cereal preparations	12.3	3.5	8.1	118.7	1.6	1.8	6.2	1.2	56.5	100.0
6	01.106	Macaroni, spaghetti, related foods	146.8	216.7	188.6	111.5	2.1	980.2	287.4	0.7	43.1	100.0

Appendix Table 14.4. Continued

			Colombia	France	Germany, F.R.	Hungary	India	Italy	Japan	Kenya	U.K.	U.S.
7	01.111	Fresh beef, veal	47.4	86.5	24.0	2.9	0.4	80.2	5.8	9.4	49.9	100.0
8	01.112	Fresh lamb, mutton	38.8	197.6	0.0	46.5	9.2	93.6	4.0	29.3	635.8	100.0
9	01.113	Fresh pork	16.0	99.2	148.5	92.0	0.6	51.6	45.3	0.5	34.3	100.0
10	01.114	Fresh poultry	7.6	78.6	19.6	68.5	1.3	61.2	18.7	1.1	42.9	100.0
11	01.115	Other fresh meat	79.9	741.6	49.3	102.0	24.2	298.4	52.0	25.1	130.5	100.0
12	01.116	Frozen, salted meat	6.7	81.0	81.7	43.9	0.0	50.0	14.3	0.8	100.4	100.0
13	01.121	Fresh, frozen fish	5.4	191.6	28.0	42.0	72.9	108.7	353.7	28.8	79.3	100.0
14	01.122	Canned fish	13.7	110.6	69.5	6.1	0.0	97.6	510.6	2.0	74.3	100.0
15	01.131	Fresh milk	31.7	71.2	60.5	60.6	20.9	42.7	28.3	24.2	67.5	100.0
16	01.132	Milk products	14.6	256.5	80.9	50.1	3.7	139.4	14.7	4.7	121.1	100.0
17	01.133	Eggs, egg products	16.6	68.4	87.5	65.5	1.1	57.6	91.2	0.4	74.1	100.0
18	01.141	Butter	21.0	387.0	415.0	70.1	91.1	73.6	9.4	25.4	302.3	100.0
19	01.142	Margarine, edible oil	44.2	91.6	97.4	12.3	26.9	166.4	27.9	6.1	32.4	100.0
20	01.143	Lard, edible fat	18.7	0.0	0.0	1,338.9	0.0	0.0	2.1	11.6	167.0	100.0
21	01.151	Fresh fruits, tropical, subtropical	398.9	100.2	66.3	22.6	15.8	112.5	80.9	60.7	53.3	100.0
22	01.152	Other fresh fruits	1.8	267.9	141.4	238.2	1.8	392.5	80.6	0.2	58.1	100.0
23	01.153	Fresh vegetables	41.4	242.8	80.6	148.2	27.7	319.7	160.8	43.2	91.9	100.0
24	01.161	Fruit other than fresh	0.9	9.5	21.5	5.1	0.2	17.5	11.5	0.1	36.9	100.0
25	01.162	Vegetables other than fresh	11.8	28.2	31.7	9.1	13.3	12.4	33.9	3.4	55.0	100.0
26	01.170	Potatoes, manioc, other tubers	89.6	201.6	91.6	137.7	14.8	69.6	32.3	133.9	200.6	100.0
27	01.191	Coffee	25.8	51.7	67.3	16.2	1.4	29.2	4.4	1.1	27.0	100.0
28	01.192	Tea	2.2	23.1	40.9	11.7	88.1	13.2	218.4	63.7	863.8	100.0
29	01.193	Cocoa	228.2	147.8	174.9	30.0	0.0	21.5	60.9	3.6	43.8	100.0
30	01.180	Sugar	170.7	141.9	204.9	150.6	57.3	130.7	43.2	54.7	169.3	100.0
31	01.201	Jam, syrup, honey	12.9	64.1	73.2	6.8	1.3	43.4	84.0	16.0	118.7	100.0
32	01.202	Chocolate, ice cream	2.6	50.5	68.7	82.0	1.7	34.2	18.5	0.7	132.6	100.0
33	01.203	Salt, spices, sauces	78.6	27.3	11.5	164.7	109.5	101.6	445.6	10.7	41.8	100.0
34	01.310	Nonalcoholic beverages	8.4	84.2	51.3	11.3	0.6	46.4	49.9	3.5	65.1	100.0
35	01.321	Spirits	16.3	61.1	90.8	35.2	0.1	59.1	23.5	1.6	125.2	100.0
36	01.322	Wine, cider	4.6	3408.4	440.7	548.4	1.9	1,469.7	770.8	0.8	133.4	100.0
37	01.323	Beer	4.3	32.2	112.2	29.2	0.2	29.6	58.9	6.7	156.2	100.0
38	01.410	Cigarettes	12.0	55.3	57.4	67.7	0.3	55.3	45.5	3.6	82.8	100.0
39	01.420	Other tobacco	22.9	196.9	170.9	6.1	104.2	54.1	1.2	1.0	136.5	100.0
40	02.110	Clothing materials	27.4	70.0	91.4	50.2	20.1	127.6	372.6	11.9	58.2	100.0
41	02.121	Men's clothing	14.6	92.1	86.6	39.1	3.2	48.1	39.2	3.4	48.5	100.0
42	02.122	Women's clothing	2.5	24.5	37.9	16.8	2.5	9.4	30.8	0.6	36.4	100.0
43	02.123	Boys', girls' clothing	7.3	24.7	47.4	41.4	1.2	45.9	34.3	3.2	34.8	100.0
44	02.131	Men's, boys' underwear	8.8	116.5	82.7	48.0	0.2	189.2	60.7	0.6	86.9	100.0
45	02.132	Women's, girls' underwear	5.4	55.5	72.6	19.8	0.0	24.6	19.4	0.4	53.6	100.0
46	02.150	Other clothing	11.7	108.6	123.8	94.5	0.0	22.1	67.6	1.2	179.4	100.0
47	02.160	Clothing rental, repair	25.1	84.4	40.3	189.1	10.8	226.1	260.9	4.8	62.7	100.0
48	02.211	Men's footwear	21.2	75.0	63.4	51.8	1.8	69.7	37.3	9.3	91.4	100.0
49	02.212	Women's footwear	14.2	60.9	72.9	61.5	1.4	25.1	28.8	3.1	93.3	100.0
50	02.213	Children's footwear	15.2	69.1	99.4	48.1	1.2	47.9	23.6	2.9	82.5	100.0
51	02.220	Footwear repairs	26.7	100.8	482.1	110.8	2.0	170.4	26.6	3.2	164.8	100.0
52	03.110	Gross rents	10.8	62.0	63.7	17.7	3.7	51.2	37.2	2.8	55.0	100.0
53	03.120	Indoor repair, upkeep	25.4	206.2	94.8	156.1	13.9	33.3	60.8	0.3	202.7	100.0
54	03.210	Electricity	10.0	26.3	48.4	10.5	0.3	26.6	29.3	0.3	72.1	100.0
55	03.220	Gas	6.7	28.7	16.6	17.9	0.0	14.0	9.0	0.0	28.4	100.0
56	03.230	Liquid fuels	7.3	44.3	54.5	4.7	1.8	30.6	9.4	0.4	11.7	100.0
57	03.240	Other fuels, ice	26.9	237.6	270.6	1,007.3	183.3	56.3	159.6	98.0	525.9	100.0
58	04.110	Furniture, fixtures	18.8	85.1	108.7	37.6	0.3	38.9	19.2	3.1	22.1	100.0
59	04.120	Floor coverings	3.5	23.4	47.4	10.4	22.0	6.9	16.3	0.6	90.1	100.0
60	04.200	Household textiles, etc.	8.8	32.9	42.7	19.8	4.1	15.5	7.9	1.2	47.3	100.0
61	04.310	Refrigerators, etc.	2.1	37.3	37.4	11.5	0.5	15.5	21.8	0.4	18.2	100.0
62	04.320	Washing appliances	1.7	64.0	72.7	17.8	0.0	46.1	38.1	0.1	52.1	100.0
63	04.330	Cooking appliances	13.8	49.6	28.8	73.1	0.0	32.7	18.6	0.6	50.9	100.0
64	04.340	Heating appliances	2.7	43.6	49.3	20.2	0.1	15.4	38.7	0.9	43.0	100.0
65	04.350	Cleaning appliances	6.1	77.1	98.3	19.7	0.0	15.6	40.9	0.3	55.2	100.0
66	04.360	Other household appliances	3.1	62.5	115.0	18.8	0.4	20.5	86.7	0.5	14.4	100.0
67	04.400	Household utensils	8.8	101.8	163.8	44.1	5.1	47.9	65.3	9.4	88.7	100.0
68	04.510	Nondurable household goods	25.2	80.3	100.8	30.0	3.3	37.8	29.9	8.9	80.0	100.0
69	04.520	Domestic services	373.2	0.0	0.0	17.0	39.8	0.0	12.8	40.8	65.7	100.0
70	04.530	Household services	15.6	35.1	40.0	8.1	14.7	76.8	59.8	1.4	69.0	100.0
71	04.600	Household furnishing repairs	0.0	0.0	0.0	143.5	24.2	0.0	15.1	0.6	73.8	100.0
72	05.110	Drugs, medical preparations	4.6	362.5	148.1	75.3	11.0	147.9	160.9	5.2	112.6	100.0
73	05.120	Medical supplies	0.0	41.6	162.0	76.5	7.9	19.5	863.6	2.5	100.7	100.0
74	05.200	Therapeutic equipment	4.4	84.3	274.3	0.0	2.5	8.6	40.8	0.5	120.2	100.0
75	05.310	Physicians' services	26.2	82.0	112.9	111.9	10.9	73.0	66.0	7.0	66.9	100.0
76	05.320	Dentists' services	14.8	75.0	98.0	43.0	1.1	95.0	68.9	1.0	48.1	100.0
77	05.330	Services, nurses, other personnel	6.0	65.0	75.8	73.9	4.8	34.5	54.1	16.2	102.3	100.0
78	05.410	Hospitals, etc.	18.0	81.1	139.8	96.4	6.7	115.8	130.1	15.1	115.2	100.0
79	06.110	Personal cars	3.9	28.4	29.4	3.0	0.1	19.2	4.6	0.8	23.7	100.0
80	06.120	Other personal transport	0.1	15.0	13.5	18.7	0.9	6.4	9.7	0.1	8.7	100.0
81	06.210	Tires, tubes, accessories	4.7	56.0	38.2	12.0	0.3	20.0	2.3	0.8	75.2	100.0
82	06.220	Repair charges	23.6	61.5	54.1	8.1	2.1	34.5	8.5	4.3	67.9	100.0
83	06.230	Gasoline, oil, etc.	1.6	15.8	20.9	2.2	0.2	9.8	3.5	0.1	21.4	100.0

Appendix Table 14.4. Continued

			Colombia	France	Germany, F.R.	Hungary	India	Italy	Japan	Kenya	U.K.	U.S.
84	06.240	Parking, tolls, etc.	31.5	121.1	75.7	5.8	2.6	86.5	17.2	1.8	108.2	100.0
85	06.310	Local transport	177.0	125.3	84.3	131.8	20.7	150.3	1,391.7	9.2	346.8	100.0
86	06.321	Rail transport	1,169.3	1,924.2	1,620.9	1,620.9	244.5	2,252.7	3,582.6	60.6	1,215.8	100.0
87	06.322	Bus transport	81.5	462.6	538.8	556.7	308.4	396.8	285.9	255.1	110.3	100.0
88	06.323	Air transport	74.5	11.1	5.1	10.1	0.1	5.3	11.6	10.5	68.2	100.0
89	06.330	Miscellaneous transport	0.0	0.0	0.0	31.1	58.4	0.0	116.3	2.7	69.0	100.0
90	06.410	Postal communication	3.9	70.3	207.4	38.8	5.7	63.3	13.2	1.1	84.6	100.0
91	06.420	Telephone, telegraph	17.9	11.1	13.1	8.0	1.3	21.6	18.6	0.7	35.6	100.0
92	07.110	Radio, TV, phonograph, etc.	5.3	31.8	27.9	16.5	0.4	13.3	76.6	0.9	14.1	100.0
93	07.120	Major durable recreation equip.	1.1	21.5	45.8	1.4	0.0	1.3	18.6	1.8	14.2	100.0
94	07.130	Other recreation equipment	1.6	73.5	119.7	8.5	0.1	24.7	40.6	1.3	67.7	100.0
95	07.210	Public entertainment	43.3	47.6	64.9	172.1	0.5	84.4	97.6	9.4	184.2	100.0
96	07.230	Other recreation, cultural events	4.9	31.5	32.0	173.0	2.6	14.7	26.2	2.8	100.1	100.0
97	07.310	Books, papers, magazines	8.5	119.3	70.8	43.9	2.6	59.4	37.0	2.7	140.2	100.0
98	07.320	Stationery	2.1	196.2	75.2	13.1	4.2	38.8	29.3	0.1	55.0	100.0
99	07.411	Teachers, 1st, 2nd	56.9	77.9	72.1	73.0	36.4	86.7	70.9	28.6	67.2	100.0
100	07.412	Teachers, college	16.0	19.4	25.5	28.1	8.5	24.5	44.7	1.2	48.6	100.0
101	07.420	Educational facilities	4.5	21.7	58.8	39.0	0.5	14.1	25.5	2.8	46.2	100.0
102	07.431	Educational supplies	24.2	18.5	12.4	33.9	3.2	12.6	36.1	5.4	176.7	100.0
103	07.432	Other education expenditures	28.7	12.7	66.2	66.5	2.8	30.0	60.0	9.0	134.2	100.0
104	08.100	Barber, beauty shops	15.2	123.8	112.5	137.4	4.4	127.6	154.5	0.8	152.0	100.0
105	08.210	Toilet articles	10.9	74.2	50.5	38.6	1.9	27.6	57.4	0.7	40.4	100.0
106	08.220	Other personal-care goods	5.6	56.9	46.2	23.2	2.5	33.4	24.1	2.3	54.2	100.0
107	08.310	Restaurants, cafes	17.3	94.6	43.9	62.6	1.2	35.7	71.8	3.8	30.0	100.0
108	08.320	Hotels, etc.	27.0	645.8	367.9	44.3	15.6	313.0	218.4	41.7	421.5	100.0
109	08.400	Other services	47.7	6.1	10.1	30.6	3.3	4.1	79.3	3.4	57.2	100.0
111	10.100	1- and 2-dwelling buildings	36.0	59.6	35.7	41.3	8.0	106.7	129.3	10.9	94.0	100.0
112	10.200	Multidwelling buildings	12.9	442.9	503.7	117.5	20.4	143.3	150.7	3.6	99.9	100.0
113	11.100	Hotels, etc.	22.0	173.7	253.7	95.0	4.5	119.6	115.0	2.4	24.1	100.0
114	11.200	Industrial buildings	24.8	98.3	247.3	116.4	1.4	129.4	45.0	9.0	99.6	100.0
115	11.300	Commercial buildings	16.7	184.4	156.8	32.9	7.5	42.3	65.8	3.2	53.9	100.0
116	11.400	Office buildings	39.2	107.3	123.7	43.4	2.6	72.0	84.4	4.4	37.1	100.0
117	11.500	Educational buildings	18.7	62.7	83.5	31.0	1.4	24.7	74.1	4.3	61.4	100.0
118	11.600	Hospital buildings	10.5	77.1	132.6	25.0	2.2	45.9	56.2	6.9	73.4	100.0
119	11.700	Agricultural buildings	176.8	439.4	224.1	990.7	54.9	250.9	46.6	9.3	199.4	100.0
120	11.800	Other buildings	8.0	172.5	21.2	12.7	3.0	24.4	132.8	1.2	52.4	100.0
121	12.100	Roads, highways	49.0	84.4	168.1	32.9	4.6	72.1	95.1	2.5	64.1	100.0
122	12.200	Transmission, utility lines	23.3	133.7	92.7	123.1	9.7	30.5	155.3	1.8	33.2	100.0
123	12.300	Other construction	108.1	91.9	203.0	337.1	38.6	61.7	869.5	11.5	58.5	100.0
124	13.000	Land improvement	213.1	35.3	44.4	110.5	72.7	175.4	34.1	12.6	54.8	100.0
125	14.110	Locomotives	0.7	146.2	35.6	99.6	2.8	65.5	122.6	35.1	15.4	100.0
126	14.120	Other	2.3	76.3	35.0	74.9	2.0	16.4	3.7	8.3	6.5	100.0
127	14.200	Passenger cars	3.5	78.5	54.3	2.6	0.1	45.8	89.0	3.7	26.5	100.0
128	14.300	Trucks, buses, trailers	4.3	84.4	56.3	31.8	1.8	37.2	83.2	3.8	2.5	100.0
129	14.400	Aircraft	4.8	16.0	48.7	6.5	0.2	22.9	6.7	2.8	22.7	100.0
130	14.500	Ships, boats	130.7	152.5	552.8	23.9	5.5	146.0	370.7	2.1	429.7	100.0
131	14.600	Other transport	2.3	13.9	6.8	394.3	8.6	83.6	218.7	4.2	359.7	100.0
132	15.100	Engines and turbines	4.8	29.9	25.4	27.2	1.8	22.0	105.5	4.1	5.4	100.0
133	15.210	Tractors	5.5	138.7	69.1	49.3	1.5	30.3	17.3	4.3	35.0	100.0
134	15.220	Other agricultural machinery	3.2	148.8	56.1	67.7	0.2	17.9	54.0	3.0	30.9	100.0
135	15.300	Office machinery	0.9	68.3	75.2	8.3	0.1	9.8	56.7	0.6	22.5	100.0
136	15.400	Metalworking machinery	9.3	103.8	139.2	38.6	1.2	59.3	102.3	1.4	86.9	100.0
137	15.500	Construction, mining	6.2	124.3	80.3	35.2	0.5	14.3	95.1	2.9	78.6	100.0
138	15.600	Special industrial	13.4	249.4	210.8	147.8	2.3	63.8	374.0	10.0	135.3	100.0
139	15.700	General industrial	10.0	126.0	330.4	46.2	3.7	64.2	203.0	6.5	338.7	100.0
140	15.800	Service industrial	0.4	11.4	17.0	6.0	0.3	10.3	20.4	1.1	9.2	100.0
141	16.100	Electrical transmission	6.1	298.5	266.8	27.1	3.5	146.8	216.4	5.6	153.4	100.0
142	16.200	Communication equipment	2.9	72.2	109.1	27.5	1.8	20.9	90.7	1.0	61.9	100.0
143	16.300	Other electrical	77.0	202.7	194.7	20.2	3.3	327.6	161.6	5.9	214.7	100.0
144	16.400	Instruments	4.4	174.8	178.2	46.1	0.8	30.4	63.5	1.2	63.2	100.0
145	17.100	Furniture, fixtures	5.0	84.7	109.0	93.6	0.1	31.1	87.8	1.7	49.3	100.0
146	17.200	Other durable goods	4.4	90.6	86.5	4.5	1.8	45.6	39.7	4.1	5.0	100.0
147	18.000	Increase in stocks	45.9	532.1	379.8	307.1	33.3	164.8	580.6	26.1	104.8	100.0
148	19.000	Exports less imports	—	—	—	—	—	—	—	—	—	
149	20.100	Blue-collar, unskilled	92.8	39.7	67.8	274.5	184.0	220.3	377.7	503.0	793.9	100.0
150	20.210	Blue-collar, skilled	3.1	47.3	40.8	2.6	2.7	18.9	174.4	2.8	20.1	100.0
151	20.220	White-collar	13.6	61.2	106.4	35.8	30.8	54.9	35.5	5.8	80.4	100.0
152	20.300	Professional	11.8	37.6	13.6	23.6	5.3	6.0	19.9	5.3	22.0	100.0
153	21.000	Government expenditure on commodities	4.5	33.5	63.4	25.0	3.0	18.9	18.7	2.0	29.4	100.0

Notes:

1. The net expenditure of residents abroad, line 110 in the binary tables, has been consolidated with other services (line 109) in the multilateral comparisons. Thus there are 152 categories in this table. See page 70.

2. The quantity ratios for line 148 are not printed because they would not have a clear economic meaning. The international dollar values are given in Table 14.5.

Appendix Table 14.5. Quantities per Capita Valued at International Prices, 1970 (I$)

No.	Code	Item	Colombia	France	Germany, F.R.	Hungary	India	Italy	Japan	Kenya	U.K.	U.S.
1	01.101	Rice	12.9	2.0	1.9	2.1	51.6	2.6	83.9	0.9	0.5	3.0
2	01.102	Meal, other cereals	5.8	2.2	8.6	12.5	33.6	2.3	1.3	33.0	3.1	9.0
3	01.103	Bread, rolls	2.4	32.9	32.0	34.5	0.1	27.0	5.7	1.1	25.4	10.4
4	01.104	Biscuits, cakes	0.9	19.3	13.3	5.2	0.0	9.5	25.9	2.3	31.9	23.9
5	01.105	Cereal preparations	0.9	0.3	0.6	8.9	0.1	0.1	0.5	0.1	4.2	7.5
6	01.106	Macaroni, spaghetti, related foods	2.8	4.2	3.6	2.2	0.0	18.9	5.5	0.0	0.8	1.9
7	01.111	Fresh beef, veal	36.6	66.7	18.5	2.2	0.3	61.9	4.4	0.8	16.7	77.2
8	01.112	Fresh lamb, mutton	1.0	5.2	0.0	1.2	0.2	2.5	0.1	0.8	9.3	2.6
9	01.113	Fresh pork	4.3	26.9	40.2	24.9	0.2	14.0	12.2	0.1	13.2	27.1
10	01.114	Fresh poultry	2.3	24.2	6.0	21.1	0.4	18.8	5.8	0.4	4.6	30.8
11	01.115	Other fresh meat	2.8	26.4	1.8	3.6	0.9	10.6	1.8	0.9	51.5	3.6
12	01.116	Frozen, salted meat	3.4	41.6	41.9	22.5	0.0	25.6	7.3	0.4	5.3	51.3
13	01.121	Fresh, frozen fish	0.4	12.7	1.9	2.8	4.8	7.2	23.5	1.9	4.9	6.6
14	01.122	Canned fish	0.9	7.3	4.6	0.4	0.0	6.4	33.5	0.1	26.0	6.6
15	01.131	Fresh milk	12.2	27.4	23.3	23.4	8.0	16.4	10.9	9.3	22.2	38.5
16	01.132	Milk products	2.7	47.1	14.8	9.2	0.7	25.6	2.7	0.9	15.3	18.3
17	01.133	Eggs, egg products	3.4	14.1	18.0	13.5	0.2	11.8	18.8	0.1	21.8	20.6
18	01.141	Butter	1.5	27.9	30.0	5.1	6.6	5.3	0.7	1.8	6.7	7.2
19	01.142	Margarine, edible oil	9.1	18.8	20.0	2.5	5.5	34.2	5.7	1.2	3.4	20.6
20	01.143	Lard, edible fat	0.4	0.0	0.0	27.0	0.0	0.0	0.0	0.2	3.5	2.0
21	01.151	Fresh fruits, tropical, subtropical	26.2	6.6	4.4	1.5	1.0	7.4	5.3	4.0	3.5	6.6
22	01.152	Other fresh fruits	0.2	24.1	12.7	21.4	0.2	35.2	7.2	0.0	5.2	9.0
23	01.153	Fresh vegetables	6.6	38.6	12.8	23.5	4.4	50.8	25.5	6.9	14.6	15.9
24	01.161	Fruit other than fresh	0.3	2.8	6.4	1.5	0.1	5.2	3.4	0.0	25.2	45.8
25	01.162	Vegetables other than fresh	5.4	12.9	14.5	4.2	6.1	5.7	15.5	1.6	16.0	7.9
26	01.170	Potatoes, manioc, other tubers	7.1	16.0	7.3	10.9	1.2	5.5	2.6	10.6	16.0	29.1
27	01.191	Coffee	7.5	15.1	19.6	4.7	0.4	8.5	1.3	0.3	7.9	1.9
28	01.192	Tea	0.0	0.4	0.8	0.2	1.7	0.3	4.2	1.2	16.6	1.2
29	01.193	Cocoa	2.8	1.8	2.2	0.4	0.0	0.3	0.8	0.0	0.5	8.6
30	01.180	Sugar	14.7	12.2	17.7	13.0	4.9	11.3	3.7	4.7	14.6	5.6
31	01.201	Jam, syrup, honey	0.7	3.6	4.1	22.0	0.1	2.4	5.0	0.2	35.6	26.8
32	01.202	Chocolate, ice cream	0.7	13.6	18.4	10.7	0.4	9.2	29.0	0.7	2.7	6.5
33	01.203	Salt, spices, sauces	5.1	1.8	0.7	1.8	7.1	6.6	7.7	0.5	10.1	15.5
34	01.310	Nonalcoholic beverages	1.3	13.1	8.0	7.8	0.1	7.2	5.2	0.4	27.9	22.3
35	01.321	Spirits	3.6	13.6	20.2	16.2	0.1	13.1	22.8	0.0	4.0	3.0
36	01.322	Wine, cider	0.1	100.0	13.0	9.3	0.1	43.5	18.7	0.0	49.6	31.7
37	01.323	Beer	1.4	10.2	35.6	38.6	0.2	9.4	25.9	2.1	47.2	56.9
38	01.410	Cigarettes	6.8	31.5	32.7	0.3	5.0	31.5	0.1	0.0	6.6	4.8
39	01.420	Other tobacco	1.1	9.5	8.2	6.1	2.4	2.6	45.2	1.4	7.1	12.1
40	02.110	Clothing materials	3.3	8.5	11.1	22.0	1.8	27.0	22.0	1.9	27.3	56.2
41	02.121	Men's clothing	8.2	51.7	48.6	19.3	2.9	10.7	35.3	0.7	41.7	114.6
42	02.122	Women's clothing	2.8	28.0	43.4	11.4	0.3	12.7	9.4	0.9	9.6	27.6
43	02.123	Boys', girls' clothing	2.0	6.8	13.1	7.0	0.0	27.6	8.8	0.1	12.7	14.6
44	02.131	Men's, boys' underwear	1.3	17.0	12.1	8.4	0.0	10.5	8.2	0.2	22.8	42.5
45	02.132	Women's, girls' underwear	2.3	23.6	30.9	12.5	0.0	2.9	9.0	0.2	23.7	13.2
46	02.150	Other clothing	1.6	14.4	16.4	5.2	0.3	6.3	7.2	0.1	1.7	2.8
47	02.160	Clothing rental, repair	0.7	2.3	1.1	6.5	0.2	8.8	4.7	1.2	11.5	12.6
48	02.211	Men's footwear	2.7	9.4	8.0	6.5	0.2	8.8	4.7	1.2	14.8	15.9
49	02.212	Women's footwear	2.3	9.7	11.6	9.8	0.2	4.0	4.6	0.5	8.8	10.7
50	02.213	Children's footwear	1.6	7.4	10.6	5.1	0.1	5.1	2.5	0.3	2.9	1.8
51	02.220	Footwear repairs	0.5	1.8	8.5	2.0	0.0	3.0	0.5	0.1	2.9	1.8
52	03.110	Gross rents	39.8	227.8	233.8	65.0	13.5	188.1	136.7	10.4	202.0	367.2
53	03.120	Indoor repair, upkeep	3.5	28.8	13.2	21.8	1.9	4.7	8.5	0.0	28.3	14.0
54	03.210	Electricity	6.2	16.4	30.2	6.5	0.2	16.6	18.3	0.2	45.0	62.5
55	03.220	Gas	3.3	14.3	8.3	8.9	0.0	7.0	4.5	0.1	14.1	49.9
56	03.230	Liquid fuels	2.7	16.3	20.1	1.7	0.7	11.3	3.5	0.1	4.3	36.9
57	03.240	Other fuels, ice	1.1	9.6	11.0	40.8	7.4	2.3	6.5	4.0	21.3	4.0
58	04.110	Furniture, fixtures	10.6	47.7	61.0	21.1	0.2	21.8	10.8	1.7	12.4	56.1
59	04.120	Floor coverings	0.5	3.1	6.3	1.4	2.9	0.9	2.2	0.1	12.0	13.3
60	04.200	Household textiles, etc.	4.5	17.0	22.0	10.2	2.1	8.0	4.1	0.6	24.4	51.6
61	04.310	Refrigerators, etc.	0.5	8.3	8.4	2.6	0.1	3.5	4.9	0.0	6.9	13.3
62	04.320	Washing appliances	0.2	8.5	9.6	2.4	0.0	6.1	5.0	0.1	5.3	10.4
63	04.330	Cooking appliances	1.4	5.2	3.0	7.6	0.0	1.5	3.6	0.1	4.1	9.4
64	04.340	Heating appliances	0.3	4.1	4.7	1.9	0.0	0.8	2.0	0.0	2.7	4.9
65	04.350	Cleaning appliances	0.3	3.8	4.8	1.0	0.0	1.1	4.8	0.0	0.8	5.5
66	04.360	Other household appliances	0.2	3.4	6.3	1.0	1.1	10.1	13.8	2.0	18.7	21.1
67	04.400	Household utensils	1.9	21.5	34.6	9.3	1.2	13.5	10.6	3.2	28.5	35.6
68	04.510	Nondurable household goods	9.0	28.6	35.9	10.7	1.6	0.0	0.5	1.6	2.7	4.0
69	04.520	Domestic services	15.1	0.0	0.0	0.7	2.7	14.1	11.0	0.3	12.6	18.3
70	04.530	Household services	2.9	6.4	7.3	1.5	1.0	0.0	0.6	0.0	3.0	4.0
71	04.600	Household furnishing repairs	0.0	0.0	0.0	5.8	1.0	0.0	0.6	0.0	3.0	4.0
72	05.110	Drugs, medical preparations	1.4	109.1	44.6	22.6	3.3	44.5	48.4	1.6	33.9	30.1
73	05.120	Medical supplies	0.0	1.9	7.2	3.4	0.4	0.9	38.5	0.1	4.5	4.5
74	05.200	Therapeutic equipment	0.3	5.1	16.5	0.0	0.1	0.5	2.4	0.0	7.2	6.0
75	05.310	Physicians' services	7.4	23.2	32.0	31.7	3.1	20.7	18.7	2.0	19.0	28.3
76	05.320	Dentists' services	2.4	12.2	15.9	7.0	0.2	15.4	11.2	0.2	7.8	16.2
77	05.330	Services, nurses, other personnel	1.2	13.3	15.5	15.1	3.1	7.1	11.1	3.3	20.9	20.4

Appendix Table 14.5. Continued

			Colom-bia	France	Germany, F.R.	Hun-gary	India	Italy	Japan	Kenya	U.K.	U.S.
78	05.410	Hospitals, etc.	4.7	21.1	36.4	25.1	1.7	30.2	33.9	3.9	30.0	26.1
79	06.110	Personal cars	8.9	64.0	66.2	6.7	0.1	43.2	10.3	1.7	53.4	225.2
80	06.120	Other personal transport	0.0	4.3	3.8	5.3	0.3	1.8	2.8	0.0	2.5	28.5
81	06.210	Tires, tubes, accessories	1.4	17.4	11.9	3.7	0.1	6.2	0.7	0.3	23.4	31.1
82	06.220	Repair charges	8.5	22.0	19.3	2.9	0.7	12.3	3.0	1.5	24.3	35.8
83	06.230	Gasoline, oil, etc.	3.3	32.3	42.8	4.6	0.4	20.1	7.1	0.3	43.8	204.8
84	06.240	Parking, tolls, etc.	5.2	20.1	12.6	1.0	0.4	14.4	2.9	0.3	18.0	16.6
85	06.310	Local transport	9.9	7.0	4.7	7.4	1.2	8.4	77.7	0.5	19.4	5.6
86	06.321	Rail transport	5.9	9.7	16.6	8.1	1.2	11.3	18.0	0.3	6.1	0.5
87	06.322	Bus transport	1.4	7.8	9.1	9.4	5.2	6.7	4.8	4.3	1.9	1.7
88	06.323	Air transport	13.0	1.9	0.9	1.8	0.0	0.9	2.0	1.8	11.9	17.5
89	06.330	Miscellaneous transport	0.0	0.0	0.0	1.0	1.8	0.0	3.7	0.1	2.2	3.2
90	06.410	Postal communication	0.3	4.6	13.6	2.5	0.4	4.1	0.9	0.1	5.5	6.5
91	06.420	Telephone, telegraph	6.4	4.0	4.7	2.9	0.4	7.7	6.6	0.2	12.7	35.7
92	07.110	Radio, TV, phonograph, etc.	3.4	20.7	18.2	10.8	0.2	8.7	50.0	0.6	9.2	65.3
93	07.120	Major durable recreation equip.	0.4	7.3	15.4	0.5	0.0	0.4	6.3	0.6	4.8	33.7
94	07.130	Other recreation equipment	0.8	38.2	62.1	4.4	0.0	12.8	21.1	0.7	35.1	51.9
95	07.210	Public entertainment	8.1	8.9	12.1	32.2	0.1	15.8	18.3	1.8	34.5	18.7
96	07.230	Other recreation, cultural events	1.4	9.0	9.1	49.5	0.8	4.2	7.5	0.8	28.6	28.6
97	07.310	Books, papers, magazines	2.9	40.8	24.2	15.0	0.9	20.3	12.7	0.9	48.0	34.2
98	07.320	Stationery	0.2	23.4	9.0	1.6	0.5	4.6	3.5	0.0	6.6	11.9
99	07.411	Teachers, 1st, 2nd	34.3	47.0	43.5	44.0	22.0	52.3	42.7	17.2	40.5	60.3
100	07.412	Teachers, college	5.0	6.0	7.9	8.7	2.7	7.6	13.9	0.4	15.1	31.1
101	07.420	Educational facilities	1.7	8.4	22.6	15.0	0.2	5.4	9.8	1.1	17.8	38.5
102	07.431	Educational supplies	1.7	1.3	0.9	2.4	0.2	0.9	2.6	0.4	12.7	7.2
103	07.432	Other education expenditures	3.2	1.4	7.4	7.5	0.3	3.4	6.8	1.0	15.1	11.3
104	08.100	Barber, beauty shops	1.6	13.0	11.8	14.4	0.5	13.4	16.2	0.1	15.9	10.5
105	08.210	Toilet articles	4.1	28.0	19.1	14.6	0.7	10.4	21.7	0.3	15.3	37.7
106	08.220	Other personal-care goods	2.3	23.9	19.4	9.7	1.1	14.0	10.1	1.0	22.7	42.0
107	08.310	Restaurants, cafes	24.2	132.6	61.5	87.8	1.6	50.0	100.7	5.4	42.1	140.2
108	08.320	Hotels, etc.	2.3	54.4	31.0	3.7	1.3	26.4	18.4	3.5	35.5	8.4
109	08.400	Other services	44.3	5.7	9.3	28.4	3.1	3.8	73.6	3.2	53.1	92.8
111	10.100	1- and 2-dwelling buildings	34.2	56.7	33.9	39.3	7.6	101.4	123.0	10.4	89.4	95.1
112	10.200	Multidwelling buildings	4.4	151.2	171.9	40.1	7.0	48.9	51.4	1.2	34.1	34.1
113	11.100	Hotels, etc.	1.0	8.0	11.7	4.4	0.2	5.5	5.3	0.1	1.1	4.6
114	11.200	Industrial buildings	9.5	37.6	94.5	44.5	0.5	49.5	17.2	3.4	38.1	38.2
115	11.300	Commercial buildings	3.3	36.3	30.8	6.5	1.5	8.3	12.9	0.6	10.6	19.7
116	11.400	Office buildings	9.2	25.3	29.2	10.2	0.6	17.0	19.9	1.0	8.7	23.6
117	11.500	Educational buildings	5.7	18.7	25.3	9.4	0.4	7.5	22.4	1.3	18.6	30.2
118	11.600	Hospital buildings	1.3	9.5	16.4	3.1	0.3	5.7	7.0	0.9	9.1	12.4
119	11.700	Agricultural buildings	7.1	17.6	9.0	39.7	2.2	10.0	1.9	0.4	8.0	4.0
120	11.800	Other buildings	1.6	34.5	4.2	2.5	0.6	4.9	26.5	0.2	10.5	20.0
121	12.100	Roads, highways	19.5	33.6	66.9	13.1	1.8	28.7	37.9	1.0	25.5	39.8
122	12.200	Transmission, utility lines	12.8	73.5	50.9	67.6	5.3	16.8	85.3	1.0	18.2	54.9
123	12.300	Other construction	10.3	8.7	19.3	32.0	3.7	5.9	82.6	1.1	5.6	9.5
124	13.000	Land improvement	13.1	2.2	2.7	6.8	4.5	10.8	2.1	0.8	3.4	6.1
125	14.110	Locomotives	0.0	4.0	1.0	2.7	0.1	1.8	3.4	1.0	0.4	2.7
126	14.120	Other	0.3	8.3	3.8	8.1	0.2	1.8	0.4	0.9	0.7	10.9
127	14.200	Passenger cars	1.9	42.7	29.5	1.4	0.1	24.9	48.4	2.0	14.4	54.4
128	14.300	Trucks, buses, trailers	3.0	59.8	39.9	22.6	1.3	26.4	59.8	2.7	1.8	70.8
129	14.400	Aircraft	1.0	3.3	10.2	1.4	0.0	4.8	1.4	0.6	4.8	21.0
130	14.500	Ships, boats	4.8	5.6	20.1	0.9	0.2	5.3	13.5	0.1	15.6	3.6
131	14.600	Other transport	0.1	0.5	0.2	13.6	0.3	2.9	7.5	0.1	12.4	3.5
132	15.100	Engines and turbines	0.5	3.4	2.9	3.1	0.2	2.5	11.9	0.5	0.6	11.3
133	15.210	Tractors	0.6	15.4	7.7	5.5	0.2	3.4	1.9	0.5	3.9	11.1
134	15.220	Other agricultural machinery	0.5	24.2	9.1	11.0	0.0	2.9	8.8	0.5	5.0	16.2
135	15.300	Office machinery	0.4	28.8	31.8	3.5	0.0	4.1	24.0	0.2	9.5	42.2
136	15.400	Metalworking machinery	1.9	20.6	27.7	7.7	0.2	11.8	20.3	0.3	17.3	19.9
137	15.500	Construction, mining	1.7	35.2	22.7	9.9	0.1	4.1	26.9	0.8	22.2	28.3
138	15.600	Special industrial	2.7	51.1	43.2	30.3	0.5	13.1	76.6	2.1	27.7	20.5
139	15.700	General industrial	2.4	29.8	78.0	10.9	0.9	15.2	48.0	1.5	80.0	23.6
140	15.800	Service industrial	0.1	3.0	4.4	1.6	0.1	2.7	5.3	0.3	2.4	26.1
141	16.100	Electrical transmission	0.9	44.5	39.7	4.0	0.5	21.9	32.2	0.8	22.8	14.9
142	16.200	Communication equipment	1.1	26.3	39.7	10.0	0.7	7.6	33.0	0.4	22.5	36.4
143	16.300	Other electrical	3.0	7.9	7.6	0.8	0.1	12.8	6.3	0.2	8.4	3.9
144	16.400	Instruments	0.8	32.2	32.9	8.5	0.2	5.6	11.7	0.2	11.7	18.4
145	17.100	Furniture, fixtures	1.2	20.1	25.9	22.3	0.0	7.4	20.9	0.4	11.7	23.8
146	17.200	Other durable goods	1.4	29.1	27.8	1.4	0.6	14.7	12.8	1.3	1.6	32.1
147	18.000	Increase in stocks	10.4	120.2	85.8	69.4	7.5	37.2	131.2	5.9	23.7	22.6
148	19.000	Exports less imports	-8.0	8.9	84.3	-45.4	-1.0	2.4	38.0	-3.7	25.3	11.1
149	20.100	Blue-collar, unskilled	3.9	1.7	2.8	11.5	7.7	9.3	15.9	21.1	33.4	4.2
150	20.210	Blue-collar, skilled	1.7	26.6	23.0	1.5	1.5	10.6	98.1	1.6	11.3	56.2

Appendix Table 14.5. Continued

			Colombia	France	Germany, F.R.	Hungary	India	Italy	Japan	Kenya	U.K.	U.S.
151	20.220	White-collar	7.5	33.6	58.5	19.7	16.9	30.2	19.5	3.2	44.2	55.0
152	20.300	Professional	13.0	41.4	15.0	25.9	5.8	6.6	21.9	5.8	24.2	110.1
153	21.000	Government expenditure on commodities	16.0	120.1	227.4	89.7	10.7	67.9	67.0	7.2	105.5	358.8

Note: The net expenditure of residents abroad, line 110 in the binary tables, has been consolidated with other services (line 109) in the multilateral comparisons. Thus there are 152 categories in this table. See page 70.

Appendix Table 14.6. Per Capita Expenditures in National Currencies, 1967

			Hungary (forint)	India (rupee)	Japan (yen)	Kenya (shilling)	U.K. (pound)	U.S. (dollar)
1	01.101	Rice	48.9	111.45	16,702.	1.25	0.091	1.26
2	01.102	Meal, other cereals	231.7	76.18	360.	90.96	0.635	5.47
3	01.103	Bread, rolls	285.3	0.30	1,244.	4.75	5.843	15.14
4	01.104	Biscuits, cakes	78.3	0.35	4,671.	1.89	5.661	16.68
5	01.105	Cereal preparations	56.7	0.29	102.	0.77	0.998	7.01
6	01.106	Macaroni, spaghetti, related foods	23.1	0.29	1,428.	0.15	0.272	1.55
7	01.111	Fresh beef, veal	84.4	0.54	1,599.	28.17	7.204	58.87
8	01.112	Fresh lamb, mutton	12.7	0.98	25.	3.31	3.829	2.39
9	01.113	Fresh pork	583.4	0.19	2,289.	0.66	1.742	14.30
10	01.114	Fresh poultry	315.2	1.67	1,077.	1.39	2.468	16.12
11	01.115	Other fresh meat	20.0	2.84	447.	2.73	1.089	2.53
12	01.116	Frozen, salted meat	275.4	0.0	1,519.	2.26	11.468	32.94
13	01.121	Fresh, frozen fish	26.2	4.91	5,837.	7.45	2.286	6.87
14	01.122	Canned fish	10.2	0.0	4,315.	1.12	1.270	3.23
15	01.131	Fresh milk	269.3	18.25	2,777.	34.72	8.020	30.56
16	01.132	Milk products	91.1	2.82	587.	3.92	3.284	14.16
17	01.133	Eggs, egg products	233.6	0.79	2,882.	0.53	3.484	12.05
18	01.141	Butter	83.3	14.79	169.	5.05	2.921	4.06
19	01.142	Margarine, edible oil	27.1	14.56	784.	4.34	1.107	8.83
20	01.143	Lard, edible fat	381.8	0.0	8.	1.05	0.544	0.70
21	01.151	Fresh fruits, tropical, subtropical	56.9	4.21	2,228.	12.41	1.742	6.73
22	01.152	Other fresh fruits	296.2	0.64	2,504.	0.29	2.468	10.23
23	01.153	Fresh vegetables	221.2	10.67	5,631.	18.30	4.373	21.44
24	01.161	Fruit other than fresh	7.7	0.30	617.	0.08	2.105	17.38
25	01.162	Vegetables other than fresh	2.7	19.39	2,609.	2.96	3.466	17.52
26	01.170	Potatoes, manioc, other tubers	184.0	5.23	719.	24.32	4.010	9.67
27	01.191	Coffee	125.3	0.80	248.	1.27	0.998	9.81
28	01.192	Tea	10.9	4.00	730.	4.50	2.558	1.82
29	01.193	Cocoa	11.5	0.0	135.	0.34	0.091	0.70
30	01.180	Sugar	245.6	16.93	874.	6.91	1.923	3.78
31	01.201	Jam, syrup, honey	70.9	0.33	795.	3.46	0.998	4.21
32	01.202	Chocolate, ice cream	172.0	1.60	1,095.	2.52	7.657	12.76
33	01.203	Salt, spices, sauces	160.4	12.01	3,914.	5.16	0.817	5.89
34	01.310	Nonalcoholic beverages	22.9	0.16	896.	4.39	2.540	11.07
35	01.321	Spirits	89.6	0.11	6,874.	2.07	8.056	16.68
36	01.322	Wine, cider	281.4	1.08	407.	0.22	3.792	3.56
37	01.323	Beer	81.1	0.30	3,023.	13.85	17.328	20.89
38	01.410	Cigarettes	235.1	0.86	3,855.	13.35	23.860	41.90
39	01.420	Other tobacco	6.1	10.88	14.	0.23	3.502	4.87
40	02.110	Clothing materials	145.4	8.92	8,375.	2.59	1.089	4.76
41	02.121	Men's clothing	331.2	4.89	2,743.	5.93	6.460	41.85
42	02.122	Women's clothing	312.6	6.87	1,600.	3.49	10.524	64.13
43	02.123	Boys', girls' clothing	165.8	0.72	721.	1.84	2.105	19.74
44	02.131	Men's, boys' underwear	104.8	0.07	3,121.	0.52	3.448	9.01
45	02.132	Women's, girls' underwear	106.8	0.06	2,259.	0.44	4.536	23.63
46	02.150	Other clothing	169.9	0.03	2,434.	0.64	4.808	10.70
47	02.160	Clothing rental, repair	72.1	0.60	3,208.	0.43	0.726	3.29
48	02.211	Men's footwear	114.5	1.03	517.	2.74	2.177	9.56
49	02.212	Women's footwear	176.4	1.03	513.	0.68	2.994	12.59
50	02.213	Children's footwear	55.3	0.52	171.	0.53	1.633	9.57
51	02.220	Footwear repairs	58.5	0.15	316.	0.22	0.635	1.79
52	03.110	Gross rents	558.7	18.72	23,043.	55.43	49.481	350.61
53	03.120	Indoor repair, upkeep	126.5	1.84	3,747.	0.18	10.016	14.46
54	03.210	Electricity	123.4	0.85	3,544.	1.33	9.417	37.73
55	03.220	Gas	45.8	0.03	2,187.	0.10	4.681	25.67
56	03.230	Liquid fuels	15.3	4.61	702.	1.29	1.089	22.40

Appendix Table 14.6. Continued

			Hungary (forint)	India (rupee)	Japan (yen)	Kenya (shilling)	U.K. (pound)	U.S. (dollar)
57	03.240	Other fuels, ice	307.0	19.35	1,835.	6.58	6.677	4.34
58	04.110	Furniture, fixtures	294.8	0.28	2,964	3.91	5.716	45.02
59	04.120	Floor coverings	35.0	1.83	247.	0.64	4.627	15.29
60	04.200	Household textiles, etc.	166.9	3.52	301.	2.00	3.992	31.17
61	04.310	Refrigerators, etc.	54.4	0.55	1,649.	0.49	1.179	12.65
62	04.320	Washing appliances	39.2	0.0	747.	0.07	1.542	7.09
63	04.330	Cooking appliances	61.7	0.01	795.	0.52	1.361	7.82
64	04.340	Heating appliances	30.2	0.01	1,013.	0.47	1.270	3.80
65	04.350	Cleaning appliances	12.7	0.0	192.	0.08	0.907	2.09
66	04.360	Other household appliances	6.0	0.10	1,024.	0.20	0.272	3.00
67	04.400	Household utensils	154.3	2.92	2,458.	5.68	5.534	16.09
68	04.510	Nondurable household goods	192.6	3.41	5,354.	13.54	5.353	23.81
69	04.520	Domestic services	27.4	2.00	333.	7.43	2.450	22.53
70	04.530	Household services	31.9	2.77	188.	1.33	2.849	20.35
71	04.600	Household furnishing repairs	96.4	1.02	1,629.	0.06	0.635	6.61
72	05.110	Drugs, medical preparations	261.5	7.77	9,340.	5.19	5.153	30.32
73	05.120	Medical supplies	42.1	0.73	953.	0.41	0.889	4.13
74	05.200	Therapeutic equipment	0.0	0.21	256.	0.07	1.506	8.10
75	05.310	Physicians' services	97.1	0.93	1,521.	4.18	4.064	38.71
76	05.320	Dentists' services	7.7	0.00	343.	0.29	1.325	11.69
77	05.330	Services, nurses, other personnel	102.0	1.38	1,348.	3.73	6.841	56.23
78	05.410	Hospitals, etc.	336.3	1.46	2,956.	11.75	9.236	80.38
79	06.110	Personal cars	134.1	0.94	1,396.	10.22	13.740	125.38
80	06.120	Other personal transport	61.2	0.94	596.	0.16	0.871	10.71
81	06.210	Tires, tubes, accessories	39.2	0.47	35.	1.22	3.175	19.37
82	06.220	Repair charges	36.0	0.56	178.	2.09	2.994	29.57
83	06.230	Gasoline, oil, etc.	55.7	0.98	560.	11.93	10.034	88.67
84	06.240	Parking, tolls, etc.	9.8	0.50	253.	0.89	5.353	21.13
85	06.310	Local transport	137.0	2.25	2,906.	2.11	8.601	11.15
86	06.321	Rail transport	146.8	3.63	855.	1.32	1.996	1.04
87	06.322	Bus transport	137.0	9.41	279.	12.48	0.454	1.80
88	06.323	Air transport	14.7	0.06	79.	14.20	2.450	8.14
89	06.330	Miscellaneous transport	26.5	2.69	134.	0.21	1.633	2.99
90	06.410	Postal communication	29.9	0.64	297.	0.33	1.960	5.85
91	06.420	Telephone, telegraph	34.3	0.73	1,230.	0.82	2.468	37.91
92	07.110	Radio, TV, phonograph, etc.	169.6	0.85	3,315.	2.25	2.631	36.42
93	07.120	Major durable recreation equip.	8.2	0.07	1,635.	2.54	1.270	19.68
94	07.130	Other recreation equipment	75.2	0.12	1,408.	1.74	8.419	29.65
95	07.210	Public entertainment	171.9	0.26	453.	6.13	5.316	23.84
96	07.230	Other recreation, cultural events	221.1	1.50	7,529.	4.45	11.486	46.49
97	07.310	Books, papers, magazines	148.4	1.81	4,320.	5.42	6.550	29.67
98	07.320	Stationery	60.3	0.52	815.	0.08	1.542	8.18
99	07.411	Teachers, 1st, 2nd	407.1	9.26	2,919.	32.06	17.873	133.01
100	07.412	Teachers, college	42.9	1.26	346.	1.72	3.647	21.84
101	07.420	Educational facilities	191.2	0.60	1,276.	4.55	4.318	22.12
102	07.431	Educational supplies	19.5	0.54	375.	1.87	1.597	5.71
103	07.432	Other education expenditures	106.3	0.68	1,393.	3.09	2.903	6.39
104	08.100	Barber, beauty shops	82.2	1.02	3,984.	0.70	3.212	18.63
105	08.210	Toilet articles	97.0	2.78	4,414.	1.67	3.629	24.44
106	08.220	Other personal-care goods	145.6	2.79	1,042.	1.67	3.901	26.78
107	08.310	Restaurants, cafes	1,624.4	4.83	7,526.	12.49	13.572	116.93
108	08.320	Hotels, etc.	33.0	4.83	2,921.	13.64	8.691	7.60
109	08.400	Other services	330.6	3.16	5,987.	12.64	15.949	117.19
111	10.100	1- and 2-dwelling buildings	508.5	12.86	22,205.	22.12	16.709	96.00
112	10.200	Multidwelling buildings	428.3	12.86	6,164.	3.32	8.583	26.08
113	11.100	Hotels, etc.	82.9	0.42	918.	0.67	0.472	6.17
114	11.200	Industrial buildings	676.7	1.11	6,686.	5.28	11.849	35.22
115	11.300	Commercial buildings	82.7	2.96	3,967.	2.74	3.520	18.74
116	11.400	Office buildings	84.6	1.21	4,360.	2.39	2.304	23.03
117	11.500	Educational buildings	97.5	0.67	2,858.	5.35	5.135	35.94
118	11.600	Hospital buildings	30.5	0.40	1,053.	2.07	2.268	10.09
119	11.700	Agricultural buildings	250.1	4.43	574.	1.33	1.107	3.18
120	11.800	Other buildings	36.8	1.02	2,949.	0.89	2.722	17.47
121	12.100	Roads, highways	192.6	2.87	7,393.	10.64	4.772	44.65
122	12.200	Transmission, utility lines	743.5	8.80	12,633.	8.04	4.627	52.01
123	12.300	Other construction	277.6	4.79	5,650.	12.81	1.760	10.67
124	13.000	Land improvement	194.8	7.86	3,847.	3.75	1.651	11.70
125	14.110	Locomotives	82.3	0.64	121.	3.12	0.181	1.31
126	14.120	Other	143.4	1.27	749.	5.53	0.272	7.08
127	14.200	Passenger cars	29.6	0.41	4,611.	11.41	4.990	30.68
128	14.300	Trucks, buses, trailers	214.4	5.84	10,755.	13.07	0.526	29.14
129	14.400	Aircraft	12.3	0.35	158.	3.02	0.671	16.72
130	14.500	Ships, boats	29.3	0.54	2,599.	0.52	2.685	3.68
131	14.600	Other transport	144.6	0.91	670.	0.60	2.958	1.72
132	15.100	Engines and turbines	70.8	0.96	1,198.	1.87	0.091	5.04
133	15.210	Tractors	57.7	0.33	518.	2.06	0.744	9.45

Appendix Table 14.6. Continued

			Hun-gary (forint)	India (rupee)	Japan (yen)	Kenya (shilling)	U.K. (pound)	U.S. (dollar)
134	15.220	Other agricultural machinery	122.6	0.27	982.	2.92	1.107	12.00
135	15.300	Office machinery	71.5	0.23	1,815.	1.61	2.486	27.54
136	15.400	Metalworking machinery	225.3	1.93	3,649.	0.99	3.520	18.98
137	15.500	Construction, mining	122.6	0.39	3,611.	4.08	3.702	12.93
138	15.600	Special industrial	596.6	3.45	8,804.	8.76	6.097	15.64
139	15.700	General industrial	147.5	3.93	3,810.	8.28	16.947	16.17
140	15.800	Service industrial	39.2	0.53	2,074.	1.78	0.472	14.57
141	16.100	Electrical transmission	116.3	3.07	4,306.	3.54	5.371	12.37
142	16.200	Communication equipment	78.9	2.12	4,067.	2.52	7.022	19.64
143	16.300	Other electrical	13.9	0.74	269.	0.96	1.470	3.71
144	16.400	Instruments	130.0	0.79	722.	1.23	1.379	15.66
145	17.100	Furniture, fixtures	204.0	0.16	1,533.	1.72	1.651	16.93
146	17.200	Other durable goods	35.5	5.49	1,234.	4.59	0.381	15.55
147	18.000	Increase in stocks	1,373.4	8.93	22,907.	13.50	3.956	34.50
148	19.000	Exports less imports	-473.7	-13.91	1,018.	-8.06	-8.383	3.54
149	20.100	Blue-collar, unskilled	165.2	9.26	5,164.	33.43	17.147	13.82
150	20.210	Blue-collar, skilled	9.5	0.84	10,217.	2.36	2.123	72.12
151	20.220	White-collar	153.7	9.71	2,519.	9.14	13.591	82.97
152	20.300	Professional	139.1	7.54	3,376.	22.65	6.151	102.98
153	21.000	Government expenditure on commodities	1,162.4	19.21	8,584.	21.37	34.022	329.70

Note: The net expenditure of residents abroad, line 110 in the binary tables, has been consolidated with other services (line 109) in the multilateral comparisons. Thus there are 152 categories in this table. See page 70.

Appendix Table 14.7. Percentage Distribution of Expenditures in National Currencies, 1967

			Hun-gary	India	Japan	Kenya	U.K.	U.S.
1	01.101	Rice	0.20	17.39	3.83	0.14	0.01	0.03
2	01.102	Meal, other cereals	0.96	11.89	0.08	10.26	0.09	0.14
3	01.103	Bread, rolls	1.18	0.05	0.29	0.54	0.81	0.38
4	01.104	Biscuits, cakes	0.32	0.05	1.07	0.21	0.79	0.42
5	01.105	Cereal preparations	0.23	0.05	0.02	0.09	0.14	0.18
6	01.106	Macaroni, spaghetti, related foods	0.10	0.05	0.33	0.02	0.04	0.04
7	01.111	Fresh beef, veal	0.35	0.08	0.37	3.18	1.00	1.48
8	01.112	Fresh lamb, mutton	0.05	0.15	0.01	0.37	0.53	0.06
9	01.113	Fresh pork	2.41	0.03	0.52	0.07	0.24	0.36
10	01.114	Fresh poultry	1.30	0.26	0.25	0.16	0.34	0.40
11	01.115	Other fresh meat	0.08	0.44	0.10	0.31	0.15	0.06
12	01.116	Frozen, salted meat	1.14	0.0	0.35	0.25	1.59	0.83
13	01.121	Fresh, frozen fish	0.11	0.77	1.34	0.84	0.32	0.17
14	01.122	Canned fish	0.04	0.0	0.99	0.13	0.18	0.08
15	01.131	Fresh milk	1.11	2.85	0.64	3.91	1.11	0.77
16	01.132	Milk products	0.38	0.44	0.13	0.44	0.46	0.36
17	01.133	Eggs, egg products	0.97	0.12	0.66	0.06	0.48	0.30
18	01.141	Butter	0.34	2.31	0.04	0.57	0.41	0.10
19	01.142	Margarine, edible oil	0.11	2.27	0.18	0.49	0.15	0.22
20	01.143	Lard, edible fat	1.58	0.0	0.00	0.12	0.08	0.02
21	01.151	Fresh fruits, tropical, subtropical	0.24	0.66	0.51	1.40	0.24	0.17
22	01.152	Other fresh fruits	1.23	0.10	0.57	0.03	0.34	0.26
23	01.153	Fresh vegetables	0.92	1.66	1.29	2.06	0.61	0.54
24	01.161	Fruit other than fresh	0.03	0.05	0.14	0.01	0.29	0.44
25	01.162	Vegetables other than fresh	0.01	3.03	0.60	0.33	0.48	0.44
26	01.170	Potatoes, manioc, other tubers	0.76	0.82	0.16	2.74	0.56	0.24
27	01.191	Coffee	0.52	0.12	0.06	0.14	0.14	0.25
28	01.192	Tea	0.04	0.62	0.17	0.51	0.36	0.05
29	01.193	Cocoa	0.05	0.0	0.03	0.04	0.01	0.02
30	01.180	Sugar	1.02	2.64	0.20	0.78	0.27	0.09
31	01.201	Jam, syrup, honey	0.29	0.05	0.18	0.39	0.14	0.11
32	01.202	Chocolate, ice cream	0.71	0.25	0.25	0.28	1.06	0.32
33	01.203	Salt, spices, sauces	0.66	1.87	0.90	0.58	0.11	0.15
34	01.310	Nonalcoholic beverages	0.09	0.03	0.21	0.50	0.35	0.28
35	01.321	Spirits	0.37	0.02	1.58	0.23	1.12	0.42
36	01.322	Wine, cider	1.16	0.17	0.09	0.02	0.53	0.09

Appendix Table 14.7. Continued

			Hungary	India	Japan	Kenya	U.K.	U.S.
37	01.323	Beer	0.34	0.05	0.69	1.56	2.41	0.52
38	01.410	Cigarettes	0.97	0.13	0.88	1.51	3.31	1.05
39	01.420	Other tobacco	0.03	1.70	0.00	0.03	0.49	0.12
40	02.110	Clothing materials	0.60	1.39	1.92	0.29	0.15	0.12
41	02.121	Men's clothing	1.37	0.76	0.63	0.67	0.90	1.05
42	02.122	Women's clothing	1.29	1.07	0.37	0.39	1.46	1.61
43	02.123	Boys', girls' clothing	0.69	0.11	0.17	0.21	0.29	0.50
44	02.131	Men's, boys' underwear	0.43	0.01	0.72	0.06	0.48	0.23
45	02.132	Women's, girls' underwear	0.44	0.01	0.52	0.05	0.63	0.59
46	02.150	Other clothing	0.70	0.00	0.56	0.07	0.67	0.27
47	02.160	Clothing rental, repair	0.30	0.09	0.74	0.05	0.10	0.08
48	02.211	Men's footwear	0.47	0.16	0.12	0.31	0.30	0.24
49	02.212	Women's footwear	0.73	0.16	0.12	0.08	0.42	0.32
50	02.213	Children's footwear	0.23	0.08	0.04	0.06	0.23	0.24
51	02.220	Footwear repairs	0.24	0.02	0.07	0.02	0.09	0.04
52	03.110	Gross rents	2.31	2.92	5.28	6.25	6.87	8.80
53	03.120	Indoor repair, upkeep	0.52	0.29	0.86	0.02	1.39	0.36
54	03.210	Electricity	0.51	0.13	0.81	0.15	1.31	0.95
55	03.220	Gas	0.19	0.00	0.50	0.01	0.65	0.64
56	03.230	Liquid fuels	0.06	0.72	0.16	0.14	0.15	0.56
57	03.240	Other fuels, ice	1.27	3.02	0.42	0.74	0.93	0.11
58	04.110	Furniture, fixtures	1.22	0.04	0.68	0.44	0.79	1.13
59	04.120	Floor coverings	0.15	0.29	0.06	0.07	0.64	0.38
60	04.200	Household textiles, etc.	0.69	0.55	0.07	0.23	0.55	0.78
61	04.310	Refrigerators, etc.	0.23	0.09	0.38	0.06	0.16	0.32
62	04.320	Washing appliances	0.16	0.0	0.17	0.01	0.21	0.18
63	04.330	Cooking appliances	0.26	0.00	0.18	0.06	0.19	0.20
64	04.340	Heating appliances	0.13	0.00	0.23	0.05	0.18	0.10
65	04.350	Cleaning appliances	0.05	0.0	0.04	0.01	0.13	0.05
66	04.360	Other household appliances	0.02	0.02	0.23	0.02	0.04	0.08
67	04.400	Household utensils	0.64	0.46	0.56	0.64	0.77	0.40
68	04.510	Nondurable household goods	0.80	0.53	1.23	1.53	0.74	0.60
69	04.520	Domestic services	0.11	0.31	0.08	0.84	0.34	0.57
70	04.530	Household services	0.13	0.43	0.04	0.15	0.40	0.51
71	04.600	Household furnishing repairs	0.40	0.16	0.37	0.01	0.09	0.17
72	05.110	Drugs, medical preparations	1.08	1.21	2.14	0.59	0.72	0.76
73	05.120	Medical supplies	0.17	0.11	0.22	0.05	0.12	0.10
74	05.200	Therapeutic equipment	0.0	0.03	0.06	0.01	0.21	0.20
75	05.310	Physicians' services	0.40	0.15	0.35	0.47	0.56	0.97
76	05.320	Dentists' services	0.03	0.00	0.08	0.03	0.18	0.29
77	05.330	Services, nurses, other personnel	0.42	0.22	0.31	0.42	0.95	1.41
78	05.410	Hospitals, etc.	1.39	0.23	0.68	1.33	1.28	2.02
79	06.110	Personal cars	0.56	0.15	0.32	1.15	1.91	3.15
80	06.120	Other personal transport	0.25	0.15	0.14	0.02	0.12	0.27
81	06.210	Tires, tubes, accessories	0.16	0.07	0.01	0.14	0.44	0.49
82	06.220	Repair charges	0.15	0.09	0.04	0.24	0.42	0.74
83	06.230	Gasoline, oil, etc.	0.23	0.15	0.13	1.35	1.39	2.23
84	06.240	Parking, tolls, etc.	0.04	0.08	0.06	0.10	0.74	0.53
85	06.310	Local transport	0.57	0.35	0.67	0.24	1.19	0.28
86	06.321	Rail transport	0.61	0.57	0.20	0.15	0.28	0.03
87	06.322	Bus transport	0.57	1.47	0.06	1.41	0.06	0.05
88	06.323	Air transport	0.06	0.01	0.02	1.60	0.34	0.20
89	06.330	Miscellaneous transport	0.11	0.42	0.03	0.02	0.23	0.08
90	06.410	Postal communication	0.12	0.10	0.07	0.04	0.27	0.15
91	06.420	Telephone, telegraph	0.14	0.11	0.28	0.09	0.34	0.95
92	07.110	Radio, TV, phonograph, etc.	0.70	0.13	0.76	0.25	0.37	0.91
93	07.120	Major durable recreation equip.	0.03	0.01	0.37	0.29	0.18	0.49
94	07.130	Other recreation equipment	0.31	0.02	0.32	0.20	1.17	0.74
95	07.210	Public entertainment	0.71	0.04	0.10	0.69	0.74	0.60
96	07.230	Other recreation, cultural events	0.92	0.23	1.73	0.50	1.59	1.17
97	07.310	Books, papers, magazines	0.61	0.28	0.99	0.61	0.91	0.74
98	07.320	Stationery	0.25	0.08	0.19	0.01	0.21	0.21
99	07.411	Teachers, 1st, 2nd	1.68	1.45	0.67	3.62	2.48	3.34
100	07.412	Teachers, college	0.18	0.20	0.08	0.19	0.51	0.55
101	07.420	Educational facilities	0.79	0.09	0.29	0.51	0.60	0.56
102	07.431	Educational supplies	0.08	0.08	0.09	0.21	0.22	0.14
103	07.432	Other education expenditures	0.44	0.11	0.32	0.35	0.40	0.16
104	08.100	Barber, beauty shops	0.34	0.16	0.91	0.08	0.45	0.47
105	08.210	Toilet articles	0.40	0.43	1.01	0.19	0.50	0.61
106	08.220	Other personal-care goods	0.60	0.43	0.24	0.19	0.54	0.67
107	08.310	Restaurants, cafes	6.72	0.75	1.73	1.41	1.88	2.93
108	08.320	Hotels, etc.	0.14	0.75	0.67	1.54	1.21	0.19
109	08.400	Other services	1.37	0.49	1.37	1.43	2.21	2.94
111	10.100	1- and 2-dwelling buildings	2.10	2.01	5.04	2.49	2.55	2.42
112	10.200	Multidwelling buildings	1.77	2.01	1.41	0.37	1.19	0.65
113	11.100	Hotels, etc.	0.34	0.07	0.21	0.08	0.07	0.15

Appendix Table 14.7. Continued

			Hun-gary	India	Japan	Kenya	U.K.	U.S.
114	11.200	Industrial buildings	2.80	0.17	1.53	0.60	1.64	0.88
115	11.300	Commercial buildings	0.34	0.46	0.91	0.31	0.49	0.47
116	11.400	Office buildings	0.35	0.19	1.00	0.27	0.32	0.58
117	11.500	Educational buildings	0.40	0.11	0.66	0.60	0.71	0.90
118	11.600	Hospital buildings	0.13	0.06	0.24	0.23	0.31	0.25
119	11.700	Agricultural buildings	1.04	0.69	0.13	0.15	0.15	0.08
120	11.800	Other buildings	0.15	0.16	0.68	0.10	0.38	0.44
121	12.100	Roads, highways	0.80	0.45	1.69	1.20	0.66	1.12
122	12.200	Transmission, utility lines	3.08	1.37	2.90	0.91	0.64	1.31
123	12.300	Other construction	1.15	0.75	1.30	1.44	0.24	0.27
124	13.000	Land improvement	0.81	1.23	0.88	0.42	0.23	0.29
125	14.110	Locomotives	0.34	0.10	0.03	0.35	0.03	0.03
126	14.120	Other	0.59	0.20	0.17	0.62	0.04	0.18
127	14.200	Passenger cars	0.12	0.06	1.06	1.29	0.69	0.77
128	14.300	Trucks, buses, trailers	0.89	0.91	2.47	1.47	0.07	0.73
129	14.400	Aircraft	0.05	0.05	0.04	0.34	0.09	0.42
130	14.500	Ships, boats	0.12	0.08	0.60	0.06	0.37	0.09
131	14.600	Other transport	0.60	0.14	0.15	0.07	0.41	0.04
132	15.100	Engines and turbines	0.29	0.15	0.27	0.21	0.01	0.13
133	15.210	Tractors	0.24	0.05	0.12	0.23	0.10	0.24
134	15.220	Other agricultural machinery	0.51	0.04	0.23	0.33	0.15	0.30
135	15.300	Office machinery	0.30	0.04	0.42	0.18	0.35	0.69
136	15.400	Metalworking machinery	0.93	0.30	0.84	0.11	0.49	0.48
137	15.500	Construction, mining	0.51	0.06	0.83	0.46	0.51	0.32
138	15.600	Special industrial	2.47	0.54	2.02	0.99	0.85	0.39
139	15.700	General industrial	0.61	0.61	0.87	0.93	2.35	0.41
140	15.800	Service industrial	0.16	0.08	0.48	0.20	0.07	0.37
141	16.100	Electrical transmission	0.48	0.48	0.99	0.40	0.75	0.31
142	16.200	Communication equipment	0.33	0.33	0.93	0.28	0.97	0.49
143	16.300	Other electrical	0.06	0.12	0.06	0.11	0.20	0.09
144	16.400	Instruments	0.54	0.12	0.17	0.14	0.19	0.39
145	17.100	Furniture, fixtures	0.84	0.03	0.35	0.19	0.23	0.42
146	17.200	Other durable goods	0.15	0.86	0.28	0.52	0.05	0.39
147	18.000	Increase in stocks	5.68	1.39	5.25	1.52	0.55	0.87
148	19.000	Exports less imports	-1.96	-2.17	0.23	-0.91	-1.16	0.09
149	20.100	Blue-collar, unskilled	0.68	1.44	1.18	3.77	2.38	0.35
150	20.210	Blue-collar, skilled	0.04	0.13	2.34	0.27	0.29	1.81
151	20.220	White-collar	0.64	1.52	0.58	1.03	1.89	2.08
152	20.300	Professional	0.58	1.18	0.77	2.55	0.85	2.58
153	21.000	Government expenditure on commodities	4.8	3.0	2.0	2.4	4.7	8.3

Note: The net expenditure of residents abroad, line 110 in the binary tables, has been consolidated with other services (line 109) in the multilateral comparisons. Thus there are 152 categories in this table. See page 70.

Appendix Table 14.8. Purchasing-Power Parities per U.S. Dollar, Five Countries, and International Prices, 1967

			Hun-gary (forint)	India (rupee)	Japan (yen)	Kenya (shilling)	U.K. (pound)	Inter-national prices
1	01.101	Rice	51.9	4.78	377.	4.49	0.347	1.97
2	01.102	Meal, other cereals	16.3	3.32	242.	4.97	0.227	1.33
3	01.103	Bread, rolls	5.5	2.77	162.	2.46	0.167	0.48
4	01.104	Biscuits, cakes	24.7	8.85	268.	0.99	0.202	0.90
5	01.105	Cereal preparations	6.6	3.49	289.†	7.71	0.208	0.65
6	01.106	Macaroni, spaghetti, related foods	17.4	12.22	332.	12.83	0.357	1.39
7	01.111	Fresh beef, veal	49.0	3.94	594.	3.61	0.207	1.01
8	01.112	Fresh lamb, mutton	11.2	3.85	400.†	4.04†	0.260	0.99
9	01.113	Fresh pork	51.7	2.04	401.	6.86	0.330	2.18
10	01.114	Fresh poultry	35.9	6.30	496.	4.54	0.315	1.67
11	01.115	Other fresh meat	18.1	4.92	432.†	3.89	0.304	1.41
12	01.116	Frozen, salted meat	26.8	4.45	504.	7.54	0.330	1.29
13	01.121	Fresh, frozen fish	8.3	1.16	241.	3.89	0.360	0.80
14	01.122	Canned fish	64.6	8.16	423.	13.35	0.462	1.79
15	01.131	Fresh milk	13.2	2.87	384.	4.41	0.349	1.11
16	01.132	Milk products	24.5	5.87	382.	4.74	0.166	1.14

Appendix Table 14.8. Continued

			Hungary (forint)	India (rupee)	Japan (yen)	Kenya (shilling)	U.K. (pound)	International prices
17	01.133	Eggs, egg products	38.1	5.22	280.	6.50	0.356	1.52
18	01.141	Butter	36.1	3.63	432.	4.49	0.209	1.39
19	01.142	Margarine, edible oil	30.0	5.72	397.	7.13	0.330	1.99
20	01.143	Lard, edible fat	44.9	7.50	552.	13.19	0.452	2.68
21	01.151	Fresh fruits, tropical, subtropical	58.5	2.63	526.	2.61	0.418	1.08
22	01.152	Other fresh fruits	13.1	3.31	299.	14.21	0.346	0.96
23	01.153	Fresh vegetables	5.9	1.36	182.	1.79	0.196	0.56
24	01.161	Fruit other than fresh	57.1	5.32	337.	4.09	0.289	1.10
25	01.162	Vegetables other than fresh	29.3	7.12	461.	5.53	0.312	2.05
26	01.170	Potatoes, manioc, other tubers	13.6	3.16	312.	2.29	0.205	0.77
27	01.191	Coffee	133.0	11.69	715.	8.21	0.416	2.36
28	01.192	Tea	48.6	2.11	195.	2.36	0.142	0.73
29	01.193	Cocoa	50.0	15.29	525.†	8.11	0.295	1.89
30	01.180	Sugar	39.8	7.82	500.	5.79	0.252	2.38
31	01.201	Jam, syrup, honey	20.5	7.58	416.	4.12	0.190	1.16
32	01.202	Chocolate, ice cream	37.4	7.50	594.	25.02	0.474	1.85
33	01.203	Salt, spices, sauces	15.7	1.14	172.	3.08	0.310	0.63
34	01.310	Nonalcoholic beverages	29.6	5.80	370.	13.91	0.372	1.48
35	01.321	Spirits	29.9	7.84	319.	7.55	0.440	1.40
36	01.322	Wine, cider	15.7	14.61	292.	8.76	0.655	1.20
37	01.323	Beer	18.8	8.50	329.	8.42	0.545	1.56
38	01.410	Cigarettes	10.2	8.53	214.	6.10	0.690	1.20
39	01.420	Other tobacco	18.6	2.52	207.†	4.93	0.630	1.16
40	02.110	Clothing materials	67.7	6.93	397.	8.86	0.435	2.19
41	02.121	Men's clothing	22.3	3.14	237.	5.19	0.320	1.18
42	02.122	Women's clothing	27.6	3.50	230.	10.71	0.483	1.33
43	02.123	Boys', girls' clothing	24.4	2.65	292.	3.41	0.307	1.18
44	02.131	Men's, boys' underwear	33.4	1.72	262.	10.14	0.452	1.35
45	02.132	Women's, girls' underwear	28.0	5.54	229.	4.69	0.348	1.15
46	02.150	Other clothing	20.9	6.08	177.	5.75	0.230	0.96
47	02.160	Clothing rental, repair	8.7	1.28	101.†	3.52	0.330	0.52
48	02.211	Men's footwear	24.4	3.85	204.	2.95	0.232	1.08
49	02.212	Women's footwear	21.5	3.55	206.	1.85	0.262	1.10
50	02.213	Children's footwear	13.2	2.85	172.	1.93	0.201	0.84
51	02.220	Footwear repairs	11.8	3.49	101.	3.67	0.214	0.71
52	03.110	Gross rents	9.5	1.40	237.	5.50	0.243	0.89
53	03.120	Indoor repair, upkeep	4.9	1.22	214.	4.84	0.319	0.67
54	03.210	Electricity	35.7	6.79	334.	8.39	0.298	1.23
55	03.220	Gas	17.4	4.16	1,175.	7.78	0.855	1.57
56	03.230	Liquid fuels	56.4	12.65	470.	16.74	0.412	1.79
57	03.240	Other fuels, ice	7.8	3.91	200.	2.81	0.262	0.91
58	04.110	Furniture, fixtures	19.2	2.89	215.	4.73	0.530	1.13
59	04.120	Floor coverings	26.8	0.43	274.	9.76	0.256	0.54
60	04.200	Household textiles, etc.	35.1	2.46	318.	10.16	0.285	1.22
61	04.310	Refrigerators, etc.	66.3	8.91	656.	11.86	0.523	1.83
62	04.320	Washing appliances	25.9	7.50	270.	10.85	0.333	1.19
63	04.330	Cooking appliances	13.4	5.65	186.	9.73	0.351	0.94
64	04.340	Heating appliances	46.8	4.32	625.	14.53	0.815	2.12
65	04.350	Cleaning appliances	34.3	7.50	369.	13.54	0.801	1.71
66	04.360	Other household appliances	24.7	4.69	326.	17.09	0.601	1.38
67	04.400	Household utensils	29.0	3.89	216.	4.18	0.406	1.26
68	04.510	Nondurable household goods	31.4	4.94	264.	7.34	0.263	1.34
69	04.520	Domestic services	7.8	0.31	123.	0.83	0.197	0.32
70	04.530	Household services	13.0	1.23	241.	3.42	0.194	0.73
71	04.600	Household furnishing repairs	10.4	1.04	160.	1.98	0.139	0.65
72	05.110	Drugs, medical preparations	12.1	2.39	128.	3.63	0.138	0.71
73	05.120	Medical supplies	24.1	2.56	181.	4.49	0.202	0.98
74	05.200	Therapeutic equipment	2.9	1.09	70.	1.94	0.174	0.64
75	05.310	Physicians' services	2.2	0.20	59.	1.53	0.157	0.32
76	05.320	Dentists' services	1.6	0.02	44.	2.57	0.247	0.46
77	05.330	Services, nurses, other personnel	2.5	0.49	44.	0.41	0.119	0.32
78	05.410	Hospitals, etc.	4.3	0.26	28.	0.97	0.100	0.31
79	06.110	Personal cars	65.8	11.45	398.	11.72	0.524	1.33
80	06.120	Other personal transport	26.0	6.59	526.	11.36	0.591	1.49
81	06.210	Tires, tubes, accessories	33.4	7.94	287.	11.85	0.222	1.08
82	06.220	Repair charges	18.1	1.24	340.	1.80	0.175	0.80
83	06.230	Gasoline, oil, etc.	36.4	7.90	617.	8.56	0.563	1.32
84	06.240	Parking, tolls, etc.	3.2	2.34	418.	5.66	0.279	0.89
85	06.310	Local transport	10.9	1.60	62.	2.44	0.239	0.55
86	06.321	Rail transport	15.0	2.46	136.	3.38	0.608	0.97
87	06.322	Bus transport	22.5	2.80	216.	4.00	0.250	1.16
88	06.323	Air transport	36.5†	7.65	284.	14.54	0.453	2.12
89	06.330	Miscellaneous transport	23.5	1.97	118.	3.14	0.705	1.03
90	06.410	Postal communication	12.1	3.04	330.	6.66	0.336	1.04
91	06.420	Telephone, telegraph	5.3	1.29	193.	2.92	0.181	0.76
92	07.110	Radio, TV, phonograph, etc.	50.8	7.50	230.	10.55	0.538	1.36
93	07.120	Major durable recreation equip.	19.6	7.50	171.	7.74	0.328	0.99

Appendix Table 14.8. Continued

			Hungary (forint)	India (rupee)	Japan (yen)	Kenya (shilling)	U.K. (pound)	International prices
94	07.130	Other recreation equipment	21.3	6.72	261.	7.26	0.341	1.13
95	07.210	Public entertainment	5.7	2.95	338.	2.91	0.149	0.55
96	07.230	Other recreation, cultural events	2.2	1.09	135.	2.95	0.222	0.41
97	07.310	Books, papers, magazines	12.3	3.14	301.	7.44	0.141	0.89
98	07.320	Stationery	33.1	1.47	263.	10.74	0.244	1.10
99	07.411	Teachers, 1st, 2nd	3.1	0.22	30.	0.60	0.185	0.24
100	07.412	Teachers, college	5.3	0.59	42.	3.11	0.265	0.54
101	07.420	Educational facilities	27.6	5.31	369.	7.96	0.378	1.40
102	07.431	Educational supplies	12.3	3.14	301.	7.44	0.141	0.87
103	07.432	Other education expenditures	24.9	4.37	378.	5.50	0.318	1.36
104	08.100	Barber, beauty shops	3.4	1.39	115.	3.31	0.136	0.46
105	08.210	Toilet articles	16.1	5.17	298.	10.82	0.310	1.22
106	08.220	Other personal-care goods	28.1	4.39	197.	6.13	0.299	1.23
107	08.310	Restaurants, cafes	14.1	3.54	122.	2.82	0.402	0.88
108	08.320	Hotels, etc.	14.6	4.28	305.	5.01	0.282	1.22
109	08.400	Other services	11.0	0.88	122.	2.58	0.216	0.72
111	10.100	1- and 2-dwelling buildings	15.7	1.66	279.	3.45	0.199	0.93
112	10.200	Multidwelling buildings	14.7	1.77	236.	3.83	0.207	0.86
113	11.100	Hotels, etc.	16.2	1.90	301.	5.14	0.406	1.07
114	11.200	Industrial buildings	23.1	2.79	581.	5.19	0.389	1.43
115	11.300	Commercial buildings	19.0	1.60	432.	3.98	0.342	1.12
116	11.400	Office buildings	12.3	1.71	284.	2.82	0.262	0.97
117	11.500	Educational buildings	14.8	1.90	208.	2.77	0.309	0.03
118	11.600	Hospital buildings	11.8	1.48†	185.	3.39†	0.246	0.84
119	11.700	Agricultural buildings	21.6	1.94	747.	2.32	0.244	1.07
120	11.800	Other buildings	21.3	1.94†	401.	3.44†	0.379	1.23
121	12.100	Roads, highways	19.0	1.76	297.	9.84	0.232	1.13
122	12.200	Transmission, utility lines	13.3	1.46	164.	7.66	0.215	0.80
123	12.300	Other construction	11.4	1.60	193.	9.53	0.328	0.88
124	13.000	Land improvement	10.1	1.36	158.	3.56	0.364	0.68
125	14.110	Locomotives	65.0	3.21	378.†	7.32	0.520	2.24†
126	14.120	Other	44.0†	7.26†	451.†	10.12†	0.620†	2.14
127	14.200	Passenger cars	68.0	8.91	422.	7.86	0.610	1.58
128	14.300	Trucks, buses, trailers	36.1	5.92†	358.†	4.91†	0.491†	1.55
129	14.400	Aircraft	42.4†	8.52	423.†	7.87	0.580†	1.31
130	14.500	Ships, boats	18.3†	1.83†	250.†	7.69†	0.334†	1.08
131	14.600	Other transport	37.6†	3.28	386.†	7.53	0.530†	1.89
132	15.100	Engines and turbines	47.5	11.21†	303.†	8.71	0.300	1.83
133	15.210	Tractors	37.5	5.93	276.†	6.43	0.320	1.39
134	15.220	Other agricultural machinery	27.1	6.10	287.†	9.06	0.352	1.39
135	15.300	Office machinery	43.4	6.69	282.†	8.46	0.427	1.29
136	15.400	Metalworking machinery	24.8	5.60	377.	4.77	0.326	1.40
137	15.500	Construction, mining	27.4	12.18	322.	9.49	0.361	1.43
138	15.600	Special industrial	32.2	5.73	238.	6.11	0.363	1.44
139	15.700	General industrial	29.2	6.88	242.	6.50	0.283	1.22
140	15.800	Service industrial	21.3	8.07	283.†	11.18	0.324†	1.25
141	16.100	Electrical transmission	19.6	9.08	292.†	5.56	0.341†	1.34
142	16.200	Communication equipment	16.9	6.26	302.†	10.70	0.352	1.27
143	16.300	Other electrical	27.2	4.39	212.	5.30	0.182	1.00
144	16.400	Instruments	26.6	3.84	286.	7.57	0.173	1.19
145	17.100	Furniture, fixtures	26.7	2.86	291.†	6.76	0.225	1.27
146	17.200	Other durable goods	35.6	6.13	295.†	6.92	0.345†	1.63
147	18.000	Increase in stocks	24.6	4.63	313.	5.96	0.361	1.44
148	19.000	Exports less imports	00.0	0.00	000.	0.00	0.000	0.00
149	20.100	Blue-collar, unskilled	5.3	0.37	144.	0.53	0.165	0.23
150	20.210	Blue-collar, skilled	5.9	0.43	120.	1.29	0.157	0.61
151	20.220	White-collar	6.1	0.61	130.	2.07	0.218	0.51
152	20.300	Professional	7.0	1.32	204.	4.63	0.311	0.83
153	21.000	Government expenditure on commodities	20.5	2.52	236.	4.38	0.295	1.00

Notes:
1. The net expenditure of residents abroad, line 110 in the binary tables, has been consolidated with other services (line 109) in the multilateral comparisons. Thus there are 152 categories in this table. See page 70.
2. The quantity ratios for line 148 are not printed because they would not have a clear economic meaning. The international dollar values are given in table 14.10.
†The PPPs for these items where price and quantity data were missing have been estimated by applying the double-weighted CPD method and are considered less reliable than direct estimates. The corresponding quantity estimates in 14.10 share the same weakness.

Appendix Table 14.9. Quantities per Capita with U.S.=100, 1967

			Hungary	India	Japan	Kenya	U.K.	U.S.
1	01.101	Rice	75.0	1,851.2	3,521.0	22.1	20.8	100.0
2	01.102	Meal, other cereals	260.0	419.1	27.1	334.4	51.2	100.0
3	01.103	Bread, rolls	339.5	0.7	50.8	12.7	230.9	100.0
4	01.104	Biscuits, cakes	19.0	0.2	104.4	11.4	167.9	100.0
5	01.105	Cereal preparations	122.5	1.2	5.0	1.4	68.5	100.0
6	01.106	Macaroni, spaghetti, related foods	85.8	1.6	278.2	0.7	49.3	100.0
7	01.111	Fresh beef, veal	2.9	0.2	4.6	0.7	59.2	100.0
8	01.112	Fresh lamb, mutton	47.7	10.6	2.6	13.3	616.5	100.0
9	01.113	Fresh pork	78.9	0.7	39.9	34.3	36.9	100.0
10	01.114	Fresh poultry	54.4	1.6	13.5	0.7	48.6	100.0
11	01.115	Other fresh meat	43.7	22.8	41.0	1.9	142.0	100.0
12	01.116	Frozen, salted meat	31.2	0.0	9.1	27.7	105.4	100.0
13	01.121	Fresh, frozen fish	46.1	61.5	352.8	0.9	92.4	100.0
14	01.122	Canned fish	4.9	0.0	316.2	27.9	85.1	100.0
15	01.131	Fresh milk	66.6	20.8	23.7	2.6	75.1	100.0
16	01.132	Milk products	26.2	3.4	10.8	25.8	140.0	100.0
17	01.133	Eggs, egg products	50.9	1.2	85.3	5.8	81.2	100.0
18	01.141	Butter	56.8	100.3	9.6	0.7	344.9	100.0
19	01.142	Margarine, edible oil	10.2	28.9	22.3	27.7	38.0	100.0
20	01.143	Lard, edible fat	1,214.5	0.0	2.1	6.9	172.1	100.0
21	01.151	Fresh fruits, tropical, subtropical	14.4	23.9	62.9	11.4	61.9	100.0
22	01.152	Other fresh fruits	221.3	1.9	81.9	70.5	69.8	100.0
23	01.153	Fresh vegetables	173.7	36.6	144.4	0.2	104.2	100.0
24	01.161	Fruit other than fresh	0.8	0.3	10.5	47.6	41.9	100.0
25	01.162	Vegetables other than fresh	0.5	15.5	32.3	0.1	63.4	100.0
26	01.170	Potatoes, manioc, other tubers	139.7	17.1	23.8	3.1	202.6	100.0
27	01.191	Coffee	9.6	0.7	3.5	109.7	24.4	100.0
28	01.192	Tea	12.3	104.1	205.0	1.6	990.6	100.0
29	01.193	Cocoa	32.7	0.0	36.9	104.7	44.0	100.0
30	01.180	Sugar	162.9	57.2	46.2	5.9	201.6	100.0
31	01.201	Jam, syrup, honey	82.1	1.0	45.4	31.6	124.6	100.0
32	01.202	Chocolate, ice cream	36.0	1.7	14.4	19.9	126.6	100.0
33	01.203	Salt, spices, sauces	173.0	178.9	386.3	0.8	44.7	100.0
34	01.310	Nonalcoholic beverages	7.0	0.3	21.9	28.5	61.7	100.0
35	01.321	Spirits	17.9	0.1	129.2	2.9	109.9	100.0
36	01.322	Wine, cider	503.3	2.1	39.1	1.6	162.5	100.0
37	01.323	Beer	20.7	0.2	44.0	0.7	152.2	100.0
38	01.410	Cigarettes	54.8	0.2	43.0	7.9	82.5	100.0
39	01.420	Other tobacco	6.7	88.7	1.4	5.2	114.2	100.0
40	02.110	Clothing materials	45.1	27.0	443.0	1.0	52.6	100.0
41	02.121	Men's clothing	35.5	3.7	27.7	6.1	48.3	100.0
42	02.122	Women's clothing	17.7	3.1	10.8	2.7	34.0	100.0
43	02.123	Boys', girls' clothing	34.4	1.4	12.5	0.5	34.7	100.0
44	02.131	Men's, boys' underwear	34.8	0.4	132.3	2.7	84.5	100.0
45	02.132	Women's, girls' underwear	16.1	0.0	41.7	0.6	55.1	100.0
46	02.150	Other clothing	76.1	0.0	128.4	0.4	195.7	100.0
47	02.160	Clothing rental, repair	252.3	14.3	968.0	1.0	66.9	100.0
48	02.211	Men's footwear	49.0	2.8	26.5	3.8	98.0	100.0
49	02.212	Women's footwear	65.2	2.3	19.8	9.7	90.6	100.0
50	02.213	Children's footwear	43.9	1.9	10.4	2.9	84.7	100.0
51	02.220	Footwear repairs	277.1	2.3	175.1	2.9	166.0	100.0
52	03.110	Gross rents	16.8	3.8	27.7	3.4	58.1	100.0
53	03.120	Indoor repair, upkeep	177.7	10.4	121.2	2.9	217.2	100.0
54	03.210	Electricity	9.2	0.3	28.1	0.3	83.8	100.0
55	03.220	Gas	10.2	0.0	7.3	0.4	21.3	100.0
56	03.230	Liquid fuels	1.2	1.6	6.7	0.0	11.8	100.0
57	03.240	Other fuels, ice	903.9	114.1	211.4	0.3	588.0	100.0
58	04.110	Furniture, fixtures	34.1	0.2	30.6	54.1	24.0	100.0
59	04.120	Floor coverings	8.5	28.0	5.9	1.8	118.0	100.0
60	04.200	Household textiles, etc.	15.2	4.6	3.0	0.4	45.0	100.0
61	04.310	Refrigerators, etc.	6.5	0.5	19.9	0.6	17.8	100.0
62	04.320	Washing appliances	21.4	0.0	39.1	0.3	65.4	100.0
63	04.330	Cooking appliances	58.7	0.0	54.7	0.1	49.6	100.0
64	04.340	Heating appliances	17.0	0.1	42.7	0.7	41.0	100.0
65	04.350	Cleaning appliances	17.8	0.0	24.9	0.9	54.2	100.0
66	04.360	Other household appliances	8.1	0.7	104.8	0.3	15.1	100.0
67	04.400	Household utensils	33.1	4.7	70.6	0.4	84.6	100.0
68	04.510	Nondurable household goods	25.8	2.9	85.1	8.4	85.4	100.0
69	04.520	Domestic services	15.6	28.8	12.0	7.8	55.1	100.0
70	04.530	Household services	12.1	11.1	3.8	39.8	72.3	100.0
71	04.600	Household furnishing repairs	141.0	14.8	154.3	0.5	69.2	100.0
72	05.110	Drugs, medical preparations	71.2	10.7	240.4	4.7	123.3	100.0
73	05.120	Medical supplies	42.3	6.9	127.4	2.2	106.7	100.0
74	05.200	Therapeutic equipment	0.0	2.4	45.2	0.4	106.7	100.0
75	05.310	Physicians' services	111.5	11.9	66.2	7.1	66.8	100.0

Appendix Table 14.9. Continued

			Hun-gary	India	Japan	Kenya	U.K.	U.S.
76	05.320	Dentists' services	41.6	1.5	66.3	1.0	45.8	100.0
77	05.330	Services, nurses, other personnel	72.8	5.0	54.1	16.0	102.3	100.0
78	05.410	Hospitals, etc.	96.2	6.9	130.9	15.0	114.9	100.0
79	06.110	Personal cars	1.6	0.1	2.8	0.7	21.0	100.0
80	06.120	Other personal transport	22.0	1.3	10.6	0.1	13.8	100.0
81	06.210	Tires, tubes, accessories	6.0	0.3	0.6	0.5	73.7	100.0
82	06.220	Repair charges	6.7	1.5	1.8	3.9	57.7	100.0
83	06.230	Gasoline, oil, etc.	1.7	0.1	1.0	1.6	20.1	100.0
84	06.240	Parking, tolls, etc.	14.7	1.0	2.9	0.7	90.7	100.0
85	06.310	Local transport	112.8	12.7	420.8	7.7	322.3	100.0
86	06.321	Rail transport	942.2	142.2	607.5	37.6	316.6	100.0
87	06.322	Bus transport	338.0	186.7	71.7	173.2	100.7	100.0
88	06.323	Air transport	4.9	0.1	3.4	12.0	66.5	100.0
89	06.330	Miscellaneous transport	37.7	45.5	37.7	2.2	77.3	100.0
90	06.410	Postal communication	42.0	3.6	15.4	0.8	99.6	100.0
91	06.420	Telephone, telegraph	17.2	1.5	16.8	0.7	36.0	100.0
92	07.110	Radio, TV, phonograph, etc.	9.2	0.3	39.6	0.6	13.4	100.0
93	07.120	Major durable recreation equip.	2.1	0.0	48.5	1.7	19.7	100.0
94	07.130	Other recreation equipment	11.9	0.1	18.2	0.8	83.2	100.0
95	07.210	Public entertainment	126.5	0.4	5.6	8.8	149.7	100.0
96	07.230	Other recreation, cultural events	214.2	3.0	119.7	3.2	111.1	100.0
97	07.310	Books, papers, magazines	40.8	1.9	48.3	2.5	156.1	100.0
98	07.320	Stationery	22.3	4.3	37.9	0.1	77.3	100.0
99	07.411	Teachers, 1st, 2nd	98.1	32.0	73.5	40.2	72.6	100.0
100	07.412	Teachers, college	37.4	9.8	38.0	2.5	63.0	100.0
101	07.420	Educational facilities	31.3	0.5	15.6	2.6	51.6	100.0
102	07.431	Educational supplies	27.8	3.0	21.8	4.4	197.9	100.0
103	07.432	Other education expenditures	66.9	2.4	57.7	8.8	142.8	100.0
104	08.100	Barber, beauty shops	127.9	4.0	185.7	1.1	126.7	100.0
105	08.210	Toilet articles	24.6	2.2	60.5	0.6	47.9	100.0
106	08.220	Other personal-care goods	19.3	2.4	19.8	1.0	48.7	100.0
107	08.310	Restaurants, cafes	98.7	1.2	52.6	3.8	28.9	100.0
108	08.320	Hotels, etc.	29.7	14.8	125.8	35.8	404.6	100.0
109	08.400	Other services	25.6	3.0	41.7	4.2	63.0	100.0
111	10.100	1- and 2-dwelling buildings	33.7	8.1	82.1	6.7	96.1	100.0
112	10.200	Multidwelling buildings	111.5	27.0	100.2	6.7	158.9	100.0
113	11.100	Hotels, etc.	82.9	3.6	49.5	2.1	18.8	100.0
114	11.200	Industrial buildings	83.2	1.1	32.7	2.9	86.6	100.0
115	11.300	Commercial buildings	23.3	9.8	49.0	3.7	54.9	100.0
116	11.400	Office buildings	29.8	3.1	66.6	3.7	38.2	100.0
117	11.500	Educational buildings	18.3	1.0	38.3	5.4	46.2	100.0
118	11.600	Hospital buildings	25.6	2.7	56.4	6.1	91.5	100.0
119	11.700	Agricultural buildings	364.6	71.8	24.2	18.0	143.1	100.0
120	11.800	Other buildings	9.9	3.0	42.1	1.5	41.2	100.0
121	12.100	Roads, highways	22.8	3.7	55.7	2.4	46.0	100.0
122	12.200	Transmission, utility lines	107.6	11.6	148.3	2.0	41.5	100.0
123	12.300	Other construction	228.1	28.0	274.3	12.6	50.3	100.0
124	13.000	Land improvement	164.2	49.2	208.6	9.0	38.8	100.0
125	14.110	Locomotives	96.8	15.3	24.4	32.6	26.7	100.0
126	14.120	Other	46.0	2.5	23.5	7.7	6.8	100.0
127	14.200	Passenger cars	1.4	0.1	35.6	4.7	26.6	100.0
128	14.300	Trucks, buses, trailers	20.4	3.4	103.1	9.1	3.7	100.0
129	14.400	Aircraft	1.7	0.2	2.2	2.3	6.9	100.0
130	14.500	Ships, boats	43.5	8.0	282.4	1.8	218.4	100.0
131	14.600	Other transport	223.9	16.2	101.2	4.7	325.2	100.0
132	15.100	Engines and turbines	29.5	1.7	78.4	4.3	6.0	100.0
133	15.210	Tractors	16.3	0.6	19.9	3.4	24.6	100.0
134	15.220	Other agricultural machinery	37.7	0.4	28.5	2.7	26.2	100.0
135	15.300	Office machinery	6.0	0.1	23.4	0.7	21.1	100.0
136	15.400	Metalworking machinery	47.8	1.8	51.0	1.1	56.8	100.0
137	15.500	Construction, mining	34.6	0.2	86.8	3.3	79.4	100.0
138	15.600	Special industrial	118.4	3.9	237.0	9.2	107.4	100.0
139	15.700	General industrial	31.3	3.5	97.4	7.9	370.6	100.0
140	15.800	Service industrial	12.6	0.5	50.3	1.1	10.0	100.0
141	16.100	Electrical transmission	48.1	2.7	119.1	5.2	127.2	100.0
142	16.200	Communication equipment	23.8	1.7	68.6	1.2	101.4	100.0
143	16.300	Other electrical	13.7	4.6	34.2	4.9	217.7	100.0
144	16.400	Instruments	31.2	1.3	16.1	1.0	50.9	100.0
145	17.100	Furniture, fixtures	45.2	0.3	31.2	1.5	43.4	100.0
146	17.200	Other durable goods	6.4	5.8	26.9	4.3	7.1	100.0
147	18.000	Increase in stocks	161.8	5.6	212.2	6.6	31.8	100.0
148	19.000	Exports less imports	-446.3	-52.4	79.9	-31.9	-663.5	100.0
149	20.100	Blue-collar, unskilled	227.6	182.2	259.4	457.4	753.4	100.0
150	20.210	Blue-collar, skilled	2.2	2.7	118.5	2.5	18.7	100.0

Appendix Table 14.9. Continued

			Hun-gary	India	Japan	Kenya	U.K.	U.S.
151	20.220	White-collar	30.1	19.3	23.4	5.3	75.1	100.0
152	20.300	Professional	19.3	5.5	16.1	4.8	19.2	100.0
153	21.000	Government expenditure on commodities	17.2	2.3	11.0	1.5	35.0	100.0

Note: The net expenditure of residents abroad, line 110 in the binary tables, has been consolidated with other services (line 109) in the multilateral comparisons. Thus there are 152 categories in this table. See page 70.

Appendix Table 14.10. Quantities per Capita Valued at International Prices, 1967 (I$)

			Hun-gary	India	Japan	Kenya	U.K.	U.S.
1	01.101	Rice	1.9	45.8	87.1	0.5	0.5	2.5
2	01.102	Meal, other cereals	18.9	30.5	2.0	24.3	3.7	7.3
3	01.103	Bread, rolls	24.6	0.1	3.7	0.9	16.7	7.3
4	01.104	Biscuits, cakes	2.9	0.0	15.7	1.7	25.2	15.0
5	01.105	Cereal preparations	5.6	0.1	0.2	0.1	3.1	4.5
6	01.106	Macaroni, spaghetti, related foods	1.8	0.0	6.0	0.0	1.1	2.2
7	01.111	Fresh beef, veal	1.7	0.1	2.7	7.9	35.1	59.2
8	01.112	Fresh lamb, mutton	1.1	0.3	0.1	0.8	14.5	2.4
9	01.113	Fresh pork	24.6	0.2	12.4	0.2	11.5	31.1
10	01.114	Fresh poultry	14.7	0.4	3.6	0.5	13.1	26.9
11	01.115	Other fresh meat	1.6	0.8	1.5	1.0	5.1	3.6
12	01.116	Frozen, salted meat	13.2	0.0	3.9	0.4	44.7	42.4
13	01.121	Fresh, frozen fish	2.5	3.4	19.4	1.5	5.1	5.5
14	01.122	Canned fish	0.3	0.0	18.3	0.2	4.9	5.8
15	01.131	Fresh milk	22.6	7.0	8.0	8.7	25.5	33.9
16	01.132	Milk products	4.2	0.5	1.7	0.9	22.5	16.1
17	01.133	Eggs, egg products	9.3	0.2	15.6	0.1	14.8	18.3
18	01.141	Butter	3.2	5.6	0.5	1.6	19.4	5.6
19	01.142	Margarine, edible oil	1.8	5.1	3.9	1.2	6.7	17.6
20	01.143	Lard, edible fat	22.7	0.0	0.0	0.2	3.2	1.9
21	01.151	Fresh fruits, tropical, subtropical	1.1	1.7	4.6	5.1	4.5	7.3
22	01.152	Other fresh fruits	21.7	0.2	8.0	0.0	6.8	9.8
23	01.153	Fresh vegetables	20.8	4.4	17.3	5.7	12.5	12.0
24	01.161	Fruit other than fresh	0.1	0.1	2.0	0.0	8.0	19.2
25	01.162	Vegetables other than fresh	0.2	5.6	11.6	1.1	22.7	35.9
26	01.170	Potatoes, manioc, other tubers	10.4	1.3	1.8	8.2	15.1	7.5
27	01.191	Coffee	2.2	0.2	0.8	0.4	5.7	23.2
28	01.192	Tea	0.2	1.4	2.7	1.4	13.2	1.3
29	01.193	Cocoa	0.4	0.0	0.5	0.1	0.6	1.3
30	01.180	Sugar	14.7	5.2	4.2	2.8	18.2	9.0
31	01.201	Jam, syrup, honey	4.0	0.1	2.2	1.0	6.1	4.9
32	01.202	Chocolate, ice cream	8.5	0.4	3.4	0.2	29.8	23.6
33	01.203	Salt, spices, sauces	6.5	6.7	14.4	1.1	1.7	3.7
34	01.310	Nonalcoholic beverages	1.1	0.0	3.6	0.5	10.1	16.4
35	01.321	Spirits	4.2	0.0	30.1	0.4	25.6	23.3
36	01.322	Wine, cider	21.5	0.1	1.7	0.0	6.9	4.3
37	01.323	Beer	6.7	0.1	14.3	2.6	49.5	32.5
38	01.410	Cigarettes	27.5	0.1	21.6	2.6	41.4	50.2
39	01.420	Other tobacco	0.4	5.0	0.1	0.1	6.5	5.7
40	02.110	Clothing materials	4.7	2.8	46.2	0.6	5.5	10.4
41	02.121	Men's clothing	17.5	1.8	13.6	1.3	23.8	49.2
42	02.122	Women's clothing	15.0	2.6	9.2	0.4	28.9	85.1
43	02.123	Boys', girls' clothing	8.0	0.3	2.9	0.6	8.1	23.2
44	02.131	Men's, boys' underwear	4.2	0.1	16.1	0.1	10.3	12.2
45	02.132	Women's, girls' underwear	4.4	0.0	11.4	0.1	15.0	27.3
46	02.150	Other clothing	7.8	0.0	13.2	0.1	20.1	10.2
47	02.160	Clothing rental, repair	4.3	0.2	16.5	0.1	1.1	1.7
48	02.211	Men's footwear	5.1	0.3	2.7	1.0	10.1	10.3
49	02.212	Women's footwear	9.0	0.3	2.7	0.4	12.5	13.8
50	02.213	Children's footwear	3.5	0.2	0.8	0.2	6.8	8.0
51	02.220	Footwear repairs	3.5	0.0	2.2	0.0	2.1	1.3
52	03.110	Gross rents	52.4	11.9	86.8	9.9	181.7	312.7
53	03.120	Indoor repair, upkeep	17.2	1.0	11.7	0.0	21.0	9.7
54	03.210	Electricity	4.3	0.2	13.1	0.2	39.0	46.6

Appendix Table 14.10. Continued

			Hun-gary	India	Japan	Kenya	U.K.	U.S.
55	03.220	Gas	4.1	0.0	2.9	0.0	8.6	40.4
56	03.230	Liquid fuels	0.5	0.7	2.7	0.1	4.7	40.2
57	03.240	Other fuels, ice	35.6	4.5	8.3	2.1	23.2	3.9
58	04.110	Furniture, fixtures	17.3	0.1	15.6	0.9	12.2	50.8
59	04.120	Floor coverings	0.7	2.3	0.5	0.0	9.8	8.3
60	04.200	Household textiles, etc.	5.8	1.7	1.2	0.2	17.1	38.1
61	04.310	Refrigerators, etc.	1.5	0.1	4.6	0.1	4.1	23.2
62	04.320	Washing appliances	1.8	0.0	3.3	0.0	5.5	8.4
63	04.330	Cooking appliances	4.3	0.0	4.0	0.1	3.7	7.4
64	04.340	Heating appliances	1.4	0.0	3.4	0.1	3.3	8.0
65	04.350	Cleaning appliances	0.6	0.0	0.9	0.0	1.9	3.6
66	04.360	Other household appliances	0.3	0.0	4.3	0.0	0.6	4.1
67	04.400	Household utensils	6.7	0.9	14.3	1.7	17.2	20.3
68	04.510	Nondurable household goods	8.2	0.9	27.2	2.5	27.3	32.0
69	04.520	Domestic services	1.1	2.1	0.9	2.8	3.9	7.2
70	04.530	Household services	1.8	1.7	0.6	0.3	10.8	14.9
71	04.600	Household furnishing repairs	6.0	0.6	6.6	0.0	3.0	4.3
72	05.110	Drugs, medical preparations	15.3	2.3	51.6	1.0	26.5	21.5
73	05.120	Medical supplies	1.7	0.3	5.1	0.1	4.3	4.0
74	05.200	Therapeutic equipment	0.0	0.1	2.4	0.0	5.6	5.2
75	05.310	Physicians' services	13.7	1.5	8.1	0.9	8.2	12.3
76	05.320	Dentists' services	2.2	0.1	3.6	0.1	2.5	5.4
77	05.330	Services, nurses, other personnel	13.2	0.9	9.8	2.9	18.6	18.1
78	05.410	Hospitals, etc.	23.9	1.7	32.6	3.7	28.6	24.9
79	06.110	Personal cars	2.7	0.1	4.7	1.2	35.1	167.3
80	06.120	Other personal transport	3.5	0.2	1.7	0.0	2.2	16.0
81	06.210	Tires, tubes, accessories	1.3	0.1	0.1	0.1	15.4	20.9
82	06.220	Repair charges	1.6	0.4	0.4	0.9	13.7	23.7
83	06.230	Gasoline, oil, etc.	2.0	0.2	1.2	1.8	23.5	116.8
84	06.240	Parking, tolls, etc.	2.8	0.2	0.5	0.1	17.1	18.8
85	06.310	Local transport	6.9	0.8	25.7	0.5	19.7	6.1
86	06.321	Rail transport	9.4	1.4	6.1	0.4	3.2	1.0
87	06.322	Bus transport	7.1	3.9	1.5	3.6	2.1	2.1
88	06.323	Air transport	0.9	0.0	0.6	2.1	11.5	17.3
89	06.330	Miscellaneous transport	1.2	1.4	1.2	0.1	2.4	3.1
90	06.410	Postal communication	2.6	0.2	0.9	0.1	6.1	6.1
91	06.420	Telephone, telegraph	4.9	0.4	4.8	0.2	10.3	28.7
92	07.110	Radio, TV, phonograph, etc.	4.5	0.2	19.7	0.3	6.7	49.6
93	07.120	Major durable recreation equip.	0.4	0.0	9.5	0.3	3.8	19.5
94	07.130	Other recreation equipment	4.0	0.0	6.1	0.3	28.0	33.6
95	07.210	Public entertainment	16.7	0.0	0.7	1.2	19.8	13.2
96	07.230	Other recreation, cultural events	41.0	0.6	22.9	0.6	21.2	19.1
97	07.310	Books, papers, magazines	10.8	0.5	12.8	0.6	41.3	26.4
98	07.320	Stationery	2.0	0.4	3.4	0.4	7.0	9.0
99	07.411	Teachers, 1st, 2nd	30.8	10.1	23.1	12.6	22.8	31.4
100	07.412	Teachers, college	4.4	1.2	4.4	0.3	7.4	11.7
101	07.420	Educational facilities	9.7	0.2	4.9	0.8	16.0	31.1
102	07.431	Educational supplies	1.4	0.1	1.1	0.2	9.8	5.0
103	07.432	Other education expenditures	5.8	0.2	5.0	0.8	12.4	8.7
104	08.100	Barber, beauty shops	11.0	0.3	16.0	0.1	10.9	8.6
105	08.210	Toilet articles	7.3	0.7	18.0	0.2	14.3	29.8
106	08.220	Other personal-care goods	6.4	0.8	6.5	0.3	16.0	32.9
107	08.310	Restaurants, cafes	101.1	1.2	53.8	3.9	29.6	102.4
108	08.320	Hotels, etc.	2.8	1.4	11.7	3.3	37.5	9.3
109	08.400	Other services	21.6	2.6	35.2	3.5	53.1	84.3
111	10.100	1- and 2-dwelling buildings	30.3	7.2	73.7	6.0	86.3	89.8
112	10.200	Multidwelling buildings	25.1	6.3	22.5	0.7	35.7	22.5
113	11.100	Hotels, etc.	5.5	0.2	3.3	0.1	1.2	6.6
114	11.200	Industrial buildings	41.9	0.6	16.5	1.5	43.7	50.4
115	11.300	Commercial buildings	4.9	2.1	10.3	0.8	11.6	21.0
116	11.400	Office buildings	6.6	0.7	14.8	0.8	8.5	22.3
117	11.500	Educational buildings	6.1	0.3	12.8	1.8	15.4	33.4
118	11.600	Hospital buildings	2.2	0.2	4.8	0.5	7.8	8.5
119	11.700	Agricultural buildings	12.4	2.4	0.8	0.6	4.9	3.4
120	11.800	Other buildings	2.1	0.6	9.0	0.3	8.8	21.4
121	12.100	Roads, highways	11.5	1.8	28.2	1.2	23.3	50.5
122	12.200	Transmission, utility lines	44.7	4.8	61.6	0.8	17.2	41.6
123	12.300	Other construction	21.5	2.6	25.9	1.2	4.7	9.4
124	13.000	Land improvement	13.0	3.9	16.6	0.7	3.1	7.9
125	14.110	Locomotives	2.8	0.4	0.7	1.0	0.8	2.9
126	14.120	Other	7.0	0.4	3.6	1.2	0.9	15.1
127	14.200	Passenger cars	0.7	0.1	17.2	2.3	12.9	48.4
128	14.300	Trucks, buses, trailers	9.2	1.5	46.6	4.1	1.7	45.2
129	14.400	Aircraft	0.4	0.1	0.5	0.5	1.5	21.9
130	14.500	Ships, boats	1.7	0.3	11.3	0.1	8.7	4.0

Appendix Table 14.10. Continued

			Hun-gary	India	Japan	Kenya	U.K.	U.S.
131	14.600	Other transport	7.2	0.5	3.3	0.2	10.5	3.2
132	15.100	Engines and turbines	0.4	0.2	2.7	7.2	0.6	9.2
133	15.210	Tractors	0.4	0.1	2.1	2.6	3.2	13.1
134	15.220	Other agricultural machinery	0.4	0.1	6.3	4.8	4.4	16.7
135	15.300	Office machinery	0.2	0.0	2.1	8.3	7.5	35.5
136	15.400	Metalworking machinery	0.3	0.5	12.7	13.6	15.1	26.6
137	15.500	Construction, mining	0.6	0.0	6.4	16.0	14.6	18.5
138	15.600	Special industrial	2.1	0.9	26.6	53.2	24.1	22.5
139	15.700	General industrial	1.6	0.7	6.2	19.3	73.3	19.8
140	15.800	Service industrial	0.2	0.1	2.3	9.2	1.8	18.3
141	16.100	Electrical transmission	0.9	0.5	8.0	19.8	21.2	16.6
142	16.200	Communication equipment	0.3	0.4	6.0	17.2	25.4	25.0
143	16.300	Other electrical	0.2	0.2	0.5	1.3	8.1	3.7
144	16.400	Instruments	0.2	0.2	5.8	3.0	9.5	18.7
145	17.100	Furniture, fixtures	0.3	0.1	9.7	6.7	9.3	21.4
146	17.200	Other durable goods	1.1	1.5	1.6	6.8	1.8	25.3
147	18.000	Increase in stocks	3.3	2.8	80.4	105.4	15.8	49.7
148	19.000	Exports less imports	−1.7	−2.8	−24.1	4.3	−35.9	5.4
149	20.100	Blue-collar, unskilled	14.8	5.9	7.3	8.4	24.3	3.2
150	20.210	Blue-collar, skilled	1.1	1.2	1.0	52.4	8.3	44.2
151	20.220	White-collar	2.3	8.2	12.9	10.0	32.1	42.7
152	20.300	Professional	4.1	4.7	16.5	13.7	16.4	85.6
153	21.000	Government expenditure on commodities	5.2	8.1	60.4	38.8	123.0	351.2

Note: The net expenditure of residents abroad, line 110 in the binary tables, has been consolidated with other services (line 109) in the multilateral comparisons. Thus there are 152 categories in this table. See page 70.

Chapter 15

Some applications of the data

A detailed analysis of the results of the ICP described in Chapters 13 and 14 is beyond the scope of the present volume, but we cannot resist the temptation now to engage in some simple analyses of the data. In part, we are curious to see what the data tell us about the structure of prices and quantities in relation to incomes. At the same time, we are interested in checking on the plausibility of our results by determining whether quantities, prices, and incomes appearing in the tables are tied together—at least approximately—in the way that economic theory would suggest.

Certain well-known elementary facts about consumption behavior in the ten ICP countries can be verified without reference to the "science" of economics: for example, that beef consumption is minimal in India; that the relatively cold countries of Western Europe consume much larger quantities of residential heating fuel than do tropical countries; that the French eat in restaurants more than do the residents of other countries; and so on. But what deeper observations can be made after a few such propositions are shown to hold? We discussed in Chapter 2 the plausibility of treating these numbers as though they were generated by a group of ten populations that share common tastes. Their tastes certainly are not truly identical, but we now wish to see if we can tell if they are similar enough for us to be able to explain a part of the differences in expenditure behavior in the ten ICP countries by differences in relative prices and relative per capita incomes.

We start out by comparing five of the 1970 ICP countries with that information which we have about them from the Gilbert-Kravis study done in the early 1950s.[1] We go on to throw light on the fundamental question of whether the hypothesis of common tastes is tenable. This is done by applying a "similarity-index" analysis, first to the five-country–two-time-point data, then to the data of the ten ICP countries of 1970. The results are sufficiently encouraging to embolden us to attempt

to estimate regressions that might loosely be called "demand functions." However, our reservations about the extent to which these crude regressions refer to actual structural relationships cause us to shrink from employing here the sophisticated methods implied by the theory of consumer behavior (for example, the Geary-Stone linear expenditure system). Nevertheless, partly to facilitate our narrative when we describe the regressions, we shall write of coefficients as price and income elasticities when it is convenient. The fairly strong tendency for the regression estimates to conform to a priori expectations, we feel, adds to the weight of evidence from the similarity-index analysis.

A. Similarity Indexes

In Chapters 13 and 14, we summarized the results of our study in terms of quantity and PPP comparisons for GDP and various subcomponents of GDP. Here, we go one step further and investigate the similarity of the countries with respect to quantity and price structures. Underlying the comparisons given in the main bodies of the previous chapters were appendix tables in which vectors of both PPPs and relative quantities were presented for each of the ten countries. The PPP vectors are representations of relative prices (with U.S. prices as the numeraire), and it is in this sense that we use them here. The quantity structures of the countries are reflected in the quantity vectors. Thus, the price and quantity vectors provide a basis for positioning the countries with respect to their degrees of similarity with one another.

FIVE COUNTRIES, 1950 AND 1970

For five of the ten countries, we have vectors of quantities and PPPs not only from the 1970 study upon which we have been reporting, but also from the 1950 study of the OEEC.[2] Although both the 1950 and 1970 studies provided considerable detail on the composition of GDP, there were differences in classification. As a

---

[1] M. Gilbert and I. B. Kravis, *An International Comparison of National Products and the Purchasing Power of Currencies* (Paris: Organization for European Economic Cooperation, 1954).

[2] See Table 1.6.

result, it is convenient for present purposes to work with a twenty-category classification consisting of sixteen consumption, two capital formation, and two government groupings.[3] Some further breakdown would have been possible, but the errors in both studies increase with disaggregation, and it was not obvious that the extra work would have been warranted. The matching of even twenty categories required a fair amount of reclassification of ICP data. It should also be borne in mind that the 1950 data referred to the consumption in the territory of the country, whereas those of 1970 referred to the consumption of residents.

First, we address relatively simple but interesting questions:

- To what extent did the quantity structures of the four European countries—France, the Federal Republic of Germany, Italy, and the United Kingdom—draw closer to that of the United States?
- To what extent did the quantity structures of the European countries draw together over the twenty-year period? (It may be seen in Table 1.6 that their per capita GDP levels in 1970 are more tightly clustered than in 1950. The coefficients of variation for 1950 and 1970 are, respectively, 0.30 and 0.17 for the ideal indexes.)
- To what extent has the price structure of the five countries come closer together over twenty years?

Comparisons of similarity indexes. We examine the degree of similarity between all the pairs of situations involving the five countries in 1950 and 1970—that is, ten pairs of different countries in 1950, ten pairs of different countries in 1970, five pairs involving the same country in the two different years, and ten pairs of different countries in different years. The index we have used as our measure of similarity between the vectors of category quantities (or prices) referring to any pair of situations is the weighted *"raw correlation"* coefficient— that is, the ratio of the cross moment to the square root of the product of the two second moments, each moment being computed relative to the origin rather than the mean. This is the same as the cosine of the angle between the two situation quantity (or price) vectors located in the commodity (or price) space.[4] Because the

quantities (and prices) are all in index form (with the United States 1970=100), the weights applied to the individual categories in calculating the raw moments were expenditures. In fact, U.S. expenditure weights have been used. In addition, the quantity (and price) indexes that make up the vectors being compared are those obtained using U.S. price (or quantity) weights in the binary comparisons.[5] The similarity indexes are invariant with respect to the units of the groupings.

This similarity measure has been applied to the quantity vectors of sixteen categories of consumption and twenty categories of GDP in order to compare each of the European countries with the United States, with the following results:

United States and	Consumption		GDP	
	1950	1970	1950	1970
France	.81	.86	.82	.86
Germany, F.R.	.86	.93	.87	.90
Italy	.83	.87	.82	.87
United Kingdom	.84	.93	.84	.94

The increase in the quantity similarity index between 1950 and 1970 in every case indicates that European consumption patterns and overall quantity patterns for GDP both have become more like that of the United States.[6] Whether this is caused by the shrinkage of the income gap or to other influences, these data alone cannot tell us.

When the same type of analysis is applied to the various pairs of European countries, the results are somewhat more equivocal. The similarity indexes for the per capita quantities, still using U.S. price and expenditure weights, are:

	Consumption			GDP		
	Germany, F.R.	Italy	U.K.	Germany, F.R.	Italy	U.K.
France						
1950	.91	.99	.86	.88	.99	.87
1970	.93	.97	.93	.95	.96	.92
Germany, F.R.						
1950		.93	.96		.90	.94
1970		.94	.95		.92	.91
Italy						
1950			.88			.89
1970			.95			.94

---

[3]The 20 categories, which represent combinations of the more detailed 152-category breakdown of earlier chapters, are: food, alcoholic beverages, tobacco, clothing and footwear, rent, fuel and power, household furnishings and operations, household and personal services, personal transport equipment, operation of personal transport equipment, public transportation, communication, recreation and entertainment, health, education, miscellaneous consumption, construction, producers' durable goods, government personnel, and government purchases of commodities and services.

[4]A similar index for the composition of imports and exports was used by H. Linneman, *An Econometric Study of International Trade Flows* (Amsterdam: North Holland, 1966), pp. 141ff.

[5]Although the subsequent analysis is in terms of these U.S.-weighted quantity (and price) similarity indexes, the results of using own-weighted and ideal quantity (and price) indexes also were examined. The similarity indexes for these quantity indexes were computed with weights derived as the geometric averages of the expenditures that were used to weight the quantity (and price) indexes of the pair of countries being compared.

[6]When the own-weighted or Fisher indexes are analyzed in a similar way, we find the changes in the similarity index are in the same direction, with only one exception—Italy, own-weighted index for consumption.

There is a clear tendency for the degree of similarity of pairs of countries to increase between 1950 and 1970 wherever it was relatively low in the earlier period. In every case in which the 1950 index was less than 0.90, the index increased by at least 0.05 over the next twenty years. On the other hand, in cases in which the similarities already were high in 1950, little further increase occurred, and in a few cases there was a slight diminution. The already great similarity in quantity patterns in 1950 and the relatively small relative income changes among the four European countries (as compared with their income changes relative to the United States) probably accounts for this result.[7]

The preceding text table indicates that the similarity in quantity patterns tends to be greater in both periods for Consumption than for GDP as a whole. This suggests that those factors which determine consumption patterns operate more consistently across countries than those factors which determine quantity patterns in capital formation and government.

When our measure of similarity is applied to the 1950 and 1970 price (PPP) data, the same kind of finding emerges. We need not present the individual similarity indexes for prices, but such a conclusion is clear from the following summary data:

Pairs of countries	Means of similarity indexes			
	Consumption		GDP	
	Quantities	Prices	Quantities	Prices
	(1)	(2)	(3)	(4)
U.S. and a European country				
1950	.835	.872	.838	.900
1970	.898	.928	.892	.940
All pairs				
1950	.887	.935	.882	.939
1970	.926	.955	.917	.961

The means of similarity indexes for the quantities (columns 1 and 3) are simple averages of the data presented in the preceding text tables. The data in columns 2 and 4 are the means of the corresponding similarity indexes (again using U.S. expenditure weights) for prices. The country price structures, like those of quantities, tended to converge between 1950 and 1970; convergence with the United States was greater than convergence among the already similar European countries. The table shows also that the similarity of price structures is greater than that of quantity structures in each pair of comparisons in the text table. With only two exceptions, a higher level of similarity indexes for prices than for quantities characterizes all the individual pairwise comparisons between the countries for both dates. This confirms a common view of international

trade theory: the international market mechanism can be expected to bring about conformance in price while leaving the structure of quantities more differentiated.

In the preceding paragraphs, we have suggested that the increased similarity in quantities and prices may be a consequence of the rise in per capita real income in Europe relative to the United States. Now we articulate a more general formulation, drawing somewhat informally on economic theory. We begin with the following strong assertion of the economist's creed: If relative prices and income are the critical determinants of economic choices, then if in two countries all relative prices are the same and their per capita incomes are the same, identity of tastes in the two countries would lead to (virtual) identity of per capita quantities.[8] This is simply a reflection of the economist's belief in the existence of systems of demand equations. Because no one would suggest seriously that prices and income are the sole determinants of choices, it is to be expected that demand equations are stochastic and, therefore, that the assertion should be interpreted in stochastic terms. A proximity version of the "quantity depends upon prices and income" proposition is as follows: *The more similar relative prices and income are in two countries, the more similar the countries' quantity compositions will be.* The stochastic character of this statement, too, should be recognized.

Regression analysis. The proximity statement can be prepared for statistical test by translating it into mathematical form. The general relationship hypothesized is given in equation (15.1)

$$(15.1) \qquad Q_{jk} = g(P_{jk}, Y_{jk}; u)$$

where Q_{jk}, P_{jk}, and Y_{jk} are measures of similarity of quantity composition, price structure and incomes per capita respectively in the jth and k^{th} countries, and u is a stochastic disturbance term. More specifically, a linear version that can be adapted to regression analysis is given in equation (15.2).

$$(15.2) \qquad Q_{jk} = \alpha P_{jk} + \beta Y_{jk} + \delta + u_{jk}$$

By using the similarity indexes defined earlier[9] for Q_{jk} and P_{jk}, and using $|Y_j - Y_k|$ as an income similarity measure, it is possible to use the five-country–two-time-point data (and, in the next section, the ten-country ICP data for 1970) to estimate the regression coefficients and make a judgment about the proximity proposition. Some specific modifications of equation (15.2) will be

---

[7]Comparable results are obtained from the own-weighted and Fisher indexes.

[8]The parenthetical insert signals that hedging should be introduced. For example, even if all individuals in both countries had the same tastes in the sense of identical preference functions, differences in the countries' distribution of income would lead to different per capita quantity selections.

[9]See the preceding page.

introduced, but basically it is this equation which will concern us throughout the rest of this section. Only one further remark need be made here: The proximity proposition is to be judged by the signs and sizes of the estimated coefficients and by the amount of noise (that is, variance of u) in the various regression equations.

We begin with the consumption categories. We work with all forty-five of the possible paired comparisons afforded by the five countries for the two time points. Because in original form the 1950 OEEC data were based on U.S. 1950=100 and the 1970 ICP data on U.S. 1970=100, they could not be compared without an adjustment of the quantity data. To place all the data on a comparable basis, a rough deflation of the U.S. data was performed so that the U.S. quantity in each of the 16 categories for 1950 could be expressed as a ratio of the corresponding U.S. quantity in 1970.[10] (For per capita consumption as a whole, the U.S. 1950 level was 64.5 percent of the 1970 level.) The 1950 quantities for the four European countries then were adjusted by the appropriate proportion for each category so that they, too, were expressed as percentages of the corresponding U.S. 1970 quantities.

For each pair of situations (each country in each year being paired with itself in the other year and with each other country in both years), we have three variables: two indexes of similarity (for quantities and prices) and an income similarity variable. For the analysis of consumption behavior, the income-difference variable is defined in terms of consumption; it is the absolute value of the difference between the two real per capita consumption indexes (based on U.S. price weights). For F.R. Germany$_{70}$/U.S.$_{70}$, for example, the consumption-difference variable is 0.32, obtained by subtracting 0.68 for the Federal Republic of Germany from 1.00 for the United States; the F.R. Germany$_{70}$/Italy$_{70}$ value is 0.13, obtained by subtracting 0.55 for Italy from 0.68 for Germany (see Table 13.17).

We rewrite equation (15.2) in the first of two forms we will examine.

(15.3)

$$Q_{jk}^{t\bar{t}} = \alpha P_{jk}^{t\bar{t}} + \beta |C_j - C_k^{\bar{t}}| + \delta + u_{jk}^{t\bar{t}}, \quad t, \bar{t} = 1950, 1970$$

where $Q_{jk}^{t\bar{t}}$ and $P_{jk}^{t\bar{t}}$ are the similarity measures for quantity and price, respectively, between the jth country in the tth year and the kth country in the $\bar{t}^{th}$ year; and $|C_j^t - C_k^{\bar{t}}|$ is the absolute value of the difference between the total per capita consumption of the jth country in

the tth year and the kth country in the $\bar{t}^{th}$ year. The proximity proposition can be thought of as an assertion about the parameter values of equation (15.3). If the proposition is true, then α should be greater than 0, β less than 0, and $\alpha + \delta$ should equal unity. (This latter restriction on the coefficients is the consequence of $P_{jk}^{t\bar{t}} = 1$ and $|C_j^t - C_k^{\bar{t}}| = 0$ together implying $Q_{jk}^{t\bar{t}} = 1$.) In addition, the importance of the economic variables relative to noneconomic ones is greater the smaller the standard error of estimate, σ_u.

An easy thing to look at first is the simple correlation matrix for the three variables given by the tableau (15.4).

	$P_{jk}^{t\bar{t}}$	$|C_j^t - C_k^{\bar{t}}|$
$Q_{jk}^{t\bar{t}}$	.81	−.67
$P_{jk}^{t\bar{t}}$		−.85

(15.4)

We expect to find the correlation between $Q^{t\bar{t}}$ and $P^{t\bar{t}}$ to be positive and the correlation between $Q_{jk}^{t\bar{t}}$ and $|C_j^t - C_k^{\bar{t}}|$ to be negative. The coefficients in the first row confirm these expectations; moreover, they are statistically significant.

The strong negative correlation between $P_{jk}^{t\bar{t}}$ and $|C_j^t - C_k^{\bar{t}}|$ should make us cautious in trying to guess the true separate effects of the variables and the extent of the combined explanatory power of the two variables. For this, we turn to the regression results given in Table 15.1. Even though each coefficient is of the right sign and is highly significant when taken alone (see regressions 1 and 2),[11] the separate effect of $|C_j^t - C_k^{\bar{t}}|$ is submerged completely in the combined regression (regression 3). We note that the hypothesized linear relationship among the coefficients referred to two paragraphs above ($\alpha + \delta = 1$) holds in regressions 1 and 3.[12]

The fact that $\bar{R}^2$ is less than 1 in Table 15.1 means that price and income variation do not by themselves explain all variation in quantity composition. The fact that $\bar{R}^2$ is significantly greater than 0 means the variables definitely make a difference. The fact that $\bar{R}^2$ is in the neighborhood of 0.50 to 0.70 means that, at the level of this kind of econometric analysis, a very substantial part of the difference in quantity compositions among countries can be explained in terms of the economic conditions in which the countries find themselves rather than of differences in taste.

---

[10] CPI component series found in U.S. Department of Commerce, *Business Statistics, 1971* (Washington: Government Printing Office, 1972) were used as deflators for the categories in Table 3 except for education, for which the annual earnings of full-time employees in public education (1950 from *U.S. Income and Output*, p. 213, and 1970 from *Survey of Current Business* [July 1973], p. 42) were used.

[11] The degrees of freedom adjustment of R^2 in Table 14.1 accounts for the small differences between the square roots of the $\bar{R}^2$ values in the table and the correlation coefficients shown in the above paragraph.

[12] The test of this statement was carried out as follows: Under the null hypothesis that $\alpha + \delta = 1$, the statistic $(1 - \hat{\beta}_1 - \hat{\beta}_0)/[\hat{\sigma}_{\hat{\beta}_1}^2 + \hat{\sigma}_{\hat{\beta}_0}^2 + 2\hat{\sigma}_{\hat{\beta}_1 \hat{\beta}_0}]$ is distributed as Student's t with 42 degrees of freedom. This statistic is less than 1 in both regressions 1 and 3, so the null hypothesis should be accepted.

Table 15.1. Regression Coefficients for Various Variants of

$$Q_{jk}^{t\bar{t}} = \alpha P_{jk}^{t\bar{t}} + \beta \, |C_j^t - C_k^{\bar{t}}| + \gamma D_{jj}^{t\bar{t}} + \lambda D_{jk}^{tt} + \delta + u_{jk}^{t\bar{t}} :$$

Comparisons of Five Countries, 1950 and 1970

Regression	$P_{jk}^{t\bar{t}}$	$|C_j^t - C_k^{\bar{t}}|$	$D_{jj}^{t\bar{t}}$	D_{jk}^{tt}	Constant	$\bar{R}^2$
(1)	1.4203* (.1590)	—	—	—	−.4577* (.1479)	.642
(2)	—	−.00265* (.00044)	—	—	.9398* (.0156)	.440
(3)	1.4903* (.3062)	.00018 (.00068)	—	—	−.5281 (.3019)	.634
(4)	1.1915* (.1531)	—	.0341 (.0205)	.0515* (.0137)	−.2719 (.1396)	.721
(5)	—	−.00214* (.00043)	.0683* (.0249)	.0573* (.0173)	.8916* (.0196)	.566
(6)	1.4095* (.2909)	.00058 (.0066)	.0280 (.0216)	.0537* (.0139)	−.4919 (.2860)	.719

$Q_{jk}^{t\bar{t}}$:   Index of similarity of consumption quantity-compositions of the jth and k^{th} countries in the t and $\bar{t}$ periods, respectively.

$P_{jk}^{t\bar{t}}$:   Index of similarity of price structures of the jth and k^{th} countries in the t and $\bar{t}$ periods, respectively.

$|C_j^t - C_k^{\bar{t}}|$:   Absolute value of the difference between per capita consumption of the jth and k^{th} countries in the t and $\bar{t}$ periods, respectively (taking U.S. 1970 as 100).

$D_{jj}^{t\bar{t}}$:   Dummy variable that takes on a value of 1 if the two country subscripts are the same and the year superscripts are different; and a value of 0 otherwise.

D_{jk}^{tt}:   Dummy variable that takes on a value of 1 if the two country subscripts are different and if the year superscripts are the same; and a value of 0 otherwise.

$\bar{R}^2$:   Coefficient of determination (adjusted for degrees of freedom).

Note: Numbers in parentheses are coefficient standard errors.
*: Coefficient is significantly different from 0 at the .05 level; one-tail test except for constant, where two-tail tests used.

Similarities for different times and for different countries. To check on the appropriateness of a simple pooling of all forty-five pairwide situations, two dummy variables are introduced to distinguish between the comparisons involving (1) the two years for the same country (for example, France 1950 and France 1970); (2) the same year for two different countries (France 1950 and the Federal Republic of Germany 1950); and (3) different countries and different years (France 1950 and the Federal Republic of Germany 1970). The dummy variables are $D_{jj}^{t\bar{t}}$, which refers to the first of these cases, and $D_{jk}^{t\bar{t}}$, which refers to the second. $D_{jj}^{t\bar{t}}$ takes on a value of 1 when the country subscripts are identical but the years are different, a value of 0 when either of these conditions is not met. $D_{jk}^{t\bar{t}}$ takes on a value of 1 when the years are the same and the country subscripts are different, a value of 0 when either of these conditions is not met. The case of different countries and different years is covered by both dummies taking on the value of 0. The empirical results appear as regressions 4, 5, and 6.[13] As before, the coefficients of $P_{jk}^{t\bar{t}}$ and $|C_j^t - C_k^{\bar{t}}|$ are of

the right sign and significant when they appear in the regression alone, but $|C_j^t - C_k^{\bar{t}}|$ becomes an insignificant variable when it appears along with $P_{jk}^{t\bar{t}}$.

The positive sign and significance of the coefficient of the two-country, same-year dummy variable, D_{jk}^{tt}, in each regression indicates that, other things being equal, two countries in the same year are more similar than they are for different years (France and the Federal Republic of Germany in 1970 are more similar, for example, than France in 1950 and the Federal Republic of Germany in 1970). The positive coefficient of the same-country, different-year dummy variable in the equations indicates—again, other things being equal—that

[13] In working with pairwise comparisons, it must be expected that the disturbance terms might not all be mutually independent. Dummy variables for individual countries were introduced into the regression, but the results were erratic. The conclusions with respect to $p_{jk}^{t\bar{t}}$ and $|C_j^t - C_k^{\bar{t}}|$ were still supported. The loss of degrees of freedom resulting from increasing the number of parameters to be estimated by nine was not warranted by the two significant country dummies that were found.

there is a tendency for greater similarity to show up between two years for the same country than between the two years for two different countries (France in 1970 is more similar to France in 1950, for example, than the Federal Republic of Germany in 1970 is to France in 1950). The effect is quite weak, however, and only in regression 5 is the coefficient significant. But the most interesting finding is the relationship between the coefficient of D_{jk}^{tt} and the coefficient of $D_{jj}^{t\bar{t}}$. Regressions 4 and 6 are directly relevant here. Regression 5 appears in the table only for completeness, because clearly $P_{jk}^{t\bar{t}}$ should be included in the regression. In both regressions 4 and 6, the coefficient of D_{jk}^{tt} is larger than $D_{jj}^{t\bar{t}}$, though the differences are not statistically significant. (The coefficient is only nine-tenths of the standard error of the difference in the first case and 1.16 times as great in the second.) This suggests—but does not prove—that, other things being equal, the five different countries tended to be more similar at a given time than individual countries were at times twenty years apart. We return to this point in the next section.

The significance of the coefficient of D_{jk}^{tt} warns against relying upon the coefficients in the correlation matrix. However, our a priori expectations of the effects of price and income, which were confirmed by the signs and significance of the correlation coefficients, still are borne out by the signs and significance of the coefficients of these variables in the equations in which the dummy variables have been added. It is unclear just how the linear restriction on the coefficients should be interpreted when the dummies are included in the regression. Because the dummy coefficients are quite small, however, the general sense of the linear restriction seems to be confirmed in regressions 4 and 6.

Perhaps this regression exercise suffers from the inadequate treatment of prices as exogenous rather than endogenous. It may be argued that although such a cavalier treatment of prices would be subject to question in a standard international demand analysis, it is not obvious that the similarity index for prices must be regarded as endogenous. We return in the next section to the problems of endogeneity.

A final point that may be made about these results relates to the claims set out earlier that international comparisons do not necessarily place any greater strain on the underlying economic rationale than comparisons for dates widely separated in time for a given country. Support for this claim already has been provided in the discussion of the regressions. There was some indication that greater similarity existed with respect to the quantity composition of consumption between countries in a given year than between the composition for a given country in different periods twenty years apart. This result was obtained holding price and income constant, but the outcome is the same when price and income are allowed to vary.[14]

Recourse once again to a table displaying the similarity indexes will make the latter result more transparent. Consider the following indexes of similarity of quantity composition:

	France 1970	Germany, F.R. 1970	Italy 1970	U.K. 1970
France				
1950	.92			
1970		.93	.97	.93
Germany, F.R.				
1950		.81		
1970	.93		.94	.95
Italy				
1950			.88	
1970	.97	.94		.95
U.K.				
1950				.87
1970	.93	.95	.95	

For each of the four countries, the 1970 quantity structure was more like the 1970 quantity structure of the other three countries than its own 1950 quantity structure.[15] The picture is mixed, however, when the United States is introduced. The U.S. 1970 quantity structure is more like the 1970 quantity structures of the Federal Republic of Germany (.93) and the United Kingdom (.93) than its own 1950 quantity structure (.92), but is less like that of France (.86) and Italy (.87).

The regressions summarized in Table 15.1 and the entire discussion surrounding them was based on the sixteen categories of consumption. We estimated similar equations adding the four categories of capital formation and government to the sixteen consumption categories. The results are so similar that it is not worth displaying them. The only notable difference is that the gap in GDP per capita turns out to be a slightly stronger variable in these regressions than was the gap in consumption per capita in the earlier ones. In the equivalent of regression (3) in Table 15.1, the coefficient of the variable measuring the difference in per capita GDP was nearly twice its standard error, whereas the corresponding coefficient in regression (3) is less than its standard error. When the variable reflecting the income gap between the two countries is taken as the only independent variable (regression 2), $\bar{R}^2$ is higher in the GDP regressions (.49) than in the consumption regressions (.44). In the other regressions, however, the $\bar{R}^2$ declines.

[14] $Q_{jk}^{t\bar{t}} = .070\,D_{jj}^{t\bar{t}} + .093\,D_{jk}^{tt} + .812,$ $\qquad\bar{R}^2 = .325$
$\qquad\quad (.031)\quad\;\; (.020)\quad\;\; (.014)$
The difference between the coefficients of $D_{jj}^{t\bar{t}}$ and D_{jk}^{tt} is 0.57 times the standard error of the difference.

[15] The same conclusion emerges if intercountry similarity indexes for 1950 are compared with the intertemporal similarity indexes for given countries (though a little less uniformly) or if own-weighted and Fisher indexes are used.

Once again, these results correspond to expectations. We would expect differences in income levels to be a more powerful influence than relative prices on the determination of the capital formation component of per capita GDP and, perhaps, of the government component as well. Thus, when the four nonconsumption categories are included in the regressions, the explanatory power of income rises and that of prices declines.

The proximity proposition does not imply a particular functional form for equation (15.1). Those alternatives to the linear forms described in Table 15.1 which were examined (for example, linear in the angles between the country vectors in the quantity and price spaces rather than linear in the cosines;[16] and also linear-in-the-logs of the cosines) led to essentially the same substantive conclusions relating to the price and income variables.

TEN COUNTRIES IN 1970

The analysis of the data for five countries in 1950 and 1970 necessarily was based on binary comparisons. Of the forty-five pairs, only eight involved the United States. The other pairs consisted of countries other than the United States whose quantity (and price) vectors were compared through use of the United States as a bridge country. As noted in Chapter 4,[17] bridge-country comparisons are subject to the distortions that we have minimized but not avoided entirely by bridging at the detailed-category level in establishing the quantity and price vectors.

In the analysis of similarities for the ten ICP countries in 1970, we are able to avoid these difficulties by drawing upon the multilateral comparisons in which pairs of countries not including the United States are on the same theoretical and statistical basis as pairs involving the United States. In calculating the similarity indexes, the various categories were weighted in accordance with their importance in "world GDP."[18] Because we were not confined by the problem of reconciling the classification used in the ICP with an earlier one, we were able to base the similarity indexes on all 152 categories in principle. In fact, however, we deleted two categories in which expenditures can be negative—Exports Minus Imports and Increases in Stocks. Thus, we were left with 150 categories, of which 109 are in consumption, 36 in capital formation, and 5 in government.

Comparisons of similarity indexes. The similarity indexes for quantities and prices are set out for GDP, consumption, and capital formation in Tables 15.2, 15.3, and 15.4. The countries are arrayed in both the lines and the columns in order of increasing size of real per capita GDP. An easy confirmation of the role of per capita income in determining the quantity compositions can be obtained merely by glancing along the lines or down the columns of the quantity matrices of Tables 15.2 and 15.3. There is a distinct tendency for the size of the similarity indexes to diminish as one moves along a line or column away from the principal diagonal—from upper left to lower right. That is, similarity in quantity composition diminishes as the per capita income gap between the countries increases. The corresponding tendency in the price matrices for GDP and consumption is clearly weaker. Table 15.4, relating to capital formation, does not show the same tendency; income differences apparently play a small role in explaining investment patterns.

The patterns exhibited by the similarity indexes in Tables 15.2, 15.3, and 15.4 can be summarized in different ways. Table 15.5 gives the averages of each country's similarity index with respect to each other country. These averages depend on the composition of the sample countries, so generalizations made from these averages strictly apply only to similarities within the sample of ten countries.

It can be seen that India has the most dissimilar quantity structure from that of the other countries in the consumption sector and for GDP as a whole. There is some tendency for countries to be more alike in the quantity composition of capital formation than in the quantity composition of consumption. But on average, the Federal Republic of Germany and France differ more from other countries in the structure of their capital formation than they do in the structure of their consumption. Once again, it can be seen that the similarity of price structure is consistently greater than the similarity in the composition of quantities. Even Kenya and India, with consumption patterns very dissimilar from the other countries, have price structures that are not so radically different. Similarities in price structure seem to be greater within capital formation than within consumption.

The sets of mean similarity indexes of Table 15.5 represent only one of a number of possible ways of setting out the relationships between the countries. Formal dimension-reducing methods for facilitating comparisons across countries can provide a visual representation of the relationships among the countries. One such nonmetric, multidimensional scaling procedure was devised by Torgerson utilizing the so-called TORSCA algorithm.[19] It is designed to position a group of entities,

[16] See page 268.

[17] See page 52.

[18] For each category of GDP, each representative country's quantity (in international dollars) was blown up to represent the corresponding supercountry's quantity. (This was done by multiplying the international dollar quantity of the representative country by the ratio of the supercountry GDP to representative country GDP.) These totals were then summed across the ten representative countries to get the category's "world" total, which could be compared with world GDP.

[19] W. S. Torgerson, *Theory and Methods of Scaling* (New York: John Wiley, 1960); P. E. Green, and V. R. Rao, *Applied*

Table 15.2. Indexes of Similarity for Quantity Structures and Price Structures for GDP, 150 Categories, 1970

	Kenya	India	Colombia	Hungary	Italy	Japan	U.K.	Germany, F.R.	France	U.S.
				Part A. Quantities						
Kenya	1.000	0.665	0.633	0.557	0.546	0.505	0.540	0.467	0.489	0.484
India	0.665	1.000	0.534	0.441	0.423	0.549	0.419	0.412	0.399	0.391
Colombia	0.633	0.534	1.000	0.759	0.836	0.833	0.820	0.690	0.763	0.750
Hungary	0.557	0.441	0.759	1.000	0.775	0.824	0.799	0.845	0.850	0.821
Italy	0.546	0.423	0.836	0.775	1.000	0.845	0.955	0.875	0.932	0.872
Japan	0.505	0.549	0.833	0.824	0.845	1.000	0.839	0.774	0.846	0.775
U.K.	0.540	0.419	0.820	0.799	0.955	0.839	1.000	0.908	0.908	0.924
Germany, F.R.	0.467	0.412	0.690	0.845	0.875	0.774	0.908	1.000	0.929	0.923
France	0.489	0.399	0.763	0.850	0.932	0.846	0.908	0.929	1.000	0.879
U.S.	0.484	0.391	0.750	0.821	0.872	0.775	0.924	0.923	0.879	1.000
				Part B. Prices						
Kenya	1.000	0.872	0.853	0.822	0.849	0.856	0.903	0.847	0.840	0.850
India	0.872	1.000	0.898	0.842	0.818	0.811	0.880	0.798	0.763	0.763
Colombia	0.853	0.898	1.000	0.798	0.785	0.769	0.846	0.778	0.759	0.763
Hungary	0.822	0.842	0.798	1.000	0.873	0.881	0.851	0.871	0.832	0.809
Italy	0.849	0.818	0.785	0.873	1.000	0.922	0.905	0.979	0.959	0.898
Japan	0.856	0.811	0.769	0.881	0.922	1.000	0.898	0.916	0.882	0.899
U.K.	0.903	0.880	0.846	0.851	0.905	0.898	1.000	0.907	0.892	0.921
Germany, F.R.	0.847	0.798	0.778	0.871	0.979	0.916	0.907	1.000	0.974	0.926
France	0.840	0.768	0.759	0.832	0.959	0.882	0.892	0.974	1.000	0.917
U.S.	0.850	0.763	0.763	0.809	0.598	0.899	0.921	0.926	0.917	1.000

each described by an n-dimensional vector within an m-dimensional space ($m < n$) in such a way that the Euclidean distance between entity points may be interpreted as a representation of their relative similarity. In the present ICP applications, we work with ten countries (entities), each described by its quantities or prices for each of the 109 consumption categories (that is, $n = 109$). We wish to pass to a two-dimensional representation (that is, $m = 2$) for each country such that the distance between country points in the two-dimensional space will indicate the relative degree of similarity between the countries with respect to quantity composition or price structure.[20]

We are interested in the spatial configuration of Figures 15.1 and 15.2 without being concerned about the coordinates (or meaning of the coordinates) of the specific points. We see in Figure 15.1 that, with respect to quantity compositions, India and Kenya are quite dissimilar and also are quite different from each of the other eight countries, including even Colombia. On the other hand, the United States, France, the Federal Republic of Germany, Italy, and the United Kingdom are all much alike. Hungary, Japan, and Colombia are dissimilar between themselves and are unlike the EEC countries and the United States to about the same degree; however, there is far greater similarity among them than there is between them and India and Kenya.

The points of Figure 15.2 represent price structures of countries. The fact that they are more widely scattered than those of the quantity points of Figure 15.1 does not mean price structures are more dissimilar. In fact, we have seen above that the opposite is true. The distances of Figure 15.1 are not comparable with the distances of Figure 15.2. Again, the same four countries of Western Europe and the United States are close together, with Japan away slightly and, off farther in the same direction, Hungary. The three developing countries are together. Interestingly enough, the United Kingdom is close relatively to its Commonwealth partners, India and Kenya.

One may expect that the degree of similarity will be in part a function of the degree of disaggregation. Substitutions are more likely to occur between similar products serving the same function than between broad categories of goods. Thus, when we compare the results of Table 15.2, based on 150 detailed categories, with similarity indexes based on a 34-category classification

---

Multidimensional Scaling (New York: Holt, Rinehart and Winston, 1972).

[20]Because the object of the present discussion is merely to provide some visual feeling for the relative closeness of the ICP countries to each other, the TORSCA method will be treated here as a black box. It involves a modified (that is, nonmetric) factor analysis, and here only the first two factors are computed and graphed. The first factor in Figures 15.1 and 15.2 appears on the horizontal axis and the second on the vertical one. The distance between any two country points is a measure of the similarity between the two countries, which reflects not only the appropriate direct similarity index of Table 15.3 but also takes account (through factor analysis) of all the indirect similarities implied by all the other entries in the table.

Figure 15.1. Relationship between Country Quantity Compositions, ICP 1970

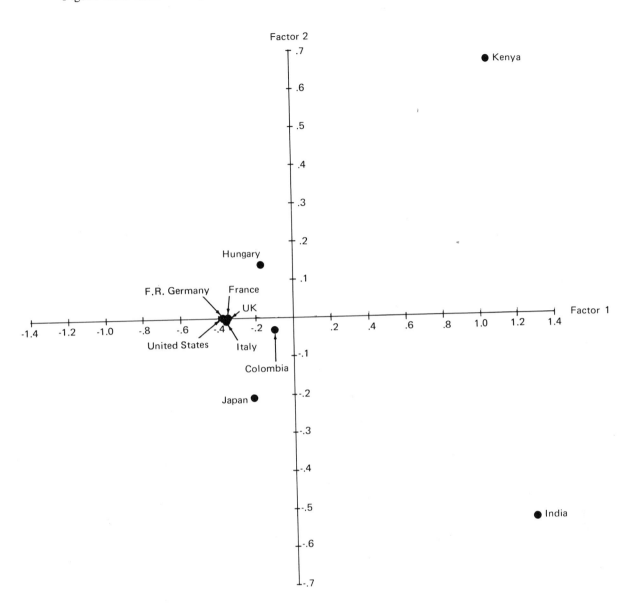

of GDP used in the summary tables of Chapter 14,[21] we find that the latter yields measures of similarity that generally are higher. Table 15.6, which presents the ratios of the 34-category indexes to the 150-category indexes, shows that the use of the more aggregative classification increased the quantity similarity most in the cases of Kenya and Hungary. Aggregation or disaggregation has smaller effects on indexes of price similarity.

[21] The thirty-four summary categories are those selected from the stubs of the summary multilateral tables in Chapter 14 so as to obtain a set of categories that account for the entire GDP without duplication and without the use of any data in the table that represent aggregations of other data in the table.

Regression analysis. The preceding paragraphs have been devoted to a description of the ten ICP countries couched in terms of our similarity indexes. Following the approach used above in the analysis of 1950 and 1970 data for five countries, we now examine by regression analysis the relationship between quantity similarity, on the one hand, and price and income similarity, on the other. Once again, the index of quantity similarity is taken as the dependent variable, and the index of price similarity and the gap in GDP per capita are treated as independent variables. The forty-five pairs that can be formed from the ten countries are our observations. The results of the regressions based on similarity indexes for 150 categories of GDP and 109 categories of consump-

Figure 15.2. Relationship between Country Price Structures, ICP 1970

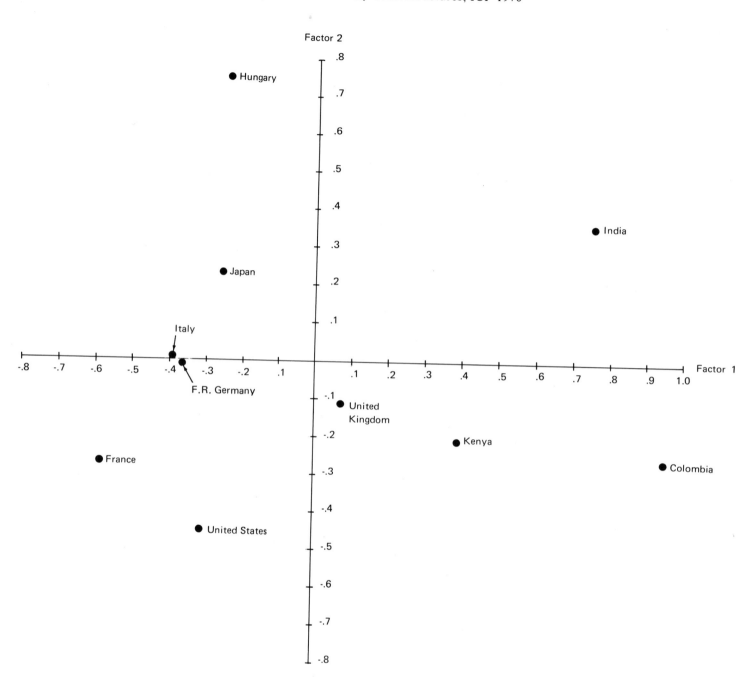

tion are presented in Table 15.7, as well as results based on similarity indexes drawn from more aggregative data (34 categories of GDP and 25 of consumption).

Once again, our expectations are confirmed by the data. In every regression the coefficient of P_{jk} is positive and that of $|G_j - G_k|$ or $|C_j - C_k|$ is negative; with only two exceptions, they are all statistically significant. Even when both price and income similarity appear in the regressions (regressions 3, 4, 7, 8, 11, 12, 15, and 16) the separate effects of the two variables show up clearly. Unmistakably, countries with similar price structures and with relatively small differences in per capita GDP

have more similar quantity structures than countries that are not so much alike in these two respects. More than that, the $\alpha + \delta = 1$ relationship also holds statistically. We observe that when the detailed categories are used (150 for GDP and 109 for consumption), the proportion of the total variation in the similarity indexes for quantities that is explained by similarities in prices and incomes is only around one-third, both for GDP and for consumption (see regressions 3 and 11). Matters are improved substantially, however, when the similarity indexes are based on more aggregated categories. Price and income similarities explain nearly one-half of the

Table 15.3. Indexes of Similarity for Quantity Structures and Price Structures for Consumption, 109 Categories, 1970

Part A. Quantities

	Kenya	India	Colombia	Hungary	Italy	Japan	U.K.	Germany, F.R.	France	U.S.
Kenya	1.000	0.664	0.612	0.562	0.505	0.466	0.482	0.479	0.479	0.455
India	0.664	1.000	0.507	0.384	0.367	0.554	0.351	0.355	0.335	0.327
Colombia	0.612	0.507	1.000	0.800	0.817	0.843	0.816	0.777	0.795	0.801
Hungary	0.582	0.384	0.800	1.000	0.798	0.852	0.798	0.796	0.854	0.781
Italy	0.505	0.367	0.817	0.798	1.000	0.862	0.966	0.974	0.969	0.938
Japan	0.466	0.554	0.843	0.852	0.862	1.000	0.867	0.862	0.884	0.851
U.K.	0.482	0.351	0.816	0.798	0.966	0.867	1.000	0.980	0.941	0.961
Germany, F.R.	0.479	0.355	0.777	0.796	0.974	0.862	0.980	1.000	0.959	0.961
France	0.479	0.335	0.795	0.854	0.969	0.884	0.941	0.959	1.000	0.931
U.S.	0.455	0.327	0.801	0.781	0.938	0.851	0.961	0.961	0.931	1.000

Part B. Prices

	Kenya	India	Colombia	Hungary	Italy	Japan	U.K.	Germany, F.R.	France	U.S.
Kenya	1.000	0.872	0.857	0.799	0.838	0.852	0.895	0.835	0.830	0.833
India	0.872	1.000	0.875	0.817	0.806	0.814	0.881	0.789	0.758	0.767
Colombia	0.857	0.875	1.000	0.765	0.776	0.779	0.853	0.778	0.767	0.784
Hungary	0.799	0.817	0.765	1.000	0.862	0.877	0.820	0.863	0.817	0.791
Italy	0.838	0.806	0.776	0.862	1.000	0.926	0.894	0.977	0.954	0.890
Japan	0.852	0.814	0.779	0.877	0.926	1.000	0.887	0.917	0.869	0.885
U.K.	0.895	0.881	0.853	0.820	0.894	0.887	1.000	0.900	0.884	0.920
Germany, F.R.	0.835	0.789	0.778	0.863	0.977	0.917	0.900	1.000	0.970	0.921
France	0.830	0.758	0.767	0.817	0.954	0.869	0.884	0.970	1.000	0.906
U.S.	0.833	0.767	0.784	0.791	0.890	0.885	0.920	0.921	0.906	1.000

variation in the similarity indexes when the similarity indexes are based on 34 categories of GDP and 25 categories of consumption (see regressions 7 and 15). These $\bar{R}^2$s (.477 and .493) are smaller than the corresponding $\bar{R}^2$s derived from the earlier analysis of the four European countries and the United States (.551 and .634), but it should be borne in mind that the earlier analysis was based on a still larger degree of aggregation (that is, on 20 categories for GDP and 16 for consumption). We find again that the regressions meet the test suggested earlier:[22] that the predicted value of Q_{jk} should be unity when P_{jk} is unity and $|G_j - G_k|$ (or $|C_j - C_k|$) is 0.

[22] See page 270.

Table 15.4. Indexes of Similarity for Quantity Structures and Price Structures for Capital Formation, 36 Categories, 1970

Part A. Quantities

	Kenya	India	Colombia	Hungary	Italy	Japan	U.K.	Germany, F.R.	France	U.S.
Kenya	1.000	0.760	0.918	0.644	0.946	0.846	0.887	0.421	0.529	0.875
India	0.760	1.000	0.830	0.840	0.864	0.867	0.779	0.715	0.832	0.808
Colombia	0.918	0.830	1.000	0.726	0.907	0.860	0.846	0.454	0.546	0.863
Hungary	0.644	0.840	0.726	1.000	0.750	0.849	0.706	0.753	0.820	0.804
Italy	0.946	0.864	0.907	0.750	1.000	0.862	0.911	0.662	0.756	0.924
Japan	0.846	0.867	0.860	0.849	0.862	1.000	0.857	0.628	0.668	0.847
U.K.	0.887	0.779	0.846	0.706	0.911	0.857	1.000	0.647	0.939	0.638
Germany, F.R.	0.421	0.715	0.454	0.753	0.662	0.628	0.647	1.000	0.939	0.752
France	0.529	0.832	0.546	0.820	0.733	0.756	0.668	0.939	1.000	0.752
U.S.	0.875	0.808	0.863	0.804	0.905	0.924	0.847	0.638	0.752	1.000

Part B. Prices

	Kenya	India	Colombia	Hungary	Italy	Japan	U.K.	Germany, F.R.	France	U.S.
Kenya	1.000	0.869	0.846	0.874	0.900	0.856	0.923	0.894	0.884	0.922
India	0.869	1.000	0.955	0.906	0.902	0.807	0.900	0.869	0.833	0.801
Colombia	0.846	0.955	1.000	0.878	0.862	0.745	0.848	0.821	0.777	0.748
Hungary	0.874	0.906	0.878	1.000	0.934	0.886	0.934	0.922	0.895	0.880
Italy	0.900	0.902	0.862	0.934	1.000	0.915	0.939	0.985	0.971	0.929
Japan	0.856	0.807	0.745	0.686	0.915	1.000	0.913	0.913	0.922	0.940
U.K.	0.923	0.900	0.848	0.934	0.939	0.913	1.000	0.919	0.906	0.926
Germany, F.R.	0.894	0.869	0.821	0.922	0.985	0.913	0.919	1.000	0.981	0.940
France	0.864	0.833	0.777	0.895	0.971	0.922	0.906	0.981	1.000	0.957
U.S.	0.922	0.801	0.748	0.880	0.929	0.940	0.926	0.940	0.957	1.000

Table 15.5. Means of Similarity Indexes†

	GDP		Consumption		Capital formation	
	Quantities	Prices	Quantities	Prices	Quantities	Prices
Kenya	.54	.85	.52	.85	.76	.89
India	.47	.83	.43	.82	.81	.87
Colombia	.74	.81	.75	.80	.77	.83
Hungary	.74	.84	.74	.82	.77	.90
Italy	.78	.89	.80	.88	.84	.93
Japan	.75	.87	.78	.87	.83	.88
U.K.	.79	.89	.80	.88	.79	.91
Germany	.76	.89	.79	.88	.65	.92
France	.78	.87	.79	.86	.73	.90
U.S.	.76	.86	.78	.86	.82	.89

†For each country, average of its indexes relative to the other nine countries.

We explored the possibility that countries linked by close cultural or political ties might have more similar quantity structures for a given level of similarity in price structures and in incomes. We inserted intercept dummies into the equations for the countries that were members of the British Commonwealth (India, Kenya, and the United Kingdom) and for countries that were members of the European Economic Community (France, the Federal Republic of Germany, and Italy). We also included three dummy variables for comparisons involving two low-income countries (that is, pairs including India, Kenya, and Colombia), for those involving two medium-income countries (Hungary, Italy, Japan, and the United Kingdom), and for those involving two high-income countries (France, the Federal Republic of Germany, and the United States). It turns out that the dummy variable for low-income countries has the great-

est explanatory power, and regressions including it appear in Table 15.7 (regressions 4, 8, 12, and 16). The dummy variable for the Commonwealth countries also proved to be significant in some cases. It had less explanatory power than the dummy for the low-income countries, however, and we have not thought it worthwhile to include it in the tables, particularly because two of the three Commonwealth countries, India and Kenya, are in the low-income group. The dummy for EEC pairs was not significant in any of the equations.

One possible reason for the significance of the dummy for pairs of low-income countries is that poor countries tend to rely largely upon traditional factors of production that reflect their particular environment and history, and they tend to transform these resources into traditional patterns of output. Only after industrialization and modernization begin do similarities in quan-

Table 15.6. Ratios of 34-Category to 150-Category Similarity Indexes

Part A. Quantities

	Kenya	India	Colombia	Hungary	Italy	Japan	U.K.	Germany, F.R.	France	U.S.
Kenya	1.000	1.355	1.145	1.266	1.249	1.424	1.252	1.276	1.288	1.258
India	1.355	1.000	1.009	1.222	1.175	1.038	1.148	1.053	1.065	1.056
Colombia	1.145	1.009	1.000	1.188	1.037	1.004	1.017	1.142	1.065	1.056
Hungary	1.266	1.222	1.188	1.000	1.157	1.126	1.146	1.095	1.098	1.056
Italy	1.249	1.175	1.037	1.157	1.000	1.000	.991	1.058	1.033	1.060
Japan	1.424	1.038	1.004	1.126	1.000	1.000	1.048	1.151	1.072	1.041
U.K.	1.252	1.148	1.017	1.146	.991	1.048	1.000	1.043	1.066	1.027
Germany, F.R.	1.276	1.053	1.142	1.095	1.058	1.151	1.043	1.000	1.038	.997
France	1.288	1.065	1.121	1.098	1.033	1.072	1.066	1.038	1.000	1.034
U.S.	1.258	1.056	1.056	1.060	1.014	1.041	1.027	.997	1.034	1.000
Average	1.279	1.125	1.080	1.151	1.079	1.100	1.082	1.095	1.091	1.060

Part B. Prices

	Kenya	India	Colombia	Hungary	Italy	Japan	U.K.	Germany, F.R.	France	U.S.
Kenya	1.000	1.024	1.093	1.100	1.052	1.076	1.044	1.064	1.058	1.075
India	1.024	1.000	1.000	1.040	1.008	1.060	.977	1.016	1.023	1.015
Colombia	1.093	1.000	1.000	1.118	1.082	1.133	1.041	1.098	1.108	1.090
Hungary	1.100	1.040	1.118	1.000	1.056	1.047	1.048	1.049	1.067	1.063
Italy	1.052	1.008	1.082	1.056	1.000	1.046	1.054	1.014	1.016	1.051
Japan	1.076	1.060	1.133	1.047	1.046	1.000	1.059	1.050	1.076	1.042
U.K.	1.044	.977	1.041	1.048	1.054	1.059	1.000	1.055	1.057	1.036
Germany, F.R.	1.064	1.016	1.098	1.049	1.014	1.050	1.055	1.000	1.011	1.031
France	1.058	1.023	1.108	1.067	1.016	1.076	1.057	1.011	1.000	1.046
U.S.	1.074	1.015	1.090	1.063	1.051	1.076	1.057	1.011	1.000	1.046
Average	1.065	1.018	1.085	1.065	1.042	1.065	1.041	1.043	1.051	1.050

tities become closely geared to price structure and income similarities. An alternative explanation is that, though in all countries the individual demand functions are the same, the stochastic element has a larger variance for low-income countries. This kind of heteroscedasticity in the demand functions would lead to the need for dummies such as D in Table 15.7.

B. Quantities and the Roles of Price and Income Differences

The encouraging results concerning the explanatory power of prices and incomes for quantities lead naturally to demand analysis of the more traditional form, in which the quantity of a specific product or group of products is taken as a function of own and other prices and of income or overall level of consumption. We are handicapped in following this avenue by our having observations on only ten countries, a limitation that will be eased as additional countries are brought into the ICP system of comparisons. In order to make available without delay the basic results set out in Chapters 13 and 14, we confine ourselves here to a simple investigation involving a very loose formulation of a demand system. This continues our efforts to document our position that quantities demanded depend significantly on relative prices and income, and that commonality of tastes around the world is plausible.

At a later time, a far more elaborate econometric analysis of a system of demand relationships will be carried out. The similarity-index exploration just described constitutes a rough approach to the analysis of the full system. It involves relating—admittedly, in a very special way—*all* of the elements of the matrix of detailed category (or summary category) quantities to *all* of the entries of the matrix of detailed category (or summary category) prices and to *all* of the individual country incomes or levels of consumption. This is what is done in, say, the linear-expenditure–system approach to consumption data, though that very different system specification draws far more on the implications of the theory of consumer behavior for a single consumer.[23]

Our basic demand function takes the form of equation (15.4):

$$(15.4) \quad \ln q_{\alpha j} = \beta_{\alpha 1} \ln\left(\frac{p_{\alpha j}}{p_{cj}}\right) + \beta_{\alpha 2} \ln C_j + \beta_{\alpha o} + u_{\alpha j},$$
$$\alpha = 1, \ldots, m; \ j = 1, \ldots, 10,$$

[23] As is generally acknowledged, market demand equations *need* not meet the restrictions implied for individuals by the theory of consumer behavior. See H. Wold and L. Jureen, *Demand Analysis* (New York: John Wiley, 1953), p. 120, Theorem 1; or R. A. Pollak and T. J. Wales, "Estimation of the Linear Expenditure System," *Econometrica* 37 (October 1969), pp. 611–12.

Table 15.7. Regression Coefficients for Various Variants of $Q_{jk} = \alpha P_{jk} + \beta |G_j - G_k| + \gamma D + \delta + u_{jk}$: Comparisons of Ten Countries, 1970

Regression	P_{jk}	$|G_j - G_k|$	D	Constant	$\bar{R}^2$
	GDP: 150 Categories				
(1)	1.511* (.4246)	—	—	-.5874 (.3657)	.210
(2)	—	-.00413* (.00095)	—	.8670* (.0424)	.291
(3)	.7332 (.4898)	-.00312* (.0012)	—	.1986 (.4484)	.311
(4)	.5050 (.4592)	-.00435* (.00115)	-.2597* (.0904)	.4583 (.4238)	.412
	GDP: 34 Categories				
(5)	2.1948* (.3671)	—	—	-1.2022* (.3324)	.441
(6)	—	-.00411* (.00086)	—	.9367* (.0385)	.332
(7)	1.6340* (.4540)	-.00193* (.00097)	—	-.6227 (.4346)	.477
(8)	1.3858* (.4523)	-.00284* (.00103)	-.1643* (.0782)	-.3531 (.4372)	.516
	Consumption: 109 Categories				
(9)	1.9109* (.4925)	—	—	-.9103* (.4207)	.242
(10)	—	-.00472* (.00121)	—	.8826* (.0505)	.245
(11)	1.2650* (.5404)	-.00317* (.00133)	—	-.2496 (.4861)	.317
(12)	1.1284* (.5090)	-.00428* (.00131)	-.2781* (.1062)	-.0759 (.4602)	.400
	Consumption: 25 Categories				
(13)	2.4403* (.4224)	—	—	-1.4208* (.3821)	.424
(14)	—	-.00462* (.00103)	—	.9440* (.0429)	.305
(15)	1.8643* (.4532)	-.00262* (.00100)	—	-.8093 (.4278)	.493
(16)	1.6911* (.4495)	-.00336* (.00105)	-.1610* (.0853)	-.6166 (.4277)	.522

Q_{jk}: Index of similarity of quantity compositions of the jth and k^{th} countries.

P_{jk}: Index of similarity of price structure of the jth and k^{th} countries.

$|G_j - G_k|$: Absolute value of the difference between per capita GDP of the jth and k^{th} countries, taking U.S. as 100.

$|C_j - C_k|$: Absolute value of the difference between per capita consumption of the jth and k^{th} countries, taking U.S. as 100.

D: A dummy variable that has a value of 1 when both countries are low-income countries (Colombia, India, or Kenya); 0 otherwise.

Note: Numbers in parentheses are coefficient standard errors.
*: Coefficient is significantly different from 0 at the .05 level; one-tail test except for constant, where two-tail test used.

where *ln* stands for the natural logarithm, $q_{\alpha j}$ is the real quantity per capita of the αth good consumed in the jth country (denominated in international dollars, and given in either Table 14.5 or Appendix Table 14.5); $p_{\alpha j}$ is the PPP for the αth good in the jth country (as given in either Table 14.3 or Appendix Table 14.3), p_{cj} is the purchasing power parity for consumption in the jth

country given in line 1 of Table 14.3; and C_j is real consumption per capita in the jth country (denominated in international dollars and given in line 1 of Table 14.5). Since C is given in real terms, the demand function is homogeneous of degree zero, as it should be. Placing p_{cj} in the denominator in the price term takes account of substitution possibilities with no loss of scarce degrees of freedom. The regression coefficients $\beta_{\alpha 1}$ and $\beta_{\alpha 2}$ may (charitably) be called price and income elasticities.[24] They have been estimated by Ordinary Least Squares, one equation at a time, for each of the subaggregate groupings defined in the summary tables of Chapter 14, and also for most of the commodities defined by the detailed categories.[25] The problem of possible simultaneous equation estimation bias will be referred to below.

SUMMARY CATEGORIES

First, in Table 15.8 we present the results of the regressions obtained for the summary categories. It can be seen that the coefficient of relative price is generally negative. The price elasticity for food as a whole is positive (and insignificant), but only Oils and Fats, and Spices and Sweets, Sugar among the eight food subcomponents show a positive elasticity. Among the other categories of consumption, only Tobacco has a positive price elasticity. The elasticities are more than unity for Meat among the foods, and for Beverages, Footwear, most Transportation and Communication groupings, and Other Expenditures among the nonfoods. The consumption elasticity is uniformly positive, and, except for Bread and Cereals, it is highly significant for all the groupings in the table. Apart from Meat, the consumption elasticity for the food groups is less than one. For the other groupings, it is above one except for Household Supplies and Operations, Public Transport, and Education.

The regressions we have computed have their origins in the pioneering international cross-section analyses done by Houthakker.[26] Their specific predecessors, how-

ever, are the demand regressions of Gilbert and Associates computed for the Organization for European Economic Cooperation for 1950.[27] Our results appear with those of the OEEC in Table 15.9. The ICP consumption elasticities, based upon a quite different time period and a very different mix of countries, match the earlier results fairly closely: eleven out of eighteen are of about the same value, and fourteen out of eighteen differ by no more than one might expect from chance (at the .05 level), given the standard errors of the estimates. The estimates of price elasticities in both sets of regressions are subject to such large standard errors that the match between the two sets of regression results is less clear: in eleven out of eighteen, the two price elasticities are distinctly different from the point of view of any policy implication, but individual tests of hypotheses that they are really the same lead to acceptance of the null hypothesis in fourteen out of the eighteen cases. (The proper way to compare the two sets of regressions is through analysis of covariance applied to all of the individual observations of the 1950 and 1970 data. Our judgments, however, have been made using only the already computed regression coefficients and their standard errors.)

DETAILED CATEGORIES

Table 15.10 contains the results of applying equation (15.4) to the detailed categories.[28] In the large majority of the cases, the coefficients of the relative price and of the consumption variable correspond to expectations. The coefficient of the price variable is negative in about 80 percent of the categories. The consumption coefficient is positive in all but a handful of cases: in these few exceptional cases, the negative sign is not implausible. Commodities such as rice, meal, and macaroni, as well as public transport, may not actually be inferior goods, as the negative signs would suggest, but among countries with such a wide range of incomes, they certainly can be expected to have very low income elasticities.

Is the price elasticity of demand less for a summary category than for each of the individual detailed categories which it contains? It may be conjectured that substitution for reasons of price takes place primarily at low levels of aggregation. A comparison of the price elasticities of Table 15.8 with those of Table 15.10 lends

---

[24] These cross-section estimates, of course, should be interpreted as long-run elasticities.

[25] Two niceties of an ideal estimation process may be mentioned:

First, the so-called seemingly unrelated equation technique (A. Zellner, "An Efficient Method of Estimating Seemingly Unrelated Regressions and Tests for Aggregation Bias," *Journal of the American Statistical Association* 57 [June 1962], pp. 348-68) could be applied to the system of equations given by (15.4); in the ICP case, however, the number of product equations that can be handled in the system cannot exceed nine.

Second, because, as indicated in Chapter 5, the $p_{\alpha j}$s for the most part were estimated by CPD and the $q_{\alpha j}$s came out of the Geary-Khamis method, the available variances of the estimates should be exploited, at least in principle, in the estimation method.

[26] H. S. Houthakker, "Some Problems in the International Comparison of Consumption Patterns," *L'Evaluation et le Role des Besoins des Biens de Consommation dans les Divers Regimes Economiques* (Paris: Centre Nationale Researche Statistique,

1951); "An International Comparison of Household Expenditure Patterns, Commemorating the Centenary of Engle's Law," *Econometrica* 25 (October 1957), pp. 532-51; "The Influence of Prices and Income on Household Expenditure," *Bulletin of the International Statistical Institute* 37 (1960), pp. 1-16; "New Evidence on Demand Elasticities," *Econometrica* 33 (April 1965), pp. 277-88.

[27] M. Gilbert and Associates, *Comparative National Products and Price Levels* (Paris: Organization for European Economic Cooperation, 1958) pp. 63-74.

[28] In 34 out of 109 categories, $q_{\alpha j}$ is equal to 0 for at least one country. Because ln_0 is undefined, the regressions for those categories were not computed.

some limited support to this conjecture. Each of the twenty-four summary price elasticities was compared with the price elasticities of its own components (for example, −.9774 for Milk, Cheese, and Eggs was compared with −.6761 for Fresh Milk, 1.3551 for Milk Products, and 1.5070 for Eggs) and it was found that in almost two-thirds of all cases (significant at the .95 level) the summary category was less price elastic than its components. A similar comparison of $\bar{R}^2$s for the summary categories with the $\bar{R}^2$s of their components suggests that the summary relationships have less noise in them than do the components. (In more than four-fifths of the cases, the $\bar{R}^2$ for the summary category exceeds the $\bar{R}^2$ of the components.)

VARIABLES OTHER THAN PRICE AND INCOME

That important elements of the real world are omitted from the picture is evident. In a fuller study of demand relationships, it would be desirable to attempt to take into account some obviously relevant variables. The response of consumers to different climatic conditions, for example, clearly is important. In most cases, however, our empirical results give no clear signal of our failure to allow for this (see $\bar{R}^2$s of Tables 15.8 and 15.10). We experimented with just one noneconomic variable in connection with three of our commodity groupings to determine whether, with our very limited number of observations, we could improve our explanation of the quantity demanded. We examined the impact of country temperature on quantity of residential heating fuel consumed, as well as on both the quantity of clothing and the quantity of footwear. The regressions results (with standard errors in parentheses) were as follows:

| | Coefficients of | | | | $\bar{R}^2$/ |
	ln Price	ln Consumption	ln Temperature	Constant	SEE
Fuel	−.3100 (.3290)	.5472 (.2572)	−1.1526 (.6821)	3.7721 (4.1752)	.815 .415
Clothing	−.2118 (.3476)	1.3033 (.0989)	−.3329 (.2357)	−3.6077 (1.5255)	.989 .145
Footwear	−1.1306 (.7085)	1.2779 (.3052)	−.3291 (.8161)	−5.2297 (5.0037)	.874 .503

The three negative t values for temperature, though not individually significant, together are significant at the .95 level, confirming our expectation of the impact of temperature on demand in these groupings.[29] Because

---

[29] Under the null hypothesis that temperature does not explain the dependent variable, the average of the three t values (−1.699, −1.412, −.403) will be distributed approximately normally, with mean 0 and standard deviation somewhat greater than $1/\sqrt{3}$. ("Somewhat greater" because the t distribution with six degrees of freedom has a standard deviation greater than 1.) $\bar{t} ÷ 1/\sqrt{3} = −2.03$, which is significant at the .05 level.

temperature and level of consumption are negatively correlated in the ICP sample of countries, the omission of temperature from the regressions in Tables 15.8 and 15.10 biased the consumption coefficient upward. In effect, the contribution of temperature in explaining the dependent variables was being carried by consumption in the tables. When the separate contributions of consumption and temperature are isolated, the consumption elasticities are reduced.

To obtain a further glimpse of the potentialities of these data, we ran two more pairs of regressions. The formulation of price in equation (15.4) standardizes own prices relative to the average of all consumption-goods prices, but it does not allow for the prices of specific substitutes. We consider first Meat and Fish regressions, which allow for cross-price elasticities.

| | Coefficients of | | | | $\bar{R}^2$/ |
	$ln\,P_{meat}$	$ln\,P_{fish}$	ln Consumption	Constant	SEE
Meat	−1.1324 (.7071)	1.2183 (.5629)	1.0525 (.1925)	−3.2025 (1.3760)	.887 .495
Fish	1.3757 (1.3946)	.0741 (1.1101)	.8564 (.3796)	−4.3809 (2.7137)	.260 .977

The introduction of the substitute price slightly improved the fit of both equations. The Meat coefficients are what would be expected, though now the consumption elasticity is a little less than usually is estimated. The own-price inelasticity of Fish still shows up in the form of a trivial positive coefficient, but now we see a good-size (though not significant) cross-price effect.

Regressions of the same sort were run for Butter and Margarine. (Because quantities of butter may find their way into consumption as a result of government policies that are not sensitive to market prices—for example, school food programs or distribution to military forces—it was not surprising that $\bar{R}^2$ was relatively low for the Butter regression in Table 15.10.)

| | Coefficients of | | | | $\bar{R}^2$/ |
	$ln\,P_{butter}$	$ln\,P_{margarine}$	ln Consumption	Constant	SEE
Butter	−1.7730 (1.5005)	.2544 (2.3280)	.4725 (.8339)	−1.0713 (6.5566)	.067 1.234
Margarine	+1.2464 (1.0194)	−1.6328 (1.5815)	.3261 (.5665)	.0815 (4.4543)	.356 .838

The t value for the margarine price term in the Butter regression is trivial in size, and thus the loss of an extra degree of freedom reduces the $\bar{R}^2$ sharply. The Margarine regression is improved slightly by the addition of butter price, but still the standard errors of the coefficients are too large for the coefficients to be meaningful.

Finally, we return to the issue of the exogenous treatment of prices. In the case of products that are traded internationally, treating prices as an independent vari-

Table 15.8. Regressions of Real Per Capita Quantities on Relative Price and Per Capita Consumption, 1970 (Summary Groupings)

$$\ln q_j = \beta_1 \ln\left(\frac{p_{\alpha j}}{p_{cj}}\right) + \beta_2 \ln C_j + \beta_0 + u_j \qquad j = 1, \ldots, 10$$

	Coefficient of			
	$\ln\left(\frac{p_{\alpha j}}{p_{cj}}\right)$	$\ln C_j$	Constant	$\bar{R}^2$/SEE
1 Food, beverage, tobacco	0.1949	0.7215*	0.8275	0.9586
	(0.4660)	(13.7635)	(2.0577)	0.1428
2 Food	0.1843	0.6339*	1.2613*	0.9583
	(0.6030)	(13.9561)	(3.6872)	0.1257
3 Bread and cereals	−0.4464	0.1396	3.0959*	−0.1246
	(−0.4732)	(0.9049)	(2.8398)	0.4472
4 Meat	−1.7066*	1.2081*	−4.0063*	0.8272
	(−2.1075)	(5.4772)	(−2.4475)	0.6120
5 Fish	−0.1173	0.7708*	−3.3697	0.2523
	(−0.0852)	(2.1023)	(−1.3380)	0.9820
6 Milk, cheese, eggs	−0.9774	0.6884*	−1.1320	0.9402
	(−1.7092)	(6.5757)	(−1.4420)	0.2013
7 Oils and fats	0.8016	0.9130*	−3.7312	0.4705
	(0.7233)	(2.5690)	(−1.3118)	0.6783
8 Fruits and vegetables	−0.8248	0.6482*	−0.3890	0.8455
	(−1.8104)	(6.8310)	(−0.5748)	0.2751
9 Coffee, tea, cocoa	−0.5918*	0.8899*	−3.5773*	0.8504
	(−2.4480)	(6.4305)	(−3.5027)	0.3972
10 Spices and sweets, sugar	0.1509	0.6708*	−1.3863	0.8032
	(0.2543)	(5.6644)	(−1.5162)	0.3057
11 Beverages	−1.5221*	1.1783*	−4.5545	0.8789
	(−2.5189)	(3.0353)	(−1.5698)	0.7181
12 Tobacco	0.0390	1.1534*	−5.0298*	0.9355
	(0.1744)	(11.5112)	(−7.1125)	0.2908
13 Clothing and footwear	−0.1198	1.3976*	−5.3751*	0.9872
	(−0.3365)	(22.9010)	(−11.3466)	0.1551
14 Clothing	−0.1609	1.4114*	−5.6403*	0.9877
	(−0.4360)	(21.0865)	(−10.4482)	0.1543
15 Footwear	−1.1316	1.3792*	−7.1865*	0.8896
	(−1.7023)	(8.4784)	(−6.2552)	0.4721
16 Gross rent, fuel	−0.1350	1.2280*	−3.6962*	0.9917
	(−0.7971)	(29.5862)	(−12.7587)	0.1095
17 Gross rents	−0.0083	1.2823*	−4.3763*	0.9819
	(−0.0487)	(21.5743)	(−10.5847)	0.1680
18 Fuel and power	−0.2090	1.1205*	−4.2667*	0.9213
	(−0.6277)	(10.3389)	(−5.5192)	0.3145
19 House furnishings, operation	−0.2669	1.1194*	−3.5441*	0.9502
	(−0.5015)	(13.1509)	(−5.8781)	0.2470
20 Furniture, applicances	−0.1850	1.3855*	−6.0600*	0.9578
	(−0.4885)	(14.3240)	(−8.7818)	0.2805
21 Supplies and operation	−0.7938*	0.8908*	−2.8841*	0.9357
	(−1.9368)	(11.5111)	(−5.1659)	0.2233
22 Medical care	−0.7944*	1.3240*	−5.777*	0.9354
	(−2.4541)	(10.9346)	(−5.5920)	0.3030
23 Transport and communication	−1.3125*	1.1480*	−3.0428*	0.9489
	(−2.2275)	(10.0276)	(−3.3030)	0.2887
24 Equipment	−0.8243	1.5046*	−7.0920	0.8628
	(−1.0696)	(3.5842)	(−2.0919)	0.7152
25 Operation costs	−1.7632*	1.7503*	−8.3228*	0.8778
	(−2.1529)	(8.1565)	(−5.7344)	0.5936
26 Purchased transport	−1.5227*	0.5824*	−0.8489	0.8136
	(−3.9628)	(5.2633)	(−1.0860)	0.3207
27 Communication	−1.1977*	1.5343*	−9.2525*	0.9307
	(−2.8368)	(11.0804)	(−9.1518)	0.3920
28 Recreation and education	−0.1731	1.0294*	−2.4005*	0.9712
	(−0.9323)	(12.6271)	(−3.9213)	0.1620
29 Recreation	−0.5951	1.5259*	−6.6558*	0.9393
	(−0.9095)	(9.3825)	(−5.6753)	0.3936
30 Education	−0.3189*	0.7845*	−1.5372	0.9425
	(−2.3138)	(8.4638)	(−2.1618)	0.1461

Table 15.8. Continued

		Coefficient of			
		$ln\left(\dfrac{p_{\alpha j}}{p_{cj}}\right)$	$ln\,C_j$	Constant	$\bar{R}^2$/SEE
31	Other expenditure	−1.4185 (−1.1867)	1.2167* (8.8471)	−4.0808* (−4.2446)	0.9013 0.3953
32	Personal care	−0.4113 (−1.0189)	1.4772* (16.8362)	−7.1932 (−10.9551)	0.9841 0.1889
33	Miscellaneous services	−0.5197 (−0.4695)	1.1821* (6.6676)	−4.0541 (−3.1355)	0.8253 0.5117

Notes:
t: Student *t* value for the regression coefficient appears within parentheses.
R^2: Coefficient of determination (adjusted for degrees of freedom).
SEE: Standard error of estimate.
*: Coefficient is significantly different from 0 at the .05 level; one-tail test except for constant, where two-tail tests used.

able is quite plausible. In that case, differences in price from country to country may represent simply differences in transfer costs and government policies. No problems of simultaneous equation estimation arise in this situation. When, however, commodities or, more particularly, services are produced domestically, price should be treated as a jointly determined variable. Simultaneous equation estimation methods then are called for. Some experimentation was attempted with the use of a number of "general-purpose" exogenous variables—rate of

Table 15.9. Comparison of Price and Consumption Elasticities Obtained in a 1950 OEEC Study and Corresponding ICP Elasticities for 1970

	Price elasticity		Consumption elasticity	
	ICP	OEEC	ICP	OEEC
Food	.18 (.31)	− .27 (.27)	.63 (.05)	.54 (.05)
Breads and cereals	− .45 (.94)	− .59 (.34)	.14 (.15)	.20 (.14)
Meat	−1.71 (.81)	− .19 (.39)	1.21 (.22)	.86 (.18)
Fish	− .12 (1.38)	−1.03 (.49)	.77 (.37)	.62 (.39)
Dairy products	− .98 (.57)	− .43 (.26)	.69 (.10)	.60 (.10)
Oils and fats	.80 (1.11)	− .60 (.32)	.91 (.36)	.37 (.17)
Fruits and vegetables†	− .82 (.46)	−2.10 (.46)	.65 (.09)	.73 (.21)
Spices and sweets, sugar	− .15 (.51)	−1.62 (.55)	.67 (.12)	.42 (.25)
Tobacco	.04 (.22)	− .26 (.29)	1.15 (.10)	.88 (.28)
Clothing	− .16 (.37)	− .63 (.61)	1.41 (.07)	.84 (.15)
Footwear	−1.13 (.66)	− .62 (.20)	1.38 (.16)	1.01 (.09)
Fuel and power	− .21 (.33)	− .86 (.40)	1.12 (.11)	1.19 (.32)
Medical care	− .79 (.32)	−1.59 (.80)	1.32 (.12)	1.80 (.33)
Transport equipment	− .82 (.77)	−3.84 (1.66)	1.50 (.42)	.71 (.78)
Purchased transport	−1.52 (.38)	−1.79 (.39)	.58 (.11)	1.10 (.17)
Communication	−1.20 (.42)	− .92 (.31)	1.53 (.14)	2.03 (.20)
Recreation	− .60 (.65)	− .99 (.50)	1.53 (.17)	1.15 (.23)
Education	− .32 (.14)	− .49 (.22)	.78 (.09)	.75 (.13)

Source:
OEEC: M. Gilbert and Associates, *Comparative National Products & Price Levels: A Study of Western Europe & the United States* (Paris: Organization for European Economic Cooperation, 1958).
ICP: present study.
Note: Numbers in parentheses are standard errors.
†The OEEC study gives the elasticities separately for Fruits and for Vegetables. In the absence of the detailed OEEC data necessary for pooling the two categories, the elasticities and standard errors simply were averaged together for the purposes of this table. [Price elasticities: Fruits −2.06 (.29); Vegetables −2.15 (.64). Consumption elasticities: Fruits, .71 (.15); Vegetables, .75 (.27).]

Table 15.10. Regressions of Real per Capita Quantities on Relative Price and per Capita Consumption, 1970 (seventy-five detailed categories)

$$\ln q_{oj} = \beta_1 \ln\left(\frac{p_{oj}}{p_{cj}}\right) + \beta_2 \ln C_j + \beta_0 + u_i; \quad i = 1, \ldots, 10$$

			Coefficient of			
			$\ln\left(\dfrac{p_{oj}}{p_{ci}}\right)$	$\ln C_j$	Constant	$\bar{R}^2$/SEE
1	01.101	Rice	1.5798 (0.9998)	-0.3224 (-0.5328)	3.0652 (0.6929)	-0.0551 1.7264
2	01.102	Meal, other cereals	-1.1019 (-1.0150)	-0.8166* (-2.7422)	8.0007* (3.6947)	0.4100 0.8628
3	01.103	Bread, rolls	-1.9904* (-2.8559)	1.3772* (4.6215)	-8.3429* (-4.1074)	0.8235 0.8109
4	01.105	Cereal preparations	-2.7740* (-2.8195)	0.4146 (0.9371)	-2.6311 (-0.8129)	0.5954 1.1133
5	01.111	Fresh beef, veal	-2.2725* (-2.2876)	1.3086* (3.0729)	-6.0428 (-2.0288)	0.5455 1.2209
6	01.113	Fresh pork	0.8163 (1.2264)	2.0603* (8.1816)	-12.8175* (-7.1468)	0.8799 0.7305
7	01.114	Fresh poultry	0.0205 (0.0283)	1.5696* (6.1481)	-9.2218* (-4.6572)	0.8347 0.6599
8	01.115	Other fresh meat	-1.0696 (-0.9545)	0.6314* (2.0759)	-3.0889 (-1.4106)	0.3314 0.8595
9	01.121	Fresh, frozen fish	-0.6347 (-0.5436)	0.6547 (1.4582)	-3.1924 (-1.0007)	0.0186 1.1298
10	01.131	Fresh milk	-0.6761* (-2.1090)	0.4091* (4.6788)	-0.0003 (-0.0005)	0.7946 0.2396
11	01.132	Milk products	-1.3551 (-1.6409)	0.9603* (2.9281)	-4.5380 (-1.8862)	0.7951 0.6668
12	01.133	Eggs, egg products	1.5070 (1.8284)	2.3094* (8.7980)	-15.0642* (-7.2502)	0.9298 0.5242
13	01.141	Butter	-1.7013 (-1.3602)	0.3963 (0.9357)	-0.4591 (-0.1454)	0.1985 1.1433
14	01.142	Margarine, edible oil	-0.7879 (-0.5352)	0.4540 (0.7880)	-0.7470 (-0.1640)	0.3105 0.8673
15	01.151	Fresh fruits, tropical, subtropical	-1.2648* (-3.6115)	0.5097* (2.3511)	-1.6755 (-1.1219)	0.5755 0.5833
16	01.153	Fresh vegetables	-1.0685 (-1.3607)	0.6843* (3.3984)	-2.5115 (-1.6105)	0.5165 0.5520
17	01.162	Vegetables other than fresh	-0.2865 (-0.4651)	0.7667* (3.1559)	-2.9717 (-1.5614)	0.5677 0.6406
18	01.170	Potatoes, manioc, other tubers	-1.9742* (-5.5242)	0.2763* (2.1933)	-0.4644 (-0.5236)	0.7969 0.3646
19	01.191	Coffee	-0.4214 (-0.8877)	1.3390* (4.2432)	-7.4943* (-3.1661)	0.6895 0.8875
20	01.180	Sugar	-0.5249 (-1.1013)	0.1676 (0.8246)	1.2829 (0.8311)	0.1673 0.5074
21	01.201	Jam, syrup, honey	-1.3485* (-2.2192)	0.7673* (2.5530)	-4.5930 (-2.1039)	0.7111 0.7409
22	01.202	Chocolate, ice cream	0.0720 (0.0803)	1.8842* (4.8539)	-11.5948* (-3.5767)	0.8656 0.6970
23	01.203	Salt, spices, sauces	-3.6895* (-3.9715)	0.1750 (0.6914)	0.1969 (0.1101)	0.6157 0.7345
24	01.310	Nonalcoholic beverages	-0.2638 (-0.3134)	1.4879* (3.4669)	-9.1861* (-2.8696)	0.8438 0.6542
25	01.323	Beer	-0.2537 (-0.2942)	1.5654* (2.9333)	-8.9524 (-2.2974)	0.6661 1.0917
26	01.410	Cigarettes	-0.8098* (-2.1186)	1.5633* (6.4771)	-8.2004 (-4.7753)	0.8576 0.6802
27	02.110	Clothing materials	0.1485 (0.2189)	0.8490* (2.9580)	-4.0537 (-1.7871)	0.5177 0.6934
28	02.121	Men's clothing	0.1540 (0.1988)	1.3160* (11.3575)	-6.4305* (-7.3313)	0.9608 0.2532
29	02.122	Women's clothing	-1.4551* (-3.4804)	1.3085* (9.8546)	-5.8512* (-5.5537)	0.9577 0.3247
30	02.123	Boys', girls' clothing	0.0250 (0.0270)	1.3670* (7.0192)	-7.9029* (-5.7592)	0.8406 0.5642

Table 15.10. Continued

			Coefficient of			
			$ln\left(\frac{p_{\alpha j}}{p_{cj}}\right)$	$ln C_j$	Constant	$\bar{R}^2$/SEE
31	02.160	Clothing rental, repair	-2.3781* (-7.8080)	1.4377* (13.1858)	-10.3312* (-12.8840)	0.9536 0.2983
32	02.211	Men's footwear	-1.1526 (-1.5343)	1.1567* (5.9792)	-6.6091* (-4.8257)	0.8163 0.5545
33	02.212	Women's footwear	-0.7493 (-1.4399)	1.5150* (8.5876)	-9.2551* (-7.3898)	0.8893 0.4955
34	02.213	Children's footwear	-1.0682 (-1.5268)	1.6231* (8.8634)	-10.5320* (-7.9584)	0.8952 0.5171
35	03.110	Gross rents	0.1025 (0.4070)	1.2870* (15.1770)	-4.4828* (-7.6314)	0.9643 0.2368
36	03.210	Electricity	-1.6019* (-7.2455)	1.5924* (16.3745)	-8.4243* (-11.2615)	0.9889 0.2163
37	03.230	Liquid fuels	-1.2139 (-1.6694)	0.9755* (2.0499)	-4.7700 (-1.2860)	0.8306 0.7276
38	03.240	Other fuels, ice	-0.6645 (-0.0713)	0.4152 (1.0124)	-1.0724 (-0.3663)	-0.1048 1.1039
39	04.110	Furniture, fixtures	-2.2482 (-1.7329)	1.4809* (5.1219)	-7.6702* (-3.6869)	0.7876 0.8155
40	04.120	Floor coverings	-1.4457* (-5.1263)	1.3416* (7.1928)	-8.4893* (-6.4872)	0.8751 0.5283
41	04.200	Household textiles, etc.	-0.9108 (-1.4636)	1.1642* (6.2356)	-5.7893* (-4.1462)	0.8494 0.5117
42	04.310	Refrigerators, etc.	-0.1863 (-0.9256)	1.8238* (13.4142)	-11.9242* (-11.3810)	0.9792 0.2697
43	04.400	Household utensils	-0.4565 (-0.7625)	1.1149* (6.4576)	-5.6665* (-4.6219)	0.8531 0.4618
44	04.510	Nondurable household goods	-1.0422 (-1.2494)	0.8210* (3.2935)	-3.0106 (-1.6129)	0.8431 0.4391
45	04.530	Household services	-1.8758* (-2.0510)	1.3919* 5.1100	-8.3599* -4.2487	0.7368 0.6502
46	05.110	Drugs, medical preparations	-1.4878 (-3.1403)	1.1139* (5.3398)	-5.1785* (-3.5945)	0.8815 0.5358
47	05.310	Physicians' services	-0.1958 (-1.4362)	1.0840* (8.3744)	-5.1245* (-5.2523)	0.9046 0.3070
48	05.320	Dentists' services	0.0488 (0.3744)	1.6802* (8.0635)	-10.2355* (-6.7334)	0.9086 0.5221
49	05.330	Services, nurses, other personnel	0.0890 (0.2524)	0.9741* (3.7229)	-4.6818 (-2.1305)	0.6598 0.6632
50	05.400	Hospitals, etc.	-0.1012 (-0.4674)	1.0559* (5.9784)	-4.8734* (-3.5953)	0.7906 0.5061
51	06.110	Personal cars	-1.3168 (-1.4742)	1.4060* (2.4877)	-6.2400 (-1.3835)	0.7953 1.0140
52	06.210	Tires, tubes, accessories	-0.9520 (-0.6723)	1.3614 (1.8234)	-8.0936 (-1.4429)	0.7485 0.9859
53	06.220	Repair charges	-1.2965* (-2.0237)	1.6847* (4.8334)	-10.0348* (-3.9689)	0.7533 0.6637
54	06.230	Gasoline, oil, etc.	-0.7495 (-1.2125)	1.9928* (8.9744)	-11.1687* (-6.2330)	0.9173 0.6044
55	06.240	Parking, tolls, etc.	0.1377 (0.1462)	1.4252* (3.9643)	-8.4675* (-3.1125)	0.6639 0.9451
56	06.310	Local transport	-2.3458* (-7.1342)	1.3485* (9.0255)	-8.7903* (-7.8117)	0.9146 0.4036
57	06.321	Rail transport	-2.8520* (-2.3421)	0.7324* (1.9751)	-4.6232 (-1.7578)	0.4648 1.0751
58	06.322	Bus transport	1.3314 (1.3642)	-0.0836 (-0.3245)	2.3560 (1.2447)	-0.0153 0.7173
59	06.410	Postal communication	-2.2426* (-1.8658)	1.3497* (5.8070)	-9.0119* (-5.5622)	0.8399 0.6389
60	06.420	Telephone, telegraph	-1.4140* (-2.5437)	1.5887* (7.4125)	-10.2007* (-6.4860)	0.8547 0.5878

Table 15.10. Continued

			Coefficient of			
			$ln\left(\dfrac{p_{\alpha j}}{p_{cj}}\right)$	$ln\,C_j$	Constant	$\bar{R}^2$/SEE
61	07.110	Radio, TV, phonograph, etc.	−1.2408* (−1.9454)	1.3524* (4.4824)	−6.6658* (−2.7420)	0.8857 0.6218
62	07.210	Public entertainment	−0.9290 (−1.1968)	1.3942* (3.6131)	−8.0152* (−2.9454)	0.5918 1.1179
63	07.230	Other recreation, cultural events	−1.1984* (−3.0656)	1.4688* (6.9608)	−8.9886* (−5.8248)	0.8427 0.5921
64	07.310	Books, papers, magazines	−0.9086* (−2.8169)	1.3391* (12.1590)	−7.0177* (−9.0231)	0.9714 0.2559
65	07.411	Teachers, 1st, 2nd	−0.1531 (−1.4952)	0.4993* (5.5758)	−0.0041 (−0.0057)	0.9032 0.1207
66	07.412	Teachers, college	−0.6824* (−4.6925)	1.2801* (10.9402)	−7.1719* (−8.6383)	0.9291 0.3138
67	07.420	Educational facilities	−0.5315 (−0.3582)	1.4247* (3.6534)	−8.0425* (−2.5620)	0.7923 0.7383
68	07.431	Educational supplies	−1.1213 (−1.0336)	0.7127* (1.8768)	−4.5429 (−1.6985)	0.4867 0.8903
69	07.432	Other education expenditures	0.4839 (0.2328)	1.0288* (2.7222)	−6.0716 (−2.0072)	0.4809 0.8839
70	08.100	Barber, beauty shops	−1.2886* (−3.5636)	1.7096* (11.8156)	−11.1280* (−10.7967)	0.9452 0.4193
71	08.210	Toilet articles	−0.8936 (−1.7388)	1.2754* (5.3679)	−6.5537* (−3.5856)	0.9632 0.3116
72	08.220	Other personal-care goods	0.0657 (0.2798)	1.3668* (17.9598)	−7.4666* (−13.6755)	0.9729 0.2197
73	08.310	Restaurants, cafes	−0.8717 (−1.2897)	1.3553* (6.4648)	−5.8934* (−3.9853)	0.8288 0.6054
74	08.320	Hotels, etc.	−2.7291 (−1.8099)	0.6273 (1.7680)	−2.0542 (−0.5186)	0.6367 0.7913
75	08.400	Other services	0.8034 (0.3539)	0.5842 (0.8930)	−0.9899 (−0.1853)	0.0924 1.3067

Notes:

t: Student t value for the regression coefficient appears within parentheses.

$\bar{R}^2$: Coefficient of determination (adjusted for degrees of freedom).

SEE: Standard error of estimate.

*: Coefficient is significantly different from 0 at the .05 level; one-tail test except for constant, where two-tail tests used.

growth of real output, proportion of the population in the labor force, and proportion of population to arable land—to apply the estimating method known as Two-Stage Least Squares. With such a small number of observations, however, the price elasticity estimates varied over an extremely wide range depending upon just which combination of the three exogenous variables was introduced into the system. For the most part, the consumption elasticities were insensitive to changes in the set of exogenous variables. This indicates that the price elasticities of Tables 15.8 and 15.10 are even more imprecise than their standard errors there would suggest, but that the consumption elasticities are fairly robust (insensi-

tive) with respect to the problem of simultaneous equation bias.

Although a definitive assessment of the role of relative prices and income levels in explaining relative quantities from country to country must await a more careful formulation of the underlying model, as well as the accumulation of data from more countries, the regression coefficients in Tables 15.8 and 15.10 indicate clearly that relative prices and income levels work with sufficient power and persistence that their influence shows through—despite the imperfections of the underlying data and of the theoretical framework in which these equations are formulated.

Glossary

Additivity: The property that makes it possible to have correct country-to-country quantity relationships for each detailed category, and, at the same time, to obtain the correct country-to-country quantity relationships for any desired aggregation of categories simply by summing the quantities for the included categories. This requires that the quantities be stated in value terms so that (1) the values for any category are directly comparable between countries and (2) the values for any country are directly comparable between categories.

Binary comparison: A price or quantity comparison between two countries without regard to the consistency of this comparison with comparisons of each of the countries with any third countries. (See **Circularity or transitivity.**)

Bridge-country binary comparison: A price or quantity comparison between a pair of countries derived from the comparison of each country with a third country. For example, if we have $I_{j/k}$ and $I_{l/k}$, the bridge-country method of obtaining $I_{j/l}$ is to divide $I_{j/k}$ by $I_{l/k}$, where I is a price or quantity index and j, k, and l are countries. (See also **Original-country binary comparison.**)

CEP (consumption expenditures of the population): The ICP concept of "consumption" that includes both household expenditures and expenditures of government on such categories as health and education. (See Table 13.15.)

Characteristicity: The property whereby the sample of prices or quantities and the weights used in an international comparison conform closely to a representative sample of items and to the weights of each of the countries included in the comparison.

Circularity or transitivity: There is circularity or transitivity if the indexes expressing the price or quantity relationships between any two among three or more countries are the same whether derived (1) from an original-country comparison between them or (2) from the comparison of each country with any third country. In the case of three countries, where I is a price or quantity index and j, k, and l are countries, the circular test is satisfied if: $I_{j/k} = I_{j/l} \div I_{k/l}$. When this test is satisfied, there is a unique cardinal scaling of countries with respect to relative quantities and prices.

Country-product–dummy (CPD) method: A generalized bridge-country method employing regression analysis to obtain transitive price comparisons for each detailed category. The basic data for a given category consist of all the prices available for the various specifications for the entire collection of countries. The prices are regressed against two sets of dummy variables; one set contains a dummy for each specification; the second set, a dummy for each country other than the numeraire country. The transitive price comparisons are derived from the coefficients of the country dummies. (See Chapter 5.)

Country-reversal test: This test is satisfied if, when country j is taken as the base country, the price or quantity index for countries j and k is the reciprocal of the index when country k is the base country. For example, $I_{j/k} \cdot I_{k/j} = 1$, where I is a price or quantity index.

Detailed categories: The subdivisions of final expenditure for which the first aggregation of price (or quantity) ratios for individual specifications or items takes place. (See appendix tables of Chapters 13 and 14.)

Direct price or quantity comparison: One made by comparing for two or more countries the prices or quantities for a representative sample of equivalent commodities. (See also **Indirect price or quantity comparison.**)

Double-weighted CPD: A weighted CPD method in which the weights are the products of (1) the importance of each cell in the column in which it falls (the percentage of the country's expenditure) and (2) the importance of the cell in the row in which it falls (the percentage of the total quantity of the category in the ten countries). The double-weighted CPD is used to obtain PPPs for categories for which no price comparisons were made. The CPD is applied in this case to the matrix of PPPs in which the columns represent countries and the rows detailed categories. (See **Country-product–dummy method.**)

Exchange-rate–deviation index: The ratio of the real GDP per capita relative to the United States as estimated by the ICP to the GDP per capita relative to the United States when the exchange rate is used to convert nondollar currencies to dollars.

Equal weighting: Used in the ICP to refer to the practice of applying simple or unweighted averages to all the price ratios within a category to derive the PPP for the category. (See **Item weighting**.)

Factor-reversal test: The condition that, for any given item, category, or aggregate and for any given pair countries, the product of the price ratio (or index) and the quantity ratio (or index) be equal to the expenditure ratio.

Final products: Products purchased for own use and not for resale or for embodiment in a product for resale; those purchased by households, by government, or by business on capital account.

Fisher, or "ideal," index: The geometric mean of two indexes, one the harmonic mean of price (or quantity) relatives weighted by the numerator country's expenditures, the other, the arithmetic mean weighted by the denominator country's expenditures.

Frequency-weighted CPD: The CPD method applied to a detailed category with each price weighted by $1/n_j$, where n_j is the number of price observations for country j. (See **Country-product–dummy method**.)

GCF (gross capital formation): Includes fixed capital formation, change in stocks, and net exports. Definitions of these three components correspond to SNA concepts, although the SNA does not include net exports in its definition of GCF.

Geary-Khamis method: An aggregation method in which category international prices (reflecting relative category values) and country PPPs (depicting relative country price levels) are estimated simultaneously from a system of linear equations. (See pp. 68–70.)

GFCE (government final consumption expenditure): The SNA concept of "government" which includes public expenditures on education, health, and similar categories. (See Table 13.15.)

ICP: International Comparison Project

"Ideal" index: See **Fisher, or "ideal," index**.

Index spread: The ratio of a U.S.-weighted quantity index to an own-weighted quantity index.

Indirect price or quantity comparison: A comparison made by dividing the price or quantity ratio into the expenditure ratio. That is, the indirect quantity comparison between country j and country k for commodity i, $\frac{q_{ij}}{q_{ik}}$, is obtained from: $\frac{\rho_{ij}}{\rho_{ik}} \frac{q_{ij}}{q_{ik}} \div \frac{\rho_{ij}}{\rho_{ik}} = \frac{q_{ij}}{q_{ik}}$, where the ρs are the commodity prices. (See also **Direct price or quantity comparison**.)

International prices: Average prices based on the prices of the ten included countries, each weighted by the GDP of the supercountry to which it is assigned.

International dollars (I$): Dollars with the same purchasing power over total GDP as the U.S. dollar, but with a purchasing power over subaggregates and over detailed categories determined by average international prices rather than by U.S. relative prices.

Item weighting: The assignment of individual weights to each specification for which prices are compared within a detailed category. (See **Equal weighting**.)

Multilateral comparison: A price or quantity comparison of more than two countries simultaneously that produces consistent relations among all pairs; that is, satisfies the circular test or the transitivity requirement.

Original-country binary comparison: A price or quantity comparison between two countries based on the data of the two countries and no others. (See also **Bridge-country binary comparison**.)

Own weights: The weights of the numerator country: that is, the weights of country j in the index $I_{j/k}$. We use the term to refer mainly to the weights of a country other than the United States in comparisons in which the United States is the base country, k.

PFC (public final consumption expenditure): The ICP concept of "government" that excludes public expenditures for education, health, and like categories. (See Table 13.15.)

PFCE (private final consumption expenditure): The SNA concept of "consumption" that excludes public expenditures on education, health, and similar categories. (See Table 13.15.)

PPP: See **Purchasing-power parity**.

Price index: The price level for a category or aggregate of goods in one country expressed as a percentage of the price level for the same category or aggregate in another country, when prices in both countries are expressed in a common currency, usually the U.S. dollar, with the official exchange rate being used for currency conversions. A price index may be derived from a purchasing power parity by dividing by the exchange rate. (See **Purchasing-power parity**.)

Price ratio or price relative: The purchasing power parity for a single specification.

Purchasing-power parity (PPP): The number of currency units required to buy goods equivalent to what can be bought with one unit of the currency of the base country, usually the U.S. dollar in the present study.

Quantity index: The quantity per capita of a category or aggregate of goods in one country expressed as a percentage of the quantity per capita in another country.

Quantity ratio: The quantity of a particular commodity in one country as a percentage of the quantity of the same commodity in another country.

Real product or real quantity: The final product or quantity in two or more countries which is valued at common prices and, therefore, valued in comparable terms internationally.

Representative country: One of the ten included countries regarded as a representative of a larger group of countries that together with it form a supercountry. All the countries in the world are assigned to one of the ten supercountries. (See also **Supercountry**.)

Similarity index: The weighted "raw correlation" coefficient between the price (or quantity) vectors of two countries. Expenditures are used as the weights. The coefficient is the ratio of the cross moment to the square root of the product of the two second moments, where each moment is computed relative to the origin rather than to the mean.

Specification: A description of an item for which a price comparison is to be made. The description is designed to ensure that goods of equivalent quality are compared.

Supercountry: A group of countries assumed to have the price and quantity structure of the representative country. The aggregate GDP of the supercountry is used to weight the prices of the representative country in the process of deriving average international prices. (See also **Representative country**.)

Transitivity requirement: See **Circularity or transitivity**.

Index

THE JOHNS HOPKINS UNIVERSITY PRESS

This book was set in Press Roman text and display type
by Jones Composition Company, from a design by
Susan Bishop. It was printed on Westvāco 60-lb. Clear
Spring paper and bound in Columbia Bayside cloth by
Universal Lithographers, Inc.